STRATEGIES
AND TECHNIQUES
IN FAMILY THERAPY

STRATEGIES AND TECHNIQUES IN FAMILY THERAPY

Edited by

JAMES C. HANSEN

*State University of New York
at Buffalo*

and

DAVID ROSENTHAL

*University of Iowa
Iowa City, Iowa*

CHARLES C THOMAS • **PUBLISHER**
Springfield • Illinois • U.S.A.

616.8915
S 898

Published and Distributed Throughout the World by
CHARLES C THOMAS • PUBLISHER
Bannerstone House
301-327 East Lawrence Avenue, Springfield, Illinois, U.S.A.

© *1981, by* CHARLES C THOMAS • PUBLISHER
ISBN 0-398-04154-7 (paper)
0-398-04451-1 (cloth)
Library of Congress Catalog Card Number: 80-22378

With THOMAS BOOKS careful attention is given to all details of manufacturing and design. It is the Publisher's desire to present books that are satisfactory as to their physical qualities and artistic possibilities and appropriate for their particular use. THOMAS BOOKS will be true to those laws of quality that assure a good name and good will.

Library of Congress Cataloging in Publication Data

Main entry under title:

Strategies and techniques in family therapy.

    Bibliography: p.
    1. Family psychotherapy.   I. Hansen, James C.   II. Rosenthal, David.
RC488.5.S77   616.89′156   80-22378
ISBN 0-398-04154-7 (paper)
      0-398-04451-1 (cloth)

Printed in the United States of America
PS-R-1

CONTRIBUTORS

Harry J. Aponte
Arthur M. Bodin
Luigi Boscolo
Ivan Boszormenyi-Nagy
Murray Bowen
Kenneth Bruce Bower
Elizabeth Carter
Gian Franco Cecchin
William C. Coe
Larry L. Constantine
Richard M. Eisler
Craig A. Everett, Ph.D.
Larry B. Feldman
Richard Fisch
Lawrence Fisher
David S. Freeman
Robert Friedman
Neal Gansheroff
Michael Geddes
Herta A. Guttman
James C. Hansen
Rachel T. Hare-Mustin
James L. Hawkins
Michel Hersen
Bonnie S. Himes
Paulette M. Hines

Carter Jefferson
Bradford P. Kenney
David V. Keith
Luciano L'Abate
Ronald F. Levant
Robert Liberman
Carmen Lynch
John Matrullo
Joan Medway
Augustus Y. Napier
Mara Selvini Palazzoli
Peggy Papp
Giuliana Prata
Uri Rueveni
Robert B. Rutherford
Virginia M. Satir
Robert S. Schachter
Olga Silverstein
Carlos E. Sluzki
Michael A. Solomon
Patricia H. Soper
Paul Watzlawick
John H. Weakland
Carl A. Whitaker
Gerald H. Zuk

INTRODUCTION

Family therapy is generally based on the belief that the family is a system and the therapeutic process involves treating the whole family system or individuals and subsystems regarding their interaction with the whole family. There are numerous conceptual strategies to family therapy and a variety of specific techniques that can be used in the process. A strategy is a plan for achieving an end, and in family therapy the therapist's strategy is the general and specific guidelines for promoting change in the family. The specific behaviors in implementing the changes are the techniques of family therapy. This book presents several prominent strategies followed by sections concentrating on practical techniques.

This book is intended to provide easy access to literature on the procedures of family therapy. The articles were selected for their practical nature. The papers in the strategy section may be called theoretical positions, but they show how the strategy can be used. The technique sections contain papers that describe the technique or concept and how it applies in the therapeutic process. The book is intended to be a textbook or a supplementary book of readings for students and professionals in psychology, psychiatry, social work, and other human service fields.

The book is divided into two major parts. The first part is titled Strategies and contains eight articles describing prominent strategies in family therapy. These articles have been authored by prominent individuals explaining their approach to therapy. These articles meet the definition of the term strategy and provide the reader with guidelines to follow in working with a family.

The second part is titled Techniques and is subdivided into areas focusing on specific processes and techniques. The first section involves Initiating Family Therapy. This section discusses the goals of therapy and examines many of the procedures that are helpful in engaging the family in the process. The second section covers Diagnosis and Assessment in Family Therapy. The therapist's understanding of the family is an integral part of therapy, and the articles in this section present some dimensions and paradigms to use. The third section focuses on the Therapist as a Technique and concentrates on the therapist's involvement as an important aspect of the process. The fourth section, Behavioral Techniques, presents articles on charting, contracting, and the behavioral approach to interacting with families. The fifth section contains articles covering Family Sculpture Techniques. The sixth section covers a variety of Nonverbal Techniques. These articles highlight the relatively stable patterns of verbal and nonverbal communication and illuminate focal points for intervention. The seventh section, Paradoxical Interventions, provides the concepts, directions, and examples of paradox techniques. The eighth section discusses Stages in Family Therapy and the techniques used by therapists during these stages. The last section examines the Legal, Values, and Ethical Considerations that arise for the family theapist.

A book of this nature represents the efforts of many individuals. We wish to thank the authors and publishers of the selections for permission to utilize their original material.

CONTENTS

ix

STRATEGIES
AND TECHNIQUES
IN FAMILY THERAPY

Part I
STRATEGIES

STRATEGIES FOR FAMILY THERAPY

Most therapists begin working with individuals and groups and then modify their conceptions of problem behaviors and how people change to focus on the family. The therapist's concept of the functional and dysfunctional families will certainly affect the therapeutic process. While family therapy is rooted in the basic psychological science, it is an applied field and the task of therapists is to define how behavior change is brought about in the context of the family. This suggests that the therapist's role is in part determined by theoretical orientation. A theory serves four major functions. It serves to synthesize a particular body of knowledge and attempts to put separate findings into a meaningful and useful package. Second, by ordering and demonstrating which pieces of information are most important, it increases the understanding of the knowledge. Third, it acts as a guide to making predictions and pathways that are possible and indicates what may occur if certain routes are followed. Fourth, it stimulates research to substantiate, reject, or revise the predictions. Many of the prominent positions in the family therapy do not fulfill all the requirements for a good theory. Many positions are still in the process of development. For a therapist, the most important aspect of a theory is the third function in which it serves as a guide in understanding what behaviors to expect and what pathways to follow. It is this function that may be described as a strategy. A strategy is the plan the therapist uses to promote change in the family. The articles in this section of the book were selected to provide this practical aspect of a theory.

Levant's article is an excellent lead article for this section because it presents a review of several attempts to classify theorists in family therapy. The comments regarding the various concepts of family therapy will be helpful in examining the following strategies.

Aponte presents therapy in terms of the family structure. He describes therapy in which the therapist helps the family members agree on the problem, identifies individuals related to the problem, and then helps them change the structure of the family interaction.

The article by Bowen is the classical presentation of his position. Bowen covers his theory of the family as a system and then his conceptualization of the therapeutic process.

Virginia Satir believes the symptom of a family member is a comment on a dysfunctional family system, however, her strategy differs from the structural or Bowen approach. She focuses on the analysis of family communication and then on changing communication which will lead to appropriate outcomes for individuals.

Liberman presents the concepts and techniques of the behavioral

5

approach to family therapy. He gives a behavioral model and then uses several case studies to illustrate this strategy.

Brief therapy, developed by Weakland, Fisch, Watzlawick, and Bodin, is a pragmatic strategy to resolve interpersonal problems. This article follows a six-stage schema for brief therapy and also offers some evaluation of the approach.

Gerald Zuk develops a conceptualization of value systems in families and the relationship of values to family problems. He goes on to discuss his basic therapist functions of go-between, side-taker, and celebrant in working with the value systems.

Rueveni describes the strategy of network family therapy. This approach helps families reconnect with a larger support network to mobilize problem solving in family crises. He covers the six phases in this strategy as well as the roles of the therapist throughout the process.

Chapter 1

A CLASSIFICATION OF THE FIELD OF FAMILY THERAPY: A REVIEW OF PRIOR ATTEMPTS AND A NEW PARADIGMATIC MODEL

Ronald F. Levant

In the early days of family therapy, the relative merits of family therapy were compared with individual psychotherapy (typically, psychodynamically oriented therapy), as if family therapy were a unitary, homogeneous form of therapy. In the past 25 years we have seen a proliferation of theories and techniques in the family therapy field. Today it is clear that there are numerous types of family therapy, so it is important to attempt to bring some order to the field—to characterize and classify the approaches to family therapy in order to have a better idea of what it is we are offering our clients.

In this regard we can learn from the individual psychotherapy research literature. Bergin (1971), in an analysis of the existing outcome studies, concluded that, on the average, individual psychotherapy has had a modestly positive effect. But, he went on to observe, the averages on which this conclusion was based obscure the fact that some clients gain a great deal, some gain a modest amount, some show no change, and some deteriorate after a course of psychotherapy. He pointed out that psychotherapy is not a unitary phenomenon—there is a wide range of theories and practices and great diversity in the practitioners. What is vitally important to know, then, is: "*what* treatment, by *whom*, is most effective for *this* individual with *that* specific problem, and under *which* set of circumstances" (Paul, 1967, p. 111).

It is reasonable to expect that this question, and the principle of specificity upon which it rests, should be equally important to the field of family therapy.

The preparation of a classification of the various family therapy approaches is a necessary first step in the process of a fine-grained examination of the outcome of family therapy. This will be a somewhat difficult undertaking because—due to the openness and flexibility with which the field has evolved—there has been a great deal of cross-fertilization and exchanging of concepts and techniques among

7

theoretically distinct groups. As a result there is a lot of eclecticism, and it is somewhat difficult to discern the "pure strains" within the array of family therapy approaches. At a more serious level, it has been questioned whether the schools of family therapy derive from comprehensive and consistent theoretical bases or are, rather, a "hodge podge of techniques and part-theories" (Zuk, 1976, p. 299). One of the aims of this paper is to examine the issue of whether a set of distinct, theoretically based approaches to family therapy exists.

Alexander (1963), in an early attempt to describe the field of family therapy, called attention to three current practices of mental health agencies regarding the involvement of the families of their clients. The first of these is *collaborative* treatment, used by the child guidance clinics, in which one or more members of the primary client's family is also in therapy, usually with a different therapist. The typical practice in the child guidance clinics is for the child (primary client) to be seen by a psychiatrist and for the mother to be seen by a social worker. The second practice is *concomitant* treatment, used in marriage counseling, wherein the same therapist sees both the husband and the wife individually, with joint sessions held rarely, if at all. The third is *conjoint* treatment, in which the entire family, or a relevant subunit, is seen regularly in therapy. It is this third practice which has evolved into the field of family therapy as we know it today, which will be the focus of this paper. However, it should be noted that, as the field has evolved, there has been increasing variation regarding which family members participate in therapy. Current practice includes seeing an individual family member, a dyad (marital partners or parent-child dyad), a triad (parents and child), a set of siblings, the nuclear family, or the multigenerational extended family.

EARLY ATTEMPTS TO CLASSIFY THE FIELD

There have been a number of attempts to characterize and classify the schools of family therapy. One of the earliest consisted of a set of amusing caricatures provided by the inimitable satirist of the field, Jay Haley (1962). This appeared in the lead article of the first issue of *Family Process*, of which Haley was then editor. Haley first described three schools concerned with the families of moderately disturbed child patients: The *Dignified School of Family Therapy* (J. E. Bell), in which the therapist does not take sides in family conflict; the *Dynamic Psychodynamic School of Family Diagnosis* (N. W. Ackerman), in which the therapist takes sides with different family members at different times, gets pulled in many different directions and often wishes that he could flee the room; and the *Chuck It and Run School* (C. Fulweiler), in which the therapist does just that, leaving the family members to confront each other in an observation room equipped with recording devices. Haley then described two schools concerned with more disturbed families in which there is a schizophrenic member. Whereas, in the *Great Mother School* (V. Satir), the therapist emanates a benevolent concern for family members and attempts to create a more friendly family atmosphere, the *Stonewall School* (D. Jackson) therapist bedevils the family into health.

> Just as a fat man is often called Skinny, the *Stonewall School of Family Therapy* derives its name from the activities of a slippery therapist who takes charge of the family in such a way that no one can come to grips with him. A characteristic of this school is the way it sprains the brains of family members. Often they leave a session batting themselves alongside the head to clear it. The therapist insists that all family members are absolutely right and absolutely wrong and that love is hate, criticism is complimentary, disloyalty is undying affection, and leaving home is really staying. Whatever direction the family members are going, in their aimless way, is accepted by the therapist but re-labeled as actually some other direction, so that the family must become less aimless to find out what the devil is really going on. (Haley, 1962, p. 76)

Finally, Haley enumerated four *Multiplication Schools* which utilized more than one therapist: *The Eyebrows School* (R. D. Laing in England), which used two therapists; the *Brotherly Love School* (A. S. Friedman and associates at the Philadelphia Psychiatric Center), in which dual therapists met the family in the home; the *Total Push in the Tall Country School* (R. MacGregor and associates of the Multiple Impact Therapy Program in Texas), in which every family member got a therapist; and the *Hospitalize the Whole Damn Maelstrom School* (M. Bowen), which flung all of the family members into the hospital together.

The Committee on the Family of the Group for the Advancement of Psychiatry (GAP, 1970) conducted a survey of the field of family therapy in 1965-66. The report identified three theoretical positions. Position A therapists are psychodynamically-oriented individual therapists who view family therapy as one method within their therapeutic repertoire. They will occasionally see families but retain a focus on their individual patient. The family is seen as a stress factor with which their patient must cope. As would be expected, Position A therapists tend to emphasize history-taking, diagnosis, expression of affect and insight.

Position Z therapists use a family system orientation exclusively. They see family therapy not as a method, but as a fundamentally new orientation to mental health. All therapeutic interventions are seen as family interventions. The issue is whether or not therapists are aware of the family implications and consequences of their work. Instead of viewing the individual-in-distress as the patient, the Position Z therapist sees him or her as the "identified patient" or "symptom bearer" who is expressing the dysfunction within the family system. Position Z therapists are ahistorical, focusing on present interaction. They tend to eschew diagnosis, based as it is in an individual nosology.

The expression of affect is seen as needless torture. Instead of forcing family members to disclose their unpleasant feelings about each other, the Position Z therapist will work toward resolving the underlying relationship problems which are producing the unpleasant feelings.

Position M therapists are in the middle ground—they tend to blend psychodynamic and family systems concepts.

The report noted that "family theory combines two bodies of knowledge: personality dynamics and multipersonal system dynamics. The thorough integration of these two systems levels into a comprehensive theory is a long-range task" (GAP, 1970, p. 31). The report went on to observe that some proponents of family theory advocate it as a replacement for, rather than an addition to personality theory. It prognosticated that the future may see the emergence of ideological struggles based on either/or rather than synthesis. The polarization which was forseen was already being reflected in data they had collected on the preference of the three mental health disciplines for specific theoretical orientations. This data showed psychiatrists and social workers to be fairly well polarized, preferring either psychodynamic or family theory. In contrast, psychologists' preferences were more evenly distributed among six theoretical orientations: psychodynamic, family theory, behavioral, learning, small group and existential.

Zuk (1971), observed an intensification of this ideological struggle during the period 1964-70. He listed Wynne, Boszormenyi-Nagy and Framo as representative of the psychodynamic camp, and Haley, Jackson and himself as representative of the systems orientation.

Beels and Ferber (1969) took a somewhat different tack in their attempt to classify family therapists. They focused on the personality style of the therapist, with particular attention to the dominance dimension. They made a distinction between "conductors" and "reactors." Conductors are dominant and participate in a group by leading it. They tend to maintain themselves on the senior side of the generational hierarchy. They are movers, in Kantor and Lehr's (1975) terminology. Reactors respond to events within the family group. In Kantor and Lehr's terms, they may follow the flow of family interaction, oppose particular family members on a symmetrical, same-generational basis or bystand family process by moving to the perifery of the family group when they consult with their cotherapists.

The distinction between conductors and reactors is based to a large extent on the charisma of the therapist: "Many of the conductors are vigorous personalities who can hold audiences spellbound. . . . The reactors have, on the whole, less compelling public personalities" (Beels and Ferber, 1969, p. 286).

Beels and Ferber place the conductor-reactor dimension in a superordinate relationship to the analyst/systems theorist distinction, by subsuming both theoretical orientations within the reactor group. As conductors they include: Ackerman and Satir as the "East and West

Coast charismatic leaders," respectively (p. 286); Bowen and Minuchin who are "artful stage directors;" Tharp and MacGregor of the Multiple Impact Therapy Group in Galveston, Texas; and N. Paul and J. E. Bell. As reactors-analysts they include people who explicity subscribe to psychoanalytic theory as well as people who utilize cotherapists. This includes Wynne's group; Boszormenyi-Nagy, Framo and associates in Philadelphia; and Whitaker. The reactors-systems purists include Jackson, Haley and Zuk, who, though active, have covert agendas in their work.

Foley (1974) compared five leading family therapists (Ackerman, Bowen, Jackson, Haley and Satir) in terms of three issues: "What is a family?" "What should the outcome of family therapy be?" and "How does a family change?" He also examined the therapists in terms of the emphasis given to eight specific aspects of therapy: history, diagnosis, affect, learning, values, conscious vs. unconscious, transference and therapist as teacher. Finally, he attempted to integrate the Group for the Advancement of Psychiatry's (1970) classification system (based on theoretical orientation) with Beels and Ferber's (1969) classification of family therapists according to the role played in therapy. He came up with the two-dimensional model displayed in Figure 1-1, although he did not attempt to place current approaches within the frame of reference of his model.

Guerin (1976) pointed out that the emphasis on the style of the therapist (conductor-reactor or active-observant) reflected an antitheory trend of the late 1960s and early 1970s. The antitheory stance emerged partly in response to the excesses of the ideological struggle taking place between the analysts and the systems people. Although the antitheorists

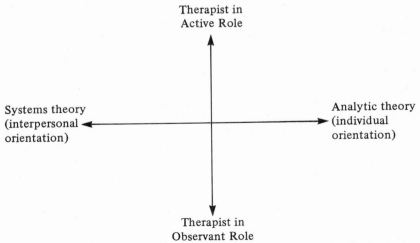

Figure 1-1: Foley's two-dimensional model for classifying family therapists (Foley, 1974, p. 132).

swung too far to the opposite extreme in asserting that theory was merely a rationalization for the practices of a given therapist, they did make a significant contribution in calling our attention to the need for a careful consideration of the relationship between theory and practice.

For his part, Guerin (1976) is more interested in developing a comprehensive theoretical classification of the schools of family therapy. Using the GAP schema as a starting point, he divided therapists into two basic groups—psychodynamic and systems—and then sketched in more fully the variety of approaches within each group. He divided the psychodynamic group into individual, group, experiential and Ackerman-type approaches. The individual subgroup is represented by dynamically-oriented therapists who occasionally see families. This is basically the Position A therapist of the GAP schema. Practitioners of family group therapy, such as J. E. Bell, Wynne and Beels use a psychodynamic group therapy orientation in which the family is defined as a particular type of group (a natural group as contrasted with an artifical group of strangers brought together for the purpose of therapy). He includes in the experiential subgroup therapists such as Whitaker and Ferber. Ackerman-type therapists include Nathan and Norman Ackerman and Israel Zwerling. The systems group includes three subgroups: strategic family therapy (Haley, Jackson, Watzlawick, Weakland); structural family therapy (Minuchin); and Bowenian family systems theory and therapy.

As Guerin pointed out, the style of the therapist is less important as a classificatory criterion than theoretical orientation. The question of the relationship between theory and practice should be examined, but on a school-by-school basis, after the schools have been classified according to their theoretical orientations. However, the classification of theoretical orientations in family therapy along a single dimension, with individually-based psychodynamic theory at one end and multipersonal systems theory at the other, does not do justice to the full range of theoretical positions. For example, Guerin's inclusion of the experiential therapists within the psychodynamic group ignores the fact that experiential therapists draw their theoretical orientation from existentialism and phenomenology rather than psychoanalysis.

Although classifying family approaches along a single dimension will not do, classifications such as Steidl's and Wexler's (1977), which simply describes several schools of therapy (communications, psychodynamic, structural and the Bowen theory) without attempting to systematically describe the differences and similarities between them are also unsatisfactory.

RITTERMAN'S PARADIGMATIC CLASSIFICATION SCHEME

Ritterman (1977) attempted the much more ambitious task of developing a paradigmatic classification of family therapy theories. She differentiated two of the systems schools—communicational and structural—in terms of their "pretheoretical assumptions" or commitments to philosophical world views.

Ritterman starts by describing two world views—the "mechanistic" and the "organismic"—in terms of their "corollary model issues," which are contextually determined concepts which "shape any less general theoretical model derived from a world view" (p. 30). The mechanistic or Newtonian-Gallilean world view will demonstrate commitments to the primary corollary model issue of *elementarism* (the analysis of a phenomenon by breaking it down to its most fundamental or irreducible elements) and the secondary corollary model issue to *antecedent-consequent causality* (in which change is "represented as determined *not* by the form or organization of the phenomena at hand but by antecedent stimulation" p. 30). The organismic world view, derived from biology, will demonstrate commitments to the primary corollary model issue to *holism* (the position that the whole is greater than the sum of the parts due to its organization) and to the secondary corollary model issue of *reciprocal causality* (which "provides for a dialectical analysis of the relationships between part-processes in what is called the 'organized complexity' of the whole" p. 31).

Ritterman argues that the two systems theories under consideration—communicational and structural—demonstrate assumptions consistent with the corollary model issues of the mechanistic and organismic world views, respectively.

The communications systems theorists of the Mental Research Institute (Haley, Jackson, Watzlawick, Weakland) are committed to the methods of elementarism in their approach. This is evident from the most fundamental aspects of their approach, namely their tendency to analyze the family system by breaking it down to its most irreducible units—bits of communication or messages. Pathology is seen as the result of particular sequences of observable messages in which A leads to B leads to C, etc. (antecedent-consequent causality). Effective treatment is aimed at the removal of symptoms or the solving of problems (Haley, 1976) rather than the restructuring of the family system (Minuchin, 1974). Treatment consists of identifying the communicational sequences which maintain the symptom or problem and devising strategies for interrupting these sequences. The focus is on the use of messages with a particular content (often counter-paradoxical, e.g., Selvini-Pallazzoli et al., 1978) in order to disrupt sequences of messages with a particular content (often malignantly paradoxical).

In contrast, Minuchin's structural school demonstrates a commitment to a holistic approach:

> In essence, the structural approach to families is based on the concept that a family is more than the individual biopsychodynamics of its members. Family members relate according to certain arrangements, which govern their transactions. These arrangements, though usually not explicitly state or even recognized, form a whole—the structure of the family. The reality of the structure is of a different order from the reality of the individual members (Minuchin, 1974, p. 89).

Rather than analyzing sequences of messages, communication is observed in order to infer the hypothetical structure of the family. Structural family therapists move away from the observable, toward the inferential; away from content, toward form; away from the particular sequence of behavioral events, toward the organization of the whole. The aim of therapy is the restructuring of the family rather than the removal of symptoms. Treatment consists of three processes: 1) joining the family in a position of leadership to form the therapeutic system; 2) evaluating the family experientially, by participating in its processes, in order to derive an interactional diagnosis; and 3) restructuring the family system. In regard to the third step, note the contrast between the approach of the structural school, which often uses symptoms in order to change structure, and that of the communications school, which changes patterns in order to solve problems.

Extension of the Schema

Ritterman's schema could be extended to take into account other schools of family therapy. This broadened schema would classify schools of family therapy along two dimensions: whether they adhere to an elementaristic-analytic or a holistic approach; and whether they focus on the internal subjective states of the individual members of the family or on the external behavior of the multipersonal family group. This scheme is presented in Figure 1-2.

Psychodynamic family therapy is in Quadrant I as the main representative of elementaristic-analytic theories which focus on the internal subjective states of individual family members. Psychodynamic family therapy is based on psychoanalytic theory. Psychoanalytic theory is concerned with the search for the fundamental elements of experience, which are seen as rooted in the conflict between sexual and aggressive drives and societal restraints against their expression. All experience may be reduced to this fundamental dilemma. A creative act, for example, may be analyzed by examining the transformation of basic sexual drives by certain ego defense mechanisms (i.e., sublimation). Personality structure and development is analyzed in terms of the vicissitudes of the conflict between instinctual drive and societal restraint (as represented by ones' parents) as it is played out during the first five years of life.

Psychodynamic family therapy is concerned with the unconscious aspects of family members' relationships to each other. Particular reference is made to object relations theory, which holds that we internalize (introject) images (objects) of the nurturing but frustrating parents of our infancy in order to control them. We hold on to these images or objects long after they cease to be appropriate, in order to avoid the pain of losing them. These introjected objects of the past have enormous importance in the present; we seek representatives of them in our present lives, to whom we relate, in part, as if they were these objects. This is known as a "narcissistic relationship," similar to transference phenomena in therapy. Family systems are seen as interlocking

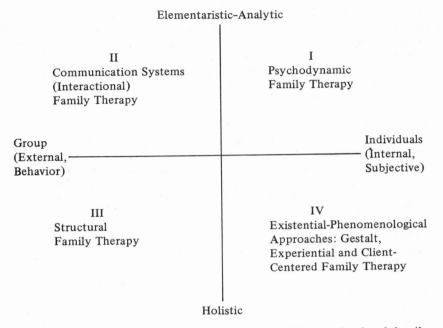

Figure 1-2: Two dimensional schema for classifying schools of family therapy according to the nature of the theoretical orientation (elementaristic-analytic vs. holistic and focus on individual vs. group).

networks of bilateral narcissistic relationships. Therapy is a working-through process analogous to psychoanalytically-oriented individual therapy. The transference of family members to each other and to the therapists is interpreted with the aim of helping individual family members give up their attachments to introjected objects, thus clearing the way for less distortion in their relationships with family members and others.

A number of workers have contributed to the development of psychodynamic family therapy. These include Wynne and associates at the National Institute for Mental Health (NIMH) and later at the University of Rochester; Lidz and associates at Yale University; Ackerman and associates in New York; Framo and associates at the Eastern Pennsylvania Psychiatric Institute (EPPI); Friedman and associates at the Philadelphia Psychiatric Center; Zinner and Shapiro at NIMH; Searles at Chestnut Lodge; Paul in Boston; Beels in the Bronx; and Epstein and associates in Montreal.

In Quadrant II are elementaristic-analytic approaches which focus on the external behavior of the family group. The primary representative is communication systems family therapy (also known as interactional family psychotherapy—Greenberg, 1977). The communication systems school developed on the West Coast. It grew out of Bateson's research project on communication in families with a schizophrenic member and was based at the Mental Research Institute (MRI), founded in Palo Alto, California, in 1959 under the leadership of Jackson. Satir joined during the first year. She was followed three years later by Haley, Weakland and Watzlawick. In the same year, MRI and Ackerman's Family Institute cofounded *Family Process*, the first professional journal of the field.

In the mid and later 1960s MRI suffered several major losses. Haley left to work with Minuchin at the Philadelphia Child Guidance Clinic. Satir left to become the first director of training at the Esalen Institute in Big Sur, California. The type of therapy for which she has become known represents a blending of a concern with communication with a humanistic frame of reference. In 1968, Jackson died. With the loss of these three major figures, the importance of MRI receded until the mid 1970s when, under the leadership of Watzlawick, Weakland and Fisch (1974), it became known for a refined form of the earlier approach to family therapy. This is a brief, problem-focused therapy which shares many elements in common with Haley's (1976) recently developed problem-solving therapy.

In Quadrant III are holistic theories concerned with the external behavior of the family group. The primary representative of this type of family therapy is structural family therapy; developed by Minuchin and associates at the Wiltwyck School in New York and later at the Philadelphia Child Guidance Clinic.

In Quadrant IV are the existential-phenomenological theories of family therapy, as the representative of holistic theories concerned with the internal subjective states of individual family members. There are several variants of this type of family therapy. First, there is Gestalt family therapy. The best known practitioner and conceptualizer of this approach is probably Kempler (1974), who was an associate of Perls at Esalen and now has his own institute in Southern California. However, in recent years a number of other workers have contributed to this approach (Hatcher, 1978; Kaplan and Kaplan, 1978; Rabin, in Levant et al., 1980).

Experiential family therapy was developed by Whitaker and associates at Emory University in Atlanta and, from 1965 on, at the University of Wisconsin. This approach to family therapy is probably the most atheoretical of all (Whitaker, 1976). In fact, the only real theoretical foundation this group has is psychodynamic theory, in which they were trained. This school represents, for the most part, a highly developed intuitive form of therapy, relying on the "left-hemisphere craziness" of its practitioners (which also include Warkentin, Malone, Napier and Ferber).

Client-centered family therapy is the newest entrant into the field. Drawing chiefly from the theories of Rogers (1951, 1972), an attempt has been made to extend client-centered thinking into the area of the family.

This approach has conceptualized the family system as an internal subjective phenomenon inherent in each family member. The chief workers in this area are van der Veen at the Institute for Juvenile Research in Chicago (Raskin and van der Veen, 1970) and Levant (1978a, 1978b) at Boston University.

The progression of schools of family therapy from Quadrant I to Quadrant II to Quadrant III to Quadrant IV represents a chronological sequence, and also a dialectical process. Psychodynamic family therapy can be seen as thesis, in so far as it was an extension of the psychoanalytic thinking which held sway in the field in the 1940s and 1950s. Communication systems theory can be viewed an antithesis, analogous to the role played by behavior modification in relation to psychoanalysis in the field of individual therapy. Structural family therapy represents, to a limited extent, the synthesis, in so far as it takes into account the defensive structures of the individuals in the family. Existential-phenomenological approaches have not contributed much to the clash of ideologies, coming onto the scene later and also playing a role analogous to that of Third Wave (Maslow) played by humanistic theories in the field of individual therapy.

Analysis of the Schema

Ritterman's (1977) schema, with this extension of it, is useful for some purposes, but there are some problems with it. First of all, the model loses credibility when Ritterman portrays one theory as inherently less valid than the other because it is based on an older world view. She makes the mistake of assuming that a philosophy or world view which is associated with a particular theory in the natural sciences—one which is accepted as more valid and inclusive than older theories in the natural sciences—is necessarily more valid when applied to the social sciences. Although it would be ideal to have a scientific theory that is so generally valid that it is able to explain phenomena as diverse as the behavior of subatomic particles and the dynamics of family systems, science has not progressed to that point at this time.

In our era, the social sciences remain considerably less developed than the natural sciences. Whereas the natural sciences have a relatively unified body of general theory, the social sciences have a cacophony of theories and conceptual frameworks for which we are not even able to specify with precision the domains of their application. What is needed in the social sciences now is less emphasis on the promotion of particular theoretical orientations and more emphasis on the empirical determination of the actual range of application of particular theories. With regard to theories of family therapy we need to know *which* approach rendered by *whom* is the most effective for *this* family with *that* specific dysfunction in *this* context and under *these* circumstances (Paul, 1967).

A second problem with this model is that it exaggerates the difference between communication systems and structural family therapy. Although it may be true that the two theories differ dramatically in their commitments to certain world views, it is unlikely that this has a tremendous bearing on the operational theories of the two schools. Remember that Haley contributed to the development of both approaches, and that there is much overlap between them. Although there are pragmatic consequences to distinguishing elementaristic from holistic theories with regard to the individually-oriented schools, the pragmatic importance of this distinction shrinks when viewed in relation to the group-oriented theories. Therefore, this dimension of pretheoretical assumptions gives a somewhat distorted picture and may not be the most useful way to characterize family therapy theories.

A third problem with the model is that, although it improves upon earlier schemata, it still does not do justice to the full range of family therapy theories. In particular, it is difficult to know where to place Bowen's multigenerational theory. One could make a case for placement in Quadrant III, along with Minuchin's structural theory, because of its treatment of the structural aspects of families in a holistic manner. But then, what about Bowen's emphasis on individuals? This is seen both in his theory of the family, in which the concept of differentiation of self is a central one, and in his approach to therapy, which emphasizes the increasing differentiation of individual family members. Bowen's theory is actually a synthesis of individual and multipersonal systems perspectives, one which parallels very closely a psychodynamic frame of reference with regard to individuals, but which operates out of a holistic perspective. Bowen has commented on this in terms of his concept of detachment:

> When it was possible to attain a workable level of interested detachment, it was then possible to begin to defocus the individual and to focus on the entire family at once . . . Once it was possible to focus on the family as a unit, it was like shifting a microscope from the oil immersion to the low power lens, or like moving from the playing field to the top of the stadium to watch a football game. Broad patterns of form and movement that had been obscured in the close-up view became clear. The close-up view could then become more meaningful once the distant view was also possible (Bowen, 1960, p. 351).

Boszormenyi-Nagy's intergenerational theory presents a similar dilemma with regard to placement in the model. Fundamentally a psychodynamically oriented approach, it is able to adopt a systemic frame of reference. In addition, it admires significant elements of existential phenomenology (Boszormenyi-Nagy and Spark, 1973).

Thus, despite its promise, the schema has several serious flaws: It portrays some theories as inherently less valid than others; it exaggerates the differences between certain theories; and it does not easily accommodate certain important theories of family therapy.

A NEW PARADIGMATIC MODEL

At this point a fresh approach was needed. Nearly 15 years have passed since the GAP report predicted the blending of psychodynamic and systems concepts. This has occurred to a significant extent. Moreover, in the 25 years since the beginning of the family therapy movement, concepts have been borrowed from all sorts of places and integrated with disparate models and theories. The important thing to notice is that the process of theory construction took place in response to the tremendous wealth of new data and experience which emerged from the unprecedented phenomenon of working clinically with whole families.

Given this state of affairs, it seemed much more appropriate to examine inductively the models that have been elaborated to explain the new data than to impose external categories (such as world views) on the field deductively. Using a qualitative factor analytic method to first determine if the schools of family therapy clustered into conceptually, and pragmatically meaningful groups, and then to determine the factors which distinguished these groups, one first order factor and one second order factor emerged. The first order factor concerns the time perspective taken in working with the family, whether oriented to the past (historical) or the present (ahistorical). The second order factor pertains only to the present-oriented or ahistorical group. It concerns whether the therapy focuses on changing the structure or process of the family as a social organization, or on providing an intense affective experience for the members of the family. The three clusters of family therapy schools are: historical approaches; structure/process approaches; and experiential approaches. These clusters constitute therapeutic paradigms.

The historical paradigm includes the psychodynamic (Wynne, Lidz, Ackerman, Framo, Friedman, Zinner, Shapiro, Searles, Paul, Beels and Epstein), multigenerational (Bowen), and intergenerational (Boszormenyi-Nagy and Spark) schools of family therapy. These approaches are concerned with the person within the system, with particular attention to those elements of his/her interpersonal functioning which represent attachments to figures in the past and which will be transmitted to future generations. In these approaches there is a fundamental commitment to psychodynamic theory. Yet, through the integration of systemic concepts, the perspective has broadened so that it can include the larger picture of the interactional patterns—and transmission of interactional patterns over generations—of a family of individuals (each of whom is viewed in psychodynamic of psychodynamic-compatible terms).

In general, the approach to therapy in these schools involves freeing individuals from their excessive attachments to the previous generation. This occurs through a process of uncovering these attachments, gaining insight into their inappropriateness and gradually giving them up. The therapist's role involves facilitation of this process, either through the interpretation of the relationship between past attachments and present behavior or through "coaching" (Bowen) clients as they attempt to form more appropriate, present-oriented, adult relationships with members of their families of origin.

The structure/process paradigm includes the communication systems or interactional (Jackson, Haley, Watzlawick, Weakland), problem-solving (Haley), brief problem focused (Watzlawick, Weakland, Fisch), strategic (Rabkin), triadic (Zuk), structural (Minuchin) and behavioral (Patterson) schools of family therapy, as well as the work of family therapists such as V. Satir, R. Bandler, J. Grinder, M. Selvini-Palazzoli, L. Hoffman and P. Papp. These approaches are concerned with the current patterns of interaction of the family and the relationship of these patterns with the symptoms or presenting problem of the index patient. There is some variation among these schools in whether the interactional patterns are viewed from a structural (Minuchin) or process (Satir) perspective, whether the primary aim is to change the structure or remove the symptom, and whether the orientation is drawn from systems theory or learning theory. But as a group they differ sharply from the historical approaches in dismissing history-taking, uncovering, interpretation and insight as irrelevant to the treatment process, and in focusing at the system level with little or no consideration given to the psychology of the individual. They also contrast sharply with the experiential therapists in playing down the importance of affect in the treatment process.

The approach to therapy involves reordering the family system in order to remove the dysfunctional elements which produced or maintain the symptom. The therapist's role is that of expert; his or her job is to diagnose the dysfunctional elements of the system and plan a series of interventions which will alleviate them. Directives, often paradoxical ones, are used as means toward this end.

It is interesting to compare these two therapeutic paradigms (the historical and the structure/process) in terms of the time required for therapy. The historical paradigm is notoriously long-term, so only exceptionally well-motivated families and individuals are able to undergo the entire process. On the other hand, the structure/process paradigm has been able to achieve dramatic results with symptom relief in a very short period of time. Compare, for example, the two statements below. The first is from a psychodynamic family therapist; the second is from a structural family therapist.

> There are centers in the country who see a family for only several months, offering a family therapy program which does not go beyond what we consider the preliminary phases of treatment. (Framo, 1965, p. 166)

*   *   *   *

Family transformation does not follow a single intervention

but requires a continuous involvement in the direction of the therapeutic goal. But many therapists spend years meandering in the middle phases of therapy because they have lost the sense of direction that a family map makes explicit. (Minuchin, 1974 p. 14)

The experiential paradigm includes Gestalt (Kempler, Rabin, Hatcher, the Kaplans), experiential (Whitaker, Warkentin, Malone, Napier, Ferber), and client-centered (van der Veen, Levant) school of family therapy. These approaches are concerned more with enhancing the quality of life of the individuals in the family than with alleviating symptoms or changing the family system. These schools are based principally on existential-phenomenological theoretical orientations.

In general the approach to therapy in these schools involves providing an intensified affective experience for family members, in order that their own restorative and self-actualizing processes will take hold. The therapist's role is facilitative, following and reflecting the process of family interaction and joining the family process as a genuine and nondefensive person. Some go into the therapy intent on having a growth experience for themselves, knowing that this will stimulate the family to do the same.

Summary

In summary, the new paradigmatic model proposes a classification of the field of family therapy in terms of three therapeutic paradigms: the historical, the structure/process and the experiential. These three paradigms are mutually exclusive, but taken together form an inclusive classification of existing schools of family therapy. They are more general than schools or theories of family therapy, as each paradigm subsumes several schools of family therapy. These groups of schools share certain formal characteristics, particularly in regard to their operational premises concerning the nature of family dysfunction and the process of therapeutic change.

It is hoped that this paradigmatic model will be helpful in terms of providing both an orientation to the field for newcomers and a basis for evaluative comparisons of distinct approaches to family therapy.

REFERENCES

Alexander, I.E. Family therapy. *Marriage and Family Living*, 1963, 25, 146-154.
Beels, C.C. and Ferber, A. Family therapy: A view. *Family Process*, 1969, 8, 280-332.
Bergin, A.E. The evaluation of therapeutic outcomes. In A.E. Bergin and S.L. Garfield (Eds,), *Handbook of Psychotherapy and Behavior Change*. New York: John Wiley & Sons, 1971.
Boszormenyi-Nagy, I. and Spark, G.M. *Invisible Loyalties*. Hagerstown,

Md.: Harper & Row, 1973.

Bowen, M. A family concept of schizophrenia. In D.D. Jackson (Ed.), *The Etiology of Schizophrenia.* New York: Basic Books, 1960.

Foley, V.D. *An Introduction to Family Therapy.* New York: Grune & Stratton, 1974.

Framo, J.L. Rationale and techniques of intensive family therapy. In I. Boszormeny-Nagy and J.L. Framo (Eds.), *Intensive Family Therapy: Theoretical and Practical Aspects.* Hagerstown, Md.: Harper & Row, 1965.

Greenberg, G.S. The family interactional perspective: A study and examination of the work of Don D. Jackson. *Family Process,* 1977, 16, 385-412.

Group for the Advancement of Psychiatry. *Treatment of Families is Conflict: The Clinical Study of Family Process.* New York: Jason Aronson, 1970.

Guerin, P.J., Jr. Family therapy: The first twenty-five years. In P.J. Guerin, Jr. (Ed.), *Family Therapy: Theory and Practice.* New York: Gardner Press, 1976.

Haley, J. Whither family therapy. *Family Process,* 1962, 1, 69-100.

Haley, J. *Problem Solving Therapy.* San Francisco: Jossey-Bass, 1976.

Hatcher, C. Intrapersonal and interpersonal models: Blending Gestalt and family therapies. *Journal of Marriage and Family Counseling,* 1978, 4(1), 63-68.

Kantor, D. and Lehr, W. *Inside the Family: Toward a Theory of Family Process.* San Francisco: Jossey-Bass, 1975.

Kaplan, M.L. and Kaplan, N.R. Individual and family growth: A Gestalt approach. *Family Process,* 1978, 17, 195-206.

Kempler, W. *Principles of Gestalt Family Therapy.* Salt Lake City: Deseret Press, 1974.

Levant, R. Family therapy: A client-centered perspective. *Journal of Marriage and Family Counseling,* 1978, 4(2), 35-42. (a)

Levant, R. Client-centered approaches to working with the family: An overview of new developments in therapeutic, educational and preventive methods. *International Journal of Family Counseling,* 1978, 6(1), 31-44. (b)

Levant, R., Longin, E., Doyle, G., and Rabin, M. *The Field of Family Therapy: A Paradigmatic Classification and Presentation of Three Major Approaches.* Symposium presented at Annual Convention, American Personnel and Guidance Association, Atlanta, March, 1980.

Minuchin, S. *Families and Family Therapy.* Cambridge: Harvard University Press, 1974.

Paul, G.L. Strategy of outcome research in psychotherapy. *Journal of Consulting Psychology,* 1967, 31, 109-118.

Raskin, N.J. and van der Veen, F. Client-centered family therapy: Some clinical and research perspectives. In J.T. Hart and T.M. Tomlinson (Eds.), *New Directions in Client-Centered Therapy,* Boston: Houghton Mifflin, 1970.

Ritterman, M.K. Paradigmatic classification of family therapy theories. *Family Process,* 1977, 16, 29-48.

Rogers, C.R. *Client-Centered Therapy.* Boston: Houghton Mifflin, 1951.

Rogers, C.R. *Becoming Partners.* New York: Dell, 1972.

Selvini-Palazzoli, M., Cecchin, G., Prata, G., and Boscolo, L: *Paradox and Counter-Paradox: A New Model in the Therapy of the Family in Schizophrenic Transaction.* New York: Jason Aronson, 1978.

Steidl, J.H. and Wexler, J.P. What's a clinician to do with so many approaches to family therapy? *The Family,* 1977, 4, 59-66.

Watzlawick, P., Weakland, J., and Fisch, R. *Change: Principles of Problem Formation and Problem Resolution.* New York: W.W. Norton & Co., 1974.

Whitaker, C. The hindrance of theory in clinical work. In P.J. Guerin, Jr. (Ed.), *Family Therapy: Theory and Practice.* New York: Gardner Press, Inc., 1976.

Zuk, G.H. Family therapy: 1964-1970. *Psychotherapy: Theory, Research and Practice,* 1971, 8, 90-97.

Zuk, G.H. Family therapy: Clinical hodgepodge or clinical science? *Journal of Marriage and Family Counseling,* 1976, 2(4), 299-303.

ORGANIZING TREATMENT AROUND THE FAMILY'S PROBLEMS AND THEIR STRUCTURAL BASES

HARRY J. APONTE

In a structural approach to family therapy the therapist works to change the structural organization of systems.[1] He conceptualizes the problems presented to him by the family as products of the way the family structure is functioning. He thinks of therapy as a "structural means of resolving conflicts, inconsistencies, and ambiguities that arise between the different elements of the . . . structure."[2]

The family system is made up of a complex of subsystems. Each system or subsystem includes two or more family members organized around a family related function. Two family members make up different systems according to the purpose of their relationship at any given moment. For example, two adults in a family can form both a parent subsystem and a spouse subsystem, and at various times their cooperative behavior may be guided more by the rules of one system or the other. The structures these systems are based on are specific to each relationship. The structure refers to the rules that order the manner in which persons in a system organize the various elements that go into the relationship they are forming.[3] A man in a spouse system may be a dominating tyrant and may be accepted as such, if not happily, by his wife. That spouse system is founded, in part, upon the qualities that make up this dominant husband—accepting wife relationship, which means that this spouse system will tend to produce certain predictable behaviors in various situations specifically related to that particular structure. To guess what movie they will attend on a Friday night one need only know what movie the husband wants to see, since it is his wish that will be satisfied.

Systems depend on systems and the couple's system depends on both larger systems (e.g., community) and smaller systems (e.g., individual

From H.J. Aponte, Organizing Treatment Around the Family's Problems and Their Structural Bases, *Psychiatric Quarterly*, 48:209-22. Courtesy of Human Sciences Press, New York.

personalities). Let us say that the wife in this particular spouse system had been a very young and sheltered woman when she first married. Let us also say that she matures with age and experience and becomes increasingly depressed about her lack of self-expression in the marriage. The couple becomes unhappy because of the wife's depression and asks for help. The therapist may remedy the situation by helping the two change the structure of the spouse relationship so that the husband is less dominant and the wife more assertive. The wife's wishes would consequently be more attended to, and she would no longer be depressed. And, if the husband learns to enjoy his more self-expressive wife, the spouse system would be happy based on a different, more equitably balanced structure.

This is a gross oversimplification of what happens between couples, and certainly of the more complex situation encountered in families with children. However, the point has been made, and we can proceed to some examples of how a therapist determines the structural bases of family systems that have produced problems serious enough to warrant a request for therapy from the family.

The therapist is meeting with the family for one purpose—to solve these problems. He wants to know concretely from each of the family members what specific *problems* he or she is bringing to him for solution. The identification of the problem will permit the therapist to relate himself to the issues for which the family members have some motivation to change. The more specific the definition of the problem, the more specific can be the definition of its structural base.

The therapist needs to elicit a statement of the problem from each of the family members, and to have them interact with one another around the issue of their problems in order to begin assessing what the family structure is and how the relationships between the members or *participants* are creating the problem for which they seek help.[4] He needs to know how each family member is participating in the problem so that he can understand the structural underpinnings of the problem. But he needs to know the participants—not just to understand who is helping to create the problem, but also to know who can contribute to resolving it. This inquiry may certainly move the therapist not only to look at smaller subsystems within the family, but also outside of the nuclear family organization and into the extended family and larger social organizations. A whole set of overlapping systems can contribute to the development of a problem as well as to its solution. Just as relatives and friends can make a couple suffer, they can also contribute to the solution of a specific marital problem that a couple has. How narrowly or broadly a therapist will go in defining those systems specifically related to maintaining or eradicating a problem will depend on the nature of the problem and on the kind of system he is trained to work with. He may work primarily with the nuclear family or with a large network.[5] The therapist working with the larger network does not negate the operation of the smaller systems, but he does see and work with the ties among many more and broader systems. He would be more likely to say to relatives and friends, "If you are not part of the solution, you are part of the problem." By not acting to change it they are in fact supporting its maintenance. Or he may concentrate on the structure of the nuclear family—and should a change in a related larger system be required, he may seek to create a ripple effect by supporting the change of the smaller unit as the fuse that will set off the other, larger system to change.

According to the nature of the problem and its host structure, the therapist will engage a specified number of participants and seek to obtain commitments from them to help change certain structural relationships of which they are a part. In these commitments lie the *pledges* for change in treatment. The pledges or contracts are commitments by members of a system to seek agreed-upon changes through agreed-upon means. A pledge may, for example, involve family tasks, tailored specifically to the structural changes called for.

CASES

In the examples that follow, the author will attempt to present material organized conceptually according to problems, participants, and pledges based on the structural viewpoint of family functioning. The examples will not attempt to discuss the interviewing techniques of the therapist nor his process with the family outside of the aspects of the work which we are abstracting for the thesis of this paper.

The R. family brought in their 12-year-old boy as their delinquent. The boy himself joined dutifully in accusing himself as the deviant in their family system. Yet their evidence for grievous misdeed was indeed shallow. Their overreadiness to nail the delinquent label on him suggested to the therapist early in the first interview that the deviance-labeling itself was more the immediate issue than anything else.[6] The family members with the cooperation of the 12-year-old had organized to make him their point of stress, their steam vent.

The therapist responded to the family's request to stop the boy's delinquency by focusing attention on the family's other problem areas from which the stress on the boy was being displaced, thereby beginning to remove the deviant or delinquent label from the 12-year-old. Within 10 minutes of the first interview, the therapist sought implicitly to begin changing the boy's scapegoat function by offering to give his interest and concern to the problems of the other members of the family. Within this context he learned that the mother of the "delinquent" felt harassed and inadequate as a mother, the 14-year-old brother was maintained homebound as his mother's helper, and the 10-year-old sister was being spoiled and protected as mother's pet, creating a feeling of jealousy in the other siblings. The therapist effectively gave these issues more importance than the delinquent's sins and simultaneously offered support and hope for solutions for these problems. The family members responded by beginning to talk with the therapist as if these were the problems for which they had come for help. This contract was never explicitly made but the therapist's extending of his interest and the family's responsiveness was a contract, nevertheless, to deal with the structures in the family that were creating these other problems.

This contract eventually paid off for them in a reorganization of the family structure that provided the mother with more support and help at home from her children and a chance to feel some freedom from her household and family duties. Their pledges made possible the release of the 14-year-old from his homemaking enchainment and a more realistic treatment of the 10-year-old (which was not quite so appreciated by her, however). In the process the delinquent stopped being a delinquent without effort directed specifically by the therapist toward changing the boy's so-called bad behavior.

The reidentification of the problem was in itself the cornerstone of the cure of the 12-year-old's misbehavior. It meant spreading the stress in this family system throughout the structure and away from one of the participants in the problem. Towards the end of the treatment the therapist did spend some time with this boy alone to help him consolidate his new position. He also met the boy and his mother to help clarify and dispel some of the stigma attached to the question of who his father was, wherein apparently lay the foundation for the beginnings of the deviant position of the boy vis-a-vis the family. The boy suspected but did not know that his father was not the same as the other children's and was of a race other than the rest of the family's.

The therapist also tried to intervene in the boy's school system to help remove him from his scapegoat classification there. The therapist failed with the school, but the boy eventually worked himself out of this position with the strengths that he gained from the change in his position within the family structure.

The therapist's approach to the problems of the R. family can be outlined according to the systems and subsystems implicit in the identification of the participant groupings.

1. *problem*— a 12-year-old "delinquent"
   participants— the boy, his family and his school
   pledges— the boy and his family will work on other family problems with the therapist
   a pledge between the school and the family would have been useful, but the school would not work with the boy, his family and the therapist; therefore no pledge was made
   a. *problem*— an overburdened mother
      participants— the mother and children
      pledges— mother and children will work with therapist to re-distribute more of the household responsibilities among the

children, and to establish a more appropriate generational distance
between the mother and her children

b. *problem*— a 14-year-old homebound boy
participants—the boy, his mother and his siblings
pledges— mother and boy will work with the therapist on the
boy's assuming the responsibility and independence of the oldest
in sibling group and he will join the 12-year-old in more peer
activities

c. *problem*— a favored and pampered 10-year-old girl
participants— the girl, her mother and her siblings
pledges— girl and mother will work with therapist to achieve
a little more distance between mother and girl and to have girl
become more a part of her sibling subgroup

This ordering of the problems roughly follows the evolution of
the pledges in the therapy. While the family came in asking to make a
contract for #1, the 12-year-old's "delinquency," pledges a, b, and c were
implicitly agreed upon as part of the treatment package. These pledges
were all arrived at about the same time. In terms of the order in which
problems were worked on, a, b, and c preceded #1. The three problems
under a, b, and c were linked together by the common factor of the
family's structural enmeshment and disorganization.[7] There was no
generational boundary between mother and children and few personal
boundaries around each person's individual system. This threesome of
problems had its own relative autonomy and needed to be focused on
directly. The 12-year-old's scapegoat problem had relatively little
autonomy or steam of its own. It depended so much on the existence of
the other problems that with the solution of these other family
problems, it ceased to exist as an issue. After the rest of the family
problems were concluded, the therapist talked with the 12-year-old and
his mother about the boy's paternal origins to further solidify the boy's
new inclusion in the family. He stressed the boy's successful behavior in
school and at home to further reinforce his new position as a "good"
member of the family. In this last step, the therapist focused on the
mother-son subsystem.

In the second family, as in the first, we have interdependent problems,
two of which, however, were dealt with simultaneously. In the B. family
the 7-year-old's mother called the clinic to say that he kept running away
from home, probably because of his grandmother's recent death. He had
been close to her. With the problem identified as the running away, the
family was asked to come in as a group. The mother and son came
without the father. (They had not told him about the appointment.)
They proceeded to talk about the father as having mistreated the boy,
suggesting that this was the reason he ran away. They thus redefined
the participants in the problem of the running away as the father and
son, instead of the deceased grandmother and the boy.

The therapist would not agree on this definition of the problem and its participants without the father's input. The interview with the mother and son had been videotaped. With the mother's permission, this tape was shown to the father before the interview which the therapist held with the father and son. In this interview a problem between the father and the son was identified. The boy reacted to his father with a feeling of strangeness and the father's gruff manner with him also frightened the boy. The father, the boy and the therapist agreed to begin working on this father-son subsystem immediately. The father would try to communicate to the boy in a more gentle manner and would try to spend at least 15 minutes per day playing with him. The boy readily agreed to cooperate with this pledge.

In planning out this task, the father talked of his anticipation that the mother would interfere as she had done with almost everything he tried to do with the boy. He also told of how she had been responsible for a sizeable cut on the boy's forehead, and how he had to protect the boy from her after he had last run away from home. The therapist and the father tentatively agreed on the identification of another problem, the mother's interposing herself between the father and son, a structural problem in the mother-father-son system.

With the father's agreement a videotape of the interview of him with his son was shown to the mother the next time they returned. Then the mother and father met with the therapist. The videotape made possible the presentation by all family members of their respective perceptions of their problems. The third interview, which brought both parents together, gave them a chance to interact in relation to their respective perceptions. In talking about the father's statement that the mother interfered with his son and him, the therapist and the parents identified another problem, the intense power struggle between the parents. The parents agreed that as the parents had fought more the mother moved closer to her son. And consequently as the father withdrew from the mother, he also withdrew from his son, who had become more her son. The mother's bad temper with the boy was also touched on in the interview. Both these problems however, were seen as rooted in the power struggle between the parents—a problem related to the marital system. The parents and the therapist agreed that this issue, the marital struggle, must take a prominent position in the treatment.

The problem of the father-son relationship had some of its basis in the father's lack of a fathering model in his own childhood, and for this reason this father-son problem had some autonomy of its own. Therefore the father-son relationship was worked on parallel to the work being done by the couple and the therapist on the marriage. The marital problem, however, clearly took the greater concentration on the couple's part. The couple achieved a significant degree of resolution of the marital conflict. The parenting difficulties changed even more dramatically.

The evolution of the treatment contracts related to the various systems and subsystems in the B. family can be outlined as follows:

1. *problem*— 7-year-old boy running away from home
   participants— both parents and their son
   pledge— family will see problem as involving all three and will work with therapist accordingly
   a. *problem*— boy fears father
      participants— boy and father
      pledge— father will spend more time with son and will be more gentle
   b. *problem*— mother beating son
      participants— mother, son and father
      pledge— with father's support mother will stop hitting son and allow father to discipline him more
   c. *problem*— mother interposing self between father and son
      participants— father, mother and son
      pledge— mother will make room for father to care for son and parents will deal directly with one another about their differences and not through son
2. *problem*— power struggle between parents
   participants— the couple
   pledge— the couple will work on problem by talking with the therapist and by engaging in various tasks prescribed by therapist—e.g., on alternate weeks each spouse will assume responsibility for making all decisions relating to their relationship

This outline presents the problems roughly in the order they were identified by the therapist and the family members in the interviews. Problem #1 was never dealt with in the treatment after its initial identification because of its total dependence on the other problems. Problem #1a, related to the father-son subsystem, was explicitly worked on throughout the treatment. While it was dependent on the issues that follow it, it also had a certain degree of its own autonomy in that it was partly related to the father's somewhat aggressive manner and lack of personal experience with a father of his own. Problems #1b and #1c were so dependent on problem #2, the marital struggle, that they hardly had to be dealt with after the initial pledges for change in problem #2 were reached. Problem #2, the power struggle in the spouse subsystem, had its own autonomy from the other issues and was also the most stubbornly resistant to change. It took most of the energy and attention of the couple and the therapist, but it was focused on simultaneously with the father-son subsystem.

In the third family example we again look at a family treatment in which there are parent-child problems and marital problems which are worked on simultaneously. In the S. family, however, the parent-child problems took prominence equal to the marital problems during the first phase of treatment, in contrast to the B. family where the marriage was the preeminent issue.

The mother of a 13-year-old boy called the therapist to ask for help with the boy with whom she was in a continual struggle. The therapist asked her to come in with her family. She had said she was separated but to the therapist's surprise she came in with her husband. Their 12-year-old daughter also came. The father's obvious involvement in what was happening at home prompted the therapist in the first session to ask whether he was really living outside of the home. He was.

All four members of the family agreed on the presenting problem as the conflict between mother and son. In exploring the nature of the problem and the roles of its participants, however, it became clear that the father was an active participant in the power struggle between mother and son. The mother would call on the father repeatedly to enforce one of her rules. The father would proclaim his support. He would state to the boy his alliance with the mother about the issue, but then would remain quiet when the boy disobeyed. All the S. family members acknowledged that the father seldom agreed with his wife's rules or manner of trying to enforce them. It was a major factor in their separation. The father formed the triangle to the mother-son relationship, allying himself with the boy against the mother.

However, the physical separation of the parents did not alter the basic structures of the family system. The therapist identified the participants in the problem of the mother-son conflict as both parents and the boy. The family agreed. To decide on the treatment contract, however, they needed to clarify what family structures they wanted. If the mother were to handle her son in the manner of a fully independent, separated woman, she would need to participate in the treatment with her son, and herself assume the burden of the solution of the problem. If she wished to share the responsibility with her separated husband, then the parental couple would have to agree to work on the problem together even though they remained physically apart. The definition of these issues was the substance of the first interview. The father would need to de-triangulate either by allying himself with the mother in the discipline of their son, or else by disassociating himself from the disciplining of the boy.

The second interview occurred two weeks later (a delay caused by holidays). When the family returned they announced that the parents had reunited. They had been separated seven months. They not only wanted to work together on the problem with their son, but they also wanted help with their marriage. The parents chose to reform their alliance. The therapist and the family agreed on two-stage sessions to start; first, father and mother to discuss their marital problems, and second, the parents and the boy to deal with parent—child conflict. This structure of the sessions permitted the parents to build a fence around their marital relationship that would prevent their son from interposing himself between the pair, and it also provided a forum wherein they would have the opportunity to work together in relation to their son.

As the family began to look more closely at the mother-son conflict, however, it became apparent to all that a problem of equal seriousness existed between mother and daughter. The conflict between mother and son was one of an open conflict of wills. (The mother, an insecure person, tended to control everyone around her, a problem related not only to her past but also to the uncertain marital situation she had lived in for years.) The daughter was in the meantime disengaged from the home and from school, but no one seemed aware or concerned. Once given the opportunity, she told of feeling of no importance to anyone. It bothered her most that her mother, to whom she had been closely attached when younger, was now preoccupied with the son in the family and the husband. In the treatment time, therefore, that had been allotted for the mother-son conflict, the family and the therapist also involved themselves in the mother-daughter conflict. The father, of course, was involved in both issues as he was fighting the mother through the son and was competing with the daughter for the mother's attention. The son was also competing with his sister for the mother's interest. The father was triangulating with the son against mother, and with the mother against daughter. The son was likewise trying to gain closeness to the mother through an intensely negative relationship which excluded his sister.

As with the B. family, the S. family also resolved its parent-child problems more quickly than the husband-wife conflicts. The parent-child problems had a degree of structural autonomy from the spouses' difficulties and so had to be attended to directly. The couple's marital conflict was not so essentially related to their difficulties in managing the children as to prevent them from making some changes in their handling of the children before improvement became very evident in the marriage. This phase of the treatment was terminated before the work with the married couple was brought to a conclusion.

The development of the treatment contracts with the S. family can be outlined as follows:

1. *problem*— mother-son conflict over control
   participants— mother, son and father
   pledge— with cooperation of mother and son, and the support of the therapist, the father will attempt not to fight mother through son and will himself take more responsibility for son
2. *problem**— many-leveled husband-wife conflict
   participants— husband and wife

---

*The children could be included in this formulation of the marriage problem, since by this time they were actively participating in the problem as conduits of mother-father attacks and as individuals seeking their own ends by aligning themselves with one or another parent. They are not included because their contribution to the marital struggle was decidedly secondary to what the marital couple was itself contributing to it.

pledge— agreement by both to seek change with therapist in how they act in regard to one another and to selves in marital relationship

3. *problem*— mother-daughter alienation
   participants— all four family members
   pledge— with the therapist, father and son will work at not competing so much with daughter for mother; mother will work on closing gap between daughter and herself.

As with the outlines for the R. and B. family problems, the problems of the S. family are listed in the order that they were identified and pledges were arrived at by family and therapist. Numbers 1 and 3 were dealt with as a package since they were so closely interwoven with one another in this parent-child sub-system. The parent-child problems had momentum of their own although they could not be conceptualized as separate from the marital friction. Because of the relative autonomy of the parent-child problems, these problems had to receive attention of their own. Because of the urgency of these parent-child conflicts, they needed to be worked on from the beginning along with the marriage conflict which was uppermost in the parents' minds. In this family, one has two sets of problems that have some autonomy while also being interdependent within the family system. The two sets of problems have an urgency which is comparable. This required that they be worked on at the same time, but when the parent-child problems were resolved, the marriage was attended to alone and for a considerable amount of time after the conclusion of the work on the child-related issues.

DISCUSSION

The *problems, participants,* and *pledges* have been illustrated in three examples. The examples themselves, however, warrant some further comment.

In the examples the autonomy and interdependence of problems, and their related structures to other problems and related structures in the family system, were often alluded to. While each of the problems listed in our examples was dependent on other family problems, the extent of its autonomy from the other problems varied from case to case. In our illustrations, the more dependent problems were resolved without special attention as the family and therapist found solutions to other problems on which these issues were dependent. For example, in problem #1 of the R. family, the scapegoat position of the 12-year-old ceased to be an issue when the rest of the problematic structures of the family were changed. On the other hand, there were problems which were quite autonomous from other issues in the family for their maintenance. These problems required attention and work in their own right even after other related problems in the family were resolved. An example here is the marital conflict, problem #2 in the B. family which, although intertwined with the parent-child problems, had a history of its own and required attention long after the parent-child problems were taken care of. The question of *autonomy or dependence* of problem-structures has relevance in determining which problems should be focused on first or given greater emphasis. In addition, however, the *degree of urgency* was also a factor in considering the order or emphasis that particular problems called for.

With respect to the concept of participants, it should be emphasized that this had to do with the *current participants* in maintaining the structures a problem was built on, not the participants in a past structure to which the problem was related. Also, the participants in maintaining the problem need to be distinguished from those who pledge participation in the solution. For example, the therapist was always a participant in the pledge though not a participant in the problem and not everyone who is part of the family structure that is feeding a problem will participate in its solution. Certainly, the closer one arrives at having unanimous participation of the members of the family system, and often these familial and social systems are the key to assisting a family change its internal problem-producing structures.

In thinking about the pledges of family members with the therapist, one must also realize that the pledges to work on a problem were not always explicitly made. They were understood at some level of awareness and perhaps were never overtly alluded to by the therapist or the family. This is exemplified in the R. family, in which the contracts to work on the problems in the scapegoat's family, problems, a, b, and c, were never overtly stated by either the therapist or the family members. The burden is on the sensitivity of the therapist to determine when he does have a contract to work. In fact, the family may sometimes enunciate an explicit pledge to which they are not really committed. The pledge, then, has not been made. One might add that this point about *implicitness* and *explicitness* can just as readily be made about the issues of what are the problems and who are the participants. Verbal acknowledgment may not only be unnecessary, but misleading with respect to the conviction of those making the acknowledgment of a problem or participation in its solution.

Finally, some further emphasis should be made about the therapist in the process of identifying problems and participants, and in the making of pledges. The therapist takes a very active part in this process. He, with the family members, forms a new unit, a new system, one in existence for the purpose of making changes in the family. It is this new structure which goes through the change process called therapy.

SUMMARY

The author has attempted in this paper to conceptualize family treatment in structural terms. He has described a therapeutic process in which the therapist helps members of a family system to agree on the *problem* they wanted to solve, the *participants* in the family structure to which the problem was related and, finally, the *pledges* of the participants in the structure to work on changing the structural basis of the problems presented by the family.

REFERENCES

1. Minuchin, S.: Structural family therapy. In: American Handbook of Psychiatry. Vol. III. Revised Edition. G. Caplan, editor. Basic Books. New York. 1972.
2. Lane, M.: Introduction. In: Introduction to Structuralism, p. 16. M. Lane, editor. Basic Books. New York. 1970.
3. Piaget, J.: Introduction. In: Structuralism, p. 5. C. Maschler, trans. and editor. Basic Books. New York. 1970.
4. Personal Communication from Jay Haley.
5. Speck, R.V., and Rueveni, U.: Network therapy—A developing concept. vol. VIII, No. II. In· Family Process. p. 182. Sept. 1969.
6. Hoffman, L.: Deviation—Amplifying process in natural groups. In: Changing Families, p. 295. J. Haley, editor. Grune and Stratton, New York, 1971.
7. Minuchin, S. et al.: The disorganized and disadvantaged family: Structure and process. In: Families of the Slums, pp. 192-242. Basic Books. New York. 1967.

Chapter 3

THE USE OF FAMILY THEORY
IN CLINICAL PRACTICE

Murray Bowen

In little more than one decade, family psychiatry has evolved from the relative unknown to a position of recognized importance on the psychiatric scene. The term "family therapy," or some variation of it, is known to the informed lay person. What is the origin and current status of the "family movement"? I believe it is a "movement," which I shall attempt to convey in this paper. Since there is disagreement even among leaders of the family movement about some of the critical theoretical and therapeutic issues, any attempt to explain or describe the family movement will represent the bias and viewpoint of the author. In this paper I shall present some of my ideas about circumstances that gave rise to the family movement and some ideas about the current status and future potential of the movement. The main body of the paper will be a presentation of my own theoretical orientation, which provides a blueprint for the clinical use of family psychotherapy.

I believe that the family movement began in the early and mid-1950s and that it grew out of an effort to find more effective treatment methods for the more severe emotional problems. In a broad sense, I believe it developed as an extension of psychoanalysis which had finally achieved general acceptance as a treatment method during the 1930s. Psychoanalysis provided useful concepts and procedures for the mass need of World War II, and a "new" era in psychiatry began. Within the course of a few years psychiatry became a hopeful, promising speciality for thousands of young physicians. Membership in the American Psychiatric Association increased from 3684 in 1945 to 8534 in 1955. Psychoanalytic theory had explanations for the total range of emotional problems, but standard psychoanalytic treatment techniques were not effective with the more severe emotional problems. Eager young psychiatrists began experimenting with numerous variations in the

---

From Murray Bowen, The Use of Family Theory in Clinical Practice, *Comprehensive Psychiatry*, 7: 345-74, 1966. Reprinted by permission of Grune & Stratton, Inc. and Murray Bowen.

treatment method. I believe the study of the family was one of these new areas of interest.

There are those who say the family movement is not new and that it goes back 25 years or more. There is some evidence to support the thesis that current family emphasis evolved slowly as the early psychoanalytic formulations about the family were put into clinical practice. In 1909 Freud reported the treatment of "Little Hans,"[1] in which he worked with the father instead of the child. In 1921 Flugel published his well-known book, *The Psycho-analytic Study of the Family.*[2] There was the development of child analysis and the beginning of the child guidance movement in which it became standard procedure for a social worker or second therapist to work with parents in addition to the primary psychotherapy with the child. Later, the child guidance principles were adapted to work with adults, both in inpatient and outpatient settings, in which a social worker or second therapist worked with relatives to suplement the primary psychotherapy with the patient. With these early theoretical and clinical awarenesses of the importance of the family, there is accuracy to the statement that "family" is not new. However, I believe that the current family direction is sufficiently important, new, and different to be viewed as a movement. I shall review some of the theoretical and clinical issues that seem important in this development.

Psychoanalytic theory was formulated from a detailed study of the individual patient. Concepts about the family were derived more from the patient's perceptions than from direct observations of the family. From this theoretical position, the focus was on the patient and the family was outside the immediate field of theoretical and therapeutic interest. Individual theory was built on a medical model with its concepts of etiology, the diagnosis of pathology in the patient, and treatment of the sickness in the individual. Also inherent in the model are the subtle implications that the patient is the helpless victim of a disease or malevolent forces outside his control. A conceptual dilemma was posed when the most important person in a patient's life was considered to be the cause of his illness, and pathogenic to him. Psychiatrists were aware that the model did not quite fit and there were attempts to tone down the implicit starkness of the concepts, but the basic model remained. For instance, the concept of the unconscious postulated that the parent could be unconsciously hurtful while trying to help the child. This was different from what it would be if the hurt had been intentional or an irresponsible act of omission, but it still left the parent as "pathogenic." There were efforts to modify the diagnostic labels and there were even suggestions that labels be discarded, but a *patient* requires a *diagnosis* for his *illness* and psychiatry still operates with a medical model.

One of the most significant developments in the family movement, which distinguishes it from previous "family" work, is a change in the basic treatment process. Since the beginning of psychoanalysis, the analysis and resolution of the transference has been viewed as the primary therapeutic force for the treatment of emotional illness. Though modified by different "schools," the "therapeutic relationship" is the basic therapeutic modality used by most psychiatrists. The confidential, personal, and private nature of the relationship is considered essential for good therapy. Over the years there have been methods, rules, and even laws to guard this privacy. Since the beginning of the child guidance movement there have been efforts to involve the family in "treatment," but the "therapeutic" patient-therapist relationship was protected against intrusion and the family assigned secondary importance. Among those who initiated the current family movement were psychiatrists who, in addition to the patient's dilemma, began to pay more attention to the family side of the problem.

I believe the current family movement was started by several different investigators, each working independently, who began with either a theoretical or clinical notion that the family was important. As the focus shifted from the individual to the family, each was confronted with the dilemma of describing and conceptualizing the family relationship system. Individual theory did not have a conceptual model for a relationship system. Each investigator was "on his own" in conceptualizing his observations. One of the interesting developments has been the way investigators first conceptualized the system and the way these concepts have been modified in the past ten years. There were terms for the distortion and rigidity, the reciprocal functioning, and the "interlocking," "binding," "stuck togetherness" of the system. The following illustrates some of the terms used by a few of the early investigators. Lidz and Fleck used the concept "Schism and Skew,"[3] and Wynn and his co-workers used the concept "Pseudomutuality."[4] Ackerman, one of the earliest workers in the field, presented a conceptual model in his 1956 paper, "Interlocking Pathology in Family Relationships."[5] He also developed a therapeutic method which he calls "Family Therapy," which might be described as observing, demonstrating, and interpreting the "interlocking" to the family as it occurs in the family sessions. Jackson and his co-workers used a different model with the concept of the "Double Bind."[6] As I perceived his original position, he used communication theory to account for the relationship system and individual theory to account for functioning in the individual. His "Conjoint Family Therapy," which I interpret as the joining of individuals in family therapy, would be consistent with his conceptual scheme. I conceived of a preexisting emotional "stuck togetherness," the "Undifferentiated Family Ego Mass," and developed a therapeutic method for which I have used the term "Family Psychotherapy," which is designed to help individuals differentiate themselves from the "mass." Other investigators used a spectrum of slightly different terms to describe and conceptualize the same family phenomenon. As the years pass, the original concepts tend to be less "different."

CURRENT STATUS AND POSSIBLE FUTURE OF THE FAMILY MOVEMENT

The family movement is currently in what I have called a "healthy, unstructured state of chaos." The early investigators arrived at "family therapy" after preliminary clinical investigation and research. There may have been one exception to this general statement, recounted by Bell,[7] one of the earliest workers in the field. He misinterpreted a statement about psychotherapy for the family, following which he worked out his own plan to begin seeing family members together. After the idea of "family therapy" was introduced, the number of family therapists began to multiply each year. Most went directly into family therapy from their orientation in individual theory. Group therapists modified group therapy for work with families. As a result, the term "family therapy" is being used to refer to such a variety of different methods, procedures, and techniques that the term is meaningless without further description or definition. I consider this "healthy," because once a therapist begins seeing multiple family members together, he is confronted with new clinical phenomena not explained by individual theory, he finds that many previous concepts have become superfluous, and he is forced to find new theoretical concepts and new therapeutic techniques. The increasing number of family conferences become forums for discussion of experiences and acquiring new ways to conceptualize the family phenomenon.

A high percentage of therapists are using the term "family" to designate therapy methods in which two or more generations (usually parents and children) attend the sessions together, the term "marital therapy" when two spouses are seen together, and "individual therapy" when only one family member is seen by the therapist. The one most widely held concept of "family therapy," both within the profession and by the public, is that of entire families (usually parents and children) meeting together with the therapist while the family acquires the ability to verbalize and communicate thoughts and feelings to each other, with the therapist sitting alongside to facilitate the process and to make observations and interpretations. This I have called "family group therapy." In my experience, this can be amazingly effective as a short-term process for improving family communication. Even a slight improvement in communication can produce dramatic shifts in the feeling system, and even a period of exhilaration. I have not been able to use this as a long-term method for resolving underlying problems.

Although the family movement may continue to focus on "therapy" for many years to come, I believe the greatest contribution of "family" will come from the theoretical. I think the family movement rests on solid ground, that we have hardly scratched the surface in family research, and that "family" will grow in importance with each passing generation. The study of the family provides a completely new order of theoretical models for thinking about man and his relationship to nature and the universe. Man's family is a *system* which I believe follows the laws of natural systems. I believe knowledge about the family system may provide the pathway for getting beyond static concepts and into the functional concepts of systems. I believe that family can provide answers to the medical model dilemma of psychiatry, that family concepts may eventually become the basis for a new and different theory about emotional illness, and that this in turn will make its contribution to medical science and practice.

THEORETICAL AND CLINICAL ORIENTATION
OF THE AUTHOR

The primary goal of this presentation is to describe a specific theoretical and therapeutic system in which family theory serves as a blueprint for the therapist in doing family psychotherapy and also as a useful theoretical framework for a variety of clinical problems. A family orientation is so different from the familiar individual orientation that it has to be experienced to be appreciated. It is difficult for a person who thinks in terms of individual theory, and who has not had clinical experience with families, to "hear" family concepts. Some are better able to hear abstract theoretical ideas while others hear simple clinical examples. The first part of this section is designed as a bridge between individual and family orientations. To provide a variety of bridges, it will include a spectrum of clinical observations, broad abstract ideas, theoretical concepts, and some of my experiences as I shifted from an individual to a family frame of reference.

My family experience covers 12 years and over 10,000 hours of observing families in family psychotherapy. For the first five years of family practice I also did some individual psychotherapy and I had a few patients in psychoanalysis. The term "family psychotherapy" was reserved for the process when two or more family members were seen together. The technical effort was to analyze the already existing emotional process between the family members and toward keeping myself emotionally disengaged, which I called "staying out of the transference." This will be discussed later. During those years I used the term "individual psychotherapy" for the process when only one family person was seen. I had not dealt with my own emotional functioning sufficiently nor developed techniques to avoid a transference and there was the "either-or" distinction between family and individual psychotherapy. I considered it *family* when the emotional process could be contained within the family, and *individual* when this was not possible. During those years, another evolutionary process was taking place.

After having spent thousands of hours sitting with families, it became increasingly impossible to see a single person without "seeing" his total family sitting like phantoms alongside him. This perception of one person as a segment of the larger family system had governed the way I thought about and responded to the individual, and it had changed my basic approach to psychotherapy. For the past seven years my practice has been devoted entirely to "family" psychotherapy, although about one-third of the hours are spent with only one member of a family. The volume of clinical experience has been in private practice where an average clinical load of 40 families are seen with a maximum of 30 hours per week. In past years only a few families have been seen more than once a week, and an increasing number do well with less frequent appointments. It has been difficult to communicate the notion of avoiding a transference and "family" psychotherapy with only one family member. It is my hope that this can be better clarified in this paper.

A number of facets of the human phenomenon come into view in observing family members together that are obscured with any composite of individual interviews. Any person who exposes himself to daily observations of families as they "relate to" and "interact with" each other is confronted with a whole new world of clinical data that does not fit individual conceptual models. I use the terms "relate to" and "interact with" because these are a few of the inadequate terms that have been used to describe the family phenomenon. Actually, family members are *being*, and *doing*, and *acting*, and *interacting*, and *transacting*, and *communicating*, and *pretending*, and *posturing* in such a variety of ways that structure and order are hard to see. There is something wrong with any single term that has been used. To this point, family research has gone toward selecting certain areas for detailed, controlled study. In 1957 one of my research associates did a study called "The Action Dialogue in an Intense Relationship,"[8] which was an attempt to blank out words and do a coherent "dialogue" from one period of gross action between a mother and daughter. Birdwhistell and Scheflen[9,10] have made a significant contribution in their precise definition of "kinesics," a "body language" system, automatic in all relationships. One of the popular areas for study has been "communication," which on the simplest level is verbal communication. There have been the linguistic studies and the different communications that are conveyed by nuances in tone of voice, inflection, and ways of speaking—communications that each person learns in infancy and uses without "knowing" he knows it. Bateson and Jackson and co-workers, from analysis of verbal communication, developed their concept of the "double bind," which has to do with conflicting messages in the same statement. There is also the area of nonverbal communication and extrasensory perception which operates with fair accuracy in some families. There is an advantage in using terms such as "communication" or "transactional" system in that each lends itself to more precise research analysis. The disadvantage is in the narrowness of the concept and the necessity of using a broad interpretation of the concept. For instance, under "communication" theory it become necessary to assume the full range of verbal, action, nonverbal, extrasensory and feeling communication, plus other modalities such as a visceral response in one family member to anxiety or a mood shift in another. However one approaches the family, each investigator has to choose his own way of conceptualizing the family phenomenon.

One striking group of clinical patterns, present to some degree in all families, will provide a brief view of the family relationship system. These follow the general pattern of the family process that diagnoses, classifies, and assigns characteristics to certain family members. Observations may prove reasonably consistent, periodically consistent, or inconsistent with the family pronouncements about the situation. The "family projection process" by which a family problem is transmitted to one family member by years of nagging pronouncements, and then fixed there with a diagnosis, has been discussed in detail in another paper.[11] Family assignments that overvalue are as unrealistic as those that devalue, though the ones that devalue are more likely to come within the province of the psychiatrist. The diagnosed one may resist the family pronouncement and precipitate a family debate; or he may alternately resist and accept; or he may invite it, at which time the assigned characteristic becomes an operational *fact*. Family debates on subjects such as "rejection," "love," and "hostility" will force the therapist to reevaluate his own use of such terms. As I see "rejection," it is one of the most useful mechanisms for maintaining equilibrium in a relationship system. It goes on constantly between people, usually unmentioned. At one point in the family process someone makes a fuss about "rejection" and the debate starts. At a point when rejection is present throughout the family, the one who claims "rejection" is usually more rejecting of the other, rather than the obverse being true. Positive statements about the presence or absence of "love," with reactions and counterreactions, can occupy the scene while there is no objective evidence of change in "love" within the family. Whatever love *is*, it is factual that many family members react strongly to statements about it. The misuse and overuse of the concept "hostility" is another in the same category. The same can apply to terms such as "masculine," "feminine," "aggressive," "passive," "homosexual," and "alcoholic."

The use of the term "alcoholic" provides a good example. In one family, two generations of descendants referred to a grandfather as alcoholic. He had been successful and fairly responsible except to his wife, who was a very anxious woman. He found reason to stay away from her and he did drink moderately. The wife's label was accepted by the children and transmitted to the grandchildren. A recent consultation with another family illustrates another aspect of the problem. A wife had presented the details of her husband's alcoholism. I asked for the husband's view of the problem. He agreed he had a real drinking problem. When asked how much he drank, he flared with, "Listen, Buster! When I tell you I have a drinking problem, I mean it!" When asked how many days he had lost from work because of drinking, he said, "One! But I really hung one on that time." It can be grossly inaccurate to assign *fact* to statements such as, "He was an alcoholic." It can be accurate and also convey a *fact* about the relationship system if such statements are heard as, "One family member *said* another was an alcoholic." This applies to the entire spectrum of terms used in the family relationship system.

I would like to present the concept of the family as a system. For the moment I shall not attempt to say what kind of system. There is no single word or term that would be accurate without further qualification, and qualification would distort the *system* concept. The family *is* a system in that a change in one part of the system is followed by compensatory change in other parts of the system. I prefer to think of the family as a variety of systems and subsystems. Systems function at all levels of efficiency from optimum functioning to total dysfunction and failure. It is necessary also to think in terms of overfunction, which can range from compensated overfunction to decompensated overfunction. An example of this would be the tachycardia (overfunctioning heart) of an athlete in strenuous physical activity, to tachycardia that precedes total heart failure and death. The functioning of any system is dependent on the functioning of the larger systems of which it is a part, and also on its subsystems. On a broad level, the solar system is a subsystem of the larger system, the universe. The molecule is one of the smallest defined subsystems. On another level, the process of evolution is a system that operates slowly over long periods of time. There is sufficient knowledge about evolution to recognize the general patterns of its function, but there is much less knowledge about the larger systems of which evolution is a subsystem. We can look back and make postulations about the factors that influenced past evolutionary change, but our lack of knowledge about the larger systems reduces us to guessing about the future course of evolution.

From observing families I have attempted to define and conceptualize some of the larger and smaller family functioning patterns as they repeat and repeat, and as old patterns tone down and new ones become more prominent. The research started with schizophrenia in which one family member was in a state of total dysfunction and collapse, and the patterns so intense they could not be missed, but it required work with the entire range of human dysfunction to see the patterns in broader perspective. One of the most important aspects of family dysfunction is an equal degree of overfunction in another part of the family system. It is factual that dysfunctioning and overfunctioning exist together. On one level this is a smooth working, flexible, reciprocating mechanism in which one member automatically overfunctions to compensate for the dysfunction of the other who is temporarily ill. Then there are the more chronic and fixed states of overfunctioning and dysfunction in which flexibility is lost. An example would be the dominating (overfunctioning) mother and passive father. The overfunctioning one routinely sees this as necessary to compensate for the poor functioning of the other. This might be valid in the case of temporary illness in one spouse, but in the chronic states there is evidence that the dysfunction appears later to compensate for overfunction in the other. However it develops, the overfunction-dysfunction is a reciprocating mechanism. In previous papers[12,13] I called this the "overadequate-inadequate reciprocity." Symptoms develop when the dysfunction approaches nonfunctioning. Families often do not seek help until flexibility of the system is lost and the functioning of one member is severely impaired. When the mechanism advances beyond a certain point, anxiety drives the mechanism toward panic and rapid increase in both overfunction and dysfunction. The increased pressure can "jam the circuits" of the disabled one into paralyzed collapse. Even at this point, recovery can begin with the slightest decrease of the overfunctioning, or a slight decrease in the dysfunction.

Some of the main functional patterns observed in families have been formulated into component concepts that comprise the family theory of emotional illness. It would be more accurate to say "family dysfunction." The broad family patterns of emotional illness are also present in physical illness and social dysfunction such as irresponsible behavior and delinquency. The component concepts (subsystems) are among those I believe to be the most critical variables in human dysfunction. Symptoms in any part of the family are viewed as evidence of dysfunction, whether the symptoms be emotional, physical, conflictual, or social. There have been most promising results from the effort to view all emotional symptoms as evidence of family dysfunction rather than as intrapsychic phenomena.

The "therapist" also fits into this concept of the family as a system. This is a combination theoretical-therapeutic system in which theory determines therapy, and observations from therapy can in turn modify the theory. The original design, reported in another paper,[14] has been continued, although both the theory and therapy have been constantly modified. From the early days of the research there was increasing emotional detachment from the families. The more one observes families, the easier it is to detach from the narrow conceptual boundaries of individual theory; and the more one detaches from individual theory, the easier it is to see family patterns. The early family psychotherapy was predominantly observational, with questions to elicit more information about the observations. Over the years, "research" families have done better in family psychotherapy than those for whom the primary goal was "therapy." This helped establish a kind of orientation which has made all families into "research" families. It has been my experience that the more a therapist learns about a family, the more the family learns about itself; and the more the family learns, the more the therapist learns, in a cycle which continues. In the observational process with early families, some were able to restore family functioning without much "therapeutic intervention." The most successful families followed remarkably consistent courses in accomplishing this. Thereafter, it was possible to "intervene" and tell new families about successes and failures of former families and to save the new families endless hours and months of "trial and error" experimentation. In broad terms, the therapist became a kind of "expert" in understanding family systems and an "engineer" in helping the family restore itself to functioning equilibrium.

The overall goal was to help family members become "system experts" who could know the family system so well that the family could readjust itself without the help of an outside expert, if and when the family system was again stressed. It is optimum when the family system can begin a shift toward recovery with the important members of the family attending the hours. There were those in which the family became "worse" during the therapy, the "helpless one" becoming more helpless in response to the overfunctioning of the other. Some would struggle through this period and then move toward recovery; others would terminate. In these situations, it was found to be more profitable to work with one side of the reciprocity, until the family was able to work together without increasing the "bind." It is far easier for the overfunctioning one to "tone down" the overfunctioning than for the poorly functioning one to "pull up." If the overfunctioning one is motivated, I see this one alone for a period of "family" psychotherapy in which the goal is to free the immobilized system and restore enough flexibility for the family to work together. From my orientation, a theoretical system that "thinks" in terms of family and works toward improving the family system *is* family psychotherapy.

With this theoretical-therapeutic system, there is always the initial problem of the therapist establishing the orientation of the system. Most families are referred with a diagnosis for the dysfunction. They think in terms of the medical model and expect that the therapist is going to change the diagnosed family member, or the parents may expect the therapist to show or tell them how to change the child without understanding and modifying their part in the family system. With many families, it is surprisingly easy for the therapist to establish this family orientation in which he stands alongside to help them understand and take steps to modify the system. To help establish this orientation, I avoid the diagnosis of any family member and other medical model concepts such as "sick" or "patient." I persistently oppose the tendency of the family to view me as a "therapist." Instead, I work toward establishing myself as a "consultant" in family problems for the initial interviews, and as a "supervisor" of the family effort for the long-term process. When the therapist allows himself to become a "healer" or "repairman," the family goes into dysfunction to wait for the therapist to accomplish his work.

From this discussion of the family as a system, I have avoided saying what kind of a "system." The family *is* a number of different kinds of systems. It can accurately be designated a social system, a cultural system, a games system, a communication system, a biological system, or any of several other designations. For the purposes of this theoretical-therapeutic system, I think of the family as a combination of "emotional" and "relationship" systems. The term "emotional" refers to the force that motivates the system and "relationship" to the ways it is expressed. Under relationship would be subsumed communication, interaction and other relationship modalities.

There were some basic assumptions about man and the nature of emotional illness, partially formulated before the family research, that governed the theoretical thinking and the choice of the various theoretical concepts, including the notion of an "emotional" system. Man is viewed as an evolutionary assemblage of cells who has arrived at his present state from hundreds of millions of years of evolutionary adaptation and maladaptation, and who is evolving on to other changes. In this sense, man is related directly to all living matter. In choosing theoretical concepts, an attempt was made to keep them in harmony with man as a protoplasmic being. Man is different from other animals in the size of his brain and his ability to reason and think. With his intellectual ability he has devoted major effort to emphasizing his uniqueness and the "differences" that set him apart from other forms of life, and he has devoted comparatively little effort to understanding his relatedness to other forms of life. A basic premise is that what man thinks about himself, and what he says about himself, is different in many important ways from what he *is*. Emotional illness is seen as a disorder of man's emotional system, and man's emotional system is seen as basically related to man's protoplasmic being. I view emotional illness as a much deeper phenomenon than that conceptualized by current psychological theory. There are emotional mechanisms as automatic as a reflex and that occur as predictably as the force that causes the sunflower to keep its face toward the sun. I believe that the laws that govern man's emotional functioning are as orderly as those that govern other natural systems and that the difficulty in understanding the system is governed more by man's reasoning that denies its existence than by the complexity of the system. In the literature there are discrepant views about the definition of and the relatedness between *emotion* and *feelings*. Operationally I regard an emotional system as something deep that is in contact with cellular and somatic processes, and a feeling system as a bridge that is in contact with parts of the emotional system on one side and with the intellectual system on the other. In clinical practice, I have made a clear distinction between feelings, which have to do with subjective awareness, and opinions, which have to do with logic and reasoning of the intellectual system. The degree to which people say, "I feel that . . ." when they mean, "I believe that . . ." is so commonplace that many use the two words synonymously. However valid the ideas behind the selection of these concepts, they did play a major part in the choice of concepts.

An attempt has been made to keep terminology as simple and descriptive as possible. Several factors have governed this. The effort to think of the family as a fluid, ever-changing, functional system was impaired by the use of the static, fixed concepts conveyed by much of conventional psychiatric terminology. Early in family research, the loose use of psychiatric term, such as "depressed," "hysterical," and "compulsive," interfered with accurate description and communication. An effort was made to prohibit the use of psychiatric jargon within the research staff and to use simple descriptive words. This was a worthwhile discipline. It is difficult to communicate with colleagues without using familiar terms. An effort was made to bridge this gap by the sparing use of familiar terms. In the early years I worked toward some kind of correlation of family concepts with psychoanalytic theory. In writing and professional communication, the use of certain familiar terms would evoke vigorous discussion about the proper definition and use of terms. When the discussions went beyond productive exhanges of views and into nonproductive cyclical debates that consumed both time and energy, I elected to describe the family phenomenon in terms that did not stir up debates, to advance the research as far as possible, and to leave integration of individual and family concepts for some future generation. Although there are inaccuracies in the use of the term "family psychotherapy," I have retained it as the best working compromise between the theory and the practice, and for describing it to the professions to which it is related.

THE FAMILY THEORY

The central concept in this theory is the "undifferentiated family ego mass." This is a conglomerate emotional oneness that exists in all levels of intensity—from the family in which it is most intense, to the family in which it is almost imperceptible. The symbiotic relationship between a mother and child is an example of a fragment of one of the most intense versions. The father is equally involved with the mother and child, and other children are involved with varying lesser degrees of intensity. The basic notion to be conveyed at this moment is that of an emotional process that shifts about within the nuclear family (father, mother, and children) ego mass in definite patterns of emotional responsiveness. The degree to which any one family member may be involved depends on his basic level of involvement in the family ego mass. The number of family members involved depends on the intensity of the process and the functional state of individual relationships to the central "mass" at that moment. In periods of stress, the process can involve the entire nuclear family, a whole spectrum of more peripheral family members, and even nonrelatives and representatives of social agencies, clinics, schools, and courts. In periods of calm, the process can remain relatively contained within a small segment of the family, such as the symbiotic relationship in which the emotional process plays back and forth between mother and child with the father isolated from the intense twosome.

The term "undifferentiated family ego mass" has been more utilitarian than accurate. Precisely defined, the four words do not belong together, but this term has been the most effective of all in communicating the concept so that others might "hear." Also, the four words, each conveying an essential part of the concept, have provided latitude in theoretical extension of the idea. Clinically, the best examples of the relationship system within the undifferentiated family ego mass are conveyed by the more intense versions of it, such as the symbiotic relationship or the "folie a deux" phenomenon. The emotional closeness can be so intense that family members know each other's feelings, thoughts, fantasies, and dreams. The relationships are cyclical. There is one phase of calm, comfortable closeness. This can shift to anxious, uncomfortable overcloseness with the incorporation of the "self" of one by the "self" of the other. Then there is the phase of distant hostile rejection in which the two can literally repel each other. In some families, the relationship can cycle through the phases at frequent intervals. In other families the cycle can stay relatively fixed for long periods, such as the angry rejection phase in which two people can repulse each other for years, or for life. In the rejection phase, each can *refuse* into a similar emotional involvement with another family member or with certain other people outside the family. Within the family emotional system, the emotional tensions shift about in an orderly series of emotional alliances and rejections. The basic building block of any emotional system is the triangle. In calm periods, two members of the triangle have a comfortable emotional alliance, and the third, in the unfavored "outsider" position, moves either toward winning the favor of one of the others or toward rejection, which may be planned as winning favor. In tension situations, the "outsider" is in the favored position and both of the emotionally overinvolved ones will predictably make efforts to involve the third in the conflict. When tension increases, it will involve increasing outside members, the emotional circuits running on a series of interlocking emotional triangles. In the least involved situations, the emotional process shifts about in a subtle process of emotional responsiveness, which might be compared to an emotional chain reaction. These mechanisms can be defined in the later stages of family psychotherapy in which it is possible to analyze the family emotional system. For instance, a smile in one family member might initiate an action response in another, and this initiate a reverie about a dream in another, which is followed by a "change the subject" joke in another.

There are three major theoretical concepts in the theory. The first has to do with the degree of "differentiation of self" in a person. The opposite of differentiation is the degree of "undifferentiation" or "ego fusion." An attempt has been made to classify all levels of human functioning on a single continuum. At one end of the scale is the most intense version of the undifferentiated family ego mass in which "undifferentiation" and "ego fusion" dominate the field and there is little "differentiation of self." The symbiotic relationship and the "folie a deux" phenomenon are examples of clinical states with intense ego fusion. At the other end of the scale the "differentiation of self" dominates the field and there is little overt evidence of ego fusion. People at this end of the scale represent the highest levels of human functioning. Another concept has to do with the relationship system *within* the nuclear family ego mass and the *outside* emotional forces from the extended family emotional system and from the emotional systems of work and social situations that influence the course of the process within the family ego mass. Important in this concept is the "family projection process" by which parental problems are transmitted to their children. The patterns of this process have been incorporated into a third concept which deals with the multigenerational interlocking of emotional fields and parental transmission of varying degrees of "maturity" or "immaturity" over multiple generations. For practical purposes, the term "family ego mass" refers to the nuclear family which includes the father, mother, and children of the present and future generations. The term "extended family" refers to the entire network of living relatives, though in the everyday clinical situation this usually refers to the three-generation system involving grandparents, parents, and children. The term "emotional field" refers to the emotional process in any area being considered at the moment.

The Differentiation of Self Scale is an attempt to conceptualize all human functioning on the same continuum. This theory does not have a concept of "normal." It has been relatively easy to define "normal" measurements for all areas of man's physical functioning, but attempts to establish a "normal" for emotional functioning have been elusive. As a baseline for this theoretical system, a detailed profile of "complete differentiation of self," which would be equivalent to complete emotional maturity, has been assigned a value of 100 on a scale from 0 to 100. The lowest level of "no self," or the highest level of "undifferentiation," is at the bottom of the scale. Some of the broad general characteristics of people at the various levels of the scale will be presented.

People in the lowest quarter of the scale (0 to 25) are those with the most intense degree of "ego fusion" and with little "differentiation of self." They live in a "feeling" world, if they are not so miserable that they have lost the capacity to "feel." They are dependent on the feelings of those about them. So much of life energy goes into maintaining the relationship system about them—into "loving" or "being loved" or reaction against the failure to get love, or into getting more comfortable—that there is no life energy for anything else. They cannot differentiate between a "feeling" system and an "intellectual" system. Major life decisions are based on what "feels" right or simply on getting comfortable. They are incapable of using the "differentiated *"I"* (I am— I believe—I will do—I will not do) in their relationships with others. Their use of "I" is confined to the narcissistic, "I want—I am hurt—I want my rights." They grew up as dependent appendages of their parental ego masses and in their life course they attempt to find other dependent attachments from which they can borrow enough strength to function. Some are able to maintain a sufficient system of dependent attachments to function through life without symptoms. This is more possible for those in the upper part of this group. A "no self" who is sufficiently adept at pleasing his boss might be considered a better employee than if he had some "self." This scale has nothing to do with diagnostic categories. All in the group have tenuous adjustments, they are easily stressed into emotional disequilibrium, and dysfunction can be long or permanent. The group includes those who manage marginal adjustments and those whose efforts failed. At the extreme lower end are those who cannot exist outside the protective walls of an institution. It includes the "dead enders" of society, many of the lower socioeconomic group, and those from higher socioeconomic groups with intense ego fusions. I would see the hard core schizophrenic person at 10 or below on the scale, and his parents at no more than 20. In family psychotherapy, I have yet to see a person in this group attain a higher "basic" level of differentiation of self. Many attain reasonable alleviation of symptoms, but life energy goes into getting comfortable. If they can gain some symptom relief and a dependent attachment from which they can borrow strength, they are satisfied with the result.

People in the second quarter of the scale (25 to 50) are those with less intense ego fusions and with either a poorly defined self or a budding capacity to differentiate a self. This has to be in general terms because a person in the 30 range has many of the characteristics of "lower scale" people, and those between 40 and 50 have more characteristics of a higher scale. This scale provides an opportunity to describe "feeling" people. From 50 down it is increasingly a *feeling* world except for those at the extreme lower end who can be too miserable to feel. A typical *feeling* person is one who is responsive to emotional harmony or disharmony about him. Feelings can soar to heights with praise or approval or be dashed to nothingness by disapproval. So much life energy goes into "loving" and seeking "love" and approval that there is little energy left for self-determined, goal-directed activity. Important life decisions are based on what feels right. Success in business or professional pursuits is determined more by approval from superiors and from the relationship system than the inherent value of their work. People in this group do have some awareness of opinions and beliefs from the intellectual system but the budding "self" is usually so fused with feelings that it is expressed in dogmatic authoritativeness, in the compliance of a disciple, or in the opposition of a rebel. A conviction can be so fused with feeling that it becomes a "cause." In the lower part of this group are some fairly typical "no selfs." They are transilient personalities, who, lacking beliefs and convictions of their own, adapt quickly to the prevailing ideology. They usually go along with the system that best complements their emotional system. To avoid upsetting the emotional system, they use outside authority to support their position in life. They may use cultural values, religion, philosophy, the law, rule books, science, the physician, or other such sources. Instead of using the "I believe" of the more differentiated person, they may say, "Science has shown . . ." and it is possible to take science, or religion, or philosophy out of context and "prove" anything. It is misleading to correlate this scale with clinical categories, but people in the lower part of this segment of the scale, under stress, will develop transient psychotic episodes, delinquency problems, and other symptoms of that intensity. Those in the upper range of the scale will develop neurotic problems. The main difference between this segment and the lower quarter of the scale is that these people have some capacity for the differentiation of selfs. I have had a few families in the 25 to 30 range who have gone on to fairly high levels of differentiation. It is a situation of *possibility* but *low probability*. Most in this range will lose motivation when the emotional equilibrium is restored and symptoms disappear. The *probability* for differentiation is much higher in the 35 to 50 range.

People in the third quarter of the scale (50 to 75) are those with higher levels of differentiation and much lower degrees of ego fusions. Those in this group have fairly well-defined opinions and beliefs on most essential issues, but pressure for conformity is great and under sufficient stress they can compromise principle and make feeling decisions rather than risk the displeasure of others by standing on their convictions. They often remain silent and avoid stating opinions that might put them out of step with the crowd and disturb the emotional equilibrium. People in this group have more energy for goal-directed activity and less energy tied up in keeping the emotional system in equilibrium. Under sufficient stress they can develop fairly severe emotional or physical symptoms, but symptoms are more episodic and recovery is much faster.

People in the upper quarter of the scale (75 to 100) are those I have never seen in my clinical work and I rarely meet in social and professional relationships. In considering the overall scale, it is essentially impossible for anyone to have *all* the characteristics I would assign to 100. In this group I shall consider those that fall in the 85 to 95 range which will include most of the characteristics of a "differentiated" person. These are principle-oriented, goal-directed people who have many of the qualities that have been called "inner directed." They begin "growing away" from their parents in infancy. They are always sure of their beliefs and convictions but are never dogmatic or fixed in thinking. They can hear and evaluate the viewpoints of others and discard old beliefs in favor of new. They are sufficiently secure within themselves that functioning is not affectd by either praise or criticism from others. They can respect the self and the identity of another without becoming critical or becoming emotionally involved in trying to modify the life course of another. They assume total responsibility for self and are sure of their responsibility for family and society. They are realistically aware of their dependence on their fellowman. With the ability to keep emotional functioning contained within the boundaries of self, they are free to move about in any relationship system and engage in a whole spectrum of intense relationships without a "need" for the other that can impair functioning. The "other" in such a relationship does not feel "used." They marry spouses with equal levels of differentiation. With each a well-defined self, there are no questions or doubts about masculinity and femininity. Each can respect the self and identity of the other. They can maintain well-defined selfs and engage in intense emotional relationships at the same time. They are free to relax ego boundaries for the pleasurable sharing of "selfs" in sexuality or other intense emotional experience without reservation and with the full assurance that either can disengage from this kind of emotional fusion and proceed on a self-directed course at will.

These brief characterizations of broad segments of the scale will convey an overall view of the theoretical system that conceives all human functioning on the same continuum. The scale has to do with *basic* levels of differentiation. Another important aspect has to do with *functional* levels of differentiation which is so marked in the lower half of the scale that the concept of *basic* levels can be misleading. The more intense the degree of ego fusion, the more the "borrowing" and "lending" and "giving" and "sharing" of self within the family ego mass. The more the shifting of "strength" within the ego mass, the more likely the marked discrepancies in functional levels of self. The occasional brief shifts are striking. One of the best examples of this is that of the regressed schizophrenic person who pulls up to resourceful functioning when his parents are sick, only to fall back when they have recovered. Other shifts are so fixed that people wonder how one spouse so strong would marry another so weak. A striking example of this is the overadequate husband who might function well in his work at perhaps 55 on strength from a wife housebound with phobias, excessive drinking, or arthritis and a functioning level of 15. In this situation, the basic level would be about 35. Fluctuations in the upper half of the scale are present but less marked and it is easier to estimate basic levels. People high on the scale have almost no functional shifts. Other characteristics apply to the entire scale. The lower the person on the scale, the more he holds onto religious dogma, cultural values, superstition, and outmoded beliefs, and the less able he is to discard the rigidly held ideas. The lower a person on the scale, the more he makes a "federal case" of rejection, lack of love, and injustice, and the more he demands recompense for his hurts. The lower he is on the scale, the more he holds the other responsible for his self and happiness. The lower he is on the scale, the more intense the ego fusions, and the more extreme the mechanisms such as emotional distance, isolation, conflict, violence, and physical illness to control the emotion of "too much closeness." The more intense the ego fusions, the higher the incidence of being in touch with the intrapsychic of the other, and the greater the chance that he can intuitively know what the other thinks and feels. In general, the lower the person on the scale, the more the impairment in meaningful communication.

Relationship System in the Nuclear Family Ego Mass

An example of a marriage with spouses in the 30 to 35 range will convey an idea of several concepts in this theoretical system. As children, both spouses were dependently attached to parents. After adolescence, in an effort to function autonomously, they either denied the dependence while still living at home, or they used separation and physical distance to achieve autonomy. Both can function relatively well as long as they keep relationships distant or casual. Both are vulnerable to the closeness of an intense emotional relationship. Both long for closeness but both are "allergic" to it. The marriage for each duplicates essential character-istics of former ego masses. They fuse together into a "new family ego mass" with obliteration of ego boundaries and incorporation of the two "pseudo selfs" into a "common self." Each uses mechanisms, pre-viously used in their families of origin, in dealing with the other. For instance, the one who ran away from his own family will tend to run away in the marriage. The most common mechanism is the use of sufficient emotional distance for each to function with a reasonable level of "pseudo self." The future course of this new family ego mass will depend on a spectrum of mechanisms that operate *within* the family ego mass, and others that operate *outside* in their relationships within the extended family system.

Within the family ego mass, spouses use three major mechanisms to control the intensity of the ego fusion. (1) *Marital conflict* in which each spouse fights for an equal share of the common self and neither gives in to the other. (2) *Dysfunction in one spouse.* A common pattern is a brief period of conflict followed by one spouse who reluctantly "gives in" to relieve the conflict. Both spouses usually see self as "giving in," but there is one who does more of it. In another pattern, one spouse volunteers to be the "no self" in support of the other on whom they become dependent. The spouse who "loses self" in this mechanism may come to function at such a low level that they become candidates for physical, emotional, or social illness. There are some marriages that continue for years with one functioning well and the other chronically ill. (3) *Transmission of the problem to one or more children.* This is one of the most common mechanisms for dealing with family ego mass problems. There are a few families in which ego mass problems are relatively contained within one of the three areas. There are a few with severe marital conflict but no impairment of either spouse and no transmission to the children. There are also a few with no marital conflict, no dysfunction in either spouse and in which the entire weight of the marital problem goes into one child. There may be no significant symptoms until after adolescence, when the child collapses in psychotic dysfunction or other dysfunction of comparable degree. In most families, the problem between the spouses will be "spread" to all three areas. The few families in which the problem remains contained in one area are important theoretically. The fact that there are some families with intense marital conflict and no impairment of children is evidence that marital conflict does not, within itself, cause problems in children. The fact that serious impairment of children can develop in calm, harmonious marriages is further evidence that impairment of children can occur without conflict. The degree of the problem between the spouses can be assigned quantitative measures. The system operates as if there is a certain amount of "immaturity" to be absorbed by the system. Large quantities of this may be "bound" by serious dysfunction in one family member. One chronically ill parent can be a kind of "protection" against serious impairment of children. In the area of transmission to children, the family projection process focuses on certain children and leaves others relatively uninvolved. There are, of course, families in which the "quantity" of immaturity is so great that there is maximum marital conflict, severe dysfunction in one spouse, maximum involvement of children, conflict with families of origin, and still free-floating "immaturity."

The mechanisms that operate *outside* the nuclear family ego mass are important in determining the course and intensity of the process *within* the nuclear family. When there is a significant degree of ego fusion, there is also a borrowing and sharing of ego strength between the nuclear family and the family of origin. In periods of stress the nuclear family can be stabilized by emotional contact with a family of origin, just as the nuclear family can also be disturbed by stress in the family of origin. In general, the intensity of the process in a nuclear family is attenuated by active contacts with the families of origin. There is one striking pattern illustrated by the following example: The father separated himself from his family when he left for college. There was no further contact except infrequent, brief visits and occasional letters and

Christmas cards. He married a wife who maintained close contact with her family, including frequent exchanges of letters and gifts, regular family reunions, and visits with scattered members of the clan. Five out of six of the father's siblings followed the same pattern of separating from the family of origin. The mother was one of five siblings, all of whom married spouses who were brought into the emotional orbit of her family. This pattern is so common that I have called these *exploding* and *cohesive* families. The spouse who separates from his family of origin does not resolve the emotional attachment. The old relationship remains "latent" and can be revived with emotional contact. Through the "active" relationship with the cohesive family, the nuclear family system is responsive to emotional events within the cohesive extended family. There are other nuclear families in which both spouses detach themselves from families of origin. In these the spouses are usually much more dependent on each other, and the emotional process in the family tends to be more intense. The average family in which both spouses are emotionally separated from families of origin tend to become more invested in the emotional systems of work and social situations. An example is a family in which the principal outside emotional tie was the father's long-term emotional dependence on his boss at work. Within weeks after the sudden death of the father's boss, a teen-aged son was in serious dysfunction with a behavior problem. A brief period of "family" psychotherapy with the father alone restored the family emotional equilibrium sufficiently for the parents to work productively together toward resolution of the parental interdependence. Knowledge of the relationship patterns in the extended family system is important in understanding the overall problem and in devising a family psychotherapy program.

Multigenerational Transmission Process

One of the important concepts of this theoretical system is the pattern that emerges over the generations as parents transmit varying levels of their immaturity to their children. In most families the parents transmit part of their immaturity to one or more children. To illustrate this multigenerational pattern in its most graphic and extreme form; I shall start with parents with an average level of differentiation and assume that in each generation the parents project a major portion of their immaturity to only one child, thereby creating maximum impairment in one child in each generation. I shall also assume that in each generation one child grows up relatively outside the emotional demands and pressures of the family ego mass and attains the highest level of differentiation possible in that situation. It would be essentially impossible for this pattern to occur generation after generation, but it does illustrate the pattern. The example starts with parents at 50 on the scale. They have three children. The most involved child emerges at 35 on the scale, much lower than the basic level of the parents and a fairly maximum degree of impairment for one generation. Another child emerges with 50, the same basic level of the parents. A third grows up relatively outside the problems of the family ego mass and emerges with a level of 60, much higher than the parents. In considering the child at 35 who marries a spouse in the 35 range, the personality characteristics of this marriage would vary according to the way this family ego mass handles its problems. A maximum projection family would have a calm marriage and almost total preoccupation with the health, welfare, and achievement of the most involved child, who could emerge with a level as low as 20. They could have another who grew up outside the family ego mass with a level of 45, much higher than the parents. To have two children, one at 20 and another at 45, is hardly probable. The child at 20 is already in the danger zone and vulnerable to a whole spectrum of human problems. In his early years he might be an overachiever in school, and then in the postadolescent years go into an emotional collapse. With special help he might eventually finish school, spend a few aimless years, and then find a spouse whose "needs" for another are as great as his. At this level of ego fusion the problems are too great to be contained in one area. They will probably have a variety of marital, health, and social problems, and the problem will be too great for projection to only one child. They might have one child at 10, another at 15, and another who grows up outside the family mass to a level of 30, much above the basic level of the parents. The ones at 10 and 15 are good candidates for total functional collapse into states such as schizophrenia or criminal behavior. This illustrates former statements that it requires at least three generations for a person to acquire the level of "no self" for a later collapse into schizophrenia. In the average situation the immaturity would progress at a much slower rate. Also, in every generation there are children who progress up the scale, and in the average family the upward progression is much slower than illustrated in this example.

It is emphasized that the scale level figures used in the preceding examples are to illustrate the broad principles of the theoretical system. The shift in functional levels in the lower half of the scale is so responsive to such a variety of hour-to-hour and week-to-week shifts, through good years and bad, that approximate levels can be established only after having awareness of the particular variables most operative over a period of time for a given family. It is the general level and the pattern that are most important in the clinical situation. The levels in the multigenerational concept are strictly schematic and for illustrative purposes only. The postulations for this concept were derived from historical material covering three to four generations on approximately 100 families, and ten or more generations on eight families.

There is one other theoretical concept that I have combined with my own work that is used with every family in psychotherapy. These are the personality profiles of the various sibling positions as presented by Toman in *Family Constellation*.[15] I consider his work one of the significant contributions to family knowledge in recent years. He presents the thesis that personality characteristics are determined by the sibling position and the family constellation in which one grows up. I have found his personality profiles to be remarkably accurate, especially for people in the mid-scale range of my Differentiation of Self Scale. Of course, he did his study on "normal" families and made no attempt to estimate other variables. He also did not consider the personality alterations of the child who was the object of the family projection process. An example of the shift is a family of two daughters. The older, the one most involved in the family emotional system, emerged with the profile of a younger "baby." The younger daughter, who was less involved in the emotional system with the parents, emerged with more of the characteristics of an older daughter. Most of his profiles contain a mixture of the adult and the infantile characteristics. The higher a person on the scale, the more the adult qualities predominate; the obverse is also true.

CLINICAL USE OF FAMILY PSYCHOTHERAPY

I hope that the theoretical concepts help the reader think more in terms of family systems rather than diagnostic categories and individual dynamics. Each point in the theory has application in clinical evaluation and in family psychotherapy. This section will be presented in three main parts: (1) Survey of the family fields, (2) the process of "differentiation of self" in family psychotherapy, and (3) family psychotherapy principles and techniques.

Survey of the Family Fields

This is a term used to designate a family "evaluation" process used in the initial interview with every family I see. It is designed to get a volume of factual information in a brief time. The information is used with the family theory for a formulation about the overall patterns of functioning in the family ego mass for at least two generations. The formulation is used in planning the psychotherapy. Initially, it required a number of hours to get this information. With practice, and the careful structuring of the interview, and an average uncomplicated family, it is possible to do a survey adequately for planning the psychotherapy in one hour. This is different from the kind of "evaluation" in which the therapist may spend several hours with all family members together to observe the workings of the family relationship system. In the training of young therapists, considerable experience in observing multiple family members together is essential. It is not possible to *know* family without direct clinical observation, and it is not advisable to work with segments of families until one has a working knowledge of the whole. For the average family, the initial interview is with both parents, who can usually provide more information than one. In addition, it provides a working view of the marital relationship. If there is evidence that martial discord might interfere with the fact gathering, I often ask to see the one parent who has the most knowledge about the family. Some interesting developments come from this. Most families seek help when there is dysfunction in one or more of the three main stress areas of the nuclear family system: (1) marital conflict, (2) dysfunction in a spouse, or (3) dysfunction in a child. To illustrate this survey, I shall use a family referred for a behavior problem in a teen-age child.

In surveying the family fields, I first want to know about the functioning in the nuclear family field and then how the functioning of the extended family field intergears with the nuclear field. A good starting point is a chronological review of the symptom development in the teen-aged child, with specific dates and circumstances at the time of each symptom eruption. Many symptomatic eruptions can be timed exactly with other events in the nuclear and extended family fields. The parents might report the child first played hooky from school "in the eighth grade," but it would convey much about the family system if one knew the day he played hoooky was the day his maternal grandmother was hospitalized for tests for a feared cancer. Information about feeling and fantasy systems of other family members on that day would be helpful if it could be obtained.

The second area of investigation is the functioning of the parental ego mass since marriage. This emotional unit has its own system of internal dynamics that change as it moves through the years. The internal system also responds to the emotional fields of the extended families and to the reality stresses of life. The goal is to get a brief chronological view of the internal system as it has interresponded with outside forces. This might be compared to two constantly changing magnetic fields that influence each other. The internal functioning is influenced by events such as closeness or distance and emotional contact with extended families, changes in residence, the purchase of a home, and occupational success or failure. Major events that influence both emotional fields are births within the central ego mass and serious illness or death in the extended family. Functioning within the ego mass can be estimated with a few questions about stress areas, which are marital conflict, illness or other dysfunction, and projection to a child. A change in stress symptoms might be related to internal dynamics or external events. The dates of changes are important. A change from a calm to a conflictual relationship might be explained by the wife as, "The time I began to stand up to him," when it would in fact be timed exactly with a disturbance in an extended family.

Important ego mass changes accompany the birth of children. The birth of the first child changes the family from a two-person to a three-person system. At an important event such as this, it is desirable to do a "fix" on the entire family system, including place, date, ages of each person in the household and the functioning of each, and a check on the realities in the extended families. It is desirable to get readings on the feeling-fantasy systems of various family members at stress points, if this is possible. A check on the family projection process is often easy by asking about the mother's fantasy system before and after the birth of the child. If it is a significant projection process, her worries and concerns have fixed on the child since the pregnancy, her relationship with this one has been "different," she has long worried about it, and she is eager to talk about it. An intense, long-term, projection process is evidence of a deeper and more serious problem in the child. A projection process that started later, perhaps following the death of an important family member, is much less serious and much easier handled in family psychotherapy. A projection process, usually between mother and child, *changes* the internal functioning of the family system. This much psychic energy from mother to child will change the psychic energy system in the family. It might serve to reduce marital conflict, but it might also disturb the husband to the point he would start spending longer hours at work, or he might begin drinking, or have an affair, or become emotionally closer to his parents. This survey is followed to the onset of symptoms in the child for which there are already nodal points that may be connected with dates and events in the parental relationship. The survey provides a picture of general functioning levels, responsiveness to stress, and evidence about the flexibility or rigidity of the entire system. It also provides a notion about the more adaptive spouse who is usually the more passive. The adaptive one is much more than one who "gives in" on a controlled surface level. This involves the entire fantasy, feeling, and action system. A spouse who develops physical symptoms in response to an emotional field is in a "cell to cell" adaptiveness that is deep.

The next area of investigation is the two extended family fields in either order the therapist chooses. This is similar to the nuclear family survey except it focuses on overall patterns. Exact dates, ages, and places are very important. The occupation of the grandfather and a note about the marital relationship and the health of each grandparent provides key clues to that family ego mass. Information about each sibling includes birth order, exact dates of birth, occupation, place of residence, a few words about spouse and children, a note about overall life course, and frequency and nature of contact with other family members. From this brief information, which can be obtained in five or ten minutes, it is possible to assemble a fairly accurate working notion about the family ego mass, and how the nuclear parent functioned in the group. Siblings who do best are usually least involved in the family emotional system. Those who do poorly are usually most involved. Distance from other family members and quality of emotional contacts with family provides clues about the way the person handles all emotional relationships and whether this tends toward an "exploding" or "cohesive" family. A high incidence of physical illness often occurs in those with low levels of differentiation of self. The sibling position is one of the most important bits of information. This, plus the general level of family functioning, makes it possible to postulate a reasonably accurate personality profile to be checked later. In general, a life style developed in the family of origin will operate in the nuclear family and also in family psychotherapy.

Surveys of the family fields follow the same pattern for other problems, except for different emphases. Certain areas may require detailed exploration. It is always helpful to go back as many generations as possible. The overall goal is to follow the total family through time with a focus on related events in interlocking fields. The lower the general level of differentiation in a family, the greater the frequency and intensity of the related events. A secondary dividend of a family field survey is the family's beginning intellectual awareness of related events. The family emotional system operates always to obscure and misremember and to treat such events as coincidental. Family replies to an effort to get specific dates might go, "That was when he was about . . . 11 or 12 years old," and, "He must have been in the fifth grade," or "It was about five or six years ago." It requires persistent questioning and mathematical computation to get specific information. The obscuring process is illustrated by a family in family psychotherapy. Ten days after the wife returned from her mother's funeral, her daughter developed nephritis. Some weeks later the wife was insisting that the daughter's illness preceded her mother's death. The husband's memory and my notes were accurate. In theoretical thinking, I have never been willing to postulate causality or go beyond noting that such events have a striking time sequence. I believe it may have to do with man's denial of dependence on his fellowman. I avoid glib dynamic speculations and record the family explanations as, "The family member *said* . . ." I have never been able to use the related events early in psychotherapy. Early in family psychotherapy there was the temptation to show this to the family after the initial interview. Some families found reason to never return. My goal is to keep asking questions and let the calendar "speak" when others are able to "hear."

The family field survey is primarily for the therapist in knowing the family and how it operates, and in planning the psychotherapy. If the symptoms develop slowly in the nuclear family, it is likely to be the product of a slow buildup in the nuclear family. If the symptoms develop more quickly, the situation deserves a thorough exploration for disturbance in the extended family. If it is a response to the extended family, it can be regarded as an "acute" situation and it is fairly easy to restore the family functioning. The following is an example of multiple acute problems following a disturbance in the extended family.

A 40-year-old woman was referred for a depression for which hospitalization had been suggested. Her husband belonged to a "cohesive" family of six siblings, all of whom lived within a few hundred miles of their parents. Two months before, his 65-year-old mother had a radical mastectomy of breast cancer. Two weeks after the operation, one of the husband's sisters had a serious automobile accident which required months of hospitalization. Six weeks after the operation, one of the husband's brothers had a son arrested for a series of delinquent acts, the first of which had occurred two weeks after the operation. After an initial interview with the depressed wife alone, the husband and wife were seen together. A few hours with the process focused on feelings about the mother brought rapid relief of the depression and set the stage for long-term family psychotherapy with both together.

The Process of Differentiation of a Self

The basic effort of this therapeutic system is to help *individual* family members toward a higher level of differentiation of self. An emotional system operates with a delicately balanced equilibrium in which each devotes a certain amount of being and self to the welfare and well-being of the others. In a state of disequilibrium, the family system operates automatically to restore the former togetherness equilibrium, though this be at the expense of some. When an individual moves toward a higher level of differentiation of self, it disturbs the equilibrium and the togetherness forces oppose with vigor. In larger emotional systems, an individual may seek an ally or group to help oppose the forces of the system, only to find self in a new undifferentiated oneness with his allies (even a sect or minority group within the larger system) from which it is harder to differentiate than from the original oneness. Any successful effort toward differentiation is for the individual alone. Some of the forces that oppose the "differentiation of self" will be described later. When the individual can maintain his "differentiation" stand in spite of opposition, the family later applauds.

One of the important concepts in this theoretical system has to do with "triangles." It was not included with the other concepts because it has more to do with therapy than the basic theory. The basic building block of any emotional system is the "triangle." When emotional tension in a two-person system exceeds a certain level, it "triangles" a third person, permitting the tension to shift about within the triangle. Any two in the original triangle can add a new triangle. An emotional system is composed of a series of interlocking triangles. The emotional tension system can shift to any of the old preestablished circuits. It is a clinical fact that the original two-person tension system will resolve itself automatically when contained within a three-person system, one of whom remains emotionally detached. This will be discussed under "detriangling the triangle."

From experience with this therapeutic system, there are two main avenues toward a higher level of "differentiation of self." (1) The optimum is differentiation of a self *from* one's spouse, as a cooperative effort, in the presence of a potential "triangle" (therapist) who can remain emotionally detached. To me, this is the "magic" of family psychotherapy. They must be sufficiently involved with each other to stand the stress of "differentiation" and sufficiently uncomfortable to motivate the effort. One, and then the other, moves forward in small steps until motivation stops. (2) Start the differentiation alone, under the guidance of a supervisor, as a preliminary step to the main effort of differentiating a self *from* the important other person. This second avenue is a model for family psychotherapy with one family member. A third avenue is less effective: (3) the entire process under the guidance of a supervisor who coaches from the sidelines. Direct use of the "triangle" is lost, the process is generally slower, and the chances of an impasse are greater. As a general comment about "differentiation," the highest level of differentiation that is possible for a family is the highest level that any family member can attain and maintain against the emotional opposition of the family unit in which he lives.

Family Psychotherapy Principles and Technique

My optimum approach to any family problem, whether marital conflict, dysfunction in a spouse, or dysfunction in a child, is to start with husband and wife together and to continue with both for the entire period of family psychotherapy. In most families, this "optimum" course is not possible. Some 30 to 40 per cent of "family" hours are spent with one family member, mostly for situations in which one spouse is antagonistic or poorly motivated, or when progress with both is too slow. The method of helping one family member to "differentiate a self" will be discussed later. The method of working with the two parents evolved from several years of experience in which both parents and symptomatic child (usually postadolescent behavior and neurotic problems) attended all sessions together. An average course would continue a year or more. Family communication improved, symptoms disappeared, and the families would terminate, much pleased with the result. There was no basic change in the pattern of the parental relationship, postulated to be fundamental in the origin of the problem. On the premise that the entire family system would change if the parental relationship changed, I began asking such parents to leave the child at home and to focus on their own problems. These have been the most satisfying results in my experience. Many of the children who initiated the family effort were never seen, and others were seen only once. The parents who achieved the best results would continue about four years at once a week for a total of 175 to 200 hours with better results than could be achieved with any other psychotherapeutic method in my experience. The children were usually symptom free in a few weeks or months, and changes have gone far beyond the nuclear family into the extended family system. The time has been so consistently in the four-year range that I believe it might require this amount of time for significant differentiation of self. Some people can spend a lifetime without defining themselves on numerous life issues. I am now experimenting with less frequent appointments to reduce the total amount of time.

The basic process of working with husbands and wives together has remained very much the same over the years with some different emphases and modifications in theoretical concepts. In the past I stressed the communication of feelings and the analysis of the unconscious through dreams. More recently, it has been a process of watching the step-by-step process of externalizing and separating out their fantasy, feeling, thinking systems. It is a process of knowing one's own self, and also the self of the other. There have been comments such as, "I never knew you had such thoughts!" and the counterresponse, "I never dared tell anyone before, most especially *you!*"

The following is an example of two small "differentiation" steps with the emotional response of the other. One wife, after many hours of private thinking, announced, "I have decided to take all the thoughts, time and energy that I have devoted to trying to make you happy and to put it into trying to make myself into a more responsible woman and mother. Nothing I tried really worked anyway. I have thought it out and I have a plan." The husband reacted with the usual emotional reaction to an "I" position by the other. He was angry and hurt. He ended with, "If I had realized it would come to this after 15 years, I can tell you one thing, there never would have been a wedding!" Within a week he was happy with his "new" wife. Some weeks later, after much thinking by the husband, he announced, "I have been trying to think through my responsibilities to my family and to work. I have never been clear about this. If I worked overtime, I felt I was neglecting my family. If I spent extra time with the family, I would feel I was neglecting my work. Here is my plan." The wife reacted with emotion about his real selfish lack of concern finally showing its true color. Within a week that had subsided.

As spouses change in relation to each other, they disturb the emotional equilibrium in families of origin where there are the same emotional reactions and resolutions as between themselves. Most of these spouses have become the most responsible and respected in both extended family systems. The emotional opposition to change also occurs in social and work emotional systems. The main point to be communicated here is that a change in "self" disturbs the emotional equilibrium and evokes emotional opposing forces in all interlocking emotional systems. If two spouses can make the primary changes in relation to each other, it is relatively easy to deal with the other systems.

One of the most important processes in this method of psychotherapy is the therapist's continuing attention to defining his "self" to the families. This begins from the first contact which defines this theoretical and therapeutic system and its differences from others. It proceeds in almost every session around all kinds of life issues. Of importance are the "action" stands which have to do with "what I will do and will not do." I believe a therapist is in poor position to ask a family to do something he does not do. When the family goes slowly at defining self, I begin to wonder if there is some vague ambiguous area of importance about which I failed to define myself.

At this point, I shall describe *family* psychotherapy with one family member. The basic notion of this has to do with finding a way to start some change in the deadlocked family; with finding a way to get into contact with family resourcefulness and strength and to get out of contact with the sickness morass; and with getting some differentiation to rise out of the family quagmire. Actually, if it is possible to get some differentiation started in one family member, it can loosen up the entire family system. Communication of this idea has been difficult. To those who use a medical model and consider the therapeutic relationship the basic healing force in emotional illness, the idea is erroneous. I have used several different concepts in trying to write about the idea and a number of different angles in trying to teach it. There are those who heard it as "treating the healthiest family member instead of the patient, on the grounds that the healthiest is more capable of modifying behavior." This is an accurate description of the goal but it uses a "health" concept in the place of "sickness," which is still a medical model. A therapist who attempts to "treat" the healthiest with his medical orientation could either drive him away or make him into a "patient."

The conflictual marriage provides one of the best examples of working with one spouse. This is a clinical situation in which the emotional system is already fairly well locked in dysfunction before they seek help. A fair level of overt conflict is "normal" and it has to reach a relative state of dysfunction before they seek help. The marriage began with an almost idyllic model in which each devoted a high percentage of "self" to the happiness and well-being of the other. This I have called a "fraudulent" emotional contract in which it was realistically impossible for either to live up to the agreement. With this arrangement, the functioning of self *is* dependent on the other and, in that sense, any failure in happiness or functioning *is* the fault of the other. The emotional investment in each other continues; only it shifts into negative energy that accuses, indicts, and diagnoses. I believe the conflictual marriage is an enduring one because of the energy investment. The amount of *thinking* time that goes into the other is probably greater than calm marriages. With the intensity of emotional interdependence and the ability to utilize conflict, the conflictual spouses usually do not seek help until adaptive mechanisms are jammed. In a high percentage of conflictual marriages, I see one spouse alone for a few months to a year before calm working together is possible. Choice about the one to see first is easy when one is motivated and the other antagonistic. It is a little different when both are seen together and the repetitious "accuse the other—excuse self" continues in the interview. If they have any capacity to stop the cycle and look at the pattern, I continue with both together. If a vigorous effort to help them contain the cycle is not successful, I say that I consider this cyclical and nonproductive, that I am not willing to spend time this way, and that I want to see the healthiest, best-integrated one alone for a period of time to help this one gain some objectivity and emotional control. A request for the "healthiest" establishes a different orientation and changes their long-term diagnosing, "You are the sick one who needs a psychiatrist." I do not see spouses alternately. It invites "triangling," neither really works at the problem, each expects the other to do it, and each justify self justify self to the therapist. My "I" stands, all based on experience, are in terms of what I will do and will not do, and are never in terms of "what is best."

Since the process of working with one family member alone is similar in all situations, I shall describe the effort with the conflictual spouse in some detail. The early sessions go into a detailed communication of an orientation with the use of clinical examples and a blackboard for diagrams. In broad terms, the concept is one of withdrawing psychic energy from the other and investing it in the poorly defined ego boundaries. It involves the idea of "getting off the back" of the other by reducing the "other directed" thinking, verbal, action energy which is designed to attack and change the other, and directing that energy to the changing of self. The changing of "self" involves finding a way to listen to the attacks of the other without responding, of finding a way to live with "what is" without trying to change it, of defining one's own beliefs and convictions without attacking those of the other, and in observing the part that self plays in the situation. Much time is devoted to establishing the therapist's self in relation to the one spouse. These ideas are passed along for their possible use in defining a "self." They are told that others have found some of them helpful, that the effort will fail if they try them without incorporating them into "self" as their own beliefs, that they would be unrealistic to try something they could not really believe in, and it will be their responsibility to find other ideas and principles if these do not fit with their own "selfs." They are assigned the task of becoming "research observers" and told that a major part of each hour will go into their report on their efforts to see self. I tell them about the predictable stages they can expect if their efforts are successful in defining "self" and containing the critical actions, words, and thoughts that have been trying to direct the life of their spouse. If they are successful at this, the first reaction will be a version of, "You are mean, selfish and vicious; you do not understand, you do not love, and you are trying to hurt the other." When they can listen to the expected attack without reacting, a milestone will have been passed. Then they can expect a withdrawal from the other which emphasizes, "To heck with you, I do not need you." This will be the most difficult stage. They might get depressed and confused and develop a whole spectrum of physical symptoms. This is the reaction of one's psyche and soma as it cries out for the old dependence and togetherness. If they can live with the symptoms without reacting, they can expect the other to make a new and different bid for affection on a higher level of maturity. It is usually many days after that before the other spouse asks to take the therapy hour, and often not many hours before they can finally work together.

The life style of this low level of "differentiation" is the investment of psychic energy in the "self" of another. When this happens in the therapy, it is transference. A goal of this therapy is to help the other person make a research project out of life. It is important to keep "self" contained with the therapist as the other spouse. If the person understands the life-goal nature of the effort and that progress will slow down or stop with energy invested in the "self" of the therapist, he is in a better position to help keep the energy focused on the goal. If progress does stop, the family psychotherapy is shifted to a similar effort with the other spouse. It is not possible to use this "differentiation of a self" approach with two spouses. It results in intense "triangling."

Work with one sick spouse depends on the problem and which one seeks help. If the well one seeks help, the "sick" one is near collapse. With these I work toward avoiding a relationship with the sick side of the family, and work toward relating to the well one about his problems with the sick one. Some of these families achieve remarkable symptom relief with a few appointments, but these people are not motivated for more than symptom relief. When the "sick" one seeks help, I maintain a detached, "Let's examine this and understand your part in the family problem." The cells of the "sick" spouse literally go into dysfunction in the presence of the other spouse, especially in those with severe introjective and somatic dysfunctions. If the other spouse is brought in too early, the therapy effort may terminate within a few hours. A goal is to propose "family" early and wait until the "self" of the sick one can operate in the presence of the other without going into dysfunction. There have been some excellent long-term results which include about six months with the sick one and some two years with both. Problems such as impotence and frigidity belong more in the area of relationship functioning. These can usually be converted to "family" within a few hours and the response has been good. Impotence often disappears within a few weeks and frigidity is rarely mentioned after a few months. Most of these go on with long-term family therapy for two years or more.

The problem of the "triangled" child presents one of the most difficult problems in family psychotherapy. From the initial family survey can come a fair estimate of the intensity of the process. If it is not too severe, the parents can focus on their own problems immediately, they almost forget about the child and, suddenly, he is symptom free. Even with severe "triangling," I do a "trial run" with both parents together to test the flexibility in the parental relationship. In the severe "triangling" or projection of the parental problems to the child, the parents are not able to leave the child out of their feelings, thoughts, and actions. There are the less severe versions in which parents try hard to work on their problem but the relationship between them is dull and lifeless. Life and self is invested in the child. The "gut reaction," in which a parent's "insides tie into knots" in response to discomfort in the child, is common. After several years of symptom-relieving methods, including working with various combinations of family members, I began what I have called "detriangling the triangle." This is too complex for brief discussion but it involves helping one parent to establish an "I" position and to "differentiate a self" in the relationship *with the child*. If there is another "magic" in family psychotherapy, it is the family response when one parent can begin to "differentiate a self" from the amorphous "we-ness" of the intense undifferentiated family ego mass. One bit of clearly defined "self" in this area of amorphousness can bring a period of amazing calm. The calm may quickly shift to other issues, but the family *is* different. The other parent and child fuse together into a more intense oneness that alternately attacks and pleads with the "differentiating parent" to rejoin the oneness. If the differentiating one can maintain a reasonable "I" for even a few days, there is an automatic decrease in the intensity of the attachment between the other two and a permanent decrease in the intensity of the triangle. The second stop involves a similar effort by the other parent to "differentiate a self." Now the parental relationship has come a little more to life. Then there is another cycle with each parent separately, and then still more life and zest between the parents. Differentiation proceeds slowly, at this level of ego fusion, but there have been a few of these families that have gone on to reasonable levels of differentiation.

There are several other configurations of family psychotherapy with one family member, but this provides a brief description of the basic principles. It is used when the family system is so stalled that efforts to work with multiple family members increases the dysfunction, or when work with multiple members reaches a cyclical impasse. The effort is to help one family member to a higher level of functioning which, if possible, can restore function to the family system.

SUMMARY

Presented here is a family theory of emotional illness and its component system of family psychotherapy, which is one of several different theoretical approaches to the family, and one of many different kinds of "family therapy" that have come on the psychiatric scene in little more than one decade. A brief review of the family movement attempts to put this system into a kind of perspective with the overall family movement. Since this system places maximum emphasis on "family" as a theoretical system, the theory has been presented in some detail. The shorter section of family psychotherapy presents both broad principles and specific details about the usefulness of family concepts in clinical practice.

REFERENCES

1. Freud, S.: Analysis of a phobia in a five year old boy. *In:* Collected Papers. Vol. III. London, Hogarth Press, 1949, pp. 149-289.
2. Flugel, J.C.: The Psycho-Analytic Study of the Family. London, Hogarth Press. 10th Impr., 1960.
3. Lidz, T., Cornelison, A., Fleck, S., and Terry, D.: The intrafamilial environment of the schizophrenic patient: II. Marital schism and marital skew. Amer. J. Psychiat. 114:241-248, 1957.
4. Wynne, L., Rykoff, I., Day, J., and Hirsch, S.: Pseudo-mutuality in the family relations of schizophrenics. Psychiatry 21:205-220, 1958.
5. Ackerman, N.: Interlocking pathology in family relationships. *In:* Changing Concepts in Psychoanalytic Medicine (Sandor Rado and G. E. Daniels, Eds.). New York, Grune & Stratton, 1956.
6. Bateson, G., Jackson, D., Haley, J., and Weakland, J.: Toward a theory of schizophrenia. Behav. Sci. 1:251-264, 1956.
7. Bell, J.E.: Family Group Therapy. Public Health Monograph 64. 1961.
8. Dysinger, R.: The action dialogue in an intense relationship. Paper read at Annual Meeting. American Psychiatric Association, Chicago, 1957.
9. Birdwhistell, R.: Introduction to Kinesics. Louisville, Ky., University of Louisville Press, 1952.
10. Scheflen, A.: The significance of posture in communication systems. Psychiatry 26:316-331, 1964.
11. Bowen, M.: Family psychotherapy with schizophrenia in the hospital and in private practice. *In:* Intensive Family Therapy (Ivan Boszormenyi-Nagy and J.L. Framo, Eds.). New York, Harper and Row, 1965.
12. Bowen, M.: Family relationships in schizophrenia. *In:* Schizophrenia—An Integrated Approach (Auerback, Ed.). New York, Ronald Press, 1959.
13. Bowen, M.: A family concept of schizophrenia. *In:* The Etiology of Schizophrenia (D. Jackson, Ed.). New York, Basic Books, 1960.
14. Bowen, M.: Family psychotherapy. Amer. J. Orthopsychiat. 30:40-60, 1961.
15. Toman, W.: Family Constellation. New York, Springer Publishing Co., 1961.

Chapter 4

THE FAMILY AS A TREATMENT UNIT

Virginia M. Satir

Using the family as a treatment unit in therapy seems to be the inevitable outcome of experience and research in which new knowledge about human behavior has suggested different approaches to the meaning and causation of behavior and consequently made different treatment procedures possible.

Treating the family as a unit means having all family members present at the time in the same place with a single therapist or with male and female cotherapists. The whole family is then viewed and treated as a system originally developed by the male and female adults who were the "architects" of the family.

The symptom of any family member at a given time is seen as a comment on a dysfunctional family system. The wearer of the symptom, the identified patient, is seen as signalling distortion, denial, and/or frustration of growth. Simultaneously, he is signalling the presence of pain, discomfort, or trouble in his survival figures. (Survival figures are those people who have provided and continue to provide nurture, economic support, and directing functions for him.) The major treatment tool in family therapy is the application of concepts and procedures relating to interaction and communication.

To begin to look to a family system, one can remind oneself that each member of any family is unavoidably committed to the system of his family, if only because that is where he had his beginnings. If the system is an open one, he can use it for his growth. He continues to move in and eventually out of his family system as his maturity develops. Then he himself becomes an architect in developing a further branch of the system, interacting with other people in other situations.

To exist as an open system, the family needs rules which allow it to meet changes openly, directly, clearly and appropriately. Ability for expansion and reshaping is needed for three kinds of changes that inevitably occur because of the nature of life and living. These are:

From V.M. Satir, The Family as a Treatment Unit, *Confinia Psychiatrica*, 8: 37-42, 1965. Courtesy of S. Karger AG.

1. changes within the individual members; for example, *changes which occur between birth and maturity in the use and perception of authority, independence, sexuality, and productivity;*

2. changes between family members; for example, *between adults and a child from birth to maturity, between husband and wife before they have a child and after the coming of a child, the illness or injury of one or the advancing age of both husband and wife;* and

3. changes which are demanded by social environment; for example, *war, a new job, school, neighborhood or country, or new laws.*

If the family system is a closed one, the family will handle these inevitable changes by attempting to maintain the status quo, and thus by denying or distorting the change. This creates a discrepancy between the presence of change and the acknowledgment of change, and presents a dilemma which must be dealt with before life and relationships can continue.

Because changes must be coped with, a family system which does not have functional ways to assimilate it will have dysfunctional ways. Generally speaking, a system which has rules requiring that the present be seen in terms of the past will be dysfunctional. If the rules of the system can be changed to meet the present, it will become functional. The dysfunctional family, when confronted with change, produces symptoms.

The precursors to what we call symptoms, to modern clinical entities, are the physically ill person, the witch, the pauper, the idiot, and the criminal. It was not until relatively recently that it was recognized that all of these entities had something in common. Family therapy is concerned with all of them.

Initially the treatment of behavior problems—of deviant behavior—centered around the person wearing the symptom. This was true until the advent of child guidance clinics, where the mother was seen along with the child who wore the symptom. Fathers were not discovered until relatively recently in the child guidance clinics. Sometime later, marital counseling or marital therapy including both husband and wife was initiated.

Now we have ideas about family therapy which include people as individuals, and in their respective roles: marital, parental, filial, and sibling. Furthermore, we see that the conclusions drawn from experience in the family of origin are connected with the selection of spouse, and with the blueprint for childrearing practices. The symptom is regarded as a report about the individual wearing it, about his family, and about the rules of the family system; and to understand the symptom, one must understand not only the symptom-wearer, but also his family, and the family system.

This means that a symptom such as psychosis in either parent indicates dysfunction in the marital relationship, as well as in child rearing practices. By the same token, symptoms in a child indicate dysfunction in the marital relationship. Thus by seeing the whole family together, we can serve both treatment and preventative functions.

We believe that by observing and learning to understand communication in a family we can discover the rules that govern each individual's behavior. The family system has rules about 1. self and manifestation of self, or "how I may report", 2. self and expectation of other, or, "what I may expect from you", and 3. self and the use of the world outside of the family, or "how I may go outside the family". Family members are not necessarily aware of these rules. We believe the rules are shaped by interactional experience and acquired as each person attempts to survive, grow, get close to others, and produce.

Because each person comes into the world without a blueprint for interacting in these ways, he must develop it as he grows from birth. The beginning of this blueprint will of necessity be shaped by those who surround him. These are the adults who attempt to insure his survival—through nurture and economic support, through directing his actions, and through providing a model for what he can become.

Most adults have little notion about their importance as models for a child. They behave as though the child sees and hears only that which he is directed to see and hear. If the way in which adults behave with each other and with the outside world, and the way in which the child is asked to behave are incongruent, the child will perceive this. Because the child is confined by the rules about what he may report, by his inability to judge and by his lack of a complete enough set of reporting symbols, the adult is deluded into believing that he is successfully labelling what the child sees and hears. The parent believes, in other words, that the child does not see or hear that which the parent does not directly direct him to see and hear. We believe that children's symptoms are a distorted but obvious comment on the discrepancies which they have experienced are experiencing. The child cannot grow if he must deal with important discrepancies upon which he may not comment openly. Clues to the nature of the discrepancies may be found in the way the family communicates.

We approach the analysis of communication by observing and understanding the *means* of communication—the giving, receiving, and checking out of meaning with another, as it is revealed through the use of words, the tone and pace of voice, facial expressions, and body tonus and position. Then we look at the outcome: what actually happens in the communication process, and what kinds of joint decisions or understandings occur.

Next, we examine certain processes to shed light on how these outcomes evolved. We ask: 1. how is the uniqueness and individuality of each person manifested? 2. how are decisions made, and 3. how is differentness reacted to? In other words, we are attempting to discern the rules for: 1. manifesting self and validating to the other uniqueness and individuality, 2. making decisions, and 3. acknowledging the presence of, reacting to, and using differentness.

Our goals, in therapy, are also related to this analysis of family communication. We attempt to make three changes in the family system. First, each member of the family should be able to report congruently, completely, and obviously on what he sees and hears, feels and thinks about himself and others, in the presence of others. Second, each person should be addressed and related to in terms of his uniqueness, so that decisions are made in terms of exploration and negotiation rather than in terms of power. Third, differentness must be openly acknowledged, and used for growth.

When these changes are achieved, communication within the family will lead to appropriate outcomes. "Appropriate outcomes" are decisions and behavior which fit the age, ability, and role of the individuals, which fit the role contracts and the context involved, and which further the common goals of the family.

I would like to give you a simple example of the relationship between communication rules and behavior. Suppose that right now you are committed to taking back a report of what I have to say, but you can't get my meaning. And, you have rules that you can't ask about my meaning, for fear of *exposing* you or me (making a conclusion of badness, sickness, stupidity, or craziness about you or me). If these conditions are present, you will probably lay blame somewhere; there will be three places to point your finger: to yourself, to me, or to the situation.

You will undergo some form of personal discomfort; you will feel anxiety, hostility toward me, and helplessness toward the situation—(anxiety: "I am no good", hostility: "You are no good", helplessness: "I am little and weak"). You will probably experience all three feelings, roughly in that order—anxiety, hostility, and helplessness. They will have been occasioned by the fact that you could not keep your *commitment* to yourself. And your inability to keep your commitment to yourself will have been caused by our *rules* about what kind of questions you can ask.

If you have rules which permit you to risk exposure and seek clarity, in the presence of confusion or lack of clarity, you can save yourself these feelings of anxiety, hostility, and helplessness. Risk requires a perception of your ability to survive in the face of pain, anger, and hurt in another and the perception that the other will not die from his experience of being pained, angered and/or hurt—(pain: "I am injured", anger: "You injured me", and hurt: "I don't count").

A direct question is often regarded as a "risk runner". The infrequent use of direct questions is one of the signals of inability to communicate in a troubled family; another is the infrequent use of first names.

It should be clear, by now, that I believe that human beings are continually searching to make things fit. Lack of success in making things fit becomes manifest in symptoms. Inability to explore by asking direct questions and making accurate reports does not stop the search; it only makes the search come out in a confused, indirect or unclear way, which may show up in symptoms, or inappropriate outcomes.

Thus the analysis of a symptom starts with an analysis of communication, and a documentary of the outcome. Then comes the exploration of the family system, which makes explicit the rules for maintaining the system, and points out the individual processes which implement these rules.

SUMMARY

Family therapy centers around the application of concepts of interaction and deals with the present rules and processes of individuals by exploring the family system. Theories relating to behavior to interactional processes are far from new. Freud used this idea in his treatment of little Hans; Sullivan, Moreno, Ackerman, Lidz, Fleck, Bowen, Bateson, Jackson and Berne—to mention a few—have used interactional concepts to understand human behavior. At present theories of human behavior which include interactional phenomena are more widely embraced and are getting to be better understood. Using the family as a treatment unit is a further way to both use and develop the theory.

REFERENCES

Ackerman, N.; Beatman, F. and Sherman, S.W. (Eds.): Exploring the Base for Family Therapy (Family Service Ass., New York 1961).

Brodey, W.M.; Bowen, N.M.; Dysinger, G. and Basamania, B.: Some family operations of schizophrenia: a study of five hospitalized families each with a schizophrenic member. A.M.A. Arch. gen. Psychiat. *1*:379-402 (1959).

Jackson, D.D. (Ed.): Etiology of Schizophrenia (Basic Books, New York, 1960).

MacGregor, R.; Ritchie, A.M.: Serrano, A.C. and Schuster, F.P., Jr.: Multiple Impact Therapy with Families (MacGraw Hill, New York 1964).

Overton, A.; Tinker, K.H.: Casework Notebook (Family Centered Project, St. Paul, Minn. 1959).

Satir, V.: Conjoint Family Therapy (Science and Behavior Books, Palo Alto, Calif. 1964).

Chapter 5

BEHAVORIAL APPROACHES TO FAMILY AND COUPLE THERAPY

Robert Liberman

The current splurge of couple and family therapies is not simply an accident or passing fad. These increasingly used modes of treatment for psychiatric problems are anchored in a sound foundation and are not likely to blow away. The foundation of these newer therapies lies in the opportunity they offer to induce significant behavioral change in the participants by a major restructuring of their interpersonal environments.

Couple and family therapy can be particularly potent means of behavior modification because the interpersonal milieu that undergoes change is that of the day-to-day, face-to-face encounter an individual experiences with the most important people in his life—his spouse or members of his immediate family. When these therapies are successful it is because the therapist is able to guide the members of the couple or family into changing their modes of dealing with each other. In behavioral or learning terms, we can translate "ways of dealing with each other" into consequences of behavior or *contingencies of reinforcement.* Instead of rewarding maladaptive behavior with attention and concern, the family members learn to give each other recognition and approval for desired behavior.

Since the family is a system of interlocking, reciprocal behaviors (including affective behavior), family therapy proceeds best when each of the members learns how to change his or her responsiveness to the others. Family therapy should be a learning experience for all the members involved. For simplification, however, this paper will analyze family pathology and therapy from the point of view of the family responding to a single member.

Typically, families that come for treatment have coped with the maladaptive or deviant behavior of one member by responding to it over the years with anger, nagging, babying, conciliation, irritation, or

From R. Liberman, Behavioral Approaches to Family and Couple Therapy, *American Journal of Orthopsychiatry, 40:*106-18. Copyright © 1970 the American Orthopsychiatric Association, Inc. Reproduced by permission.

sympathy. These responses, however punishing they might seem on the surface, have the effect of reinforcing the deviance, that is, increasing the frequency or intensity of the deviant behavior in the future. Reinforcement occurs because the attention offered is viewed and felt by the deviant member as positive concern and interest. In many families with a deviant member, there is little social interaction and the individuals tend to lead lives relatively isolated from each other. Because of this overall lack of interaction, when interaction does occur in response to a member's "abnormal" behavior, such behavior is powerfully reinforced.[14]

Verbal and nonverbal means of giving attention and recognition can be termed *social reinforcement* (as contrasted with food and sex, which are termed *pimary reinforcement*). Social reinforcement represents the most important source of motivation for human behavior.[6, 19] Often massive amounts of such "concern" or social reinforcement are communicated to the deviant member, focused and contingent upon the member's maladaptive behavior. The deviant member gets the message: "So long as you continue to produce this undesirable behavior (symptoms), we will be interested and concerned in you." Learning the lesson of such messages leads to the development and maintenance of symptomatic or deviant behavior and to characterological patterns of activity and identity. Sometimes, the message of concern and interest is within the awareness of the "sick" member. Individuals with a conscious awareness of these contingencies are frequently termed "manipulative" by mental health professionals since they are adept at generating social reinforcement for their maladaptive behavior. But learning can occur without an individual's awareness or insight, in which case we view the maladaptive behavior as being unconsciously motivated.

Massive amounts of contingent social reinforcement are not necessary to maintain deviant behavior. Especially after the behavior has developed, occasional or *intermittant reinforcement* will promote very durable continuation of the behavior. Laboratory studies have shown that intermittant reinforcement produces behavior that is most resistant to extinction.[6]

Many family therapists[7, 8, 21] have demonstrated that the interest and concern family members show in the deviance of one member can be in the service of their own psychological economy. Maintaining a "sick" person in the family can be gratifying (reinforcing) to others, albeit at some cost in comfort and equanimity. Patterson[15] describes how this reciprocal reinforcement can maintain deviant behavior by using the example of a child who demands an ice cream cone while shopping with his mother in a supermarket. The reinforcer for this "demand behavior" is compliance by the mother, but if she ignores the demand, the effect is to increase the rate or loudness of the demand. Loud demands or shrieks by a child in a supermarket are aversive to the mother; that is, her noncompliance is punished. When the mother finally buys the ice cream cone, the aversive tantrum ends. The reinforcer for the child's tantrum is the ice cream cone. The reinforcing contingency for the mother was the termination of the "scene" in the supermarket. In this reciprocal fashion, the tantrum behavior is maintained. I shall return to this important aspect of family psychopathology—the mutually reinforcing or symbiotic nature of deviance—in the case studies below. Indeed, the balance between the aversive and gratifying consequences of maladaptive behavior in a member on the other family members is the crucial determinant of motivation for and response to treatment.

Changing the contingencies by which the patient gets acknowledgment and concern from other members of his family is the basic principle of learning that underlies the potency of family or couple therapy. Social reinforcement is made contingent on desired, adaptive behavior instead of maladaptive and symptomatic behavior. It is the task of the therapist in collaboration with the family or couple to (1) specify the maladaptive behavior, (2) choose reasonable goals which are alternative, adaptive behaviors, (3) direct and guide the family to change the contingencies of their social reinforcement patterns from maladaptive to adaptive target behaviors.

Another principle of learning involved in the process of successful family therapy is modeling, also called imitation or identification. The model, sometimes the therapist but also other members of the family, exhibits desired, adaptive behavior which then is imitated by the patient. Imitation or identification occurs when the model is an esteemed person (therapist, admired family member) and when the model receives positive reinforcement (approval) for his behavior from others.[3] The amount of observational learning will be governed by the degree to which a family member pays attention to the modeling cues, has the capacity to process and rehearse the cues, and possesses the necessary components in his behavioral experience which can be combined to reproduce the more complex, currently modeled behavior.

Imitative learning enables an individual to short-circuit the tedious and lengthy process of trial-and-error (or reward) learning while incorporating complex chains of behavior into his repertoire. Much of the behaviors which reflect the enduring part of our culture are to a large extent transmitted by repeated observation of behavior displayed by social models, particularly familial models. If performed frequently enough and rewarded in turn with approval by others, the imitated behavior will become incorporated into the patient's behavioral repertoire. The principles of imitative learning have been exploited with clinical success by researchers working with autistic children,[12] phobic youngsters,[4] and mute, chronic psychotics.[18] How modeling can be used in family therapy will be illustrated in the cases cited below.

I will limit the scope of the case examples to couples and families;

however, the same principles of learning apply to group therapy[11,17] and with some modification to individual psychotherapy.[9] Although learning theory has been associated in clinical psychiatry with its systematic and explicit application in the new behavior therapies, it should be emphasized that learning theory offers a generic and unitary explanation of the processes mediating change in all psychotherapies, including psychoanalytic ones.[1,13]

TECHNIQUE

Before getting to the case material, I would like to outline the main features of an application of behavior theory to family therapy. The three major areas of technical concern for the therapist are (1) *creating and maintaining a positive therapeutic alliance;* (2) *making a behavioral analysis of the problem(s);* and (3) *implementing the behavioral principles of reinforcement and modeling in the context of ongoing interpersonal interactions.*

Without the positive therapeutic alliance between the therapist and those he is helping, there can be little or no successful intervention. The working alliance is the lever which stimulates change. In learning terms, the positive relationship between therapist and patient(s) permits the therapist to serve as a social reinforcer and model; in other words, to build up adaptive behaviors and allow maladaptive behaviors to extinguish. The therapist is an effective reinforcer and model for the patients to the extent that the patients value him and hold him in high regard and warm esteem.

Clinicians have described the ingredients that go into this positive therapist-patient relationship in many different ways. Terminology varies with the "school" of psychotherapy to which the clinician adheres. Psychoanalysts have contributed notions such as "positive transference" and an alliance between the therapist and the patient's "observing ego." Reality therapists call for a trusting involvement with the patient. Some clinicians have termed it a "supportive relationship" implying sympathy, respect, and concern on the part of the therapist. Recent research has labeled the critical aspects of the therapist-client relationship: nonpossessive warmth, accurate empathy, and genuine concern.[20] Truax and his colleagues[20] have been able to successfully operationalize these concepts and to teach them to selected individuals. They have further shown that therapists high on these attributes are more successful in psychotherapy than those who are not. Whatever the labels, a necssary if not sufficient condition for therapeutic change in patients is a doctor-patient relationship that is infused with mutual respect, warmth, trust, and affection.

In my experience, these qualities of the therapeutic alliance can be developed through a period of initial evaluation of the patient or family. The early therapist-family contacts, proceeding during the first few interviews, offer an opportunity to the therapist to show unconditional warmth, acceptance, and concern for the clients and their problems.

Also during the first few sessions, while the therapeutic relationship is being established, the therapist must do his "diagnostic." In a learning approach to family therapy, the diagnostic consists of a *behavioral* or *functional analysis* of the problems. In making his behavioral analysis, the therapist, in collaboration with the family, asks two major questions:

1. What behavior is maladaptive or problematic—what behavior in the designated patient should be increased or decreased? Each person, in turn, is asked, (1) what changes would you like to see in others in the family, and (2) how would you like to be different from the way you are now? Answering these questions forces the therapist to choose carefully *specific behavioral goals.*

2. What environmental and interpersonal contingencies currently support the problematic behavior—that is, what is maintaining undesirable behavior or reducing the likelihood of more adaptive responses? This is called a "functional analysis of behavior," and also can include an analysis of the development of symptomatic or maladaptive behavior, the "conditioning history" of the patient. The mutual patterns of social reinforcement in the family deserve special scrutiny in this analysis since their deciphering and clarification become central to an understanding of the case and to the formulation of therapeutic strategy.

It should be noted that the behavioral analysis of the problem doesn't end after the initial sessions, but by necessity continues throughout the course of therapy. As the problem behaviors change during treatment, so must the analysis of what maintains these behaviors. New sources of reinforcement for the patient and family members must be assessed. In this sense, the behavioral approach to family therapy is dynamic.

The third aspect of behavioral technique is the actual choice and implementation of therapeutic strategy and tactics. Which interpersonal transactions between the therapist and family members and among the family members can serve to alter the problem behavior in a more adaptive direction? The therapist acts as an educator, using his value as a social reinforcer to instruct the family or couple in changing their ways of dealing with each other. Some of the possible tactics are described in the case studies below.

A helpful way to conceptualize these tactics is to view them as "behavioral change experiments" where the therapist and family together re-program the contingencies of reinforcement operating in the family system. The behavioral change experiments consist of family members responding to each other in various ways, with the responses contingent on more desired reciprocal ways of relating. Ballentine[2] views the behavioral change experiments, starting with small but well-defined successes, as leading to (1) a shift toward more optimistic and hopeful expectations; (2) an emphasis on doing things differently while giving the responsibility for change to each family member; (3) "encouragement of an observational outlook which forces family members to look closely at themselves and their relationships with one another, rather than looking "inside" themselves with incessant why's and wherefores"; and (4) "the generation of empirical data which can be instrumental to further change, since they often expose sequences of family action and reaction in particularly graphic and unambiguous fashion."

The therapist also uses his importance as a model to illustrate desired modes of responding differentially to behavior that at times is maladaptive and at other times approaches more desirable form. The operant conditioning principle of "shaping" is used, whereby gradual approximations to the desired end behavior are reinforced with approval and spontaneous and genuine interest by the therapist. Through his instructions and example, the therapist teaches shaping to the members of the couple or family. Role playing or behavioral rehearsal are among the useful tactics employed in generating improved patterns of interaction among the family members.

The therapist using a behavioral model does not act like a teaching machine, devoid of emotional expression. Just as therapists using other theoretical schemas, he is most effective in his role as an educator when he expresses himself with affect in a comfortable, human style developed during his clinical training and in his life as a whole. Since intermittent reinforcement produces more durable behavior, the therapist may employ trial terminations, tapering off the frequency of sessions prior to termination and "booster" sessions.[1] The strategy and tactics of this behavioral approach to couples and families will be more clearly delineated in the case studies that follow. A more systematic and detailed outline of the behavior modification approach is presented in Table 5-I. The specification and implications of the items in this outline can be found in the manual by Reese.[16]

CASE #1

Mrs. D is a 35-year-old housewife and mother of three children who had a 15-year history of severe, migranous headaches. She had had frequent medical hospitalizations for her headaches (without any organic problems being found), and also a 1½-year period of intensive, psychodynamically oriented, individual psychotherapy. She found relief from her headaches only after retreating to her bed for periods of days to a week with the use of narcotics.

After a brief period of evaluation by me, she again developed intractable headaches and was hospitalized. A full neurological workup revealed no neuropathology. At this time I recommended that I continue with the patient and her husband in couple therapy. It had previously become

Table 5-I
A Behavioral Model for Learning
(adapted from E.P. Reese[16])

1. Specify the final performance (therapeutic goals):
   • Identify the behavior.
   • Determine how it is to be measured.
2. Determine the current baseline rate of the desired behavior.
3. Structure a favorable situation for eliciting the desired behavior by providing cues for the appropriate behavior and removing cues for incompatible, inappropriate behavior.
4. Establish motivation by locating reinforcers, depriving the individual of reinforcers (if necessary), and withholding reinforcers for inappropriate behavior.
5. Enable the individual to become comfortable in the therapeutic setting and to become familiar with the reinforcers.
6. Shape the desired behavior:
   • Reinforce successive approximations of the therapeutic goals.
   • Raise the criterion for reinforcement gradually.
   • Present reinforcement immediately, contingent upon the behavior.
7. Fade out the specific cues in the therapeutic setting to promote generalization of acquired behavior.
8. Reinforce intermittantly to facilitate durability of the gains.
9. Keep continuous, objective records.

clear to me that the patient's headaches were serving an important purpose in the economy of her marital relationship: headaches and the resultant debilitation were the sure way the patient could elicit and maintain her husband's concern and interest in her. On his part, her husband was an active, action-oriented man who found it difficult to sit down and engage in conversation. He came home from work, read the newspaper, tinkered with his car, made repairs on the house, or watched TV. Mrs. D got her husband's clear-cut attention only when she developed headaches, stopped functioning as mother and wife, and took to her bed. At these times Mr. D was very solicitous and caring. He gave her medication, stayed home to take care of the children, and called the doctor.

My analysis of the situation led me to the strategy of redirecting Mr. D's attention to the adaptive strivings and the maternal and wifely behavior of his wife. During ten 45-minute sessions, I shared my analysis of the problem with Mr. and Mrs. D and encouraged them to reciprocally restructure their marital relationship. Once involved in a trusting and confident relationship with me, Mr. D worked hard to give his wife attention and approval for her day-to-day efforts as a mother and housewife. When he came home from work, instead of burying himself in the newspaper he inquired about the day at home and discussed with his wife problems concerning the children. He occasionally rewarded his wife's homemaking efforts by taking her out to a movie or to dinner (something they had not done for years). While watching TV he had his wife sit close to him or on his lap. In return, Mrs. D was taught to reward her husband's new efforts at intimacy with affection and appreciation. She let him know how much she liked to talk with him about the day's events. She prepared special dishes for him and kissed him warmly when he took initiative in expressing affection toward her. On the other hand, Mr. D was instructed to pay minimal attention to his wife's headaches. He was reassured that in so doing, he would be helping her decrease their frequency and severity. He was no longer to give her medication, cater to her when she was ill, or call the doctor for her. If she got a headache, she was to help herself and he was to carry on with his regular routine insofar as possible. I emphasized that *he should not, overall, decrease his attentiveness to his wife, but rather change the timing and direction of his attentiveness.* Thus the behavioral contingencies of Mr. D's attention changed from headaches to housework, from invalidism to active coping and functioning as mother and wife.

Within ten sessions, both were seriously immersed in this new approach toward each other. Their marriage was different and more satisfying to both. Their sex life improved. Their children were better behaved, as they quickly learned to apply the same reinforcement principles in reacting to the children and to reach a consensus in responding to their children's limit-testing. Mrs. D got a job as a department store clerk (a job she enjoyed and which provided her with further reinforcement— money and attention from people for "healthy" behavior). She was given recognition by her husband for her efforts to collaborate in improving the family's financial condition. She still had headaches, but they were mild and short-lived and she took care of them herself. Everyone was happier including Mrs. D's internist who no longer was receiving emergency calls from her husband.

A followup call to Mr. and Mrs. D one year later found them maintaining their progress. She has occasional headaches but has not had to retreat to bed or enter a hospital.

CASE #2

Mrs. S. is a 34-year-old mother of five who herself came from a family of ten siblings. She wanted very badly to equal her mother's output of children and also wanted to prove to her husband that he was potent and fertile. He had a congenital hypospadius and had been told by a physician prior to their marriage that he probably could not have children. Unfortunately Mrs. S was Rh negative and her husband Rh positive. After their fifth child she had a series of spontaneous abortions because of the Rh incompatibility. Each was followed by a severe depression. Soon the depressions ran into each other and she was given a course of 150 EST's. The EST's had the effect of making her confused and unable to function at home while not significantly lifting the depressions. She had some successful short-term psychotherapy but again plunged into a depression after a hysterectomy.

Her husband, like Mr. D in the previous case, found it hard to tolerate his wife's conversation, especially when it was taken up mostly by complaints and tearfulness. He escaped from the unhappy home situation by plunging himself into his work, holding two jobs simultaneously. When he was home, he was too tired for any conversation or meaningful interaction with his wife. Their sexual interaction was nil. Although Mrs. S tried hard to maintain her household and raise her children and even hold a part-time job, she received little acknowledgment for her efforts from her husband who became more distant and peripheral as the years went by.

My behavioral analysis pointed to a lack of reinforcement from Mrs. S's husband for her adaptive strivings. Consequently her depressions, with their large hypochondriacal components, represented her desperate attempt to elicit her husband's attention and concern. Although her somatic complaints and self-depreciating accusations were aversive for her husband, the only way he knew how to "turn them off" was to offer sympathy, reassure her of his devotion to her, and occasionally stay home from work. Naturally, his nurturing her in this manner had the effect of reinforcing the very behavior he was trying to terminate.

During five half-hour couple sessions I focused primarily on Mr. S, who was the mediating agent of reinforcement for his wife and hence the person who could potentially modify her behavior. I actively redirected his attention from his wife "the unhappy, depressed woman" to his wife "the coping woman." I rightly recommended to him that he drop his extra job, at least for the time being, in order to be at home in the evening to converse with his wife about the day's events, especially her approximations at successful homemaking. I showed by my own example (modeling) how to support his wife in her efforts to assert herself reasonably with her intrusive mother-in-law and obnoxious neighbor.

A turning point came after the second session, when I received a desperate phone call from Mr. S one evening. He told me that his wife had called from her job and tearfully complained that she could not go on and that he must come and bring her home. He asked me what he should do. I indicated that this was a crucial moment, that he should call her back and briefly acknowledge her distress but at the same time emphasize the importance of her finishing the evening's work. I further suggested that he meet her as usual after work and take her out for an ice cream soda. This would get across to her his abiding interest and recognition for her positive efforts in a genuine and spontaneous way. With this support from me, he followed my suggestions and within two weeks Mrs. S's depression had completely lifted.

She was shortly thereafter given a job promotion, which served as an extrinsic reinforcement for her improved work performance and was the occasion for additional reinforcement from me and her husband during the next therapy session. We terminated after the fifth session, a time limit we had initially agreed on.

Eight months later at followup they reported being "happier together than ever before."

CASE #3

Edward is a 23-year-old young man who had received much psychotherapy, special schooling, and occupational counseling and training during the past 17 years. He was diagnosed at different times as a childhood schizophrenic and as mentally subnormal. At age 6 he was evaluated by a child psychiatry clinic and given three years of psychodynamic therapy by a psychoanalyst. He had started many remedial programs and finished almost none of them. He, in fact, was a chronic failure—in schools as well as in jobs. His parents viewed him as slightly retarded despite his low normal intelligence on IQ tests. He was infantilized by his mother and largely ignored or criticized by his father. He was used by his mother, who was domineering and aggressive, as an ally against the weak and passive father. When I began seeing them in a family evaluation, Edward was in the process of failing in the most recent rehabilitation effort—an evening, adult high school.

The initial goals of the family treatment, then, were (1) to disengage Edward from the clasp of his protective mother, (2) to get his father to offer himself as a model and as a source of encouragement (reinforcement) for Edward's desires and efforts towards independence, (3) to structure Edward's life with occupational and social opportunities that he could not initiate on his own. Fortunately the Jewish Vocational Service in Boston offers an excellent rehabilitation program based on the same basic principles of learning that have been elucidated in this article. I referred Edward to it and at the same time introduced him to a social club for ex-mental patients which has a constant whirl of activities daily and on weekends.

During our weekly family sessions, I used modeling and role-playing to help Edward's parents positively reinforce his beginning efforts at the J.V.S. and the social club. After three months at the J.V.S., Edward secured a job and now after another seven months has a job tenure and membership in the union. He has been an active member of the social club and has gone on weekend trips with groups there—something he had never done before. He is now "graduating" to another social club, a singles' group in a church, and has started action on getting his driver's license.

The family sessions were not easy or without occasional storms, usually generated by Edward's mother as she from time to time felt "left out." She needed my support and interest (reinforcement) in her problems as a hard-working and unappreciated mother at these times. Because of the positive therapeutic relationship cemented over a period of nine months, Edward's parents slowly began to be able to substitute positive reinforcement for his gradually improving efforts at work and play instead of the previous blanket criticism (also, paradoxically, a kind of social reinforcement) he had received from them for his failures. I encouraged the father to share openly with Edward his own experiences as a young man reaching for independence, thereby serving as a model for his son.

The parents needed constant reinforcement (approval) from me for trying out new ways of responding to Edward's behavior; for example, to eliminate the usual nagging of him to do his chores around the house (which only served to increase the lethargic slothful behavior which accrues from the attention) and to indicate instead pleasure when he mows the lawn even if he forgets to rake the grass and trim the hedge. They learned to give Edward approval when he takes the garbage out even if he doesn't do it "their" way. And they learned how to spend time listening to Edward pour out his enthusiasm for his job even if they feel he is a bit too exuberant.

Our family sessions were tapered to twice monthly and then to once a month. Termination went smoothly after one year of treatment.

CASE #4

Mr. and Mrs. F have a long history of marital strife. There was a year-long separation early in their marriage and several attempts at marriage counseling lasting three years. Mr. F has paranoid trends which are reflected in his extreme sensitivity to any lack of affection or commitment toward him by his wife. He is vey jealous of her close-knit relationship with her parents. Mrs. F is a disheveled and unorganized woman who has been unable to meet her husband's expectations for an orderly and accomplished homemaker or competent manager of their five children. Their marriage has been marked by frequent mutual accusations and depreciation, angry withdrawal and sullenness.

My strategy with this couple, whom I saw for 15 sessions, was to teach them to stop reinforcing each other with attention and emotionality for undesired behavior and to begin eliciting desired behavior in each other using the principle of *shaping*. Tactically, I structured the therapy sessions with an important "ground-rule.": No criticism or harping were allowed and they were to spend the time telling each other what the other had done during the past week that approached the desired behaviors. As they gave positive feedback to each other for approximations to the behavior each valued in the other, I served as an auxiliary source of positive acknowledgment, reinforcing the reinforcer.

We began by clearly delineating what specific behaviors were desired by each of them in the other and by my giving them homework assignments in making gradual efforts to approximate the behavioral goals. For instance, Mr. F incessantly complained about his wife's lack of care in handling the evening meal—the disarray of the table setting, lack of tablecloth, disorderly clearing of the dishes. Mrs. F grudgingly agreed that there was room for improvement and I instructed her to make a start by using a tablecloth nightly. Mr. F in turn was told the importance of his giving her positive and consistent attention for her effort, since this was important to him. After one week they reported that they had been able to fulfill the assignment and that the evening meal was more enjoyable. Mrs. F had increased her performance to the complete satisfaction of her husband, who meanwhile had continued to give her positive support for her progress.

A similar process occurred in another problem area. Mr. F felt that his wife should do more sewing (mending clothes, putting on missing buttons) and should iron his shirts (which he had always done himself). Mrs. F was fed up with the home they lived in, which was much too small for their expanded family. Mr. F resolutely refused to consider moving to larger quarters because he felt it would not affect the quality of his wife's homemaking performance. I instructed Mrs. F to begin to do more sewing and ironing and Mr. F to reinforce this by starting to consider moving to a new home. He was to concretize this by spending part of each Sunday reviewing the real estate section of the newspaper with his wife and to make visits to homes that were advertised for sale. He was to make clear to her that his interest in a new home was *contingent* upon her improvements as a homemaker.

Between the third and sixth sessions, Mrs. F's father—who was ill with terminal lung cancer—was admitted to the hospital and died. During this period, we emphasized the importance of Mr. F giving his wife solace and support, I positively reinforced Mr. F's efforts in this direction. He was able to help his wife over her period of sadness and mourning despite his long-standing antagonism toward her father, Mrs. F in turn, with my encouragement, responded to her husband's sympathetic behavior with affection and appreciation. Although far from having an idyllic marriage. Mr. and Mrs. F have made tangible gains in moving closer toward each other.

DISCUSSION

There is too much confusion in the rationales and techniques underlying current practices in family therapy. Although attempts to convey the method of family therapy always suffer when done through the written word, I do not share the belief that "the vital communications in all forms of psychotherapy are intuitive, felt, unspoken, and unconscious."[7] Although this article is not meant as a "how to do it" treatise for family therapists, I do intent it as a preliminary attempt to apply a few of the basic principles of imitative learning and operant conditioning to couple and family therapy.

Although the rationalized conceptualization of family therapy practiced by psychoanalytically oriented therapists differs from the learning and behavioral approach described here, closer examination of the actual techniques used reveals marked similarity. For example Framo,[7] in explaining the theory behind his family therapy, writes: "The overriding goal of the intensive middle phases consists in understanding and working through, often through transference to each other and to the therapists, the introjects of the parents so that the parents can see and experience how those difficulties manifested in the present family system have emerged from their unconscious attempts to perpetrate or master old conflicts arising from their families or origin. . . . The essence of the true work of family therapy is in the tracing of the vicissitudes of early object-relationships, and . . . the exceedingly intricate transformations which occur as a function of the intrapsychic and transactional blending of the old and new family systems of the parents. . . ."

Despite the use of psychoanalytic constructs, Framo describes the actual process of family therapy in ways that are very compatible within a learning framework. He writes: "Those techniques which prompt family interaction are the most productive in the long run. . . . It is especially useful to concentrate on here-and-now feelings; this method usually penetrated much deeper then dealing with feelings described in retrospect. . . . As we gained experience in working with families we became less hesitant about taking more forceful, active positions in order to help the family become unshackled from their rigid patterns."

Framo goes on to give illustrations of his work with families in which differential reinforcement for behavior considered more desirable and appropriate is given by the therapists. In dealing with angry and aggressive mothers, "we learned to avoid noticing what they did (e.g. emotional in-fighting) and pay attention to what they missed in life." Trying to activate passive fathers, "the therapists make every conscious effort to build him up during the sessions. . . . A number of techniques have been tried: forcing more interaction between the husband and wife; assigning tasks; having a female therapist give encouragement in a flattering way; occasional individual sessions with the father." Zuk[23] describes his technique of family therapy in ways that fit into a reinforcement framework. He views the cornerstone of the technique the exploration and attempt "to shift the balance of pathogenic relating among family members so that new forms of relating become possible." Zuk further delineates the therapist's tactics as a "go-between" in which he uses his leverage to "constantly structure and direct the treatment situation."

It should be emphasized that the behavioral approach does not simplistically reduce the family system and family interaction to individualistic or dyadic mechanisms of reinforcement. The richness and complexity of family interaction is appreciated by the family therapist working within a behavioral framework. For instance, Ballentine[2] states: ". . . behavior within a system cannot be so easily modified by focusing on the behavioral contingencies existing within any two-person subsystem, since one person's behavior in relation to a second's is often determined by behaviors of others within the system . . . the behavioral contingencies within a family system are manifold and constitute a matrix of multiple behavioral contingencies."

The complexity of family contingencies is exemplified by a transient problem which arose in Case #3. As Edward developed more independence from his parents and spent less and less time at home, his parents began to argue more angrily. Edward had served as a buffer between them—taking sides, being used as a scapegoat for their hostility, and serving as a "problem child" who required joint parental action and solidarity. With their buffer gone, the husband-wife relationship intensified and friction developed. Since the therapeutic goals were limited to Edward's emancipation from his parents and since it seemed that the parents were sufficiently symbiotic to contain a temporary eruption of hostility, the therapist's major efforts at this point were aimed at protecting Edward from backsliding in response to guilt or family pressure. The strategy worked, and within a few weeks the parents had reached a new modus vivendi with each other while Edward continued to consolidate and extend his gains.

A behavioral and learning approach to family therapy differs from a more psychoanalytic one. The therapist defines his role as an educator in collaboration with the family; therefore, the assigning of "sickness" labels to members, with its potential for moral blame, does not occur as it does under the medical model embodied in the psychoanalytic concept of underlying conflict or disease. There is no need for family members to acknowledge publicly their "weaknesses" or irrationality since insight per se is not considered vital.

The behavioral approach, with its more systematic and specific guidelines, makes it less likely that a therapist will adventitiously reinforce or model contradictory behavior patterns. The behavioral approach, consistently applied, is potentially more effective and faster. When patients do not respond to behavioral techniques, the therapist can use his more empirical attitude to ask why and perhaps to try another technique. The orientation is more experimental and "the patient is always right," with the burden on the therapist to devise effective interventions. In the psychoanalytic approach, the tendency has been for the therapist to decide that their failures are caused by patients who were inappropriate for the technique rather than viewing the technique as needing modification for the particular patient.

The work of behaviorally oriented family therapists is not restricted to the here-and-now of the therapy sessions. As the cases described reveal, much of the effort involves collaboration and involvement with adjunctive agencies such as schools, rehabilitation services, medication, and work settings. Family therapists are moving toward this total systems approach.

The advantages of behavioral approaches to family therapy sketched in this paper remain to be proven by systematic research. Such research is now proceeding.[5, 10, 15, 22] Much work will go into demonstrating that family processes are "essentially behavioral sequences which can be sorted out, specified and measured with a fair degree of accuracy and precision."[2] Hopefully, further clinical and research progress made by behaviorally oriented therapists will challenge all family therapists, regardless of theoretical leanings, to specify more clearly their interventions, their goals, and their empirical results. If these challenges are accepted seriously, the field of family therapy will likely improve and gain stature as a scientifically grounded modality.

REFERENCES

1. Alexander, F. 1965. The dynamics of psychotherapy in the light of learning theory. Internat. J. Psychiat. 1:189-207.
2. Ballentine, R. 1968. The family therapist as a behavioral systems engineer . . . and a responsible one. Paper read at Georgetown Univ. Symp. on Fam. Psychother. Washington.
3. Bandura, A., and Walters, R. 1963. Social Learning and Personality Development. Holt, Rinehart and Winston, New York.
4. Bandura, A., Grusec, J., and Menlove, F. 1967. Vicarious extinction of avoidance behavior. Personality and Soc. Psychol. 5:16-23.
5. Dunham, R. 1966. Ex post facto reconstruction of conditioning schedules in family interaction. *In* Family Structure, Dynamics and Therapy, Irvin M. Cohen, ed.: 107-114. Psychiatric Research No. 20, Amer. Psychiat. Assn., Washington.
6. Ferster, C. 1963. Essentials of a science of behavior. *In* An Introduction to the Science of Human Behavior, J.I. Nurnberger, C.B. Ferster, and J.P. Brady, eds. Appleton-Century-Crofts, New York.
7. Framo, J. 1965. Rationale and techniques of intensive family therapy. *In* Intensive Family Therapy, I. Boszormenyi-Nagy, and J.L. Framo, eds. Hoeber Medical Division, New York.
8. Handel, G. (ed.). 1967. The Psychosocial Interior of the Family. Aldine, Chicago.
9. Krasner, L. 1962. The therapist as a social reinforcement machine. *In* Research in Psychotherapy, H. Strupp, and L. Luborsky, eds. Amer. Psychol. Assn., Washington.
10. Lewinsohn, P., Weinstein, M., and Shaw, D. 1969. Depression: a clinical research approach. *In* Proceedings, 1968 Conference, Assn. Advan. Behav. Ther., San Francisco. In press.

11. Liberman, R. 1970. A behavioral approach to group dynamics. Behav. Ther. In press.
12. Lovaas, O., et al. 1966. Acquisition of imitative speech by schizophrenic children. Science, 151:705-707.
13. Marmor, J. 1966. Theories of learning and psychotherapeutic process. Brit. J. Psychiat. 112:363-366.
14. Patterson, G., et al. 1967. Reprogramming the social environment. Child Psychol. and Psychiat. 8:181-195.
15. Patterson, G., and Reid, J. 1967. Reciprocity and coercion: two facets of social systems. Paper read at 9th Ann. Inst. for Res. in Clin. Psychol. Univ. of Kansas.
16. Reese, E. 1966. The Analysis of Human Operant Behavior. Wm. C. Brown, Dubuque, Iowa.
17. Shapiro, D., and Birk, I. 1967. Group therapy in experimental perspectives. Internat. J. Group Psychother. 17:211-224.
18. Sherman, J. 1965. Use of reinforcement and imitation to reinstate verbal behavior in mute psychotics. J. Abnorm. Psychol. 70:155-164.
19. Skinner, B. 1953. Science and Human Behavior. Macmillan, New York.
20. Truax, C., and Carkhuff, R. 1967. Toward Effective Counseling and Psychotherapy: Training and Practice. Aldine, Chicago.
21. Vogel, E., and Bell, N. 1960. The emotionally disturbed child as the family scapegoat. *In* A Modern Introduction to the Family, N.W. Bell, and E.F. Vogel, eds. Free Press, New York.
22. Zeilberger, J., Sampen, S., and Sloane, H. 1968. Modification of a child's problem behaviors in the home with the mother as therapist. J. Appl. Behav. Anal. 1:47-53.
23. Zuk, G. 1967. Family therapy. Arch. Gen. Psychiat. 16:71-79.

Chapter 6

BRIEF THERAPY:
FOCUSED PROBLEM RESOLUTION

JOHN H. WEAKLAND, RICHARD FISCH,
PAUL WATZLAWICK, AND ARTHUR M. BODIN

I n the last few years, brief treatment has been proliferating—both growing and dividing. As Barten's (2) recent collection of papers illustrates, "brief therapy" means many different things to many different therapists. The brief therapy we wish to present here is an outgrowth of our earlier work in that it is based on two ideas central to family therapy: (a) focusing on observable behavioral interaction in the present and (b) deliberate intervention to alter the going system. In pursuing these themes further, however, we have arrived at a particular conceptualization of the nature of human problems and their effective resolution, and of related procedures, that is different from much current family therapy.

We have been developing and testing this approach at the Brief Therapy Center over the past six years. During this period the Center, operating one day a week, has treated 97 cases, in which 236 individuals were seen. (We have also had extensive experience using the same approach with private patients, but these cases have not been systematically followed up and evaluated.) These 97 cases reached us through a considerable variety of referral sources, and no deliberate selection was exercised. As a result, although probably a majority of our cases involve rather common marital and family problems, the sample covers a wide range overall. We have dealt with white, black, and oriental patients from 5 to over 60 years old, from welfare recipients to the very wealthy, and with a variety of both acute and chronic problems. These included school and work difficulties; identity crises; marital, family, and sexual problems; delinquency, alcohol, and eating problems; anxiety, depression, and schizophrenia. Regardless of the nature or severity of the problem, each case has been limited to a maximum of ten one-hour sessions, usually at weekly intervals. Under these circumstances, our

From J.H. Weakland, R. Fisch, P. Watzlawick, and A.M. Bodin, Brief Therapy: Focused Problem Resolution, *Family Process*, *13:*141-68, 1974. Courtesy of *Family Process*.

treatment has been successful—in terms of achieving limited but significant goals related to the patients' main complaints—in about three-fourths of these cases. We have also demonstrated and taught our approach to a number of other therapists in our area.

We present our approach here for wider consideration. Any form of treatment, however, is difficult to convey adequately by a purely verbal account, without demonstration and direct observation. We will, therefore, begin by discussing the significance and nature of our basic premises in comparison with other forms of treatment. Hopefully, this will provide an orienting context for the subsequent description—supplemented with illustrative case material—of our interrelated concepts, plan of treatment, specific techniques, and results.

PSYCHOTHERAPY—PREMISES AND PRACTICES

In characterizing treatment approaches, although some over-simplification may result, outlining basic premises may make their nature—and especially, their implications—more plain. Often, attention is concentrated on what is explicit and detailed, while what is common and general is neglected. Yet, the more general an idea, the more determinative of behavior it is—especially if its existence is not explicitly recognized. This holds for interpersonal influence as well as individual thinking and behavior; Robert Rosenthal's (21) experiments demonstrate how the beliefs, assumptions, expectations, and biases of an experimenter or interviewer have a profound effect on his subjects. Similarly, the beliefs and theories held by a therapist may strongly influence not only his technique but also the length and outcome of his treatments—by affecting his patient's behavior, his evaluation of that behavior, or both.

For instance, if schizophrenia is conceptualized as a gradual, irreversible mental deterioration involving loss of contact with reality, then attempts at psychotherapeutic contact make little sense, and the only reasonable course of action is long-term hospitalization. The hospitalized patient is then likely to react in a way that clearly justifies this initial "preventive" action. Alternatively, if schizophrenia is seen as a manifestation of a dysfunctional structure of family relationships, the outlook is different and more hopeful, although basic restructuring of the family system is now likely to be seen as necessary. Again, in terms of the postulates of classical psychoanalytic theory, symptom removal must perforce lead to symptom displacement and exacerbation of the patient's condition, since it deals only with manifestations of deeper problems. The premises of the theory permit no other conclusion, except the alternative of claiming that the problem must not have been a "real" one (22). On the other hand, in therapies based on learning or deconditioning theories, symptom manipulation is consistent with the theoretical premises. This enables the therapist is try very different interventions—and, to some extent, constrains him to do so.

That is, all theories of psychotherapy (including our own) have limitations, of practice as well as conception, that are logically inherent in their own nature. Equally important, these limitations are often attributed to *human* nature, rather than to the nature of the theory. It is all too easy to overlook this and become enmeshed in unrecognized, circular explanations. Stating the basic premises of any psychotherapeutic theory as clearly and explicitly as possible at least helps toward perceiving also its implications, limitations, and possible alternatives.

Our Brief Therapy—Bases and Comparisons

Much of the shorter-term treatment that has recently developed in response to the pressure of patient needs and situational limitations consists essentially of briefer versions of conventional forms of individual or family therapy. The same basic assumptions are involved, and, correspondingly, the methods used are similar, except for limited adaptations to the realities of fewer sessions (3, 5, 20). This is expectable, as the usual frameworks naturally offer more restraints to innovation than encouragement and guidance. Within their terms, new methods are apt to appear strange and unreliable (15). Consequently, "brief therapy" ordinarily connotes an expedient that may be necessary when a preferred treatment is not available or is considered not feasible—since the "best" therapies often require patients equipped with rather exceptional resources of time, money, intelligence, persistence, and verbal sophistication. The goals of such brief therapy correspondingly are conceived as limited "first aid"—such as relief of some pressing but not fundamental aspect of the patient's problem, or a supportive holding action until really thorough treatment becomes possible.

We recognize and value the practical and economic advantages for patients and society of shortening treatment. We do not, however, see our own kind of brief treatment as an expedient, nor is brevity in itself a goal to us, except that we believe setting time limits on treatment has some positive influence on both therapists and patients. Rather the nature of our therapy, including its brevity, is primarily a consequence of our premises about the nature and handling of psychiatric problems.

Our fundamental premise is that regardless of their basic origins and etiology—if, indeed, these can ever be reliably determined—the kinds of problems people bring to psychotherapists *persist* only if they are maintained by ongoing current behavior of the patient and others with whom he interacts. Correspondingly, if such problem-maintaining behavior is appropriately changed or eliminated, the problem will be resolved or vanish, regardless of its nature, origin, or duration (24, 26). Our general principles and specific practices of treatment all relate closely to these two assumptions.

This view, like any other, must be judged by its fruits rather than by its seeds. Yet, a brief consideration of two areas of shared prior experience and interest that appear to have had major implications for our present joint position may clarify it and give some due acknowledgment.

Our present brief therapy is visible first as pursuing further two main aspects of family therapy, in which we have all been extensively involved. A decade-and-a-half ago family therapy began to focus attention on observable behavioral interaction and its influence, both among family members and between them and the therapist, rather than on long-past events or inferred mental processes of individuals (10). In line with this, we now see disturbed, deviant, or difficult behavior in an individual (like behavior generally) as essentially a social phenomenon, occurring as one aspect of a system, reflecting some dysfunction in that system, and best treated by some appropriate modification of that system. We differ, however, with those family therapists who consider the dysfunction involved to be necessarily a fundamental aspect of the system's organization and requiring correspondingly fundamental changes in the system. Instead, we now believe that apparently minor changes in overt behavior or its verbal labeling often are sufficient to initiate progressive developments. Further, while we recognize that along with its obvious disadvantages symptomatic behavior usually has some recognizable advantages or "pay-offs"—such as providing leverage in controlling relationships—we no longer consider these especially significant as causes of problems or obstacles to change.

Family therapy also has prompted greater activity by therapists. Once family interaction was seen as significant for problems, it followed that the therapist should aim to change the going system. Extending this, we now see the therapist's primary task as one of taking deliberate action to alter poorly functioning patterns of interaction as powerfully, effectively, and efficiently as possible.

On the matter of *how* the therapist can actively influence behavior effectively—the strategy and techniques of change—we are especially indebted to the hypnotic work of Milton Erickson and his closely related psychotherapy.[1] Two points have been particularly influential. First, although Erickson is much concerned with how overt behavior affects feelings or states of mind, his moves to change existing behavior usually depend upon implicit or indirect means of influence. Even when behavior is explicitly discussed, his aim often is not to clarify the "reality" of a situation but to alter and ameliorate it by some redefinition. Second, both as hypnotist and therapist, Erikson has emphasized the importance of "accepting what the client offers," and turning this to positive use—in ways we will illustrate later—even if what is "offered" might ordinarily appear as resistance or pathology.

---

[1] *The work of Jay Haley (11, 12, 13) has been valuable in making Erickson's principles and practices more explicit, as well as in providing additional ideas from Haley's own work in family therapy and brief treatment.*

While our present approach thus derives directly from basic family therapy, in part, and from Erickson's work, in part, it also differs from both. For example, many family therapists attempt to bring about change largely by explicit clarification of the nature of family behavior and interaction. Such an attempt now seems to us like a family version of promoting "insight," in which one tries to make clear to families the covert rules that have guided them; we ordinarily avoid this. Meanwhile, our conceptualization of problems and treatment appears at least more general and explicit than Erickson's and probably different in various specific respects.

On the other hand, similarities as well as differences are observable between our treatment approach and other approaches with which we have had little interaction. For example, within the general field of family therapy, we share with crisis-intervention therapy of Pittman, Langsley, and their co-workers (18) beliefs in the importance of situation change for the onset of problems and of both directive measures and negotiation of conflicts in promoting better functioning in family systems. Minuchin and Montalvo (16), together with a number of their colleagues at the Philadelphia Child Guidance Clinic, have increasingly emphasized active intervention aimed at particular reorderings of family relationship structure to achieve rapid problem resolution; we often pursue similar aims. Other family therapists than ourselves, notably Bowen, assign patients homework as part of treatment. Work with families similar to our own is also being developed abroad, for instance, at the Athenian Institute of Anthropos under Dr. George Vassiliou and at the Istituto per lo Studio della Famiglia in Milan, under Prof. Dr. Mara Selvini Palazzoli. In addition, the behavior modification school of therapy involves a number of ideas and interventions rather parallel to ours, although that field still appears to give little attention to systems of interaction. Furthermore, as noted later, a number of the techniques of intervention we utilize have also been used and described, though usually in a different conceptual context, by other therapists.

In sum, many particular conceptual and technical elements of our approach are not uniquely ours. We do, however, see as distinctive the overall system of explicitly stated and integrated ideas and practices that constitute our approach.

MAIN PRINCIPLES OF OUR WORK

1. We are frankly symptom-oriented, in a broad sense. Patients or their family members come with certain complaints and accepting them for treatment involves a responsibility for relieving these complaints. Also, since deviant symptomatic behavior and its accompanying vicious circles of reaction and counter-reaction can themselves be so disruptive of system functioning, we believe that one should not hasten to seek

other and deeper roots of pathology. The presenting problem offers, in one package, what the patient is ready to work on, a concentrated manifestation of whatever is wrong, and a concrete index of any progress made.

2. We view the problems that people bring to psychotherapists (except, of course, clearly organic psychiatric syndromes) as situational difficulties between people—problems of interaction. Most often this involves the identified patient and his family; however, other systems such as a patient's involvement with others in a work situation may be important at times.

3. We regard such problems as primarily an outcome of everyday difficulties, usually involving adaptation to some life change, that have been mishandled by the parties involved. When ordinary life difficulties are handled badly, unresolved problems tend increasingly to involve other life activities and relationships in impasses or crises, and symptom formation results.

4. While fortuitous life difficulties, such as illness, accidents, or loss of a job sometimes appear to initiate the development of a problem, we see normal transitional steps in family living as the most common and important "everyday difficulties" that may lead to problems. These transitions include: the change from the voluntary relationship of courtship to the commitment of marriage, and from this to the less reversible commitment when the first child is born; the sharing of influence with other authorities required when a child enters school, and with the child himself and his peers in the adolescent period; the shift from a child-oriented marital relationship back to a two-party system when children leave the home, and its intensification at retirement; and return to single life at the death of one spouse. Although most people manage to handle these transitions at least passably well, they all require major changes in personal relationships that may readily by mishandled. This view is similar to that of Erickson and Haley (12).

5. We see two main ways by which "problems" are likely to develop: if people treat an ordinary difficulty as a "problem" or if they treat an ordinary (or worse) difficulty as no problem at all—that is, by either overemphasis or underemphasis of difficulties in living.

The first appears related to utopian expectations of life. There are countless difficulties which are part and parcel of the everyday business of living for which no known ideal or ultimate solutions exist. Even when relatively severe, these are manageable in themselves but can readily become "problems" as a result of a belief that there should or must be ideal, ultimate solution for them. For instance, there apparently has been a "generation gap" for the past 5000 years that we know of, but is difficulties only became greatly exacerbated into a "problem" when many people became convinced that it should be closed.

Inversely, but equally, "problems" can arise out of the denial of manifest difficulties—which could be seen as utopian assertions. For instance, the husband and wife who insist their marriage was made in heaven, or the parents who deny the existence of any conflicts with their children—and who may contend that any one seeing any difficulty must be either bad or mad—are likely to be laying the foundation for some outbreak of symptomatic behavior.

Two other aspects of this matter need mention. First, over- or under-emphasis of life difficulties is not entirely a matter of personal or family characteristics; this depends also on more general cultural attitudes and conceptions. While these often may be helpful in defining and dealing with the common vicissitudes of social life, they can also be unrealistic and provoke problems. For example, except for the death of a spouse, our own culture characterizes most of the transitions listed earlier as wonderful steps forward along life's path. Since all of these steps ordinarily involve significant and inescapable difficulties, such over-optimistic characterization increases the likelihood of problems developing—especially for people who take what they are told seriously. Second, inappropriate evaluation and handling of difficult situations is often multiplied by interaction between various parties involves. If two persons have similar inappropriate views, they may reciprocally reinforce their common error, while if one over-emphasizes a difficulty and another under-emphasizes it, interaction may lead to increasing polarization and an even more inappropriate stance by each.

6. We assume that once a difficulty begins to be seen as a "problem," the continuation, and often the exacerbation, of this problem results from the creation of a positive feedback loop, most often centering around those very behaviors of the individuals in the system that are intended to resolve the difficulty: The original difficulty is met with an attempted "solution" that intensifies the original difficulty, and so on and on (26).

Consider, for instance, a common pattern between a depressed patient and his family. The more they try to cheer him up and make him see the positive sides of life, the more depressed the patient is likely to get: "They don't even understand me." The action meant to *alleviate* the behavior of the other party *aggravates* it; the "cure" becomes worse than the original "disease." Unfortunately, this usually remains unnoted by those involved and even is disbelieved if any one else tries to point it out.

7. We view long-standing problems or symptoms not as "chronicity" in the usual implication of some basic defect in the individual or family, nor even that a problem has become "set" over time, but as the persistence of a *repetitively* poorly handled difficulty. People with chronic problems have just been struggling inappropriately for longer periods of time. We, therefore, assume that chronic problems offer as great an opportunity for change as acute problems and that the principal difference lies in the usually pessimistic expectations of therapists facing a chronic situation.

8. We see the resolution of problems are primarily requiring a substitution of behavior patterns so as to interrupt the vicious, positive feedback circles. Other less destructive and less distressing behaviors are potentially open to the patient and involved family members at all times. It is usually impossible, however, for them to change from their rigidly patterned, traditional, unsuccessful problem-solving behavior to more appropriate behavior on their own initiative. This is especially likely when such usual behavior is culturally supported, as is often the case: Everyone *knows* that people should do their best to encourage and cheer up a loved one who is sad and depressed. Such behavior is both "right" and "logical"—but often it just doesn't work.

9. In contrast, we seek means of promoting beneficial change that works, even if our remedies appear illogical. For instance, we would be likely to comment on how sad a depressed patient looks and to suggest that there must be some real and important reason for this. Once given some information on the situation, we might say it is rather strange that he is not even *more* depressed. The usual result, paradoxical as it may seem, is that the patient begins to look and sound better.

10. In addition to accepting what the patient offers, and reversing the usual "treatment" that has served to make matters worse, this simple example also illustrates our concept of "thinking small" by focusing on the symptom presented and working in a limited way towards its relief.

We contend generally that change can be effected most easily if the goal of change is reasonably small and clearly stated. Once the patient has experienced a small but definite change in the seemingly monolithic nature of the problem most real to him, the experience leads to further, self-induced changes in this, and often also, in other areas of life. That is, beneficent circles are initiated.

This view may seem insensitive to the "real," "big," or "basic" problems that many therapists and patients expect to be changed by therapy. Such goals are often vague or unrealistic, however, so that therapy which is very optimistic in concept easily becomes lengthy and and disappointing in actual practice. Views of human problems that are either pessimistic about change or grandiose about the degree of change needed undermine the therapist's potentially powerful influence for limited but significant change.

11. Our approach is fundamentally pragmatic. We try to base our conceptions and our interventions on direct observation in the tratment situation of *what* is going on in systems of human interaction, *how* they continue to function in such ways, and *how* they may be altered most effectively.

Correspondingly, we avoid the question *"Why?"* From our standpoint, this question is not relevant, and involvement with it commonly leads toward concerns about "deeper" underlying causes—historical, mental, familial—of problem behavior and about "insight" into these.

That is, the question "Why?" tends to promote an individualistic, voluntaristic, and rationalistic conception of human behavior, rather than one focused on systems of interaction and influence. Moreover, since underlying causes inherently are inferential rather than observable, concern about them distracts a therapist from close observation of the present problem and what behavior may be perpetuating it.

On the basis of this general conception of problems and their resolution, which is discussed more fully in Watzlawick, Weakland, and Fisch (25), we can now describe the overall practical approach and specific techniques that we utilize.

OPERATION OF THE BRIEF THERAPY CENTER

The Brief Therapy Center was established as one of the projects at the Mental Research Institute in January, 1967. Since the termination of our founding grants, we have continued our work on a somewhat reduced scale on volunteered time. Some direct operating expenses have been met by donations from patients, although we provide free treatment where appropriate.

Our working quarters consist of a treatment room and observation room, separated by a one-way viewing screen, with provision for simultaneously listening to and tape-recording sessions. There is also an intercom phone between the two rooms. At the outset of our work, a therapist and an official observer were assigned, in rotation, to each case. More recently, we have been working as an overall team, with several observers of equal status usually present.

Our handling of all cases follows a six-stage schema, although in practice there may be some overlap among these:
1. Introduction to our treatment set-up.
2. Inquiry and definition of the problem.
3. Estimation of behavior maintaining the problem.
4. Setting goals of treatment.
5. Selecting and making behavioral interventions.
6. Termination.
Each of these will now be considered in order.

Introduction to Our Treatment Set-Up

Patients intentionally are accepted with no screening. A first appointment is set by the project secretary whenever an applicant calls and there is a vacancy in our schedule. No waiting lists are kept; when we have no vacancy, people are referred elsewhere.

At the first meeting, our secretary has the patient or family fill out a form covering basic demographic data and brings him or them to the treatment room. The therapist begins by explaining the physical and organizational arrangements, mentioning the potential advantages for treatment of the recording and observation, and requests written consent to this. Only two patients have ever declined to proceed on this basis. The therapist also tells the patient at once that we work on a maximum of ten sessions per case; this helps to set a positive expectation of rapid change.

Definition of the Problem

Since our treatment focus is symptomatic, we want first to get a clear and explicit statement of the presenting complaint. Therefore, as soon as the therapist has taken a brief record of the referral source and any previous treatment, he asks what problem has brought the patient to see us. If a patient states a number of complaints, we will ask which is the most important. In marital or family cases, since viewpoints may differ, although they often are plainly interrelated, we ask each of the parties involved to state his own main complaint. From the beginning, then, we are following a form of the general principle, "Start where the patient is at."

Fairly often, the patient will give an adequate answer—by which we mean a clear statement referring to concrete behavior. In many cases, however, the response will leave the presenting problem still in doubt. Further inquiry is then needed to define more clearly this point of departure for the entire treatment. For example, patients with previous treatment experience or psychological sophistication are likely, after only the briefest mention of any present behavioral difficulty, to launch into discussion of presumed underlying matters, especially intrapsychic factors and family history, presenting these as the "real problem." We then press the question of what particular difficulties in living have brought them to see us *now*. To make things more specific, we often ask such questions as "What do you now do because of your problem that you want to stop doing, or do differently?" and "What would you like to do that your problem interferes with doing now?" Such inquiries also begin to raise the related question of treatment goals.

Other patients, especially younger ones, may state their complaints in vague terms that lack reference to any concrete behavior or life situation: "I don't know who I really am"; "We just can't communicate." Such patients can be particularly difficult initially. We find it important not to accept such statements as appropriate and informative but to continue inquiry until at least the therapist, if not the patient, can formulate a concrete, behavioral picture of the problem—of which such attachment to vague and often gradiose thinking and talking may itself be a major aspect.

Estimation of Behavior Maintaining the Problem

Our view, as mentioned earlier, is that problem behavior persists only when it is repeatedly reinforced in the course of social interaction between the patient and other significant people. Usually, moreover, it is just what the patient and these others are doing in their efforts to deal with the problem—often those attempts at help that appear most "logical" or unquestionably right—that is most important in maintaining or exacerbating it.

Once behavior is observed and considered in this light, the way this occurs is often rather obvious: The wife who nags her husband and hides his bottle in her efforts to save him from his alcohol problem and succeeds only in continually keeping drinking uppermost in his mind; the forgiving husband who never criticizes his wife until she feels he doesn't care anything about her, whatever she does, and becomes depressed—and he is forgiving of that too; the parents of a child dissatisfied with school who "encourage" him by talking all the more about how important and great education is—instead of it being a necessary drag. In other instances, of course, the reinforcements may be more difficult to perceive, either because they are subtle or complex— nonverbal behaviors, contradictions between statements and actions, different behaviors by several persons—or because even therapists are conditioned to accept cultural standards of logic and rightness without examining whether things really work that way.

In practice, the therapist first simply asks the patient and any family members present how they have been trying to deal with the problem. This alone may lead rapidly to a view of what keeps things going badly. If not, the inquiry, aiming always at concrete behavior, can be pursued at more length and in more detail, but sympathetically—the therapist's aim is to get enough information to understand what is happening, for which he needs cooperation, not to confront people with their mistakes. In addition to what the patient or others state explicitly, it is important to note *how* they discuss the problem and its handling, including their interaction. Such inquiry is likely to disclose a number of things that play some part in maintaining the problem, but working briefly demands choosing priorities. On the basis of observation and experience, one must judge which behavior seems most crucial.

Setting Goals of Treatment

Setting a goal both acts as a positive suggestion that change is feasible in the time allotted and provides a criterion of therapeutic accomplishment for therapist and patient. We, therefore, want goals stated clearly in terms of observable, concrete behavior to minimize any possibility of uncertainty or denial later. If parents bring us a child because he is failing in school, we ask for an explicit criterion of satisfactory progress—because we want to avoid subsequent equivocations such as "He is getting B's now instead of F's, but he isn't really learning enough." Also, we steer toward "thinking small" for reasons already discussed. Therefore, our usual inquiry is something like "At a minimum, what (change in) behavior would indicate to you that a definite step forward has been made on your problem?''

Concerning goals espeically, however, patients often talk in vague or sweeping terms, despite our efforts to frame the question in terms of specific behavior. We then try to get more concrete answers by further discussion, clarification, and presentation of examples of possible goals for consideration. With vague, grandiose, or utopian patients, we have found it helpful to reverse our field, bringing them down to earth by suggesting goals that are too far out even for them. This again involves accepting what the patient offers, and even enlarging on this, in order to change it. For example, a student who was already in his mid-20's and was still being supported by a working mother told us he was studying "philosophical anthropology" in order to bring the light of India and China to bear on the West. He also, however, mentioned some interest in attending a well-known school of Indian music. It was then pointed out to him that this represented a rather limited aim compared to his concern to unite the spirituality of India with the practical communism of China and use both to reconstruct Western society. He then said that, since he was not doing well in his studies and was short of money, if he could secure a scholarship and really learn Indian music, this would be quite enough accomplishment for the present.

We usually are able, directly or indirectly, to obtain a stated goal that appears sufficiently explicit and appropriate to the problem. In some cases, however, we have not been able to do so. Either the patient persisted in stating only vague, untestable goals, or, rarely, the patient stated and stuck to an explicit goal which we judged inappropriate to his problem. Then we do not dispute what the patient insists on but privately set our own goal for the case by joint staff discussion of what sort of behavior would best exemplify positive change for the particular patient and problem. In act, some such discussion occurs for all cases; at the least, the staff must always judge whether the patient's statement of his goal is adequate. Also, there is always staff discussion of intermediate behavioral goals; how does the patient—or his family members—need to behave so that the specific goal of treatment will follow?[2]

Our aim is to have a definite goal established by the second session, but gathering and digesting the information needed for this sometimes takes longer. Occasionally, we may revise the original goal in the course of treatment or add a secondary goal.

Selecting and Making Interventions

Once we have formed a picture of current behavior central to the

---

problem and estimated what different behavior would lead to the specific goal selected, the task is one of intervening to promote such change. This stage must be discussed at some length, since it ordinarily constitutes the largest, most varied, and probably most unusual part of our treatment.

Change and "insight." We have already stated that our aim is to produce behavior change and that we do not see working toward insight, at either an individual or a family level, as of much use in this. In fact, working toward insight can even be counter-productive. Simple, practical-minded patients are often put off by this, since they want action and results, while more intellectually minded patients are likely to welcome such an approach but use it to delay or defeat any change in actual behavior. However, in addition to suggesting or prescribing changes in overt behavior, we do utilize interpretations. Our aim, though, is simply the useful relabeling of behavior. Patients often interpret their own behavior, or that of others, in ways that make for continuing difficulties. If we can only redefine the meaning or implications attributed to the behavior, this itself may have a powerful effect on attitudes, responses and relationships. Such interpretation might look like an attempt to impart insight, but it is not. Using interpretation to promote insight implies that truth can helpfully be disclosed and recognized. This is not our aim or our belief. Rather, our view is that redefining behavior labeled "hostile" and "concerned interest," for example, may be therapeutically useful whether or not *either* label is "true," and that such truth can never be firmly established. All that is observable is that some labels provoke difficulties, while others, achievable by redefinition, promote adjustment and harmony—but this is enough.

Such relabeling may be especially important with rigid patients. It does not require overt behavior change, and it may even be accomplished without the need for *any* active cooperation by the patient or any family member. If the therapist's redefinition of an action or situation is not openly challenged—which can usually be arranged—then the meaning and effects of that behavior have already been altered.

Use of idiosyncratic characteristics and motivation. We attempt early in treatment to determine what approach would appeal most to the particular patient—to observe "where he lives" and meet this need, whether it is to believe in the magical, to defeat the expert, to be a caretaker of someone, to face a challenge, or whatever. Since the consequences of any such characteristic depend greatly on the situation in which it operates and how this is defined, we see these characteristics of different individuals not as obstacles or deficiencies, but as potential levers for useful interventions by the therapist.

For example, certain patients appear inclined toward defeating therapists, despite their request for help. This may be indicated by a history of unsuccessful treatment, repeated failure to understand explanations or carry out instructions, and so on. In such cases, the easiest and most effective course may be for the therapist to insist that the patient cannot possibly resolve his problem and that treatment can at most help him to endure it better. The patient is then likely to defeat *this* stance by improving.

A middle-aged widow first came to us with a complaint about the behavior of her 18-year-old son: delinquency, school failures, anger, and threatened violence toward her. She stated this was her only problem, although she also mentioned that she was an epileptic and was unable to use her right arm as a result of a work injury. Both mother and son had had about two years of previous therapy. We first suggested directly that her son was acting like a difficult, provoking, overgrown kid and, accordingly, she might gain by handling him more firmly in a few simple ways. She quickly thwarted such suggestions by increasing claims of helplessness: Now the epilepsy was emphasized; there was trouble with the other arm, too; a hysterectomy and appendectomy were also reported, along with childhood rheumatic fever, bleeding gums, troubles with her former husband and with her mother-in-law, constant worsening financial crises, and much more. In short, she was already a woman carrying on bravely amidst a sea of troubles that would have totally swamped anyone else; how could we ask her to do more yet? We then changed our approach to utilize this characteristic opposition. We began to insist to her that she was being unduly optimistic, was minimizing her troubles in an unrealistic way, and was not recognizing that the future very probably held even greater disasters for her, both individually and in terms of her son's behavior. It took some doing to surpass her own pessimistic line, but once we were able to do so, she began to improve. She started to oppose our pessimism—which she could only do by claiming and proving that she was not *that* sick and helpless—and to take a much more assertive attitude with her son, to which he responded well.

Directed behavior change. One of our main stated aims is to change overt behavior—to get people to stop doing things that maintain the problem and to do others that will lead toward the goal of treatment. While we are willing to issue authoritative directions, we find compliant patients rather rare. After all, most patients have already been exposed to lots of advice. If it was good, they must have some difficulty about profiting from advice; if it was bad, some preparation is needed for them to respond to quite different advice. Moreover, again, it is often just that behavior that seems most logical to people that is perpetuating their problems. They then need special help to do what will seem illogical and mistaken. When sitting on a nervous horse, it is not easy to follow the instructor's orders to let go of the reins. One *knows* the horse will run away, even though it is really the pull on the reins that is making him jump.

Behavioral instructions therefore are more effective when carefully framed and made indirect, implicit, or apparently insignificant. When requesting changes, it is helpful to minimize either the matter or the manner of the request. We will suggest a change rather than order it. If the patient still appears reluctant, we will back off further. We may then suggest it is too early to do that thing; the patient might think about it but be sure not to take any action yet. When we do request particular actions, we may ask that they be done once or twice at most before we meet again. We may request only actions that will appear minor to the patient, although in our view they represent the first in a series of steps, or involve a microcosm of the central difficulty. For example, a patient who avoids making any demands of others in his personal relationships may be assigned the task of asking for one gallon of gasoline at a service station, specifically requesting each of the usual free services, and offering a twenty-dollar bill in payment [*sic*].

This example also illustrates our use of "homework" assignments to be carried out between sessions. Homework of various kinds is regularly employed, both to utilize time more fully and to promote positive change where it counts most, in real life outside the treatment room.

Paradoxical instructions. Most generally, paradoxical instruction involves prescribing behavior that appears in opposition to the goals being sought, in order actually to move toward them. This may be seen as an inverse to pursuing "logical" courses that lead only to more trouble. Such instructions probably constitute the most important single class of interventions in our treatment. This technique is not new; aspects and examples of it have been described by Frankl (8, 9), Haley (11), Newton (17) and Watzlawick, *et al.* (24). We have simply related this technique to our overall approach and elaborated on its use.

Paradoxical instruction is used most frequently in the form of case-specific "symptom prescription," the apparent encouragement of symptomatic or other undesirable behavior in order to lessen such behavior or bring it under control. For example, a patient who complains of a circumscribed, physical symptom—headache, insomnia, nervous mannerisms, or whatever—may be told that during the coming week, usually for specified periods, he should make every effort to increase the symptom. A motivating explanation usually is given, e.g., that if he can succeed in making it worse, he will at least suffer less from a feeling of helpless lack of control. Acting on such a prescription usually results in a *decrease* of the symptom—which is desirable. But even if the patient makes the symptom increase, this too is good. He has followed the therapist's instruction, and the result has shown that the apparently unchangeable problem can change. Patients often present therapists with impossible-looking problems, to which every possible response seems a poor one. It is comforting, in turn, to be able to offer the patient a "therapeutic double bind" (4), which promotes progress no matter which alternative response he makes.

The same approach applies equally to problems of interaction. When a schizophrenic son used bizarre, verbal behavior to paralyze appropriate action by his parents, we suggested that when he needed to defend himself against the parents' demands, he could intimidate them by acting crazy. Since this instruction was given in the parents' presence, there were two paradoxical positive effects: the son decreased his bizarreness and the parents became less anxious and paralyzed by any such behavior.

Not infrequently, colleagues find it hard to believe that patients will really accept such outlandish prescriptions, but they usually do so readily. In the first place, the therapist occupies a position of advice-giving expert. Second, he takes care to frame his prescriptions in a way most likely to be accepted, from giving a rationale appropriate to the particular patient to refusing any rationale on the grounds that the patient needs to discover somethings quite unanticipated. Third, we often are really just asking the patient to do things they already are doing, only on a different basis.

We may also encourage patients to use similar paradoxes themselves, particularly with spouses or children. Thus, a parent concerned about her child's poor school homework (but who probably was covertly discouraging him) was asked to teach the child more self-reliance by offering incorrect answers to the problems he was asking help in solving.

Paradoxical instructions at a more general level are often used also. For example, in direct contrast to our name and ten-session limit, we almost routinely stress "going slow" to our patients at the outset of treatment and, later, by greeting a patient's report of improvement with a worried look and the statement, "I think things are moving a bit too fast." We also do the same thing more implicitly, by our emphasis on minimal goals, or by pointing out possible disadvantages of improvement to patients, "You would like to do much better at work, but are you prepared to handle the problem of envy by your colleagues?" Such warnings paradoxically promote rapid improvement, apparently by reducing any anxiety about change and increasing the patient's desire to get on with things to counteract the therapist's apparent overcautiousness.

On the same principle, when a patient shows unusually rapid or dramatic improvement, after acknowledging this change we may prescribe a relapse, on the rationale that it further increases control: "Now you have managed to turn the symptom off. If you can manage to turn it back on during this next week, you will have achieved even more control over it." This intervention, similar to Rosen's "re-enacting the psychosis" (18) and related techniques of Erickson, anticipates that in some patients improvement may increase apprehension about change and meets this danger by paradoxically redefining any relapse that might occur as a step forward rather than backward.

Since we as therapists are by definition experts, giving authoritative instructions on both thinking and acting, another pervasive element of paradox is created by the fact that ordinarily we do so only tentatively, by suggestions or questions rather than direct orders, and often adopt a "one-down" position of apparent ignorance or confusion. We find that patients, like other people, accept and follow advice more readily when we avoid "coming on strong."

Utilization of interpersonal influence. Although many of our treatment sessions include directly only one therapist and one patient, we consider and utilize more extended interpersonal relationships constantly in our work. First, even when we see only the "identified patient," we conceive the problem in terms of some system of relationships and problem-maintaining behavior involving his family, his friends, or his work situation. Therefore, we believe that any interventions made with the patient must also take their probable consequences for others into account. Equally, however, useful interventions may be made at any point in the system, and frequently it appears more effective to focus our efforts on someone other than the identified patient. Where a child is the locus of the presenting problem, we very commonly see the whole family only once or twice. After this we see the parents only and work with them on modifying their handling of the child or their own interaction. With couples also, we may see the spouses separately for the most part, often spending more time with the one seen by them as "normal." Our point is that effective intervention anywhere in a system produces changes throughout, but according to what the situation offers, one person or another may be more accessible to us, more open to influence, or a better level for change in the system.

Second, the therapist and the observers also constitute a system of relationships that is frequently used to facilitate treatment. With patients who find it difficult to accept advice directly from a real live person, an observer may make comments to the therapist over the intercom phone to be relayed to the patient from this unseen and presumably objective authority. When a patient tends to disagree constantly, an observer may enter and criticize the therapist for his "poor understanding" of the case, forming an apparent alliance with the patient. The observer can then often successfully convey re-phrased versions of what the therapist was offering originally. With patients who alternate between two different stances, two members of the treatment team may agree, separately, with the two positions. Then, whatever course the patient takes next he is going along with a therapist's interpretation, and further suggestions can be given and accepted more successfully. Such therapist-observer interaction strategies can bring about change rapidly even with supposedly "difficult" patients.[3]

---

[3]Team work facilitates such interventions but actually is seldom essential. A single therapist who is flexible and not unduly concerned about being correct and consistent can

As may be evident, all of these techniques of intervention are means toward maximizing the range and power of the therapist's influence. Some will certainly see, and perhaps reject, such interventions as manipulative. Rather than arguing over this, we will simply state our basic view. First, influence is an inherent element in all human contact. Second, the therapist's functioning necessarily includes this fact of life, but goes much further; professionally he is a specialist at influence. People come to a therapist because they are not satisfied with some aspect of their living, have been unable to change it, and are seeking help in this. In taking any case, therefore, the therapist accepts the assignment of influencing people's behavior, feelings, or ideas toward desirable ends. Accordingly, third, the primary responsibility of the therapist is to seek out and apply appropriate and effective means of influence. Of course, this includes taking full account of the patient's stated and observed situation and aims. Given these, though, the therapist still must make choices of what to say and do, and equally what not to say and do. This inherent responsibility cannot be escaped by following some standard method of treatment regardless of its results, by simply following the patient's lead, or even by following a moral ideal of always being straightforward and open with the patient. Such courses, even if possible, themselves represent strategic choices. To us, the most fundamental point is whether the therapist attempts to deny the necessity of such choices to himself, not what he tells the patient about them. We believe the better course is to recognize this necessity, to try whatever means of influence are judged most promising in the circumstances, and to accept responsibility for the consequences.

Termination. Whether cases run the limit of ten sessions or goals are achieved sooner, we usually briefly review the course of treatment with the patient, pointing out any apparent gains—giving the patient maximum credit for his achievement—and noting any matters unresolved. We also remark on the probable future beyond termination, ordinarily in connection with reminding patients that we will be contacting them for a follow-up interview in about three months. This discussion usually embodies positive suggestions about further improvement. We may remind patients that our treatment was not intended to achieve final solutions, but an initial breakthrough on which they themselves can build further. In a minority of cases, however—particularly with negativistic patients, ones who have difficulty acknowledging help from anyone, or those fond of challenges— we may take an opposite tack, minimizing any positive results of treatment and expressing skepticism about any progress in the future. In both instances, our aim is the same, to extend our therapeutic influence beyond the period of actual contact.

---

also utilize similar techniques—for example, by stating two different positions himself.

In some cases, we encounter patients who make progress but seem unsure of this and concerned about termination. We often meet this problem by means of terminating without termination. That is, we say we think enough has been accomplished to terminate, but this is not certain; it can really be judged only by how actual life experience goes over a period of time. Therefore, we propose to halt treatment, but to keep any remainder of the ten sessions "in the bank," available to draw on if the patient should encounter some special difficulty later. Usually, the patient then departs more at ease and does not call upon us further.

EVALUATION AND RESULTS

If psychotherapy is to be taken seriously as treatment, not just an interesting exploratory or expressive experience, its effectiveness must be reliably evaluated. But this is far from easy, and rather commonly therapists offer only general clinical impressions of their results, with no follow-up of cases after termination, while researchers present ideal study designs that seldom get implemented.

We certainly cannot claim to have resolved this problem fully, even though we have been concerned with systematic evaluation of results from the outset of our work. Our method of evaluation still involves some clinical judgments and occasional ambiguities, despite efforts to minimize these. Until very recently, we have not had the resources needed to repeat our short-term follow-ups systematically after longer periods. And our evaluation plan is apt to seem overly simple in comparison with such comprehensive schemes as that of Fiske, *et al.* (6). At most, we can claim only that our method of evaluation is simple, avoiding dependence upon either elaborate manipulation and interpretation of masses of detailed data or elaborate theoretical inference; that it is reasonably systematic and practicable; and most important, that it is consonant with our overall approach to problems and treatment.

We see the essential task of evaluation as systematic comparison of what treatment *proposes* to do and its observable *results*. Our treatment aim is to change patients' behavior in specific respects, in order to resolve the main presenting complaint. Given the brevity of our work, the past refractoriness of most of the problems presented, and our frequent observation of behavior change immediately following particular interventions, we feel fairly safe in crediting observed changes to our treatment. Our evaluation then depends on answers to the two questions: Has behavior changed as planned? Has the complaint been relieved?

In our follow-up, the interviewer, who has not participated in the treatment, first inquires whether the specified treatment goal has been met. For instance, "Are you still living with your mother, or are you living in your own quarters now?" Next, the patient is asked the current status of the main complaint. This is supplemented by inquiring whether any further therapy has been sought since terminating with us. The patient is also asked whether any improvements have occurred in areas not specifically dealt with in treatment. Finally, to check on the supposed danger of symptom substitution, the patient is routinely asked if any new problems have appeared.

Ideally, such evaluation would divide our cases into two neat piles: successes in which our goal of behavior change was met and the patient's problem completely resolved, and failures in both respects. In reality, our treatment is not perfect; while results in these terms are clear for a majority of cases, several sources of less clear-cut outcomes remain: (a) Fairly often we have had cases in which our goal was reached or approached and considerable improvement was evident, but complete resolution of the presenting problem or problems was not attained. (b) Occasionally we have failed to formulate a goal explicit and concrete enought to check on its achievement with certainty. (c) In a very few cases, achievement of the planned goal and reported relief of the problem have been inversely related—hitting our target of change did not lead to relief, or we somehow got results in spite of missing our specific target.

In terms of our basic principles, all such mixed cases must be considered as failures of either conception or execution that demand further study. In the patients' terms, on the other hand, some of these cases have been completely successful, and many others represent quite significant progress. For the more limited and immediate purpose of evaluating the general utility of our approach, therefore, we have classified our cases into three groups according to practical results, recognizing that these correlate generally but not completely with achievement of our specific goals of behavior change. These groups represent: (a) complete relief of the presenting complaint; (b) clear and considerable, but not complete, relief of the complaint; and (c) little or not such change. For simplicity, the one case in which things were worse after treatment is included in the third group. We have not broken down our sample into sub-groups based on common diagnosis, since the conventional system of diagnostic categories and our conception of problems and their treatment are based on different assumptions and the nature of the presenting problem has appeared to make little difference for our rate of success or failure. It should also be noted that this evaluation refers directly only to the major presenting complaint. However, in none of our cases in which this complaint was resolved was there any report of new problems arising, and in many of these improvements in additional areas were reported. On this basis, then, our overall results for 97 cases, involving an average of 7.0 sessions, are:

Success	39 cases	40 per cent
Significant improvement	31 cases	32 per cent
Failure	27 cases	28 per cent

These results appear generally comparable to those reported for various forms of longer-term treatment.

CONCLUSION: IMPLICATIONS

In this paper we have set forth a particular conception of the nature of psychiatric problems, described a corresponding brief treatment approach and techniques, and presented some results of their application. Clearly, further clinical research should be done, as important problems obviously remain; goals are still difficult to set in certain types of cases, the choice of interventions has not been systematized, evaluation is not perfected. Concurrently, though, there should also be more thinking about the broader significance of these ideas and methods. Our results already give considerable evidence for the usefulness of our general conception of human problems and their practical handling. Since this is both quite different from more common views and potentially widely relevant, we will conclude with a tentative consideration of some broad implications of our work.

The most immediate and evident potential of our work is for more effective use of existing psychiatric facilities and personnel. This could include reduction in the usual length of treatment and a corresponding increase in the number of patients treated, with no sacrifice of effectiveness. In fact, our approach gives promise of more than ordinary effectiveness with a variety of common but refractory problems, such as character disorders, marital difficulties, psychoses, and chronic problems generally. Further, it is not restricted to highly educated and articulate middle-class patients but is applicable to patients of whatever class and educational background.

In addition, our approach is relatively clear and simple. It might therefore be feasible to teach its effective use to considerable numbers of lay therapists. Even if some continuing supervision from professionals should be necessary, the combination of brief treatment and many therapists thus made possible could help greatly in meeting present needs for psychological help. Although this kind of development would have little to offer private practice, it could be significant for the work of overburdened social agencies.

Taking a wider view, it is also important that our model sees behavioral difficulties "all under one roof" in two respects. First, our model interrelates individual behavior and its social context instead of dividing them—not only within the family, but potentially at all levels of social organization. Second, this framework helps to identify continuities, similarities, and interrelations between normal everyday problems, psychiatric problems of deviant individual behavior, and many sorts of socially problematic behavior, such as crime, social isolation and anomie, and certain aspects of failure and poverty. At present, social agencies attempting to deal with such problems at the individual or family level are characterized by marked conceptual and organizational divisions—between psychological vs. sociological, supportive vs. disciplinary orientations, and more specifically, in the division of problems into many categories that are presumed to be distinct and discrete—reminiscent of the "syndromes" of conventional psychiatry. At best, this results in discontinuity; ineffective, partial approaches; or reduplication of efforts. At worst, it appears increasingly likely that such divisions themselves may function to reinforce inappropriate attempts at solution of many kinds of problems, as suggested by Auerswald (1) and Hoffman and Long (14). Our work thus suggests a need and a potential basis for a more unified and effective organization of social services.

Finally, our work has still broader implications that deserve explicit recognition, even though any implementation necessarily would be a very long-range and difficult problem. Our theoretical viewpoint is focused on the ways in which problems of behavior and their resolution are related to social interaction. Such problems occur not only with individuals and families, but also at every wider level of social organization and functioning. We can already discern two kinds of parallels between problems met in our clinical work and larger social problems. Problems may be reduplicated widely, as when concern about differences between parents and children becomes, in the large, "the generation gap problem." And conflicts between groups—whether these groups are economic, racial, or political—may parallel those seen between individuals. Our work, like much recent social history, suggests very strongly that ordinary, "common-sense" ways of dealing with such problems often fail, and, indeed, often exacerbate the difficulty. Correspondingly, some of our uncommon ideas and techniques for problem-resolution might eventually be adapted for application to such wider spheres of human behavior.

REFERENCES

1. Auerswald, E., "Interdisciplinary vs. Ecological Approach," *Fam. Proc.*, 7:202-215, 1968.
2. Barten, H. (Ed.), *Brief Therapies*, New York, Behavioral Publications, 1971.
3. Barten, H., and Barten, S., (Eds.), *Children and Their Parents in Brief Therapy*, New York, Behavioral Publications, 1972.
4. Bateson, G., Jackson, D., Haley, J., and Weakland, J., "Towards a Theory of Schizophrenia," *Behav. Sci.*, 1:251-264, 1956.
5. Bellak, L., and Small, L., *Emergency Psychotherapy and Brief Psychotherapy*, New York, Grune and Stratton, 1965.
6. Fiske, D., Hunt, H., Luborsky, L., Orne, M., Parloff, M., Reiser, M., and Tuma, A., "Planning of Research on Effectiveness of Psychotherapy," *Arch. Gen. Psychiat.*, 22:22-32, 1970.
7. Frank, J., *Persuasion and Healing*, Baltimore, Johns Hopkins Press, 1961.
8. Frankl, V., *The Doctor and the Soul*, New York, Alfred A. Knopf, 1957.
9. Frankl, V., "Paradoxical Inteventions," Amer. J. Psychother., 14:520-535, 1960.
10. Jackson, D., and Weakland, J., "Conjoint Family Therapy: Some Consider-

ations of Theory, Technique, and Results," *Psychiatry,* Supplement to 24:2: 30-45, 1961.

11. Haley, J., *Strategies of Psychotherapy,* New York, Grune and Stratton, 1963.

12. Haley, J., *Uncommon Therapy: The Psychiatric Techniques of Milton H. Erickson, M.D.,* New York, W.W. Norton, 1973.

13. Haley, J. (Ed.), *Advanced Techniques of Hypnosis and Therapy: Selected Papers of Milton H. Erickson, M.D.,* New York, Grune and Stratton, 1969.

14. Hoffman, L., and Long, L., "A Systems Dilemma," *Fam. Proc.,* 8:211-234, 1969.

15. Krohn, A., "Beyond Interpretation," (A review of M.D. Nelson, *et al., Roles and Paradigms in Psychotherapy). Contemporary Psychology,* 16:380-382, 1971.

16. Minuchin, S., and Montalvo, B., "Techniques for Working with Disorganized Low Socioeconomic Families," *Amer. J. Orthopsychiat.,* 37:880-887, 1967.

17. Newton, J., "Considerations for the Psychotherapeutic Technique of Symptom Scheduling," *Psychotherapy: Theory, Research and Practice,* 5:95-103, 1968.

18. Pittman, F.S., Langsley, D.G., Flomenhaft, K., De Young, C.D., Machotka, P., and Kaplan, D.M., "Therapy Techniques of the Family Treatment Unit," pp. 259-271 in Haley, J. (Ed.), *Changing Families: A Family Therapy Reader,* New York, Grune and Stratton, 1971.

19. Rosen, J., *Direct Analysis,* New York, Grune and Stratton, 1953.

20. Rosenthal, A., Report on brief therapy research to the Clinical Symposium, Department of Psychiatry, Stanford University Medical Center, November 25, 1970.

21. Rosenthal, R., *Experimenter Effects in Behavioral Research,* New York, Appleton-Century-Crofts, 1966.

22. Saizman, L., "Reply to the Critics," *Int. J. Psychiat.,* 6:473-478, 1968.

23. Spiegel, H., "Is Symptom Removal Dangerous?" *Amer. J. Psychiat.,* 123: 1279-1283, 1967.

24. Watzlawick, P., Beavin, J., and Jackson, D., *Pragmatics of Human Communication,* New York, W.W. Norton, 1967.

25. Watzlawick, P., Weakland, J., Fisch, R., *Change: Principles of Problem Formation and Problem Resolution,* New York, W.W. Norton, 1974.

26. Wender, H., "The Role of Deviation-Amplifying Feedback in the Origin and Perpetuation of Behavior," *Psychiatry,* 31: 317-324, 1968.

Chapter 7

VALUE SYSTEMS AND PSYCHOPATHOLOGY IN FAMILY THERAPY

GERALD H. ZUK

In the early days of family therapy—meaning in the early 1950s—when its major thrust was to investigate family dynamics associated with schizophrenia, and to test its efficacy as a therapy of schizophrenia, the problem of values in family therapy and dynamics was considered of subsidiary importance and given little consideration. The two major factions in family therapy in the fifties, the analytically-oriented therapists and the communicationists, hardly addressed the problem.

MAJOR ACHIEVEMENTS IN FAMILY THERAPY

From 1950 through the early 1960s

Of advances in this period, there are four that seem most significant: (1) A confirmation of Harry Stack Sullivan's view that it took longer to "learn" schizophrenia than infancy and early childhood, but that adolescence and young adulthood were also important stages in causation, and that the family was a key source of systematic reinforcement for the kind of learning necessary to produce the illness. (2) The double-bind hypothesis, conceived by the Palo Alto Group (Bateson et al., 1956), although not the complete explanation of schizophrenia they had hoped, nor effective as a treatment method, was the most original, creative concept of the period in that it showed how families systematically reinforced irrational modes of thinking in members prone to schizophrenia. (3) While family therapy proved neither more not less effective as a treatment method than other psychotherapies, it did produce some remarkable instances of symptom reduction in schizophrenics—sometimes in a remarkably brief period. (4) Family therapy experience confirmed the notion that schizophrenia was an illness of

From G. Zuk, Value Systems and Psychopathology in Family Therapy, *International Journal of Family Therapy, 1*:133-51, 1979. Courtesy of Human Sciences Press, New York.

diverse origins which clearly ran different courses in individuals.

The intense focus of the 1950s on schizophrenia may itself have contributed to a disinterest in the problem of values in family therapy, for it is such a dramatic phenomenon that it tends to mute others. In their work with families, the analytically-oriented therapists maintained the traditional neutral stance toward values, and the communicationists practically duplicated their attitude. When values were mentioned, they seemed to basically reflect the white, middle class family value system. Only one of the early workers in the field (Midelfort, 1957) suggested it was helpful if the therapist was familiar with the ethnic and religious origins of the psychiatric patient and his family; or even that he be a member of the same ethnic-religious group.

From the mid-1960s through mid-1970s

With the advent of the community mental health movement in the mid-1960s, family therapy underwent a radical change. For the first time therapists began to see a wide range of families presenting diverse problems. Many referrals were made as "behavior problems" bearing little if any relation to accepted psychiatric nosology. In my opinion the five major advances of the period have been as follows: (1) A commitment to crisis-oriented, short-term or brief family therapy as opposed to other models, due mainly to the fact that this was the model that *families* would accept. (2) A commitment to the problem of how to engage families in therapy, due to the fact that so many were lost during attempts to engage them. Once engagement "took," it appeared that various short- and long-term therapy models could be successful. (3) A commitment to exploring the value systems by which families operated, due to the growing conviction that the family value system was among the most important determinants of whether a family would become engaged in therapy. (4) A focus on values expressed by the *therapist* and on values attributed by the *family to the therapist,* such as might be related to their expectations about the therapy or its outcome. Analytically-oriented therapists in the 1960s were suggesting that beginners should undergo a personal experience in family therapy or a study of their own families. Although this never did gain much acceptance, in the 1970s it became obvious that therapists had to be more sensitive to the family values which might restrict or limit their readiness for therapy. (5) A focus on the *nuclear* family rather than three or more generations, particularly on the marital couple, due to the difficulty of involving more than two generations in therapy and the large increase in referrals presenting a discordant marriage. I think it is also true that even in cases where children had been identified as symptomatic, therapists increasingly came to focus on the marital couple as the "source" of the symptoms.

FAMILY VALUE SYSTEMS

Goal and Definition

The aim of this section is to present a system of values used by families. In the next section, "Technique in Family Therapy," there will be an attempt to relate values to family therapy technique.

There are many definitions of the word value, but here it will mean *an attitude, belief or way of evaluating events that typifies a* person or group. The focus on value reflects my belief that it is a central issue in any broadly-based theory of family therapy.

Conflict in Families

Elicitation of conflict often consumes a major portion of family interviews, and rightly so because conflict provides rich material for the therapist. The issues over which family members quarrel probably number in the hundreds. Therapists listen to arguments over family finances, child-rearing practices, relations with extended family and friends, job commitment of the husband versus his expected duties at home, and so on. These are the "contents" of some of the manifold quarrels, but conflict can also be viewed from the perspective of the "parties" involved. In family therapy, because the nuclear family is present in most instances, there are three main "parties": (1) males versus females, especially husbands versus wives; (2) the older versus younger generation, especially parents versus children; and (3) the nuclear family versus other, usually larger social units, such as the extended family, the neighborhood or institutions.

In family interviews husbands and wives can and do accuse each other of all sorts of misdeeds, bad intentions, or lies. Sometimes this is done in an open manner, sometimes not. Another male versus female conflict is that between brother and sister. Conflict between parents and children is also common in family interviews. It may be over the disarray of the child's bedroom. Or it may be about the selection of the first "date" of the adolescent, or the hour he or she is expected home from dates. Still later it may be about the choice of careers. Generational conflict may also exist between parents and *their* parents. It may, for example, arise when parents' parents remind them of supposed duties or obligations to other family members. Conflict between the nuclear family and other social units is commonly observed in family interviews. In some instances there is squabbling with neighbors because children have trespassed property. A family receiving welfare payments may be challenged to show why payments should be continued. Parents may be upset with the school which sends home a poor report card on a child. Or a child may be brought home by police after being picked up on suspicion of delinquency.

Two Value Systems in Families

Observation in family interviews suggests that, with respect to values expressed towards each other, the "parties" do not enter into conflict in a completely random manner. For example, in conflict between husbands and wives, wives are more likely to express certain values than their husbands. These I have referred to elsewhere (Zuk, 1975) as "continuity" values. The values expressed by husbands were designated "discontinuity" values. Furthermore, I suggested that the "continuity-discontinuity" polarity held with respect to values expressed in conflict between parents and their children, with children commonly expressing the "continuity" values, parents the "discontinuity" values. And in conflict between the nuclear family and other social units, the nuclear family expressed "continuity" values while charging other social units, such as the neighborhood, with holding "discontinuity" values. When a wife had conflict with her husband, she took the "continuity" position; but when there was conflict between parents and children, she then joined her husband in maintaining "discontinuity" values. So it was possible for a family member, depending on which "parties" were in conflict, to switch sides from the "continuity" to "discontinuity" position. To know specifically what the "continuity" and "discontinuity" value systems are composed of, Table 7-I is reproduced (from Zuk, 1975, p. 29).

There are four categories listed within the two value systems: (1) the affective/attitudinal; (2) the moral/ethical; (3) the cognitive/perceptual; and (4) tasks/goals. The affective, attitudinal category distinguishes those affects, emotions, or attitudes that may be labeled empathic, sympathetic or "warm" from those that may be labeled distant, reserved or "cool." The former are "continuity", the latter "discontinuity". The moral/ethical category distinguished anticonformist, idealistic and egalitarian values ("continuity") from values expressed by the disciple of law, order and codes, and pragmatic and elitist values ("dis-

Table 7-I
Categories of Contrasting Values Expressed in Family Interviews

Categories	Values	
	"Continuity"	"Discontinuity"
1. Affective/Attitudinal	Empathic, Sympathetic	Distant, Reserved, "Cool"
2. Moral/Ethical	Anticonformist, Idealistic, Egalitarian	Disciple of Law & Codes, Pragmatic, Elitist
3. Cognitive/Conceptual	Intuitive, Holistic	Analytic, Systematic
4. Tasks/Goals	Nurturing, Caretaking	Achieving, Structuring

continuity"). The tasks/goals category distinguishes the values of nurturing and caretaking ("continuity") from those expressed by the desire for achievement and structure ("discontinuity").

As an example of how the table applies to family life, let us consider the very common conflict over child-rearing practices. When we hear arguments between husband and wife over the raising of children, typically it is the wife who accuses the husband of misunderstanding the situation due to his distance, reserve and acting too "cool". She may simply accuse him of not caring, of being uninvolved. The husband, on the other hand, typically responds (retaliates may be the more appropriate word) that his wife is the victim of her emotions when it comes to the children: she is too sympathetic, too "warm." He says she lacks proper perspective. This is an example of the "continuity-discontinuity" division of values expressed along the affective/attitudinal axis. Of course, there are exceptions to the rule (as in clinical work there are always exceptions), but the pattern exists.

In a child-rearing conflict in which the parents and children are at odds, more commonly the children accuse the parents of holding "discontinuity" values, and the parents accuse the children of holding "continuity" values. The argument, for example, may be over the time the children are expected home for dinner. The parents have set the time and the children persistently are tardy and give weak excuses. When the issue is confronted, the children typically charge the parents as too rule-and-regulation oriented. The parents maintain that the children are disobedient or rebellious and anticonformist. The conflict is typically waged along the moral/ethical dimension of the "continuity-discontinuity" value system structure.

In child-rearing conflict in which the nuclear family and other social units such as the neighborhood are engaged, more commonly the nuclear family takes the "continuity" position, the neighborhood the "discontinuity" position. An example is the neighbor who complains to parents that their children are making too much noise, or have damaged property. The parents are inclined to defend their children by insisting that all children are noisy or break things and that the neighbors should make allowances. The neighbors reply that good parents discipline their children for misbehavior, and that the attractiveness of the neighborhood must be maintained. Here again is the "continuity-discontinuity" dispersion mainly expressed along with the ethical/moral dimension.

The nuclear family versus other social unit conflict can itself be further broken down into conflict over race, ethnic origin, religion, social class level, and even political association. For example, in family interviews with blacks, it is not uncommon to hear whites described as too achievement oriented, too impersonal, too rational. On the other hand, with whites, blacks are described as implusive, lacking in orderliness. The whites are usually assigned the "discontinuity" values, the blacks the "continuity" values.

In interviews with families of southern European origin, persons of northern European origin will be labeled too reserved, too controlled, too orderly. Southerners will be described by Northerners as impulsive, over-emotional. In interviews with middle class families, lower class families will be described as impulsive, unorganized, over-emotional. Lower class families will refer to the middle class as too rigid, overcontrolled, too orderly and systematic. Gentiles will refer to Jews as too achievement-oriented, too conscious of material well-being; while Jews will criticize Gentiles for being wishy-washy, hypocritical in their ideals and methods. Families whose politics are conservative will describe those with liberal politics as wishy-washy, prone to idealize; whereas liberal families will criticize conservatives as too rational, too rigid. In these comparisons also there is a nonrandom assignment of values according to the "continuity-discontinuity" system.

Two clinical examples may be useful here to highlight the opposition of the two value systems in family conflict:

Case 1: I had been seeing the K family, even though the parents had been divorced many years. Kenny, 10, the youngest of six children, was doing poorly in school and had been placed in a class for learning-handi-capped children. The bitterness and rancor of the parents were immediately evident. Mr. K was especially harsh in his criticism of his wife. She was careless, didn't know how to discipline the children, and was impulsive. Mr. K prided himself on his methodical approach to problems. He was a self-made man, even though at the time in a dilemma concerning future employment, and he prided himself on his efficiency and orderliness. He insisted his wife undermined his efforts to help the children be better behaved and achieve more in school and at jobs.

An important therapeutic step was, after a few interviews, to insist that the recriminations stop during interviews. It was not easy to establish this rule but after a few more meetings the parents responded to the therapist's direction. Shortly thereafter, they reported improvements in the conduct of the children. Kenny, the only child attending meetings, was calmer and more helpful at home.

Clearly Mr. K was an exponent of "discontinuity" values, and attributed "continuity" values to his wife. In their marriage they failed to resolve their value orientations peacefully. The circumstances of their lives added fuel to the kindling fire. Mr. K wanted desperately to succeed at his job and deeply resented his wife's failure to use birth control. His job required extensive travel, which facilitated his withdrawal from wife and children, and he began to drink heavily while away from home. Mrs. K became resentful of her husband's absences, his drinking, and his failure to discipline the children.

Case 2: Ron and his wife constrast with the K family in that both were professionally trained, there were no children, and they were younger than Mr. and Mrs. K when first seen in therapy. I saw Ron and his wife for several months before the breakup of their marriage of six years. He was the only son of Jewish parents residing in an Canadian city; she was from a German-Catholic family in a Midwest city. They met while Ron was at a university where both obtained degrees.

About a year before I began to see them Ron persuaded his wife that, since their sexual relationship seemed inadequate, perhaps sexual experimentation with others might improve it. Far from being good for the marriage, this arrangement seemed to doom it. Ron's wife decided to leave him and seek a divorce, and she declined to continue in couple therapy.

Ron was agitated by his wife's decision to leave him and asked me to continue to see him alone, and I agreed. I saw him regularly for about one year, then irregularly for another. During the period in which I saw him alone, he changed jobs and the divorce became final. I asked him to cooperate with me in two ways: (1) to find a job that offered him responsibilities commensurate with his level of training and experience, and to stay with it for at least two years no matter what the frustrations were; and (2) to form a serious relationship with a woman with the intention to share his life on a permanent basis.

With the first task Ron more or less complied, but with the second he did not. He formed *numerous* brief relationships with women during the time I saw him. None seemed to him to match his ex-wife. He mourned the end of that relationship, even as he recognized how he had helped end it. I think Ron grew up a bit during the time I saw him. I concentrated on trying to help him deal constructively with frustrations at work and discouraged him from becoming over-manipulative in his relationships with women.

Ron and his wife were a more "modern" couple than Mr. and Mrs. K; that is, they were more geographically mobile, less bound by traditional family obligations, more socially sophisticated, and freer to establish their own rules for their marriage. They had greater flexibility in regard to the expression of "continuity" and "discontinuity" values. I believe the failure of the marriage resulted from a failure to accept limits to the flexibility.

The Power Concept in Relation to Values

In an interesting paper, Distler (1970) contends that there is a revolution among youth due to a culture shift from what he terms a patristic-instrumental culture to a more matristic-expressive culture. He refers to hippies as prime example of a youth group which has adopted values of their mothers. He cites Adler to the effect that in the history of Western society there have been shifts between the patristic-instrumental and matristic-expressive. He also cites Keniston and

Gutmann's formulation that alienated, uncommitted young men were in effect "living out" their mother's unresolved identity crisis.

In a brilliant paper written originally in German in 1932, Fromm (1970) indicates the likelihood of the change from the patriarchal to a matriarchal structure of society. Fromm cites the theory of J.J. Bachofen, the German sociologist-philosopher, who in 1861 first published "Mother Right." According the Bachofen, the matriarchal principle is that of life, unity and peace. Through caring for her infant, the mother extends her love beyond herself to others with the aim of preserving and beautifying the existence of others. While the matriarchal principle is that of universality, the patriarchal principle is that of restrictions. Along with Distler, Fromm notes that certain matriarchal tendencies can be observed in radical youth, and he cites other evidence of an increasing matriarchal trend in Western society today. Referring to the fact that in history matriarchy and patriarchy have frequently clashed, Fromm says that in other instances they have formed a creative synthesis, as in the case of the Catholic Church and Marx's concept of socialism. But when they are opposed to each other, dire consequences for the individual can result:

> the matriarchal principle manifests itself in motherly overindulgence and infantilization of the child, preventing its full maturity; fatherly authority becomes harsh denomination (sic) and control, based on the child's fear and feelings of guilt. . . . The purely matriarchal society stands in the way of the full development of the individual, thus preventing technical, rational, artistic progress. The purely patriarchal society cares nothing for love and equality; it is only concerned with man-made laws, the state, abstract principles, obedience. (p. 83)

I would refer the reader to Table 7-I at this point, because there is more than a passing resemblance between the "continuity" value system and what Fromm and Bachofen described for the matriarchal system, and between the "discontinuity" value system and what they described for the patriarchal system.

Has there been a shift from the patriarchal to the matriarchal in recent decades, as Fromm suggested? Parsons (1955) and his colleagues suggest and provide evidence that the nuclear family has emerged as the dominant family form in recent decades. I have suggested (Zuk, 1971) that under the pressures of American society, the nuclear family is inevitably one in which the mother assumes an increasingly central role with her children, the father an increasingly peripheral role. The tendency of children is to over-learn or over-identify with the values expressed by their mothers, with the result that they are poorly adapted to the values dominant in society which are primarily male values. I prefer the terms "continuity" and "discontinuity" rather than matriarchal and patriarchal (or expressive and instrumental, following Parsons), because I believe they are more inclusive, but my conclusion regarding the fate of children in present-day society is the same as that of

Fromm and the others. Because they are so identified with the values of their mothers ("continuity" values), and because these values differ from those held by their fathers ("discontinuity" values) children, particularly males, are bound to have a difficult transition as they make their way into a society still dominated by male ("discontinuity") values.

Thus I agree with Fromm and the others when they suggest that Western society has shifted in the direction of the matriarchal principle, but do not think this should be taken to mean that Western, specifically American, society *is* matriarchal. On the contrary, it is still overwhelmingly patriarchal (although I would prefer to say that it overwhelmingly reflects "discontinuity" values). Yet in that essential unit of society which is the nuclear family, "continuity" values have become dominant. Children and their mothers are allied against and antagonistic toward fathers and society, and the result for the individual in society reflects this condition of stress. The peculiar dilemma of fathers is that they have been caught between what Alvin Toffler has referred to as "future shock" and a further gradual weakening of their position in the nuclear family as a result of declining ties with the extended family. I think these factors are interrelated: rapid technological advance has required greater mobility on the part of the nuclear family, which has weakened ties with extended family (which validated and confirmed the importance of the father's role in the nuclear family), and the result is a decline in the father's role.

Generally speaking, those who take the "continuity" position in conflict situations tend to think of themselves and be though of as less powerful than those who take the "discontinuity" position. Less powerful can refer to physical or numerical strength, or to material wealth. For instance, women as wives tend to think of themselves as less powerful than men as husbands. Children tend to think of themselves as less powerful than parents. And the nuclear family believes itself to be less powerful than other social units. Historically women, children and the nuclear family *have* been less powerful when compared to men, parents and other social units. In times past, the power differential was significantly greater than it is today, and I would surmise that the evolution of value systems in society has played a prominent role in reducing the power differential. As men and women, parents and children, and the nuclear family and other social units have related to each other over the centuries, have struggled with one another and sought to resolve those struggles, and as a result of powerful pressures, brought to bear by technological and other cultural innovations, the effect of new values, in my opinion, has been to reduce the power differential between the groups, although not totally erasing it.

Values and Psychiatric Nosology

In the previous section citations were made (Fromm was an example) of deleterious effects on offspring of dominance of the matriarchal principle in society, or the patriarchal principle. Infantilization was given as one of the effects of matriarchal dominance. Table 7-II is a summary of the connections I visualize between various psychiatric entities and the "continuity-discontinuity" family value system structure. It is based on listening extensively to what family members say about themselves and others in family therapy interviews.

At the neurotic level, one will hear the family member who engages in so-called antisocial behavior (various delinquencies including drug use, heavy drinking, runaway behavior, sexual promiscuity) describe himself or herself, or be described by other family members, as having a hard time controlling emotions, as being impulsive, perhaps even as too idealistic or naive with respect to the motives of influential friends. I would classify (and do so in Table 7-II) this description as consistent with the "continuity" position. On the other hand, the member who under stress and anxiety reacts with so-called psychosomatic symptomatology (e.g., gastric, circulatory, respiratory or orthopedic complaints with or without organic basis) is frequently described as well-behaved, almost too "good," a perfectionist, a person who "holds everything in" emotionally. These are judgments that, according to my schema in Table 7-II, fall within the "discontinuity" system.

At the characterologic level of psychiatric disorder, the family member who responds to stress with an hysteric reaction is frequently described by himself or other family members as too emotional, as naive or immature, as either over- or underresponsive to others. This is the person who can become overdependent, then suddenly seeks isolation from others. In Table 7-II, the individual falls within the "continuity" system. Then there is the obsessive-compulsive who cannot tolerate disorder, dust or dirt, and may create rituals to avoid them. The behavior of such an individual is more in accord with the "discontinuity" system.

At the psychotic level of psychiatric disorder, we find the individual who reacts to stress radically—he or she falls into a catatonic state or becomes somewhat hebephrenic. In family interviews these individuals are often described as overemotional or as naive and idealistic, as too easily influenced by others, and so on. In other words, they are described

Table 7-II
Value Systems in Relation to Psychiatric Nosology

Psychiatric Disorder	Values	
	"Continuity"	"Discontinuity"
1. Neurotic Level	Delinquent Behavior	Psychosomatic
2. Characterologic Level	Hysteric	Obsessive-Compulsive
3. Psychotic Level	Catatonic or Hebephrenic	Paranoid

in terms that fit within the "continuity" system. Another radical response to stress is the paranoid reaction. This individual has systematized his suspicions about persons or events and sometimes responds violently when his suspicions are triggered. In family interviews these individuals may be described as ordinarily ones who hide their emotions, are hard workers, neat, orderly, somewhat perfectionistic, and shy of persons, especially strangers. In Table 7-II, they fall within the "discontinuity" system.

TECHNIQUE IN FAMILY THERAPY

I have previously laid out (Zuk, 1971, 1975) what seemed to me the basic functions of the family therapist which, taken together, constitute the whole of his role: (1) when he acts as go-between; (2) when he acts as side-taker; and (3) when he acts as celebrant. But I have not pointed to an interrelation of these role functions with the "continuity-discontinuity" value system structure, and will do so here. I hope to show that within each of the role functions the therapist responds basically in either of two ways: either in accord with the "continuity" position, or the "discontinuity" position. In carrying out his role, the therapist is always expressing values of one sort or another, and I think it is helpful if he recognizes that these values are essentially of the two types considered at some length in this paper.

As go-between the therapist mediates or facilitates discussion with and within the family, or he sets limits and imposes rules which are intended to regulate discussion. As indicated in Table 7-III, when the therapist mediates or facilitates discussion, he is espousing "continuity" values. When he sets limits and imposes rules, he is espousing "discontinuity" values.

Table 7-III
Values in Relation to the Therapist's Role

Role Functions of Therapist	Values	
	"Continuity"	"Discontinuity"
1. Go-Between	Mediator, Facilitator of Communication	Sets limits, Imposes Rules or Regulations on Communication
2. Side-Taker	Sides with Wife against Husband, Children against Parents, Nuclear Family against Community	Sides with Husband against Wife, Parents against Children, Community against Nuclear Family
3. Celebrant	Espouses Mercy, Compassion, Forgiveness	Espouses Justice, Upholds Law, Codes, Regulations

As side-taker, the therapist aligns himself with one party or another in the family; he is, so to speak, for or against certain family members in disputes that arise in interviews. If, for example, he sides with a wife against her husband, or with a child against parents, or with the nuclear family against another social unit, he is espousing "continuity" values. If he sides in the opposition direction in the combinations mentioned above, then he is espousing "discontinuity" values.

As celebrant, the therapist certifies family events or happenings as either important or unimportant, relevant or irrelevant, and may comment on the nature or meaning of the event or happening for the family presently and in the future. When as celebrant the therapist expresses compassion, or speaks on behalf of mercy or forgiveness in the face of the event or happening, and asks family members to do likewise, then he is espousing "continuity" values. When, on the contrary, he expresses moral indignation, is stern and insists that justice be done in the face of the event or happening, then he is espousing "discontinuity" values.

Short-term Therapy; The Engagement Process

In the past several years the trend in the field of family therapy toward short-term technique has been one of the notable events. The positive results of short-term work (Leventhal and Weinberger, 1975) are reasonably persuasive. Among the reasons given for the good results, one of the most significant is that the majority of families allow the therapist access for a limited amount of time. *Good results flow from the fact that the therapist does not abuse the brief time limit established by the majority of families.* It is odd that many therapists who are proponents of short-term methods appear quite oblivious to this. Rather they seem entrapped in the old argument with the advocates (usually psychoanalytically-oriented therapists) of the long-term approach in psychotherapy, based on the view that personality change was the major goal and that such change obviously required an extensive period of time. Many short-term advocates are preoccupied with proving, for example, how useless insight is in producing change, thus fail to see that the majority of families will simply not tolerate long-term contact with a therapist.

In my view short-term methods work well, perhaps best, in family therapy because they are consistent with the expectations of the majority of families. The majority does not want a long-term contact, for such a prospect frightens most and is a major precipitant of premature termination. In the past few years I have concentrated on an aspect of therapy technique that seemed to me critical—the technique of engaging families who are poorly motivated for therapy or whose motivation is mixed. Quantitative reports by Sager et al. (1968), Shapiro and Budman (1973) Solomon (1969) and Slipp et al. (1974) highlight the need to find means to engage families of diverse origins.

Family values play a significant role in the effectiveness of short-term methods because values affect the expectations of families about therapy. Generally speaking, if therapy is expected to work—whether it be short-term or long-term—it works. But values play an especially significant role in whether or not families will become *engaged* in therapy. My experience actually leads me to the following statement: once families are engaged, the outcome is likely to be successful regardless of whether the succeeding method used is short-term or long-term. I have come to the conclusion that establishing the engagement is about half the battle. I am not a strict proponent of the short-term method in family therapy, even though it is the most appropriate method for the majority of cases. Therapists should encourage families to continue so long as they are willing to deal with issues affecting their lives, and so long as they are responsive to the therapist's direction. In numerous cases, particularly with lower class families, poor minority groups and families seen at the point of crisis, symptomatic relief may be obtained during the engagement itself (symptomatic relief during the engagement also is not uncommon in well-motivated, white, middle class families). But with the lower class, poor minority and crisis-type families, once symptomatic relief has been obtained, there is a tendency to quit therapy even when its continuation is encouraged by the therapist. From the point of view of the therapist, the therapy may be judged a failure; but from the family's point of view it was successful in that it produced the desired result in the desired time.

Studies are showing that change in brief therapy is frequently of a relatively permanent nature. Not only does the patient feel that help has been obtained, but relief and improvement are maintained over a significant period of time. Of course, certain psychoanalytic workers have objected that even though short-term methods appear effective, they are superficial; and that in order to produce so-called dynamic change, the long-term method is required. But a recent report by Malan et al. (1975) from the Tavistock Clinic in London, casts doubt on this line of reasoning. These workers, who are psychoanalytic in orientation, reported on a group of eleven neurotic individuals who appeared improved "psychodynamically" after only one or two psychiatric interviews. These individuals, followed up over periods of from two or more years, seemed substantially improved in overall functioning, to have insight into factors responsible for their improvement, and to have a sense that they were more in control of their lives than they had been when they sought help. Following an initial evaluation interview or two with a psychiatrist (some of these patients judged not acceptable for or likely to be amenable to psychotherapy), the individual felt relieved and were able to make use of friends for aid and advice in a way they were unable to previously. At follow-up they cited the initial interview or two as critical for producing an immediate change upon which they were able to build over time.

I have found that even a single interview or two with a family can have a therapeutic effect that persists and develops with time, despite the fact that the family leaves treatment for one reason or another. The therapist may be disappointed with what he considers a premature termination, but the family may be grateful beyond words for the experience.

Family Bias Versus Therapist Bias

Any definition of the family must include the fact that, because it is an agent that transmits value, it has prejudices and biases. Prejudices and biases are values of a certain kind which will be leveled against the therapist as they are toward any outsider. In my experience as therapist and training supervisor, the three major biases exhibited by families against therapist are: (1) the therapist is female; (2) the therapist is young; and (3) the therapist is black. (The presumption, of course, is that the family is one of the majority in the United States: white, from a part of the middle class, and that the parents are in their late thirties or early forties.)

Today, fortunately, the majority of families do not possess such deep-set prejudice that being female, young or black rules out effective work as a therapist. In the great majority of cases, such therapists can be effective, although a training supervisor would be less than diligent to forget to advise the trainee of possible adverse family reactions. In certain instances prejudice *is* deep-set and, after a suitable period of exploration, the therapist would be well advised to refer the family elsewhere. This is not a reflection on the therapist's skill, but simply an acknowledgment that all families impose some limitations on what may transpire in therapy, or even if therapy is to occur.

With black families the *white* therapist is at a disadvantage and in certain one-parent families (with father absent) it may be advantageous if the therapist is a *middle-aged female or older.* Some young couples today will react poorly to an older male therapist whom they regard as "not with it." These are cases in which the advantage is to the female, young or black therapist.

The other side of the coin is that, as human beings who grew up in families, *therapists* have biases and prejudices which may interfere with effective work with families. In the case of female, young or black therapists, I think there is a tendency to side with "continuity" values against "discontinuity" values. Simply being female, young or black tends to produce this type of allegiance. Now when these therapists work with the garden variety type of problem in American family life—namely, the coalition of mother and children against father and/or community producing stress that leads to symptoms in a family member—they are somewhat at a disadvantage. This all too common problem in families results in the erosion of "discontinuity" values represented by the father and community. If therapists begin therapy allied too strongly with the "continuity" values, then they cannot set right the imbalance between the one value system and the other, and consequently their therapy will be less effective. Training supervisors are responsible for spotting these special allegiances that interfere with effective work. Obviously being white, older and male does not protect the therapist from biases which may also require correction.

The issue of therapist-family match along age, gender, racial and religious lines (to mention only a few of the more obvious relevant factors) is one on which there has been a major deficiency of studies. The reason is probably that it is deemed too "sensitive", and it is indeed my experience that it elicits strong emotional reaction in trainees and supervisors when it is raised. Still I believe there is no avoiding the issue in the long run because it is a major contributor to the high loss-rate early in family therapy.

REFERENCES

Bateson, G., Jackson, D., Haley, J. & Weakland, J. Toward a theory of schizophrenia. *Behavioral Science*, 1956, *1*, 251-265.

Distler, L. The adolescent "hippie" and the emergence of a matristic culture. *Psychiatry*, 1970, *33*, 362-371.

Fromm, E. *The crisis of psychoanalysis.* New York: Holt, Rinehart, Winston, 1970.

Leventhal, T., & Weinberger, G. Evaluation of a large-scale brief therapy program for children. *American Journal of Orthopsychiatry*, 1975, *45*, 119-133.

Malan, D., Heath, E., Bascal, H. & Balfour, H. Psychodynamic changes in untreated neurotic patients: II. apparently genuine improvements. *Archives of General Psychiatry*, 1975, *32*, 110-126.

Midelfort, C. *The family in psychotherapy.* New York: McGraw-Hill, 1957.

Parsons, T. The American family: Its relation to personality and social structure. In T. Parsons & R. Bales (Eds.), *Family, socialization and interaction process.* Glencoe, Ill.: Free Press, 1955, 3-33.

Sager, C., Masters, Y., Bonall, R. & Normand, W. Selection and engagement of patients in family therapy. *American Journal of Orthopsychiatry*, 1968, *38*, 715-723.

Shapiro, R. & Budman, S. Defection, termination and continuation in family and individual therapy. *Family Process*, 1973, *12*, 55-67.

Slipp, S., Ellis, S. & Kressel, K. Factors associated with engagement in family therapy. *Family Process*, 1974, *13*, 413-427.

Solomon, M. Family Therapy dropouts: resistance to change. *Canadian Psychiatric Association Journal*, 1969, *14*, 21-29.

Zuk, G. *Family therapy: a triadic-based approach.* New York: Behavioral Publications, 1971.

Zuk, G. *Process and practice in family therapy.* Haverford, Pa.: Psychiatry and Behavior Science Books, 1975.

THE FAMILY THERAPIST
AS A SYSTEM INTERVENTIONIST

URI RUEVENI

A s family therapists we often aim to develop strategies which can help the dysfunctional family change. Experience with families in emotional crisis (e.g., attempted suicides, "psychotic" manifestations, self-destructive symbiotic bonds, severe marital strife, family disorganization and depression) indicates that therapeutic strategies which help family members reconnect with additional sources of emotional support and strength are effective in crisis resolution and in the development of temporary support structures. (Rueveni and Speck, 1969; Speck and Rueveni, 1969, 1977; Rueveni, 1975, 1976. Rueveni and Weiner, 1976).

These social and family support networks consisting of family, relatives and friends can be mobilized and activated to become involved with the concerns of the nuclear family members, aiding in the development of alternative options in solving the family crisis.

An increasing number of family therapists of various orientations have written both on the clinical and theoretical aspects of the extended family system as the potential source of support available for families. (Attneave, 1976; Bell, 1962; Boszormenyi-Nagy and Spark, 1973; Bowen, 1972; Caplan, 1975; Curtis, 1973; Garrison, 1974; Pattison, 1976; Speck, 1967, 1973; Tolsdorf, 1976).

An important part of this modality of intervention is the skills and therapeutic strategies that the team of therapists utilize during the network sessions. This paper attempts to discuss a number of roles that the therapists undertake in working with the nuclear family and its extended system.

THE NETWORK PHASES AND INTERVENTION GOALS

Each network, if fully mobilized, usually evolves six distinct phases:

From U. Rueveni, The Family Therapist as a System Interventionist, *International Journal of Family Therapy*, 1:63-75, 1975. Courtesy of Human Sciences Press, New York.

Retribalization, Polarization, Mobilization, Depression, Breakthrough, and Exhaustion-Elation. The Retribalization phase is the period of initial building and rebuilding of ties among network members who meet together to help solve a problem. This phase is followed by Polarization, a period characterized by increased tensions, conflicting points of view, disagreement and divisiveness among the network members. Mobilization is the phase whereby a collaborative exploration begins, leading toward additional investments of energy that facilitate active involvement particularly on the part of the network "Activitists." A Depression phase is the period where the network members experience a setback, little progress, and a sense of impass in their efforts toward solving a crisis. This phase is usually followed by a Breakthrough period where solutions can begin to be formulated, and an Exhaustion-Elation phase, characterized by a feeling of satisfaction and accomplishment.

Any one network session can either evolve all six phases or only some of them. Some sessions end in a Depression phase, indicating further need for a second session leading toward a Breakthrough. Inasmuch as these phases can be found within any group that assembles for a period of time seeking to solve a particular concern, experience with family network intervention indicates that the skills of the network therapist are critical in fully mobilizing the system for crisis resolution.

Family network intervention functions best when a small team of two or three professionals can assist the network therapist. Members of such a team usually are skilled in family, group, and psychodramatic techniques. These members can be therapists, or non-therapists whose backgrounds may not be in therapy but have considerable experience, understanding, and appreciation for family dynamics and group process.

The Therapist as a System Convenor

The therapist and members of the team function as network convenors primarily during the home visit or the retribalization phase. While the responsibility for assembling a network is primarily that of the family members, the therapist functions as a helpful resource in outlining ways of developing family maps, lists for assembling the extended system of relatives, friends, and neighbors. When the task of convening the extended system becomes difficult for some families due to little remaining family, the therapist helps in considering the convening of friends' networks, and friends of friends' networks. In one case the request for convening a network came from Mrs. Nash who was interested in exploring the possibilities of assembling a network to help her in dealing with her thirty-two year old daughter labelled "paranoid schizophrenic" who was living at home with her and causing her a great deal of anguish. She could not assemble more than a dozen family and relatives since many in her family including her own husband had died. The therapist offered this family an opportunity to participate in an upcoming workshop on networks which was to be convening in town the following week. The fifty network participants became a "family" support group for one day. Most of them returned to participate in a second network session the following week making additional efforts in providing support and help for resolving her crisis.

The Jones family network is another example of how the therapist provides for help in his role as network convenor. A network meeting was about to take place in the Jones' home in an attempt to help both parents deal with their twenty-nine year old daughter who had barricaded herself in the front vestibule, refusing to leave, eat, or sleep. Only twenty people showed up for the meeting. The team leader went outside and recruited a number of neighbors who were willing to convene and participate in helping the family at their time of crisis. The therapist and his team were also able to call on the local minister and members of his congregation to come immediately following the service that Sunday afternoon to participate in the network session. The outcome of the network resulted in a development of a support system for the young woman who was then able to move out and live with her aunt.

Another, more direct role of the therapist as a network convenor can be observed during the beginning of the main network session. During the retribalization phase the therapist's task is to provide network members the opportunity to interact, share, and get acquainted with each other. People mill around the room, some have not seen each other for quite some time, others wonder why they were invited, there may be cliques, the initial activity may be that of a small group interaction. During this period, the need is for an increased collaborative development of the network energy level which will enhance further network energies for involvement. The therapist needs to develop a sequence of activities, some verbal and others nonverbal which will allow for the development of the retribalization phase to take place rapidly. He does that by providing network members with an opportunity to engage in such energizing activities as milling around, stamping their feet, screaming, singing in unison, followed by more relaxing activities such as standing in a circle, holding hands, closing their eyes and humming silently.

The therapist's role is of a network convenor working to increase a network's "energy level" and state of readiness for further involvement in the network process. It is entirely possible that during this phase and perhaps during the entire network process the network therapist is perceived as taking the role of a celebrant, a term coined by Zuk (1975) connoting a role traditionally given by family members to clergy for initiating a healing ceremony.

Additional experiences with various forms of retribalization indicate the potential usefulness of this phase for bringing on powerful emotions to the surface in a cathartic fashion. A similar experience is reported by Katz (1976) in his interesting description of the healing ceremonies on the !Kung Zhan/Twasi healing dance ceremony, a collaborative effort which involves the whole community to release healing energy.

Another example from the Blum family network further details this convening role of the network therapist. The therapist and his team began the retribalization phase by suggesting to members of the immediate family that they could lead the entire network in a favorite medley of their choice. They chose the theme song "Sunrise, Sunset" from the show *Fiddler on The Roof*. As the rest of the network joined in, mother began sobbing and was held by her husband as the rest of the network was getting ready to deal with the unfolding of family problems.

The therapist can oftentime encourage other network members to help him and his team as network convenors. In a network assembled on Friday evening at the home of a Jewish family seeking to stop their son's ongoing suicidal attempts, the retribalization phase began by the son's cousin, a rabbincal student, who was asked by the team leader to initiate the meeting by lighting the candles and offering the blessing, followed by the traditional welcoming of the Sabbath melody sung by the entire network. The cousin, utilizing the traditional Jewish religious ritual, was able to quickly retribalize the network.

The Therapist as a System Mobilizer

Little can be achieved during any network session unless the network can become mobilized for action. The therapist and his team can, and should be able to, stimulate and encourage maximum participation and disclosures, sharing of conflicting points of view, and open dialogue by the network membership. In doing so, the therapist cannot be passive or uninvolved. To rapidly mobilize the network, the therapist oftentimes takes sides, confronts family or network members, and encourages clear comunications and disclosures of painful feelings or secrets.

During the mobilization phase where the potential exists for the formation of the network activists, the therapist needs to provide further support for additional exploration of the crisis. When the network members seem "stuck" or feel that their contributions are not being taken constructively by members of the immediate family, a temporary phase of depression develops. During this phase the therapist needs to structure additional experiences that will lead toward a deeper exploration of the crisis.

The following vignettes further elaborate on this role of the therapist. During a recent network session members of the immediate family had some difficulty in sharing their concerns openly. They spoke in generalities and were unable to outline specific issues. The therapist queried the family as to whether or not there were any secrets in the family. One of the uncles indicated that he wished he could share some but his wife prohibited him from doing so. The therapist and his team insisted on discussing this issue, whereby the uncle was able to disclose the absence of one family member who was not invited, and also to bring out the issue of his own feeling of being exluded from important family events. The therapist helped both the uncle and the network mobilize their resources to deal with that specific issue.

During another network session some of the relatives felt uncomfortable with the process. One uncle threatened to punch the therapist in the nose. When invited to do so he left the room and then came back and shared his initial frustration and anxiety. An aunt seemed unable to speak directly to the patient and had to be reminded by the therapist on numerous occasions to speak directly to him, in the first person, with no lecturing. At another point during the same session, an argument developed between two cousins as to the nature of previous help provided by each, and their past interests in the family's problems. The therapist encouraged self-expression. At one point he took sides with one at another point showed appreciation for the effects of the other. When a group of activitists began to form around the young man who was labelled "psychotic," the therapist and his team had to repeatedly encourage and remind the group to deal with feelings, avoid scapegoating, and to provide specific alternatives for discussion.

The Quincy case provides another example. The Quincy network assembled to help the divorced mother, her five children, and their father to deal with the difficulty they all had in relating to the fourteen year old daughter who lately refused to attend school, take a bath, or cooperate with the family. She remained in the garage most of the time, causing a great deal of stress on all other family members. When the team visited the home prior to the network session, the woman was tied with a rope to the garage door, refusing to participate in the session. She was told that the network was going to be held with or without her, and that she was welcome to attend if she so chose. During mid session she was standing below in the basement listening to the events taking place upstairs. At the same time, one team member found a typed note on this young woman's bedroom door requesting from the network members various specific actions she would like to see take place in her life. The team arranged for a support group to go down into the basement and work further on the issues with her. The network was mobilized around these events, particularly when it became evident that the requests dealt with tutoring, moving away from home, and making social contacts.

The Therapist as System Choreographer

Papp (1976) describes family choreography as a method of actively intervening in the nuclear and extended family by realigning family relationships through physical and movement positioning. She further states that choreography allows the therapist to draw the system with space, time, sight, hearing, energy, and movement. This role is quite similar to what the network therapist is involved with during the intervention process. To facilitate transition from one network phase to another, the therapist needs to be aware of two interacting systems; the nuclear family system, and the extended family system. When members of either one of these two systems seem to have difficulty during the network process, the therapist and the team members need to develop active and dramatic techniques which can mobilize the network for further involvement in providing additional opportunity for a deeper exploration of the crisis. These active intervention techniques oftentime involve direct encounter, family sculpturing, and psychodrama which can provide family members a setting for restructuring and realigning of dysfunctional and self-destructive patterns. These patterns can be examined within the supportive network atmosphere where trust levels can be achieved and public sharing of such interpersonal concerns can be dealt with in an open manner.

The following vignettes clarify this role of the therapist as network choreographer. The Blum network was assembled to help the family members develop alternative options in dealing with their oldest daughter's frequent suicidal attempts following her divorce, many in the family and the network felt depressed and unable to make progress in their efforts to help. The suicidal daughter and her sister seemed angry but afraid to confront their mother. The therapist and his team felt that a confrontation between mother and daughter could mobilize the network for further involvement and action. A sequence of activities was developed to help bring the confrontation about. First, the daughter was asked to step on a chair and look around the room for people she would trust. She mentioned a few people excluding her mother. Mother, sitting below and looking up at her daughter, began sobbing, sharing her feelings of loss of a relationship and her need to love her daughter. The daughter, while standing on the chair, was helped by the therapist and the team to confront her mother directly and seek specific issues that she could fight over with her mother. Standing on the chair, physically "higher" than her mother, the young woman looked at her mother and then expressed feelings of resentment toward her. When both faced each other later on, an intense exchange of feelings took place. The daughter, supported by the therapist, pointed her finger at her mother and yelled that she needed to be herself and she would not care to do what her mother wanted her to do. The mother screamed back at her daughter and then reached toward her in an attempt to hug her, crying that she did not want to lose her. At that point the team separated them and asked the family members to realign themselves either beside the mother or the daughter. Mother was joined by some of her friends, while the daughter was joined by her father and sister. The sixteen year old son refused to join either and hid in the kitchen. This confrontation helped both family and network members explore further the nature of the relationship and the crisis that was related to it.

Another example of how the therapist functions as a network choreographer comes from the Gross network. When the therapist and the team staged a "funeral ceremony" where the son was asked to lie on the floor and declared dead, his mother and later on the rest of the network members were asked to share their own feelings about him.

This "death ceremony" was choreographed by the therapist to bring out the grief feelings mother had to face in separating from her son. It also provided an opportunity for the network system to offer direct help to both the mother and the son in their efforts to disengage from each other.

Recent experiences with simulating family "death ceremonies" are encouraging in that they seem to elicit a great deal of energy oftentime revealing intergenerational conflicts and "hidden agendas" not previously brought to the surface. Katz (1966) reporting his experiences with the !Kung tribe quotes their view that to heal one must die and be reborn. My experience with "death scenes" during family network sessions suggests that it can be a powerful tool that should be used selectively and timed for a specific purpose.

A final example comes from a simulated network assembled to help a depressed wife who was having difficulty in relating to her husband who she claimed was too "close to his own mother." The wife perceived that relationship as interfering with her own marriage. The therapist choreographed an experience that helped mobilize the network for involvement and action. The first experience was created around the wife who revealed that she never felt loved by her own mother. Her two sisters were asked to kneel beside her while she attempted to create a dialogue with her dead mother sitting in the chair in front of her. The experience was further developed by the local minister who came to comfort the wife together with her two sisters, and a group of network activists joining them to consider additional support and ways of dealing with her concerns. The second experience concerned the husband's relationship to his own mother. Some of the network members felt that both should be able to examine their relationship openly. The therapist was approached by the father for help in dealing with the issue. The therapist tied a rope around the man's waist and asked his mother to hold on to the other end of the rope. Many in the network, including the team, confirmed that the situation depicted precisely how both were relating to each other. When the man finally was able to remove the rope, he began sharing his feelings toward his mother that in the past he could not or would not allow himself to share. The support groups assembled around the father and his own mother made some constructive suggestions for their future relationships.

The Therapist as a System Resource Consultant

Network members are able to begin and formulate alternative courses of action in dealing with family crisis by forming into support groups. The therapist and the network team encourage the formation of such support groups. Team members usually are expected to provide the initial leadership in forming such groups, but are not required to actively become members of such groups unless they, themselves, choose to do so. When these support groups form, usually toward the end of the first network session, they meet in between sessions and following the completion of the network meetings for various periods of time. The team is available for members of such support groups serving as resource consultant on a variety of issues that members of such groups struggle with. The following are some examples of this role of the therapist.

Toward the end of a network session assembled to help both parents with their suicidal daughter (the Blum network), the therapist suggested that the network members form into three support groups, one for the daughter, and one for each of the parents, where each member could take a stand supporting the family member of his choice. Many in the network felt uneasy in taking sides. "We like all three of them" and "We would like to help them all" were not uncommon comments. The therapist and the team members insisted on the formation of the three groups. When the support groups formed, arrangements were made by the members to meet during the week. A support group coordinator was selected who kept in contact with the therapist and his team during the week to consult on a variety of issues relating to the support group's ongoing commitments of work with the family members they were supporting. During the week another team member met with the daughter, serving in a resource-consultant role, reviewing the network progress and her own future involvement concerning the second network meeting. The result of this meeting with the daughter was that she was able with the help of the team members to further elaborate her needs from her parents and from the network membership. These included her feeling that many in the network provided her with new social contacts which helped lessen her suicidal feelings and increase her need for additional friends, a new job, and continued support. Following the completion of the second network meeting, members of all three family support groups met for a number of months keeping in contact with team members to provide ongoing suggestions and feedback.

Following the completion of the Gross network, assembled to help the mother and her son cut their mutual self-destructive symbiotic relationship, the support group assembled for the son had only a few family members. Most members were professionals and friends who felt they could be of help. The support group consulted frequently with members of the team concerning housing, further therapy, and social contacts. The commitment of the members was quickly put to a test by the young man who was encouraged to find a place to stay away from home. He took an apartment in the local YMCA returning home later only to find that the locks on the doors of his mother's house had been changed by his mother on the advice of her support group members. The son paced outside of the house pleading to get in but finally returned to the YMCA. He further attempted to put pressure on his support group members to convince them that he needed to be taken care of in a hospital setting. The following evening he called the local suicide prevention center claiming he had overdosed and that he was a patient of a certain psychiatrist. The psychiatrist was alerted and being aware of the support group's involvement, he called on them for action. One of the support group members, a psychiatric resident, took it upon himself to visit the young man and found him not be a medical emergency. The support group members continued their efforts for a number of months providing social and financial help. For a period of over one year following the network there was improvement with no hospitalization or suicidal attempts on his part. The mother's and sister's support groups continued making additional efforts at helping both mother and daughter.

The Therapist as a Strategist

The therapist's roles elaborated in this paper are all roles that mandate that the therapist be an effective strategist. The task of the therapist in family network intervention, and to a great extent in family therapy, is to be an effective clinical strategist. In family therapy the clinical strategy depends on the background and frame of reference within which the therapist operates. Most clinicians utilize strategies to help their clients change. The therapist serving as the leader of the network intervention team employs his clinical skills to develop intervention strategies which will lead toward the resolution of the family crisis.

The concept of the therapist as a strategist implies that the therapist be aware of his own need to shift ground, to mobilize parts of himself which may need to be activated and reactivated. The therapist cannot remain inactive during the intervention efforts. His energies are directed in collaboration with the team toward a rapid mobilization of the family system and to achieve this goal he may need to utilize himself, his own skills, energies, talents, acting ability, and resourcefulness if he intends to be an effective interventionist.

REFERENCES

Attneave, C.L. Y'All come: Social networks as a unit of intervention. Philip

Guerin (Ed.), *Family Therapy: Theory and Practice.* New York: Gardner Press, 1976.

Bell, N.W. Extended family relations of disturbed and well families. *Family Process,* 1962, *1,* 175-193.

Boszormenyi-Nagy, I., and Spark, G.M. *Invisible Loyalties.* Hagerstown Md.: Harper and Row, 1973.

Bowen, M. Towards Differentiation of Self in One's Own Family of Origin. In Francis D. Andres (Ed.), *Georgetown Family Symposium: A Collection of Selected Papers,* 1971-1972, *1,* 77-95.

Caplan, G., and Killilea, M. *Support Systems and Mutual Help.* New York: Grune and Stratton, 1975.

Curtis, W.R. Community human service networks, new roles for mental health workers. *Psychiatric Annals,* 1973, *3, 7,* 23-42.

Garrison, J. "Network techniques: Case studies in the screening-linking-planning conference method. *Family Process,* 1974, *13,* 337-353.

Katz, R. The Painful Ecstasy of Healing. *Psychology Today,* December, 1976, pp. 81-96.

Papp, P. Family Choreography. In P. Guerin (Ed.), *Family therapy: Theory and practice.* New York: Gardiner Press, 1976.

Pattison, E.M. *A theoretical empirical base for social systems therapy.* Paper presented at the 23rd Annual Conference of the American Group Psychotherapy Association, Boston, Mass., February 1976.

Rueveni, U. Family networks healing families in crisis. *Intellect,* 1976, *104,* 580-582.

Rueveni, U. Network intervention with a family crisis. *Family Process,* 1975, *14,* 193-204.

Rueveni, U., and Speck, R.V. Using encounter group techniques in the treatment of the social network of the schizophrenic. *International Journal of Group Psychotherapy,* 1969, *19,* 495-500.

Rueveni, U., and Wiener, M. Network intervention of disturbed families: The key role of network activists. *Psychotherapy: Theory, Research and Practice,* 1976, *13*(2), 173-176.

Speck, R.V. Family Therapy in the Home. *Journal of Marriage and Family Living,* 1964, *26,* 72-76.

Speck, R.V. Psychotherapy of the social network of a schizophrenic family. *Family Process,* 1967, *6,* 208-214.

Speck, R.V., and Attneave, C. *Family Networks.* New York: Vintage Books, 1973.

Speck, R.V., and Rueveni, U. Treating the family in time of crisis. In Jules H. Masserman (Ed.), *Current Psychiatric Therapies.* New York: Grune & Stratton, 1977, *17,* 135-142.

Speck, R.V., and Rueveni, U. Network therapy—a developing concept. *Family Process,* 1969, *8,* 182-191.

Tolsdorf, C.C. Social networks and coping: An exploratory study. *Family Process,* 1976, *15*(4), 407-417.

Zuk, G.H. *Process and practice in family therapy.* Haverford, Pa.: Psychiatry and Behavioral Science Books, 1975.

Part II
TECHNIQUES

INITIATING FAMILY THERAPY

Regardless of one's theoretical approach the initial sessions are crucial. First contact is typically made by telephone, and it is at that point that family therapy begins. The therapist must now make decisions that may have an impact on the entire family counseling process. Specifically: (1) Do I see the whole family together? (2) Who presented the concerns? and (3) What are the presenting concerns? are questions that must be examined.

Following the telephone contact, initial family interviews should be used for (a) further assessment, (b) establishing rapport, and (c) providing a positive atmosphere for future exploration. Some family therapists also believe that the intial interview should be used to compile an extensive family history. One of the therapist's goals during these early sessions should be to define the family's concerns as extensively as possible and hypothesize future directions for treatment.

The articles in this section highlight several points: (1) who controls the therapy will be an issue during the initial counseling sessions; (2) the issue of why the family has initiated treatment must be explored by all family members; and (3) one of the main concerns a therapist will have in the early sessions is to assess coalitions, alliances, rules, roles, and communication patterns. While these articles describe different methods for initiating the family therapy process, they all appear to emphasize the previously mentioned points.

The article by Feldman suggests that goal setting by the therapist can facilitate the therapeutic process. The establishment of clear goals for the therapy will result in clear interventions toward appropriate conclusions.

Napier explores the initial stages of treatment as they relate to resistance and the family's struggles with therapist. He views the family's resistance as being quite different from what traditionalists have described as resistance and considers that much of the struggle is related to the family's anxiety about change. In this article Napier also presents a series of recommendations for therapists initiating treatment with families.

Many therapy styles do not give individuals or families the feeling that they are capable of or responsible for change. Friedman presents some specific techniques for working through the family's initial manipulations and getting at the core issues. He presents a variety of "typical" attitudes and comments directed at the therapist and then suggests ways to work with those concerns in an effective and affective manner.

During the initial sessions the family therapy should be assessing the family's alliances and coalitions. This type of assessment strategy should allow the therapist to intervene most effectively. Slerzki initially argues that by his/her attendance the therapist will not be able to avoid involvement in coalitions. However, the therapist must be aware of these alliances, attempting not to get enmeshed in any particular coalition while remaining open to all family members. By shifting from alliance to alliance, the therapist uses his/her power and presence to change or modify existing patterns in the family.

All of the articles in this section focus on getting the entire family into treatment and involving them in the change process quickly. The ability of the therapist to assess the family and move beyond the intial struggles is crucial if the therapy is going to have a positive outcome.

GOALS OF FAMILY THERAPY

LARRY B. FELDMAN

During the past two decades, family therapy has emerged as a major innovative force in the field of mental health. Published reports (e.g., Burks & Serrano, 1965; Cutter & Hallowitz, 1962; Langsley & Kaplan, 1968; Minuchin, et al., 1967; Safer, 1966) have attested to the efficacy of the family therapy approach with a wide variety of clinical problems, and numerous descriptions of family therapy strategies and techniques have appeared (e.g., Beels & Ferber, 1969; Bell, 1961; Boszormenyi-Nagy & Framo, 1965; Haley, 1963; Minuchin, 1974). In the present report, attention will be directed to the objectives or goals of family therapy. A variety of different goals will be reviewed and discussed, and an integrative framework for conceptualizing these goals will be presented.

What is family therapy? A number of writers (e.g., Bell, 1971; Haley, 1971) have suggested that family therapy is any form of therapy which is guided by a family systems conceptualization of psychopathology, and that the definition of family therapy is not dependent on who is actually seen for therapy. For example, when Bowen (1967) meets with individuals and "coaches" them regarding visits to their family of origin, he is conducting a form of family therapy. Nonetheless, in practice family therapy has generally come to mean conjoint family therapy, in which two or more members of a family meet (either by themselves or with a group of other families) with one or more therapists. Family therapy with a marital couple (marital therapy) is sometimes distinguished from family therapy with two or more generations. In the present report, family therapy will be defined as any form of therapy with one or more members of a family which is guided by a family systems conceptualization of psychopathology. No attempt will be made to differentiate between the goals of family therapy with groups of families, single families, multigenerational families, marital couples,

From L. Feldman, Goals of Family Therapy, *Journal of Marriage and Family Counseling*, 2:103-12, 1976. Courtesy of American Association for Marriage and Family Therapy.

individuals. This approach is based on the writer's belief that certain groups of goals are common to all of the different forms of family therapy and that the construction of a general framework is essential.

In discussing family therapy goals, it is important to distinguish between the goals of the family and the goals of the therapist. When families begin therapy, they bring a set of ideas (more or less clear and more or less conscious) about what they hope to get from the therapy. Often, these ideas are focused on one member of the family who is the "identified patient." An important part of the early work of therapy consists of a search by the family and the therapist for a mutually acceptable set of therapeutic goals. As therapy progresses, the therapist and/or the family may want to revise the original goals or add new ones, in which case the issue of the goals of therapy would have to be renegotiated.

Another issue which arises in considering the goals of family therapy is that the goals of individual family members may not all be the same. For example, in one family seen by the writer, the wife wanted help for her children during the process of adjusting to the pending divorce between her and her husband while the husband wanted to work on the marriage in hope of avoiding the divorce. Resolving discrepancies between the goals of individual family members is an important part of the early work in family therapy. At times, it may not be necessary to actually resolve such discrepancies, provided that techniques can be devised which allow for simultaneous attainment of several seemingly discrepant goals.

In considering the therapist's goals, it is important to distinguish between outcome goals and process goals. Outcome goals are those objectives that the therapist hopes will be achieved by the time therapy is over. Process goals are objectives that may have to be reached before it is possible to achieve an outcome goal. For example, suppose an outcome goal is the disappearance of an adolescent girl's suicidal behavior. The therapist meets with the entire family and identifies a pattern of unclear, incongruent, and indirect communication which he believes is highly correlated with the daughter's suicidal behavior. The initial goal of the therapy may become improved communication, seen as a means to the outcome goal of symptomatic improvements in the daughter. As this example illustrates, process goals often become outcome goals. Improved communication is a desirable end in its own right, in addition to being a means for achieving symptomatic improvement.

SPECIFIC GOALS FOR SPECIFIC FAMILIES

In recent years, increasing attention has been paid to the importance of specificity in the assessment of psychotherapy outcome. Kiesler (1971) has criticized much of the existing psychotheapy outcome research on the basis of what he called the "uniformity myth"—that is, the myth that all patients or clients are alike. He notes that, contrary to the uniformity myth, constructive change for different individuals "may represent change in different directions on the same variables, or change on different dimensions, or different patterns of change on the same variables—or different degrees of these various changes (p. 40)."

With regard to family therapy, specificity of goal setting has been emphasized by a number of writers. Weakland, et al., (1974) have argued that the major goal of family therapy should be the improvement or resolution of whatever problem or problems the family wishes to work on. They note that "patients or their family members come with certain complaints and accepting them for treatment involves a responsibility for relieving these complaints . . . The presenting problem offers, in one package, what the patient [family] is ready to work on, a concentrated manifestation of whatever is wrong, and a concrete index of any progress made (p. 147)." Liberman (1970) has indicated that in his behavioral approach to family therapy, one of the first tasks which must be undertaken by the therapist and family is a behavioral or functional analysis of the problems. In making a behavioral analysis, the therapist addresses the following questions: What behavior is maladaptive or problematic; what behavior should be increased or decreased? Each person, in turn, is asked: 1) what changes would you like to see in others in the family, and 2) how would you like to be different from the way you are now?

Answering these questions forces the therapist to choose carefully *specific* behavioral goals. Kramer (1968) takes the position that a necessary goal of therapy with any family is the reduction or elimination of the presenting problems. He sees this as a major goal of the first phase of therapy, and notes that about two-thirds of the families he has treated have decided to terminate once this goal has been reached. Termination at the end of first phase in *not* viewed as failure or "flight into health" but rather as the successful achievement of an important set of family therapy goals. If the family decides to continue into middle phase, the work will be directed toward an additional set of goals, mutually agreed upon by the family and the therapist.

GENERAL GOALS

In addition to those therapy goals which are specific for a particular family, there are also a variety of general goals which are widely applied in various combinations to the therapy of all or most families. These general goals can be grouped into two major categories: 1) Family Interaction; and 2) Systems and Character Traits of Individual Family Members. In the following sections, the goals in each of these categories will be reviewed.

Family Interaction

The idea that therapeutic intervention should be directed toward altering the nature of family interactions is a basic concept of family therapy. In attempting to conceptualize this area, it is useful to distinguish two aspects of family interaction: 1) Family Structure; and 2) Family Processes.

Family structure. The structure of any system is the manner in which the elements of that system are organized or interrelated (Random House, 1968). Since the elements of the family system are the individual family members, the structure of a family is the overall form or pattern of intra-familial relationships. With regard to the goals of family therapy, two aspects of family structure have received major attention: a) family rules and programs; and b) family roles and boundaries.

a) Family rules and programs. Family rules are relationship agreements which prescribe and limit family members' behaviors over a wide variety of content areas. Although the term "agreement" is used in this definition, it does not necessarily imply conscious agreement; most relationship rules are probably outside of awareness (Jackson, 1965). The existence and nature of the family rules are inferred from the family's observable patterns of recurrent behavior (redundancies). Such patterns, or "family behavior programs" (Beels & Ferber, 1969), are a fundamental aspect of family structure.

Change in the nature of family rules and family behavior programs has come to be widely regarded as a major goal of family therapy. Watzlawick, Weakland, and Fisch (1974) have labeled such change "second order change" and have contrasted it with first order change, in which outward appearances are altered, but fundamental premises are left intact. Haley (1963) has indicated that in working with married couples his primary objective is to provoke a change in the rules by which the couple keep the marital system stable. Langsley and his colleagues (1968) attempt to intervene at times of family crisis in such a way that hospitalization of the symptomatic family member can be avoided. In their view, hospitalization of the identified patient is a homeostatic pattern which frequently leads to the continuation of pathological behavior. Their goal in working with families in crisis is to help the family find other patterns of equilibration so that hospitalization can be avoided.

b) Family roles and boundaries. Another dimension of family structure which has received considerable attention from family therapists is that of family roles and boundaries. Minuchin (1974) emphasizes the importance of intrafamilial role boundaries, and visualizes most families who come for therapy as falling at one of two extremes on a continuum of boundary rigidity-flexibility. In families with overly rigid sub-system boundaries ("disengaged" families), "communication across sub-systems becomes difficult, and the protective functions of the family are handicapped . . . Members of disengaged sub-systems or families may function autonomously but have a skewed sense of independence and for requesting support when needed (pp 54-55)." In families with overly diffuse sub-system boundaries ("enmeshed" families), "the differentiation of the family diffuses . . . (and) the heightened sense of belonging requires a major yielding of autonomy (p 55)." In many families, the structure is a combination of disengagement and enmeshment. For example: "A highly enmeshed sub-system of mother and children . . . can exclude father, who becomes disengaged in the extreme (p 55)." In Minuchin's view, a major goal of family therapy is improving family structure by re-calibrating sub-system boundaries. He notes that the therapist often functions as a boundary maker, clarifying diffuse boundaries and opening in appropriately rigid boundaries. In this way, boundaries become clear enough to allow sub-system members to carry out their functions without undue interference but are permeable enough to allow contact between the members of the sub-system and others.

Another major goal of family therapy in the area of role relations is role flexibility. Haley (1963) has emphasized the goal of role flexibility with regard to power and control in family therapy with marital partners. He anticipates a change from a rigid system of role relations which, for example, the husband always assumes the dominant role and the wife always assumes the submissive role, to a more flexible pattern, with both spouses periodically assuming the dominant and submissive roles. Whitaker (1974) has extended the goal of role flexibility to include parent-child as well as marital roles. He notes that:

> . . . individuation in a healthy family makes possible such mobility that any member can function in any role. The four year old boy can 'mother' his own father; the 40 year old mother can be a little girl to her son or her daughter and this flexibility is available in response to a situation and the impulse or creative moment taking place within the family (p 2).

It is important to distinguish inter-generational role flexibility (in which each family member is free to assume *temporarily* any familial role) from the quite different phenomenon of chronic blurring of inter-generational role distinctions. Often, when families come to theapy, the role relations between one or both parents and one or more of the children are more like those of spouses than parent-child. Likewise, the parents often relate to each other as parent-child instead of co-equal adults. When this is the case, a major goal of family therapy is the reduction of inter-generational blurring of roles (Haley, 1963).

Family processes. A process is a systematic series of actions directed to some end (Random House, 1968). In regard to family interaction, the most basic processes are morphostasis and morphogenesis; communication; and conflict resolution.

(a) Morphostasis and morphogenesis. Morphostasis (homeostasis) is the process whereby a system maintains internal stability and organization; morphogenesis is the process whereby a system alters or changes its structure (Speer, 1970). Morphostasis is accomplished by means of negative (deviation counter-acting) feedback while morphogenesis is accomplished by means of positive (deviation amplifying) feedback. Speer (1970) has suggested that dysfunctional families are characterized by high morphostasis and low morphogenesis, and that a major goal of family therapy should be a shift away from morphostasis and toward morphogenesis. Another way of putting this is that dysfunctional families are locked into rigid repetitions of the same patterns of family interaction, and are unable to alter their own structure in response to changing circumstances (e.g., growth and development of children). A major goal of family therapy, then, is to help such families develop the capacity to observe and change themselves, rather than rigidly maintaining familiar (albeit painful) homeostatic patterns of interaction.

b) Communication. Improved communication has been defined by family therapists is a variety of ways. Satir (1967) has written that as a result of successful family therapy, communication should become more clear, congruent, non-contradictory, direct, and honest. Ackerman (1961) and Bell (1961) have indicated that there should be more open and spontaneous expression of feelings, wishes, ideals, goals, and values among family members as a result of family therapy. A number of other writers have also highlighted one or more of these dimensions (e.g., Bach & Wyden, 1968; Boszormenyi-Nagy, 1965; Minuchin, et al., 1967). In the following sections the notions of clarity, congruence, and consistency (non-contradictoriness) will be discussed together because their meanings tend to overlap. Following this, the concepts of openness and directness will be considered.

i) Clarity, congruence, consistency. Riskin and Faunce (1969) have defined clarity as existing when "the words in the speech make sense to the observer and the affect (tone, inflection, etc.) fits (i.e., is congruent with) the idea or feeling which the words express (p 25)." Goldfarb and his colleagues (1966) sub-divide the clarity concept into 15 distinct variables. Among these are: 1) denotative clarity—the extent to which the literal expressions of ideas, facts, and references to emotions that are conveyed by words are clear; 2) connotative clarity—the extent to which ideas and emotions communicated by vocal inflection, amplitude, rate, rhythm, and tone of speech, facial expression, body movement, and posture are clear; 3) consistency—the extent to which ideas and feelings are presented in a congruent and non-contradictory manner; and 4) relevance—the extent to which the content of the message is related to the context. Wynne and Singer (1963) define a number of concepts which are closely related to clarity, congruence, and non-contradictoriness although these authors do not use these terms. Instead, they speak of "patterns of handling attention and meaning" and cluster variables into three groupings—closure problems, disruptive behavior, and peculiar verbalizations. Closure problems include the following dimensions, among others: 1) speech fragments; 2) unintelligible remarks; 3) contradictory information, inconsistent references, and incompatible alternatives. Disruptive behavior includes, among others: odd, tangential, or inappropriate responses. Peculiar verbalizations includes, among others: 1) peculiar word usages, constructions, and pronunciations; and 2) peculiar logic.

ii) Openness and directness. Bach (1968) has defined communication as "open" when the participants' messages are "overt, transparent, and not disguised; when participants mean what they say and the meaning is obvious (p 164)." Beaver, et al., (1972) focus on the ability of family members to express *emotions* openly. They have constructed a five-point rating scale which categorizes familial expression of emotions as either: 1) open and direct; 2) direct despite some discomfort; 3) obviously restricted with regard to some feelings; 4) although some feelings are expressed, there is masking of most feelings; or 5) no expression of feelings. Epstein, et al., (1968) classify communications as "direct" when "the message is aimed at the person for whom it is intended (p 6)." This is contrasted with "displaced" communications which are aimed at someone other than the one for whom they are actually intended. Bach and Beavers et al., have similar definitions of the directness—displacement dimension.

c) Conflict resolution. Changes in the frequency, quality, and methods of handling intra-familial conflicts are cited by many writers as a major goal of family therapy. Ard (1969) and Tharp (1966) suggest that successful family therapy will lead to fewer intra-familial conflicts. On the other hand, Haley (1963) and Boszormenyi-Nagy (1965) note that for some families (those who have difficulty expressing conflict openly) the goal is just the opposite—namely, an *increase* in the frequency of conflicts. More accurately, the goal with "conflict-avoidant" families is to increase the frequency of *overt* expression of conflict while simultaneously decreasing the frequency of *covert* conflict expression. When conflict is expressed overtly, the possibility of a constructive resolution exists. With covert conflict expression, issues cannot be resolved because they cannot be discussed.

What are the ingredients of constructive conflict management? Ard (1969) suggests that one ingredient is a willingness to consider and accept responsibility for one's own part in the conflict. Related to this is Ackerman's (1961) statement that a goal of family therapy is the reduction of "fruitless and vindictive forms of blaming (p 64)." Boszormenyi-Nagy (1965) suggests that family members need to learn to state their points of view about issues of disagreement more specifically and less generally. For example, being told by one's spouse that he or she did not like the fact that you drank so much at a particular party is very different from being told that "you're impossible at parties." The former statement, if delivered in a non-destructive manner, can be the basis for negotiation; the latter is simply an insult.

The issue of destructiveness is also discussed by Boszormenyi-Nagy (1965) who notes that in successful family therapy conflicts become less personally destructive. In a coding scheme developed by the present writer, "personally destructive" behaviors are defined as acts which are hurtful (either physically or psychologically) and which do *not* promote communication or negotiation. Examples of personally destructive acts are sarcasm, denigration, namecalling and physical attack.

Spiegel (1957) emphasizes the importance of compromise in the process of conflict management. When family members are able to "settle" for something less than what they wanted initially, and not resent doing so, the family is well on its way to more satisfactory functioning. In order for this step in the process to take place, the previous steps—willingness to consider one's own part in the conflict, specificity, and non-destructiveness—are essential.

Once a compromise or change has been agreed to, the next step is implementation. It is one thing to agree to change, but quite another to actually do so. In order for lasting change to take place, each partner must receive positive reinforcement in response to behavioral changes. The specific forms of behavior which function as reinforcers vary from family to family. For example, in some families praise will be experienced as encouraging, while in other families, it will be experienced as infantilizing. Whatever specific forms of reinforcement are appropriate, it is important that they be consistent and reciprocal (See Liberman, 1970, for more on reciprocal reinforcement.)

Symptoms and Character Traits of Individual Family Members

The family is a vehicle for individual growth and development—it is not an end in itself. In fact, a number of writers (e.g., Jackson, 1965; Wynne, et al., 1958) have noted that one important characteristic of pathological families is that the growth and development of individual family members is sacrificed to the maintenance of the family as a unit. In family therapy, outcome goals are very often individual ones, with changes in family interaction being viewed as necessary for the attainment of specific individual goals. In the following sections, the individual goals of symptomatic improvement, increased differentiation, increased empathy, and increased mature dependency will be reviewed.

Symptomatic improvement. A symptom is most broadly defined as "deviant or disturbed behavior (GAP, 1966; p 270)." This definition is necessarily vague because, as noted by Redlich and Freedman (1966), what constitutes manifest behavior disorders depends on the culture or value system; there is no sharp line of demarcation between normal and abnormal behavior—only marked deviations can be clearly recognized. In actual practice, most clinicians appear to define behavior as abnormal or symptomatic when it is seriously disabling, frustrating, and deviates from established cultural norms. Haley (1963) has highlighted the interpersonal significance of symptomatic behavior, and describes the ways in which symptoms function as homeostats within the context of the family system.

What, then, is symptomatic improvement? According to many writers (e.g., Ackerman, 1961; Haley, 1963; Boszormenyi-Nagy, 1965) symptomatic improvement means reduction in the frequency and/or intensity of symptoms or the complete disappearance of symptoms. Bell (1961) adds the additional notion that often in successful family theapy there is a reinterpretation of symptoms by the family with consequent lessening of their disturbing effects on the symptomatic one and on the other members of the family. In studies of family therapy outcome, improvement has been noted in a wide variety of symptoms, including those of the psychoses (e.g., Burks & Serrano, 1965; Esterson, et al., 1965; Langsley & Kaplan, 1968); character disorders (e.g., Cutter & Hallowitz, 1962; Schreiber, 1966; Minuchin, et al., 1967); and neuroses (e.g., Kaffman, 1963; Pittman, et al., 1968).

Increased differentiation. The idea that family members should become more differentiated (autonomous, self-responsible) as a result of successful family therapy appears in many of the reviewed sources (e.g., Ard & Ard, 1969; Bowen, 1967; Framo, 1965; Satir, 1967; Winer, 1971). Framo (1965) states that when family therapy is successful ". . . Each individual becomes more free to explore an individual definition of self, which may be quite different from his role as formerly viewed by the family (p 206)." Bowen (1967) defines differentiation as a process in which a person comes to assume responsibility for his or her own happiness and comfort, and avoids thinking that tends to blame and hold others responsible for one's own unhappiness or failure. He describes his approach to family therapy as being directed toward the primary goal of increased differentiation for each family member.

Increased empathy. To empathize with another is to attempt actively to experience and share the internal states (thoughts and feelings) of that other. It implies a capacity for concern (caring about other's needs as well as one's own) and for frustration tolerance (empathy is an active and, at times, frustrating process; it seldom "just happens"). The goal of increased empathy has been particularly emphasized by Paul (1967) who writes that in his approach to conjoint marital therapy "exposure of affects related to disappointments, frustration, and internal pain . . . is designed to generate reciprocating empathic responses (p 187)." Paul notes that the therapist's ability to empathize with each family member is an important factor in promoting increased empathy among the family members themselves. In addition to the work of Paul, increased empathy has been used as an outcome criterion in a number of studies of family therapy (e.g.,Fitzgerald, 1969; Landes & Winter, 1966; Reding, et al., 1967).

Increased mature dependency. The concept of mature dependency has not been written about much by family therapists, but is included here because it is the writer's belief that it is an important general goal of family therapy. In order to be involved in an intimate relationship with another person, one must be able to allow oneself to be "taken care of" at times. When feeling overwhelmed by events, one must be able to cry, to lament, to express feelings of hopelessness and helplessness. In many ways, mature dependency is a counterpart of empathy—in order for the partner to be empathic, one must be able to reveal feelings for him or her to be empathic to. In my experience, many families who come for therapy are not able to allow themselves to reveal their feelings in this way. In these families, anxiety about becoming "one-down" to other family members is so strong that enormous quantities of energy are wasted in the effort to remain "one-up." In such a situation, one goal of family therapy is to reduce this anxiety enough so that a healthy level of mature dependency can become available for all members of the family.

DISCUSSION

Having conceptualized family therapy goals in terms of family interaction and individual symptoms and character traits, a model for integrating these two sets of goals will now be discussed. The most basic concept of this model is that the family and the individual represent two levels in a hierarchical arrangement which includes the biological level of cells, organs, and organisms, the individual level of psychological processes, the interpersonal level of family and group processes, and the transcultural level of intergroup processes. Since the systems at each of these levels (cells, individuals, families, et cetera) are relatively open, events at one level influence, and are influenced by, events at each of the other levels. Thus, changes in family interaction produce changes in individual family members' symptoms and character traits, and vice versa. This model of circular causality includes intrapsychic events which, in the writer's opinion, represent a highly significant level in the hierarchy. As individuals develop, their behavior is increasingly stimulated and reinforced by wishes, fears, images, and expectations. These events influence and are influenced by the interpersonal context in which they presently occur and carry with them the residues of the interpersonal context in which they developed (i.e., the family).

The connections between intrapsychic events, individual behavior, and family interaction are illustrated by the relationship of structural family boundaries to individual autonomy, empathy, and mature dependency. Families at the disengaged end of the structural spectrum are characterized by overly rigid and impermeable system boundaries and great interpersonal distance. The individuals in such families behave as if they were deathly afraid of intimacy. They may function with a high degree of autonomy, but show very little empathy or mature dependency. In families at the enmeshed end of the spectrum, just the opposite is observed—boundaries are overly flexible and permeable, with excessive interpersonal closeness. Individuals in enmeshed families behave as if they were deathly afraid of separation. They may function with a high degree of empathy and mature dependency, but are underdeveloped in the area of autonomy. The concepts of disengagement and enmeshment, then, encompass three levels of events: intrapsychic (anxiety about intimacy or separation); characterological (autonomy, empathy, mature dependency); and familial (rigid and impermeable or overly flexible and permeable boundaries). Changes in any one of these three levels lead to changes in each of the others. These changes, in turn, re-influence the level in which the initial change took place. In successful family therapy, these changes are mutually reinforcing, creating growth-promoting positive feedback loops which allow for continuing and self-perpetuating change.

Clinical Implications

The beginning phase of family therapy is in many ways the most important, since it sets the stage for all later work. At the same time, it is often the most difficult phase, especially for beginning family therapists. The quantity of information that the therapist must perceive and integrate at the beginning of family therapy is enormous. In addition, the family outnumbers the therapist, creating potential difficulties around the crucial issue of control of the therapy. The therapist brings to the therapy his or her personal strengths and weaknesses, a greater or lesser amount of experience working with families, and a set of concepts (of which the therapist may or may not be consciously aware) of how families work and how family therapy works. It is in this last-named area that the conceptual schema which has been presented in this report is of potential clinical utility. In many ways, the most important initial task for the family therapist is goal-setting. Unfortunately, this process is often not carried out. In too many instances, family therapists (especially beginning family therapists) start to "intervene" before having formulated (in conjunction with the family) a clear set of goals for the therapy. As a consequence, the therapy often gets bogged down, meanders aimlessly, or is precipitously terminated. In the writer's opinion, part of the reason that explicit goal setting is often ignored is that any effort to think about the great variety of potential family therapy goals is apt to be confusing and frustrating without the benefit of a coherent conceptual schema for systematically organizing one's thoughts. The present schema provides such a framework, and is easily applicable to actual family therapy cases. What is required of the therapist is the systematic assessment of each of the major categories (Family Structure, Family Processes, Individual Symptoms, and Individual Character Traits) and sub-categories (Family Rules and Programs, Family Roles and Boundaries, Morphostasis and Morphogenesis; Communication; Conflict Resolution, Symptoms; Differentiation; Empathy; and Mature Dependency) and a decision, for each subcategory, and whether change in this area ought to be a goal for therapy with this family. The therapist's thinking should be guided, for the most part, by the explicit and implicit goals of the family members. Often, a discussion about goals between the therapist and the family will be indicated; at times, this may not be necessary. In either case, it is imperative that the therapist have a clear conceptualization of his or her goals for the therapy, so that interventions are directed toward clear ends, rather than being aimless.

Goals for the Family and Goals for the Therapist

In addition to the goals that the therapist has for the family, he or she also has a set of goals for himself or herself which may be conscious or unconscious. As with the family, the therapist's goals will be a reflection of his or her system of values. Examples of the kinds of goals that therapists may have for themselves include: a) increased differentiation from own family of origin; b) increased integration of own childhood experiences; c) increased self-esteem; d) resolution of anxiety-producing conflicts; e) keeping families together at all costs because of own familial experiences. In order to function effectively with families, it is imperative that the therapist be able to "tune in" to his or her own goals, including those that are initially out of awareness. Once the therapist is aware of these personal goals, those that are reasonable can be retained and those that do not seem reasonable can be discarded. The fact that the therapist hopes to derive some personal benefits from the therapy is not a sign of destructive countertransference. In fact, Whitaker has suggested (1974) that therapy works best when the therapist is "trying to . . . become a person and is utilizing his work with the family as a means to this end (p 3)."

REFERENCES

Ackerman, N. "A dynamic frame for the clinical approach to family conflict." In Ackerman, et al., (Eds.), *Exploring the base for family therapy*, New York: Family Service Association of America, 1961.

American Psychoanalytic Association. *A glossary of psychoanalytic terms and concepts.* New York: American Psychoanalytic Association, 1968.

Ard, B.N., & Ard, C.C. *Handbook of marriage counseling.* Palo Alto: Science & Behavior Books, 1969.

Bach, G., & Wyden, P. *The intimate enemy.* New York: William Morrow & Co., 1968.

Beavers, W.R., et al. "Development of family evaluation scales." *Timberlawn Foundation Report No. 72*, Dallas, Texas, 1972.

Beels, C., & Ferber, A. "Family therapy: A view." *Family Process*, 1969, *8*, 280-318.

Bell, J. *Family group therapy.* Public Health Monograph 64, U.S. Dept. Health, Education and Welfare, 1961.

Boszormenyi-Nagy, I. "Intensive family therapy as process." In Boszormenyi-Nagy and Framo (Eds.), *Intensive family therapy*, New York: Harper & Row, 1965.

Bowen, M. "Toward the differentiation of a self in one's own family." In Framo (Ed.), *Family interaction*, New York: Springer, 1967.

Burks, H., & Serrano, A. "The use of family therapy and brief hospitalization." *Diseases of the Nervous System*, 1965, *26*, 804-806.

Cutter, A., & Hallowitz, D. "Diagnosis and treatment of the family unit with respect to the character-disordered youngster." *Journal of the American Academy of Child Psychiatry*, 1962, *1*, 605-618.

Epstein, N., et al. "*Family categories schema.*" Unpublished manuscript. Dept. of Psychiatry, Jewish General Hospital, Montreal, Quebec, 1968.

Fitzgerald, R. "Conjoint marital psychotherapy: An outcome and follow-up study." *Family Process*, 1969, *8*, 261-271.

Framo, J. "Rationale and techniques of intensive family therapy." In Boszormenyi-Nagy and Framo (Eds.), *Intensive family therapy*, New York: Harper and Row, 1965.

Goldfarb, W., et al. In Goldman and Shapiro (Eds.), *Developments in psychoanalysis at Columbia University: Proceedings of the twentieth anniversary conference, psychoanalytic clinic for training and research, Columbia University*, New York: Hofner, 1966.

Group for the Advancement of Psychiatry. *Psychopathological disorders in childhood*. GAP publication *62*, 1966.

Group for the Advancement of Psychiatry. *The field of family therapy*. GAP publication *78*, 1970.

Haley, J. *Strategies of psychotherapy*. New York: Grune & Stratton, 1963.

Haley, J. "Approaches to family therapy." In Haley (Ed.), *Changing families*, New York: Grune & Stratton, 1971.

Jackson, D. "The question of family homeostasis." "Psychiatric Quarterly Supplement, 1957, *31*, 79-90.

Jackson, D. "The study of the family." *Family Process*, 1965, *4*, 1-21.

Kaffman, M. "Short term family therapy." *Family Process*, 1963, *2*, 216-234.

Kanfer, F. & Phillips, J. *Learning foundations of behavior therapy*. New York: Wiley, 1970.

Kiesler, D. "Experimental designs in psychotherapy research." In Bergin and Garfield (Eds.), *Handbook of psychotherapy and behavior change*. New York: Wiley, 1971.

Kramer, C. *Psychoanalytically oriented family therapy*. Chicago: The Family Institute of Chicago, 1968.

Landes, J., & Winter, W. "A new strategy for treating disintegrating families." Family Process, 1966, *5*, 7-20.

Langsley, D., & Kaplan, D. *The treatment of families in crisis*. New York: Grune & Stratton, 1968.

Liberman, R. "Behavioral approaches to family and couple therapy." *American Journal of Orthopsychiatry*, 1970, *40*, 106-118.

Minuchin, S., et al. *Families of the slums: An exploration of their structure and treatment*. New York: Basic Books, 1967.

Minuchin, S. *Families and family therapy*. Cambridge: Harvard University Press, 1974.

Paul, N.: "The role of mourning and empathy in conjoint marital therapy." In Zuk and Boszormenyi-Nagy, (Eds.), *Family therapy and disturbed families*. Palo Alto: Science & Behavior Books, 1967.

Pittman, F., et al. "Work and school phobias: A family approach to treatment." *American Journal of Psychiatry*, 1968, 124, 1535-1541.

Random House Dictionary of the English Language. New York: Random House, 1968.

Reding, G., et al.: "Treatment of the couple by a couple, II. Conceptual framework, case presentation, and follow-up study." *British Journal of Medical Psychology*, 1967. 40, 243-252.

Redlich, F., & Freedman, D. *The theory and practice of psychiatry*. New York: Basic Books, 1966.

Riskin, J., & Faunce, E. *Family interaction scales scoring manual*. Palo Alto: Mental Research Institute, 1969.

Ryder, R. "The factualizing game: A sickness of psychological research." *Psychological Reports*, 1966, *19*, 563-70.

Safer, D. "Family therapy for children with behavior disorders." *Family Process*, 1966, 5, 243-255.

Satir, V. *Conjoint family therapy*. Palo Alto: Science and Behavior Books, 1967.

Schreiber, L. "Evaluation of family group treatment in a family agency." *Family Process*, 1966, 5, 21-29.

Sigal, J., et al. "Indicators of therapeutic outcome in conjoint family therapy." *Family Process*, 1967, 6, 215-226.

Speer, D. "Family systems: Morphostasis and morphogenesis, or 'is homeostasis enough?" *Family Process*, 1970, *9*, 259-279.

Spiegel, J. "The resolution of role conflict within the family." *Psychiatry*, 1957, *20*, 1-16.

Tharp, R., & Otis, G. "Toward a theory for therapeutic intervention in families." *Journal of Consulting Psychology*, 1966, *30*, 426-434.

Watzlawick, P. *Charge: Principles of problem formation and problem resolution*. New York: Worton, 1974.

Weakland, J., et al. "Brief therapy: Focused problem resolution." *Family Process*, 1974, *13*, 141-169.

Wells, R., et al. "The results of family therapy." A critical review of the literature." *Family Process*, 1972, *11*, 189-209.

Whitaker, C. "Process techniques of family therapy." Unpublished manuscript. University of Wisconsin Dept. of Psychiatry, Madison, Wisconsin, 1973.

Winer, L. "The qualified pronoun count as a measure of change in family psychotherapy." *Family Process*, 1971, *10*, 243-249.

Wynne, L., et al. "Pseudomutuality in the family relations of schizophrenics." *Psychiatry*, 1958, *21*, 205-220.

Wynne, L., & Singer, M. "Thought disorder and family relations of schizophrenics: I. A research strategy." *Archives of General Psychiatry*, 1963, *9*, 191-198.

Chapter 10

TECHNIQUES FOR RAPID ENGAGEMENT IN FAMILY THERAPY

ROBERT FRIEDMAN

The techniques and tactics presented in this paper are useful in facilitating rapid and decisive engagement in family therapy. These techniques are based on an eclectic communication model emphasizing the experiential more than the cognitive, and are designed to cut through an overly intellectual approach to family problems, attempted manipulation of the therapist, or the "dumping" of responsibility for problem solving on the therapist. They require active participation by family members, and convey quickly the view that the family is capable of change.

The techniques have been used in child guidance clinics and in private practice with families from diverse socioeconomic and ethnic backgrounds, having varying degrees of therapy sophistication. They presuppose a presenting complaint of a child's behavioral or learning difficulty.

THE INTRODUCTORY QUESTION

To determine the family's perception of their therapy needs, each family member is asked at the first session, "Why did the family come here today?" This question is pursued until each person gives a relevant reason. If the family consists of one child and one or two parents, the child is asked first, then the parent(s). If the "problem" child does not know (or says he does not know), the child is asked to inquire of the parent. When other children are present, they are questioned first, beginning with the youngest (age 3 or more). This takes the onus from the child who has been labeled the problem, and refocuses attention on the family unit. The problem child who arrived tense, defensive or withdrawing can then relax and be more available to treatment. Parents sometimes resist requiring an answer from a preschool child, on the

From R. Friedman, Techniques for Rapid Engagement in Family Therapy, *Child Welfare*, 16:509-17, 1977. Courtesy of Child Welfare League of America.

basis that the child is unable to respond, is too nervous or bashful, or is too young to understand. Experience demonstrates, however, that very young children understand and are able to participate meaningfully in therapy. When a younger, "normal" child does not respond, the anxiety of the parents about this child often increases their motivation for therapy.

Most families can establish during the first session why they are there. Using the single question for the interview quickly reveals the family communication style (both overt and covert), and the direction of therapy may be established. The way in which the question is answered yields significant information about family communication patterns, family dynamics, and process. The negative effect of the family's way of communicating becomes clear to the parents when the children exhibit confusion, hostility or controlling behavior in their answers. When Johnny Smith's problem is relabeled and accepted as a Smith family problem, a firmer basis for family therapy has been established.

Some parents can give straight answers and can get their children to follow suit. A more typical response is parental inability or unwillingness to be direct and confront a child with the seriousness of the presenting complaint. Resentment toward therapy frequently surfaces, as do transactions between the parents that contribute to the problem. Sometimes it turns out that one of the "nonproblem" children has a more critical emotional difficulty than the identified patient.

Drawing all family members into the communication process quickly undermines the tendency of family dyad or triad groups to sit back expecting the therapist to work with the identified problem child. A family secret or a destructive homeostasis is harder to conceal when the focus is on the family unit and not on one member.

A good deal of heat as well as light may be generated by this technique; the family sometimes reacts to a persistent directive with irritation or even anger. Although many parents tell children a reason for the visit in advance, children may distort, forget, tune out or repeat an explanation that may not be the real reason. When a child balks at giving the reason after the parent has told it to him, feelings of embarrassment, irritation, anger or consternation build up. The target of these feelings may be the parent, child or therapist. The family must be made aware that the therapist is willing to stick to a point until it is settled, and able to accept expressions of annoyance or hostility from family members to the therapist or to each other. The therapist demonstrates a willingness to be involved at a "gut" level at the very start of treatment.

EXPECTATIONS: THE FAMILY SCHOOL

A central idea useful to convey to parents in family therapy is that children do what their parents expect them to do. When possible, this comment is made in connection with an event during the therapy hour or in the context of the diagnostic, structured family interview described in another publication [1:85-107]. When this flat statement is made, the reaction from parents is often skepticism or anger. Parents have their own explanations for their child's behavior and a competing thought may not be welcome, particularly if the parent thinks that the child is not behaving according to expectations. The elements of expectation are defined to the parents as demand and prediction. However, the parent often expresses expectations that are conflicted, unclear or phrased in unconvincing language. The parent's prediction of what the child will do in the session, at home or in school is nearly always directly opposed to the parent's expressed desire. When the demand is convincing and the prediction consistent with the demand, the child will do what the parent expects. The outcome of a negative prediction can be presented to the parent in this way: "You are predicting that Johnny will not answer the question, and he obediently is fulfilling your prediction."

Parents should experience the power of a convincing demand and a positive prediction after this concept has been presented in the session. They can be asked to give the child a series of simple tasks, as a vehicle for parental practice in clear and convincing communication. This demonstration is often necessary to help integrate this concept into parental behavior.

The concept of the "family school" also is useful in explaining what is meant by expectations. For example, if the presenting problem is school learning difficulties, an important concept to explain to the parents is that they are the child's first teachers. It is in the "family school" that the child first relates to authority and establishes work habits. If the child has not learned in the family the behavior essential for mastering the three Rs, learning disability can result.

The child's school performance may appear to contradict the parents' perception of their expectations. However, an examination of these expectations often reveals a concealed message of permission or even encouragement for the child to fail, as well as a prediction of failure. These messages may include rationalizations offered by the parent for not holding the child responsible for his school performance, such as hyperactivity, perceptual problems, brain damage, heredity and poor teaching. The child responds accordingly, and the parents' prophecy of failure is fulfilled.

Parents also seem to prefer cultural cliches for interpretation of their child's behavior: "Boys will be boys." "He's just like his uncle." These cliches serve to absolve the child of responsibility for the behavior, thereby relieving the parent of the need to confront the child.

The therapist can indicate to parents that they can learn to have realistic expectations of the behavior necessary for learning and can implement such behavior in the family. For example, a parent can insist that the child learn to listen in the family. It is then realistic for the parent to predict that the child will listen in school: the youngster will loyally carry out the parent's fair, prediction-supported demand, i.e., the parent's expectation.

"CAN'T" AND "WON'T": THE K FAMILY CASE

Therapists often hear these statements in an interview: "I can't relate to him." "I want a better relationship with her, but I just can't get through to her." "He won't give me a chance to express myself." "Can't" and "won't" are frequently expressed by family members who feel pain and frustration in relationships within the family. Rather than devoting therapy time to analyzing or discussing the complexities of a particular relationship, an ahistoric, directive approach may be more effective.

In the K family, where the presenting complaint was an adolescent's truancy and impending expulsion from school, Mr. K came to the first session with a skeptical attitude, but declared he had come to therapy to achieve a better relationship with his son. Mr. K detailed their mutual hostility, lack of warmth, and inability to communicate, and stated that he didn't think communication with Tim was possible: "He just won't listen." Mr. K's sincerity and potential for movement, and also his position as the emotional pivot of this family, were apparent early in the session. He appeared to be the key to the family's progress in treatment. Therefore the response to his "can't" message was: "Mr. K, you want to communicate with your son and have a better relationship; that's what we'll work on now." The rest of the session was spent working on the barrier between father and son. By utilizing Mr. K's growing determination to reach his son and Tim's own pain at the lack of closeness, this barrier was broken. This breakthrough involved the father in treatment sufficiently to withstand another incident of truancy several weeks later. Therapy sessions dealt with other relationships and feelings within the family, but the fulcrum of change remained the father/son relationship. This truancy problem was successfully resolved and the relationship between father and son was substantially improved. Therapy was terminated after the sixth session. A followup interview 18 months later indicated that Tim was attending school regularly and that the improved father/son relationship continued.

By immediately challenging the "can't" and "won't" attitudes, the therapist opposes the negative, infuses hope, and actively involves family members in uncovering communication barriers and resolving problems. Frequently, "can't" and "won't" become "can" and "will," with the result that the family experiences early success in the therapy. The therapist also is perceived as responsive to the family's perception of their needs. Rather than accepting the family view of "can't" and "won't" as obstacles, this view can be used to provide rapid engagement of the family.

BEHAVIOR CHANGE VERSUS ATTITUDE CHANGE

"I want Jane to enjoy school." "We have such trouble with Cliff and the trash; he always has such a sour face when we make him take it out." "Sarah is always angry when I tell her to get off the phone." One reaction to this type of complaint is to let parents know that the therapist understands their complaint, but can't help them with it. This response is based on the position that a change in the child's attitudes and feelings to match the desires of the parent is not an appropriate goal of therapy unless the child wants the same change. Behavior change, on the other hand, is an appropriate, realizable goal. Parents can therefore be asked what they really want. Do they want Jane to enjoy school (this would require a change in attitude), or to learn to read (a behavior change)? Do they want Cliff to take out the trash regularly without being reminded (behavior), or do they want him to enjoy the chore (attitude)? After all, why does he have to like it? By helping parents to refocus goals quickly and decisively, unrealistic expectations can be given up with a minimum of lost time. This shift can be facilitated by pointing out that children are more likely to be receptive to the values parents wish them to acquire if family relationships are first improved by changing the behavior that is producing negative family feelings.

"EXPERT" DECLINED

A frequently encountered attitude regarding the etiology of the presenting complaint and its expected resolution is: "You're the 'expert'; tell us why and how to . . ." The therapist may be tempted to give explanations and advice, but the motive of the questioner may be to shift parental responsibility onto the therapist. The popularization of psychological terminology and ideology also leads parents to expect a "deep," complicated interpretation of behavior before change is possible.

The role of "expert" can be rejected by pointing out that the family has more experience with the problem than the therapist. If psychodynamic concepts are advanced by the parents, they can be rejected as too complex. Repeating the "simple" clarification—"Children do what their parents expect them to do"—can help parents focus on their own potential as change agents. A discussion and demonstration of the point may then follow.

Assigning the therapist the role of expert and demanding complicated explanations usually represent resistance to change and an attempt to manipulate the therapist and control the therapy. An early challenge can be made to the premise that the problem is complex and therefore requires long, involved treatment, with success dependent on the expertise of the therapist. It is thus made clear that treatment outcome depends on how the family works in therapy, and that primary responsibility for change rests with the family.

ASK THE CHILD

Although the parents often come to family therapy with an exasperated, blaming attitude toward a misbehaving child, exploration of the parents' behavior often reveals that they do not hold the child responsible for his actions. One technique that helps parents make the child accountable for his own behavior is to redirect their questions of the therapist to the child. The parent asks, "Why does Johnny cut school? Why did he break his sister's bicycle?" The therapist can reply, "Ask Johnny; he knows why." Parents often resist this suggestion on the basis that the child doesn't know or won't tell.

The parents are directed to obtain explanations from the child, and are encouraged not to accept explanations they consider invalid. After many unsuccessful attempts, the parents may conclude that Johnny indeed either doesn't know or won't tell. The therapist can say to the parent, "I guarantee that Johnny knows and that if you really expect him to answer, he will tell you the reason." This stance may lead to a discussion of expectations, so that the parent is redirected to continue the questioning.

When the parent perseveres, the child or teenager does give a concise, valid explanation, e.g.: "I cut school because the work is too hard and it's boring. I'd rather be with my friends at the beach." "I broke her bike because she 'finked' on me about cutting school." These simple, direct answers provide the opportunity to discuss such issues as the relation of feelings to action, alternative ways of expressing feelings, and responsibility for one's actions.

THERAPIST ABSENCE

A primary goal of therapy is to make the family less dependent on the services of the therapist. Some of the tactics useful in facilitating consolidation of family strengths are: increasing the time between sessions, providing homework, and reducing the therapist's activity. A helpful approach is to leave the office for a time during the session. This works best when the family members are comfortable with the therapist, have made some progress in treatment, and will not become unduly anxious or threatened by the therapist's leaving the office. This approach introduced the concept that the therapist need not always be present.

In preparation for this development, the family members can be told that is is important to see how they deal with an issue at hand in the absence of the therapist. In other instances, the therapist may only ask the family to continue whatever is going on, or ask that some specific therapy work take place. What parents are told when the therapist leaves is based on the perception of the degree of anxiety this tactic might create. Anxiety can be reduced by stating how long the therapist will be gone: "I'd like you to work on this for 5 minutes without me." When the therapist returns to the office, parents can be asked what it was like to work alone, or to report on what took place.

This technique has produced favorable results. The threapist's absence usually does not inhibit and frequently enhances meaningful exchange, and the family's growing awareness of strength is reinforced. The absence interval can be lengthened and may become part of the termination process as the family gains confidence in their own potential for dealing with their problems.

In the few cases where the session stalls, the lapse uncovers useful diagnostic information about the dependency status of the family, and allows for refocusing the session on an uncovered resistance to change, i.e., the feeling of inadequacy.

COMMENT

The techniques described facilitate rapid engagement of the family in therapy and lead to positive growth. They involve the whole family at an affective level and place major responsibility for change with the family, in the context of providing early opportunities to experience their potential for change. The techniques are applicable in many family therapy cases and are an efficient use of therapy time.

REFERENCE

1. Friedman, Robert. "Structured Family Interviewing in the Assessment of School Disorders," in *Family Roots of School Learning and Behavior Disorders*, edited by Robert Friedman. Springfield, Ill: Charles C Thomas, 1973.

Chapter 11

BEGINNING STRUGGLES WITH FAMILIES

Augustus Y. Napier

Anyone who has worked therapeutically with families is acutely aware of an experience of struggle and conflict between therapist and family as one attempts to get the process of treatment under way. The family puts up a predictable but highly variable series of barriers to the smooth and productive beginning of therapy. While resistance to treatment is an old and thoroughly-documented phenomenon in psychoanalytic literature (Langs, 1973), there has been relatively little written about a similar phenomenon in family treatment (Solomon, 1794). This paper presents a series of recommendations for the therapist in dealing with the "struggle" with the family in the initial interviews, though this conflict with family is viewed in a different way than is the traditional concept of resistance.

Psychoanalytic writing about resistance seems to imply that the patient engages in a form of neurotic misbehavior. Who, after all, would not avail themselves of help if they were not suffering from some internal blockage? This formulation implies that the basic initiative for treatment must be with the therapist, since the patient "resists treatment"—as though refusing to take a therapeutic pill.

The author prefers to see the family's "struggle over treatment" as basically *anxiety concerning change*. The family is anxious about the prospect of exposing their most intimate support network to a stranger, and anxious at the thought of possible unpredictable changes in this valued network. In the face of this uncertainty, the family may have many unverbalized but pressing questions about the therapist's adequacy, approach, or philosophy, as well as questions about the nature of the therapeutic process. Their struggling with the therapist can be seen as a kind of "behavioral question," therefore, through which they attempt to find out more about the person[1] of the therapist and the nature of therapy. This paper presents several of the most common intuitive questions asked by families and suggested responses to the

From A. Napier, Beginning Struggles with Families, *Journal of Marriage and Family Counseling*, 2:3-11, 1976. Courtesy of American Association for Marriage and Family Therapy.

questions.

The author's approach to family therapy might be termed "experiential" in that a therapeutic encounter process is stressed rather than rational understanding or technical, structural intervention. The therapist is seen as a co-therapy team, and change in the family's qualitative experience is the treatment aim. Models of process created within the co-therapy team or between the therapy team and the family provide the direction for change. Work with families tends to be long-term and is an intensive experience involving both therapists and family, with therapists moving from symbolic figures in the initial stages to personally-meaningful, real-time relationships in the later stages. Extended family is often brought into the therapy, and emphasis is on the family's general emotional growth rather than on symptom relief.

As soon as the suggestion of family therapy is made, most families become anxious about the process of meeting as a whole family with a therapist. Whether the suggestion is made by the referring source or by the therapist over the telephone, the first question seems to arise:

DO WE DARE EXPOSE OUR FAMILY TO THIS STRANGER?

There are two main components in the question: "our family" and "this stranger." The family is intuitively aware of its vulnerability in exposing this most crucial network to a relative stranger. Members usually are quite suspicious about both the process of family therapy and the person of the family therapist. They know, for example, that the pull of the interaction process may force them to reveal themselves in ways they cannot control, and everyone fears being exposed in a negative light. They also worry about what the therapist might do to the family: Would he or she break up meaningful coalitions, promote open hostility, expose closely-guarded secrets? Is the therapist a person to whom they can trust their most sacred belonging—however hateful the process of their living together might feel—the family?

One way the family can attempt to delimit its anxiety and also find out about the therapist is to attempt from the very first contact to control the therapy. While taking control can be quite beneficial in later stages, the family that attempts to control therapy by determining the membership at the initial meetings may make successful therapy impossible. The therapist may be defeated from the start if important members are absent. How, then, can the therapist "take over" the beginning process and establish an adequate quorum for the meetings without angering the family? The following guidelines may provide a rough index for the therapist's initial contacts.

A. Use the telephone contact as the first interview. Therapy actually begins when the patient calls for an appointment, and the therapist is well-advised to pay careful attention to this contact. The caller is the family's "scout" into pioneer country and will carry important information to the remainder of the family about therapy and the therapist. The therapist should also learn a number of things by the end of the call:

1. the major complaint.
2. previous therapists.
3. the structure of the family, including all the residents of the immediate household as well as the contiguity of extended family.
4. the family's attitude toward family therapy.
5. specific persons in the family who may resist coming.

While on the telephone, the therapist should make an initial decision about a beginning structure, explain its rationale to the caller if necessary, and insist on that structure as a prerequisite for beginning. It is a very difficult art to make an instant appraisal and to feel sure enough of it to negotiate with the family about a certain membership, but it indeed seems necessary to do so.

B. Choose a structure that does not have built-in liabilities. The traditional first move for the family therapist is to insist on the entire nuclear family, or at least that portion living under one roof, as a minimum for the first interview. One might say, "My practice is limited to family therapy, and I only work with entire families. I would be glad to see you if the entire family will participate." One begins optimally in this case with the family deferring to the therapist's leadership and with the basic family unit as the patient or client. In some instances, however, the optimal is not possible. Husband may confess over the telephone that he has been having an affair with someone and has not told his wife yet; to insist that he bring his teenage children to the first interview with this announced agenda may invite premature defeat. Or one may have come gradually to the realization that one's individual client needs the family's involvement if therapy is to succeed. Family therapy thus begins with a prior involvement with one person. Certain deviations from the optimal seem to be particularly difficult, however, and should be avoided where possible:

1. Meeting alone with one of the spouses. Even one interview with one of the spouses tends to bias the therapist, and it certainly biases the excluded spouse's view of the therapist.
2. Accepting the parents-and-scapegoat-child triangle. Parents who insist on excluding their supposedly non-symptomatic children from theapy are indicating their unwillingness to look at themselves or to relinquish the scapegoating process. They thus challenge from the outset some of the basic tenets of the family therapy process. While it is certainly possible to work with those families, they may have a very poor prognosis if they refuse to bring all the children to at least the first interview.
3. Attempting to shift from established individual therapy to family therapy without special arrangements. The individual therapist

is usually thoroughly biased in favor of his client, and simply adding the family to this relationship usually results in early termination. The original therapist could add a co-therapist who deliberately establishes an early bias by meeting alone with the members of the family who have been absent from the previous therapy. Whoever the therapist was, if one of the spouses has had considerably more individual therapy experience than the other, it may provide a difficulty in family treatment, and the therapist should be alert to this "inequality."

Perhaps the most general guideline in establishing structure is to attempt to *keep each generation intact*, avoiding splitting the marital pair or the children. A typical pattern in working with less than the entire family is to begin with the couple, adding later all the children, still later the grandparents from both sides, and perhaps even siblings from the family of origin.

C. Be prepared to wait. If the family, or certain members of the family, are reluctant to come, ask the caller to talk further with them. Explain carefully the need for the "reluctant" person, documenting it as a technical mistake for the therapist to meet without an important person present. Offer to talk with this person about therapy over the telephone: "Tell your husband to call me if he has any questions about why we need him." Do not engage in a power struggle with the caller, but define the need to wait until the needed individual is ready. Deferring the interview at the time of crisis is a very powerful tool, and while it must be used carefully where there is a suicidal individual involved, it usually results in establishing a structure that conforms with the therapist's wishes.

D. Be confident! More important than what the therapist does is the way he or she does it. The client is interested in knowing about the person of the therapist. They wish to know if the therapist is a humane person, someone reasonably wise about living; and, most crucially for the initial interviews, they wish to know if the therapist is strong enough to handle the family's stresses. If the therapist is sure and confident about what he wants, it is enormously reassuring to the family. They need to know that the therapist has a professional plan which he believes in and insists on, and they need evidence of the therapist's self-confidence from the initial telephone contact.

WHO IS IN CHARGE HERE?

The family's implicit questions about the therapist's strength and leadership ability usually surface before therapy has actually begun, during the telephone contact. Hopefully the entire nuclear family appears at the first interview with the beginnings of a transference relationship, having deferred to the therapist's requirement for structure. Even if the family begins the first interview by deferring to the therapist's official status, however, he still needs to assert active leadership of the initial session. Adequate evidence exists that a passive stance by the therapist in the early interviews is a serious mistake (Shapiro & Budman, 1973). The following steps may guide the therapist in leading the first interview:

A. Chair the meeting. Call on individuals to state their view of the family and its problems; direct the conversation, keep the meeting on task.

B. Make a personal contact with every family member. During the hour, the therapist should attempt to "hear" with direct attention the view of every family member, even young children, and pre-verbal children should be acknowledged in some way. Special attention should be paid to the father—since he is usually the most distant from the family and likeliest to withdraw from therapy—or to other individuals whom the therapist is aware of from the telephone contact as being resistant to therapy.[2] A subtle amount of "political persuasiveness" may help mitigate some of the anxiety of these individuals. Save the mother's comments for a while, because the power of her involvement may dominate the session if she enters the discussion too early.

C. Stop arguments and diversions. There will be plenty of time for the family to get into its usual conflicts, and they need to come away from the first interview with more than a repetition of their habitual conflict cycle.

D. Ask questions! The therapist should ask many questions, attempting to learn as quickly as possible about the family from a number of points of view. If the therapist can *selectively* "think out loud" with the family as he questions, clarifying his own confusion, exploring areas that interest him, the family can see how the therapist thinks about a system.

E. Build a central hypothesis. The questioning process allows the therapist an opportunity to try out tentative hypotheses concerning the hidden agenda in the family, and the therapist can note as he proceeds how the family deals with the attempt to reinterpret their dilemma. By the end of the meeting the therapist needs to have at least one fairly well-developed interpretative comment for the family. This process of hypothesis-building is discussed further below.

F. Resist challenges to the therapist's leadership. Often the family will not allow the calm process of questioning and reflective thought. They are too anxious and too uncertain of the therapist's strength and must challenge this leadership. Mother will attempt to take over the questioning, father will interpret for the daughter, or husband will try to conduct an almost clinical interview with his wife. Teenage daughter will storm angrily out of the room. The five-year-old will have a temper outburst just as the parents start to talk about a tense issue.

In all these instances, the therapist should calmly and firmly reassert control. Often a careful mixture of strength and tact (and sometimes humor) is needed: mother can be gently asked to let the therapist be the therapist, father can be asked to wait a moment until daughter speaks, the partner can be softly kidded about "being a therapist." The family can be sent to retrieve the daughter who flees the room. The therapist can turn and help the child who is anxious about the parents' stress, then turn back to their conflict after dealing with the cause of the disruption.

Sometimes the stress in the challenge to the therapist is quite high, and gentler methods are to no avail. Then the therapist may need to meet the challenge to his leadership with a kind of "binding confrontation," in which he communicates his intent to help at the same time that he cites directly the need to be in charge if he is to be able to help. Sometimes a quietly spoken willingness to be defeated by the family in the first interview will reestablish the therapist's faltering control: "Perhaps the family really doesn't want to change anything here."

Whatever the therapist's tactics, an overall strategy of leading the first interview firmly seems appropriate; and a mixture of willingness to be assertive yet tactful usually provides a healthy balance.

WHAT IS WRONG WITH US?

Members of the family feel mystified by their dilemma, and the fact that they must ask for help often seems degrading to them. Thus they conceal their puzzlement and anxiety in a pseudo-diagnosis of their problems, a diagnosis whose function is largely defensive. They seem to be asking for help with an individual, someone who agrees to be "sick" or "bad" in order to provide the family with an organizational focus for a wider, systemic stress. They obviously need to get beyond seeing their problems as revolving around one overtly stressed member, but the fact of their needing to see their problems in a new and more complex light does not mean that they *want* this experience of enlightenment. In fact, the family members often will resist fiercely any attempt by the therapist to redefine the family's problems, at the same time that they seem to require such a redefinition. Their struggle over this issue is basically a product of low self-esteem and is a protective mechanism against flooding by feelings of self-blame. The major problem then is in how the therapist deals with the family members' anxiety about the "awful things" they may discover about themselves, at the same time trying to be honest about what he or she sees.

While there are many different types of family crisis, the situation in which an adolescent is an "identified patient" is a common source of referral for family therapy and provides an illustrative framework here.

The Family with an Adolescent in Crisis

A central problem in the family whose stress is organized around one of the children is that the origin of the "extra" stress on the child is often located in the older generations, specifically in the marital pair and in their conflicts with each other and with their own parents and siblings. Because there is a real power differential between the child and the parents, the child often is driven in self-defense to indirect and desperate strategies in order to withstand the parents' power, e.g., suicide, running away, and anti-social acts in the wider community. Furthermore, the triangular nature of the conflicts is usually quite covert. Both parents usually have quite subtly "double-teamed" the child, one parent covertly supporting a rebellion which the other parent then punishes. Or both parents blame or criticize the adolescent in a way that feels confusing and overwhelming. What the family usually reports is that the adolescent defies *one* of the parents. The parents want the therapist's help in establishing more control and compliance in the adolescent. They often are so defensive and so indignant at the child's behavior that they are reluctant to look at their own individual problems, the problems in the marriage, or the problems in their families of origin. Thus the family members with the most "real" power may feel so threatened that they are unwilling to look at themselves.

The therapist's initial problem is that if the family is to "hear" his redefinition of their dilemma—and some redefinition seems to be necessary if the family is to do more than continue to scapegoat the adolescent—he must speak to the family in a way that does not alienate either "side" of a very polarized equation. The therapist's alliances must be carefully established in the initial interviews (Sluzki, 1975). While there is not a sure formula for solving this dilemma, the following guidelines may assist the therapist in the initial interviews:

1. Build a developmental history of the family. Attempt to gather a brief history of the family, with some attention to the shifts in the experience of closeness in the family. A usual sequence involves close rapport and teaming between the couple during the early years, with much supporting and "parenting" of each other. Though one may have to listen carefully to hear evidence of it, a growing separation between the couple often ensues as the marriage evolves, a disillusionment with the "helping" function in marriage often being a central factor. As life-stresses accumulate, the couple discovers that they cannot help each other as much as each would like. Growing demands on each other also stimulate a panic about symbiosis in the family, precipitating separation as a way of dealing with the panic. The adolescent becomes involved as mediator in the usually covert marital war, later becoming an "agent" in the family's attempt at individuation. The fact that the adolescent's rebellion is self-defeating and abortive only exposes the lack of a viable model for individuation. A few tentative test questions at this phase may allow the therapists to sample the family's defensiveness: "Do you think you've been too close as a family at times?" and "Were you worried the family was going stale before this crisis came up?"

2. Define the presenting problem as a cycle. The family members usually can see that the events they are so distressed by follow a predictable pattern, and that everyone contributes their particular "step" to the "dance." If they can each admit that they cannot seem to resist saying the same thing every time, doing the same thing every time, this admission takes them one step toward admission of the problem as being family-wide.

3. Outline a family-wide "togetherness" as an underlying problem. The "real" problem, the therapist then asserts, is a quality of group power or togetherness (symbiosis is too technical a word) which prevents the individuals from having the freedom to disconnect themselves from the cycle of interaction in the family. Dad "can't help" getting furious, and mom "can't help" defending son when dad attacks, and son "can't help" running away. Or at least they *think* they cannot resist the pull of those forces! Usually the family can feel the magnetic pull of the conflict cycle if stopped and asked about it as they are being drawn into another fight: "Can you feel the power of this thing pulling on you?" the therapist asks. Thus the *process of the family's relatedness* becomes the focus, rather than any particular person's behavior. The therapist's positive suggestion can be that the family members all need to have more sense of themselves as separate individuals, with less need to be the slaves of a repetitive interaction process.

4. Ask *sympathetically* about the older generations. The parents of the troubled adolescent do not need to be blamed for their child's problems—they already covertly blame themselves. But it can be quite useful to ask with genuine interest about the problems in the older generation. Perhaps the best way to begin is to ask about *their* parents: "Dad, tell me about your family—the one you grew up in. What was it like?" Getting the adult talking about his or her family of origin is a good way to "induce" them gently into the patient role—suddenly the father is talking about how his father was hard on him, and the therapist can see the human side of the parent and feel a bit softer toward him. The therapist's tone of voice and the authenticity of his concern is a. central issue in this move: The therapist needs to be able to "see" with a kind of parental perspective the stresses of the parents, not always an easy job, especially for the young therapist. Questions regarding the family of origin should be bilateral if time permits. Sooner or later the therapist will wish to ask about the marriage, but better later than sooner. Give time during the interview for some relationship with the family to build. Even then, the way in which the therapist asks is crucial: "Do you have a feeling for what the stresses are between the two of you? I'm assuming every marriage has at least *some* stress." And a further question: "How about the stresses *within* each of you? Do you think you understand or have some feeling for each other's stresses?" Phrasing, intonation, and delicate choice of words may permit the therapist to tread lightly in very threatening territory, though one should be

prepared for the couple's anxiety and for some point beyond which they cannot go.

5. Define therapeutic or growthful aspects of their dilemma. The family feels shamed by having to come to therapy, and it may help them to see that what they see as their "failure" may have healthy components. This move contains several thrusts: Allowing the family to feel less ashamed, helping the scapegoat feel less unworthy, and leading toward a look at the older generation's problems. The therapist should attempt to find a "healthy" side in the adolescent's rebellion. On the most general level, the crisis can be seen as an individuation move, the pull away from the family and the defiance of the parental authority representing an attempt to "become a separate person." But depending on the family's dynamics, other interpretations may be more successful:

"Maybe John by fighting with his mother is trying to teach Mother to be stronger so she can fight better with Dad."

"Maybe John is rebelling against Dad to help him learn how to stand up to *his* old man."

"Maybe John gets elected to go out in the world and have an adventure and bring it back to the family so things won't stay too cool here."

"Perhaps John is afraid the two of you are drifting apart, and he wants to give you someting to get you together. It certainly seems to happen that way!"

"John got elected to find help for the family."

"John wants to make sure the two of you don't have to worry about whether you would have a second honeymoon—and he just expresses his concern by making sure you have him to take care of."[3]

Whatever the comment, the therapist needs a twinkle in his or her eye and a good sense of humor to make some of these methaphorical "realignments" tolerable by the family. It may help the agree with the parents that "John may not be going about his project in the most satisfactory way," but he does seem important to help the parents and the adolescent see that all the turmoil and the activity by the young person has a kind of psychological validity. The adolescent is not just "misbehaving" but is struggling to achieve a goal—albeit usually struggling unproductively.

It seems important that the family see that not only is the scapegoat "up to something" with creative possibilities, but that it is not strictly an individual initiative. To some degree the family colludes to make the crisis possible, and they need not be blamed for helping make the dilemma, but rewarded: "It takes courage to let things get this desperate, so that something *has* to change." Thus, contrary to their expectations, the family is congratulated on its willingness to attempt to break out of an impasse through the mutual creation of a crisis.

The question then remains of their *means* of solving their dilemma. Their end or goal is seen as basically positive. The family can be gently coached on the members' need to improve their *approach* to each other:

"John may decide that the drug scene isn't the best way to get what he's after." Or: "Maybe you can collaborate with your parents on this leaving home thing, John, rather than waste all your energy and theirs in having a war."

6. Defuse the control issue. In many families the issue of discipline and control by the parents is the central surface concern, though many other covert agendas hover around it. Lacking adequate rapport with the adolescent, the parents attempt to use coercion when they see the young person leaving home prematurely, failing in school, striking back at them, or engaging in self-sacrificial behavior. While these disciplinary tactics might "succeed" with a younger child, or if the parents had higher self-esteem, or if they had better rapport with their child, they usually fail. And they fail because the parents have an unconscious agenda that *requires* that they fail. To paraphrase Voltaire: "We all get what we want. But we don't know what it was we wanted until after we've gotten it!"

In addition to exposing the covert agendas in the family, the therapist should attempt to defuse potentially damaging confrontations in the early phases of treatment by down-playing the coercive process. To the parents: "It feels to me as if you're asking too much of yourselves to feel like you have to *control* Johnny. There's just too much to control—your jobs, the other children, the house, the car. I'm not sure it can work by control. How can you *make* somebody his age and size do *anything* he doesn't want to? Seems to me if this family works, it will have to be by cooperation, not force." To Johnny: "The question of who wins is a pretty deadly question. If you work at it, you can probably wreck your parents' lives, and they can wreck yours." To the family: "Maybe what you need is a new *feeling* in the family, a new attitude. And a new language for talking to each other. Maybe it can be the language of persuasion rather than the language of power."

The family often is delighted by permission from the therapist to discontinue temporarily its conflicts, though members also may become alarmed at the other possibility, the chance of warmth emerging in the family. The adolescent in particular may be anxious that increased warmth will trap him in the family. The permission to defuse control issues will not solve the conflicts, but they can then reemerge later in therapy after more relationship with the therapist has been established.

7. Suggest new alliances. The family often feels locked into stereotyped relationship patterns. Son fights with mother and never speaks to father. Mother talks warmly with daughter and ignores son. The parents never talk except when the scapegoat intervenes. The scapegoat never relates to his siblings. The therapist can begin to initiate change without precipitating conflict by suggesting new "positive alliances." Siblings who never relate can be coached on getting to know each other. Son can be urged to try to "reach" father as an alternative to always fighting with mother. The couple can be given implicit permission to

be "irresponsible" and elope for a weekend together. These structural realignments can provide the family with a sense of exhilaration with minimum trauma in the initial stages of treatment.

SOME GENERAL ISSUES

This early phase of treatment, which could be called an "engagement" phase, is the attempt by family and therapist to make an intuitive contract with each other to begin therapy. Such negotiating is probably best left implicit rather than explicit, in that the family may feel suspicious if the therapist attempts to get them to agree to an explicit contract. The therapist works—perhaps for only one interview, but often for two or three—for that point when he senses a kind of subjective relief. This relief is a signal that the family has decided to "be in therapy." While other issues quickly become active, one phase of the struggle is at an end.

It is important throughout this phase to keep in mind some general goals: the therapist is attempting to make the family as a whole the client or patient, and any sense of "fault" or "error" is best seen as residing in their process of relating, in the way the family is organized, or in a family-wide stress or morale issue. It is critical to make clear to the family—by demonstration, not statement—that the therapist is fair to everyone and available as the whole family's therapist. Sidetaking or scapegoating by the therapist alarms the family and often results in early termination. On the other hand, the therapist cannot just be "nice." He must be willing to be assertive, to press an issue if needed, and to cut through unproductive or dissimulating talk. A kind of humane assertiveness is perhaps the best stance, though it is sometimes a difficult posture to achieve.

As the family balks at certain points, becomes argumentative with the therapist or refuses to consider an alternative or idea suggested by the therapist, one should be free to metacommunicate about the treatment process. Wife gets very defensive as therapist asks about her anxiety and therapist replies: "It felt like you thought I was accusing you. I wasn't intending to do that." Couple becomes indignant when therapist asks about their marriage so therapist says, "I wasn't implying that there *was* something wrong with the marriage. I was just trying to help you take a look at it as part of the whole situation." Therapist to father, joking: "You sure are sensitive to criticism!" In fact, a sense of humor—a warm light touch at these delicate moments—often allows everyone to breathe easier and for therapy to resume its course.

SUMMARY

As the family begins therapy, the members usually are quite anxious and they usually do not trust the therapist. They challenge the therapist about structure, procedure, or approach, but their questions about therapy are usually asked indirectly. Often they are not aware of the questions they want to ask about family therapy. The therapist should focus intently on the initial interviews, beginning with the telephone contact, trying to respond to the family's anxiety by demonstrating firmness, insight, and sensitivity.

The most difficult problem is in getting the family to shift the focus from the identified patient to the family as a whole without the members becoming too threatened. The therapist should be aware of family members who are particularly threatened by the therapy and should attempt to reach them first. The most affectively charged areas in the family—the mother-scapegoat relationship and the marriage—should be approached later, and with both strength and sensitivity.

The key in getting the family to shift the focus away from blaming the scapegoat may be in their discovering their unconscious attempts at growth. What the family perceives as a devastating failure may be an attempt to solve a problem. Thus the family may be able to agree to work on its whole organization by discovering that they have more strengths than they had thought, as well as more complicated problems than they had thought.

REFERENCES

Langs, R. *The technique of psychoanalytic psychotherapy.* New York: Jason Aronson, 1973.

Solomon, M. Resistance in family therapy: Some conceptual and technical considerations. *The Family Coordinator, 23,* 159-164, 1974.

Sluzki, C. The coalitionary process in initiating family therapy. *Family Process, 14,* 67-78, 1975.

Shapiro, R., & Budman, S. Defection, termination, and continuation in family therapy. *Family Process, 12,* 55-68, 1973.

Slipp, S., Ellis, S., & Kressel, K. Factors associated with engagements in family therapy. *Family Process, 13,* 413-428, 1974.

FOOTNOTES

[1]The author feels that the most adequate therapist for the family is a male-female cotherapy team. For the sake of simplicity and with some deference to habit, the therapist is sometimes spoken of in the masculine gender.

[2]For a discussion of factors involved in early termination, vs. engagement, see Shapiro and Budman (1973) and Slipp, et al., (1974).

[3]The author is indebted to Carl Whitaker, MD, for the phrasing of some of these metaphorical statements, and for the insight behind the phrasing.

Chapter 12

THE COALITIONARY PROCESS IN INITIATING FAMILY THERAPY

CARLOS E. SLUZKI

In the human species, the socialization process includes the transmission of a huge code that involves the mastery of different *channels* of communication—verbal-linguistic, verbal-nonlinguistic (tones, rhythm), and non-verbal (facial expressions, body gestures and posture, physical distance, etc.)—and different *levels* of communication—rules about usage of signs, and rules about those rules. Most of the pragmatic norms that govern interpersonal communication are learned and mastered without ever having been explicitly taught. Even more, certain *metarules*—i.e., rules about rules—specify that there are communicational events that should *not* be openly acknowledged nor explicitly discussed. In the long run, human beings learn to exchange a huge variety of information and to exert a wide range of interpersonal influences chiefly at an implicit level (conveyed through means other than the explicit content of the language proper) and manage to keep these processes at least partly out of awareness in spite of the intensity of emotions they may arouse.

This implicit modality of transmission of information is characteristic of the process by which relationships between people are negotiated and defined. To Gregory Bateson (2) belongs the credit for the first interactional description of these processes. Jay Haley (6, 7) further formalized them:

> When one person communicates a message to the other, he is by that act making a maneuver to define the relationship. By what he says and the way he says it he is indicating, "This is the sort of relationship we have with each other." The other person is thereby posed the problem of either accepting or rejecting that person's maneuver. He has a choice of letting the message stand, and thereby accepting the other person's definition of the relationship, or countering with a maneuver of his own to define it differently. . . . It must be emphasized that no one can avoid

From C. Sluzki, The Coalitionary Process in Initiating Family Therapy, *Family Process, 14*:67-77, 1975. Courtesy of *Family Process.*

being involved in a struggle over the definition of the relationship with someone else. Everyone is constantly involved in defining the relationship or countering the other person's definition (6, pp. 323-324)

This description, referring to a *general class of processes* aiming at the *definition of relationships,* can be applied point by point to one member of that class, namely *the coalitionary process.*

A coalition is an *agreement of alliance* established for the mutual benefit of the allies *vis-à-vis* a third party. It is arrived at by explicit negotiation and/or by implicit clues provided by the context and by the interaction proper.

The coalitionary structure contains two types of links, with opposite "signs": ally to ally and allies versus the third party, or relationships of inclusion and of exclusion.[1] The excluded third—or sometimes one of the allies—may, in fact, not be present on the scene or may even be an abstract component such as an ideology, but its realness for the other two completes the minimal, three-party system.

Triangular phenomena of this sort can be expected when any aspect of power and its use is examined. Any interpersonal system can be described as a complex network of overlapping coalitions, some of them stable and solid and some transient, some activated in one context and some in another, some resistant to any third-party attempt at disrupting them and some labile. The process of negotiation and establishment of coalitions in a family can be closely related to the vicissitudes of the power relationships within that family system.

When we interview a family, some coalitions between members appear from the start to be already established; they are usually stable alliances that have survived many tests and end up by being incorporated into the basic rules of that interrelationship.[2] Intimacy, for instance,

---

[1]The terms "inclusion" and "exclusion," as applied to the complementary interlocked components of this process, are utilized, within the framework of a sociological scrutiny of human interaction, in one of the most elegant papers I have read in recent years (Weitman, 11, 12). The core of the paper is a series of three propositions aiming at a theory of processes related to *intimacy:* (a) "Social passions (i.e., the passions whose objects of consummation are other people) tend to be aroused by, and in turn to give further rise to, processes of social inclusion and processes of social exclusion"; (b) "The very same activities which are, to those privileged to partake in them, unambiguous acts of social inclusion, are at the same time liable to represent to those who are not so privileged equally unambiguous acts of social exclusion"; and (c) "Acts of social inclusion in general are potentially just as provocative of hostile retaliation as are 'naked' acts of social exclusion" (12, pp. 225, 228, and 229).

[2]Lyman C. Wynne was referring, in all likelihood, to these stable links when he described the "emotional organization" of family systems:

An *alignment* can be defined as the perception or experience of two or more persons that they are joined together in a common endeavor, interest, attitude, or set of values, and that in this sector of their experience they have positive feelings toward one another. A *split* is here defined as a comparable perception or experience of opposition, difference, or estrangement, with associated negative feelings. The alignments and splits within a social system define to a considerable extent, the emotional organization of the system. (14, p. 96)

necessarily includes a coalitionary component. The maintenance of generational boundaries also requires stable, intrageneration coalitions. But when we examine the ongoing interaction of the triadic or larger system constituted by the family and a therapist, especially in the context of a trying situation such as a first interview, we can detect an affect-laden process in which coalitions are being proposed, accepted, modified, locked, tested, qualified, broken, rejected, and betrayed in a constantly changing flow.

Coalitions can be observed in every family. It is the *when* and the *how* of their formation that are critically significant; the structure, sequential order, intensity, persistence, and style of coalitions observed during, or triggered by, a family interview provide key information in determining areas of family conflict, in discovering the family's homeostatic functions, and in orienting the treatment strategy.

The theme of family coalitions has been frequently advanced, from different perspectives and under different nomenclature, by leading authors in the field of family. An incomplete list of these contributors follows. Murray Bowen's theoretical concept of *triangles* (3; see also Framo, 5) corresponds very closely to the coalitionary phenomenon described in this paper. Lyman C. Wynne (14) produced a well-known paper centered on the issue of stable *alliances and splits*. Nathan W. Ackerman frequently placed his emphasis on scapegoating processes (1), with explicit references to the correlation between that phenomenon and family alliances. Gerald Zuk's description of the *go-between process* (15) includes the evaluation and active use of the coalitionary field. More recently, Salvador Minuchin (8) included coalitions among the variables in developing a "mapping" of structural family conflicts and the subsequent development of treatment strategies. There have also been a number of experimental studies dealing with this theme, most of which follow the lead of Fred L. Strodtbeck (9) both in general design and instruments. All of these contributions have allowed a progressive insight into the theme revisited in this paper, which will be focused primarily on the coalitionary process that takes place in the initial family interviews.[3]

Inasmuch as the therapist is an expert called upon to help the family in distress, it could be argued that there should be an *a priori*

---

[3]This paper, it should be added, is centered on the *process proper* and not on the *phenomenology of the emotions* displayed through this process. Also, no distinctions will be drawn here between "diagnostic" and "therapeutic" interviews: in order to explore interpersonal patterning, the interviewer must probe any suspected stereotype through attempts at introducing changes in its pattern, at least in order to test the stability of the trait, the family system's tolerance for change, and its defensive styles. If a pattern changes after a therapist's intervention, that change acquires both a *diagnostic/prognostic* and a *therapeutic* value, regardless of whether it took place in the first or last interview of a treatment.

"therapeutic alliance" between each family member and the family therapist without an activation of the processes of inclusion and exclusion. But, in "real life" situations of family therapy, even the first moves are loaded with propositions and assumptions related to coalitions. The therapist, needless to say, is not only included in those negotiations but actively operates at that level from the very beginning.[4]

Throughout family therapy, and even more so during the first interviews, the therapist conveys many norms that will govern the interaction that takes place during the session proper. Some "rules of the game" are proposed explicitly by him (e.g. "Please be prompt; other wise you will miss part of the session since I have to end at the scheduled time," or, "I do not allow physical violence here"). But most of the rules are conveyed implicitly—i.e., metacommunicated—by the therapist's behavior. That is the case of those messages establishing rules about coalitions. These rules are tested by the participants—through defying them, for instance—and acquire weight when consistently followed and, therefore, reinforced by the therapist.

The chief rule about coalitions is that *the therapist is going to establish only shifting, instrumental coalitions without binding himself to stable,* aprioristic *ones or following the culturally established pattern of negotiation.*

Let us consider the first contact of therapy, the phone call made in order to arrange the appointment. Whoever makes it tends to assume that this move gives him leverage toward a coalition with the therapist. That person considers himself the "known one," the propeller of treatment and, consequently, the healthy one. He takes for granted that the therapist will be on his side and use him as an informant, if not as a co-therapist. Similar preferential treatment seems to be expected by members who consider themselves in the same age bracket as the therapist. Family members who are in their own professional life psychologists, social workers, psychiatrists, or general physicians also assume, quite in line with the attribution of other family members, a sort of professionals' coalition. This is even true of members who have been in therapy and therefore declare themselves to be experts in such matters. These assumptions are tested in the first interview by all family members from the moment that one person greets the therapist with a different style from the rest of the group.

The effect of the label of "patient" should also be considered. Quite frequently during the first interviews, the "well" members of the family

---

[4]I am referring throughout this paper to a one-therapist treatmnt situation and *not to co-therapy,* as that system has characteristics of its own. In fact, many co-therapists explicitly sustain their preference for the latter modality on the basis that each co-therapist is freer to establish relatively stable identification and coalitions with one family member, counting on the other to do the same with another member: by sex, age, or cross-sex pairing.

present the configuration of a conjoint coalition versus the "sick" one and invite the therapist to enter the coalition. In turn, the identified patient can hopelessly accept (or even actively favor) the other members' maneuvers toward coalescing the therapist, or he may very well attempt to establish his own coalition with the therapist through accusations against the others. What happens only rarely, if ever, is the maintenance of equidistance between family members and the therapist.

The therapist's side of this process deserves special scrutiny. Regardless of his efforts, the therapist will simple not be able to avoid getting involved in negotiations about coalitions. The reason is contained in one of the basis premises of human communication: *one cannot not communicate* (Watzlawick, Beavin, Jackson, 10). This rule is valid at both the content and the relationship levels of interaction. Therefore, it is not possible not to communicate about coalitions when, in a previous step of the interactional chain, a proposition about the coalition was raised. Even a refusal to acknowledge such a proposition is a statement about it.

To evaluate the coalitionary process accurately in any given context, it is necessary to take a *double reading*—one of the situation and one of the messages proper. Examples of information stemming from the situation are the attributions and assumptions of coalition on the part of the one arranging the appointment, the "healthy" member, the professional, or the "expert-as-patient," already mentioned.

From the very beginning of the first interview, these situational coalitions are tested, questioned, sabotaged, counter-offered, qualified and disqualified by all the participants in a steady struggle that takes place, as already pointed out, through messages sent in channels other than the content proper: *tones and inflections of voice* denoting accusations or defenses, sacrifices or contempt; *body postures and gestures* indicating a victim or a hero; *rhythms of speech* that inform of strength or weakness; *silences* that are accusatory or defensive; *choice of wordings* that put forward a "professional" or a "naive" self image; *interruptions and yieldings*, etc.[5]

In a first interview, for instance, the member who starts to talk in an accusatory or martyr-like tone about the victimizing character of another member's behavior or symptoms is proposing to the therapist to take his side. The proposition acquires more strength if that person

---

[5]To an enumeration of channels and modes should be added the information transmitted by the combination of signs sent *simultaneously* through different channels (i.e., what phrase with what tone and what gestures at what moment) as well as *sequentially* within each channel (i.e., what tone after what tone, what body distance after what body distance). The overall effect of messages is gained through a process of codification that includes not only a "dictionary" of signs but also an extremely complex set of rules about *diachronic* (sequential) and *synchronic* (simultaneous) *combinations* of signs.

acknowledges some responsibility and even willingness to change for the other's sake. The accused member proposes in turn a coalition when, in his silence, he looks at the therapist and, as the therapist happens to look at him, he lifts his eyes to heaven, implying "Do you realize what I have to put up with every day!" A coalition between members of a couple versus the therapist can simply *be there* from the start or can be sought in the session through whatever means, such as the case of the husband who states in a sweet voice, interrupting his wife's first mention about marital disagreements, "Let's not get into the dirty laundry, dear; we *all* have our flaws, don't we?" a blackmailing intervention that freezes her participation and transforms her into a bland, unthreatening ally.

Considering that the coalitionary process will necessarily take place from the start, what strategies can the expert adopt in order to use it therapeutically? Under what conditions should a therapist denounce the proposal of a coalition? Under what conditions should he enter into one? Let us examine some options in detail.

Coalitions cannot be comfortably negotiated overtly in the presence of the excluded member(s). Therefore, one way of neutralizing, or at least of threatening seriously the success of any proposal for a coalition, is through speaking about it, i.e., through making *explicit the implicit.* It must be kept in mind, however, that the amount of paranoid anxieties aroused by the therapist's mention of an intention of coalition with him on the part of any member can seriously jeopardize the therapy, especially in the initial phases of the treatment: a metacommunicational rule of social interaction is that these types of messages are *not* to be labeled as such. When that rule is infringed upon, it dislocates the addressee's position in the system. In addition, an overtone of admonition is almost invariably attributed to the therapist's statement.

The threatening nature of this explicit intervention is mitigated by special circumstances. They are: (a) during therapy with families that have already had conjoint experience as patients and are therefore aware of some "rules of the game" of therapy; (b) when the explicit comment could be addressed to the whole family group due to a clearcut concurrence of coalitional propositions on the part of different members to the therapist (i.e., "Each of you seems to be trying hard to convince me that I should be on your side, that the other ones are crazy"); (c) when the coalition is established within the family group *in toto* as a resistance maneuver excluding the therapist. That resistance may be difficult to overcome, the extreme case being the type of family described by Wynne, *et al.* (13) as "pseudomutual"; and (d) when another previously useful coalition between the addressee and the therapist already exists, and it is preserved and used as a base in order to reduce the impact of the explicit intervention.

This last situation deserves further comment. Sometimes, in the course of therapy, a temporary coalition between one family member and the therapist is sought and established. In that situation, a message that contains further coalitionary pleas stemming from that member can be rejected without threatening the pre-existing coalition. This has the effect of decreasing the effect of the plea on the other family members (i.e., reassuring the other members that this request will not be met) without losing the pre-existing link. For example, in the course of the session, an adolescent switches from considering herself the excluded fifth *vis-à-vis* the rest of her family and the therapist to enjoying a temporary, privileged coalition with the therapist, a move favored by the latter in order to counter-balance the parent's barrage. Suddenly, the adolescent initiates a heavy attack against her parents and sibling that ends in a silence in which the fate of the therapy seems to be at stake. The therapist's intervention, addressed to the adolescent, is that she seems to be ganging up with him against all the other family members and that she must be feeling quite isolated from the rest of her family in order to do that. That intervention dissolves the tension and re-equilibrates the distances without threatening the participation of any member.[6]

The four types of situations listed above are those in which the coalitionary propositions can be made explicit without too much risk. Otherwise, it *may* make sense to keep the dialogue of the negotiation at the implicit level.[7]

Let us examine the situation in which the therapist decides to maintain his participation in the coalitionary process at the *implicit level*. Once a coalition has been proposed, the therapist has obviously only two possible alternatives: to reject the proposal (and ignoring *is* a way of signaling refusal) or to enter into the coalition (and engaging in negotiations *is* already a way of signaling willingness to coalesce).

The therapist's *refusal* in no way ends the process: whenever he rejects a coalition proposed by a member—and *especially* if this is done at the implicit level—the family interprets this refusal as an invitation to another member to attempt a coalition. For that reason, when the therapist rejects a coalitionary proposition, he must prepare himself for a series of similar propositions. This will end when the metamessage has reached all the participants that *in the context of the sessions* (a) *they cannot count on a traditional way of dealing with coalitions;* (b) *there are no stable coalitions;* and (c) *the therapist is basically equidistant.*

---

[6]Another component of that intervention should be acknowledged: that of redefining the *intentions* attributable to the adolescent from meanness or anger to a situation of isolation (which contains a flavor of "attenuating circumstance").

[7]Issues related to the coalitionary process and/or affects derived from it tend to come to our focus of attention also under other special circumstances: when some of the tacit rules of negotiation are broken, when expectations are flagrantly betrayed or at least not met, and when attention is centered on that process *a priori* (as can be the case when somebody who has just finished reading this paper wishes to explore these dimensions in his own interpersonal space.)

The other option, that of the therapist entering fully into a coalition, is especially valuable as a means of neutralizing a strong coalition previously identified by all the family as existing between one given member of sub-group and the therapist. In order to obtain this counterbalancing effect, a coalition is (implicitly) proposed or accepted between the therapist and the member who is judged to be the excluded one and lasts until the distinct message detailed in the previous paragraph has reached all members of the group. This strategy is consistent with the observation, generally agreed upon by family therapists, that a therapist cannot take the same side consistently without endangering the very continuity of the treatment.

To reject a coalition or to enter into one, are, as can be seen, two complementary sides: the mere fact that one is refused may be perceived as the establishment of another, and *vice versa*.

This characteristic can be illustrated by the events of the first conjoint session with a couple. The therapist knew the woman from a series of six individual therapeutic interviews held a year earlier because of a depressive episode. In those interviews much was said about the ups and downs of her marriage. Without looking at her husband, she began the first conjoint session forcefully, stating that she was exhausted, that she put too much effort into the relationship and her husband showed only indifference. She narrated several situations in which a recurrent sequence found her expecting something, her husband not complying, and she blowing her top. Several references to her previous therapy, as well as her tone of voice and the expansive use of office space (i.e., where and how she left her overcoat and handbag) concurred in giving the distinct impression that she felt in her own territory and that both she and her husband took for granted her coalition with the therapist. The therapist's first intervention was said with worry, "From the way you describe yourself, you must be quite unbearable to your husband. You are conveying the notion that from his side you must be experienced as a terrible bitch." She paused, looking bewildered, and protested, "Yes, maybe so, but I have my legitimate motives . . . etc." The interesting thing was to observe the change in her husband. He reappeared from the depths of his armchair and started to participate. He began, however, with a sort of man-to-man talk that in turn was met by an intervention from the therapist who, quite descriptively, stated that it sounded to him like man-to-man "solidarity" talk about somebody who was not there (i.e., the excluded third, his wife). That sequence taught something to the couple, as both "leveled from that point on throughout the interview.

Another example pertinent to this issue can be drawn from the first series of sessions with a family composed of the parents and three adolescent offspring. The youngest one, the identified patient, is an active homosexual who tends to behave in a paranoid, aggressive manner. Twice he started and abandoned individual therapies aimed manifestly at dealing with his hostility and covertly at dealing with his homosexuality, as well as with his economic exploitation of the parents. The family brought him to family therapy under the pressure of extreme economic reprisals, and he participated with open declarations of protest. What was clear from the start was that the identified patient as well as the other members were convinced that the therapist was going to establish a firm coalition with all but the former. In order to break this stereotype, the therapist placed himself consistently in coalition with the identified patient, a move that dislocated everyone, including his new ally. This lasted some six sessions, progressively fading into equidistance as the therapist observed the coalitionary maneuver balance the previously asymmetrical structure. This move, obviously, affected not only the process of the sessions but the whole family style.

Dealing with with coalitionary process may constitute, in some cases, the core of the family treatment. In others, it may represent mainly preliminary work before treatment. But, figure or ground, it is always present throughout family therapy.

The family therapist can expand his scope and leverage by integrating this level of analysis into the general treatment strategy and enrich his technical repertoire by dealing consciously—even though not necessarily explicitly—with the powerful and yet labile field of coalitions.

REFERENCES

1. Ackerman, N.W., *Treating the Troubled Family*. New York, Basic Books, 1966.
2. Bateson, G. Chapters 7, 8, 9 and 10 in J. Ruesch and G. Bateson (Ed.), *Communication: The Social Matrix of Psychiatry*. New York, Norton, 1951.
3. Bowen, M. "Family Psychotherapy," *Am. J. Orthopsychiat.*, 31: 40-60, 1972.
4. Ferreira, A.J. and Winter, W.D., "Family Interaction and Decision-Making," *Arch. Gen. Psychiat.*, 13: 214-223, 1965.
5. Framo, J.L. (Ed.), *Family Interaction*, New York, Springer, 1972, pp. 111-173.
6. Haley, J. "An Interactional Description of Schizophrenia," *Psychiatry*, 22: 321-332, 1959.
7. Haley, J., *Strategies of Psychotherapy*, New York, Grune & Stratton, 1963.
8. Minuchin, S. *Structural Family Therapy*, Boston, Harvard University Press, 1974.
9. Strodtbeck, F.L., "The Family as a Three-Person Group," *Am. Social. Rev.*, 19: 23-29, 1954.
10. Watzlawick, P., Beavin, J.H., and Jackson, D.D., *Pragmatics of Human Communication*, New York, Norton, 1967.

11. Weitman, S.R. "Intimacies: Notes Toward a Theory of Social Inclusion and Exclusion," *Arch. Europ. Sociol.*, 11: 348-367, 1970.

12. Weitman, S.R., *ibid.* in A. Birenbaum and E. Sagarin (Eds.), *People in Places: The Sociology of the Familiar*, New York, Praeger, 1973.

13. Wynne, L.C., Ryckoff, I.M., Day, J. and Hirsch, S.I., "Pseudo-Mutuality in the Family Relations of Schizophrenics," *Psychiatry*, 21: 205-220, 1958.

14. Wynne, L.C., "The Study of Intrafamilial Alignments and Splits in Exploratory Family Therapy" in Ackerman, N.W., *et al.* (Ed.) *Exploring the Base for Family Therapy*, New York, Family Service Association, 1961.

15. Zuk, G., "The Side-Taking Functioning in Family Therapy," *Am. J. Orthopsychiat.* 38: 553-559, 1968.

DIAGNOSIS AND ASSESSMENT IN FAMILY THERAPY

Assessment of a family's concerns and patterns should be part of the ongoing family counseling process. In family therapy the use of labels, i.e. scapegoat, identified patient, only serves to reinforce existing patterns. Observing the family together allows the therapist to examine the coalitions, alliances, communication patterns, and family rules as they relate to the symptomatic behavior of that identified patient. As the assessment process continues, the therapist is then able to illustrate to all family members how their behaviors have contributed to one member of that system being labeled "sick." Therefore, as the total system is examined, family members are made aware of their patterns of behavior, and change of the total system becomes possible. Thus one can easily see how assessment can lead to the formulation of treatment strategy, on the part of the therapist, and future client change. Without a coherent strategy for assessing the total family system, the therapist can only work with "gut" reactions.

Craig Everett describes a model that has evolved out of clinical work with adolescents. The author focuses upon developmental phase-specific tasks and examines them within the context of the family's dynamics. This assessment process, according to Everett, allows the clinician to identify patterns that have the potential for being constructive as well as dysfunctional.

The article by Lawrence Fisher provides a critical review of family assessment. He offers a listing of criteria for assessment, then attempts to provide linkage between the assessment process and a theoretical model of family functioning. A significant contribution of the article is the author's grouping of assessment dimensions. Hopefully, this description of dimension will lead to the introduction of coherent and systematic family diagnostic process.

Hansen and Himes offer a cyclical model for understanding family conflicts. This model proposes that the issues between family members come into open conflict when something triggers their feelings. If they are not able to resolve their differences, the issues may remain latent until the next triggering event. The therapist can examine the triggering events, the conflict behaviors, and the consequences of the conflict in understanding the real issues in the family.

Keeney presents an argument for a diagnostic system related to the ecological and systems approach to therapy. This model avoids the psychiatric medical model of labeling and replaces it with a descriptive evolving method related to the context of the therapy. Keeney's model examines the interrelatedness of the objects within the system. An example of this would be a description of how two individuals relate. However, according to Keeney, if one examines systems in a hierarchical fashion they are not using the ecosystemic epistemological approach. Thus, is this system the therapist is seen as part of the system being diagnosed.

The articles offer some commonalities and ideas for practicing family therapists. First, it appears that the real understanding of a family's dynamics comes about when the therapist is able to discern cyclical patterns. Second, while individual assessment often focuses upon intrapsychic activities, family assessment describes the client as a system of interrelated parts. How these individuals respond to each other and the structure of the system is an important feature present in family assessment. Finally, as with any type of assessment, these authors have placed some emphasis on the relationship between diagnosis and treatment. They all argue that a diagnostic strategy is necessary for clinical strategy. The results of using technique without some coherent plan or hypothesis can often result in chaos and confusion.

Chapter 13

FAMILY ASSESSMENT AND INTERVENTION FOR EARLY ADOLESCENT PROBLEMS

CRAIG A. EVERETT

The period of adolescence has been characterized frequently as one of intense transition and upheaval—a sudden convergence of biological and emotional changes with increasing sociocultural pressure. Adolescents have been described as this society's "surplus people" (Nye & Barado, 1973); caught between the games of childhood and the responsibilities of adults, with few areas of defined functional utility. The present society has institutionalized only limited structures through which adolescents can become productive economic resources. As a part of the presently changing adult attitudes toward child bearing, adolescents are viewed often as emotional and economic liabilities. Parents have become frustrated in their attempts to manage their adolescents' struggle for independence, and the deviance from family norms often accompanying this period.

It is acknowledged, both theoretically and clinically, that the primary developmental task of adolescence is to achieve a sense of autonomy in the milieu of family ties and peer influences. The intensity of this task is most apparent in early adolescence—13 to 16 years. For clinicians involved treating adolescent problems, the traditional boundaries delineating normative developmental issues and serious deviancy become unclear and transitory. The result is often frustrated therapists (not unlike parents) who either lose interest in working with adolescents or who resort to simplistic patch-work techniques. This paper will discuss a clinical assessment model for initiating treatment with early adolescents and their parents which has been operationalized and evaluated in a community mental health setting.

THE DEVELOPMENTAL MILIEU OF ADOLESCENT BEHAVIOR

An analysis of adolescent developmental issues is inseparable from a

From C. Everett, Family Assessment and Intervention for Early Adolescent Problems, *Journal of Marriage and Family Counseling,* 2:155-65, 1976. Courtesy of American Association for Marriage and Family Therapy.

recognition of family interactional patterns. The now cliched concept of a generation gap was anticipated by Kingsley Davis (1940) who identified the adolescent's growing physical and emotional prowess as occurring simultaneously with a waning of these factors, as well as those of economic potential and occupational status, for their adult parents. However, this relatively universal characteristic of parent-adolescent interaction occurs within a multidimensional milieu of family, individual, and peer dynamics.

Bernard Farber (1964) has raised the issue of exactly how much autonomy from one's family of orientation is it necessary for an adolescent to achieve. He has identified categories of "sponsored" and "unsponsored" independence which reflect the parents' relative approval of the adolescent's independent activities. Conflict arises when the adolescent fails to perform independently those activities which the parents sponsor, or when the adolescent independently performs acts which the parents oppose. The goal of sponsored independence toward self-reliance places the adolescent's developmental task of achieving autonomy within the dimension of family interaction.

However, these interactional processes must be evaluated relative to the simultaneous personal and intrapsychic dynamics of the adolescent. Psychoanalytic theory has identified in this period the resurgence of formerly latent psychosexual forces (e.g., Pearson, 1958; Freud, 1958). Specifically, Blos (1967) has identified adolescence as a "second individuation" process characterized by a heightened personality vulnerability and an urgency for congruence between psychic and maturational changes. This parallels the attainment of object consistency in the third and fourth year, and is accompanied by an emotional disengagement from internalized infantile objects and contemporary parental objects. Similarly, Erickson observed:

> In their search for a new sense of continuity and sameness, adolescents have to refight many of the battles of earlier years, even though to do so they must artificially appoint perfectly well-meaning people to play the roles of adversaries (Erickson, 1950, p. 253).

These factors tend to intensify, particularly for early adolescents (13-16 years), the inherent intrafamilial struggles.

The extrafamilial component for the adolescent involves an increasing reliance on the peer culture. Erikson's developmental theory has been utilized to emphasize the importance of the adolescent-peer group dynamics. The assumption made often is that adolescents must develop a peer group affiliation in order to gain a sense of ego identify and self esteem. This has been operationalized clinically by advocates for the use of peer group therapy in treating adolescent problems (Berkovitz, & Sugar, 1975; Brandes, & Gardner, 1973; Rachman, 1975). It is at this issue of the relative importance of family and peer ties that a variety of data converge to offer further a refinement of assessment and treatment strategies.

Erickson's (1959) view of normative development is epigenetic—a sequential process involving task resolution. From this view, a stratification of tasks throughout the adolescent period can be identified. Early adolescents must deal with the more dramatic onset of puberty, associated physiological changes, recurrent psychosexual impulses, emerging peer attachments, and heterosexual fantasies. As experience with these issues provides some resolution, later adolescents (17-21 years) will deal with tasks of heterosexual attachments, disengagement from parental dependency, and a solidification of identity. Of course, idiosyncratic differences in maturity and experience will create a certain overlap in the resolution of these issues.

For the clinician, a careful analysis of phase-specific dynamics for the adolescent is essential to effective assessment and intervention. To assume that a problematic client, simply by virtue of being an adolescent, is prepared to struggle with ego identity issues through peer group affiliation may be justifiable only for later adolescents. The routine placement of early adolescents in peer group therapy may intensify prematurely the parent-adolescent control issues and result in an inadequate resolution of the secondary individuation process. In fact, Whitaker (1975) views many problematic adolescents as ones who have separated precipitously and unsatisfactorily from their families of origin. This tends to create situations of more profound dependence and unresolvable ambivalence for both the adolescent and the parents. The resultant treatment strategy would involve a process of re-entry for the adolescent into the family toward the goal of achieving a more satisfactory separation. Similarly, Adelson (1964) has evaluated peer group experiences as inhibiting differentiation and growth for the adolescent. Individual tensions and conflicts tend to be displaced to or discharged within the peer group resulting in impersonal conformity and pseudo-adaptive resolutions.

ADOLESCENT-FAMILY ASSESSMENT ISSUES

The prior theoretical discussion has been intended to identify phase-specific tasks and to support the strategy of clinically assessing early adolescents within the context of their family dynamics. Typically, adolescents referred for treatment display a broad range of symptomatology. The analysis of these problems as a derivative of phase-specific developmental issues and dysfunctional family interaction offers a sound approach for developing interventive strategy and ongoing treatment goals.

Family assessment will enable the clinician to identify both enduring and emerging patterns of adolescent-parent interaction. These patterns will represent a blend of both dysfunctional and potentially constructive elements. In cases of severe deviancy where children have been scapegoated (see Vogel, & Bell, 1968) at an early age, the emergence of adolescence can intensify potentially destructive behavior and a more abrupt sensation from the family. Reciprocally, where scapegoating cannot be sustained, this period can precipitate decompensation in the parents' marital relationship.

In other family situations, it is recognized clearly that the emergence of puberty in a child can reactivate in parents their own unresolved adolescent struggles. Parents may attempt to handle their anxieties over these latent conflicts by further scapegoating the adolescent or externalizing the conflicts onto the adolescent (Counts, 1967). In another respect, inherent fears of fantasied erotization of the parent-adolescent relationship can produce dramatic distancing mechanisms or overt involvement by the parents in the sexuality of their adolescent (Williams, 1973). Further reciprocal issues of adolescent-parent complementarity become clear in situations where the adolescent's deviant or "unsponsored" behavior serves to stabilize both his/her own internal operations and that of the family interaction. The adolescent's fear of parental object loss can involve him/her in a collusive support of the parents' defensive organization against their own anxieties (Williams, 1973; Zinner, & Shapiro, 1972).

DESCRIPTION OF THE MODEL

This model evolved out of several years of treating adolescents in a community mental health setting. Prior to its inception, a variety of professionals had utilized individual, large and small peer group, and parent treatment methods. The need for a more efficient assessment-intervention approach was recognized, and the strengths and frustrations of the prior experiences were incorporated into this model.

The goals are twofold: 1) clinical assessment; and 2) therapeutic intervention. The former provides an analysis of the adolescent's symtomatology in the context of both developmental needs and family influences and an evaluation of the parents at personal, marital, and parental levels. The intervention provides a means of stabilizing both the adolescent's behavior and the parent-adolescent conflict so that new interactional patterns can be evolved and recommendations for further treatment can be facilitated. This therapeutic intervention is viewed as being more comprehensive than that of the traditional crisis intervention model of returning family members to a pre-crisis state of equilibrium. To expect equilibrium in this context is inappropriate when the underlying issues are recognized as developmental. In fact, such a "holding operation" would be viewed as counter-productive to the natural evolution of new interactional methods and problem solving techniques (Nichols, & Rutledge, 1965; Malouf, & Alexander, 1974).

The model is diagramatically outlined in Figure 3-I. It is essentially a combined collaborative and conjoint treatment approach utilizing cotherapists (see Green, 1963). The first and second interviews separate

Figure 13-1

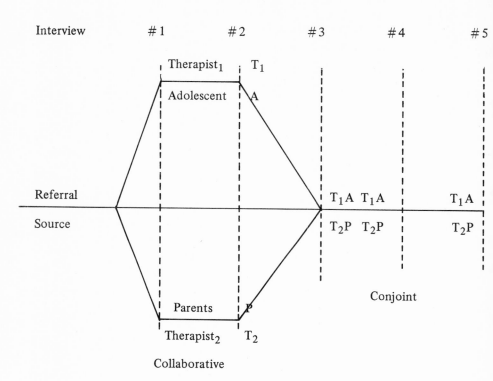

Collaborative—Conjoint Assessment Model

the adolescent and the parents with their own therapists. The third, fourth, and follow-up sessions are planned to be conjoint, i.e., involving adolescent, the parents, and both therapists. One hour sessions are conducted weekly with two to four weeks between the fourth and follow-up session. The initial two collaborative sessions are conducted simultaneously so the adolescent and parents arrive for their appointments together. The collaborative meetings between the two therapists are crucial and are scheduled following each therapy session. The following is a brief sequential description of the clinical process:

Session #1. Statements regarding precipitating issues are solicited and evaluated in terms of individual dynamics and family interaction patterns. The therapists's goals are threefold: 1) to function actively and directly, facilitating a model of open and honest interaction with the client(s); 2) to assess the client's particular role in the family structure; and 3) to evolve a potentially supportive alliance with the client(s) that will provide access to the family system.

The post-session collaboration is essential for checking congruency between the adolescent's and parents' reporting of problem issues and interaction patterns. This provides an early clue to the nature of the family's functioning as well as an indicator of therapeutic strategy and prognosis. If the reporting has been seriously incongruent, initial movement in the next session must be to gain a more realistic and consistent perception of the family from both sides. If the reporting is fairly congruent, the therapists will move to further clarify roles and needs, and to reinforce their interaction with the client(s) and access into the system. They will evaluate their initial impressions of the family's dynamics and evolve a clear strategy for the next session.

Session #2. Here the respective therapists will clarify and/or challenge incongruities, if any, and begin to engage their client(s) to examine alternate ways of interacting to alleviate family turmoil. These alternatives are tested with the therapist from the perspective of planning to verbalize and negotiate them in the upcoming conjoint family session. The post-session collaboration evaluates the family's relative flexibility for change, and formulates practical goals and/or behavior changes to be explored in the conjoint session. It is important to recognize areas of potential threat to the family system that may become intensified in the conjoint session.

Session #3. This is the initial conjoint session. The focus is on evolving interaction among the family members and between the family and the therapists. The former informs the therapists of role and interaction patterns; the latter allows the therapist to participate in the system. Depending on the therapists' particular styles at this point, activity may revolve around the stated problems, expectations for change, affective considerations, or interaction within the session. Issues and dynamics may be dramatized by a therapist assuming the role of an advocate for his/her client(s) or even challenging the client from within the context of their established alliance. The goal of this interaction is to evolve alternative actions, whether they be new roles or interaction patterns, to alleviate the family stress and provide new resources for problem solving. The therapists may formulize such an alternative in the form of a family assignment, prescription, behavioral contract, et cetera (see Parson & Alexander, 1973; Malouf & Alexander, 1974).

The post-session collaboration updates the therapists' evaluation of the family's potential for change, assesses the extent of dysfunctional family interaction and/or role behavior, and identifies positive forces to mobilize within the family. The potential for sabotaging of the assignment by certain family members must be anticipated and alternate interventions planned.

Session #4. The goal of this session is to explore feedback and consequences of the assignment over the prior week. It is important to reinforce even minimal successes with the assignments so that the family experiences the problems as manageable. The therapists continue to facilitate open interaction, affirm successes, and gradually relinquish control of the session to the ongoing family interaction. It is important that the therapists believe in the family's ability to restore itself to a functioning and adapting state. The session is concluded by reinforcing the assignments, summarizing progress, and stressing that the family has now learned to manage some of its problems in new ways. The family will be on its own for the next two to four weeks. Of course, if the conflict remains unmanageable, additional conjoint sessions should be scheduled. The post-session collaboration evaluates overall family movement, potentials for further growth, and identifies specific components of the family that will require further attention.

Session #5. The follow-up session reinforces progress and reviews the family's handling of new situations or crises. At this point, the therapists should be prepared to make specific recommendations for the continuation of treatment. If the situation has stabilized and there appears potential for building upon prior therapy experiences, the same conjoint format may be recommended. Other children in the family may be considered for entering treatment. If little interventive progress has been made beyond the assessment, the therapists may recommend individual or peer group therapy for the adolescent; individual, marital, or parent group treatment for the parents; or combinations of several of these. Generally, where treatment is recommended with the adolescent on an individual basis, the parents on an individual or marital basis, or with the family unit, the same therapists continue with the case. Following the recommendation, the treatment process and its impact on the family is evaluated by both the family members and the therapists.

TWO CASE STUDIES

A 16 Year-Old Male

The adolescent from a single child family was referred by juvenile court prior to adjudication for charges of sexually molesting a 10 year-old female. This was identified later as an isolated incident of fondling the girl's genitals with no physical force being involved. In the individual sessions with the adolescent, a pattern of social isolation was identified in his limited contact with only younger children in his neighborhood. This pattern had evolved three years earlier at a time when he experienced increasing difficulty handling his emerging sexual impulses and fantasies. He identified feelings of parental rejection during this period. His therapist, a female, discussed openly with him developmental needs in terms of fantasies, uses of masturbation, and his need for further contact with his own peer group.

The parents, in their mid-forties, were viewed as emotionally controlling though not overly punitive, rather protective in their view of their son as immature, and uninformed of his developmental needs. In their individual sessions, it became apparent that their controlling behavior had become intensified three years earlier out of their concern about his "growing up too fast." His developmental changes had triggered some latent issues regarding the mother's premarital pregnancy, and a general uneasiness in both of their backgrounds in dealing with sexual matters. As their only child, there were additional issues of "letting him go." Considerable distancing had resulted in their relations with him. This was true particularly between him and the father, who had shared a considerable interest in mechanical projects up until three years ago.

The collaborative sessions served to clarify historical and present interactional patterns, and to establish a therapeutic alliance with the adolescent and his parents. The strategies for the conjoint sessions were clearly toward more open interaction, identifying separation anxieties, evolving some reintegration of the son into the family at a more appropriate phase-specific level, and developing opportunities for more "sponsored" independent activities of the adolescent with his peer group. Dynamically, the adolescent's therapist used her supportive alliance both to model for him interaction with the parents and to encourage him toward more direct interaction himself. The parents' therapist utilized his relationship to help them manage their anxieties so as to allow the son to re-enter a relationship with them at a more mature level, and to affirm and encourage his independent acitivites with peers.

These goals were initiated and moving toward resolution in three conjoint sessions. This movement was attributed to Kaffman's (1963) "snowballing" phenomenon where the intervention broke the dysfunctional cycle and allowed for mutual shifts in the parent-adolescent relationship. The follow-up session after one month confirmed continued healthy interaction and further involvement by the son in his peer group. At this point, with the mutual agreement of the parents and son, the family treatment was terminated. The adolescent was seen by his therapist on an individual basis periodically over the following three months to reinforce his movement and to handle additional developmental issues that arose.

A 14 Year-Old Female

This adolescent was referred by her family's minister following a year of chronic abuse of amphetamines and barbiturates. She had been living with relatives the prior year during the divorce of her parents and subsequent remarriage of her mother. The drug abuse coincided with her return to her mother and new step-father. In the initial individual sessions, her female therapist experienced her as distrustful and highly manipulative. While she appeared unresponsive generally to the therapist's offer of support, she tested limits continually and responded to gestures of firmness. The mother and step-father appeared to have a good relationship, yet were experiencing their own adjustment concerns in the new marriage. They were uneasy about her role in the marriage and were intimidated by her behavior. The adolescent's three-year older sister had not displayed similar adjustment difficulties. The therapists anticipated that the adolescent's anger would dominate the conjoint sessions as a re-enactment of her manipulation and search for limits within the family. Since the behavioral problems appeared limited to the past year, the therapists decided not to probe for formerly latent psychosexual feelings that were triggered apparently by the divorce and remarriage of the mother, and entry of the step-father. The strategy for the conjoint sessions was directed at the parental control issue and re-entry of the daughter into the new family structure.

As anticipated, the adolescent dominated the conjoint sessions, and resisted all efforts to interact with the parents. Toward the end of the second session, the parents' therapist identified this situation and firmly, without overt punitiveness, asked the adolescent to leave the therapy session with her own therapist. This dramatization was utilized to shift the balance of control away from the adolescent both within the therapy and within the family. Care was exercised to preserve and reinforce her relationship with her own therapist. This follows Minuchin's (1974) identification of the need for differentiating clear parental boundaries in the family system.

The parents were seen in marital therapy for four months to clarify issues of their new relationship, to learn to implement firmer controls in the family, and to support the daughter's re-entry. The adolescent was seen individually by her therapist throughout this period. She responded well to the firmer guidelines and clearer expectations from her parents. During this period she became involved in a non-drug oriented peer group in her school. Toward the end of her treatment, she acknowledged to her therapist that formerly she had felt abandoned by her parents and unwanted in her mother's new marriage.

EVALUATION OF THE MODEL

This model has been evaluated throughout its development and following its implementation with 50 treatment cases over a two year period. Participating therapists have been interdisciplinary teams of psychiatrists, psychologists, pastoral counselors, social workers, psychiatric nurses, and graduate students representing most of these fields. The evaluation process was conducted at two levels: 1) the self-reports of the adolescents, parents, therapists, and their supervisors; and 2) an exploratory statistical comparison of these initial 50 cases with the last 50 adolescents treated at the Center immediately prior to the model's initiation. In general, the study cases involved a broad range of typical adolescent referral problems, e.g., drug abuse, sexual delinquency, runaway behavior, school adjustment, et cetera. No cases of overt psychotic behavior in the adolescent were treated during this period. The social status of the families represented slightly more from middle income than lower income levels, and 75% of the families were Caucasian. Twenty-five percent of the cases were treated with only one parent present, some of these represented divorced parents or unco-operative spouses.

Self-Report Evaluations

Several clear advantages of this model's approach have been dis-covered for the participants. The *adolescent* appears to benefit from having a therapist of his/her own. The therapist is viewed both as an advocate, i.e., one who offers support and is able to express the adolescent's feelings and perceptions to his parents, and as one who can challenge the adolescent from within the rapport of their separate relationship (see Schwartzberg, & Hammer, 1968; Solow, & Cooper, 1975). The adolescent feels and learns that the focus for the presenting problems is upon the family as a whole and not merely on himself/herself. The motivation to attend sessions is increased by the awareness of its directed and time-limited structure.

The *parents*, as the adolescent, appear more willing to make an initial commitment to the therapy because of its time-limited and contractual nature. The relative short-term definition of the assessment-intervention process appears to stabilize the conflicts, and place them in a perspective of being manageable and not irreparable. With their own therapists, the parents may discuss related problem areas that they might be reluctant to reveal in front of their children, i.e., sexual issues, extended family conflicts, et cetera. The new alternative interactions learned in these sessions appear to facilitate continuity in recommendations for further treatment (e.g., marital therapy), and to be readily employed and generalized with other family members.

The *therapists* indicate a greater willingness to work with adolescent problems in the context of a time-limited model and the shared responsibility with a co-therapist. With the responsibility for quickly assessing problem situations and interactional dynamics, the therapists must work intensely, actively, and directly to engage their client(s) and the family system. By the third session, the therapists can evaluate the extent of interventive change which will be realistically acceptable to the family. The division of the therapist's responsibilities between adolescent and parents defined alliances and relieves the frequently covert struggle for coalitions when only one therapist is involved. This process most often alienates the adolescent who brings an inherent suspicion of an "adult" therapist, frequently expecting him/her to "sell-out" to the parents. The brief period between the fourth and follow-up sessions is valuable in assessing the adaptive potentials of the family and their operationalization of alternative interactions. In several cases in which the dysfunction was severe and therapists reluctantly allowed this intervening period, considerable adaptive stabilization did occur. This appears in line with the "snowball" phenomena (Kaffman, 1963) mentioned previously. However, while intervention may break the vicious cycle and induce mutual interactional shifts, succeeding clinical changes do not necessarily parallel the intensity of therapy as in this interventive phase.

Statistical Evaluations

The exploratory statistical evaluation compared this model's initial 50 cases with the 50 adolescent cases treated at the Center immediately prior to the initiation of the model. The latter group represented similar early adolescent referral problems, and had been treated by many of the same professionals in individual, small group, or large group therapy. The two groups were compared for consistency of appointments kept and the relative continuity of treatment. The former was evaluated on the basis of the number of missed or cancelled appointments out of the first five scheduled sessions. The family assessment-intervention model indicated a rate of only 2.5% missed/cancelled appointments, compared to a rate of 28% in the traditional treatment group. Continuity of treatment was evaluated on the basis of the number of cases which withdrew from treatment after at least one appointment and prior to the fifth appointment. This is in contrast to cases terminated or referred as a result of the therapist's decision. The family model indicated a rate of only 6% (3 cases) that withdrew from treatment compared to 36% (18 cases) in the traditional treatment group.

Discussion of the Model

The relative strengths of this model for assessing and intervening in early adolescent problems reflect both theoretical and technical considerations. The underlying orientation of the therapist to phase-specific adolescent issues in the context of re-establishing supportive family ties. To have placed them initially in peer group treatment may have precipitated further alienation from the family and inadequate resolution of essential developmental tasks. As was illustrated, the resolution of these tasks within a supportive family milieu resulted in the adolescents' natural movement toward "sponsored" independent activities with their peers.

The ability of the therapist to function at both assessment and interventive levels is important, as is his/her view toward identifying and facilitating ongoing therapy needs beyond this initial phase of treatment. Technically, the time-limited, contractual nature of the model facilitated greater initial commitment on the part of both the adolescent and the parents, which in turn facilitated continuation in ongoing treatment following the recommendation session. The use of collaborative methods facilitated early assessment of individual and situational dynamics, and established therapeutic alliances. The conjoint method refined the assessment process and provided the setting for interventive treatment to stabilize parent-adolescent functioning so that they could "hear" the recommendations and continue their commitment to the treatment process.

Since this study's completion, the model has been utilized in several other capacities. In an intervention program for juvenile first offenders, the adolescents were referred by local police juvenile officers immediately following a "station adjustment" procedure. These adolescents were involved in minor first offenses in which charges were not filed. The treatment teams were composed of a variety of social service professionals and paraprofessionals. The model was easily teachable and particularly adaptable where the intervention was conducted in the families' homes.

This model has been utilized also in the Center's clinical training programs. The supervisor and the student become the treatment team. The collaborative process allows the supervisor to experience practically his/her student's clinical skills as well as teaching by the demonstration of his/her own skills.

Such a model as this, of course, may not be fully applicable to other clinical settings. Variables regarding the flexibility of an agency's treatment orientation and the therapists' skills with adolescent and family interaction dynamics will be important. The reporting of such a model is intended as a place to begin in broadening the parameters of clinical adolescent assessment and refining pursuant treatment strategies.

REFERENCES

Adelson, J. The mystique of adolescence. *Psychiatry*, 1964, *27*, 1-5.

Berkovitz, I., & Sugar, M. Indications and contraindications for adolescent group psychotherapy. In M. Sugar (Ed.), *The adolescent in group and family therapy*. New York: Brunner/Mazel, 1975.

Blos, P. The second individuation process of adolescence. *The Psychoanalytic Study of the Child*, 1967, *22*, 162-186.

Brandes, N., & Gardner, M. Therapeutic approaches. In N. Brandes and M. Gardner (Eds.), *Group therapy for the adolescent*. New York: Jason Aronson, Inc., 1973.

Counts, R. Family crisis and the impulsive adolescent. *Archives of General Psychiatry*, 1967, *17*, 64-71.

Davis, K. The sociology of parent-youth conflict. *American Sociological Review*, 1940, *5*, 523-535.

Erickson, E. *Childhood and Society*. 2nd Edition. New York: W.W. Norton, 1963.

Erikson, E. *Identity and the life cycle*. New York: International Univesities Press, 1959.

Farber, B. *Family: Organization and interaction.* San Francisco: Chandler Publishing Co., 1964.

Freud, A. Adolescence. *Psychoanalytic Study of the Child,* 1958, *13,* 255-278.

Green, R. Collaborative and conjoint therapy combined. *Family Process,* 1963, *2,* 90-98.

Kaffman, M. Short term family therapy. *Family Process,* 1963, *2,* 216-234.

Malouf, R., & Alexander, J. Family crisis intervention: A model and technique of training. In R. Hardy and J. Cull (Eds.), *Therapeutic needs of the family.* Springfield: Charles Thomas, 1974.

Minuchin, S. *Families and family therapy.* Cambridge: Harvard University Press, 1974.

Nichols, W., Jr. & Rutledge, A. Psychotherapy with teen-agers. *Journal of Marriage and the Family,* 1965, *27,* 166-175.

Nye, F.I., & Bernardo, F.M. *The family: Its structure and interaction.* New York: Macmillan, 1973.

Parsons, B., & Alexander, J. Short-term family intervention: A therapy outcome study. *Journal of Consulting and Clinical Psychology,* 1973, *40,* 223-231.

Pearson, G. *Adolescence and the conflict of generations.* New York: W.W. Norton, 1958.

Rachman, A. Identity group psychotherapy with adolescents. In G. Williams and S. Gordon (Eds.), *Clinical child psychology.* New York: Behavioral Publications, 1974.

Schwartzberg, B., & Hammer, E. Joint interview sessions with adolescent girls and their mothers as a family treatment tool. *Family Coordinator,* 1968, *17,* 75-77.

Solow, R., & Cooper, B. Co-therapists as advocates in family therapy with crisis-provoking adolescents. In M. Sugar (Eds.), *The adolescent in group and family therapy.* New York: Brunner/Mazel, 1975.

Vogel, E., & Bell, N. The emotionally disturbed child as the family scapegoat. In N. Bell and E. Vogel (Eds.), *A Modern Introduction to the Family.* New York: The Free Press, 1968.

Whitaker, C. The symptomatic adolescent—an AWOL family member. In M. Sugar, (Ed.), *The adolescent in group and family therapy.* New York: Brunner/Mazel, 1975.

Williams, F. Family therapy: Its role in adolescent psychiatry. In S. Feinstien and P. Giovacchini (Eds.), *Adolescent psychiatry,* Vol. II. New York: Basic Books, 1973.

Zinner, J., & Shapiro, R. Projective identification as a mode of perception and behavior in families of adolescents. *International Journal of Psychoanalysis,* 1972, *53,* 523-529.

DIMENSIONS OF FAMILY ASSESSMENT: A CRITICAL REVIEW

Lawrence Fisher

For more than 20 years family therapists have been engaged in the process of family assessment of one form or another. Whether the therapist specifically starts with a critical period of family evaluation and diagnosis or, as Ackerman and Behrens (1974) suggest, the process is continuous and ongoing throughout treatment, family practitioners implicitly utilize a series of underlying dimensions or foci. Some explicitly focus their evaluation in terms of family conflict, some aim toward an understanding of need or role complementarity, and some deal more with issues of boundary and social context. Yet each therapist employs a conceptual schema, a model, a personal point of view of family functioning which is useful in helping him or her understand the family and therefore work as the therapeutic agent.

The details of such schema are often difficult to specify for they are tied to therapeutic style, training experience, type of agency, and personality of the therapist, to name but a few variables. Nevertheless, these frameworks of assessment comprise a rich area for investigation, since they provide the conceptual format for how the therapist operates.

This paper is an attempt at reviewing the content and methodology of existing clinical and experimental research on family assessment dimensions. Of interest here is a critical review of descriptions of family dimensions and the methods used in the generation of these dimensions, whether clinically or empirically oriented. The paper focuses on dimensions utilized in clinical work—the more pragmatic aspects of clinical assessment—as opposed to differences in theories of family functioning (e.g., Hill & Hansen, 1960) or differences in strategies of family theory systemization (e.g., Hill, 1971). In an attempt to provide somewhat concise comparisons among the dimensional units of a variety of investigators, the liberty has been taken at times of condensing

From L. Fisher, Dimensions of Family Assessment: A Critical Review, *Journal of Marriage and Family Counseling*, 2:367-82, 1976. Courtesy of American Association for Marriage and Family Therapy.

concepts or rephrasing dimensions to fit the format of presentation, while attempting to adhere to the intent of the original author.

This paper attempts a review, not a definitive integration. The field is wide, diffuse, and confusing, and we are not yet at a point where a definitive integration can be successfully undertaken. The purpose of this paper is to pull together relevant literature so as to accelerate the integration process.

TYPES OF ASSESSMENT SCHEMAS

From a review of articles on family assessment, a condensed listing of criteria for assessment was obtained (See Table 14-I). An overview of these dimensions and approaches to assessment allowed the tentative classification of the articles into roughly four general assessment strategies, each reflecting a particular type of orientation: single concept notions, theoretical notions, broadly based clinical lists, and empirically devised approaches. Each is discussed more fully in the following sections.

Table 14-I
Family Dimensions

Ackerman (1958)
    1) Failure of reciprocity of satisfaction
    2) Conflict
Ackerman & Behrens (1974)
    1) Destructive foci of conflict & how it is handled
    2) Identification of role relationships and complementary patterns in:
        a) self esteem
        b) need satisfaction
        c) shared search for conflict resolution
        d) buttressing of defenses against anxiety
        e) support of growth and creative development
    3) Can the family balance its multiple functions
    4) Family identity, stability, integrity
    5) Capacity for change and growth
Chagoya & Guttman (1971) and *Epstein* (1968)
    1) Presenting problem: instrumental problem vs. affective problem
    2) Problem identification or how the problem emerges
    3) Problem solving: who and how
    4) Affective expression: range expressed & range accepted
    5) Affective involvement or type of closeness
        a) absence
        b) interest without emotion
        c) empathic
        d) narcissistic
        e) symbiotic
    6) Communication patterns: direction, clarity, etc.
    7) Role behavior
    8) Autonomy of person boundaries
    9) Mode of behavior control and pattern of impulse control:

Table 14-I continued

    a) rigid
    b) flexible
    c) laissez-fair
    d) chaotic
  10) Family rules

Ehrenwald (1962, 1963, & 1968)
  1) Patterns of sharing
  2) Patterns of resistence or rebellion
  3) Patterns of complementarity
  4) Patterns of contagion

Family Service Association (1965)
  1) Family vulnerability and strength
  2) Family roles and ability to alter or change them
  3) Family goals including values and aspirations
  4) Patterns of communication and their dynamics
  5) Need-response patterns

Fine (1974)
  1) Problem identification
  2) Problem solving capabilities
  3) Child rearing practices
  4) Communication of feelings and information
  5) Role assignments
  6) Acceptance of autonomy
  7) Distribution of power
  8) Behavioral controls of parents on children

GAP (1970)
  1) Presenting problem
  2) Composition of family
  3) Intergenerational context
  4) Relationship to extended family
  5) Developmental background of parents
  6) Description of courtship
  7) Course of family development
  8) Family relations
  9) Formulation
  10) Changes during treatment
  11) Predictions
  12) Development after treatment

Gehrke & Moxon (1962)
  1) Conflict in masculine and feminine roles
  2) Sado-masochistic conflict
  3) Detached, demanding conflict
  4) Oral-dependent conflict
  5) Neurotic illness conflict

Grunebaum, Christ, & Neiberg (1969)
  1) Commitment to marriage
  2) Locus of symptoms
  3) Duration of symptoms

Handel (1965)
  1) Way of viewing the external world
  2) Way of viewing the self
  3) Source of family goals
  4) Nature of action
  5) Nature of heterosexuality

Table 14-I continued

Hess & Handel (1959)
    1) Separateness vs. connectedness of members
    2) Congruence of images of family numbers
    3) Family concerns or themes
    4) Boundaries between internal and external worlds
    5) Significance of biosocial issues
Kaldushin (1971)
    1) Stage of life cycle
    2) Effectiveness of parenting
    3) Adequacy of managing economic issues
    4) Socioeconomic mobility
    5) Family Cohesiveness
    6) Communication: overt vs. covert, mixed etc.
    7) Leadership and power
    8) Grouping, pairing, splits, alliances
    9) Giving & taking
    10) Presence or absence of myths
    11) Possibility of role confusion
    12) Affective climate: depressive, anxious, etc.
    13) Theoretically defined causes for problem
Kluckholn (1958)
    1) Cultural values and styles: ways of being
Leik & Northwood (1964)
    1) Conflict: family styles and types
Meyer (1959)
    1) Role conflict
    2) Social interaction
    3) Culture conflict
    4) Intergenerational family structure
Minuchin (1974)
    1) Structure: preferred transactional patterns
    2) System flexibility and capacity for restructuring
    3) System resonance: enmeshed vs. engaged
    4) Family life context ecology
    5) Developmental stage
    6) How family uses patient's symptoms to maintain status quo
Otto (1963)
    1) Satisfaction of physical and emotional needs
    2) Sensitivity of family members
    3) Ease of communication
    4) Supportiveness of members
    5) Ability to permit growth
    6) Positiveness of extra-family contacts
    7) Ability to grow with children
    8) Flexibility of roles
    9) Respect and individuality
    10) Growth from crisis
    11) Family loyalty
Pollak (1964)
    1) Family personality styles
    2) Location of family weakness
    3) Developmental appropriateness of independence-dependence dimensions
    4) Membership deficit: excess or absence

Table 14-I continued

5) Distribution of family power incorporating cultural norms
6) Interpersonal pathology vs. incompatibility

Pollak & Brieland

1) Range of family members' needs
2) Members power positions
3) Members strengths
4) Interaction roles
5) Family Roles
6) Relationships between family members and those outside the family

Ravich, Deutsch, & Brown (1956)

1) Sharing: alternated same routes
2) Dominating and submitting: one partner always won
3) Inconsistent: no stable agreement reached
4) Intensely competitive: both fight to win
5) Disjunctive: played independently of each other

Ryder & Goodrich (1966)

1) Conflict and usage of power:
   a) affective vs. rational
   b) verbal fluency
   c) husband vs. wife assertiveness
   d) style of error making

Scherz (1965)

1) Family problem identification
2) Social and economic conditions
3) Family interaction clarified: strengths, roles, goals, communication patterns, need-response patterns

Schreiber (1966)

1) Communication: clarity, directness, etc.
2) Role: acceptance, appropriateness to developmental stage
3) Individual responsibility accepted
4) Integration of differences among family members
5) Unity and cohesion within the family

Stuart (1973)

1) Identification of goals of behavior change in others
2) Identification of goals of behavior change in self
3) Assessment of resources for change
4) Assessment of degree of understanding
5) Increase of power distribution
6) Increase of congruence of priorities
7) Increase of communication effectiveness
8) Increase of sexual satisfaction
9) Increase of congruence of child management
10) Increase of general satisfaction

Titchner & Emerson (1958)

1) Acceptance of role allocations
2) Adoptions of similar traits in other family members
3) Closeness vs. remoteness of members
4) Communication: quality, tone, volume, etc.
5) Methods of conflict resolution

Weiss & Monroe (1959)

1) Presenting problems
2) Agency contacts
3) Social psychological situation

Table 14-I continued

4) Social history
5) Cultural background
6) Environmental stress
7) Social roles
8) Dominance patterns
9) Family goals
10) Family satisfaction
11) Psychodynamics of members

Wells & Rabiner (1973)
I. Diagnostic Interview
  1) How primary family functions are performed
  2) How members see each other's role performance
  3) Affective involvement of members with each other
  4) Behaviors seen as provocative
  5) Effectiveness of need communication
  6) Capability of other's satisfying the needs of the identified patient
II. Index
  1) Psychological mindedness
  2) Sympathetic-hostile reaction to patient
  3) Tension over primary family functions
  4) Family centeredness-cohesion
  5) How well each sees other's role performance
  6) How well each sees his own role performance
  7) A list of provocative behaviors seen in family
  8) Overall positive or negative effect of each member to each other member
  9) Degree of involvement with other members
  10) Extent to which each member gratifies patient's needs
  11) Power distribution
  12) Ability to express needs
  13) Ability to recognize needs of others
  14) Acceptance of interviewer's formulation
  15) Acceptance of interviewer's treatment plan

Winter & Ferreira (1970)
  1) Good adjustment: mutual sharing, common interests
  2) Task orientation: degree of task completion efficiency
  3) Silence: degree of verbal underproduction
  4) Emotionality: emotion as opposed to task oriented approach to problems
  5) Inefficiency: rating of "normality"
  6) Pathological Productivity: degree of unevenness of responding to each other
  7) Dependency: inability to make decisions

Zelditch (1964)
  1) Power: distribution and use of power within the family

Single Concept Notions

Several assessment schema place strong emphasis on a very limited range of parameters, or they reorganize and redefine a broad range of dimensions as varieties of a single concept. The primary single concepts used to assess families, as identified in this review, are power, conflict, and conflict resolution.

The great emphasis on power and conflict within the family makes sense in light of several issues. First, many families and couples come for treatment because of intra-familial conflict or because of conflict between the family and extra-family agents. Resolving conflict, therefore, may become the therapeutic goal. Second, as the study of the family has developed into a clinically useful therapeutic technique, it has brought with it the sociological and anthropological tradition of family research and evaluation. Third, conflict resolution both as individual concepts and manifestations of power within the family have clear conceptual boundaries, are amenable to a variety of research designs, and are easily operationally defined.

Zelditch (1964) reviewed the literature in sociology pertaining to family life and reported that the use and distribution of power has been the dominating focus of family theory and classification within that academic discipline. He identifies two primary parameters of power within the family: 1) the number of power structures within the family, i.e., is there one dominating structure or does the structure vary with the content of the issue; and 2) the distribution of power across individuals, i.e., does power reside in one person exclusively without input from others or is power shared more equitably. A variety of power arrangements leading to several different kinds of power structures are described.

Ryder and Goodrich (1966) note that early literature tended to focus on husband versus wife power and the expectations for power-based behavior within the marriage. They felt that one way to assess more concretely the utilization and structure of power operations within the marriage was to observe the ways couples discuss, argue, or battle in response to differences of opinion. Using Goodrich and Boomer's color matching procedure, they identified four dimensions of the resolution process. Power, therefore, can be assessed in terms of the manifestation of conflict and the process of conflict resolution.

Using an electronic two-person bargaining game, Ravish, Duetsch, and Brown (1965) combined notions of cooperation and competition in marital dyads into what may be termed an exercise in conflict resolution. Couples were given a road map along with the game board made up of single and multiple lane roads. Husbands and wives had then to contract with each other as to who would pass first or whether they would choose alternative routes in which they had little or no contact. Five styles of handling potential conflict were identified.

Leik and Northwood (1964) identified eight types of family conflict by dividing three dimensions into bipolar descriptors: is the marital issue over which conflict is displayed personally valued or not personally valued, required or not required by external conditions, and is it valued or not valued by the spouse. The resulting 2 x 2 x 2 table leads to eight cells, each of which implies a specific type of treatment. They used the dimensions of value of the content of the problem, and the reality of external conditions as the primary categorizing variables. Gehrke and Moxon (1962) also have categorized marital discord in terms of the content of the conflict.

Power, conflict, and conflict resolution are clearly the most prominent and widely studied of the single concept notions of family assessment. There are, however, a number of other single concept approaches. Otto (1962, 1963) has focused on the assessment of family strength as opposed to conflict; Handel (1965) has emphasized the assessment of underlying covert, clinical themes: and Kluckholn (1958) has described cultural values and styles.

Watzlawick (1965) has proposed an inexpensive, brief, clinical as opposed to research, procedure to reveal the "family's dynamics and patterns of interaction." A highly structured interview technique has been developed for use during the first interview. It is composed of roughly five exercises utilizing individual, parental, and family interviews. For example, each individual is privately asked what he or she believes are the main problems in the family, and then the entire family is asked to discuss this issue together. The groupings are aimed to tapping into primary family functions and the exercises are geared toward revealing characteristic patterns of interaction around specified topics.

Theoretical Orientation

Several authors have created family assessment procedures or criteria based upon theories or partial theories (Hill, 1971) of family functioning. Most often these assessment schema are based on bits and pieces from a number of theories of family behavior. Titchner and Emerson (1958), for example, cite Parsons, Bateson, Ackerman, Kluckholn, Spiegel, and Lidz as providing the theoretical background for the establishment of clinical family assessment variables. These authors appear to have taken those aspects of partial family theory which were easily translatable to the clinical situation and combined them into formal assessment procedures.

Since there is as yet no thorough, well integrated, general theory of family behavior, one may be forced to employ partial theories from a number of sources. While the use of partial theories (such as role, values, compatibility, et cetera) allows the clinician and researcher to draw upon existing thinking within well-defined contexts, it does create a need for linkages among the partial-theories so that some sense of an integrated assessment procedure can be developed. The major problem facing many theoretically oriented assessment batteries is the difficulty in relating how one part of the battery fits in with all the others. Although there is clearly some degree of clinical sensitivity as to how, for example, role behavior relates to values or norms within the family, there is as yet no conceptual bridge between and among these multiple concepts. Clearly, there is an increasing need to focus more on the relationships among assessment criteria than on the creation of the criteria themselves.

Minuchin and his colleagues at the Philadelphia Child Guidance Clinic may have circumvented the problem by developing a theory of family therapy without getting into the quicksand of theorizing about family functioning. (Notice the title of the approach; "Structural Family *Therapy*"). Reviewing both Camp's (1973) elucidation of the approach along with Minuchin's original writings (1974), it becomes clear that the "structuralist" clinician is concerned with here and now behavior and not with "family dynamics" as one might define them theoretically. The task of the therapist is to modify existing structural patterns defined by coalitions, splits, alliances, and so forth, and not to enter into issues of awareness, past history, individual dynamics, and the traditional concepts with which theoreticians have been concerned, although these are not entirely excluded. Minuchin's list of areas of assessment, as presented in Table 14-I, focuses only on the structural aspects of the family.

A more direct approach to the problem of operationalizing theoretical notions of family functioning into formal assessment paradigms has been taken by behaviorists and learning theorists (Hammerlynck, Handy, & Mach, 1973; Knox, 1971; Liberman, 1972; Patterson, 1971, Stuart, 1973). Although there is a good deal of variation among behaviorally oriented practitioners, their general stance is to focus on the identification of specific behaviors brought into focus by family members themselves, rather than by the clinician creating a theoretical picture of his own as to where the pathology "really lies." Spouses are asked to pinpoint specific "annoying" behaviors and to describe the frequency and setting of their occurrence. Roles, splits, dynamics, and so forth, need not be contemplated in this approach, as emphasis is placed on concrete, observable behaviors—identified by the individual family member. The approach permits the utilization of self-rating scales and questionnaires, thus heavily involving the family member in the assessment process. It assumes that any person can modify his or her own behavior upon learning appropriate responses to the needs and demands of the immediate environment (Stuart, 1973).

The behavioral approach to family assessment clearly avoids the problem of theoretical organization of constructs by focusing on a technique of treatment rather than on a theory of family functioning. While certainly not atheoretical in the Skinnerian sense of the term, learning theory approaches to family treatment are highly structured, well organized, and systematically oriented to gather appropriate kinds of data to undertake treatment without falling into abstract theoretical and linkage problems.

In summary, because a theory of family behavior is not yet available, assessment strategies based upon family theory have run into two primary problems. First, they have become somewhat abstract and not easily translatable to the clinical setting in a repeatable and uniform manner. Second, the utilization of partial theories for the development of assessment criteria has left us with the problem of linking concept to concept to create an integrated series of procedures.

Clinical Lists

Many of the papers reviewed listed a number of dimensions that were derived from clinical experience and found to be useful in the clinical assessment of families. Although tied to some underlying family model, or at least to an unspecified segment of a model, such schema were developed out of years of clinical and agency experience and are felt by their authors to be particularly useful in family assessment. In addition, these schema often reflect the author's ideas of which variables should be included in a family evaluation.

Typical of such schemas is an early listing by Ackerman (1954), who presents a seven-point topic outline, with several headings under each. Besides listing major variables of family dynamics and structural material, he lists past history and psychodynamics of each family member, including intrapsychic formulations and defense structures. Ackerman clearly attempted to list all of those variables which he felt were important in the assessment process, including theoretical, family based, socially oriented, and individually based headings.

A similar listing is presented in a recent GAP report (1970) and is included in Table 14-I. Although tied to theoretical material to a limited extent, the 12-point outline can be seen as an attempt at systematizing the traditional case history for use in family assessment.

Epstein, Sigal and Rakoff (1968) and later Chagoya and Guttman (1971) present a highly systematized outline of family assessment. Their approach can be seen as typifying the clinical listing method of assessment in that only a minimal effort is made to tie assessment criteria to underlying theory. Instead, the scheme is constructed for use as a practical tool, not as an abstract series of concepts. It taps into a number of different areas of family functioning, and it attempts to be broadly based without being over-exhaustive.

Similar listings have been made by Ackerman and Behrens (1974), Family Services Association (1965), Fine (1974), Kadushin (1971), Pollack (1964), Pollak and Brieland (1961), Weiss and Monroe (1959), and Scherz (1965) (*see* Table 14-I.) All share the goal of providing the practitioner with a useable format for family assessment without the added complication of "theoretical formulating." In this respect, they serve their purpose well. The major problem with the clinical listing approach to the establishment of assessment criteria has to do with the sheer length of the lists. The GAP report includes 12 assessment areas and Ackerman's early scheme includes at least double that amount. Although the individual listing of criteria of assessment highlights important areas with which the clinician needs to be familiar, the list at times becomes so long as to become unworkable for the experienced clinician or overwhelming for the novice. On the other hand, the shorter lists sometimes tend to be somewhat limiting and restrictive. In an effort to abbreviate, they often lose the richness of clinical data, which is especially crucial to the inexperienced family practitioner.

An additional problem with the clinical listing type of scheme is that it does not aid the practitioner in the development of a unified, somewhat coherent picture of the family taken as a whole. Often, such lists are compiled by experienced clinicians who because of their own style and case load have found certain aspects of the assessment process particularly useful. While the identification of criteria is useful in adding to the body of family assessment knowledge, the process is often idiosyncratic to particular styles of clinical work and, as such, clinically oriented lists do not add to the broader issues of family functioning. Such schemas often are clinic specific and it may be that the best way to make effective use of them across the broad range of clinical cases is to work in depth with their creators or to attend workshops and training programs within the respective settings.

Perhaps the best balance has been achieved in the Family Categories Schema devised by Epstein, et al., (1968) and his colleagues. The 10 areas are clear and distinct, yet they are easily combined into a smaller number of workable generic categories: family problems, affective aspects, communication issues, and what might be called a series of structural criteria. In the manuals and guides prepared to instruct users of the schema, the author provides detailed definitions, each with illustrations to insure proper usage. Hence, the Family Categories Schema tends to bridge the gap between sufficient detail for clinical usage and overloading the evaluator by requiring too long an assessment listing.

Empirical Methods

Several authors have experimented with factor analytic and other scaling procedures in an effort to generate assessment criteria. The usual practice is for the investigator to administer a series of scales to either the family itself or to observers who then watch the family perform in a variety of exercises or clinical sessions. Other approaches utilize a series of rational or empirical variables to assess outcome.

Ehrenwald (1952, 1958, 1963) established an inventory of 30 traits which were grouped into 10 clusters or triads. Examples include "giving-supportive-effective," and "cooperative-permissive-indulgent" behavior. The traits are closely interrelated and somewhat dimensional, and although not comprehensive, they are intended to pinpoint certain variables which assess the broad range of family behavior. Clinical observers were asked to rank order each two-person relationship as to which cluster appeared from most to least representative or descriptive of the pair. (In other studies by Ehrenwald, raters were asked to select two to five clusters rather than using the rank order approach). A profile was then created for each dyad and an averaging process was used to create a family profile. In addition, the observers were asked to rate each dyad along the three trait continuum for each cluster. Four rational as opposed to statistical factors or interaction patterns have been created using this format (see Table 14-I). The patterns have been established using the results of the cluster ratings on several clinical cases. Ehrenwald presents considerable theoretical and other empirical data to support the factorial breakdown.

Rather than focusing on family pathology, Otto (1962, 1963) established a family strength questionnaire. A number of marital pairs were asked to list their strengths as a family. The couples then met for 12 sessions in a group format to discuss the strengths so as to utilize them more effectively. The sessions were tape recorded and the data generated from them were combined with the questionnaire material collected earlier. After collating the data, Otto identified 12 areas of strength which he felt would be useful in making a contribution to the development of effective programs to strengthen family life (see Table 14-I).

Grunebaum, Christ, and Neiberg (1969) proposed three dimensions that are helpful from their experiences in determining treatment modality. Based upon non-empirical data, they suggest four possible treatment approaches: a) individual treatment for each spouse with two therapists; b) individual treatment for each spouse by the same therapist; c) conjoint treatment by one or two therapists; and d) couples group treatment.

Three levels of assessment are required to determine which modality is appropriate: 1) If the couple appears uncommitted to the marriage, then individual treatment by separate therapists is suggested. 2) If there is commitment, then, an evaluation as to locus of symptoms is undertaken. If symptoms are seen as occurring both within the marriage and outside of the marriage as well, individual treatment for each spouse by the same therapist is suggested. If symptoms occur only with the marriage, two choices are open. 3) If problems are acute and their history is short, conjoint therapy is suggested. If, on the other hand, problems are chronic and have become a way of family life, couples group therapy is recommended.

Grunebaum's et al., proposals are somewhat unique in two ways. First their assessment criteria are limited to a specific area of decision making as part of the clinical enterprise. Rather than focusing on broadly based dimensions of family functioning, these authors have narrowed in on specific areas of clinical concern. Second, the usefulness of the dimensions themselves is testable empirically. That is, these proposals can be assessed in terms of outcome measures of treatment effectiveness. Hence, groups assigned to different treatment modalities could provide an assessment of the validity of their proposals. These authors, then, have established assessment criteria for specific kinds of clinical decision making.

Winter and Ferreira (1970) collected a variety of data from several triads made up of a mother, father, and child. The triads were classified as having children who were normal, neurotic, schizophrenic, or delinquent. Three major data sources were used: 1) Extra-experimental materials came from a review of demographic data. 2) The technique of revealed differences was administered in which the three members of each family were asked for their likes and dislikes individually across a variety of areas. Then the triad was asked to complete the same questionnaire jointly and a number of interaction and "resolution of differences" variables were recorded. 3) Conjoint TAT stories were also gathered. All of these data were then subjected to a factor analysis and seven factors were identified. These are presented in Table 14-I and were used to compare the four groups of triads.

Schreiber (1966) and Wells and Rabiner (1973) similarly used rating scales and interviews to establish assessment dimensions (see Table 14-I).

The studies reviewed in this section attempt to generate dimensions of assessment using some form of empirical data. Considering the variety of structured and semistructured scaling techniques and the variety of rational and statistical methods of data reduction, the similarity of the dimensions is surprising. Clearly, the results of these studies are colored by the kinds of tasks employed. Since most of them emphasize style of task completion or conflict resolution, it is understandable that some of the resulting dimensions are based upon family interaction variables related to these issues (see Riskin and Faunce (1972) for a more detailed review of this area).

Otto's approach of having the family establish its own dimensions, so to speak, is intriguing. One might extend this argument by suggesting that families by their own variability, establish their own dimensions of effective family behavior and it might be profitable to focus future research in gathering more idiographic, single family data using formalized scaling procedures. The emphasis on self-perceptions of family members and the detailing of family rules and norms of competent behavior may be of value in balancing present trends of devising criteria from external sources. Rather than going through family history or clinical experience, it might be profitable to provide experiences to enable the family to present its own criteria for behavior without being biased by the family assessor's conceptual framework. Similar work has been done in other settings (Fisher & Rubenstein, 1975) and it would seem to have applicability in the family area as well.

AN OVERVIEW OF ASSESSMENT STRATEGIES

One of the primary purposes in reviewing existing clinical assessment schemas was to compile a brief, integrated summary list of the most frequently used assessment criteria. From such a brief list, a linkage among criteria would be attempted so that the assessment process could be tied to some kind of limited theoretical model of family functioning. Such an approach, presumably, would bridge the gap among the various strategies outlined above and perhaps eventually lead to a meaningful family classification system.

Unfortunately, the number of relevant criteria is large and the varieties of alternatives within criteria expand in geometric proportion. One feels caught, then, between Scylla of simplication and the Charybdis of over-inclusiveness. Even if the dimensions were grouped into categories, as Epstein has done, there is as yet no empirical and theoretical basis for creating one or another category system. Most likely clinical preference will determine which areas practitioners will emphasize in the assessment process.

Clearly, a summary or generic grouping of assessment dimensions would be useful, as long as the dimensions by their very existence did not limit the scope of thinking in the area. The development of a diagnostic system, for example, can place a static limit to an extension and reorganization of thinking over time. Hence, any overview must be seen as an overview, not as an imposition of struture which cannot be modified or discarded as need requires.

There is surprising comparability among the large number of dimensions presented in Table 14-I. Although different authors tend to focus in one direction or another, an overview of this extensive listing indicates at least five generic areas into which dimensions can be grouped. These are listed in Table 14-II. These generic dimensions were derived on a strictly rational basis and no attempt was made to document independence among the categories. An attempt was made to organize the extensive listing of dimensions by creating categories which would include most if not all of the dimensions listed in Table 14-I. While clearly simplistic, these categories represent one attempt to summarize the major trends in the family assessment literature.

Many authors have focused quite extensively on the formal structure of the family, borrowing terms and concepts from a variety of areas. Minuchin has placed greatest emphasis in this area. The terms one uses in the description of a family structure varies from author to author, but in the review of Table 14-I, there appears to be some consensus. The six sub-headings within the structural category reflect the major areas of interest in terms found most frequently in the literature. These terms are not ordered into any hierarchy. Structural descriptors are, however, most frequently listed as the primary dimension of family assessment.

An evaluation of controls and sanctions also emerges as an area many authors consider central to the assessment process. This category of dimensions reflects the patterns of rule enforcement within the family and the exercise of power in terms of resolution of conflict. While clearly tied to many of the structural aspects of the system, there appeared to be some separateness of these areas in the studies reviewed.

The third category of assessment dimensions relates to the emotional climate of the family and the satisfaction of needs for individual family

Table 14-II
An Overview of Family Assessment Dimensions

I) Structural Descriptors
    1) role: complementarity, acceptance, confusion, adequacy
    2) splits, alliances, scapegoating
    3) boundaries: internal and external
    4) patterns of interaction and communication: rules and norms of relating
    5) conflicts and patterns of resolution
    6) family views of life, people, and the external world
II) Controls and Sanctions
    1) power and leadership
    2) flexibility
    3) exercise of control
    4) dependency—independency
    5) differentiation—fusion
III) Emotions and Needs
    1) methods and rules for affective expression
    2) need satisfaction: giving and taking
    3) relative importance of needs vs. instrumental tasks
    4) dominant affective themes
IV) Cultural-Aspects
    1) social position
    2) environmental stresses
    3) cultural heritage
    4) social and cultural views
V. Developmental Aspects: appropriateness of structural, affective, and cultural aspects to developmental stage.

members. It is here where individual dynamics and family concepts appear to interface, for while there are often powerful affective themes underlying entire families, individual needs and feelings need to be dealt with if a family is to maintain its integrity. Several authors, therefore, separate emotional issues and individual need satisfaction from the system based dimension described above.

Fourth, many authors emphasize cultural and environmental stresses as well as the more subtle aspects of cultural influence. Also within this area, one might include issues of cultural heritage and orientation to the world based on social values and social class strivings. It might be worth noting at this point that of the five dimensional groupings, cultural influences, as defined here, appeared to be the most frequently mentioned and at the same time, the most poorly articulated assessment dimension. From subjective impression, most family schemas acknowledge extra-familial issues but concentrate their energies on describing scaling internal family dimensions.

Fifth, over the past 10 years or so there has been increasing emphasis placed on seeing the family from a development point of view. Descriptions in this area tend to focus on how all of the dimensions mentioned above relate to the family's life stage and the ability of the family to deal with particular kinds of age appropriate life tasks.

These five areas, therefore, can be viewed as summary groupings of dimensions of family assessment. Because the field has been plagued by difficulties in linking dimensions so as to form some overall conceptual structure for family assessment, an ordering of these five categories of dimensions into a kind of hierarchy which will provide a conceptual link among them is needed.

An attempt in this direction is presented in Table 14-III where the five areas are ordered by two levels into a linkage system. The underlying premise is that Level A variables provide the context for the understanding of Level B variables. Cultural influences, broadly defined, provide the major background against which the family is viewed. Indeed, most clinic intake forms yield information which describes social class, race, heritage, urban versus rural or suburban setting, and so forth, in an effort to place the family into some contextual matrix and to understand these factors in light of their origin.

The second major contextual variable designated in Level A relates to the developmental stage of the family. Several authors (Grunebaum & Bryant, 1966; Haley, 1971; Solomon, 1973; Worby, 1971) have suggested an epigenetic, family stage, or developmental family task model for viewing family psychopathology. Briefly, families are seen as going through a series of developmental stages, each posing a specific family task and each creating a family crisis. The successful completion of each stage forces a rearrangement of certain major cultural aspects of the family. For example, the birth of a child into a newlywed family adds a series of new roles and responsibilities, just as the emergence of a child into adolescence requires a re-working of boundaries and rules of extra-familial contact.

The passing of the family from one stage to the next also requires an alteration in the kinds of sanctions and controls a family uses to maintain its normative structure. Families with older and younger children are forced to provide variable sanctions appropriate to the child's age. Families with adolescent children may find their norms and rules for behavior challenged openly and a successful adaptation to these demands is needed for developmental progress to be maintained.

Last, each stage can force an alteration in the effective tone of the

TABLE 14-III		
A Hierachy of Assessment Dimensions		
Level A	Cultural Aspects (IV)	
	Developmental Aspects (V)	
Level B	Structural Descriptors (I)	Controls & Sanctions (II)	Emotions & Needs (III)

family as a whole and the satisfaction of needs in individual family members. The menopausal woman, the retiring breadwinner, and the family with its first child leaving the nest are examples of how changes in development affect family climate. Also, a family's ability to satisfy needs varies in kind and intensity over time. Some families can handle the need for autonomy in adolescent children easier than they can the need for support and succorance in young children. For other families, the situation can be reversed.

Level B variables, then are clearly effected by the more static aspects of cultural demands and the more dynamic and continuously changing pressures of development through the life cycle. Perhaps the three Level B dimensions can serve as a framework for family assessment taken within the context of cultural background and developmental stage. In other words, Level A variables may provide a base line or a conceptual starting point against which the continuously changing Level B variables can be assessed. It is suggested that such an approach might provide a clinical strategy and a conceptual tool for family assessment.

CONCLUSIONS

In terms of directions for the future, several points can be made. First, the variety of orientations to family evaluation has led to an extensive list of assessment dimensions which often are not clearly related to each other theoretically or methodologically. The conceptual model presented above is an attempt to clarify this situation. It would appear, however, that future work should center more directly on the relationships among assessment dimensions rather than on the establishment of additional indices.

Second, many authors report on the development of rating scales and factorially derived evaluative procedures which demonstrate reasonable reliability and outcome usefulness. Unfortunately, there has been as yet no attempt to compare these scales on a variety of populations in different clinical settings. What has emerged, therefore, are several clinical scales with little generalizability across setting or clinical population. Many of these scales have demonstrated substantial usefulness as clinical instruments, and it is suggested that it might be wise in the short run to utilize these existing procedures more broadly, rather than creating additional scales which will most likely assess similar areas of family functioning.

Last, the clearer description and assessment of relevant dimensions should ultimately lead to the beginning of a meaningful family diagnostic system. Several of the articles reviewed in this paper suggest diagnostic groupings based upon rather general and diffuse assessment dimensions. The danger here is that in the rush to establish a nosological framework, we need to be careful to construct a reproducible and well defined support system made up of scaleable dimensions that have clinical usefulness.

REFERENCES

Ackerman, N.W. The diagnosis of neurotic marital interaction. *Social Casework*, 1954, *35*, 139-147.

Ackerman, N.W., & Behrens, M.L. Family diagnosis and clinical process. In S. Arieti (Ed.), *American handbook of psychiatry, Vol. II*, New York: Basic Books, 1974.

Camp, H. Structural family therapy: An outsider's perspective. *Family Process*, 1973, *12*, 269-277.

Chagoya, L., & Guttman, H. A guide to assess family functioning. Unpublished manuscript, 1971.

Ehrenwald, J. Neurotic interaction and patterns of pseudo-heredity in the family. *American Journal of Psychiatry*, 1958, *115*, 134-142.

Ehrenwald, J. Family diagnosis and mechanisms of psychosocial defense. *Family Process*, 1952, *2*, 121-130.

Ehrenwald, J. *Neurosis in the family and patterns of psychosocial defense.* New York: Harper & Row, 1963.

Epstein, N.B., Sigal, J.J., & Rakoff, V. Family categories schema. Unpublished manuscript, 1968.

Family Diagnosis and Treatment Committee. *Casebook on family diagnosis and treatment.* New York: Family Service Association of America, 1965.

Fine, S. Troubled families: Parameters for diagnosis and strategies for change. *Comprehensive Psychiatry*, 1974, *15*, 73-77.

Fisher, L. & Rubenstein, G. The assessment of competence in children at high risk for schizophrenia. Unpublished manuscript, 1975.

Gehrke, S., & Moxon, J. Diagnostic classification and treatment techniques in marriage counseling. *Family Process*, 1962, *1*, 253-264.

Group for the Advancement of Psychiatry. *The case history method in the study of family process*, 1970, *6*, No. 76.

Grunebaum, H., & Bryant, C. The theory and practice of the family diagnostic: Theoretical aspects and resident education. *Psychiatric Research Reports*, 1966, *20*, 150-162.

Grunebaum, H., Christ, J., & Neiberg, N. Diagnosis and treatment planning for couples. *International Journal of Group Psychotherapy*, 1969, *19*, 185-202.

Haley, J. A review of the family therapy field. In J. Haley (Ed.), *Changing families: A family therapy reader.* New York: Grune & Stratton, 1971.

Hammerlynck, L.A., Handy, L.C., & Mach, E.J. *Behavioral change: Methodology, concepts, and practice.* Champaign, IL: Research Press, 1973.

Handel, G. Psychological study of whole families. *Psychological Bulletin*, 1965, *63*, 19-41.

Hess, R.D., & Handel G. *Family worlds: A psychosocial approach to family life.* Chicago: University of Chicago Press, 1959.

Hill, R. Payoffs and limitations of contemporary strategies for family theory systematization. Paper presented to National Council on Family Relations, Estes Park, Colorado, 1971.

Hill, R., & Hansen, D.A., The identification of conceptual frameworks utilized in family study. *Marriage and Family Living*, 1960, *22*, 299-312.

Kadushin, T. Toward a family diagnostic system. *Family Coordinator*, 1971,

20, 279-289.

Kluckholn, F.R. Family diagnosis: I. Variations in the basic value of family systems. *Social Casework*, 1958, *39*, 63-72.

Knox, D. *Marriage happiness: A behavioral approach to counseling*. Champaign, IL: Research Press, 1971.

Leik, R.K., & Northwood, L.K. The classification of family interaction problems for treatment purposes. *Journal of Marriage and the Family*, 1964, *26*, 288-294.

Liberman, R.P. Behavioral approaches to family and couple therapy. In C.J. Sager and H.S. Kaplan (Eds.), *Progress in group and family therapy*, Cambridge: Harvard University Press, 1974.

Minuchin, S. *Families and family therapy*. Cambridge: Harvard University Press, 1974.

Otto, H. The personal and family resource development programmes: A preliminary report. *International Journal of Social Psychiatry*, 1962, *2*, 329-338.

Patterson, G.R. *Families*. Champaign, IL: Research Press, 1971.

Pollak, O. Issues in family diagnosis and family therapy. *Journal of Marriage and the Family*, 1964, *26*, 279-287.

Pollak, O., & Brieland, D. The midwest seminar on family diagnosis and treatment. *Social Casework*, 1961, *42*, 319-324.

Ravich, R.A., Duetsch, M., & Brown, B. An experimental study of marital discord and decision-making. *Psychiatric Research Reports*, 1965, *10*, 19-94.

Riskin, J.M., & Faunce, E.E. An evaluative review of family interaction research. *Family Process*, 1972, *11*, 365-456.

Ryder, R.G., & Goodrich, D.W. Married couples responses to disagreement. *Family Process*, 1966, *5*, 30-42.

Scherz, F.H. Exploring the use of family interviews in diagnosis. *Social Casework*, 1965, *45*, 209-215.

Schreiber, L.E. Evaluation of family group treatment in a family agency. *Family Process*, 1966, *5*, 21-29.

Solomon, M.A. A developmental, conceptual premise for family therapy. *Family Process*, 1973, *12*, 179-196.

Stuart, R.B. *Marital pre-counseling inventory and marital precounseling inventory counselors guide*. Champaign, IL: Research Press, 1973.

Titcher, J., & Emerson, R. Some methods for the study of family interaction and personality development. *Psychiatric Research Reports*, 1958, *72*, 72-88.

Watzlawick, P. A structured family interview. *Family Process*, 1965, *5*, 256-271.

Weiss, V.W., & Monroe, R.R. The framework for understanding family dynamics: Part I. *Social Casework*, 1959, *40*, 3-8.

Wells, C.F., & Rabiner, E.L. The conjoint family diagnostic interview and the family index of tension. *Family Process*, 1973, *12*, 127-144.

Winter, W.D., & Ferreira, A.J. A factor analysis of family interaction measures. *Journal Projective Techniques and Personality Assessment*, 1970, *34*, 55-63.

Worby, C. The family life cycle: An orienting concept for the family practice specialist. *Journal of Medical Education*, 1971, *46*, 198-203.

Zelditch, M., Jr., Family, marriage and kinship, In R.E.L. Faris (Ed.). *Handbook of modern sociology*. Chicago: Rand McNally, 1964.

Chapter 15

APPLICATION OF A CYCLICAL DIAGNOSTIC MODEL WITH FAMILIES

JAMES C. HANSEN AND BONNIE S. HIMES

Although diagnostic procedures take up considerable time in the usual therapeutic setting, traditional diagnosis is generally abandoned when family therapy is introduced (Haley, 1975). Diagnostic categorization of a family member is not productive and can handicap the therapist's thinking about therapeutic intervention. Even so, to develop an intervention strategy, the therapist must understand the family members. As the whole family interacts, the therapist strives to understand the individuals and their interactions. This article discusses the application of a conceptual model that has helped us understand families, that is, diagnose family interactions.

Walton (1969) proposed a cyclical diagnostic model pertaining to third party consultation between two people having conflicts in an industrial interaction. Marriage and family problems are essentially interpersonal conflicts and this model can be helpful in understanding the people and that situation.

Figure 15-I suggests that the family may occasionally engage in an overt conflict and at other times the issues will represent only a covert conflict. Something occurs that triggers opposition between the people and they engage in conflict relevant behaviors. They experience the consequence of their interchange and then the conflict between them becomes covert again.

Interpersonal conflicts tend to be dynamic and may escalate or deescalate from one cycle to the next. The figure shows that if the people do not understand the problem and resolve it, the conflict may go on and be repeated. As the figure suggests, to diagnose a family situation, the therapist must search for the issues involved in the problem, the triggering event which sets off the conflict, the interpersonal conflict behaviors, and the outcomes or consequences of the conflict. We can closely examine each phase of this model as it applies to a family.

From J. Hansen and B. Himes, Application of a Cyclical Diagnostic Model with Families, *Family Therapy*, 6:101-107, 1979. Courtesy of Libra Publishers, Inc.

Figure 15-I

A Cyclical Diagnostic Model

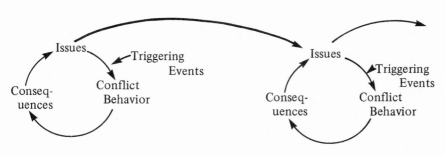

Incident 1   Incident 2

A mother brought her fourteen-year-old son for counseling. The presented problem was the son's effeminate behavior and his poor relationships within the family. The intake interview yielded the following description of the family.

The father was 45 years old and maintained an unsatisfying and low paying job as a salesman. He did not relate well to any of the sons and behaved differentially to them. The marital relationship was not happy and there was considerable arguing between husband and wife. The wife was 41, enjoyed maintaining a home, but also maintained a satisfying job with a substantial income. The sons had felt close to her but she had some difficulty with discipline.

The oldest son, 18, was just graduated from high school and had turned down an opportunity to go away to college. He was bright, aggressive, and bossy with peers and adults alike. He seemed to identify with his father. The middle son, 16, was quiet, reserved and passive-aggressive in behavior. He played a neutral position with parents and rejected both brothers. The youngest son, 14, had immature and feminine behaviors. He was passive and seemed to identify with his mother. He was frequently picked on by his brothers. Considerable fighting, verbal and physical, occurred among the siblings.

A decision was made to see the family together to gain a better perspective regarding their interaction and the problem situation. Application of the cyclical model assisted in understanding the family.

Triggering Events

According to the figure, the issues which cause problems between people can and do exist as covert conflict for periods of time. This latent period is maintained by barriers to overt conflict but there are circumstances which can precipitate open conflict. Frequently one family member will begin presenting a problem by describing the precipitant event and then describe the conflict behaviors between himself and another. Understanding the triggering events and conflict behaviors help the therapist and family come to understand the real issues in the conflict situation.

Various barriers can prevent a person from initiating or reacting to a triggering situation. A person may be inhibited from confronting the situation or another person by internal forces such as his own attitudes, values, needs, fears or habitual behaviors, perceptions of other's vulnerability or his/her own vulnerability. Despite these barriers, some events or circumstances can precipitate open conflict. With the underlying issue always present, a vigorous disagreement, problem solving interchange or candid confrontation may serve as a triggering event to break through the barriers and establish conflict behaviors.

With the family seen in family therapy we noted a routine set of triggering events which evolved around the father's behaviors. It was often the father's demanding, domineering attitude and inconsistent behaviors which triggered conflicts with the other members of the family. The father's attitude that he was boss and everything had to go his way clearly triggered the mother's exasperation which would eventually be ventilated. In some cases the father became involved in activities with his sons but became frustrated when they did not perform as he instructed them. At times the father's plans with the family fell through because he was late, thus disappointing and/or upsetting several members of the family. Most of the time the very presence of the father in the home was enough to trigger conflict in the youngest son. The father was particularly critical of that son's behavior. Events which triggered conflicts for the father occurred when anyone did not behave the way he wanted.

It is important to understand the types of barriers that are customarily used and what triggers the open conflict. This level of understanding can be used in several ways to handle the conflict. *First,* each individual can learn to manage the conflict if he/she understands the barriers he/she and the other individual uses as well as what triggers the conflict. One is better able to choose the right time and place as well as an appropriate issue for dealing with the conflict. If the preference is to avoid an open conflict, at least temporarily, one can take steps to bolster the barriers and head off triggering events. *Second,* an analysis of the events which surround and precede a conflict may provide cues regarding the primary issues in a recurring conflict. *Third,* the frequency of conflict may be controlled by operating on the barriers or triggering events.

Each member of the family handled these triggering events in different ways. Barriers were frequently used to keep conflict from occurring or continuing. The father's presence stimulated conflict in the youngest son. In order to avoid this conflict the son attempted to stay away from his father. Most of his interaction occurred with his mother. He frequently encouraged her to plan things without the father.

The middle son felt a great deal of disappointment when his father didn't keep his word. This position was one of neutrality so he did not express his negative feelings toward his father or reveal them to his mother.

We found the oldest son identifying with the father, agreeing with him and taking his side. This served as a barrier to the conflicting feelings felt for the father. At the same time, the son hassled the mother regarding her behaviors and attitudes. He also assumed a domineering attitude with the other brothers, which of course triggered conflicts among the brothers.

The mother attempted a quiet position of understanding and support. She agreed with the father and obliged him until she could no longer contain her resentment, anger and hostility.

The father used his position of dominant figure in the family as his primary barrier. He argued with each member and expected resolution on his terms. He expected everyone to understand and accept his position. At times, when the resolution did not occur as smoothly as he anticipated, he would leave the house.

Conflict Behavior

Conflict behaviors involve the tactics used as well as the resolution overtures. The conflict tactics may include expressions of feelings as anger, attack, or avoidance and rejection. The behaviors also include competitive strategies intended to win the conflict such as blocking, interrupting, depreciating others, forming alliances, and out-maneuvering the other. These are sometimes demonstrated by arguing in front of neutral individuals, criticizing the other person, blaming the other person for the problem, challenging that person's judgment, and forming an alliance with someone in a superior position.

Another part of the conflict behaviors includes the overtures toward a resolution. These involve cooperative strategies intended to end the conflict such as a search for integrated solutions. These behaviors include agreeing to meet, listening to the other side, expressing regret about the difficulty and acknowledging fault.

The diagnostic aspect of the conflict behaviors involves helping each member understand his own feelings and behaviors when the conflict comes into the open as well as developing an understanding of the other person's feelings and behaviors. This approach to diagnosis contributes to insight into oneself and others in family interactions and can lead to behavior change.

The members of the family seen in family therapy presented varying forms of conflict behavior. The youngest son frequently bore the brunt of verbal assaults. The other members of the family teased him, joked about him and picked on him. These behaviors were often instigated by him or prefaced by childlike behaviors such as giggling, loud talking, joking about himself and nervous body movements in close contact with another person. Any alliance formed was with his mother.

The middle son maintained a neutral position between the parents. At times he responded to his mother's upset behavior by defending his father's behavior in an effort to create a superficial balance. When hassled by the oldest son he responded with verbal or physical fighting.

The oldest son displayed aggressive conflict behaviors with most of the members of his family. He argued with his mother and refused to follow her directions or respond to her disciplinary approaches. He wrestled and fought with both of his brothers. He often blamed and criticized others' behaviors, rejecting them and praising himself. He made a place for himself in the family that prevented anyone from feeling comfortable with him.

At the time when the mother could no longer tolerate the tension or contain her feelings, she exhibited overt conflict behaviors. She became upset, yelled, threw objects, and slammed doors. These most often ended in crying and rejecting of the family member(s). The mother was the only one who genuinely made offers of resolution. She tried to resolve conflicts with the father and between the boys.

The father became annoyed, impatient and frustrated when things were not done the way he preferred. He yelled insults, made demands and rejected another's position. He often challenged the judgments of other members of the family. His response to tension and lack of control was threats of leaving.

Consequences

The therapist and family members must understand the consequences of the conflict. They need to be aware of the potential costs and benefits of conflict which affect each member of the family. An appreciation of the magnitude of the costs and benefits is essential. Does the risk of improvement justify the risk in trying? An analysis of the particular consequences of a recurrent conflict will provide an understanding of why the conflict is escalating or de-escalating.

The most apparent consequence was the scapegoating of the youngest son. Everyone dumped on him and he had learned to act accordingly. The other sons were constantly on edge, concerned about hassles with parents and yet hassling each other. The mother's behavior gave only temporary relief. Her anger and rejection of others soon left her guilt-ridden. This led to her offers for resolution. The father wanted to be perceived by the family as the dominant figure with the ultimate authority. He tried to present the image of a strong, adequate man. However, the family did not accept or respect his behavior. The overall consequences for the family was the lack of resolution and continued overt and covert periods of conflict.

Issues

A major distinction is made between substantive and emotional conflicts. Substantive issues involve disagreements over politics, practices, and rules while emotional issues involve negative feelings between the individuals. Substantive issues are basically cognitive while emotional conflicts are effective. The family and therapist should not focus on one aspect of an issue while ignoring the other. Issues of conflict between an adolescent and his/her parents regarding rules and regulations of behavior may appear to be substantive; however, there may be emotional issues as well.

Diagnosing the conflicts requires a discrimination between issues which are basic and those which are merely symptomatic, representing a proliferation of the primary issues. A person may inject a second or substitute issue into a conflict because it provides a more socially acceptable issue for a conflict. A primary issue sometimes risks so much embarrassment for one or both individuals that they use a symptomatic issue for the conflict which only reflects the basic issue. In some cases the eventual resolution of the symptomatic issue may lead to a resolution of the primary issue as well.

When the issues are defined, there is a better understanding by the individuals in the situation. Substantive conflicts require bargaining and problem solving among the family members. Emotional conflicts require a restructuring of one or more of the individual's perceptions and then working through the feelings between the individuals involved.

Until the family entered therapy only the mother had a hint of understanding of the central issues. There was such a proliferation of issues, it was difficult to find a resolution.

The basic issue involved the father's insecurity regarding his job. His work had provided a major part of his positive self-concept; but as the job deteriorated, so did his self-concept. In addition, the job was a source of insecurity in his relationship with his wife who was earning considerably more money. The pressure the father felt from raising three teenaged sons was increased when the sons gave him a hard time or did not meet his standards. The youngest son, who displayed immature and feminine behaviors, presented particular problems for him because his behavior reflected on him and threatened his own masculinity.

The father wished to maintain the role of the aggressive, dominant man which triggered conflict in the family and resulted in withdrawal or alienation in some form. He was not successful in achieving this position for himself with his family. The consequences were increased insecurity about his masculine image.

An understanding and appreciation of the issues involved can enable the family and therapist to identify outcomes that are desirable and realistic and map strategies for achieving such outcomes. Unless diagnosis leads to a plan for change, it is irrelevant. This model suggests that the basic issue is affective and will involve the father gaining self insight and restructuring his behavior accordingly. Some of this may be done individually as well as in the family sessions. The process will take some time, though some substantive issues can be handled immediately. The therapist can assist the family members to negotiate and evolve problem solving policies, practices and rules in the home that can improve the way they relate to each other. Change is predicated on the degree to which the members can be helped to alter their disordered interactions by changing those aspects of their thinking, feeling, and acting that are contributing to the family's dysfunctioning.

REFERENCES

Haley, J. "Why a Mental Health Clinic Should Avoid Family Therapy," *Journal of Marriage and Family Counseling*, 1975, Vol. 1, No. 1, Pp. 3-13.
Walton, R. *Interpersonal Peacemaking: Confrontations and Third-Party Consultation.* Reading, Massachusetts: Addison-Wesley, 1969.

Chapter 16

ECOSYSTEMIC EPISTEMOLOGY: AN ALTERNATIVE PARADIGM FOR DIAGNOSIS

BRADFORD P. KEENEY

The shift in therapeutic focus from isolated individual monads to ecological relationship systems has resulted in the need for an appropriate diagnostic paradigm. Although there are expanding networks of clinical literature related to diagnosis in family therapy, "there is no widely accepted conceptual scheme for family diagnosis in a formal sense" (16, p. 224). This paper attempts to mark a beginning in establishing a theoretical framework for diagnosis that resonates with the ecological and systems approach to therapy. Traditionally, clinical diagnosis has been tied to the process of ascribing a label to an individual in order to signify the particular pathology and class of symptoms exhibited. The argument of systems-oriented therapists, particularly Jackson (27), is that psychiatric nomenclature is inseparable from the underlying assumption that an individual is the receptor of lineal causal effects and hence the site of pathology. Furthermore, this nonsystemic perspective may hinder the process of inducing change in any relationship system.

This paper argues that diagnosis must be reframed in order to avoid the "diagnostic impasse" that grips family therapists who identify diagnosis with the psychiatric medical model. An attempt is made to place diagnosis within the paradigm represented by the ideas of cybernetics, ecology, and systems theory. This alternative paradigm for diagnosis is tagged "ecosystemic epistemology."

DIAGNOSIS AND EPISTEMOLOGY

The etymological meaning of diagnosis is literally "to know" (43). From this meaning it follows that anytime a therapist strives to know about a given problematic situation, that person can be characterized as

From B. Keeney, Ecosystemic Epistemology: An Alternative Paradigm for Diagnosis, *Family Process*, *18*:117-29, 1979. Courtesy of *Family Process*.

"diagnosing." Minuchin (37) has appropriately noted, "any type of diagnosis is merely a way of arranging data" (pp. 131-132).

In the epilogue of his book *Naven*, Bateson (4, p. 281) depicts his work as a "weaving of three levels of abstraction." He depicts the most concrete level to be the ethnographic data, a more abstract level as the arranging of the data to create "various pictures of the culture," and the still more abstract "self-conscious discussion of the procedures by which the pieces of the jigsaw are put together." Diagnosis can also be viewed as a process of weaving several levels of abstraction. One begins with the observed data, then on a more abstract level creates various maps or descriptions of the situation, and then on a still more abstract level arranges the data in a particular way.

The last level of abstraction is within the realm of epistemology that Auerswald (2) defines as "how a person or a group of persons processes information" (p. 684). Accordingly, one's epistemology leads to a particular way of arranging observed data, i.e., diagnosing. Auerswald (2) has noted that although different therapists may seem to seek the same information and behave in similar ways, what is not observable is that "the information extracted is being ordered differently according to the epistemological base in use by the clinician" (pp. 699-700).

All therapists diagnose in accordance with their form of epistemology. A therapist cannot *not* have an epistemology. Bateson (13) elaborates this point.

> All descriptions are based on theories of how to make descriptions. You cannot claim to have no epistemology. Those who so claim have nothing but a bad epistemology. And every description is based upon, and contains implicitly, a theory of how to describe. [13, p. 147]

Thus, whether or not a therapist is conscious of his epistemological base, his descriptions or maps of the problematic situation contain an implicit epistemology. Auerswald (2, p. 699) has divided family therapists into three classes according to their epistemological point of view: (a) those who follow "traditional linear epistemology"; (b) those who follow an "ecological epistemology"; and (c) those who are in transition from the former to the latter.

Traditional linear epistemology is exemplified by psychiatric nomenclature and the classical medical model of psychopathology. It is depicted as atomistic, reductionistic, and anticontextual and follows an analytical logic concerned with combinations of discrete elements. Ecological epistemology, or what Wilden (55, p. 274) more specifically terms "ecosystemic epistemology,"[1] emphasizes ecology, relationship and whole systems. In contrast to linear epistemology, it attunes itself to interrelation, complexity, and context.

---

[1] Wilden's "ecosystemic epistemology" is also similar to what Bateson (12, 14) loosely calls "double bind epistemology."

Ecosystemic epistemology can now be defined for diagnosis as a way of knowing problematic situations through the epistemological framework or paradigm representing cybernetics, ecology, and systems theory. The therapist who desires to intervene in an ecological and systemic fashion must see and know situations in an ecosystemic way. Diagnosis based on ecosystemic epistemology refers to such a way of seeing and knowing.

FOUNDATIONS OF AN ECOSYSTEMIC EPISTEMOLOGY FOR DIAGNOSIS

Several issues must be addressed before we can go beyond the problems and confusion associated with traditional linear epistemology. In addition, some basic theoretical statements concerning ecosystemic epistemology as it pertains to the process of diagnosis will be delineated. They initiate steps toward an alternative paradigm for diagnosis grounded in cybernetics, ecology, and systems theory.

The Meaning of System

Historically, family therapists and theorists have been troubled by how to view systems conceptually. Much theoretical controversy has centered on determining the appropriate "system level" to study, diagnose, and treat.[2] "System levels," however, are referred to by such terms as individual, dyad, family and social network. These terms do not arise from the vocabulary of systems theory but are linguistic markers for levels of social organization.

Observing social units larger than the individual does not necessarily mean one is viewing a system; i.e., "system" isn't equivalent to "social organization." It is possible for one to observe a family and never see the family system. On the other hand, one can view an individual as a system. Accordingly, Wynne (56) has objected to any individual-family dichotomy and suggests that systems theory should be "based upon the principal of *open linked* systems, in which two (but not the only two) systems which can be linked are individual personality systems and family systems" (p. 154).

Issues over appropriate level(s) of system or social organization often obscure the more basic problem of whether one is utilizing a linear or ecosystemic epistemology. Seeing systems is a function of one's epistemology. An epistemology based on systems theory enables one to order the phenomenal field so that "systems" can be identified.

Confusion arises when one thinks linearly and still attempts to

---

[2]See Wertheim (51) for a historical review of this controversy. Also, Keeney and Cromwell (31, 32) have dealt specifically with the issue of "system levels" as it pertains to family diagnosis.

identify and explicate a relationship system. For example, when one considers a relationship system as a combination of discrete properties (e.g., roles, values, and motivations), one is using a linear, non-ecosystemic epistemology. This is exemplified by therapists who claim to derive diagnoses of whole families through assessing individual family members. The systems axiom of nonsummativity asserts that diagnostic information obtained from isolated parts of the system cannot be summed to represent the whole system.

The meaning of "system" that arises from ecosystemic epistemology diminishes issues concerned with the levels of system or social organization. As Bateson (8) put it, "the polarization of opinion then will not be simply between practitioners of individual therapy and practitioners of family therapy but between those who think in terms of systems and those who think in terms of lineal sequences of cause and effect" (p. 243). Perhaps the tendency of such therapists as Haley (23) and Watzlawick (50) to deemphasize "family" when describing their recent work reflects their primary concern with epistemological shifts.

Ecosystemic epistemology defines "system" as a *cybernetic network that processes information*, or as Bateson (8) puts it, "any unit containing feedback structure and therefore competent to process information" (p. 243). The therapeutic situation can be seen as a system. For this system, the cybernetic network refers to the context of complexly intertwined human relationships in which the relevant information processed includes symptomatic and therapeutic communications. This type of system is referred to as an *ecological relationship system*.

The use of nouns describing the therapeutic system (e.g., "therapist," "family," and "symptom") implies a linear epistemology based on metaphors of substance. Ecosystemic epistemology, on the other hand, is concerned with patterns of relationship that are described by metaphors of form and pattern. Watts (48, p. 17) suggested that we come to see "substantive nouns" and "things" instead of "processual verbs" and "patterns of relationship" because of the limitations of our senses or our instruments to discriminate highly complex patterns.

Hence, when we encounter sufficient complexity (e.g., networks of human relationship), our sensory limitations lead us to committing what Whitehead (54) called "the fallacy of misplaced concreteness." Bateson (10) is correct in noticing that when we use a linear epistemology "we abstract from relationship and from the experiences of interaction to create 'objects' and to endow them with characteristics" (pp. XV-XVI). Ecosystemic epistemology requires that we undo these substantive abstractions and begin seeing patterns of relationship.[3]

---

[3]Along these lines, the cybernetician Anatol Holt (cited in 15, p. 63) created the idea for a bumper sticker that would read: HELP STAMP OUT NOUNS.

For the therapist, the ecological relationship system necessarily includes what has been traditionally called the identified patient, symptom, therapist, and larger social context. Ecosystemic epistemology reframes these descriptions in terms of information and relationship. The "patient's symptom" and the therapist's interventions" are seen as communications in an informational network of human relationships.

What becomes critical in diagnosis is knowing how the cybernetic network is interlinked or structured. This idea follows the basic rule of systems theory described by Bateson (8): "If you want to understand some phenomenon or appearance, you must consider that phenomenon within the context of all *completed* circuits which are relevant to it" (p. 244). The "relevant completed circuits" for the therapist refer to the network of complexly intertwined human relationships in which symptomatic communication has a function. When this network is identified, therapeutic communications can be issued that attempt to restructure the network. An appropriate restructuring of the network results in the alleviation of symptomatic communication.

The Symptom's Presence in the System

A major contribution of the family therapy movement has been the observation that symptoms are inextricably a part of relationship systems such that the site and nature of symptom manifestation may shift. Generalizations that have been made include:

1. Difficulties in any part of the relationship system may give rise to symptomatic expression in other parts of the system.
2. Symptomatic relief at one part of the system may result in a transfer of symptomatic expression to another site.
3. Significant change, e.g., second-order change as Watzlawick et al. (50) call it, in any part of the system may result in change in other parts of the system—what Speck (44) has called "ripple effects."

These principles from family therapy suggest that symptoms be viewed as relationship metaphors—communications about relationship. The major implication for the therapist is the s/he should look for the communicative function of symptoms within an ecological relationship system. When a symptom is viewed as a communicative function, it becomes an indicator or sign for the ecology of relationships.

This view of the symptom's presence in the system has been exemplified by Haley's work. For example, he has described a woman with a "real" pain in the neck that has no organic cause as a wife who is metaphorically giving her opinion of her interpersonal situation (23, p. 95). For the somatic metaphor to change, the woman's situation must change. If she is relieved of symptomatic expression and the situation remains the same, someone else in that situation may begin symptomatic communication. In this sense, the goal of therapy becomes changing the ecological relationship system so that the metaphors of relationship change.

On the other hand, to view a symptom in terms of its etiology and pathology (i.e., through linear epistemology) is to reify the relationship metaphor. As Watzlawick et al. (49, p. 22) warn, "a monadic view of man" inevitably leads to a "reification of what now reveal themselves more and more as complex patterns of relationship and interaction." The reification of symptoms perpetuates the myth of their having exclusive substantive locus within the boundaries of individuals.

The cybernetic network representing a family system (not individuals within a family but patterns of relationship) includes governing loops or circuits that keep the system in check. These governing loops help to maintain family stability and have accordingly been called "homeostatic cycles" by Hoffman (24). When the homeostatic cycle serves to prevent a *necessary change* (e.g., during developmental transitions[4]), the family members can be seen as experiencing a problem.

According to Hoffman (24), this type of homeostatic cycle is what family therapists attempt to disrupt. She notes (p. 502) that "when experienced family therapists find this cycle, they direct an intervention toward it with the precision of a laser beam." This homeostatic cycle is seen as a cyclical sequence of behaviors that includes a piece of behavior tagged "irrational" or "symptomatic." Since the function of the cycle is to maintain homeostatis, "getting one element to change would only cause the other elements to readjust so that the outcome was the same."

When an ecological relationship system is described in cybernetic terms, the description depicts the symptom as a message in an interconnected relationship network with feedback structure. This form of interconnectedness allows for the symptomatic message to shift from various individual sites. As we've seen, the cybernetic loop of which the symptomatic message is a part can be described as having a homeostatic function. The obvious implication for the therapist is that he should diagnose and treat the relationship network rather than focus exclusively on any isolated part.

Perhaps the first formal diagnostic statement made by the therapist should be one of redefining the symptom/problem in interpersonal terms. This has the advantage of helping both the clients and therapist(s) to see the symptom as part of a relationship system rather than exclusively located within one individual.

A selection from one of Minuchin's (37) case studies exemplifies this redefining task:

> ... the diagnosis of Mr. Smith as an agitated, depressed individual gives the psychiatrists treating him limited directions for therapy and a poor prognosis. The family therapist's first, transitory diagnosis for Mr. and

---

[4]Milton Erickson's therapy, according to Haley, suggests the view that "the symptom is a signal that a family has difficulty in getting past a stage in the life cycle," (21, p. 42).

Mrs. Smith as an interacting couple is that Mrs. Smith is in need of Mr.
Smith's help in overcoming her sexual problem. [37, p. 132]
In this example, Minuchin changed the problem site from Mr. Smith to
Mrs. Smith and insisted that Mrs. Smith needed Mr. Smith's help. This
therapeutic maneuver uses a formal diagnostic statement to help both
the clients and therapist relate to the social context of symptomatic
communication.

The idea of seeing symptoms as communications about the ecological
condition of whole systems is not new. Some members of the American
Indian culture have long subscribed to an epistemology that sees
symptoms in this way (17). For example, when the Navaho medicine
man encounters an individual expressing a symptom, his choice of
action is to treat the whole tribe in order to bring it back into harmony.
In this way individuals are relieved of symptomatic discomfort through
treatment of the whole ecosystem.

The shift toward a more ecosystemic epistemology involves moving
away from blaming the identified patient for his idiosyncrasies and/or
blaming etiological factors for causing symptoms. Seeing symptoms as
metaphoric communications about the ecology of relationship systems
leads one to a stage of awareness Bateson (5) depicts as "humility" and
"loneliness." This "loneliness of liberation," as Watts (48) calls it, arises
when there is no longer any person, group, or etiological factor to blame
and be angry with.

The Therapist's Presence in the System

The work of Rosenthal (40) has repeatedly indicated the obtrusiveness
of the human investigator or observer. A dramatic example of the effect
of intervening into a system is provided by Halbert (cited in 34, p. 298),
who found that a single drop of blood taken from a mouse's tail disturbs
the animal's circadian rhythm of certain blood cells for several days. It
follows that therapists and their ways of diagnosing affect the systems
they are treating. As Bateson (cited in 18) put it, "The probe we stick into
human material always has another end which sticks into us" (p. 26).

This Heisenberg-like hook[5] between the observer and the observed
has led Rollo May (36) to state: "We don't study nature, we investigate
the investigator's relationship to nature." These ideas support Sullivan's
(45) notion that the therapist is always a part of the field being observed
in diagnosis. In view of this, Haley (20) has insisted that the "therapist
include himself in the description of a family" (p. 161). Ways of
describing the therapist's presence in the system he diagnoses and treats
will now be examined.

---

[5] Heisenberg's famous "Uncertainty Principle" states that the observer constantly alters
what he observes by the obtrusive act of observation.

The Therapist as "Power Broker"

The therapist's obtrusive presence in the system he treats is very often described by family therapists in terms of metaphors of "power." Whitaker speaks of gaining enough power to battle the family system, and Haley speaks of power and control games between therapist and client(s). This view of the therapist sees him as a kind of "power broker" who controls the ways in which power is distributed and used in the family. This form of description, however, overlooks an admonition from Bateson (9):

> In principle all metaphors derived from a physical world of impacts, forces, energy, etc., are unacceptable in explanations of events and processes in the biological world of information, purpose, context, organization and meaning. The 'power' metaphor . . . must be looked at, as a functioning falsehood or error, causing what pathologies? [9, p. 26]

Bateson has long viewed Haley's use of the metaphor of power as an epistemological error that is self-validating and potentially pathological. He recently stated, "Haley slides too lightly over the very real epistemological differences between himself and me. . . . I believed then—and today—that the *myth* of power always corrupts because it proposes always a false (though conventional) epistemology" (11, p. 106).

Haley has never adequately responded to Bateson's criticism. In a footnote concerning the development of double-bind theory he briefly refers to the issue.

> The issue of power and control was always a problem within the project. . . . I was trying at that time to shift observation of the individual to the observation of a system and to view a power struggle as a product of the needs of a system rather than the needs of a person. I still prefer that view. . . . [22, p. 78]

At the same time, Haley agrees with Bateson that to say that people "attempt control" over one another is "not a way of describing two individuals *relating*," but is "putting a 'need' into them as individuals" (p. 78).

Haley therefore implies a contradiction in logical types when he describes the presence of the therapist in the ecosystem. In other words, he resorts to using a metaphor from linear epistemology to describe relationship. Perhaps Haley's use of the metaphor of power arises from his depiction of the notion of "hierarchy." He (23) comments that "creatures that organize together form a status, or power ladder in which each creature has a place in the hierarchy with someone above him and someone below him" (p. 101). His conception of hierarchy is in terms of a *linear* progression of power levels.

Auerswald (3) suggests that the notion of hierarchy, which involves higher and lower levels, seems to be "a linguistic hangover from the Newtonian version of 'reality.'" Auerswald, along with contemporary cyberneticians, is implying that such framings of hierarchy arise from a non-ecosystemic epistemology. This supports Varela's (47) contention that if one looks at a system in a linear, hierarchical way, one cannot see the *whole* system.

Bateson (9) argues that the main criterion separating the metaphor "power" from ecosystemic epistemology involves the matter of transitivity—that more power will always be more powerful. However, this idea is anti-ecological. Ecological goods are often intransitive so that goods become toxic if they become greater than optimum (e.g., population, oxygen, protein, money).

We now suspect that our planet faces certain "points of no return" owing to social policy created through an epistemology containing "power" metaphors. What ecological pathologies are being caused by therapists who implement strategic action on relationship systems through an epistemology containing the metaphors of "power" and "control"? Bateson has continuously issued warnings in this regard.

The Therapist as an "Ecological Part"

Bateson (9) suggests that the metaphor of power be replaced by the ecological metaphor, *"part in an ecosystem."* A crucial individual in a system (e.g., therapist) is always a *part* of that system and "is therefore subject to all the constraints and necessities of the particular part-whole relationship in which he exists" (p. 27). This terminology describes the therapist's obtrusive presence in the ecosystem he treats as "part in" or "part of" rather than outside/spectator, manipulator, or power broker.

It is apparent now that if one examines systems through the linear idea of hierarchy one can impose linearly organized levels (e.g., levels of status or power). This approach, however, is not part of an ecosystemic epistemology, and attempts to describe a therapist's relation to the system he treats in terms of metaphors of power are fundamentally anti-ecological. On the other hand, if "whole systems" are examined through a strict ecosystemic epistemology, one sees interrelated ecological parts. From this perspective, the therapist is always seen as part and parcel of the system he diagnoses and treats.

Perhaps the most important idea in cybernetics and systems theory today is that mutual, reciprocal, simultaneous interactions define, identify, and constitute whole systems (see 25, 46, 47). This view follows the axiom of ecology and systems theory that all parts within a system simultaneously act on one another. For example, as the therapist acts on the identified patient, the identified patient acts on the therapist in simultaneous fashion. It is the *simultaneous interactions* between therapist and identified patient (and all other parts of the therapeutic situation) that characterize a whole system. In this interactional sense, the therapist is always a part of the system he attempts to diagnose and help change.

The therapeutic situation is therefore a whole system consisting of the simultaneous interactions of all parts. These simultaneous interactions self-referentially identify, define and constitute the whole system. This emphasis on "self-referential systems" has been called the "cybernetics of the second order" by von Foerster (25, 47)—not the cybernetics of observed systems, but the cybernetics of observing systems.

The idea that simultaneous interactions identify, define, and constitute whole systems has been stated by various theoreticians in different ways. Bateson (6), for example, depicts the simultaneous interactions between organism and environment as constituting the basic evolutionary unit. Pask's (39) theory of the p-individual sees the situation in which there is a teacher and a taught as one in which both have to learn simultaneously. Land (33) has responded in a similar way to the classical philosophical question—does the tree exist without the observer? He states that "the tree exists as part and parcel of the interaction between the part of the cosmos and our part of the cosmos, namely the 'We' which has evolved over many centuries to be a partner with the tree" (p. 9). In the case of therapy, we have argued that the therapist and identified patient interact simultaneously and that these simultaneous interactions constitute a whole system.

The major implication for diagnosis is that the therapist can come to know the properties of a whole system *only* by interacting with it. Varela (47, p. 28) suggests that "we interact with a system by poking at it, throwing things at it, and shouting at it and doing things like that, in various degrees of sophistication." These perturbations or constraints on the stability of a system result in the system either "compensating" or "not compensating."[6]

When a therapist interacts with a system such that the system compensates, the system can be said to have integrated the therapist as part of its previously structured relationship network—morphostasis or homeostasis is achieved. When the therapist's interactions with a system cannot be compensated, however, the system restructures its relationship network so that the therapist can be a part of a new pattern—change or morphogenesis is achieved. The goal of therapy is the establishment of new relationship networks within the ecological relationship system such that symptomatic communication is not necessary.

Along these lines, Haley (19) suggests that the family therapist is "interested in diagnosing how the family responds to his therapeutic interventions" (p. 282). Minuchin, (37, p. 131) calls this form of diagnosis "interactional diagnosis." As he notes: "Interactional diagnosis constantly changes as the family assimilates the therapist,

---

[6]We are using Varela's (47) terms "compensating" and "not compensating" to refer to what has been classically called "morphostatis" (stabilizing processes) and "morphogenesis" (change processes), respectively.

accommodates to him, and restructures, or resists restructuring interventions." The family system can either compensate or change in the course of these interactions with the therapist. Interactional diagnosis is equivalent to what Haley sees as "diagnosing how the family responds to therapeutic interventions." Interactional diagnosis therefore suggests that diagnosis and therapy are inseparable.

Watzlawick, et al. point out that there is a time factor limiting successful therapeutic intervention.

> It seems to be in the nature of human relationships that the therapist has a rather limited period of grace in which to accomplish this goal. Relatively soon the new system itself consolidates to the point where the therapist is almost inextricably caught in it and from then on is much less able to produce change. [49, p. 236]

This refers to the system's battle to compensate for the perturbations on the system that arise from the therapist's interactions. If the system's stability is compensated, the therapist becomes impotent.

For diagnosis and therapy, the whole system includes therapist, identified patient, symptom, and other components of the problematic situation in mutual, simultaneous interaction. This system is self-referential in that the simultaneous interactions identify, define, and constitute the system. Diagnosing or knowing the problematic situation can only occur through interacting with it. Furthermore, the way in which one interacts, and thereby becomes part of the system, determines whether change will occur.

The Ecological Relationship System in Diagnosis

The evolution of family diagnosis and therapy has been partly characterized by an expanding view of the identified patient's relational field—from partial families to whole families, intergenerational families, and extended social networks. Jackson and Satir (28) referred to this as "horizontal expansion," in which "more members have been included, more cultures and more socioeconomic data" (p. 267). This expansion reflects the idea that the individual who is symptomatic represents the apex of a particular relationship system. In effect, the expanding relational field of the identified patient has reframed the symptom from being contained within the boundaries of an individual's skin to being a part of a larger social context.

Besides this "horizontal expansion," there has been an expanding awareness of the therapist's own relational field. The relational field of the therapist includes his professional network (e.g., colleagues and institutions) as well as his family and neighborhood. Auerswald's "intersystems conference" (1,2), Speck and Attneave's "network intervention team" (44), Selvini Palazzoli's team of therapists (42), and Whitaker's use of cotherapists (53) demonstrate the design and use of specific forms of elaborated therapeutic networks. Particularly interesting is Selvini Palazzoli's team of therapists who are principally concerned with shifting from a linear to an ecosystemic epistemology and use one another to correct epistemological errors. We could call these examples of expanding the therapist's relational field another form of horizontal expansion.

The ecological relationship system that emerges in the process of diagnosis can be seen as the interweaving of two major relational fields whose nodal points are represented by the "identified patient" and "identified therapist." The term "identified therapist" is used to imply that the role of therapist can be as flexible and indeterminate as the role of identified patient.

Whitaker's rationale for using cotherapy asserts that the therapist needs this form of flexibility. Cotherapy helps the therapist to alternate between the relational fields of the family and the therapist. More specifically, it allows for one therapist to act as a sort of lifeguard for the other therapist who may otherwise drown while exploring the sea of family patterns. Whitaker (53) maintains that the therapist must join the family and experience himself as part of that system in order to adequately know the relationship system he treats. This is similar to Minuchin's (37, p. 134) "interactional diagnosis" in which the "therapist's data and his diagnoses are achieved experientially in the process of joining the family."

The experience of oneself as part of the system one wishes to know is what Maslow (35) describes as "becoming and *being* what is to be known" (p. 50). Maslow identifies the consequence of this type of experiential knowledge for the therapist as the "ability to inflict pain without fear, without guilt, without conflict or ambivalence" (p. 59). A tenet of Whitaker's approach to therapy is that this form of experiential knowledge leads to decisive and effective action.

The diagnostic situation is therefore an ecological relationship system that is another form of the self-referential systems described above. In other words, the *simultaneous interactions* between therapist, identified patient, and other components of the relational fields identify, describe, and constitute the ecological relationship system. The two relational fields can thus be seen as two patterns that interact to create a new pattern or whole system.

This view of the intertwining relational fields of the therapist and identified patient are comparable to moire patterns where two independent patterns interact to create an emergent new pattern. Bateson's (30) latest thinking has been concerned with such interweavings: "My hunch is that if you walk around with pattern A and you encounter pattern B all you get is your pattern A and a hybrid of A and B. You never see B" (p. 28).

If Bateson's hunch is accurate and comparable to the intertwining relational patterns of therapist and identified patient, then definite implications ensue for diagnosis. The therapist and the identified patient know directly only their own relational fields and the hybrid of the two relational fields. Thus, it is in the hybrid field—what is analogous to the moire pattern—where both therapist and identified patient meet. This hybrid relationship network constitutes what we have called the ecological relationship system in diagnosis.

The Relation Between Ecosystemic Epistemology and the Process of Diagnosis

Diagnosis can now be seen as how one comes to know the ecological relationship system that emerges in the process of diagnosing—what Maslow (35) termed "Being-cognition" . . . "being what is known." This way of diagnosing is Taoistic—one does not purposively seek information in any strict programmed format, but one becomes receptive to the experience. In other words, the experience happens instead of being made to happen. Maslow (35) describes "Taoistic knowing" as a "receptive openness . . . a finding of order rather than an ordering" (p. 98). This way of diagnosing or knowing shifts constantly and does not constitute a separate component of the therapeutic process. Minuchin (37, p. 131) calls this an "evolving diagnosis related to the context," whereby "diagnosis and therapy become inseparable."

In his essay "The Hindrance of Theory in Clinical Work," Whitaker (52) argues that theories get in the way of "Being" or Taoistic knowing. What he means by "theory" is a set of systematic procedures regarding how to think and *do* therapy. The idea that one needs a systematic guide for diagnosis and/or therapy arises from a linear epistemology, whereas ecosystemic epistemology is in tune with a Taoistic, nonpurposive, process-oriented way of knowing.

Bateson (7), in comparable fashion, maintains that "mere purposive rationality"—that which emerges on our "screen of consciousness"—can only deal with a skewed sample of events of the total system of which we are a part. What this means is that if we confine our ways of knowing to purposive rational knowing, the descriptions we create will take into account only a fragment of the ecological relationship system we are attempting to know. Only through a nonpurposive, Taoistic, eco-systemic approach can one come to know the whole circuit or system of which one is a part. Bateson (7, p. 146) refers to this "sense or recognition of the fact of circuitry" or the "whole system" as "wisdom."

The task for the beginning therapist, therefore, is to learn how to know or diagnose in this ecosystemic way. Minuchin (38) describes this process of learning as similar to that required of the *samurai* swordsman who must initially spend great amounts of time learning skills and techniques. After much rigorous training, the pupil is instructed to go meditate in the mountains. When he forgets all that he has learned, he can return and *Be* the sword.

When one can forget theory and technique, abandon purposive

knowing, and attend to the "doing of non-doing" or the *Wu-Wei* of the Taoist, one can then diagnose in an ecosystemic way. This is certainly what Jung[7] had in mind, however muddled his terminology and epistemology, when he advised: "Wait for what the unconscious has to say about the situation. A way is only *the* way when one finds it and follows it oneself. There is no general prescription for 'how one should do it'" (29, pp. 31-32).

Although among family therapists, Whitaker's way of diagnosing or knowing, which he has called "nontechnical and nontheoretical family psychotherapy" (52), more nearly reflects an underlying ecosystemic epistemology, his theoretical statements occasionally use metaphors and ideas from linear epistemology (e.g., "power"). The explicit formalization of the epistemology inherent in Whitaker's as well as in all therapists' work is the task of what Bateson calls the "circularistic scientist." Bateson (41) distinguishes this scientist from the therapist or "humanist."

> The humanist, like the artist, can act spontaneously out of his own integrity and need not always stop to determine exactly what he is saying. On the other hand, the humanist will never create a cumulative science, for he cannot clearly transmit his wisdom to his successors. . . . the artist must always leave his own systems of codification implicit and unexamined. The precise and even compulsive examination of such systems is the task of the scientist. [41, pp. 270-271]

It is not unusual that a paradigm for a new form of diagnosis would appear after the new way of diagnosing has been accepted clinically. Family and systems therapists have been describing various ecosystemic ways of diagnosing—e.g., Whitaker's way of experiential knowing and the contributions of Auerswald, Haley, Hoffman, Minuchin, Selvini, Palazzoli, Speck and Attneave, and Watzlawick—but the theories generated to account for ecological and systems approaches to therapy have often involved ideas and metaphors from linear epistemology.

This paper represents a beginning effort to make explicit the epistemological framework (based on the ideas of cybernetics, ecology, and systems theory) that underlies the ecological and systems therapist's alternative paradigm for diagnosis or knowing. It must be remembered, however, that such a framework can never be complete. The metalogue between theory and practice is such that "the theorist can only build his theories about what the practitioner was doing yesterday. Tomorrow the practitioner will be doing something different because of these theories." (41, p. 272)

---

[7]Bateson (30) has noted that Jung's work reflected an ecosystemic epistemology up until he wrote *Answer to Job*. Bateson (15) has even used the Jungian terms, "pleroma" and "creatura" to distinguish between the two paradigms referred to in this paper as linear and ecosystemic epistemology, respectively.

REFERENCES

1. Auerswald, E., "Interdisciplinary Versus Ecological Approach," *Fam Proc.* 7:202-215, 1968.
2. ———, "Families, Change, and the Ecological Perspective," in A. Ferber, M. Mendelsohn, and A. Napier (Eds.), *The Book of Family Therapy*, Boston, Houghton Mifflin, 1973.
3. ———, Personal communication, Nov. 28, 1977.
4. Batseon, G., *Naven* 2d ed.,Stanford, Calif., Stanford University Press, 1958.
5. ———, "Language and Psychotherapy—Frieda Fromm-Reichmann's Last Project," *Psychiatry* 21:96-100, 1958.
6. ———, "Pathologies of Epistemology," Reprinted in G. Bateson, *Steps to an Ecology of Mind*, New York, Ballantine Books, 1972, originally published 1971.
7. ———, "Style, Grace and Information in Primitive Art," Reprinted in G. Bateson, ibid.
8. ———, "A Systems Approach," *Int. J. Psychiat.* 9:242-244, 1971.
9. ———, "Draft: Scattered Thoughts for a Conference on 'Broken Power,'" *Co-Evolution Quart.* 4:26-27, 1974.
10. ———, "Foreward: A Formal Approach to Explicit, Implicit, and Embodied Ideas and to Their Forms of Interaction," in C. Sluzki and D. Ransom (Eds.), *Double Bind: The Foundation of the Communicational Approach to the Family*, New York, Grune and Stratton, 1976.
11. ———, "Comments on Haley's History," in C. Sluzki and D. Ransom (Eds.), ibid.
12. ———, "Afterword," in J. Brockman (Ed.), *About Bateson*, New York, E.P. Dutton, 1977.
13. ———, "The Thing of It Is," in M. Katz, W. Marsh and G. Thompson (Eds.), *Explorations of Planetary Culture at the Lindisfarne Conferences: Earth's Answer*, New York, Harper and Row, 1977, pp. 142-155.
14. ———, Personal communication, Oct. 28, 1976.
15. Bateson, M., *Our Own Metaphor: A Personal Account of a Conference on the Effects of Conscious Purpose on Human Adaptation*, New York, Alfred A. Knopf, 1972.
16. Bodin, A., "Conjoint Family Assessment," in P. McReynolds (Ed.), *Advances in Psychological Assessment*, vol. 1, Palo Alto, Science and Behavior Books, 1968.
17. Boyd, D. *Rolling Thunder*, New York, Dell, 1974.
18. Framo, J., *Family Interaction: A Dialogue Between Family Researchers and Family Therapists*, New York, Springer, 1972.
19. Haley, J., "Family Therapy: A Radical Change," in J. Haley (Ed.) *Changing Families*, New York, Grune and Stratton, 1971.
20. ———, "Beginning and Experiencing Family Therapists," in A. Ferber, M. Mendelsohn, and A. Napier (Eds.), op. cit.
21. ———, *Uncommon Therapy*, New York, W.W. Norton, 1973.

22. ———, "Development of a Theory: A Historical Review of a Research Project," in C. Sluzki and D. Ransom (Eds.), op. cit.

23. ———, *Problem-Solving Therapy*, San Francisco, Jossey-Bass, 1976.

24. Hoffman, L., "Breaking the Homeostatic Cycle," in P. Guerin (Ed.), *Family Therapy: Theory and Practice*, New York, Gardner Press, 1976.

25. Howe, R. and Foerster, H., "Introductory Comments to Francisco Varela's Calculus for Self-Reference," *Int. J. General Systems* 2:1-3, 1975.

26. Jackson, D., "The Individual and the Larger Context," *Fam. Proc.* 6: 139-154, 1967.

27. ———, "Schizophrenia: The Nosological Nexus," in P. Watzlawick and J. Weakland (Eds.), *The Interactional View*, New York, W.W. Norton, 1977.

28. Jackson, D. and Satir, V., "A Review of Psychiatric Developments in Family Diagnosis and Family Therapy," in D. Jackson (Ed.), *Therapy, Communication, and Change*, Palo Alto, Science and Behavior Books, 1973.

29. Jung, C., *The Integration of Personality*, New York, Rinehart, 1939.

30. Keeney, B., *Dialogue with Gregory Bateson*, Unpublished manuscript, 1977.

31. Keeney, B. and Cromwell, R., "Systemic Diagnosis," *Fokus pa Familien*, 3:52-60, 1978.

32. Keeney, B. and Cromwell, R., "Toward Systemic Diagnosis," *Family Therapy* 4:225-236, 1977.

33. Land, E., "Process as Reality," Phi Beta Kappa Oration, Harvard University, June 14, 1977.

34. Luce, G., *Body Time*, New York, Bantam Books, 1971.

35. Maslow, A., *The Psychology of Science*, Chicago, Henry Regnery, 1969.

36. May, R., "Opening Remarks at Session One of the Association for Humanistic Psychology Theory Conference," Tucson, Arizona, April 4, 1975.

37. Minuchin, S., *Families and Family Therapy*, Cambridge, Mass., Harvard University Press, 1974.

38. Minuchin, S., Personal communication, Nov. 5, 1977.

39. Pask, G., *Conversation, Cognition and Learning*, Chicago, Aldine, 1973.

40. Rosenthal, R., *Experimenter Effects in Behavioral Research*, New York, Appleton-Century-Crofts, 1966.

41. Ruesch, J. and Bateson, G., *Communication: The Social Matrix of Psychiatry*, New York, W.W. Norton, 1968.

42. Selvini Palazzoli, M., Boscolo, L., Cechin, G., and Prata, G., *Paradosso e Controparadosso*, Milano, Feltrinelli, 1975.

43. Skeat, W., *A Concise Etymological Dictionary of the English Language*, New York, Capricorn Books, 1963.

44. Speck, R. and Attneave, C., *Family Networks*, New York, Pantheon Books, 1973.

45. Sullivan, H., *The Interpersonal Theory of Psychiatry*, New York, W.W. Norton, 1953.

46. Varela, F., "A Calculus for Self-Reference," *Int. J. General Systems* 2:5-24, 1975.

47. Varela, F., "On Observing Natural Systems," *CoEvolution Quart.* 10:26-31, 1976.

48. Watts, A., *Psychotherapy East and West*, New York, Ballatine Books, 1961.

49. Watzlawick, P., Beavin, J., and Jackson, D., *Pragmatics of Human Communication*, New York, W.W. Norton, 1967.

50. Watzlawick, P., Weakland, J., and Fish, R., *Change: Principles of Problem Formation and Problem Resolution*, New York, W.W. Norton, 1974.

51. Wertheim, E., "Family Unit Therapy and the Science and Typology of Family Systems," *Fam. Proc.* 12:361-376, 1973.

52. Whitaker, C., "The Hindrance of Theory in Clinical Work," in P. Guerin (Ed.), *Family Therapy: Theory and Practice*, New York, Gardner Press, 1976.

53. Whitaker, C., "A Systems Approach to Family Therapy," Unpublished transcript of presentation given for the Family Study Center, University of Missouri, Kansas City, 1976.

54. Whitehead, A., *Science and the Modern World*, New York, The Free Press, 1953.

55. Wilden, A. and Wilson, T., "The Double Bind: Logic, Magic, and Economics," in C. Sluzki and D. Ransom (Eds.), op. cit.

56. Wynne, L.C., Discussion in D. Jackson, "The Individual and Larger Contexts," *Fam. Proc.* 6:139-154, 1967.

For reprints: Bradford, P., Keeney, M.A., Box 829, The Menninger Foundation, Topeka, Kansas 66601.

THE THERAPIST AS A TECHNIQUE

The family therapist faces issues related to self-disclosure, authenticity, and establishing client-counselor rapport, as does any therapist. In addition, family therapists face other specific issues related to (a) getting caught up in the family's system, (b) observing interactional behaviors, and (c) choosing a co-therapist. This section concentrates on these issues and suggests concerns the therapist should consider before therapeutic decisions are made.

The articles in this chapter do not cover all issues related to the process of family therapy and the role of the therapist. One must remember that family therapy is a relatively new treatment modality with few accepted procedures followed by all practitioners. While the current situation leaves a great deal of the interpretation to the individual practitioner, systematic strategies can only enhance the clinican's ability to work with families.

James Hawkins presents a systematic approach to the issues of counselor activity, confrontation, and involvement with couples and families. Establishing client-counselor rapport and methods of confrontations are also discussed. Underlying the strategies discussed in the article are the notions that family counselors are more active than other types of counselors and counselors should examine the family's process and content messages during therapy.

Carmen Lynch provides the therapist with guidelines for not getting caught up in the family system. The article describes specific counselor behaviors that indicate to the counselor that he/she is obeying the family rules and has become "trapped" in the family's system. "Trapped" described the counselor who invests so much energy that it appears that he/she is doing all the work and has thus become less effective.

Keith and Whitaker point out that a therapist's impotence cannot be ignored, and they offer suggestions for wrestling with inadequacy. In addition, they use examples to show how absurdity and acting-in can be used as tools by the therapist.

The articles in this chapter are all concerned with therapists using their own selves as tools in the therapeutic process. Since family therapists have been described as being more active than other counselors, one can easily see the importance placed on the relationship between the behavior of that therapist and counseling outcome.

Chapter 17

COUNSELOR INVOLVEMENT IN MARRIAGE AND FAMILY COUNSELING

JAMES L. HAWKINS

The idea that marital and family counselors and somehow more "active" than other types of counselors is repeated again and again in the literature. It is also true that the entire field of psychotherapy has been exploring the virtues and pitfalls of greater therapist involvement. At least since Rogers' early works, psychotherapists have been emphasizing the therapist-patient relationship as possibly the most important factor in the psychotherapeutic equation. Johnson (1961) made this a major theme in his book on marital counseling techniques. Minuchin (1974) makes the case for family therapy by emphasizing the importance of the therapist joining the family in treatment, creating family crises, and forming coalitions to bring about system change. While many available works show by example or metaphor when and how to involve oneself with clients, none suggest a rationale for when or when not to get involved in particular ways, and what the hazards of various counselor behaviors might be.

The primary purpose of this paper is to present a systematic approach to the issues of counselor activity, confrontation, and involvement with couples and families. The conditions are outlined under which four basic categories of counselor communication behavior—conventional, controlling, speculative, and contactful—are likely to be fruitful, harmful, or inconsequential in marriage and family counseling. The discussion is couched in a communications framework, which allows a description of the style of the counselor's behavior with his clients. There is a central concern with the counselors demeanor, style, or process, regardless of the content of his speech, i.e., the interest is not in what he says, but how he says it.

From J. Hawkins, Counselor Involvement in Marriage and Family Counseling, *Journal of Marriage and Family Counseling*, 2:37-47, 1976. Courtesy of American Association for Marriage and Family Therapy.

FOUR BASIC COMMUNICATION STYLES

The four basic communication styles (cf. Hill, 1965) listed previously can be derived from the degree to which a speech is either high or low in disclosure, and open or closed to other's reality (see Table 17-I).

Table 17-I

Openness	*Disclosure*	
	High	Low
Open	Contactful	Speculative
Closed	Controlling	Conventional

Speculative Behavior

Wondering aloud about the clients, who they are, their problems, and strengths, is open, low-disclosure activity on the part of the counselor. It is aimed at understanding the clients by getting them to produce sufficient information about themselves to allow the counselor to apprehend their inner experience, family myths, rules, et cetera, hence, to comprehend that on which the clients are final authority—their own experience. Epistemologically, of course, the counselor can do nothing else, since he stands outside the client (Egan, 1971). If he arbitrarily imputes an inner experience to the client or fails to recognize the meaning of a client's productions, we say he lacks empathy, he fails to understand. That counselors, even the best, fail to understand their clients at times is evident. This happens—can happen—because the counselor must view the world in his own terms. In short, he is biased. Speculative techniques are helpful in keeping therapist bias to a minimum. Speculative activity is the haven for which counselors can always head when the natural bias of the counselor's "alienated" *standpunkt* blocks his comprehension of the couple or family.

Contactful Behavior

It is hard to imagine a time or a therapeutic orientation that would bar from the counseling hour low-disclosure counselor activity, such as in speculative behavior; but perhaps having grown up in a post-Rogerian era truncates our historical vision. Nevertheless, it is abundantly clear in this present day that high-disclosure activities have not yet been fully accepted as legitimate tools of the counseling trade.

The idea that feedback is essential to personal growth and change has gained considerable currency in the emerging fields of human relations and sensitivity training. The external position of the counselor permits him a point of view against which the clients themselves are biased. The clients must depend on others—and the counselor is a special other—for information as to how they are experienced. Of course in marriage and family counseling, feedback from other family members is equally important. Contact level behavior is open, high-disclosure activity in which the counselor uses himself to help overcome the natural bias of the clients against understanding what others feel and think about them.

Conventional Activity

This activity glosses over or avoids the internal realities of feelings, motives, values. Information revealed is often already public, such as biographical data or social space markers. The intent of the speech seems to be for purposes of sociability only, or at least the speech may be delivered in a light sociable manner. Cocktail party banter or water-cooler chit-chat are socially typical forms of conventional communications, as is discussion of the weather, gardening, and so on. Although something is said, the intent seems to be to maintain ignorance of others' private views and to keep others in the dark about one's own views, unless they are non-controversial or socially bland, acceptable. From a counseling point of view, this style may be described as being in "idling gear."

Controlling Behavior

A closed attitude and high-disclosure characterize verbalizations at the controlling style. An unfriendly or negative emotional tone is sometimes present. Or there may be other indicants of verbal attack, such as sarcasm or "put-down" words. But verbal attack may not be present at all. In fact, tone of voice and other non-verbal qualities may be quite positive and approaching in nature. Presence or absence of verbal attack leads to a further division of this category into two subtypes: 1) negative controlling activity and 2) non-negative controlling activity.

The essence of controlling style is summed up in its name; acts in this category, no matter how "positive" they may seem, nonetheless have the apparent intent of defining the way things are or will be, regardless of other's point of view.

Since there is high disclosure, one usually knows where the speaker stands and how strongly he feels about an issue. Persons often praise such actions for their honesty or candor, even when accompanied by verbal attack. Sometimes the closed nature of the speech, the lack of respect, or even interest in other's point of view, makes candor onerous, since there is no negotiation permitted, only further battle or submission. On the other hand, high disclosure moots many points, because previously erroneous assumptions are sometimes dispelled, and agreement is discovered where disagreement had previously been assumed.

Sometimes a spouse will exclaim, "I've even wished he'd hit me once. At least I'd know something I did mattered." Apparently, in some situations even acts of violence are preferred to no response at all. Clearly also, few persons approve of, let alone have the ability to live with, a continuous barrage of unfriendly, negative, inflexible, non-listening behavior.

Speculative activity on the part of the counselor seems to be widely accepted by most theoretical schools: contact level involvement is less accepted. Two other basic categories of communication behavior resulting from the marriage of open-closed and high-low disclosure enjoy considerably less acceptance as legitimate tools of the counselor's trade.

CONFRONTATION AS THERAPEUTIC ACTIVITY

The idea of the counselor using his person actively in counseling entered the literature in the context of what has increasingly come to be called confrontation. Confrontation of the client by the counselor has been receiving growing attention in the clinical and research literature, as Egan's excellent extensive review testifies. While speeches in any style may be confrontive, I believe there is a growing consensus as to what constitutes the best or most effective confrontive style.

Berne (1966) defines confrontation in terms of transactional analysis:

> In confrontation the therapist uses information previously elicited and specified, in order to disconcert the patient's Parent, Child, or contaminated Adult by pointing out an inconsistency. The patient is stirred up and his psyche is thrown out of balance and this tends to cause a redistribution of cathexis . . .
>
> To the patient's Child, a confrontation may represent a Parental move in a game that stimulates defensive operations learned early in life . . . To his Adult, it may represent an intellectual challenge for which he is grateful ("I never noticed that before."). To his Parent it may represent an incursion on Parental authority . . . (p. 235).

Shorn of its transactional trappings, the core feature of Berne's definition is the effort of the therapist to impress the patient with a new way of looking at things (which may be more realistic or mature, as defined by the transactional analysis framework). As in all communication-oriented therapies, Berne emphasizes the importance of feedback from therapist to patient. He also notes that often the client finds confronting remarks "disconcerting."

Douds, et al., (1967) describe confrontation in much the same way, but go on to specify some specific integrative situations where it is especially appropriate. They also note the therapeutic goal of self-integration and wholeness to which confrontation as a technique is directed, according to their concept of therapy. The essence again seems to consist of providing alternate and, hopefully, growthful points of view about oneself.

> Direct confrontation . . . is initiated by the therapist, based on his core understanding of the client. It brings the client into more direct contact with himself, his strengths and resources, as well as his self-destructive behavior. The purpose of confrontation is to reduce the ambiguity and incongruities in the client's experiencing and communication. In effect, it is a challenge to the client to become integrated; that is, at one with his own experience. It is directed at discrepancies within the client (his ideal versus real self); between what the client says and does (insight and action); and between illusion and reality (the therapist's experience of the client versus the client's expression of his experience of himself and the therapist). The therapeutic goal is nondestructive and emerging unity with the client. It implies a constructive attack upon an unhealthy confederation of miscellaneous illusions, fantasies, and life avoidance techniques in order to create a reintegration at a higher level of health (p. 171).

The question of confrontation, its meaning and its use as a counseling technique, is not new; and in marriage counseling literature has been the subject of explicit discussion at least since Johnson (1961, pp. 142-146, 137-138). For Johnson, a confronting comment "is one that tends to bring a client face to face with some aspect of his problem or behavior that he has not recognized, or at least not verbalized."

Egan's (1970) definition emphasizes the wide variety of confrontational techniques, as well as the point that some of these are helpful and some are harmful to clients:

> Generally, confrontation takes place when one person (the confronter), either deliberately or inadvertently, does something that causes or directs another person (the confrontee) to advert to, reflect upon, examine, question, or change some particular aspect of his behavior. In other words, some act on the part of the confronter—whether he is aware of it or not—acts as a stimulus to the confrontee; it challenges him, "pulls him up short", directs him to reflect upon or change some aspect of his behavior (behavior, that is, in the wide sense: overt acts, inaction, attitudes, moods, etc.). I believe that confrontation must be described or defined as generally as this if it is to include all behavior that is referred to in the literature as confrontational. Moreover, if it is defined this generally, it becomes quite easy to see that there are many different forms (both growthful and destructive) and many different degrees of confrontation (p. 293-4).

Throughout all of these definitions and accompanying discussions, the authors cited emphasize the desirability of bringing to the client's awareness new points of view, values, perceptions, behaviors. Ideally, they say, this should be done in a "constructive" manner, which I take to mean in a context of respect, positive regard, and empathy. Such behavior by the counselor constitutes a real sharing of himself as a person, a reaching out and a caring about his client, a definitive disclosure of self in what we have called "contactful" style, i.e., open with high disclosure. What most writers define as the best, "most therapeutic," form of confrontation seems identical with the style of interaction termed here contactful involvement. Confrontation at its best is contactful. Seen in this context, the active, involved counselor is quintessentially a confronting counselor. Helpful, growthful confrontation becomes identified with therapeutic action at its best, not confrontation in the controlling sense, but involvement in the contactful sense.

There is no mystery about confrontation, for it is nothing more nor less than the active intervention of the marriage or family therapist in the life of the client couple; loving, encouraging, cajoling, supporting, persuading, questioning, arguing, jarring them toward new and more satisfying constructions of reality. Confrontation of the couple can be carried out in any of the four basic communication styles. The speculative efforts of the counselor to try genuinely to understand motivations, his wonderings about what might happen if . . ., or the simple empathic reflection of a feeling, can provoke reflection, insight, and change. Even an offhand (conventional) comment or a joke can bring one up short with a realization not previously articulated. We are sometimes surprised by the potent effect of a seemingly innocuous remark, either by the counselor or one of the spouses.

High disclosure styles are more often confrontive in effect. Contactful involvement is the apex of effective therapeutic intervention. Since it combines both high disclosure and an open acceptance of the couple, it combines highly potent "disconcerting" potential in a spirit of warmth, understanding, and caring. Controlling confrontation, particularly of the verbal attack variety, may possess destructive potential that does not inhere in any of the other styles, and required additional discussion below.

Early writers asked when to be confrontive. The pertinent question today is not when but how. In what way can the counselor, in his brief moments with the couple or family, get them to grapple with their world? How can he make his personhood available effectively now? The issue of confrontation is simply the question of how the counselor can involve himself most effectively with his clients. Correct use of self in this manner demands attention to the state of the relationship among clients and between clients and counselor.

GAUGING CLIENT AND COUNSELOR READINESS

The kind of confrontation that will be helpful to the client is directly related to what the client himself is prepared to deal with. The sort of receptivity present in the client will determine, in part, whether counselor activity of one kind or another is likely to be helpful, or at least not harmful. Both ways of looking at the matter are important. But how do you measure the clients' ability to use or, at worst, tolerate the counselor's frequently awesome presence?

The answer, I believe lies precisely in their communication behavior. In the marital or family counseling setting, the counselor can observe each family member in interaction with the other, as well as with himself. The usual sequence begins with conventional style, which may consist of no more than initial pleasantries at the beginning of evaluation or at the opening of an hour, and then proceeds to the speculative level, with the counselor early on asking many questions or reflecting feelings or ideas, as he attempts to gain an understanding of the couple's view of themselves and their marriage. The counselor at this stage is attempting to develop rapport with the client-couple. This is developed when the counselor and the client can put together, not just a sentence or two but extended sequences of open, low-disclosure, speculative interaction. That is, both counselor and client, in dialogue, are open in the special sense described previously, as they attempt to speculate about or question the marital or family situation. Often, the counselor in this situation is engaging in a great deal of support— facilitating, reflecting, inviting disclosure, clarifying, and the like— while both the clients and counselor are wondering about, searching into, and analyzing the marital or family situation.

The counselor must be very clear on this point. The client may be revealing a great deal about his marriage, himself, and his spouse and family. He may be "leveling." The client may very well move almost immediately into contact level behavior, even in the first few minutes of the very first counseling hour. Sometimes counselors feel gratified about being successful in getting or allowing such a cooperative person to bore right into the heart of the matter. Such "good fortune" is not always what it seems, however, and the client or other members of his family may be far from ready for contact level reciprocity from the counselor. Ordinarily it is better for the counselor to be conservative at this point, placing the bulk of his verbalizations into reflecting and clarifying the client's productions, in order to test the client's ability to respond in dialogue with the counselor. The next testing steps usually will involve more active efforts to promote intimacy, such as mind-reading with checkout, documenting impressions with (here-and-now) specific examples, and so on. Such testing may reveal the client's readiness to move into continuing contactful *relationship* with the counselor; but often the client becomes shocked at how intimate he has allowed himself to become and would like to back off, but has no place to go where constructive work can be done. The job of building rapport still remains to be done. Clients who bare their soul so early often fall into silence, retreat to conventional behavior, or turn to highly abstract discussions of emotions or family life in general.

The counselor should not mistake for rapport the "cooperative" client, who willingly and literally *tells* what is wrong with his marriage or family life. Here, the client engages freely in dialogue, perhaps of an extended nature, telling the counselor and/or other family members the "facts" of the case—how the husband acts, what the wife does, how things should be but most definitely are not. The conversation may go on for many minutes, and although the counselor surely learns an enormous amount about how the client sees his marriage, not one shred of rapport may appear. For while each speech of the counselor may have been a model of support or analysis, the intervening client comments have been models not of analysis, but of controlling style. When the telling quality lacks signs of verbal attack—indeed, it may even appear friendly—the danger is especially great that the counselor may mistakenly believe rapport to have developed.

But such assertive productions by clients make the perceptive counselor want to cry out, "Won't you take responsibility for anything in this marriage?" Can the client claim ownership of his own feelings, thoughts, and perceptions? Can he come to use language that accepts the possibility of other points of view and legitimates differences of opinion and response? Until he can do this, rapport, as we define it, is not yet firmly established.

By observing the client's language behavior and utilizing the communication categories described previously, the counselor can attain quite reliable, even almost quantitative, estimates of the state of rapport—high, medium, or low—at any given time. Low rapport is characterized in some clients by long silences and in others by extended reporting in repetitive, almost legendary, manner of the facts of the case. Others will use their counseling hour to attack and berate the spouse, or the whole world. Still others wax philosophical, weaving extensive theories of marriage and family life. Others may treat the hour as a social time at the local Elk's club. And so on.

In a marital or family counseling situation, minimal rapport may be assumed if one or more family members show agreement with the counselor in a controlling way. That is, a mother may say to her son, "Go ahead, Johnny, speak up. The doctor wants you to talk to him." Minuchin (1974) sees this kind of behavior as indicating initial moves by the family or family members to permit the counselor to "join" the family. Any efforts by a client aimed at clarifying (speculative style) a counselor statement, or something said by another family member, constitute beginnings of rapport. For a therapist like Minuchin, these are also indications that the counselor is beginning to be allowed to "join" the family.

Moderate rapport has been achieved when the client can begin to analyze himself and his family relationships in terms of some cause-effect scheme, even if this scheme is not one the counselor prefers. So long as it cannot be classed as cliche, role stereotype, proverb, et cetera, and deals instead with specific qualities of these specific persons or this specific marriage or family, and so long as it is done in a tentative open way, then speculative work has begun. When the family members can put together with each other and/or the counselor sequences of reciprocal exploration and tentative analysis of his/their problems in comfort, then moderate rapport is well established.

If the client is now able, with reasonable comfort, to prick the counselor's selfhood with probing questions and receive back comfortable, genuine replies, then rapport may be said to have ascended to very high peaks indeed.

Table 17-II shows in an abbreviated way the effects on the client of counselor activity in each of the several communication styles in terms of the degree of rapport present. Both low disclosure styles (Conventional, which is closed, and Speculative, which is open) are seen to be virtually harmless, regardless of the degree of rapport, in the sense that at worst, the client will not be helped. The major counseling problem with both Conventional and Speculative styles is that they can be overdone, thus preventing or retarding growth and change. Many counselors probably engage in too much exploring, analyzing, and clarifying. Speculative activity is not the be-all or end-all of counselor-client interactions. Central as it is to effective counselor activity, open, low disclosure activity (i.e. speculative activity) must be seen as only one tool which has its place in the counselor's repertoire.

I believe that *once rapport has developed,* the counselor is remiss in his duty if he fails to reveal his own perceptions, thoughts, and feelings about the clients and his relationship to them. The counselor, after all, is or can be a significant source of feedback to his clients about how they affect each other. Thus, the counselor must reveal his person to the clients in order to be maximally helpful. Such revelation is best done, it would seem, in the contactful style. Not to do this is to renege, to give the client less than the best. To become involved may be the counselor's greatest gift.

To jump in indiscrimately or too forcefully too early could result in overwhelming the client and leading to withdrawal to non-work communication behavior, or in an over-dependence on the counselor who may be allowed by the client to take over all expression of feeling. In any event, progress in therapy is blocked until the analytical tools of at least minimal rapport are put together.

Fortunately, with the tools of language analysis presented here, the dilemma of too-early versus too-late can be managed relatively easily. As soon as the first clear signs of comfortable speculative activity emerge

Table 17-II

Therapist Style	Rapport Absent	Moderate Rapport	Full Rapport
Conventional (closed-low disclosure)	Harmless "idling gear"— May have to demonstrate counselor is a "good Joe" before rapport is possible.	Harmless, but overuse retards growth.	Usually waste of time, but client and counselor may both enjoy it. "Buddies"
Controlling Verbal Attack (closed-high disclosure; negative)	Dangerous, destructive.	Probably harmless, but usually not growthful.	Almost always harmless, may lead to therapist growth as well as client growth.
Controlling without Verbal Attack (closed-high disclosure; non-negative)	May be the only device to get client response, but can lead to round-robin conflict with client.	Harmless, and may produce client response for further processing.	Used often for emphasis when teaching skills: Mixes naturally into work styles.
Speculative (open-low disclosure)	Almost always appropriate.	Used as base point for contactful efforts.	Can be overdone; counselor "in his head" too much.
Contactful (open-high disclosure)	Can be threatening, leading to withdrawal or over-dependence. But again, may be only stimulus to work.	Leads to dramatic (usually growthful) response.	Real growth and change results.

from a client, it is no longer too early to challenge a family myth or to reveal a feeling produced in the counselor by a client behavior. That is, it is no longer too early to try to get involved. The results of the trial should encourage speculative efforts to deal with it. If the couple or family manage it well, the stage is set for further trials such that the counselor monitors progress on a moment-by-moment basis, ready to get more involved or back off, as indicated by his assessment of the client's productions. The counselor is not merely dependent on his powers of observation, because the clients' response can itself become a matter for discussion, "Was that a pretty heavy message?" "Maybe we need to let that go for a little while and come back to it when we've thought about it some more. What do you think?" "I notice you've been silent more than usual in the last few minutes. Does it have anything to do with the feelings I reported to you a while ago? Are you just thinking hard, or did I touch a tender spot? How would you like to deal with that now?" Note the return to the querying mode, with effort aimed at making sense out of figuring out a procedure for dealing with the situation. Possibly, the procedure will involve backing off for now. The counselor should be comfortable with this option. To say it as strongly as possible, the counselor must allow himself to be controlled by the clients' behavior.

The belabor a point made earlier, the thrust of the counselor's effort is toward getting involved. To get there, he may need to detour many times, but the goal is clear. Dramatic, rapid change is the pay-off. Theorists who oppose the use of high-disclosure activity altogether, on the grounds that it may become (in my terms) a controlling action by the counselor, in my opinion throw the baby out with the bath.

Controlling counselor behavior, enmeshed with signs of verbal attack, whether with words or tone of voice (or both), is the only counselor behavior that has the potential of being downright harmful and destructive. But destructiveness is most likely to result from negatively controlling behavior *only* where rapport is altogether lacking. When counselor and client have no basis for engaging in work of any sort, the client can neither talk about his own reactions to the counselor's assertive confrontation, nor reflect openly on the counselor's behavior. The best responses are to attack back, raise defensive armament, or flee. Emotional disorganization of a much more serious nature has been shown to accompany such counselor behavior in the absence of rapport (Lieberman, Yalom, & Miles, 1973).

However, when rapport already has been established between counselor and client, controlling verbal attack is, I think, much less likely to be serious (see Table 17-II). In the presence of moderate rapport, it is unlikely that the clients will make the counselor's outburst a matter of discussion, but they will be open to the counselor reintroducing the episode at a later time. Probably, such an outburst is clear indication of the need for the counselor to seek consultation with a colleague regarding his own motivations. At any rate, the rapport already developed allows the process to return to business as usual rather quickly, with no real damage done. In the presence of full rapport, the counselor's outburst most likely will become a topic of mutual exploration and analysis almost immediately. The clients may initiate the discussion, or the counselor himself may start the ball rolling, knowing (a) that the clients are likely to pursue it anyway and (b) that in any event, they can deal with the issue if he initiates the discussion. In the process, both clients and counselors will learn a bit about themselves, sort out the problem, and arrive at useful solutions. Because such outbursts are seized upon and made into growthful events so readily in the presence of full rapport, the counselor might even be encouraged to go ahead and be his "nasty self" for a few minutes. Of course, the better route would be to express his feelings in a contactful way. Under circumstances of full rapport, suppression of the counselor's feelings in most instances would be an antitherapeutic act.

Such a verbal attack by the therapist is thought of as lasting for a few speeches or, at most, a few minutes. It would be hard to conceive of even moderate rapport developing in response to a counselor whose activity is pervaded by an attitude of controlling aggression.

One of the most surprising things to us when we listen to our own and other active therapists' tapes, is the amount of non-negative controlling activity we engage in. Most often, in our own work, this seems to take the form of directives to "do this" or "don't do that," e.g., "Tell it to her, not me." "You're interrupting him; wait until he's finished." "You sit over there; I'll sit here." "Your last speech came across as a put-down. Say it again with some other words and try to get your feelings over without destroying Ellen." But "positive" controlling speeches also fall into other frequently used categories, such as firmly but warmly insisting that the client's interpretation is probably incorrect. "Don't be too sure!" "Impossible." Sometimes, also, we have found ourselves insisting that we will indeed make progress, or that Tom really is not as bad a person as he makes himself out to be. These latter efforts are, at best, misguided attempts at strength bombardment.

In whatever way the couple or family has been interpreting their world, one thing is clear: it has not been a satisfying or completely functional one for them. So long as they continue to use the same interpretations to deal with their world again and again, no change will occur. Somehow, they must be motivated to accept new premises for behaving, so that new behaviors can emerge. The therapeutic impasse is an ethical problem only when rapport is so low as to make high disclosure styles unattractive as behavioral options for the counselor. When rapport is absent, controlling style (without verbal attack) can lead to a roundrobin, oscillating conflict with the client and his family, which may only result in an even firmer adherence to the old interpretations as a defensive maneuver. Contact level involvement in the absence of rapport can generate feelings of being overwhelmed with the magnitude of the marital or family problem, and thus, a need to become overly dependent on the counselor. While neither of these results can be described as necessarily dangerous, they are,, nevertheless, undesirable. The counselor's choice is not an easy one, but is not so dangerous as many have suggested. High disclosure styles may, indeed, be the only hope the counselor has of starting the clients in a new, hopefully more satisfying, direction.

Giving directives in an effort to teach, or to choreograph new behavior, or to demonstrate a point, is necessary, acceptable, even expected of an expert in interpersonal relations. Likewise, challenging personal or family myths in a non-negative, controlling style may be fruitfully disconcerting, especially if the counselor "brackets" such speeches with speculative or contactful expressions. Ellis (1962) has shown the value of outright polemic in confronting dysfunctional belief systems. I believe that most controlling counselor activity is rarely harmful, mixes naturally into other styles, and frequently generates behavior that leads directly to work levels. Thus, non-negative (hopefully positive) controlling counselor behavior ranks second-best to contactful behavior among high disclosure styles. Verbally abusive controlling behavior ranks dead last among all styles.

SUMMARY

In summary, I believe that, with the exceptions noted, high disclosure therapist activity in both Controlling and Contactful styles is justified. Attention to client-counselor and couple or family communication behavior can provide reliable procedures for isolating points where high disclosure counselor behavior may be harmful, as well as marking circumstances where it would be positively helpful. I believe that the use of the communication style categories in estimating rapport will reduce misplaced over-caution when it is contra-indicated (and it usually is) and increase proper caution when that is the best choice. After all, moderate rapport, even quite extensive rapport, often develops quite early in therapy, when the counselor will allow it. There are many reasons to allow it and encourage rapport to develop. An important one is the cushion it provides for absorbing the counselor's own inevitable pratfalls.

REFERENCES

Berne, E. *Principles of group treatment*. New York: Oxford, 1966, 235.

Douds, J., Berenson, B.G., Carkhuff, R.R., & Pierce, R. "In search of an honest experience: Confrontation in counseling and life." In Carkhuff, R.R., & Berenson, B.G., *Beyond counseling and therapy*. New York: Holt, Rinehart, & Winston, 1967, 170-179.

Egan, G. *Encounter: Group processes for interpersonal growth.* Belmont, California: Brooks/Cole Publishing Company, 1970.

Ellis, A. *Reason and emotion in psychotherapy.* New York: Lyle Stuart, 1962.

Hill, W.F. *Hill interaction matrix: A method of studying interaction in psychotherapy groups.* Los Angeles: University of Southern California, Youth Study Center, 1965.

Johnson, D. *Marriage counseling: Theory and practice.* Englewood Cliffs, New Jersey: Prentice-Hall, 1961.

Lieberman, M.A., Yalom, I.D., & Miles, M.B. *Encounter groups: First facts.* New York: Basic Books, 1973.

Miller, S., Nunnally, E.W., & Wackman, D.B. *Alive and aware.* Interpersonal Communication Programs, Inc., 2001 Riverside Ave., Minneapolis MN, 55454: Printing Arts Inc., 1975.

Minuchin, S. *Families and family therapy.* Cambridge, Massachusetts: Harvard University Press, 1974.

Chapter 18

ON NOT GETTING CAUGHT UP
IN THE FAMILY'S SYSTEM

Carmen Lynch

A system is more powerful than the individuals in it—"the whole is more than the sum of its parts"—and the family therapist had best be aware of the power of the family system. The family in treatment will work hard to maintain the homeostasis of its system and in so doing may draw the therapist into its field so that he becomes a part of that system, frequently losing himself in the process. How does this happen? What clues does the therapist have that he is being "sucked in"? How does he handle it once he becomes aware of it?

One of the first signs that he is getting trapped in the family's pathological system—and new therapists are especially susceptible—is when he finds that he is working too hard, creating an imbalance of energy input between the therapist and the family members. To the onlooker it indeed appears that the therapist is doing all the talking, all the work. For the therapist, it is accompanied by a feeling of anxiety— that he is missing something, or not doing enough for the family; he frantically seeks an answer or a dramatic technique that will help the family "break through." And at the end of a session the therapist feels drained, with a sense of having worked harder than he has all week.

This phenomenon usually takes place with a family that is unable or unwilling to take responsibility for its difficulties—that conveys a message of helplessness and hopelessness. Some families can be absolutely disarming: they fix their doleful eyes on the therapist and beg him to "fix it" for them. Other families subtly let the therapist know that if he really knew what he was doing the family would be making more progress. And the therapist privately believes they are right.

While new therapists in particular are inclined to work too hard, so too are those whose self-esteem is attached to their effectiveness as therapists, and those who are working out rescue fantasies in doing therapy. A therapist who has difficulty dealing with dissatisfied

---

From C. Lynch, On Not Getting Caught Up in the Family's System, *Family Therapy*, 1:163-70, 1978. Courtesy of Libra Publishers, Inc.

patients, or accepting the possibility that a patient might leave the session feeling worse than when he arrived, is going to work too hard.

Physiological reactions give clear warning to the therapist that he is in danger of being sucked in. A headache, the sudden onrush of heaviness or fatigue, a pain in the neck, mood changes and "gut reactions"—each person has an idiosyncratic way of responding to certain family systems. One therapist may feel heavy and tired when working with a family in which there is a lot of unexpressed rage; another might respond with a headache to the same family. If a therapist begins a session feeling energetic and cheerful and twenty minutes later feels cranky and irritable, chances are he is being sucked into the system. Or, working with a family whose members are all smiling and talking about their great weekend, a therapist might experience an increasing tightness in the stomach. If he ignores the tightness throughout the session, even joining in the family's discussion of the great weekend, he's been sucked into the system.

Similarly, if a therapist finds himself acting in a way that doesn't fit him, his behavior is probably a reaction to something going on in the family. If he is usually easy-going, for example, and becomes argumentative each time he sees a particular family, his argumentativeness is a warning signal that he is responding to something such as anger or repressed fear in the family's system. Or if he feels empty and dead with a particular family, then he is probably picking up on *their* feelings of emptiness and deadness.

Some students and therapists get sucked in this way more easily than others—usually those who do not yet have a strong, clear sense of themselves. Their personal boundaries are unclear, and they are vulnerable to being manipulated or to over-extending themselves in some way. Significantly, they find family therapy, as compared to individual therapy, especially demanding and draining.

Voice tone is frequently an indicator of how the therapist is reacting to the system. With a depressed family, he may find himself speaking slower and softer; with an angry, resistant family, his voice may rise, becoming even strident and querulous. When he begins to imitate the family's behavior, then he has indeed been caught up in the family's system. The most cautious therapist may find himself blaming and attacking one or more members of the family just as the family does, or becoming very "reasonable" and intellectual, nodding and smiling and being extremely polite with a family who exhibits this kind of behavior. This phenomenon is most likely to occur when a therapist is working with a family that is like his own family of origin.

Likewise, the therapist may find himself obeying the family's *rules*, especially when the rules are similar to those he grew up with. This is one of the most difficult signs to detect, and, unlike the many ways a therapist can catch himself imitating a family's behavior, here it is what the therapist *doesn't* do or say that indicates he has been sucked in.

A common example is when the therapist obeys the family rule, "Don't confront Father". Nobody in the family disagrees with Father and the therapist doesn't either—and he isn't aware of this behavior, since it never occurred to him in his own family to disagree with Father. Similarly, therapists who have difficulty experiencing their own pain, loneliness or hurt, often obey the family rule, "Protect Mother from her sadness at all costs." Before the mother's tears have reached her eyes, the vulnerable therapist has already moved on to discuss how the family could solve the problem of Daughter's not going to school. In either case, the therapist accepts the family's protection pacts, does not comment on them or question their validity, but rather, silently agrees that if Mom started to get in touch with her pain, she'd fall to pieces, or if Father were confronted he'd blow his top and someone would be destroyed.

At times, a therapist may be sucked in because he has a specific investment in the outcome, as may happen when working with a family with a specific value structure. A therapist who is a member of the clergy, for example, may steer clear of any mention of divorce because he is so heavily invested in keeping the family together; or he may focus on a husband's extra-marital affair, ignoring the wife and her withholding behavior because he has an investment in the husband's terminating the affair as soon as possible. Some young therapists find themselves arguing with the parents over the effects of marijuana. Or a therapist who is a radical feminist may let her investment in the wife's being strong and independent impair her effectiveness with the other members of the family. The value system of the therapist is personal, but when it blocks his view of what is going on with the family as a system, then his effectiveness as a therapist is limited if not neutralized.

If while working with a family, the therapist finds himself censoring his own comments, trying to second-guess the family's reactions, chances are he has been sucked into the family's system. A new therapist may lose a lot of spontaneity because he is so busy figuring out the ramifications of any intervention he might make. Students are particularly likely to worry about whether they can handle the family's reactions, and will hold back, sticking to "safe" comments. Asked why he did not comment on an obvious process in the family, one replied, "Well, I thought if I told the mother she seemed frantic, the father and kids would get more upset and that would lead to the kids' creating a disturbance, and I didn't want *that* to happen, so I decided not to say anything."

Another common phenomenon, one that almost every family therapist has experienced, is the feeling of being totally neutralized—immobilized and thus helpless with a family. Families who themselves feel trapped and helpless in their situation, or enjoy the protectiveness of their "blame games," thus frustrating the therapist's attempts to move in a more positive direction, or who seem to be heavily invested in negative interaction, all threaten to suck in the therapist. There are times when a family's situation actually may be hopeless, but this does not mean that the therapist has to feel neutralized or helpless in working with them. He can always point out the reality of the situation and help the family members deal with their feelings about it. So long as the therapist stays with the flow and the process, he is not allowing himself to be immobilized by the system.

Sometimes a family therapist finds himself stuck in the role of some member of the family[1], becoming part of the system. It may mean fighting with the mother on behalf of the father, mothering the children for the mother, acting like a husband or wife to the other spouse. Whatever the circumstances, it certainly means forsaking the role of therapist. In working with one-parent families it is very easy for a therapist to find himself fulfilling the role of the absent parent. This seems to happen often with male therapists working with single mothers, some of whom are masters at hooking males into playing the part of the benevolent father.

Some families can describe their symptoms or life-style in such an exciting way that the therapist becomes absorbed in their story, while other families can be very seductive in describing their sexual experiences. It is sometimes difficult not to get caught up in a family's story. A teacher may pick up on this process in the student-therapist when the latter presents case material—where there is a wealth of information which stimulates more than the usual number of questions from others in the class—questions which pertain more to the intriguing nature of the case than to treatment strategy or a deeper understanding of the family dynamics. (Some classes come to resemble a group of detectives having great fun testing their skill.)

Finally, if the therapist finds himself in coalition with one or two members of the family, he has been sucked into the system. Such a coalition can develop along sex lines, with a female therapist identifying with the wife's struggle, or a male therapist with the husband's. Or, working with a family in which the parents have abused their children, it is easy for the therapist to form a coalition with the children against the parents. One of the ways in which families attempt to maintain homeostasis is to focus on the symptoms of the identified patient, and the unwary therapist may find himself also focusing on those symptoms—a sure sign he has been drawn into the system. Or if there is a person in the family who resembles the therapist in some way (for example, a depressed overweight adolescent who seems to be experiencing the same kind of loneliness as did the therapist when he was an overweight adolescent), then the therapist may be tempted to form a

---

[1]This is different from the therapist's legitimate and desirable function of acting as a model for the family members.

coalition with that member of the family. Sometimes a patient will call the therapist between family sessions to tell him some secret, explaining that now that he has finally come to trust the therapist, he can confide in him something he's never shared with anyone before. Here, the therapist is on very sticky ground and at any moment can find himself unwittingly drawn into a very powerful coalition.

How can the family therapist avoid being sucked into the system? Once hooked, how can he extricate himself?

First, *self-knowledge* is crucial. In many of the examples enumerated above, it was the interplay between the therapist and the family that led to the therapist's being drawn into the family's system. It is important that the therapist have a clear picture of his own family of origin and be able to own up to his areas of sensitivity and vulnerability *without putting himself down*. Some feeling-states are more difficult for some therapists to deal with than others. Many therapists steer clear of a family's fear and immediately feel blocked if this process emerges in the family session. Others have difficulty meeting anger head-on; a surprising number fear intimacy or the outward expression of tenderness.

Self-knowledge makes the therapist more cautious when entering his areas of vulnerability, and helps him stay clear and maintain his boundaries, thus adding to a sense of feeling in charge of himself (rather than the family being in charge of the therapist!).

Second, *good supervision* is essential, not only in the development and growth of the skilled family therapist, but also as an important tool in the development of his self-knowledge. Many of the processes by which a therapist gets sucked into the system are "out-of-awareness" processes, and it is only through feedback that the therapist can become aware of his blind spots. A good supervisor will watch for clues and recognize them. Video-tape and tape recorders are useful tools.

Perhaps the most effective way of dealing with systems is through co-therapy, preferably with a man and woman therapy team. It is unlikely that both will be sucked into the system at the same time. A smoothly functioning therapy team, trusting each other and knowing each other's vulnerable areas, can use the feedback process to add to self-knowledge. Further, they can use each other to check out reactions in the therapy session: "You seem to be working awfully hard to make something happen; you don't usually push people the way you're pushing Mrs. X." One therapist can go into areas where his partner fears to tread. If one gets drawn into a coalition, the other can balance the effect by putting out more energy to the other members of the family, or by simply pointing out what's going on. Co-therapists can support each other and each can add to the other's sense of well-being when working with a family, thus increasing their resistance to being sucked into the system.

A very effective way the therapist can extricate himself from the family system is simply to "let go." If he realizes he's working too hard, he can start taking it easier; if he finds himself obeying the family rules, or filling someone else's role in the family, he can just stop doing it. If he discovers that he's pushing in a certain direction and it's not working, he can let go of that and try something else.

Labeling and commenting on the process is another way the therapist can extricate himself: "I notice that I'm getting into an argument with you, Mom, and I did not set out to fight with you today." Or, "I realize I am afraid to mention certain words such as death or separation when I am working with you; I think I am picking up a message from all of you that it is a taboo subject in your family."

The therapist may choose to deal with being sucked in by dumping the matter back on the family, watching to see if anyone else in the family shares his experience.[2] Commenting on the process and immediately shifting it to the family is a way of opening up the system, and the more healthy members respond both to the openness and the modeling offered by the therapist. "I notice, Mr. X, that when you get very reasonable I begin to tune you out. I wonder if anyone else in the family has a similar reaction?" Or, "As I look around at you all, and see you all smiling, I'm surprised to discover that my stomach feels very tense; (to a specific member of the family) how's your stomach faring?" Again, "Gee, here I am arguing with you again. Every time I try to offer you something I end up arguing with you. Does anyone else have this trouble when they are trying to give Mom something?" And finally, "I realize that, as I'm paying a lot of attention to Bill here, I'm beginning to feel anxious, like I'm depriving someone else in the family of my time and attention (to parents) do you feel that kind of a struggle when you're giving to one of the children?"

I am aware that some family therapists believe that staying sucked into the system is a helpful therapeutic tool. My understanding of their rationale is that it parodies the family system, helps the family members see how they are interacting and helps the therapist experience the full impact of the family system. I have not seen this process used as a technique in family therapy, and I cannot imagine how it would be effective in helping the family make and sustain growth or change, since there seems to be an inherent "put-down" message to the patient in the technique.

My own experience has been that being sucked into the system has immediately reduced the therapist's effectiveness and has led to his feeling totally useless and helpless. When this happens, the family feels it on some level, and is frightened by its own power; or the therapist's being drawn into the system validates the family's internal fears and its

---

[2]It is usually the identified patient who responds to this technique and helps out the therapist.

perceptions of itself and becomes yet another issue that has to be dealt with in the course of therapy.

An effective therapist is one who can avoid getting sucked into the system.

Chapter 19

STRUGGLING WITH THE IMPOTENCE IMPASSE: ABSURDITY AND ACTING-IN

DAVID V. KEITH AND CARL A. WHITAKER

The impotence impasse is a bit like a certain dark angel: it can appear in many forms. It is the deadlock that develops when a therapist is asked to respond to the demand, "Do something to help us change." The impasse can be identified best when the psychotherapy is not working. The psychotherapist feels useless despite his best effort and concern. Most often the problem has to do with who will provide the initiative for the therapy, the patients or the therapist.

The power of grandparents to obstruct progress in family therapy is insidious. Often the source of the impotence impasse can be traced back to the grandparents and their attitudes about living and relationships. The grandparents set that we think of first is the one which belongs to the family in treatment. There is another set of grandparents that also get in the way of therapy. They are the therapists' professional progenitors, such as, Freud and the American Board of Psychiatry and Neurology.

We psychotherapists live with a tradition that goes back several generations and which binds therapists in a position of passive acceptance. Some psychotherapy models escape the tradition of passivity by turning to science and organizing a more active method around research models. Both patterns, which inhibit spontaneous activity by the therapists with the implied threat of severe damage to patients, can be frustrating and paralyzing. They make it difficult for the psychotherapist to be himself.

On the other hand, the psychotherapist is dogged by the fact that a receptive, supportive, intellectual, cautious pattern usually fails to facilitate actual change, except in very grown-up patients. Less mature patients may find an increase in understanding or a temporary relief of symptoms which reverse when the patient rejoins his family.

From D. Keith and C. Whitaker, Struggling with the Impotence Impasse: Absurdity and Acting-In, *Journal of Marriage and Family Counseling, 4*:69-77, 1978. Courtesy of American Association for Marriage and Family Therapy.

In family therapy, much time and effort makes only a small dent in the family process with its automatic tendency to deflect change. The family ends up unchanged and the therapist ends up alone and frustrated.

The therapist is psychotherapy is only a function, a two-dimensional fragment of himself. The family members are whole people though repressed, prepared for flight or fight, and protected with that rubber fence so nicely described by Lyman Wynne (Wynne, 1958). We live with the fear that if we overstep the functional restrictions of our technical training and make a move to introduce other pieces of ourselves we will become harmful, noxious participants in the treatment process, if not its victims.

It is possible to fight with grandmother (Freud), but it is never possible to change her. Our question is: how to get free of grandmother's dominations so that our own creativity can expand—(killing her is not a solution).

There are ways to recover after being castrated by the conventional posture of psychotherapy. One way is to be absurd, to push the situation to its ridiculous limit as described in "Psychotherapy of the Absurd" (Whitaker, 1975). One other way, described in this paper, is to use a process opposite to acting-out, which the authors call "acting-in" (Rosen, 1958).

THE ABSURD

Flipping the therapy situation into absurdity in any number of frustrating situations provides a way to escape the gravitational pull of reason or social convention into an expanding universe of creative craziness. The move to do this briefly places both patient and theapist in the realm of the unknown and forces a here-and-now reorganization of the treatment project.

Some critics think of the use of the absurd as nihilistic. Perhaps it is, but it has proven useful. It helps to understand that psychotherapy is not real life, it is a pilot project and when it works, it is an adventure. It is like chartering a raft trip down the dangerous rapids of the Colorado River. The guide has been there before, which is quite different from being invulnerable. His life is at stake, too. The tourist agrees to take chances, to invest himself in the trip but under the guidance of the professional. The offer to participate in the pilot project can be, and frequently is refused. "You are joking." "What is *that* supposed to mean?" Thereby, the family's obstruction to creativity is maintained, the rubber fence is undisturbed.

It is possible to avoid a confrontation by using a more structured problem solving method. This system is like watching a movie of a trip down the Colorado River. Everyone is safe, but it provides excitement and may be thought of as a form of preparation for a later adventure.

The psychotherapy described in this paper is oriented toward growth rather than adaptation. Persons and families are always growing; the therapist's job is to enhance the project. The problem solving occurs spontaneously, out of family initiative. The authors seek to help the family initiate a change process among themselves that will be ongoing. This goal is achieved by teaching the family how to be creative.

In his talk at the Beyond the Double Bind Conference (1977), Gregory Bateson described something which he had observed with porpoises. If a porpoise is taught a trick and then trained to add a trick onto the first trick and then taught a variation of the trick, the porpoise suddenly takes over and adds three more variations to the original trick. The porpoise has learned how to be creative.

The effort to be reasonable about being absurd is itself ridiculous. Few therapists talk about unusual experiences in psychotherapy. Perhaps it is difficult to talk about them because the problem of reporting these moments of active participation which seem outrageous, clumsy, indecent or irresponsible goes beyond socially acceptable language. It is difficult to delineate the entire context in which these events happen. Grandpa may misunderstand and exclude us from his will. Some therapists are more aware of their own absurdity and the absurdity of trying to be helpful. We think this makes being absurd with patients more possible.

Some case examples will illustrate the use of absurdity.

Case Example 1. Dr. E. had a difficult interview with a family with two hard-boiled parents and their 12-year-old depressed son. Dr. E. spent 30 minutes trying unsuccessfully to head off the parents' complaints about their son. He felt defeated by the family and gave up in his mind. Suddenly he had an idea. "Why don't you take him to an orphanage? You could leave him and take a little girl home . . . " The room fell silent, then the mother, father and child began to protest the idea. In the two months following the interview, the parents relaxed their overconcern abut the boy and his grades in school began to improve.

Being absurd has the effect of distorting the reality that the family and the therapist face. The family is bent upon establishing a reality with a single, unquestionable definition. Together the patients and therapist can break out of the reality situation and see it in a different way with the help of an absurd redefinition. The impulse arises out of the therapist's frustration which provides effective momentum to his intervention.

How appropriate is it to be absurd with lower socio-economic class or less sophisticated families? It seems even more appropriate. Absurdity or humor breaks the cultural barrier and evokes a common language.

Case Example 2. Bill, age 13, the youngest of six kids in a multiple-problem, lower class family, had been arrested for doing $93 worth of property damage. The school authorities were also concerned that he came to school dirty. His omnipotent behavior at school was frustrating to the teachers. The family was chaotic and there was no clear separation between generations. In fact, the parents were disappointed that the older children, now married, did not take over responsibility for the family. The county department of social services had thrown their hands up, the school was furious with the parents, felt powerless and was pushing for residential treatment. The family was referred by the juvenile court judge. Both parents looked beaten. Father was a part-time alcoholic who worked in a factory. Mother was an extremely obese woman who had had an ileo-jejunal bypass eight months before the interview. There were many medical complications and she decided to leave home and live with her sister. Someone had planted the idea that Billy needed Ritalin® and the family came to the clinic with that end in sight. Like many court-referred families, they were self protective and unwilling to reveal any secrets. They censured Bill's near-vulgar innuendos. In the second interview, father complained about being overworked at home and was angry that other family members did not help him, they did not wash dishes and no one liked his cooking. The therapist agreed, "Being a mother *is* hard . . . had you thought of joining a women's lib group?" The scapegoat chimed in, "He can't be a mother, he doesn't have, you know (he used hands to pantomime large breasts), hang-overs." "Shhhhh," hissed mother and father. The therapist ignored their outrage and said, "You mean breasts? Don't worry, they'll come with time. By the way, how many times do you think mother will need to get him pregnant to get back at him?" "How can he get pregnant?" said the scapegoat. "He's a man." The therapist replied, "Don't you think he'll maybe turn into a woman if he keeps working like a mother?" This set up an unsophisticated, easily understood metaphor that the family played with during the whole hour. It touched on roles, sexuality and anger. They started to talk with each other in terms of themselves as though the sexes had been changed. Bill had another hearing set for the day after Labor Day. An older sister said that father would not be able to attend the hearing if he went into labor. Later, one of the daughters raised her concern that dad was overworked and she was afraid that he might have a heart attack or a nervous breakdown. The mother said, "We don't know what we'd do with ~~him~~ them. Even if he did get pregnant, he wouldn't go to a hospital, he would have to have the baby at home. And *he's* such a baby, I don't know what he would do about the pain." The silliness broke up their worry about revealing the family stresses and secrets. They ended up trusting the therapist more. They continued in therapy for four months which produced a series of changes in the family, at least enough that Bill was taken off probation.

Case Example 3. The family arrived at the emergency ward in a panic of confusion about their psychotic 22-year-old son, K.L. They wanted him placed in the state hospital involuntarily. The psychiatrist, Dr. Q, found himself stuck between the patient's single-minded unwillingness to give up and the parents' single-minded urgency to hospitalize him. The therapist broke through the impasse by asking the parents to leave the room, while he interviewed K alone. Dr. Q wanted to see some initiative in K. After half an hour of interviewing, K agreed to come to the clinic daily for a week in order to avoid hospitalization. Dr. Q had conducted the whole interview in an absurd tone of voice, simultaneously lecturing three medical students who had accompanied him to the interview, about the mental examination. The content was silly, but the nonverbal statements were supportive and caring. "I want you to do what you want to do. I care about and respect your rights. I am treating you in an absurd way while I also look absurd. I am being playful."

Dr. Q: "Okay, K, I'm glad you made that decision. Now here's your problem as I see it. What really bothers your folks is that you're spending all of your time sitting on your dead ass at home. What are we going to do about your parent's uneasiness? See, your parents think it's good for a person's moral and spiritual growth to work hard. Your father is a self-made man. He can't appreciate the simple spiritual value in contemplating your navel. The folks don't know that contemplation is a much higher function than mere work. Look at me, I work ten hours a day and where is it getting me? I am bitter because my patients won't change. I get tired, I go home crabby. I drink beer. I get crabbier. I yell at the wife and kids. Now I'm inspired by guys like you who lack ambition, and that's why I want to help you. So, you and me have to work out a way for you to sit around the house that will seem just the same as working. (Two minutes of silence.) I have an idea! Here, get off the sofa and sit over here on this stool. (Dr. Q began to arrange K's body in different postures, while K passively participated. He set him up like the statue, *The Thinker*, his left arm resting on his leg, his chin in his right hand with his right elbow resting on his knee.) No-o-o-o . . . that isn't quite it. Here, I've got it. Put your hand like this. (Dr. Q raised K's right hand to eye level with his arm extended. He arranged and re-arranged K's feet and head, trying to get it just right.) See, you are a statue. We must do something about your clothes so that you have a more classical look; maybe we could get you a gold lamé jockstrap. You could get some flowers to hold in your hand. That would really be nice. Now, it will take a little while to get used to working like this. Your parents will probably think that I'm crazy for telling you to do it, but they'll get used to it. People will come over to the house and you'll be sitting there in your jockstrap with your arm extended, holding some of your mom's fresh-cut flowers. Your dad can smile proudly when they ask questions and say, 'That's my son, the statue.' You get what I mean, K?" K (protesting): "Yeah, but I should go to work. That'll be just like being dependent on my dad. I don't want to be dependent on my dad." Q (placating): "Look, it's art, my friend."

K left with his mother. Dad had returned to his construction job because of some problem with a crane. Dr. Q told mom that K had agreed to see him daily for at least a week and that Dr. Q thought of it as a better alternative than being committed to the state hospital. He told her that he worked out a treatment plan with K, part of it involved taking a small dose of medication each night that would help him sleep and part of it involved being a bit crazy. Mother said, "Thanks," winked and off they went. K came back daily. Dr. Q had given him six 100 mg Mellaril tablets with the instruction to take one each night at bedtime. K took them all the first night. He received no further medications. Each day Dr. Q listened patiently in the waiting room to talk about symptoms from K's parents. Then he would see K in one-to-one interviews which K clearly enjoyed. K began sleeping, and was less disheveled each day. His clinic visits were devoted to problems related to being a statue, and the interviews were fun for both patient and therapist. Some of the problems had to do with how his body would go soft without exercise and that he had to work out a way to do isometric exercises without moving. And what kind of foods would be necessary to eat? Dr. Q undermined all of K's objections to doing it, such as, he needed to work for money and he needed to get married and explained how difficult life could be in those conventional ways and he would probably become something of a celebrity if he could stick with being a statue. Dr. Q said later that while he had some apprehensions, the visits were fun.

K stayed at home, and, in fact, spent periods of time being a statue. The mother enjoyed it, the father was furious, especially in that he came to understand that it was part of K's treatment and K was getting better. Gradually K was getting re-integrated. By Friday, he was clean shaven, neatly dressed and bantering with the treatment team. Mother drove him to the clinic for the first three days, on the fourth visit he drove by himself. A week later Dr. V, who had worked with the family earlier, returned from vacation and along with Dr. Q began to see the whole family in psychotherapy. In the middle of the series of family interviews, father talked about paranoid episodes he had had in his young adulthood. Mother described masturbation fantasies that her beauty parlor customers had told to her. K steadily got better and appeared to have integrated himself at a better, move available level. At the last family interview, he said he didn't want any more family meetings since the family came only because of him. "It would be nice if *they* would change the way that *you* have," said Dr. Q. Dr. V asked if K had any more mysteries. K said yes, he still had some. In fact, he had a new one. "What is it?" asked Dr. V. K: "You know, looking back, I was really uptight a couple of months ago and I really felt far away from people and felt like I was getting further away. Now whenever I feel like I'm moving away, I just hold up my hand like this (he raised his extended right hand to eye level as Dr. Q had done at the first interview) and things are okay again. It feels like I return to people."

Followup: K was symptom-free for two years. During that time he married and had a child.

In therapy, four outcomes seem possible. (1) The family starts to laugh at themselves or the therapist, thereby transcending their impotence to change and the therapist's impotence to change them. (2) They laugh at the therapist, transcending the doctor-patient interpersonal block. "God, doc, you're crazier than I am," thus acknowledging their own craziness. (3) When the above perceptions occur, it gives the sightseeing patients the chance to become real patients. It is for fun, not for real. They shift gears into another order of experience, rather than simply stepping on the brake or on the accelerator. The other possibility is (4) they do not do anything with it. They may break out of their stiff reality compartment a short while, have some fun, then the old family homeostasis brings them back to reality, killing the possibility of excitement and creativity. It may be that if a porpoise is turned back into the ocean, he may forget all about how to jump and turn flips.

ACTING-IN

The other process which we want to describe is "acting-in." Psychiatry has long been concerned with the negative aspects and dangers of *acting-out*; the process utilized most frequently by adolescents and psychopaths who go AWOL or blast their way out of situational stress by escaping into social reality either in a verbal or a behavioral way. The process of escape is related to one's conviction that security is based on transference to the community or to insignificant others. Its effect is the decrease of affective involvement with his family or other intimates.

By contrast, acting-in is a routine method for increasing the level of affect and intimacy. In psychotherapy the most frequently used method of acting-in is well known; the therapist's silence. John Rosen used acting-in most effectively in an active way. In this process the therapist initiates an intensification of the relationship either by provocative behavior, provocative words or by challenging the patient and at the same time increasing his own affect.

One of the problems with learning techniques of confrontation, expanding absurdity or acting-in is that one has to practice it in order to learn how it works. Learning how to be passive is much easier because one does not become responsible, but avoids responsibility except for an internalized sense of decency. Whereas by moving into the therapy, one takes overt, specific responsibilities and these can be ominous; families leave therapy, become bitter, sue for malpractice and damage one's reputation. Misinterpretations are possible in multiple combinations. The therapist is also closer to the position of the real parent in the sense that he can choose any style of inducing change he wants. Whatever he does, the family will use it as a basis to push for their own independence by getting out from under his dominance.

Co-therapy

In family therapy the advantage of a co-therapist or consultant is that he provides opportunity for alternating between being a function and being a person. One of the reasons that we have been trained to be passive is because if a therapist, working by himself, moves from being passive to being active, he is apt to be locked into a control struggle with the family and lose. To avoid the stalemate, the therapist stops being a parent and becomes one of the children in the family scene, usually the older brother or sister. The therapist needs to recognize that this move into greater activity by confrontation, acting-in or absurdity to increase the affect flow, necessitates his clear capacity to back out again, lest he become trapped. He can do this in a number of ways: by denying his move, by confessing his personhood, by moving back into his role with enough strength so that the family recognizes that he has moved in and that he has what it takes to move out, by utilizing someone else to protect his moving in so that he can back out with their help.

Case Examples

The following examples demonstrate the use of acting-in. Like the impulse to be absurd, this process is born of the therapist's frustration. It is not something which one decides to do strategically but rather something that happens out of an impasse or a clear defeat.

Case Example 4. M.G., age 15, had overdosed on her mother's Valium® and was hospitalized for three weeks. Upon discharge, she was referred for therapy with her family. Mr. G was neurotic, intellectual and a condescending blow-hard. Mrs. G was a day care administrator and an ex-encounter groupie, who used clear, affect-free communication as a parenting model. M's 11-year-old brother was only slightly less grandiose than M. At the third interview, the two kids started playing with the therapist's telephone. Mother objected mildly by whining, "I feel uncomfortable when you play with the doctor's telephone. Would you please stop?" The two looked over their shoulders, sneered and went on playing. Their play became destructive. "Hey, you characters, I don't want you doing that to my phone," the therapist said. The kids did not even bother to sneer at the therapist, but kept right on with their work, dismantling the phone by removing the mouthpiece, the earpiece and then starting on the underside of the carriage. The therapist suddenly became angry and said, "Look, dammit, that's *my* phone, I don't want you playing with it, now put it back together and sit down!!" The two looked at the therapist, startled by his anger. They stopped their play immediately, put the phone back together and went to sit by their mother. The interview and the therapy moved on. After the hour ended, a first year psychiatry resident, acting as co-therapist, said, "Wow, what would you have done if they hadn't stopped?" The therapist raised his eyebrows and said, "I don't know. But I'll tell you one thing, I am glad they did."

This is an example of the use of the therapist's affect when he is being out-flanked by the family process. His first remark was heard as the same kind of meaningless words that the mother used. They knew about mother's anger at the therapist for implicating her passivity in the daughter's suicide attempt. The children also knew about father's anger at the therapist for implicating him in the family (the father had refused to come to the second interview and the therapist had sent them all home), and were simply following subliminal orders.

Case Example 5. G.B. was the 33-year-old heir to a family industrial fortune. His father was the corporate head. G had worked as dad's boy in the corporation, holding a series of jobs from loading trucks to high level management. He had experienced a brief psychotic episode at age 19. He had been reared in the protective way that a poodle might be by a trinity including his father, mother and Aunt Ellen. His second psychotic episode occurred at age 33 while staying at the family summer home with his wife, their two children and the aforementioned trinity. Family therapy began intensively with all three generations meeting for two-hour interviews on three consecutive days. They had a fairly good initial response. When their anxiety decreased, the family decided to return to their homes in another state. G became quite ill again and was hospitalized and the family returned for weekly family meetings. Early in the treatment, the co-therapy team made their strength clear by being both tough and caring. They had played with the younger children, had nurtured G in the way of rubbing his back and promising to take care of him, and became grandparents to the group by parenting the corporation president. The family group was discouraged by G's relapse, so the therapists suggested that they bring more people from the extended family. People from all over the map came for a three-hour session. G was extremely disruptive, clowning and clanging. The interview was disjointed and seemed useless. In the first hour, the therapists waited for the family to take charge of G. Different family members asked him to quit disrupting, but to no avail. They griped at him; it did not help. Aunt Ellen, with whom he was quite close, coaxed him into leaving the room, then she locked the door, but he created a huge ruckus and she allowed him back in. The family had so long ignored their own craziness that they had no way to handle G. Ther therapists assumed that the family could not get more than irritated at G because they needed him to keep them distracted from themselves. Assuming that the family could pay more attention to itself if G was quiet, Dr. B, one of the co-therapists, sat next to G and tenderly rubbed his back. Then G's five-year-old son came over to Dr. B and sat on his lap, recapitulating a scene from an earlier therapy hour. G became very quiet as he helped Dr. B rub his son's back. The co-therapist, Dr. E, took responsibility for conducting the interview. Suddenly, the room became a madhouse when G started an argument with his sister about a remark the sister made about mother. G became agitated and went to sit by his mother. He then took off on a sexual seductive mocking with his wife. Dr. B exploded, rose from his chair, went over to G who was standing and said, "Listen, I've had enough of this crap from you! We're trying to do some work and I'm sick and tired of you interrupting me. I want you to sit down and shut up!" Thereupon, Dr. B grabbed G by the collar, took a glass of water from G's hand, slowly emptied its contents over G's head, then sat him down in the chair. As this was happening, the patient's father said, "You know, somebody should have done that long ago!" G was furious. He grabbed Dr. B by the throat and they tussled. A male nursing assistant intervened and said that G had to go to the ward's seclusion room. Dr. B declared himself crazier than G, sentenced himself to the same seclusion room, and off they went. Mother went to the ladies room to vomit. Dr. E, the co-therapist, took over to calm the family. After a 20-minute interval, everyone returned to finish the interview.

The next family interview occurred six days later. Father was depressed and tense as the interview began. He said, "Last night, I came to the hospital to see G and I got so nervous I had to leave. I felt queasy and light-headed. I had to get out of the hospital." But G was calm and much better organized since his father's visit. He was talking straight, he was eager to leave the hospital, and G's wife, contrary to her earlier feelings, wanted him to come home. Father went on to say how he had experienced a flashback at the last family meeting. When G was 10 years old, G was being a pest at the breakfast table. Father became furious with him, picked up a bowl of Cream of Wheat and emptied it helmet style over G's head. Mother was enraged with father for having done this and the parents had a bitter fight. After he had done that to G, he had somehow been stripped of his parental rights. He had never exploded at G since and felt quite impotent to stop anything.

G left the hospital the day after the interview, and the family returned to their homes in a distant state. Care was transferred to someone else and no followup was available.

This case demonstrates the kind of intuitive tune that is possible with the family when the therapist develops intense involvement with them. This kind of event has not been uncommon in the author's experience with families. It is not unusual for the therapist to be able to rocket into the family's irrational stratosphere in the way exemplified.

A word of caution is necessary. The younger therapist needs to proceed carefully. Older, more experienced therapists can act with more initiative. The acting-in therapist has a problem similar to that of the scapegoat. He is pushing the system, but he must be careful not to push it too far lest the system come down on and extrude him. In this case, while the behavior of the therapist was extreme, it was supported by a number of family members and the co-therapist.

Acting-out is the way an isolated member of the family tries to make himself a member of the human race by carrying his need for security into the community. He relieves his anxiety by belonging to the anonymous whole, the crowd. *Acting-in* is the reverse of this, it *is the effort on the part of the psychotherapist to intensify the anxiety*, to increase the level of interpersonal stress, to bring about an experiential breakthrough into a new way of living, a new way of being in the here and now.

Rosen's model utilized massive verbal assaults, for example, ten minutes of demanding that a catatonic schizophrenic declare his own name in full. Rosen (1965) increased the intensity with his voice and posture until the patient in terror conformed to the request. Other ways of doing it include massaging a patient's neck, hand wrestling or invading the patient's feelings about the death of a relative. By reversing the role of the symptoms, the therapist produces an acting-in effect. When the therapist says it is good that the son is stealing cars since that probably keeps father from cheating on his income tax, the therapist has, in effect, reprecipitated the family's anxiety which had been relieved by their elected scapegoat.

ADAPTING THE USE OF THE ABSURD AND ACTING-IN TO EXISTING THERAPY STYLES

Clinical examples have been used to illustrate how absurdity and acting-in are utilized by the authors. These do not constitute new theories about psychotherapy, but rather are tools for the psychotherapist to add to his collection. Their most specific use is to aid in getting past he impotence impasse.

This paper began by describing the problems that arise out of the therapist's domination by his professional grandparents. Grandparents are a reality and an important one. There is a kind of safety in staying under the dominance of the grandparents while maintaining one's dignity by half-heartedly complaining about them. Therapists stay alive by facing their need to individuate. Here are some guidelines which might be helpful in times of identity crisis.

1. Discover your absurdity and take your impotence seriously. Be willing to confess these to your patients and colleagues. If the therapist has not faced his own absurdity, the methods described in this paper may take the form of an ambush; a strategic attack on the patient from a dangerous facade of robust mental health and implied over-adequacy.

2. Taking over responsibility for a family requires an intact corpus callosum. The left brain and right brain must stay awake and be able to alternate and share dominance. Hypertrophy of either hemisphere is incapacitating to the psychotherapist.

3. Therapists will have trouble with the absurd or acting-in if they have not had an affair with their own sadism and accepted its place in their own lives. Searles (1965, p. 422), after his careful work with

schizophrenics, says that sadistic impulses have at their root a healthy, playful quality. In his playful sadism with schizophrenics, he discovered what is best and healthiest in the patient's early relationship with the mother; playful, unfettered interaction. A therapist may be surprised to learn that there is a kind of confusion and chaos which is not disorganized and destructive, but like play, thoroughly pleasurable; the playful chaos which a mother and child can share.

4. Learning more active and responsible therapy skills is augmented by working with a co-therapist. The therapist who works alone has problems similar to those of the single parent. They end up either too close or too far away with little option to change the distance. It is important to have colleagues close enough to share experiences in the way that the mother and father do after the children have gone to bed.

5. Caring is the modulator of quality as the protagonist of *Zen and the Art of Motorcycle Maintenance* (Pirsig, 1974) discovered. The same holds true in psychotherapy. Caring is least well expressed by the words, "I care." It is much better defined by the therapist's personal style.

6. The impulse to become more active works best when it arises out of the therapist's frustration rather than out of strategic planning.

The problem of the psychotherapist's impotence cannot be ignored. It forces itself into his attention and effects his decision making about treatment and his career. The therapist must wrestle with his inadequacy. The struggle is for more creativity and who knows, out of it the grandparents may even become more human.

REFERENCES

Bateson, G. Paper presented at the Double Bind Conference, March 3 and 4, 1977, in New York City.

Pirsig, Robert M. *Zen and the Art of Motorcycle Maintenance.* New York: William Morrow and Company, Inc., 1974.

Rosen, John. Personal Communication, 1958.

Searles, Harold F. Schizophrenic Communication. *Collected Papers on Schizophrenia and Related Subjects,* New York: International Universities Press, 1965, 381-428.

Whitaker, Carl A. Psychotherapy of the absurd: With a special emphasis on the psychotherapy of aggression. *Family Process,* 1975, *14,* 1-16.

Wynne, L.C., Ryckoff, I.M., Day, J. & Hirsch, S.I. Pseudomutuality in the family relations of schizophrenics. *Psychiatry,* 1958, *21,* 205-220.

BEHAVIORAL TECHNIQUES

The behavioral techniques described in this chapter are all aimed at modifying observable behavior. In effect, these techniques are developed from traditional behavioral principles for use with the family. Operant conditioning, systematic desensitization, modeling, and other behavioral activities are all adapted to modify present family functioning.

The articles in this chapter emphasize the importance of environmental influences in developing and maintaining maladaptive behaviors. They also share a common belief that with reinforcement the newly acquired positive behaviors will continue. In addition, enhancing the family's ability to problem solve and communicate clearly appears to be a major focus of the therapy.

William Coe presents a case study and then relates his use of a "financial plan" to work with that family. First Coe describes the specific behaviors that indicate the need for such an approach. He then describes specifically the steps necessary to modify a client's behavior and finally offers some general rules the therapist can follow.

Eisler and Hersen focus on the use of behavioral techniques for intervening during a family oriented crisis. They also describe several cases and appropriate behavioral techniques. They suggest that an assessment can be best accomplished by observing the entire family's coping and problem-solving skills. Modeling, verbal reinforcement, and contractual arrangements are focused upon as ways of modifying behaviors and helping family members learn new ways of relating.

The concluding article in this chapter describes the use of behavioral contracting in conjoint family therapy. Rutherford and Bowen offer a rationale for use of contracts in family therapy and provide a few examples of previous contractual arrangements made by other families.

The behavioral techniques help clients focus on specific behaviors and hopefully result in modification of these observable behaviors. Once the therapist and client can specify the behavior that is to be changed, one of these techniques can be applied.

Chapter 20

A BEHAVIORAL APPROACH TO DISRUPTED FAMILY INTERACTIONS

WILLIAM C. COE

Dick's Family: A Case Study

This case study demonstrates an approach to family treatment that arose from a need for an effective, short-term therapy for latency age and adolescent children. The major complaints of these families arise from their children's misconduct. Most commonly, the complaints come from school personnel and parents, or in more serious cases, law enforcement agencies. By the time the children are referred to me as a private practioner, considerable turmoil is already observable at school including disruptive behavior, truancy, and low achievement; in the home there is constant fighting and discipline; and in the community some type of disturbance is often noticeable. The family is usually caught up in self-destructive attempts to communicate, and the child's self-esteem, whatever there was of it, is often at a low ebb. The usual family, group or individual therapies, at least in my experience, have not proven very effective. If they are, the expense is so great that an added and sometimes destructive burden is placed on the family.

Dick was referred by a school psychologist because of behavioral difficulties in school. He was 12 years old, in the sixth grade and doing quite poorly. Dick's parents accompanied him to the first meeting where I saw them alone briefly, Dick briefly, then all of them together. The following information was obtained from the two short interviews and the school psychologist.

Dick was a neurologically handicapped child (apparently from a birth defect) who had become increasingly difficult to manage as he approached adolescence. He frequently quarreled with his mother and refused to do what she asked. Temper tantrums were the major complaint. They were prolonged, involved cursing, yelling, and running away from home; he had even threatened to attack his mother with a knife.

From W. Coe, A Behavioral Approach to Disrupted Family Interactions, _Psychotherapy: Theory, Research and Practice,_ 9:80-85, 1972. Courtesy of _Psychotherapy: Theory, Research and Practice._

At school he was difficult to manage, did not get along with the other children, refused to do his lessons, and was frequently truant. The school had reached the point of limiting his attendance to two hours a day of special class and one hour per week in a recreational program. As the school psychologist put it, "He's a real tough apple."

The "hassle" at home had grown to major proportions. His parents wanted to ship him off to an institution and he was willing to leave, if only he had some place to go. They had, in fact, made contact with a residential center some 200 miles away. But in talking with Dick it was apparent that he was not an "animal" nor was he out of control. He had, however, a very low opinion of himself that was only reinforced by his negative behaviors. Dick's parents were surprisingly reasonable people, at least from what I'd been led to expect, but obviously at their wits end. Both of them vacillated between anger at his behavior and guilt over the fact that he was neurologically handicapped. It was also clear they felt both helpless and hopeless. They had already run the professional gamut—psychiatrists, neurologists, pediatricians, child guidance clinics—nothing had done much good. Dick's mother had benefited temporarily from individual therapy aimed at helping her to cope with the difficulties of raising Dick and drug therapy for him had been tried. In fact, it was still being used, but only when the dosage was large enough to sedate him did it have controlling effects on his behavior. They also felt the school system had pushed them from one alternative to another—again, with no results. I am certain that to them I was just another therapist that was going to "talk to them" and make everything okay, just another "doctor" who was going to tell them they had to expect this from a "brain-damaged" child. In sum, they were a family that had become confused, alienated, guilty, and most disheartening of all, lost all hope that they could cope with their difficulties.

I saw them all together for the last half of the first session. Their interactions reflected the distrust and alienation that had grown from their difficulties. If Dick said he was going to try and improve, his parents only looked at him knowingly—they had "heard that before." Rather than allow them to continue to hassle I intervened quite directly and began to explain what we would do.

First, I told them that what I thought was happening had little to do with Dick's neurological difficulties. They had worked themselves into circular hang-ups that were making it extremely difficult for all of them.

"In order to stop this, and to make everybody more comfortable, we're going to let Dick do essentially whatever he wants to do, which is, by the way, to behave properly. And you, his parents, are not going to have to punish him or continually ride him to have him do what you want."

Needless to say their eyebrows arched following my proclamation. Dick flashed me a knowing smile that he now "had it made" and his parents began to protest that he could not be left to his own choices.

Again I interrupted by saying that they should at least listen to my plans and my explanations before making a firm judgment against them. I went on to say that Dick was to be treated as an adult now and that he was to be given the responsibility for determining his own actions.

"To help him do this, we are *all* (I always accented each reference to total family participation) going to agree on Dick's desirable behavior and on his undesirable behavior. Then we will establish a reason for *everybody* to want to work toward change. For the next week you are going to have to continue dealing with your difficulties as you see fit, but before seeing me again the *three* of you are to agree on a list of behaviors that are satisfactory to all of you. One list will be the things that *all* of you want Dick to do, but that he has difficulty carrying out; another will be the behaviors that *all* of you do not want Dick to do; and the third will be those things that Dick values the most at present, or, things that he likes but you do not agree with."

At that point we stopped to look for some examples of each of the three behavioral classes. The first comment was by Dick's mother, "I want him to be good." My reply was, "I'm sure all of us want Dick to be good but that is too vague an idea to be very useful. One of the important parts of this program is to be sure that everyone knows *exactly* what behavior we are talking about so there is no conflict about whether or not he performs it. He has a right to know exactly what you expect of him and you have the right to know exactly what to expect from him. Therefore, we shall have to look for more specific things."

At that point Dick said that he did not want to have temper tantrums. Everybody agreed heartily and we had our first agreed-upon behavior, one that was placed in the "Don't" column. His mother then said, "I'd like him to go to school willingly." My retort was that "going to school" was useful for our purposes, however, "willingly" had no place in the system because it is impossible to tell for certain when a person is willing. It is not observable and, therefore, it leaves openings for valid arguments on both sides. Fine, they all agreed that Dick should go to school, a behavior in the "Do" column. The things he liked to do were a little easier to define; one was watching television, another was eating popcorn, and another was staying up after his bedtime (one his parents did not agree they wanted although conceded that he did). These behaviors were included under the "Reinforcers" column.

I drew the session to a close by explaining the "financial plan." Dick was to be paid in points, or whatever medium of exchange they agreed on, for all of the "Do" behaviors. That is, if he went to school he would be paid, say, ten points. On the other hand, he would have to pay for any behaviors or items in the "Don't" list. If Dick wanted to have a temper tantrum, for example, he could do so at the established price, say one point per minute. He also paid for the things that he liked, e.g., popcorn might be worth five points per bowl.

They were told to come to an agreement before seeing me next time on the number of points Dick could earn for each "Do" behavior and the cost of each behavior in the other two lists. I also explained that while this program might seem a little strange there was nothing so unusual about it—it was exactly the way adults carry out their lives—the only difference being the medium of exchange. Adults earn money for performing pre-determined activities and spend it for the things they want. Dick's response was highly positive. His parents still seemed doubtful but they reserved early judgment.

At our meeting a week later they presented me with a list of behaviors, some of which required further clarification. One reinforcing behavior, for instance, was for Dick to stay up after his nine o'clock bedtime. It was necessary to incorporate a time factor with this behavior, i.e., ten points for the first half-hour, 30 points for the next half-hour, and so on in order to prevent him from staying up all night. As always, it was necessary that he and his parents agree on a compromise before it was accepted. At any rate, by the second session a trial system for the family had been established and it was agreed that they implement it immediately. A chart for daily tabulation of Dick's earnings and expenses was to be posted in a conspicuous place. Any difficulties were to be noted, resolved to the family's satisfaction, or else be left alone until we could discuss them at our next meeting.

The third meeting brought me a great deal of gratification. Dick literally bounced into my office saying, "Dr. Coe, I'm worth 400 points!" I suspect this was the first time in some years he had felt he was anything but a misfit, neurologically-handicapped child. His parents followed, smiling and shaking their heads in disbelief. Dick has not thrown a temper tantrum all week (they had become almost a daily occurrence before) and he had been doing all of the positive behaviors. What he had done, in fact, was to save nearly all his points. He had spent only a minimal amount on reinforcing behaviors and had the rest in the "bank."

Obviously, the points by themselves were very reinforcing for Dick. I anticipated, however, that it would not be long before their attractiveness decreased and suggested that they establish a "trade-in" program. (The way it was at this point, Dick could stay up all night, eat 20 pounds of popcorn, etc.) His excess points could be traded for other things, such as money or special activities, depending upon what the family felt appropriate. They all agreed a bank trade-in was a good idea and not wanting to look a gift horse in the mouth I suggested we terminate the session. They could call me if something went wrong and we could meet to discuss it. Without thinking I added, "There's no sense running up the bill." The spontaneous look of gratitude that appeared on the parents' faces was indeed a moving sight. Dick later picked up this statement and when a problem was resolved he would say, "Well, that's that, no sense in running up the bill."

Two weeks later I received a call from Dick's mother. She was very upset because Dick had had a temper tantrum. I made an appointment for them to come in and discuss the matter but in the meantime she had his medication increased to the point that he was almost immobilized.

As it turned out, however, Dick's tantrum was a result of his mother's failure to follow the program. (So far in my experience it has always been the parent who breaks the bargain first.) Dick had asked to stay up later and pay the required points, but she had responded, "Dick I'd rather you didn't stay up tonight." He became upset, insistent, and eventually threw a "wing-dinger" of a temper tantrum. His mother recognized what had happened after we discussed it but the price of his tantrum had caused him to go quite a way into debt, essentially bankrupt. She thought the point system was finished, Dick was discouraged, and there seemed no way to remedy the situation. Quite frankly, I was somewhat baffled myself. Dick was dejected, his mother was dejected, and a mournful silence filled the room.

After a few anxious but thoughtful moments I said, "Okay, what happens to an adult when he faces bankruptcy? Well, he can either declare bankruptcy and be relieved of further indebtedness, or he can pay off his debts in some reasonable way."

We dismissed the idea of declaring bankruptcy because that would mean that Dick could "blow it" at almost any time and the system would lose its effectiveness. We decided that the best solution was to have him work off his debts. In order not to deprive him of all reinforcements in the meantime, however, he would be paid double points for his positive behaviors with 80 percent of his total earnings going toward paying off his debt, the remainder for buying reinforcements. Satisfied with the resolution, they again left (in less than a half-hour) with instructions to call me if it were necessary.

A few other incidents occurred but increasingly our meetings were further apart and shorter. In fact, some things were easily handled over the phone. Dick's parents were figuring out unique and creative ways to adapt their particular circumstances to the point system; in fact, they seemed to become quite confident that they could deal with their problems. To make matters ever better, Dick became quite adept at making his own creative contributions toward resolving conflicts.

The program was also expanded to include Dick's school work. With the cooperation of the school officials, especially his classroom teacher, it was arranged that he be awarded points for school achievement and adaptive work habits. The points he earned were recorded on his home chart daily and used to purchase reinforcers. By happenstance Dick was later placed in an educationally handicapped class using operant principles. Within one year his academic achievement level was almost to grade level, a gain of nearly three school years, and he was receiving A+'s, A's, and B's for his work.

That summer, several months after the program was instituted, the family enjoyed a vacation with Dick for the first time and he was off the point system while they were away. Over the following year Dick's family has begun to lead an entirely different life. Guilt, fear, hostility and hopelessness were being replaced with working together, respecting each other and approaching their problems in living with optimism and certainty.

Basic Concepts

A behavior modification technique is used as the vehicle in changing disruptive patterns of family interaction. The techniques that have developed from learning theory and its related research are proving to be the most effective methods of modifying behavior. The present program applies principles from operant conditioning, quite similar to token economies and adapts them to family functioning (Bandura, 1969; Schaefer & Martin, 1969).

The family program: The first step is to determine the appropriateness of this approach. This decision can probably be reached in the first half-hour after interviewing the parents alone, the child alone, and all of them together. Some of the major indications appear to be as follows: (1) The parents will present a number of behavioral complaints about their child and openly state, or clearly intimate, that they are unable to change them. (2) The parents will show that their only methods of control involve punishment or withholding of privileges. (3) The child feels he is being oppressed, that his parents are overly restrictive, and that he cannot "get through" to them. In short, he shows a need to be independent and sees his parents as preventing it. (4) The family's interactions reflect the foregoing factors. They do not seem to hear each other, there are numerous filings of cross-complaints, and hostility marks their exchanges.

Once the therapist decides to try this approach, he must introduce the program. There is no set way to begin but it is probably most effective to aim comments at their strongest needs. He could explain that their current ways of interacting are clearly not succeeding for any of them. They have formed patterns that lead to distress in both the parents and child. Next, he could indicate that he would like them to try an approach that will: (a) make it unnecessary for the parents to continually "ride" their child (this is often one of their chief complaints); and, (b) that the child will be able to do whatever he wants (often his primary need).

The next step is to introduce, and model, clear communication and problem solving. The therapist should introduce the three lists of behaviors with clear examples of each serving as teaching vehicles. Stress is placed on clarifying the exact nature of each behavior and on the family working as a unit by agreeing on the desirability or undesirability of each. Learning that they can agree-to-disagree may be the most enlightening—it is often a foreign experience to them. Their responsibility to come to agreement, the first step in problem solving, is also stressed. If they cannot agree they are to bring their problem to the therapist as a consultant. The three behavioral lists exemplified in the preceding case are as follows:

(1) The "Don'ts": behaviors that both the parents and child agree that he does, but should not do.

(2) The "Do's": behaviors that all agree the child should do, but has trouble doing.

(3) The "Reinforcers": behaviors or things that the child likes, whether or not his parents agree they like them.

The last step is to explain the "financial plan." First, the child is to receive payment, points or whatever medium of exchange the family decides upon, for all the behaviors in the "Do" column and he is to pay for all of the behaviors in the "Don't" and "Reinforcer" columns. The family establishes the specific behaviors for their needs and the price of each as homework. They must come to agreement, often through compromise, on how payment is made and charges are incurred.

Balancing income and outflow is of course critical and requires a good deal of problem solving. Some general rules, however, seem to be appropriate. (1), The income and cost of each behavior should be established on the basis of its adaptiveness to the child. Going to school, for example, usually a "Do" behavior, should bring the child many more points than setting the table. Or, temper tantrums, a "Don't" behavior, should cost much more than watching TV, a reinforcer, (2), Start by establishing the costs in the "Don't" and "Reinforcers" columns, then balance the income for the "Do" behaviors so the child can afford a reasonable amount of "Reinforcers" if he does the most important items in the "Do" column, (3), Strive for affluence rather than poverty. If the child performs all the desirable behaviors he should gain ample points to establish a "banking program." His excess points may be saved for long-term reinforcers such as trade-in for money, special outings, etc., or for adolescents, a car payment, reduced time on probation, etc. The bank trade-in items, of course, should be highly desirable in order to discourage orgies of "Don't" behaviors, (4), Stress reinforcement whenever possible. Try to make it clear that the child gains when he performs positive behaviors. If truancy is a problem, for instance, pay him highly for going to school rather than charge him if he does not. Positive behaviors should be associated with positive pay-offs, not aversive consequences. Use overt aversion only as a last resort. For example, Dick's temper tantrums were a constant threat to the program because of their high cost and the possibility of bankruptcy. We finally agreed that he could only pay for one-half hour of tantrum, then he would be spanked by his father, a very aversive contingency for him.

It should also be made clear that the program is at all times meant to be flexible. When disagreements arise within the family they should be dealt with by incorporating them in the behavioral lists. There is no need to fight and argue as long as they have the financial plan as a vehicle to help them resolve their differences.

The family members must agree to make certain commitments to the program and these should be stated clearly as often as necessary until they are willing to accept them. On the parent's side of the bargain they must agree to let their child buy *any* of the payable behaviors if he has the capital. From the child's side, he must agree to do only what he can afford. (The family can modify this part, and in my experience, the parents are usually so pleased when their child begins to change that they allow some free-of-charge activity.)

The Goals: Several goals become apparent. First, and most important, a disrupted family has a focus (the financial plan) around which they can come together and use their strengths in changing their behavior. As the system begins to work their new ways of interacting are reinforced and should eventually take on secondary reinforcing characteristics, i.e., their operant rate increases and they begin to generalize into everyday family life.

More specifically, the following patterns of family interactions are established: (1) clarity of communication so that ideally each family member knows precisely what the other means; (2) effective methods of reaching agreement through recognizing the needs of each person; and (3) direction of energy toward solving problems rather than hurting each other.

There are obvious gains to be won by the child. The increased frequency of positive behaviors is in itself adaptive. His behavior brings other rewards from the environment besides the "points" so that generalized patterns of positive behaviors are more likely to develop. Gaining independence is a more global concept that derives from the child's responsibility in staying with his commitment to the probram and performing his end of the financial plan. And, last but by no means least, the child should begin to build a positive self-image. Most of these children hold a very low opinion of themselves despite their seeming bravado at times. It is not easy for someone who has not "been there" to understand the significance that positive gains may have for a child who is used to being called "bad."

REFERENCES

Bandura, A. *Principles of behavior modification.* New York: Holt, Rinehart, and Winston, 1969.

Coe, W.C. Dick and his parents—a case study. Part of an address presented at the conference, "The Troubled Adolescent and His Family" sponsored by University of California Medical School, Mendocino, March 1970.

Coe, W.C. A family operant program. Paper presented at the annual meeting of the Western Psychological Association, Los Angeles, April 1970.

Schaeffer, H.H., & Martin, P.L. *Behavioral therapy.* New York: McGraw-Hill, 1969.

Chapter 21

BEHAVIORAL TECHNIQUES IN FAMILY-ORIENTED CRISIS INTERVENTION

Richard M. Eisler and Michel Hersen

Behavioral techniques in short-term family-oriented crisis intervention treatment are examined within the context of crisis theory and behavior modification. It is noted that both approaches emphasize the importance of environmental influences in developing and maintaining maladaptive behaviors. Methods for restructuring discordant family relationships through the use of particular behavioral techniques such as feedback, modeling, behavioral rehearsal, instructions, and behavioral contracts are outlined. Three case studies are presented to illustrate the therapeutic flexibility of these techniques with crisis-prone families. Not only are families helped with presenting complaints, but a major emphasis is placed on their learning more successful problem solving skills that are to be implemented in daily interactions.

During the past decade the mental health profession has witnessed rapid development of several alternatives to purely pschodynamic formulations of behavioral maladjustment. In the traditional model the focus has been on intrapsychic abnormalities such as excessive anxiety, poor impulse control, characterological defects, etc., in understanding psychopathology, However, increasing attention is now being paid to patterns of response within the social environment in maintaining maladaptive interactive behavior.

The use of selected positive and negative environmental consequences (operant conditioning) in changing the behavior of psychiatric patients was first tested experimentally by Lindsley[1,2] and Lindsley and Skinner.[3]

From R. Eisler and M. Hersen, Behavioral Techniques in Family-Oriented Crisis Intervention, *Archives of General Psychiatry*, 28:111-16, 1973. Copyright 1973, American Medical Association.

Principles of reinforcement derived from theories of operant conditioning were subsequently applied to clinically relevant problems by Ayllon and his associates.[4-7] Since then numerous other behavioral techniques have been applied to develop and maintain more desirable behavior in a broad range of psychiatric patients. Included among these techniques are feedback, instructions, behavior rehearsal, assertive training, modeling, and behavioral contracting.

Another clinical approach focusing on the relationship of adverse environmental and interpersonal stresses to development of psychopathology has been termed crisis intervention.[8-11] The goal of crisis intervention, encompassing a variety of therapeutic techniques, is to rapidly assess and treat psychological disequilibrium within the natural social environment. While treatment of the immediate social milieu typifies an approach previously utilized by family therapists of varying persuasions, crisis intervention focuses more on the immediate psychosocial precipitants of disorganization.

Concepts of Crisis

The significance of life crises related to increased vulnerability to acute impairment and enduring behavioral disorder was vividly depicted in Lindemann's[10] classic study of bereaved disaster victims whose relatives died in the tragic Coconut Grove fire in Boston. Caplan and his associates[11-13] subsequently formulated a view of crisis as a transitional period during which a variety of environmental stresses (e.g., death, divorce, illness, premature birth, financial difficulty) created problems of such magnitude that the individual was unable to use his normal coping skills. Thus, the course of the individual's interaction with his natural environment at strategic points was implicated in the development of unadaptive behavioral patterns. Crisis intervention, then, according to these writers involves treatment directed towards helping the individual grapple with and overcome real life stresses.

In discussing a framework for treatment of families in crisis, previous writers have borrowed from individually oriented theories. By contrast, Atherton et al[14] discuss functional vs dysfunctional role behaviors within a social system in terms of how satisfying they are on a reciprocal basis to individual members. They argue that:

> . . . the ideal state of affairs would exist when persons live with each other in a state of mutually satisfying interdependence in which those persons are able to achieve the maximum goal attainment and personal satisfaction in their relationships with each other and their institutional systems.

With respect to crisis intervention in social systems, Jones and Polak[15] and Polak[16] recommend confrontation of individuals within the system in terms of the mutual problems. It is also suggested that the therapist facilitate expression of emotion relative to the crisis as well as assisting family members to reorganize their roles around critical issues. In assessing inadequate crisis coping behavior, Polak[16] underscores the failure of leadership within the system, role conflict, and the reinforcement of maladaptive behavior.

Behavioral Approaches to Crisis Intervention

From the above discussion it appears that crisis intervention, focusing on the immediate social and environmental precipitants of disturbed family functioning, might provide behaviorally oriented clinicians a useful framework within which to apply specific techniques based on social learning theory. Therefore, the remainder of this paper will be directed towards an examination of the role of behavioral techniques in family-oriented crisis intervention. The use of particular behavioral methods in the rapid restructuring of the family system will be outlined.

Three major goals of a behavioral approach to family crisis situations will be described:

1. A primary goal is to develop new problem solving or coping behavior within the family to help members resolve the precipitating problem successfully. Instead of continuing antagonistic relationships between members of the family system, the objective is to generate cooperative behavior through a program of mutual reinforcement.

2. A second goal involves the expression of both positive and negative affect with respect to the precipitating problem. Effective communication of emotion appears to be very useful in problem solving when it is expressed appropriately and in amounts relative to the eliciting stimulus.

3. A final goal is to assist the family in the application of newly developed coping skills to other conflict-ridden situations. Not only must the family deal with the immediate crisis, but family members must learn how to use their newly acquired methods of problem solving in a variety of areas. This is known as generalization or positive transfer in learning theory parlance.

In the following sections specific behavioral techniques, as they apply to the crisis intervention model, will be described in some detail.

Feedback

Feedback, or information given to patients about the nature and effects of their behavior, appears to be an important but not fully understood element in both psychodynamic and behavioral approaches to psychotherapy. The administration of feedback to patients regarding specific aspects of their behavior has proven to effect positive changes in relevant target behaviors under study.[17-19]

With families experiencing a crisis, present clinical experience suggests that immediate feedback on their present modes of communication is often a prerequisite to changing the family's interaction patterns. Feedback in the form of therapist comments, role playing, or videotape replays of interactive sequences can all be used to give individuals information as to how their behavior affects other family members. It can also be used to show the family, as a unit, its difficulties in effective problem solving behavior. For example, some families are so confict avoidant that they discuss everything imaginable except their most difficult problems. Other families delay problem solving attempts until so much excess emotion is aroused that effective discussion is impossible. Still other families place the entire burden of a family problem on a particular individual (often the identified patient) instead of sharing the responsibility among all members. Additionally, feedback can be used to point out confused or inconsistent communications within the family. Confusion often results when there is a discrepancy between the verbal and nonverbal aspects of a communication. The purpose of initial feedback, therefore, is to clarify precisely what is effective and what is ineffective about the family's problem solving communications.

Modeling and Role Playing

Modeling is a technique based on principles of imitative learning. When used in combination with feedback and instructions, the necessity of the individual's discovering the most effective response through trial and error is eliminated. The research literature indicates that imitating behavior of a model has been useful in developing functional behaviors where serious deficits exist. Moreover, surplus conditioned responses have also been eliminated through modeling procedures. For example Lovaas et al[20] used modeling in combination with reinforcement to develop language functions in autistic children. Bandura et al[21] demonstrated the effectiveness of modeling in eliminating a maladaptive fear of dogs in young children. This was accomplished by having them observe a peer fearlessly interacting with the animals with no adverse effects.

Clinical experience with families evidencing repeated crises related to poor interpersonal functioning reveals that members are grossly deficient in their expression of affect. Either no affect is expressed or a surplus of expressed emotion is elicited by a seemingly innocuous stimulus. A further characteristic of families experiencing crises involves their rigid and stereotypic responses to one another. Often they are unable to implement alternative responses when instructed by their therapist. Rather than blaming the family for deficient motivation or ascribing the persistence of maladaptive functioning to masochistic or sadistic needs, it becomes necessary for the therapist to demonstrate alternative modes of interaction by using himself or another family member to model more adaptive responses. A number of advantages accrue as a result of using modeling techniques in dealing with a family crisis: (1) It interrupts stagnant and nonproductive forms of interaction; (2) it demonstrates precisely the verbal and nonverbal aspects of new responses; (3) family members are able to obtain some appreciation of the facilitating effects of new behaviors by observing the reactions elicited from other members; and (4) resistance to developing a different response repertoire is decreased by virtue of emulating the therapist, who presumably is a respected source of authority.

Behavioral Rehearsal

Behavioral rehearsal is a procedure whereby more desirable responses to interpersonal conflict situations are practiced under the supervision of the therapist.[22] The technique is often used as an adjunct to modeling and role playing. Behavioral rehearsal is often employed in assertive training whereby both positive and negative affective responses are practiced under therapeutic direction. In the therapy of crisis situations modeling may precede the use of behavioral rehearsal. After exposure to a model's handling of crisis relevant issues, family members might be guided into a behavior rehearsal of new modes of communication. A vareity of hypothetical crisis-like situations might also be presented to the family for their solution under therapeutic guidance. Feedback in the form of commentary by the therapist is then given to family members. At times, additional modeling may be needed until effective problem solving responses are attained and become part of the family member's behavioral repertoire.

Achieving Reciprocal Reinforcement in Families

A recent study of Eisler and Polak[8] showed that nearly one half of all patients accepted for treatment on a psychiatric crisis facility displayed severe family problems underlying their requests for admission. One third of all admissions involved separation of family members or threat of imminent separation. We have observed that problems which lead to threat of separation, divorce, child runaways, etc., occur in families that offer almost no rewards or satisfaction for participation in family life. As Stuart[23] points out in his discussion of unsuccessful marriages: ". . . few positive rewards are dispensed; positive reinforcement as a strategy for behavioral control is replaced with negative reinforcement (removal of an aversive event following the expected response)." Given the extremely low rates of reciprocal social reinforcement occurring in crisis-prone families, the ability of family members to cope with additional stresses such as financial difficulty, illness, or natural environmental problems is extremely limited. The family's difficulty in working together to solve its common problems leads to an acceleration of aversive strategies of behavioral control (e.g., threats, criticism, withdrawal). These strategies are unlikely to succeed as they obscure present problems, generate further aversive counterbehaviors, and alienate family members. A family crisis of this nature offers the therapist a situation which is amenable to a program of positive reinforcement. His therapeutic task involves an immediate restructuring of the family system by teaching individual members methods for increasing their rates of reciprocal positive reinforcement. Techniques for achieving reciprocity will be examined in the next two sections.

Instructions

In some cases instructions to families with respect to the use of reciprocal social reinforcement has led to significant therapeutic improvement. A first step in teaching families the benefits of positive reinforcement requires an explanation as to why this method should be effective. Since the family is well practiced in aversive strategies, some examples and demonstration of the effects or reciprocal reinforcement are warranted. A next step involves the clarification of needs and expectations of discordant family members. Not only should this be stated in precise behavioral terminology, but specific rewards or reinforcers for each family member should be clearly outlined. For example, a wife might state that she would like her husband to spend one-half hour each evening chatting about the day's events instead of his reading the evening paper in total disregard of her presence. Conversely, the husband may articulate his dislike of frozen dinners and might expect a "home-cooked" meal in return for his attentiveness.

Instructions in positive strategies of behavioral control lead to improved interpersonal functioning. These kinds of instructions serve to facilitate self-observation with respect to frequency to emitting reinforcing behaviors. In the more difficult cases it is often useful for individuals to actually record frequency of reinforcers obtained and issued to others. In other cases instructions to monitor instances of reinforcing behavior may, in themselves, facilitate increased rates of reciprocal reinforcement. Instructions on reinforcement also elicit the expectation that it is possible to change the behavior of other family members by first altering one's own behavior. If family members carry out instructions to reinforce one another contingent upon performance on desirable behavior, the increases in reciprocal cooperative behavior should be apparent to them in a relatively short time. However, the ultimate goal is that naturally occurring contingencies should take over once a sufficiently high degree of reciprocity has been achieved.

Behavioral Contracts

When crises occur in families where coercive problem solving strategies are employed to the exclusion of positive incentives, behavioral contracts are useful in developing an exchange of positive reinforcement among family members. Since members of these families perceive each other with mutual distrust on the basis of past failures to perform role obligations, it becomes necessary to provide some immediate reinforcing consequences for constructive problem solving behaviors. Specifically, a behavioral contract is a negotiated agreement detailing in writing the conditions under which individual X will do something for individual Y. It therefore makes explicit the relationship between an individual's functional behavior and the social consequences for that behavior. For example, a contract might specify that if the father returns home by 6 PM and spends one-half hour helping his son with his homework, the wife will then cook his favorite meal, and the son will perform specified chores. Family contractual agreements have been described in some detail by Patterson.[24] Such contracts have been used successfully in developing reciprocal reinforcement patterns in dysfunctional marriages,[23] in strengthening community control over the behavior of delinquents,[25] and in modifying drinking behavior in an alcoholic.[26] Some contracts specify the use of points or tokens that are earned contingently upon performance of outlined behaviors. Points and tokens are then exchangeable for previously specified reinforcers at some future time.

A major advantage of behavioral contracts is that role expectations of family members are clearly applied to observable behavior. Thus, when contracts are enacted, they reduce the amount of nonproductive verbal exchanges over failure of individuals to carry out prescribed roles. Instead of a father raging at his adolescent son for being lazy and stupid while the son retorts that father is "up tight" and rigid, a negotiated contract might specify an exchange whereby the son will be allotted use of the family automobile upon achieving good grades and upon completion of specific duties. The negotiation of contracts teaches crisis prone families the principles of compromise and reciprocal positive reinforcement as being effective methods of mediating interpersonal discord. Trust and positive feelings among family members are increased when particular behaviors are reciprocally reinforced in accordance with contractual clauses. With the implementation of behavioral contracting in crisis prone families, an attempt is made to rapidly modify behavior of family members, with an expectation that attitude change will follow.

Report of Cases

The use of behavioral techniques in crisis-oriented family intervention will be illustrated in three case presentations. In each case one of us and a psychology intern served as co-therapists.

CASE 1.—The Jones were a middle-class couple in their early 40s. Both had been married before. The major problem originated when Tom, Mr. Jones' 16-year-old son, came to live with the couple following the death of his natural mother two years prior to our intervention. Shortly after Tom's arrival, Mrs. Jones developed symptoms of nervousness, depression, crying spells, and "hysterical" temper outbursts. She had received individual psychotherapy, tranquilizers, antidepressants, and electroconvulsive shock treatments to no avail. When the Jones came to the Medical School Clinic their marriage was near dissolution, precipitated by Mrs. Jones' ultimatum that Tom leave the house, or she would file for divorce.

During the first treatment session, the Jones were requested to reenact a typical family conflict while being videotaped. The following scene was then obtained: "Tom had failed to return home at the appointed time for supper and had not telephoned as to his whereabouts. When he finally arrived Mrs. Jones displayed a temper outburst in which she accused the boy of being selfish and inconsiderate. Tom offered a rather weak excuse that he forgot his watch, but it was delivered rather defiantly. Mr. Jones angrily denounced his wife as being an oversensitive neurotic who never gave Tom a chance to explain. Mrs. Jones then directed her rage toward Mr. Jones while Tom excused himself from the dinner table. The scene ended with Mrs. Jones in tears and Mr. Jones leaving the table complaining that he was not appreciated at home."

The family was given videotape and verbal feedback with their attention focused on the aversive series of attacks which escalated the conflict. Mrs. Jones was specifically shown how her coercive attempts to obtain cooperation from Tom and her husband eventuated in their withdrawal. Tom was shown how his passivity increased Mrs. Jones' anger. It was pointed out to Mr. Jones that his counterattack method of defending his son offered no chance of solution to the problem. Inasmuch as Mrs. Jones was unable to approach her withdrawn and negativistic stepson, and in light of Mr. Jones' inability to mediate the conflict, the therapists modeled more positive strategies designed to elicit cooperation and problem-solving behavior. One of the therapists, in the role of Mrs. Jones, portrayed a mother who, despite her irritation at her son's tardiness for dinner, was able to convey some feelings of warmth for the boy. While modeling these responses, the therapist was able to elicit some conciliatory reactions from Tom. At that point Mrs. Jones, without the aid of role playing, was able to deal more appropriately with Tom about his being late. The second therapist, role playing Mr. Jones, then modeled the part of an active mediator. He pointed out to Mrs. Jones that she had a right to expect her stepson to be home on time for dinner, but that he did not approve of her methods in coping with the problem. A solution based on reinforcement principles was then presented by the model. Tom was to notify the family of his whereabouts should he be detained. Failure to do so would result in his losing weekend privileges. Following this rather successful demonstration of problem solving techniques, the Jones were requested to tackle other potential conflict situations at home.

Towards the conclusion of ten sessions, the therapists' participation in demonstrating positive strategies of control was markedly decreased. A follow-up visit three months after termination of treatment revealed that newly developed problem solving skills were sufficiently reinforcing to all family members to be self-sustaining.

CASE 2.—Mr. and Mrs. Mann were an upper-middle class couple with five young sons ranging from 2 to 12 years of age. They previously underwent one year of marital counseling with little apparent success. The crisis that precipitated their referral to the Medical School Clinic was a suicide attempt by Mrs. Mann following her husband's attentiveness to an amorous divorcee at a party.

An analysis of the Mann's interaction revealed that Mrs. Mann had an endless list of complaints about her husband's lack of family involvement. During repeated interchanges it was noted that Mr. Mann displayed two types of passive-avoidant modes of reacting to her complaints. At times he agreed that she was justified in her criticisms, but failed to modify his behavior. Other times he withdrew from the discussion. However, both tactics increased Mrs. Mann's rate of complaining. Mr. Mann, on the other hand, pointed out that whenever he attempted involvement with the family (activities with the children), Mrs. Mann invariably criticized his efforts.

The preceding suggested a negative pattern of interaction involving the wife's coercive attempts to obtain positive reinforcement (attention or help with the children) from her husband. He had intermittently reinforced her aversive nagging by verbally agreeing to most of her demands while actually fulfilling very few. She, however, punished his few positive attempts by being critical, thus resulting in his withdrawal and attempts to seek reinforcement outside the family. This sequence, repeated numerous times over the years, led to a relationship in which positive reinforcement from marital interaction was virtually absent. Therefore, it was decided to immediately restructure the marital relationship through a focus on specific behaviors with instructions based on principles of positive reinforcement.

In cases where there is a long history of negative expectations confirmed by deficient performance, we have found it useful to initially program the spouses to perform one or two positively reinforcing behaviors for one another. When this is accomplished on a reciprocal basis it then becomes possible to alter the chain of negative consequences. More specifically, Mr. Mann was instructed to return home at a designated time each evening. He was permitted one late night per week providing that he telephone Mrs. Mann in advance. Upon his return at home Mr. Mann was expected to spend one-half hour with his wife in conversation of a topic of her choice. In exchange, it was agreed that Mrs. Mann would prepare her husband's breakfast each morning. To ensure cooperation, the Manns were informed that continuation in treatment with us was contingent upon their performance of these homework assignments throughout the week. After this program was in effect for two weeks the bitter antagonism between the Manns had decreased to the extent that other more meaningful exchanges of reinforcing behavior could now take place.

During the course of treatment both Mr. and Mrs. Mann required brief assertive training focused on their expressing needs, expectations, and disagreements in more direct fashion. At the conclusion of eight weeks of treatment the Manns were responding more openly and more positively to each other.

CASE 3.—Mr. and Mrs. Roan, their 24-year-old married daughter Susan, and 16-year-old son Robert were seen in the Medical Center Clinic following an initial contact by Mr. Roan. During the course of routine history taking Mr. Roan, a 52-year-old computer programmer, described himself as being perfectionistic at work. However, he expressed concerns about the adequacy of his performance despite the fact that his supervisors were apparently satisfied with him. He felt that he had a good relationship with his family, but admitted that his son Robert was a disappointment to him. Robert apparently was only a mediocre student in high school which frustrated Mr. Roan's plans to send him to a good college.

In the first family session Mr. Roan expressed guilt feelings that he had failed in his paternal duties. Mrs. Roan was tearful throughout and evidenced an overprotective attitude towards Robert. Susan expressed her view that the family had done everything possible for Robert. Robert in turn was sullen and uncommunicative.

A rapid assessment of family interactions revealed two major problems. The first involved the family's inability to express angry feelings in a direct fashion. Unexpressed hostility was obviously compounded by Robert's recent arrest. Secondly, Robert probably had been scapegoated for other family problems which were not immediately in evidence. The initial strategy, then, was to elicit and reinforce expression of feelings related to specific events that had led to the present crisis. Some expression of anger was elicited by the therapist feedback on family members' nonverbal communications of anger (e.g., Robert's pouting or Mr. Roan's sarcastic tone of voice). This was followed by Mrs. Roan and Susan expressing their feelings that Robert frequently "let the family down." In addition, they felt that Mr. Roan displayed an overly "strict" attitude towards Robert. However, at this point, the two major protagonists, Robert and Mr. Roan, were still not communicating effectively with each other. As Mr. Roan became increasingly comfortable in challenging his son, Robert withdrew or made irrelevant statements. The two therapists then modeled an interaction sequence for the two whereby both positive and negative feelings were expressed. Observation of the models resulted in a less heated dialogue between

Robert and Mr. Roan. Mr. Roan was now able to express both affection and disappointment towards his son. Robert expressed a good deal of anger towards his father as being overly critical. Moreover, he pointed out to his father that he never really attended to any of his communications. Mr. Roan was surprised and apparently pleased by some of the points made by Robert, and he encouraged the boy to continue. In a later sequence, Susan was prompted and then reinforced by the therapists for mediating a conflict between her father and mother.

Six family treatment sessions were held over a three-week period. During the course of these meetings this family learned how to express both positive and negative feelings in a constructive fashion. There were indications that gains seen during treatment sessions generalized to the home situation, particularly with respect to improved communications among family members. At the conclusion of treatment Mr. Roan's symptoms had subsided and plans were being made for Robert to enter a trade school. The family was followed via telephone over the next three months, during which time they continued to make progress through their own initiatives.

COMMENT

With increasing attention being given to short-term crisis-oriented treatment, new and more flexible therapeutic techniques are required. Of necessity these techniques cannot be based primarily on an intense one-to-one therapeutic relationship where the development of insight and gross personality change is expected. Instead, crisis theorists and practitioners have found it more useful to concentrate therapeutic efforts toward an immediate restructuring of deficient interpersonal interactions within a designated target social system. As the family learns more effective means of functioning, therapeutic intervention is gradually diminished until the system is functioning successfully on its own.

The feasibility of using behavioral techniques within the crisis framework is of recent origin. Balson,[27] in a case study, described the flexibility of a variety of behavioral techniques in the rapid and successful treatment of an individual "crisis" patient. In this connection, behaviorists have shown considerable ingenuity in tailoring specific techniques to the needs of individual patients. In the last few years, there is also a growing interest in applying behavioral techniques to the more complex interactive behaviors of couples, families, and other social systems.[23,25,28-31]

As we have endeavored to point out in the case illustrations, a preliminary step in restructuring faulty interactions of a family in crisis involves a rapid behavioral assessment of current interactive difficulties. This is best accomplished through an in vivo elicitation of the family's present coping or problem solving skills. While family members are interacting around a particular issue, therapist participation should be minimal. In some cases we have observed the interactions through a one-way mirror in order to avoid influencing naturally occurring behavior. Following the elicitation of coercive, aversive, passive-avoidant, or other relatively unsuccessful modes of interaction, family members are first offered feedback with respect to their modes of dealing with one another and are taught more appropriate interactive patterns. This relearning process proceeds in a number of overlapping stages, in that feedback is alternated with the teaching of new behavioral repertoires.

In this approach it is assumed that individual family members are unable to function more successfully as they do not possess requisite interactive skills. Therefore, new interactional sequences are shaped through combinations of instructions and feedback on successive performances. Imitation of therapist models facilitates development of more successful interactive responses. Verbal reinforcement from the therapist, reciprocal reinforcement from other family members, and contractual arrangements ensure the continuation of newly acquired behavioral patterns. Not only are specific issues resolved during treatment sessions, but family members learn strategies that will permit smoother resolution of additional problems that may occur in the future. Although the generalization of problem solving skills is seen to occur naturally in some families, the vast majority require both supervised practice in the office and specified assignments that are to be carried out in the home.

REFERENCES

1. Lindsley OR: Operant conditioning methods applied to research in chronic schizophrenia. *Psychiatr Res Rep Am Psychiatr Assoc* 5:118-153, 1956.
2. Lindsley OR: Characteristics of the behavior of chronic psychotics as revealed by free operant conditioning methods. *Dis Nerv Syst* 21:66-78, 1960.
3. Lindsley OR, Skinner BF: A method for the experimental analysis of the behavior of psychotic patients. *Am Psychol* 9:419-420, 1954.
4. Ayllon T: Intensive treatment of psychotic behavior by stimulus satiation and food reinforcement. *Behav Res Ther* 1:53-61, 1963.
5. Ayllon T, Azrin NH: The measurement and reinforcement of behavior of psychotics. *J Exper Anal Behav* 8:357-383, 1965.
6. Ayllon T, Azrin NH: *The Token Economy: A Motivational System for Therapy and Rehabilitation.* New York, Appleton-Century-Crofts Inc, 1968.
7. Ayllon T, Haughton E: Control of the behavior of schizophrenic patients by food. *J Exp Anal Behav* 5:343-352, 1962.
8. Eisler RM, Polak P: Social stress and psychiatric disorder. *J Nerv Ment Dis* 153:227-233, 1971.

9. Hill R: Social stresses on the family: Generic features of families under stress. *Soc Casework* 39:139-150, 1958.
10. Lindemann E: Symptomatology and management of acute grief. *Am J Psychiatry* 101:141-148, 1944.
11. Parad HJ, Caplan G: A framework for studying families in crisis. *Soc Work* 5:3-15, 1960.
12. Caplan G: *Principles of Preventive Psychiatry*. New York, Basic Books Inc Publisher, 1964.
13. Caplan G, Mason EA, Kaplan DM: Four studies of crisis in parents of prematures. *Community Ment Health J* 1:149-161, 1965.
14. Atherton CR, Mitchell ST, Schein EB: Locating points for intervention. *Soc Casework* 52:131-141, 1971.
15. Jones M, Polak P: Crisis and confrontation. *Br J Psychiatry* 114:169-174, 1968.
16. Polak P: Social systems intervention. *Arch Gen Psychiat* 25:110-117, 1971.
17. Bernhart AJ, Hersen M, Barlow DH: Measurement and modification of spasmodic torticollis: An experimental analysis. *Behav Ther* 3:294-297, 1972.
18. Elkin T, et al: Modification of caloric intake in anorexia nervosa: An experimental analysis. *Psychol Rep* 32:75-78, 1973.
19. Leitenberg H, et al: Feedback in behavior modification: An experimental analysis in two phobic cases. *J Appl Behav Anal* 1:131-137, 1968.
20. Lovaas, OI, et al: The establishment of imitation and its use for the development of complex behavior in schizophrenic children. *Behav Res Ther* 5:171-181, 1967.
21. Bandura A, Grusec JE, Menlove FL: Vicarious extinction of avoidance behavior. *J Pers Soc Psychol* 5:16-23, 1967.
22. Lazarus AA: Behavior rehearsal vs non-directive therapy vs advice in effecting behavior change. *Behav Res Ther* 4:209-212, 1966.
23. Stuart RB: Operant-interpersonal treatment for marital discord. *J Consult Clin Psychol* 33:675-682, 1969.
24. Patterson GR: *Families: Applications of Social Learning to Family Life*. Champaign, Ill, Research Press, 1971.
25. Stuart RB: Behavioral contracting within the families of delinquents. *J Behav Ther Exper Psychiatry* 2:1-11, 1971.
26. Miller PM: The use of behavioral contracting in the treatment of alcoholism: A case study. *Behav Ther* to be published.
27. Balson PM: The use of behavior therapy techniques in crisis intervention: A case report. *J Behav Ther Exper Psychiatry* 2:297-300, 1971.
28. Tharp RG, Wetzel RJ: *Behavior Modification in the Natural Environment*. New York, Academic Press Inc, 1969.
29. Liberman RP: Behavioral approaches to family and couple therapy. *Am J Orthopsychiatry* 40:106-118, 1970.
30. Lazarus AA: *Behavior Therapy and Beyond*. New York, McGraw-Hill Book Co Inc, 1971.
31. Friedman PH: Personalistic family and marital therapy, in Lazarus AA (ed): *Clinical Behavior Therapy*. New York, Brunner/Mazel, 1971, pp 116-154.

BEHAVIORAL CONTRACTING IN CONJOINT FAMILY THERAPY

ROBERT B. RUTHERFORD, JR. AND KENNETH BRUCE BOWER

INTRODUCTION

The wide variety of family therapy systems that have evolved over the past 15 years can be grouped into three therapeutic modes. Harper (1975) identifies these as: 1) conjoint family therapy, where treatment involves all family members as a group, 2) collaborative family therapy, where family members are in separate treatment with individual therapists who may occasionally consult about family matters, and 3) concomitant family therapy, where one therapist sees each family member separately. Of these, the conjoint therapy mode appears to carry the most promise for maximizing collaborative involvement and potential for change of all members of the family system.

While numerous parallels to concomitant and collaborative therapy are found in the behavioral parent training literature (Becker, 1971; Bernal, 1971: Galloway & Galloway, 1971), only recently have behavior therapists addressed themselves to conjoint modes of family therapy (Alexander & Parsons, 1973; Liberman, 1970; Patterson, Reid, Jones & Conger, 1975; Rutherford, 1975; Stuart, 1970; Stuart & Lott, 1971).

Behavior therapy, with its emphasis upon a functional analysis of the antecedents and consequences of behaviors within the family system, has a unique potential for illustrating the effects of each member's behavior on the behavior patterns of other family members. *Behavioral contracting, whereby each member negotiates for various privileges and responsibilities within the family system* lends itself to the conjoint mode of family therapy.

BEHAVIORAL CONTRACTING

Behavioral contracting involves the systematic written negotiation

---

From R. Rutherford and K. Bower, Behavioral Contracting in Conjoint Family Therapy, *Family Therapy*, 2:215-26, 1975. Courtesy of Libra Publishers, Inc.

between all members of the family system of the behaviors to be performed within that system. Rutherford (1975) suggested several points that must be taken into account when establishing behavioral contracts. These points, as they apply to conjoint family therapy follow.

1) A behavioral analysis must be made of the behavior(s) to be contracted. Behavioral analysis involves the family therapist and the family members specifying: (a) the antecedents which will cue the contract behavior, (b) the contract behavior to be developed, and (c) the consequences which will maintain the contract behavior (see chart below).

A------------------------------- B -------------------------------C

Antecedents   Contract behavior   Consequences

Applied analysis of contract behavior.

The "antecedents" are events which are present in the environment to cue behaviors. They include those stimuli, cues, or directions that set the occasion for a given behavior and the specific, predictable consequence. Antecedent cues for practicing the piano may include access to a piano, sheet music, a quiet room and verbal instructions from mother "it's time to practice your lesson." These cues may signal that the "consequences" of completing the "contract behavior", e.g., practicing the piano for 45 minutes, will be positive. These positive consequences may be praise from parents, greater mastery on the piano and/or a specifically contracted item or event such as a homemade cupcake or a half hour of additional T.V. viewing time in the evening.

Behavioral analysis makes the assumption that consequences which are positive will result in an increase in the frequency of the desired behavior. Thus, behavior analysis involves planning before the fact and programming after the fact of a given behavior. Sound behavioral contracts specify systematically each of the three steps of the behavioral analysis model.

2) The behavioral contract should be a formal written document which specifies all privileges and responsibilities of the parties involved. It should be signed by all parties. The contract is a negotiated agreement between two or more family members which allows them to predict the consequences of the contracted behaviors. Signatures enhance the formality and commitment of the contract.

3) The behavioral contract must precisely and systematically specify all of the conditions of the contract. Dates, times, criterion behaviors, amounts and/or range of consequences, names of contractor and contractee, and names of others involved in the contract should all be included. The terms of the contract must be adhered to strictly and systematically at all times. While such attention to detail may seem petty, in the early stages of contracting, it will be precisely this attention to detail that will determine the success of the contract. For example, if

the contract states that a reward of "I'll do something nice for you" will follow a full morning of not "talking back" to mother, both the behavior "talking back" and the reward "doing something nice" are so vague and imprecise as to invite misinterpretation by the contracting parties. Thus behavioral contracts should be specifically spelled out.

4) The terms of the family behavioral contract must stress the positive. Contracts employing punishing consequences tell the contractee what he should not do, but at best only imply the desired behavioral change. Positive contracts, on the other hand, clearly specify the apporpriate behavior and the reward that will follow.

Additionally because *positive reinforcement strengthens the behavior which it follows, whereas punishment only temporarily suppresses behavior*, a contract which stipulates positive reinforcement rather than punishment will be more effective in changing the behaviors of the contracting parties.

5) Reinforcing consequences must always follow the completion of the contracted behavior and must be delivered immediately. In establishing a family contract, the opportunity should be available to receive some portion of the reinforcing consequence immediately upon completion of the contracted behavior. Contracts may be negotiated which allow for small but continuous payoffs for daily behaviors, while at the same time making a large payoff contingent upon completion of a whole series of daily behaviors.

6) Both the consequences which follow the completion of the contracted behavior (the *A clause*), and the consequences which follow the noncompletion of the contracted behavior (the *B clause*), must be specified. For example:

Clause A: Each evening Jerry completes his assigned homework, he will receive 5 points toward a weekend fishing trip with Dad.

Clause B: No points will be awarded for those evenings in which homework is not completed.

By thus specifying the consequences for completing and not completing the contract, the possibilities for misinterpretation are reduced. Inclusion of both the *A* and *B* clauses reduces the chance of error.

7) When a behavior initially exists at only a minimal level, the concept of "shaping" may be used in initiating behavioral contracts. The contract must begin at a level where all parties can succeed and must not demand perfect performance for reinforcement to occur. For example, when attendance of the entire family at dinner time is a major problem, it is unrealistic to specify that "To get a special dessert, all family members must be on time for dinner for two weeks." An alternative statement having a higher probability of success would be, "If all family members are on time for dinner three out of seven times the first week, four out of seven times the second week, and six out of seven times the third week, a special dessert will be served on Sunday evenings." Shaping, then, involves reinforcing successive approxima-

tions to the final contracted behavior(s).

8) The family behavioral contract must be fair to all of the contracting parties, thus implying the power of all parties to negotiate terms. If the terms are unfair, the contract will fail. The behaviors and the consequences must be balanced to the satisfaction of all parties with the provision, built into the contract, for renegotiation should the agreement prove unfair to any family member following its implementation.

A common difficulty in parent-child contracts is the expectation on the part of the parent for major changes in the child's behavior with little reciprocal behavioral change on the part of the parent. This imbalance may not be noted in the initial contract, and thus a renegotiation clause would allow for more equitable future agreements.

9) While behavioral contracts in many settings are adult-initiated with the intent of changing children's behavior, contracting within the conjoint family mode should view all family members as both contractors and contractees. Within this framework, children also have the right to negotiate changes in their own and other people's behavior.

The family therapist is in a position to act as arbitrator or mediator in facilitating change in parents' perceptions of children's responsibilities *and* rights within the family system and to aid children in developing negotiation skills within that system. In most contracts, both the contractor and contractee must change their behaviors. Under these circumstances the therapist facilitates fairness in the terms of the contract on behalf of all parties involved.

EXEMPLARY CONTRACTS

In this section, two case studies and subsequent contracts are given by way of illustration. The format will vary with the individual therapist, and as such, different formats have been chosen for illustrations.

Case I: The O'Shea family has been in family therapy for one month. Dr. Hasterok, the family therapist, has done a behavioral analysis of many of the behaviors as perceived by each family member. Mrs. O'Shea is basically happy with her second marriage but feels that there are some potentially serious problems in her family. She and Mr. O'Shea have been married for 11 months—this being her second marriage and his first. Since the marriage she has noted several changes in her children's behavior. Katie O'Shea, age 11, is becoming more aggressive, lax in cleaning her room, and talks back to both her father and mother. Eddie, age 9, on the other hand, seems to have withdrawn from family interactions since the marriage and now spends a great deal of time alone in his room. Mrs. O'Shea sees these changes in her children as at least indirectly related to Mr. O'Shea not spending enough time with the kids and to his strict discipline of the children.

Mr. O'Shea objects to what he views as Mrs. O'Shea's constantly nagging him about not spending enough time with the children and being too strict with them. In addition, he is unhappy because he feels he does not get to spend enough time alone with his wife. He complains that Katie is "spoiled", "unfriendly", and talks back to him and to her mother. Mr. O'Shea is frustrated because he would like to be able to spend more time with Eddie but feels that Eddie does not like him.

Katie is not unhappy with her mother but is somewhat disappointed because she does not get to go horseback riding as much as she wishes. She sees her father as "too strict" and as seldom around when she wants to talk to him. She is frustrated with Eddie because he won't stand up for himself to their father.

Eddie quietly objects to his mother's criticisms of his friends and, like Katie, he finds his father too strict. But more importantly, he wishes that he and his father could spend more time doing things together like his friends and their fathers do.

Under the direction of Dr. Hasterok, the following contract was drawn up between the O'Shea family members:

BEHAVIORAL CONTRACT

Date: _____

Mrs. Glenda O'Shea

1A. I, _____ agree to arrange for and spend the last weekend of each month alone with Rick O'Shea on a camping trip in return for his alloting half-hour separate periods for five of the seven days of the week along with both Eddie and Katie in an activity which the children designate.

1B. In the event that Frank does not spend half-hour separate periods for five of the seven days with each of the children, we will not take a camping trip at the end of each month.

2A. I, _____ agree to take Katie horseback riding one afternoon per week if her room is cleaned up four out of five school days prior to leaving the house for school.

2B. In the event that Katie does not clean her room up four out of five school days each week, we will not be able to go horseback riding that week.

3A. I, _____ agree to arrange for a "pop and popcorn" party at our home two evenings per month (first and third Fridays) for Eddie and four friends that he selects if he spends at least two hours each evening 5 out of 7 days per week with at least one other family member out of his room.

3B. In the event that Eddie does not leave his room for two hours each evening we will have no bi-monthly "pop and popcorn" parties.

Mr. Rick O'Shea

1A. I, _____ agree to allot half-hour separate periods for five of the seven days of the week alone with both Eddie and Katie for an activity that each child designates in return for which Glenda O'Shea agrees to arrange for and spend the last weekend of each month alone with me on a camping trip.

1B. In the event that I do not spend a half hour per day for five of the seven days with each of the children, we will not take the camping trip at the end of each month.

2A. I, _____ agree to take Katie to the Clairborne County Horse Show on November 14th in return for her not talking back to either her mother or me more than two times per day for the 14-day period before the horse show.

3A. I, _____ agree to spend an extra half hour a day with Eddie if he agrees to plan the specific activities that we will engage in.

3B. In the event that Eddie does not plan an activity for us to engage in, we will not spend our extra half hour together that day.

Katie O'Shea

1A. I, _____ agree to clean up my room four out of the five school days prior to leaving the house for school if Mom agrees to take me horseback riding one afternoon per week.

1B. In the event that I do not clean up my room four out of five mornings before school, we will not go horseback riding that week.

2A. I, _____ agree to reduce the number of times I talk back to Mom and Dad to no more than two times per day for the next two weeks. In return, Dad will take me to the Clairborne County Horse Show on November 14th. Talk-backs to be determined by Mom, Dad, Dr. Hasterok, and myself.

2B. In the event that I talk back to either Mom or Dad more than two times on any one day in the next two weeks, we will not go to the Horse Show.

3A. I, _____ agree to help Mom with Eddie's "pop and popcorn" parties if Eddie will initiate and plan one half-hour activity with Dad 5 out of 7 days each week.

3B. In the event that Eddie does not initiate and plan half-hour activities with Dad 5 out of 7 days each week, I will not be able to help Mom with Eddie's party.

Eddie O'Shea

1A. I, _____ agree to spend at least two hours per evening for 5 out of 7 evenings a week with at least one member of the family if Mom lets me have a "pop and popcorn" party with four of my friends every other Friday evening.

1B. In the event that I do not spend at least two hours per evening with another family member 5 out of 7 evenings per week, I will not have a "pop and popcorn" party.

2A. I, _____ agree to initiate and plan the extra half-hour activities that Dad and I spend together at least five evenings per week.

2B. In the event that I do not initiate and plan the activities, we will not spend the extra half hour together that day.

3A. I, _____ agree to initiate and plan the half-hour activities that Dad and I spend together at least five evenings each week in return for which Katie will help Mom with my "pop and popcorn" parties.

3B. In the event that I do not initiate and plan activities, Katie will not help Mom with my party.

We, the undersigned family members have read this complete contract and we agree to the terms stated. If, for any reason, any of us does not feel the terms are fair after the contract has been initiated, we reserve the right to renegotiate the contract in Dr. Hasterok's office next week.

Katie O'Shea daughter	Mrs. Glenda O'Shea mother
Eddie O'Shea son	Mr. Rick O'Shea father

Dr. Gerald Hasterok
mediator

Case II: Steve, age 17, is a junior at Central High School. Steve is currently on probation for marijuana use and curfew violations. Up until the last 8 months, Steve was a B+ student and presented no major problems at home. On his 16th birthday he asked his parents for a car and was told he "had a lot of growing up to do" before his father would allow him to own his own car.

His parents have been married for 19 years. Mr. Forness has a small farm implement business and he works 8 to 10 hours a day, 5½ days per week. Mrs. Forness was employed as a school teacher for several years immediately following their marriage but has not worked for the past nine years. She would like to be able to spend more time with her mother who lives 80 miles away and resents the fact that her husband takes no interest even in weekend trips for that purpose.

Mrs. Hixson, the family therapist, has had Mr. and Mrs. Forness and Steven in therapy for 5½ weeks. During this time she has noted that Mrs. Forness does most of the talking during the sessions and most of what she says revolves around negative comments about her son and husband. She describes Steve as "irresponsible", "a poor student", "runs around with a bad crowd", and complains that he comes home late at night and does not help out around the house. She describes her husband as "drinking too much", "spending too much time at the bar with his cronies and not getting home on time for dinner in the evening", and "sitting in front of the T.V. all weekend watching one football game after another." After several weeks of therapy, Mrs. Hixson has begun to elicit from Steve and his father their perceptions of the family's interactions. Steve sees his mother as constantly on his back, nagging him, and never giving him credit for the things he does around the house. Steve's major area of contention with his father centers around his father's unwillingness to buy Steve a car.

Mr. Forness states that he would just as soon be left alone. He sees his wife as constantly nagging him about the things he likes to do such as "having a beer with the boys" and "watching football". He essentially agrees with his wife about Steve's irresponsibility, and thus is reluctant to buy him a car. He does not see Steve's poor grades and his choice of friends as terribly important. He works hard through the week at his business and feels that he is "entitled to a little peace and quiet" on the weekends.

Based on the information she had gathered about the interactions and perceptions of the Forness family, Mrs. Hixson facilitated negotiation of the following contract.

CONTRACT

Date _____

We, the undersigned, agree to the provisions of the following contract contingent upon our right to renegotiate any part of the contract that is subsequently determined to be unfair to any of the parties.

_____

Mr. Joseph Forness   Signatures Validated by:

_____

Mrs. Glenda Forness   Mrs. Dorothy Hixson

_____

Steven Forness

Given: Mr. Forness will purchase a 1939 Ford pickup for a sum of $600 from Gene Wallace, a next door neighbor. The truck is to be placed in a garage at Mr. Forness' place of business. A total of $300 and 300 points must be earned by Steve for the purchase of the truck. The money will be earned through working at Mr. Forness' business while the points will be contingent upon contracted behaviors around the house.

Steve Forness—Joseph Forness

1A. I, _____ agree to work for my father two evenings per
(Steve)
week and on Saturday mornings and to be paid at the rate of $1.75 per hour. My responsibilities will include general clean-up, inventorying, and taking telephone orders. My wages will be applied toward the purchase of a 1939 Ford pickup, the total cost of which is $300. I will receive an itemized statement of my earnings and the remaining balance to be paid at the end of each bi-monthly pay period.

1B. I, _____ agree that in the event I do not report to work
(Steve)
I will receive no wages, and further, that if my work is not of comparable quality to that of other employees after a one-week training period, that

I may be terminated.

2A. I, _____ agree to the following schedule for earning
         (Steve)
points at home toward the purchase of the 1939 Ford pickup:

Behavior	Points
a) Complete homework each evening it is assigned.	2
b) Improve grades in each subject as compared to the previous school term.	20 (per grade change)
c) Return home prior to 10:30 Sunday through Thursday evenings.	2 (per night)
d) Other tasks at home as requested by mother (Bonus points earnable)	1-3 (to be negotiated at time of request)

2B. I, _____ agree that in the absence of the behaviors
         (Steve)
listed in 2A above, the corresponding number of points will not be issued.

3A. I, _____ agree to provide the money and points listed
         (Joseph)
in 1A and 2A above contingent upon the behaviors specified.

Glenda Forness—Joseph Forness

1A. I, _____ agree not to complain to Joseph more than
         (Glenda)
twice an evening about his being at the bar with his friends if he comes home before 6:00 PM four out of five week nights. "Complaints" are to be defined mutually by Joseph, myself, and Mrs. Hixson.

1B. In the event that Joseph does not return by 6:00 PM four out of five week nights, I will resume complaining to him about his drinking, his friends, and his not being home on time.

2A. I, _____ agree to stop complaining to Joseph more
         (Glenda)
than four times on the weekend about his weekend TV watching in return for which he will take me to my mother's house every third Saturday afternoon. "Complaints" are to be defined mutually by Joseph, myself, and Mrs. Hixson.

2B. In the event that Joseph does not take me to my mother's on the third Saturday following the commencement of this contract, I will resume complaining about his weekend TV watching.

3A. I, _____ agree to the terms listed in 1A, 1B, 2A, and 2B
         (Joseph)
above.

Steve Forness—Glenda Forness

1A. I, _____ agree to hang up all of my clothes and make
         (Steve)
my room orderly each morning before going to school in return for which mother will stop complaining about my not helping out around

the house and begin to look for, and write down, instances where I have helped out. "Complaints" are to be defined mutually by mother, myself, and Mrs. Hixson.

1B. In the event that mother continues to complain about my not helping around the house and does not keep track of instances where I have done so, I will not continue to pick up in my room before going to school.

2A. I, _____ agree to the provisions listed under 1A and
            (Glenda)
1B above.

CONCLUSION

Behavioral contracting in family therapy is an approach designed to build structure and predictability into the family system. Most families, upon entering therapy, tend to highlight the negative behaviors of other family members and are often confused about the effects of their behavior on that of others in the family, as well as the effects of others' behavior on their own. Behavioral contracting provides an initial restructuring of the family behaviors and their antecedents and consequences.

The role of the family therapist is: 1) to help the family design, initiate and negotiate contracts; 2) to assist in the identification of specific problem behaviors and consequences to be covered in the contract; the intent is to identify important individual behaviors that have a broad impact on family interactions rather than to identify all behaviors that are in need of change; and 3) to eventually facilitate the adoption of less formal verbal contracts in the later stages of therapy as written formal agreements become less necessary.

Conjoint family therapy emphasizes the unit of the family as a system. The use of behavioral contracts by the therapist provides a structured and systematic approach to intervening in the maladaptive interactions of all members of that unit.

REFERENCES

Alexander, J.F. & Parsons, B.V. "Short-term Behavioral Intervention with Delinquent Families: Impact on Family Process and Recidivism," *Journal of Abnormal Psychology*, 1973, *81*, 219-225.

Becker, W.C. *Parents are Teachers: A Child Management Program.* Champaign, Illinois: Research Press, 1971.

Bernal, M.E. "Training Parents in Child Management," in R. Bradfield (Ed.), *Behavioral Modification of Learning Disabilities*. San Rafael, California: Academic Therapy Publications, 1971.

Galloway, C. & Galloway, K. "Parent Classes in Precise Behavior Management," *Teaching Exceptional Children*, 1971, Spring, 120-28.

Harper, R.A. *The New Psychotherapies.* Englewood Cliffs, New Jersey: Prentice-Hall, 1975.

Liberman, R.P. "Behavioral Approaches to Family and Couple Therapy," in C. Sager & H. Kaplan (Eds.), *Progress in Group and Family Therapy.* New York: Brunner/Mazel, 1972.

Patterson, G.R., Reid, J.B., Jones, R.R. & Conger, R.E. *A Social Learning Theory Approach to Family Intervention,* Vol. 1: Families with Aggressive Children. Eugene, Oregon: Castalia Pub. Co., 1974.

Rutherford, R.B. "Establishing Behavioral Contracts with Delinquent Adolescents," *Federal Probation,* 1975, *39,* 28-32.

Stuart, R.B. & Lott, L.A. "Behavioral Contracting with Delinquents: A Cautionary Note," *Journal of Behavior Therapy and Experimental Psychiatry,* 1971, *3,* 161-69.

FAMILY SCULPTURE TECHNIQUES

Family sculpturing is initially a nonverbal activity that serves to unveil the family system. By experiencing feelings within the session rather than merely talking about them, family members are encouraged to become more aware of their own and others' perceptions of the family's structure.

Sculpturing is an imaginative technique and an effective way to move beyond the limitations of words. As with other nonverbal activities, it allows all family members to actively participate in the process. In addition, using the family as a "picture" allows members to visualize the family structure and feel what it is like to be placed by other family members. Since one person is typically in charge of the sculpting, that person draws his own picture, allowing others to see and feel others' perceptions of their place in the system. In this way the technique is making explicit what has often been only implied. Following the initial sculpting by family members, the technique can also be used to illustrate how members would like to see their family and focus on goals.

Constantine describes his article as being a "mere heuristic organization" of sculpting techniques. He suggests that family therapists use these techniques in a creative fashion to effectively facilitate the therapeutic process. A wide variety of strategies are described, and Constantine contends that the only limitation for continued growth is the counselor's creativity.

Jefferson proposes that spatialization can be used to get information where other verbal techniques have not been as effective. In addition, he argues that the sculpting will often result in families becoming more aware of their behaviors and thus increasing the possibility for change.

Papp, Silverstein, and Carter present sculpting as a preventive technique when working with "well" families. The use of sculpting as a prevention activity gives families the opportunity to mobilize their own healing process before the crisis begins.

Used properly, sculpting is an effective and powerful technique. It gives the family therapist the opportunity to assess the family system and engage the nonverbal as well as verbal client. Words are powerful tools and weapons for some family members, and by giving the quieter members of a family an equalizer the therapist encourages total participation and supports sharing by all members in a manner in which they are comfortable.

FAMILY SCULPTURE AND RELATIONSHIP MAPPING TECHNIQUES

LARRY L. CONSTANTINE

Family sculpture comprises a body of powerful evaluation and intervention techniques already in wide use by marriage and family
counselors and therapists, and increasingly by educators, consultants,
and organizational development specialists. Through the symbolic and
metaphorical use of real space a person can be helped to "sculpt" a
living tableau of people embodying essential features of their interrela-
tionships. Externalized as an active spatial metaphor, these insights
become available to both client and change agent.

Family sculpture is related both historically and in method to
psychodrama (Moreno, 1946) and to experiential exercises widely used
in human relations training. Its principal departure from psychodrama
is in its portrayal of symbolic processes and events through spatial
analogies; relatively infrequently are events reenacted literally as in
psychodrama. The difference is more than a mere matter of technique or
emphasis. Psychodramatic reenactment tends to promote recall of both
expressed and unexpressed affectual components of the experience.
Often a strong emotional reexperiencing and catharsis are primary aims
of such a technique, toward the end of freeing the individual from
blocked emotions in order to make new contemporary behavioral
choices. By contrast, sculpture aims toward *distancing* the client from
the emotional experience and, through this disengagement, enabling
new insight into complex relational determinants of past and present
situations. Where psychodrama may be thought of as putting the client
more centrally into experiences, sculpture seeks to "decentrate" the
client, promoting increased objectivity and insight into personal
participation in ongoing interpersonal patterns.

Sculpture was developed into its present forms by a number of
professionals, working both independently and with some interactions.

From L. Constantine, Family Sculpture and Relationship Mapping Techniques,
Journal of Marriage and Family Counseling, 4:13-23, 1978. Courtesy of American
Association for Marriage and Family Therapy.

The mainstream of family sculpture was originated by David Kantor with important early contributions and elaborations by Bunny Duhl, Fred Duhl, and their colleagues at Boston State Hospital and the Boston Family Institute. According to the Duhls, the earliest experiments utilized the placement of objects rather than people. The development was catalyzed by a visit from Virginia Satir, who demonstrated the use of people to metaphorically represent specific abstract types of family configurations. The basic reference work on the subject is Duhl, Kantor, and Duhl (1974). It has been popularized by Virginia Satir (see e.g., Satir, 1972) and others (Papp and Silverstein, 1972). Its emphasis on space as a key dimension of human process has its roots in the work of Hall (1959; 1969), as elaborated in family theory by Kantor and Lehr (1975).

Evidence from various fields of investigation strongly suggest that people sort out, map, and store understanding of the complex interpersonal systems in which they are imbedded in the form of compressed spatial metaphors. These visual, spatial, metaphorical representations (probably associated with the right or subdominant hemisphere of the brain) summarize a vast amount of information in a compact and efficient manner. They constitute maps of the world (Bandler and Grinder, 1976), working theories on which everybody manages their moves through the complicated interpersonal landscape. Hartmann's comprehensive review (1973) and synthesis of the findings on the function of dreaming sleep can be interpreted as supporting this contention on the neurophysiological level. Dreaming is the active process by which these metaphorical maps are constructed, reworked, and resolved (Swonger and Constantine, 1976). Kantor's pioneering study of families in their day-to-day affairs suggests that distance regulation is the core mechanism by which families may be understood to operate. Distance regulation is both a process in physical space and a metaphorical operation. The everyday use of spatial metaphor forms a rich vocabulary in common use. We speak, for example, of emotional distance. "If you can grasp that." "I hope that I am bridging the gap between us."

Sculpture (also known as space sculpture, family sculpture, relationship sculpture, spatialization) is a body of techniques which enables people to tap into their metaphorical maps, to make these internal realities external, visible, and accessible to study and change.

Basic Concepts and Issues

Sculptures and other spatializations may be conducted with almost any meaningful unit—with an individual, with couples, with a co-therapy or other work team, with a parent and child subsystem, with the sibling subsystem, with a whole family, with a family kinship network, or even with an entire corporation, although the staging and format will differ with the unit of choice. It has been used not only in family counseling and therapy, but in training (Constantine, 1976) and organizational development. The context may include only the sculptor and the therapist or other "monitor", or it may include all members of the system being sculpted. It may even incorporate an "audience" as in a training group or multiple family therapy group.

Sculpture is useful as both an evaluative and interventive measure. Though its most obvious function is exploratory or revelatory, the exposure or previously hidden or unarticulated dynamics has an impact on the system being sculpted. It can be a powerful antidote to blockage and dragging in therapy.

Sculpture is not a difficult technique to learn. In a very real sense, sculpture is based on a spatio-temporal, physical "vocabulary." The most important thing for the user to do is to become at ease with and conversant in this spatial "language", that is to read and speak freely in spatial metaphors and analogies. The possibility of a universal vocabulary within this spatial language has been suggested by recent work on kinesics and body language (Scheflen, 1972; Spiegel and Machotka, 1974).

Once certain fundamentals are acquired through a little practice, the therapist, counselor, or educator should become able to develop customized spatial techniques and procedures to fit contexts not anticipated by already developed "standard" forms. The most common abuse of spatial techniques is to use them only as mechanical procedures. "Sculpture is an organic part of an on-going process. It is not a mere gimmick or exercise thrown willy-nilly into an interactional heap." (Kantor, 1975). While some therapists might find only occasional uses for sculpture, there are some who can effectively make it the primary method for almost all their assessments and interventions.

Correctly done, all such sculpture involves three stages:

(1) Establishing the mapping between physical and metaphorical space.
(2) Constructing the sculpture.
(3) Processing the sculpture, or debriefing.

In some uses, the first and last stages are abbreviated, but they cannot be omitted altogether without losing much of the value. In some forms, notably the complete family sculptures discussed below, each stage may involve several distinct steps.

Establishing the Map

To make the fullest metaphorical use of space and objects and to access an individual's internal maps, it is necessary to build a bridge from external, real space to internal, metaphorical space. A bridge can be crossed in either direction. Once a mapping of physical space into metaphorical space has been established, it is easier for the sculptor (the client) to project internal reality onto external reality. This process sets the stage for the sculpture by defining the mapping (a correspondence) between one space and another. For example, the mapping might be between distance in physical space and emotional distance. The bridge might be built by having participants explore the real physical space, then inviting them to get in touch with their feelings for each other as they move about in this space, then to begin to sense their subtle feelings of comfort and discomfort as they move closer and farther away from each other.

Sculpting

A feature common to all forms of sculpture is that the sculptor uses himself, bodily, to construct the sculpture. By actually moving about in the physical-metaphorical space that has been established, touching and physically molding elements of the sculpture, the sculptor taps into information stored or accessible as kinesic, musculo-motor memories. Talking about or thinking about a sculpture is inadequate. Even sculptures that have been carefully "rehearsed" often emerge as something quite different when actually carried out. The sculpting process facilitates access to memories and process in the non-verbal right (subdominant) hemisphere (Ornstein, 1972).

Processing

Closure on the sculpting process is reached by crossing the bridge again, back into the real, here-and-now space. The sculpture is explored from multiple points of view and thoroughly discussed for its meaning, impact, implications, and ramifications. Each participant in the process, including members of the audience, has had a different emotional-cognitive experience of the sculpture and therefore has unique perspectives and insights to offer. On rare occasions, a sculpture which is simply constructed but not processed may be of value, but without a thorough debriefing, the full richness of the lode cannot be mined.

Sculptures may be classified into three groups: (1) simple spatializations, (2) boundary sculptures, (3) family (or other system) sculptures. Each of these groups has subcategories. The three stages discussed above may proceed differently in the three main groups. The main grouping is purely heuristic with little fundamental significance.

Simple Spatializations

Spatialization is a direct use of physical space to map a simple or limited personal or interpersonal construct. It is akin to constructing a graph or plot on a room-size scale with people as the markers. In a group, spatialization can rapidly reveal a large amount of information about a particular subject in a way which makes it possible for group members to assimilate the information.

The examples below are only suggestive of the range of possibilities. Spatializations can be designed to deal with almost any construct or set of constructs to fit some special need in a workshop or in therapy with a family. For example, in working with one family, a polar sculpture around an object representing "head of the household" proved very productive. The children were thus able to express their awareness of their mother's ambivalent desire to be "head of the house" yet to leave responsibility with her husband. He in turn was adamant in occupying the center, however ineffectively. All were able to relate this pattern to the same struggle between the parents and to use this awareness to explore alternative strategies for themselves.

Linear Sculpture

In a linear sculpture, the simplest form of spatialization, people place themselves along a line representing a unipolar (one way) dimension (such as "powerfulness", "frequency of jeolousy", or "risk-taking") or bipolar dimension (such as "head-oriented vs. gut-oriented", or "open vs. closed"). An especially useful form of linear sculpture is the "Power Line" wherein family or group members sculpt themselves in terms of perceived powerfulness.

Linear sculptures work best when careful attention is paid to the following steps:

(1) *Define the space*—Carefully explain the dimension on which to sculpt, giving special attention to what each of the poles (end points) represents. Delineate the physical area by walking along the line as its meaning is explained, standing at the appropriate pole when describing it. It is helpful to have signs at each pole which vividly describe the character of the pole, such as "all the time" and "never" or "heady, rational, intellectual, thoughtful" and "gutsy, emotional, empathic, feeling."

(2) Invite people to walk slowly back and forth along the entire length of the line. This must be done non-verbally. "As you walk along this line, try to get in touch with what you are feeling, especially how comfortable you are at each point. Continue to move along this line until you find a place that feels like the right spot for you." In this way preverbal, unarticulated self-perceptions are accessed.

(3) *Process in Place*—Process (debrief, discuss) the experience while people remain in position on the line; this heightens the experience, promotes "owning" one's position, and makes it easier for people to relate what others have said to where they said it from. Examples of questions: How did you end up where you are? Were you surprised? What did you feel (think) while doing this? Were you conscious of where other people were placing themselves? Who? Why? How did this influence your placement? The perceptions of people at the extremes

and those in clusters generally warrant special exploration.

(4) The sculpture may be repeated on the same dimension with a different "set" to explore: ideal self vs. real self, or future desired vs. future expected vs. present.

Matrix Sculpture

The matrix spatialization developed by the author is a straight-forward extension of the linear sculpture into two dimensions. This is an exceptionally efficient way to explore the relationship between two variables in a manner that gives everyone in a group a rich picture. After the first dimension is sculpted and processed in place, each person is asked to turn sideways to the original line and imagine themselves on a new line of their own which runs at right angles to the original. It is also this new line that each is to move and place themselves. The matrix technique has been used, for example, in workshops on jealousy to sculpt simultaneously on "frequency of jealousy" and "seriousness of jealousy as a problem."

Polar Sculpture

In a polar spatialization, people place themselves at some distance from a single reference point which may be a person, an object, or an abstract concept. A more elaborate variation has people also place themselves in relation to each other. The following specific examples serve to indicate the range of possibilities.

(1) An object is placed in the center of the room to represent "the 'center' or heart of this family, not a physical place but an abstract, the very core of this family as family." Family members are invited to "walk around it, think about it, move closer, then further away" until each finds that place which feels right for themselves, that is, represents how close or distant they feel they are from the "center of the family." The sculpture may be elaborated by next asking them to move in relation to each other until those distances feel like they really are. This often results in a continuous shifting of positions as members seek to accommodate varying perceptions.

(2) A *value sculpture* spatializes degree of comfort-discomfort or attraction-repulsion in relation to a value-laden or affect-laden state-ment. For example, on the chalk board there is a statement: "In the near future, *most* couples will permit and even value open sexual relations with other people." Then: "How do you feel about that? Move around, closer, farther from that statement. Try to get in touch with the feelings you are having. Keep moving until you find some place that feels right to you."

(3) Two chairs (or some other objects) are placed in the center of the room to represent "the family you grew up in." The sculpture is in

relation to "how much like or unlike that family you would *like* your family living situation as an adult to be." Right next to center represents identical, farther and farther away represents increasing degrees of difference. After processing in place, this can be repeated around "how much like or unlike that old family you *expect* your new family living situation will be." A date, say ten years in the future, may be specified.

Boundary Sculptures

The purpose of boundary sculpture is to explore the way in which a person (or persons) defines and experiences personal boundaries. In one sense, the boundaries as explored are perceptions of real physical distance and individual experiences of closeness, distance, intrusion, or exclusion in real physical space. In this sense, boundary sculpture is an exploration of personal kinesics and proxemics. At the same time, however, the boundary sculpture explores the metaphorical boundaries of personality, the limits of self, the means of ingress and egree across the boundaries of the self. The degree to which practical proxemics or personality structure are revealed in the boundary sculpture can be influenced by the approach of the monitor.

Individual Boundary Sculpture

Boundary sculpture as a variation of family sculpture was first conceived by Bunny Duhl (Duhl, Kantor and Duhl, 1974). Typically, the monitor begins by inviting the sculptor to explore the actual physical surroundings and, as he does, to begin to get in touch with his sense of "the space you carry with you. The edge of that area which feels as if it was you or yours, where your space leaves off and the rest of the world begins." When the sculptor indicates he has a sense of this boundary, the monitor begins to probe and investigate the nature of the boundary with the sculptor.

(1) One type of exploration involves the physical parameters of this personal space such as size, shape, variability.

(2) Personal boundaries can also be explored metaphorically in terms of color, texture, thickness, firmness, transparency, and penetrability. It is frequently helpful to have the sculptor close his eyes and imagine his boundary is actually made of some substance and to report on what material that might be or what it is like. The monitor should ask about inhomogeneities,the existence of openings, and changes with time.

(3) Dynamic exploration involves specific probes of the boundary with various manners of approach using subjects of various ages and both sexes, strangers, acquaintances, or intimates. The sculptor may have to be asked to assume that a certain person is, say, an elder stranger.

Fast, slow, aggressive, submissive, seductive, and stealthy, approaches might be tried from various directions to determine the sculptor's response, where the boundary is, and how clearly defined and how strongly defended it is. Since the number of possible probes is limitless, the monitor must rely on intuition and therapeutic knowledge in exploring significant features.

When the second type of exploration is emphasized, there usually emerges a complex but unified idiosyncratic image of the personal boundaries which models or accounts for much interpersonal behavior. To the extent that the first and third methods of investigation are emphasized by the monitor, more straightforward and less dramatic features of the normal social boundaries emerge.

Relationship Sculpture

This form of sculpture, also known as "Negotiating the Space", could be considered to be a variation of either boundary sculpture or family sculpture. It is a brief, efficient way to explore a limited relationship. In its most common application the work relationship of two or more people is explored. A space or arbitrary size and shape (usually a rectangle of about 50-80 square feet) is defined as representing the work relationship of the pair (or other group); outside of that space is all the rest of their life experience. A time limit is set (10 minutes works well) and the sculptors are directed to use that time to explore and negotiate that relationship space nonverbally. It should be made clear that the full time is to be taken even if they feel finished after a shorter period. Frequently completely new aspects of the relationship will emerge late in the process, after everyone thinks all is done. This is an especially valuable exercise for a newly formed co-therapy team and has been used in training to facilitate student team formation (Constantine, 1976).

System Sculpture

In the system sculpture, the sculptor is assisted by the monitor in utilizing a number of other people or objects to spatialize personal perceptions of an entire family or other system. System sculptures may be relatively general in scope or specifically focused. Among possible foci are: a specific problem or knot; a critical time period or event; a single dimension of family relationships, such as, power. Generally, it is at least desirable to pin the sculpture down to a particular time period.

In the "full" or most complete form of family sculpture, the sculpture builds in stepwise fashion and may take up to an hour or more. The steps are:

(1) Exploring the physical space.

(2) Getting in touch with the feel of the metaphorical family space to be represented.

(3) Defining and describing the boundaries of the family space. Here the parameters can be as rich and varied as with personal boundary sculpture.

(4) Peopling the sculpture, adding one person at a time and thoroughly exploring that person's interactions with the sculptor and previously added members.

(5) Assembling the action of each sculpted person into a composite "strategic sequence" representative of the family's operation.

(6) Ritualizing the sequence by repeating it in its entirety at least three times. The repetition, though often skipped by therapists and some-times thought of as silly, frequently leads to important additional discoveries and insights as to how a family system operates.

(7) Debriefing, beginning with the experiences of the players in the sculpture, then the contributions of the audience, and ending with the sculptor. It can often be useful to modify a sculpture by asking the sculptor to show how he would improve things.

Mini-sculptures

Two common errors therapists make in using sculpture are rushing the sculpture and pushing for premature closure. A deliberate mini-sculpture is better than an intentionally hurried full sculpture. Most commonly demonstrated sculptures are mini-sculptures. Mini-sculptures abbreviate the process, primarily by leaving out certain steps, for example, step (1); steps (1), (2), and (3) and/or step (6). In briefest form, the sculptor may simply be directed to position other members in ways that represent how he sees them in the family in relation to himself and to each other. The entire sculpture, including debriefing, might last only a few minutes. Often brevity is achieved by limiting or constraining the sculpture is some way, commonly by permitting only statis tableaux. Abbreviated system sculptures have their applications in rapid assessment of a situation or of a specialized and limited context or aspect of a system.

Dimensionalized Mini-sculpture

Kantor has recently introduced a powerful but simple variant of mini-sculpture that uses a limited but very natural spatial vocabulary. The sculptor is told to represent emotional involvement by physical closeness or distance, to represent differences in power by vertical displacements, higher being more powerful, and to show the general nature of the relationship between members by facial expression, gesture, and body orientation. In this way, the dimensions of family process—affect, power, and meaning (Kantor and Lehr, 1975; Constantine, 1974)—are all captured. This form of sculpture approaches the richness of a "full" sculpture in a fraction of the time.

Typological Sculpture

Another variation on mini-sculpture depends on limiting the sculpture to a fixed set of individual or collective options. For example, the therapist might describe several basic types of family and how to represent them spatially, asking the sculptor to choose one of these basic forms to build from. Satir (1972), for example, describes basic stances for individuals based on their preferred defended communication style which may be assumed by participants in a sculpture, as well as what she sees to be certain prototypical family configurations.

In the absence of more solid theory and and better sociological data on family types, this approach may risk too much imposition of the therapist's assumptions on the client.

Current Family

Sculpture of the current family with family members playing themselves, that is, without stand-ins, is undoubtedly the most commonly used form. This can be somewhat less effective than other forms in helping the sculptor to gain needed distance and perspective on the sculpture. Playing oneself minimizes this "analogic distance", the players inside the sculpture have difficulty seeing the whole, and the sculpturing process itself involves and can become stuck in the same dynamics as disable the family otherwise. For example, it can sometimes be impossible for family members to be directed by the sculptor. Actors might continually offer suggestions and corrections, thus invalidating the sculptor's perceptions or a major control struggle can prevent the parents from participating in each other's sculpture.

Unfortunately, stand-ins are only available in multiple family groups and in workshops. Unless the therapist is specifically interested in eliciting and exploring transference, the therapist does not usually serve as a stand-in. When this is done, it is essential that there be a co-therapist as monitor. In some cases it might be appropriate to direct that current family members be chosen by the sculptor to stand-in for each other, say in establishing the map between father and son's behavior. This functions much as role reversals do.

Under circumstances where the sculptor experiences difficulty in gaining distance and objectivity on his own sculpture, he can be asked to appoint a stand-in and to step aside to watch with the therapist.

Family of Origin

Sculpting the families of origin of adult family members can be tremendously productive, yielding much insight into origins of contemporary stuck behavior patterns and the ways members of the present family are induced into playing the parts of members of previous generations. Stand-ins for the absent members of the family of origin can be members of an ad-hoc group, such as a training seminar, or members of the current family. The latter is especially useful in revealing the mappings from the last to the present generation. Seeing their patients' families can be an especially freeing experience for children.

Multiple Sculpture

In a multiple sculpture (sometimes called consensus or composite sculpture [Duhl, Duhl, and Watanabe, 1975]), all family members simultaneously attempt to place themselves in relation to others. Usually this would be around a single dimension or simple construct, such as emotional distance. Each member tries to place himself in correct relation to all other members. Differences in needs for distance, and perceptions of relationships emerge rapidly and dramatically. If Dad sees himself as closer to Susie than she does to him, he might end up pursuing her around a pole.

A more elaborate form (introduced by the author) focuses on the self in family relationships and dramatizes individual roles in maintaining stuck patterns and in working out relationships. Each member is asked to use some gesture, movement, expression, or stance to represent how he feels in relation to each other family member, taking on these in sequence with each member one at a time. This is repeated continuously until a complicated dance is thus choreographed which could show either great order or an inability to match rhythms and actions. At some intermediate stage, the therapist might ask the family to continue their nonverbal interaction but with each member doing something slightly different to break up the pattern or attempt to work out a "fit" with the rest of the family that "feels right."

This type of sculpture might be started by having all family members standing around the space and thinking for a minute or two about what they would do in relation to each other before all begin simultaneously. If the family has difficulty doing it in this way, it can be built sequentially by adding one member at a time to the marital dyad.

Sculpture Using Objects

If family members of live stand-ins are not available, objects may be substituted. At the point where it becomes appropriate to "bring in" a family member, the sculptor can be invited to select any object in the field to substitute and to place this appropriately. It is usually productive to explore the basis of choice: "What about this reminds you of your brother? How is he like this?" The new imagery that is tapped into can more than compensate for the fact that gestures, movement, or expression are impossible. The therapist could also temporarily take the part of the missing player to elicit such nuances.

In ritualizing the strategic element of a sculpture using objects as stand-ins, the therapist may describe or talk-through the actions that have been given to the inanimate players or move them around for the sculptor.

Within one family seen by the author, although everyone had great difficulty engaging in non-verbal tasks of this sort, there was a shared love of board games. A successful family sculpture was conducted completely on a chess board using chess pieces as objects, in this way effectively using the family's own imagery. The task revealed a consensus that that the father and his alienated son had moved closer together and that the family viewed the therapists as less integral to their continued functioning. As a result, a decision was reached to proceed with terminating therapy.

Special Types of Sculpture and Spatialization

Space can be used in an endless variety of ways to metaphorize many things of interest in therapy, counseling, and education. The following are just a few of the ways in which spatialization has been employed to facilitate access to complex personal and relationship information.

Developmental Sculpture

A succession of circles or otherwise arbitrarily shaped spaces are defined on the floor, each space representing a significant period or stage in the sculptor's life, for example, living at home with parents, as a single adult, as a newlywed couple, or family with infant child. The scupltor enters each space and describes its quality, talking about significant features, and important people in the space. The nature and circumstances of the transition to the next space, and the changes in feelings are also explored.

Life Line

A line is marked the length of the room to represent the sculptor's life from birth to the present. The sculptor is directed to traverse the line and, as he does, to describe whatever occurs to him in terms of events, people, relationships, and feelings. The technique works best when a fixed time is set for completing the traversal. This keeps the sculptor from either rushing and skipping over things or filling with insignificant information. A clock should be clearly visible.

Life Space

The sculptor is told to consider the room or an arbitrary space within it to represent his current life and to identify and "place" within it anything—like a person, experience, event, or object—which he considers is significant to his current life situation. A fixed time limit is desirable.

Sculpture as Feedback

The therapist can use sculpture as a mechanism for communicating *to* clients, as well as gaining information. The monitor might, for example, suggest modifications to a completed sculpture to share his insights about the family, not as better or correct information but as an alternative perspective the clients are invited to consider. Or the sculptor (or other participants) could be instructed to experiment with different positions or movements the therapist thinks might reveal new information or offer new relational options.

On occasion the therapist might choose to be the sculptor. Working with one family that had an especially difficult time getting perspective on their situation, the author and his co-therapist sculpted using objects and family members to present their evaluation of the family system. When the family members saw the entire picture they were able to recognize their roles in the current crisis and to offer more insight and further modifications to the sculpture. Later sessions confirmed that required changes implied by the therapists' sculpting had begun to take effect.

Application and Conclusions

The purpose of this paper is not an exhaustive cataloging of sculpture techniques but a mere heuristic organization. Any attempt to index all sculpture techniques *should* be doomed at the outset. The purpose of presenting a range of techniques is not to fix the armamentarium but to spur the creativity of the therapist, counselor, consultant, or educator. By displaying themes and variations it is hoped that each professional will be freed to innovate new variations custom-fitted to the situation at hand.

Real comfort and creativity with sculpture techniques comes only from trying them out, from liberal experimentation. Experimentation can take place in almost any setting. One of the delights of sculpture is that it so seldom fails to liberate and to supply fresh inputs to almost any process. It can be used whenever

the therapist, or client—feeling inducted, bored, trapped, or at impasse—
may wish to: free up blocked, denied or ambiguous feelings and
communication; help a system resolve a conflict or reach a consensus;

discover a new emphasis or direction in the therapy; explore a previously identified "gray area", condense a great deal of information into a spatialized image; evolve a complete system map or elaborate some substructure in it; or explore the system's responses to alternate outcomes.

These specific clinical hunches, goals and strategies affect the types of sculpture used. (Kantor, 1975)

For example, within one family with a history of overt incest were certain members who had early made clear their refusal to reconsider there painful past events, denying any current relevance, while another family member attributed every negative event in their lives to those same transgressions. The therapists became effective change agents simply by leaving the sexual issues alone and concentrating on the contemporary relationship dynamics for several months. When the index patient's girlfriend—who had been responsible for exposing the incest—was to join the family for a session, the therapists planned a "power line" sculpture to enable the family to deal with current effects of the incest. Although the announced purpose of the sculpture was to explore power relationships, the daughter who had been involved with her father became physically ill in anticipation. All family members saw themselves as comparatively powerless. The girlfriend was seen as the most powerful and the index patient as least. The awkwardness of this position became painfully evident, and it was quickly discovered by the family that attributions of power were associated with an individual's ability to use knowledge, especially of the incest, as a threat. The sculpture proved to be a breakthrough, legitimizing re-examination of the incest and its present impact while spotlighting the real arena in which the family was disabled.

Even the professional's own family is a fertile and productive context in which to try out these techniques. The rewards are manifold, as when the author recently "negotiated the space" (a relationship sculpture) with his eight year old daughter. The sculpture clarified a pattern in which close contact could only be initiated by the daughter, but the author also learned that by sitting still he could signal his receptiveness, leaving the initiative to her. Both found they have since been better able to obtain the intimacy each wanted by respecting the other's style of contact.

The imagination is the only limit to new variations and applications.

REFERENCES

Bandler, R. & Grinder, J. *The structure of magic: A book about language and therapy*. Palo Alto, California: Science & Behavior, 1975.

Constantine, L.L. Dimensions of family process. Unpublished monograph, Center for Training in Family Therapy, Boston State Hospital, IRR Building, 591 Morton Street, Boston, MA 02124, 1974.

Constantine, L.L. Designed experience: A multiple goal-directed training program in family therapy. *Family Process,* 1976, *15,* (4).

Duhl, B., Duhl, F. & Watanable, S. Types of sculpture. Unpublished notes, The Boston Family Institute, 1170 Commonwealth Avenue, Boston, MA 02134, 1975.

Duhl, F., Kantor, D. & Duhl, B. Learning space and action in family therapy. Block, D. (ed.) *Techniques of family psychotherapy: A primer.* New York: Grune & Stratton, 1973.

Hall, E.T. *The silent language.* Garden City, New York: Doubleday, 1959.

Hall, E.T. *The hidden dimension.* Garden City, New York: Anchor Books, 1969.

Hartmann, E.L. *The functions of sleep.* New Haven: Yale University Press, 1973.

Kantor, D. Introduction to family sculpture. Unpublished notes, The Family Institute of Cambridge, 256 Concord Avenue, Cambridge, MA 02138, 1975.

Kantor, D. & Lehr, W. *Inside the family: Toward a theory of family process.* San Francisco: Jossey-Bass, 1976.

Moreno, J.L. *Psychodrama.* New York: Beacon, 1946.

Ornstein, R.E. *The psychology of consciousness.* San Francisco: Freeman, 1972.

Papp, P., Silverstein, O. & Carter, E. Family sculpting in preventive work with "well families". *Family Process,* 1973, *12,* (2).

Satir, V. *Peoplemaking.* Palo Alto: Science and Behavior, 1972.

Scheflen, A.E. *Body language and social order.* Englewood Cliffs, New Jersey: Prentice-Hall, 1972.

Spiegel, V.P. & Machotka, P. *Messages of the body.* New York: Free Press, 1974.

Swonger, A. and Constantine, L.L. *Drugs and therapy: The psychotherapist's handbook of psychotropic drugs.* Boston: Little, Brown, 1976.

Chapter 24

SOME NOTES ON THE USE OF FAMILY SCULPTURE IN THERAPY

CARTER JEFFERSON

Family sculpture, or spatialization, is a technique for solving problems in therapy. Jay Haley (3) has recently offered a succinct definition of what "a problem" is in systems terms.

> A problem is defined as a type of behavior that is part of a sequence of acts between several people. The repeating sequence of behavior is the focus of therapy. [3, p. 2]

Therapists use sculpture, therefore, as a means of bringing to awareness the "problem" sequence of behavior. In the Duhl, Kantor, and Duhl article that first described the theoretical basis for using sculpture (2), the authors focus on the use of sculpture to allow both family and therapists to generate options for new, more satisfactory behavior patterns. The increasingly common appearance of workshops, films, and articles of sculpture shows that it is an important new tool for therapists (1, 6, 7, 9).

At the Boston Family Institute, sculpture, or spatialization, is thoroughly integrated into the training program for therapists; faculty and students use it so frequently as both a teaching technique and a tool for group problem-solving that it easily and naturally becomes a basic part of the therapeutic style of graduates. But for therapists who learn to use sculpture only through short demonstrations, films, or articles, it is often difficult to become comfortable using it. This essay is an attempt to help therapists improve their skills at "using" sculpture to produce therapeutic change in a system.

Duhl, Kantor, and Duhl postulate the therapeutic process as follows: (a) family members are ignorant of their own behavior patterns and the sources of those patterns; (b) through sculptures, these patterns are made overt; (c) at least one family member's awareness changes enough to permit her or him to see options for more satisfying behavior if suggested; (d) the therapists encourage family members to think of new

From C. Jefferson, Some Notes on the Use of Family Sculpture in Therapy, *Family Process*, 17:69-76, 1978. Courtesy of *Family Process*.

options, and if necessary, they themselves suggest such options; and (e) through practice in and out of therapy sessions, family members take actions that change the family process. The therapist just beginning to use sculpture seems to have most difficulty in getting from point (b) to point (c). Clients often try, consciously or unconsciously, to avoid taking note of behavior patterns, even when they are made obvious, and thereby miss the chance to learn (5).

Yet therapists to whom spatialization is a familiar tool realize that apparent failure may not be failure at all; sometimes use of a technique that produces no apparent response is, in fact, a significant part of a "softening up" process. New insights are not always easy for clients to adopt; old "defenses" do not necessarily melt away at the first assault.

Sometimes, too, therapists are so intent on doing a "proper" sculpture of a process that they forget to watch the *process of the sculpture,* thus missing chances to make therapeutic moves. One of the most attractive things about spatialization, however, is its flexibility: a therapist who is alert to the smallest indication that something needs to be explored can continue the sculpture, simply filing away the information gained; he/she can miss something and not worry, for it will turn up again; he/she can stop the sculpture at any time, and, using information already gained, move in some other direction, then move back if it seems worthwhile to do so.

The descriptions that follow are meant to show some of the ways in which sculpture can be used either with other techniques or through repetition to help the therapist get past defenses and either begin the work that leads to behavior change or reinforce changes already begun. In each case I will try to explain what led one of the cotherapists to use spatialization, then to show what produced the decision to move to another technique or to use sculpture in a different way in order to produce new awareness. A reader of these histories might get the impression that the therapists always worked with one eye on their "bag of tricks" and were constantly aware of possible "next moves." Here I am making the transitions and their motivations as clear as possible for purposes of explanation, but therapists who use spatialization freely simply move with the context and only realize fully that they have "changed techniques" when they listen later to the tape of the session. With practice, one comes to ignore the mechanics of the process in order to concentrate on the goals.[1]

FROM SCULPTURE TO GUIDED FANTASY

In the following case the therapists turned to sculpture because talk

[1]Descriptions are altered and names changed to protect clients, but the processes described actually took place. My cotherapist on the Fullerton and Royce cases was Lucy Jefferson; on the O'Brien case, Ann Fields. Their cooperation in the work described was, of course, crucial.

was leading nowhere. The discussion was all highly intellectual, and the attitude of the client—the wife, in this case—was something like, "How interesting! I wonder how you're going to fix me." The sculpture made a pattern apparent to the therapists, but the client refused to accept responsibility for her own actions, actions that tended to make the pattern persist. Then, switching from spatialization to guided fantasy (4, 10), we succeeded in getting her to "own" her behavior and thus become open to new options.

Doris and Allen Fullerton were both the only children of parents who had had very little emotional support to give. They entered therapy at Doris's insistence, after eight years of marriage. She wanted help because she thought she was overcritical of her husband; he claimed he didn't see any problem but was willing to come in. Doris said in the first session that she was often depressed. Their major problem seemed to be that neither of them had learned anything at all about the nature of intimacy. Lacking close human contact, both had poured energy into work and were high achievers. Doris knew something was missing; Allen admitted during the third session that he never felt any emotion other than anger and said he thought that was probably bad.

Soon after they had reached a point at which Allen finally allowed himself to take notice of Doris's hostility, which had been surfacing in her "critical remarks," Doris announced that in fact she had no feelings whatever about Allen. She wasn't angry, she just felt a "hole" where her feelings about him should be. We talked half an hour about what that might mean, getting a lot of "I don't know's."

Finally we asked her to sculpt her relationship with Allen, just as she saw it at that time. She immediately put him outside the small office we were using and shut the door, saying brightly "Don't go away!" (One of the therapists opened the door a little so Allen could hear what went on.) Doris said she herself was sitting on a beach, facing the ocean. She sat on the floor facing a wall about four feet away. Asked how she felt, she said, "Alone, sad. . . . It's not unusual, I've felt this way before." We told her to describe the beach, which she said was deserted except for a few birds. The sun was brilliant but not very warm, and the sand was cold. "This," she said, "is what it must be like to have peace of mind." We might have asked her to place her two-year-old son somewhere in the sculpture, or we might have asked Allen how he felt, but I thought we were likely to get bogged down in more meaningless talk. So I decided to guide the fantasy she had created, to have her carry it in directions she might have avoided.

We talked a little about what she might do on the beach—"just sit"—and then told her that night was coming; it was getting dark and cold. She didn't want to leave the lonely beach because if she did she would lose the calm feeling she found there. Then:

Doris: It's funny. . . . The feeling I have—it's just—I don't want to sob [*she sobs*] but don't know why. I simply can't let myself do that.

Therapist: If you let yourself cry here on the beach, what happens?
Doris: Oh, I start asking, "What good is it going to do?"

As we discussed that, we found that she had learned during her unhappy days in boarding school that it does no good to cry.

Doris: At some point, I don't know when, the realization that no matter what you say or what you do, you have no control over it. . . . Somebody else does.
Therapist: Controls everything you do.
Doris: I feel I control some of it, I also feel that . . . I think I put it on Allen.
Therapist: So he controls you.
Doris: Yeah, because I . . . I guess so.

When Doris began the sculpture, her first move was loaded—she simply got rid of her husband. Her hostility was obvious. When she did that and put herself on the beach, the therapists had a choice to make. We could have explored the ramifications of the sculpture as it was. But Doris had, in a sense, said she didn't care what her husband said or did— she simply opted out. Her refusal to take responsibility for her actions in maintaining the relationship was one part of the pattern of "problem" behavior; her husband's willing acceptance of her actions was the other side. So we stayed with Doris, using fantasy, turning the sculpture into an ongoing drama. We "drove" her off the beach and that forced her to recognize that she felt powerless in her personal relationships. She had felt that way long before she met Allen, and all he had to do was tolerate her to earn her hostility. She herself said later that any other man she married would have drawn the same responses from her, but, of course, any other man might not have accepted her behavior so readily. Her recognition of her responsibility for her own behavior was a step toward taking control of that behavior and thus altering her unsatisfactory relationship with Allen. The sequence of techniques worked: from talk to sculpture to fantasy to awareness. Then we could go on to options and change.

FROM REHEARSAL TO SPATIALIZATION TO GESTALT

We turned to sculpture in the following case because a client simply "couldn't remember" anything much that happened before she was ten. An attempt to bring something back by having her recreate a scene in her past during which she certainly had strong feelings produced no significant memories. Trying a new kind of spatialization, kin to simple sculpture but more complex,[2] did not in itself yield the kind of opening

---

[2]At the Boston Family Institute, sculpture, which itself developed out of psychodrama, has evolved in several ways. From the older forms, usually nonverbal and relatively static, the BFI has developed a number of new forms that are both verbal and full of motion. We have, therefore, begun to speak less of sculpture and more of "spatialization." The "house

we needed to begin to effect a change in behavior patterns, but it opened the way for the use of an old, this time very effective, Gestalt technique (8).

Nora and Matthew Royce had been married for two years when they came to us because they were "fighting all the time." Nora also said that she had trouble getting along with her father, whom they saw frequently. Both were 29; Nora was earnest, high-achieving, uncomfortable when she wasn't working, while Matthew was much more easygoing. We concentrated on teaching them communications techniques and getting them to look upon each other as allies rather than rivals. Their fights decreased precipitously in frequency and intensity, and Nora said she was getting along better with her father, probably because now that she and Matthew were doing so well she didn't need her father's approval so much.

Nora opened the fourteenth session by telling us how nervous she was at her younger brother's wedding. We rapidly got her to explain that she has to do everything right and feels enormously guilty if anything goes wrong that she might have helped to go right. She hadn't properly coached her brother, so he might have done something awkward at the wedding, and so on. We asked her who told her she had to do everything right.

Nora: Nobody. On, maybe my mother . . . Oh, yes, my father made me sit in the corner once for doing something wrong, but I can't remember much about it.

Therapist: Tell us your earliest memory.

Nora [sounding rather pleased]: Oh, I can't remember anything at all before fifth grade. Not before I was ten or eleven.

Therapist: You remembered that you sat in the corner.

Nora: Yes, but I don't remember much about it.

Therapist: O.K., I want to try something. Let's take this chair [*puts chair in a corner of the room, facing the wall*] . . . Is that the way it was?

Nora: Yes.

Therapist: O.K., you come over here and sit in it. While you're there, tell us all about the room—what it looked like, what it smelled like, you know . . . [*Nora moves over and sits in the chair.*]

Nora: Well, it was kind of brown, I guess . . . [*twists her head around*] There was a big table in the middle of the room . . . I don't really remember.

Therapist: Look back at the wall. . . . Sit there a minute and try to remember how you felt sitting there that time. [*pause*] It must have been unpleasant.

---

walk-through" technique used in this case was invented by Fred and Bunny Duhl, who first presented it at the annual meeting of the American Orthopsychiatric Association in 1975.

Nora [*with a slight whine*]: Oh, I guess I was upset. I really can't remember.

The therapists spent a few more minutes trying to get Nora to recreate that childhood scene, with absolutely no success. So we switched techniques.

Therapist: O.K., look, I want to try something else. Will you stand over here? [*Nora obediently moves toward the therapist at one side of the office.*] Now, close your eyes. Can you remember the house you lived in when you were in fifth grade?

Nora: Fifth grade . . . That was . . . We moved. . . . I remember, that was when we lived on Pear Street.

Therapist: All right. Now take a few minutes and imagine you are standing in front of that house, on the sidewalk. Was there a sidewalk?

Nora: Yes.

Therapist: O.K., you're standing on the sidewalk . . . Now think of what you see. I'd like you to describe the house in detail . . . What did it look like, was it cold the day you're standing there . . .

Nora described the house rather vaguely. Then she was instructed to go up the walk, enter the house, and do whatever she would normally do. All the way, she was describing the look, the smell, the feel of the house. Inside, she put down her school books, said hello to her mother and was ignored (couldn't remember how that felt), went upstairs and changed clothes, came down to supper. Her speech was rather mechanical throughout, as if she were doing this simply because she is a good client who likes to please the therapists. There was no life in it. Then she began to describe the scene at supper.

Nora: We all sat around the table and talked, one at a time. My sisters and my brothers had to tell about the nice things we'd done for other people during the day.

Therapist: How did you feel, sitting there?

Nora: O.K., I guess. I didn't mind. I really can't remember.

Therapist: What was your father doing while you all were talking about what you'd done all day?

Nora: Oh, just sitting there. He didn't pay much attention because he was thinking. He just sat there, and then he sort of melted away . . . I guess.

Therapist: Melted away?

Nora: Yeah . . . he wasn't very interested in what we did. He was always thinking. I guess he just left the table. [*very slight tremor in her voice*] He didn't say much.

Therapist: How did you feel when he left the table?

Nora [*voice back to normal*] Oh, not much, I guess it was all right. He . . . My mother always told us not to bother him, he had too much to do. It was all right.

This could have continued until the end of the session. But we had heard that tremor; there were feelings about her father just below the surface. So we stopped the sculpture right there and told her to sit down. I put a stool in front of her and told her to put her father on it, dressed just as he had been on that night long ago, and to tell him what she would have liked to have said to him at that family dinner.

Nora: Uh, that feels funny. I don't have anything to say to him.

Therapist: Think about it for a while.

Nora: I can't think what to say. [*She sits there frowning for a moment or two.*] I really can't think of anything.

Then she began to cry, hard. Matthew went over and held her for several minutes. When the storm was over, she said she couldn't say anything to her father; it might hurt him. In the next few minutes she haltingly told us that there seemed to be a family rule that father had to be protected and children were not allowed even to think ill of their parents, much less express discontent. We suggested she bring her parents and any of her siblings who could come to a session. Unlike nearly all the other clients who hear such a suggestion, she protested not at all but agreed that it was a good idea, that she hadn't realized how much she was still involved with her anger toward her father. She immediately started planning to make the arrangements.

Once more we had reached a point unthinkable earlier. Nora became aware of the serious issues she had refused to deal with and began to deal with them. Later she recognized her own complicity in the pattern that protected her father, saw that she could change that pattern, and was willing to move.

USING SPATIALIZATION TO REINFORCE CHANGE

The decision to use spatialization in this case was almost made for us by the circumstances: the client knew what her problem was but had no idea what to do about it. By spatializing, she put herself into a position in which she was faced with options so obvious she could hardly ignore them. She began to make choices immediately. Reconstructing the sculpture again and again as she took more responsibility for her life helped her to believe more confidently in her own power to influence her environment.

Elaine Goldberg O'Brien and her husband of two years, Jack, had plenty to fight about when they came in. Elaine had three children by a former marriage and Jack had four. Jack, a teacher, was extremely articulate but never talked about his feelings. He was compulsively neat, while Elaine, much more easygoing, could put up with considerable disarray in things she considered insignificant. When they started working with us, it was their last resort; neither wanted another divorce, but they fought constantly, the kids didn't get along, and one of Elaine's boys was, she thought, on the road to spectacular delinquency. She wanted a chance to succeed at her new job as a designer, and she wanted some "real family life." Right then, she said, she was so upset by the chaos at home that her job was suffering, "family life" was a roaring farce, and Jack acted just like another child. Jack said he was just sad. He didn't know what was wrong, but everything was. We immediately saw that both had difficulty tolerating close relationships, and that neither had any confidence in his or her ability to deal with the children. We elected to see just the two of them for a while, without the children.

One of Elaine's major difficulties was her feeling that she had to be responsible for everybody's welfare, while, at the same time, she had no control over anything. During the first session we asked her to spatialize her relationships as she saw them. She took all the props in the room and arranged them in a circle: the footstool was her house, a chair was all the kids (both sets); a box of tissues represented the two dogs; another chair was Arnold, their paying guest; one therapist played her job, the other her ex-husband; Jack was himself; somebody's coat was the school. Poor Elaine was in the middle, and all the items surrounding her were picking at her and shouting, "Give me this! Give me that! Take care of me!"

We then asked her to change the sculpture to make it more like what she wanted her life to be. She first pushed two objects farther apart so that she could, if she wanted, walk out of the circle. Then she pulled Jack out of the periphery and put him inside the circle with her, so, she explained, he could take part of the pressure. But she was still troubled, she said, because Jack's "expectations" kept her from walking out of the circle.

This highly effective, very simple sculpture showed us, and Elaine, not only how Elaine saw her relationships—everything and everybody demanding her attention and giving nothing back—but that she herself couldn't even imagine anything much better. We spent some time getting her to clarify her wants and ordered her to do something to get control of at least one thing in that circle during the next week. Elaine could see as well as we could that she had to change something, and our directive merely strengthened a decision she was already prepared to make. We didn't tell her which item to take control of; that was left to her. But she had to do something. In a sense she asked for the order; she was pleased to get it; and she wanted to carry it out. A week later she came in and proudly declared that she had evicted Arnold, the guest. We immediately set up the old sculpture and had her ceremoniously take the chair that was "Arnold" and remove it from the circle. She put it way off in a corner.

As she got her priorities established and took control of her life, each time she made a move we once more set up the circle and had her symbolically remove an object or change the shape of the circle. After a while we no longer had to go through the actual motions—we, Jack, and Elaine would casually mention that something had happened in the circle: smiles all around, and Elaine felt more and more in command of her energies.

We worked with both of them in many ways: on communication, on getting Jack to express his feelings and take control of *his* life (he was at least as confused as Elaine), on how to deal with the kids. All these things somehow seemed to have effects on Elaine's circle. She learned that she could ask and receive, as well as decide to whom or what, and when, she would give. Now when she puts herself in the center of her circle, and puts Jack there with her, she seems not so much a victim under siege as a coleader running a group with her husband.

CONCLUSION

In each of these cases the cotherapists found reasons to use spatialization to get information. Either questions had failed to elicit anything of importance, or it seemed that spatialization would produce the information more quickly with more impact. In the first two examples, the spatializations themselves did not produce the openings for immediate change that we were seeking, perhaps only because the therapists did not make the most of them. The behavior patterns that were the "problems" either were not sufficiently apparent or the client was not yet ready to "own" her actions, to take responsibility for her own part in those patterns. But the spatializations did not "fail," for they gave the therapists openings to move into new modes that themselves led to behavior change. In the first case, a guided fantasy produced new awareness and led the client to accept her own responsibility as part of the problem. In the second case, neither the attempt to return the client to a stressful situation in the past nor the house walk-through was enough to get her to take responsibility for her part in patterns she refused to notice. But a slight break in her voice told us we had hit a place that could be usefully explored. Switching to a Gestalt technique finally produced the awareness we sought. In the third case, the first sculpture worked beautifully, for both therapists and clients saw Elaine's life clearly, and Elaine herself haltingly began to think of new options. But instead of simply letting go of that sculpture, we used it several more times as a reinforcer: each time Elaine took another step toward responsibility, we "celebrated," getting her to show us and herself how her life was changing, and Elaine saw clearly each time how one change in her behavior had altered the whole pattern of her life. That helped her to resolve to continue taking the risks involved in being responsible for her own behavior.

Spatialization may not immediately clarify the workings of a system, but therapists can always find something in a spatialization that will help them decide on their next moves. At best, patterns of behavior show up clearly, whereupon clients become aware of their own responsibility in maintaining those patterns and begin to see options and make choices. At worst, the spatialization moves the client toward thinking about the patterns that he or she seems to avoid noticing, and it gives the therapists openings that can be explored by the use of other techniques.

REFERENCES

1. Ackerman Institute for Family Therapy, "Making the Invisible Visible," videotape, Peggy Papp, therapist.
2. Duhl, Frederick J.; Kantor, D.; and Duhl, B.S., "Learning, Space, and Action in Family Therapy: A Primer of Sculpture," in D.A. Bloch (Ed.), *Techniques of Family Psychotherapy*, New York, Grune and Stratton, 1973.
3. Haley, Jay, *Problem-Solving Therapy*, San Francisco, Jossey-Bass, 1976.
4. Leuner, H., "Guided Affects Imagery (G.A.I.): A Method of Intensive Psychotherapy," *Amer. J. Psychother.* 23:4-22, 1969.
5. Lewis, William C., *Why People Change: The Psychology of Influence*, New York, Holt, Rinehart and Winston, 1972.
6. Papp, P.; Silverstein, O.; and Carter, E., "Family Sculpting in Preventive Work With 'Well Families,'" *Fam. Proc.* 12:197-212, 1973.
7. Papp, P., "Family Choreography," in P. Guerin, Jr. (Ed.), *Family Therapy: Theory and Practice*, New York, Gardner Press, 1976.
8. Polster, E. and Polster, M., *Gestalt Therapy Integrated*, New York, Brunner/Mazel, 1973.
9. Simon, R.M., "Sculpting the Family," *Fam. Proc.* 11:49-57, 1972.
10. Singer, J.L., *The Inner World of Day-Dreaming*, New York, Harper & Row, 1975.

Reprint requests should be addressed to Carter Jefferson, Ph.D., 6 Cazenove Street, Boston, Massachusetts 02116.

FAMILY SCULPTING IN PREVENTIVE
WORK WITH "WELL FAMILIES"

PEGGY PAPP, OLGA SILVERSTEIN, AND ELIZABETH CARTER

The project on which we will report consisted of three groups of families recruited for the community at large with the avowed purpose of meeting together to discuss family concerns. The groups were led by the co-authors of this paper, all family therapists trained at the same institute. They met once a week either in a church or in each other's homes for a period of six months. The emphasis of the program was on prevention. It was concerned with reaching families at a particular point in time—pre-crisis—and was based on the assumption that there was some awareness of tensions and barriers long before the crisis appeared. It was aimed at offering a service in a particular way that was non-threatening—one in which the family did not have to define itself as "sick" in order to obtain some relief.

Recently the American Orthopsychiatric Association surveyed its members to determine what they considered the top priority in the mental health feild. *Prevention* headed the list of twenty-five choices. Obviously, to prevent is better than to treat and yet to contemplate prevention is to have the mind take a continuing series of steps backward to an earlier starting point much like the contemplation of the beginning of the universe. Where and when does prevention begin?

Certainly most work in the mental health field can be considered preventive, and yet a prevailing doubt of the entire profession is that we begin too late with too little.

In 1971 Marc A. Nebejan, a Dutch psychiatrist, was sent to the United States on a World Health Fellowship for a two-fold purpose. One, to learn about the family therapy movement in the United States; two, to study the creation and operation of prevention programs. Although he felt he learned much about family therapy, he discovered there was almost nothing that would qualify as an authentic prevention program.

From P. Papp, O. Silverstein, and Elizabeth Carter, Family Sculpting in Preventive Work with "Well Families," *Family Process, 12*:197-212, 1973. Courtesy of *Family Process*.

"I asked all the people I visited if they knew of prevention-action centers or units that I could visit. The answer was practically always, 'No.' This surprised me because I had assumed that this field was fairly well developed in the United States."

Family therapy in and of itself can be considered preventive when it is successful in disrupting destructive, three-generational patterns. Yet "therapy" begins only after a problem has been designated as "serious" and in need of "treatment." There is no place in our communities for families to go when they first begin to feel something is going wrong that they don't understand and can't cope with—vague anxieties, uneasy togetherness, inexplicable tensions. Only after a child develops a serious symptom, parents are on the verge of divorce, or someone is designated as "disturbed" will families face the guilt and anxiety, not to mention the expense, of going to a mental health agency. Seeking professional help becomes a drastic step invariably accompanied by the underlying conviction that someone has failed, someone consequently is to blame, someone consequently will be found guilty and exposed. It is little wonder families put off treatment for years, sweeping the problems under the rug hoping they will disappear. By the time families do go for help they are usually in a state of panic or despair; a scapegoat has been chosen and accepted the role; destructive patterns have lacerated deep wounds; guilt is high and forgiveness low.

Our community groups were aimed at removing the stigma of sickness so that motivation for change did not have to be based on desperation. We also wanted to challenge the prevailing belief that unless a family is in a crisis it is unmotivated to seek change.

The program was offered to various churches and schools in the neighborhood surrounding the Institute. It was presented as being for the "average family with everyday problems, the kind that beset us all in this very hectic, pressured, and frightening time in which we live." The emphasis was on self-study rather than treatment or cure. The stated goal was to "understand how your family operates, to evaluate and revitalize family relationships." The setting of a group offered the opportunity to share this self-exploratory experience with other families.

Clergymen, headmasters, and principals were especially interested in the program because of their alarm over the increasing breakdown of families. One minister warned us, "You'd better hurry up. There are hardly any families left!" Clergymen offered their pulpits for a discussion of the program and headmasters sent urgent letters to their parents inviting them to come and hear Mrs. Papp speak.

The families were self-selected, unscreened, taken on a first come, first served basis. No evaluation interviews were given, no histories taken. Families were assigned to groups strictly on the basis of the ages of their children. In one group children's ages ranged from 7 to 10; in another from 11 to 14; and in the third from 15 to 17. When they met for the first time, therapists as well as families were strangers. The results so far have boosted our contention that there could have been no better way of selecting.

How "well" were these "well families"? Most of them had serious problems but none were in the midst of a self-defined crisis. Their motivation for volunteering was based on their awareness of the pressures they were experiencing at home. We defined our prevention as dealing with these stresses at an earlier point in time and felt this had a crucial bearing on the ability of the families to mobilize their healing powers.

The quality of the participation of the group families was noticeably different from that of the Institute families. The group families as a whole were more motivated, less resistant, and more creatively involved in the process of their own change. The incidence of lateness and absenteeism was low and often more frequent and longer sessions wee requested. We believe this was due to the difference in expectations of the families and the manner in which the program was introduced. The group families came not to be cured or blamed by the therapists but to actively participate in their own understanding and learning. The emotional temperatures of the families were low enough to permit more contemplation and consequently to gain more perspective.

The thrust of the pilot program was of necessity limited to the most accessible community surrounding the Institute; this was largely white, middle-class. Our initial conviction, however, that the program had value for a broad cross-section of families including those from poverty and minority groups was reinforced by a response to a write-up of the groups in the *New York Daily News*. Following this the Institute was deluged with telephone calls from families who represented a wide variety of economic, racial, social, and cultural backgrounds. These families expressed a particular interest in working in a group with other families. "We would like to talk to other families and maybe get some ideas." "It would be a comfort to be able to speak to parents of other teenagers." "I feel there is a great deal of value in being with other families, particularly families who have children of similar ages. I would like to share some of my feelings."

METHOD

Our method of intervention was influenced by the nature of the contract we had made with these families. The fact that they had not come to us with an overt crisis which they expected us to immediately alleviate gave us leeway to present a conceptual framework in which to view the family functioning. Our major goals were to teach families a way of observing their own interaction, of defining problems in terms of relationships rather than individuals, of developing an awareness of family themes continued from one generation to the next. We also hoped that by presenting family operations as a universal phenomenon, governed by common principles, members would be able to examine their family relationships with less fear and guilt. The idea that anything as intense and explosive as family relationships could be studied in a thoughtful and systematic way helped to create a "safe" atmosphere and allowed families to explore with a certain spirit of adventure.

Following are the six basic concepts from which we worked. (These were written up at the request of the families and each member given a copy.)

How Families Operate

I. Family Systems. The family operates as an emotional unit with no villains, heros, good people, bad people, healthy or unhealthy members. Family problems result from the way family members relate to one another and not from the behavior of any one person. What each person does affects every other person and a chain reaction is set off. These chain reactions become repetitious and predictable. If one can gain distance, one can study them, observe how they are set off, how they are reinforced, who picks up what cues, and the part each plays in the chain reaction.

II. Labeling. Each family member eventually gets programmed into a specific role in the family and labeled accordingly. Labeling serves a need in the family set-up, and each individual gains some identification from it. Each plays a part in assuming his label and continuing it. Most labels are stultifying, as they prevent growth and have little to do with the true nature of the person. It is possible for families to understand their own labeling process and modify it, thus releasing family members to fulfill more of their individual potential.

III. Collaboration. Collaboration is necessary among family members to keep conflicts going. One person cannot carry on an interaction all by himself. By studying how each person is involved in the family merry-go-round, the cycle can be interrupted by any one person changing his behavior. Much frustration can be avoided by concentrating on changing oneself rather than blaming others. The happiest people are those who take major responsibility for their own happiness.

IV. Triangles. Triangles tend to form in families because of the close, intense relationships. When one person feels hurt, angry, disappointed, or frustrated with another family member and cannot settle it with them, he tends to bring someone else into the relationship. Parents often use their children to make up for what is lacking between them. Children also involve their parents in triangles by playing one against the other. Sometimes a friend or relative is brought in from the outside to form a triangle. If one person in the triangle changes his position, the whole triangle will shift. It is preferable to have a separate relationship with each person that does not involve any other person and does not form a triangle.

V. Family Ghosts. Family ghosts are passed from one generation to another. Parents tend to assume the same emotional position in their present family as they assumed in their family of origin. They come with prejudices, anxieties, and expectations that are carried over and imposed on the members of their present families. If a parent can understand the way he was programmed into his family of origin and take a step to change it, he will pave the way to do the same thing in his present family.

VI. Change. The family system can be changed by any one person taking a different position and sticking to it.

Family Sculpting

Our main task was to personalize these concepts by illuminating the unique way in which they were experienced in each family. We had long been fascinated by family sculpting as an effective method of blending the cognitive with the experiential and decided to experiment with it as a therapeutic spine around which to unfold and re-shape the family systems.

Family sculpting is a therapeutic art form in which each family member arranges the other members in a tableau which physically symbolizes their emotional relationship with one another. Each creates a live family portrait placing members together in terms of posture and spacial relationships representing action and feelings. The essence of one's experience in the family is condensed and projected into a visual picture. This picture is literally worth a thousand words, revealing aspects of the family's inner life that have remained hidden. Vague impressions and confused feelings on the periphery of awareness are given form through physical spatial expression.

One of the major advantages of this method is the ability to cut through intellectualization, defensiveness, and projection of blame. Families are deprived of their familiar verbal cues and are compelled to communicate with one another on a more meaningful level. As triangles, alliances, and conflicts are choreographed, they are made concrete and placed in the realm of the visual, sensory, and symbolic areas where there are vastly more possibilities for communication of feelings in all their nuances.

Another advantage of sculpting is the adhesive effect it has on the families. It compels them to think of themselves as a unit with each person a necessary part of that unit affecting every other part. It is impossible to isolate any one intense relationship without seeing the reverberations of it throughout the family. While uniting the family, the sculpting at the same time individuates, as it requires each member to abstract his own personal experience, observe and interpret it. We shall now describe some of the ways in which we integrated the sculpting into our overall goals.

Re-Alignment of the Family

It was the job of the therapist to extract the meaning of the sculpting in terms of the family systems, analyze it, synthesize it, and feed it back. Whenever possible, we used the sculpting to shift the family balance within the session. By physically re-aligning the family, we produced a blueprint for a future emotional re-alignment. For example, in Peggy Papp's group all the members in one family had sculpted the father as the "Rock of Gibraltar" upon which the whole family stood. The twelve-year-old daughter placed him literally bending over backward to support the family with one hand and hold up three businesses with the other. The son had him lecturing virtuously but sternly on a platform with pointed finger. The mother placed the father on a pedestal looking up to him for guidance. When it came time for this "Rock of Gibraltar" to do his sculpting, he threw himself on the floor and said, "I'm swimming upstream in mud." He placed his wife hanging onto his feet and his twelve-year-old daughter hanging onto her feet with him pulling them both. He instructed his son to lie across his neck like a millstone, as he declared, "I sometimes feel like I'm going down for the third time." The therapist then asked the father to change the sculpting the way he would like it. He tried to get to his feet. In order to do this it became obvious he first had to throw his son off his neck and shake his wife from his heels. Wife and son then had to negotiate for new positions based on the father's freeing himself. When the father stood up, he held out his hand for his wife to join him by his side. Before she could do this however, she had to extricate herself from her twelve-year-old daughter who was hanging onto her feet and with whom she was overly involved. There followed a discussion as to whether her daughter would sink if she let her go, or whether she were old enough to do some swimming by herself now. Mother and daughter agreed she was and she let go of her mother's heels to join her brother. Mother still refused to move, waiting for her husband to pull her up. He refused to pull her up, waiting for her to join him. The basic family conflict had been physicalized. Responding to questions by the therapist that provoked thought and movement, husband and wife eventually ended up side by side holding hands, with the children in front of them but some distance away. Through this three-dimensional picture, we had created a common language and a common family goal toward which to work.

Clarification of Symptoms

We found the sculpting invaluable in involving children in the groups. It provided them with a channel for expressing feelings that would have been difficult, it not impossible, for them to express verbally. It enabled them to become involved immediately, alleviated their boredom and restlessness, and gave them a sense that their perceptions were important. The connection between certain symptoms and family interaction were sometimes dramatically clarified. In one family a nine-year-old son had developed a bewildering symptom. He was given to walking around in circles whenever he became restless, much to the dismay of the family. In sculpting his family, Jimmy placed his two sisters in one corner of the room playing jacks and ignoring him. He placed his mother and father in the other corner, quarreling, and himself alone in the center of the room. The therapist then asked him to demonstrate in movement what he did about this situation. "Well, first I go over here to my sisters, but they won't let me play with them and tell me to go away, so then I go over here to talk to mother and daddy but they tell me not to bother them, so then I go back to my sisters. ..." As he described his predicament, he began walking in circles, going round and round between his parents and siblings. This was a quiet boy who seldom expressed any thoughts or feelings. The family was made aware for the first time of his isolated position, his frustration in trying to find a place for himself in the family, and the connection between this and his walking in circles. This was eventually related to the broader family symptom of everybody "going around in circles."

Three-Generational Themes

We traced family themes back through the generations in order to give historical perspective to current family patterns. After each member sculpted his nuclear family, the parents sculpted their family of origin. This gave an overview of the emotional life of the families through time. These series of pictures spanning the generations set the stage for viewing problems in terms of a wide network of continuing relationships.

Intense feelings were often stirred up in the parents as they reconstructed their families. Thinking in terms of pictures is a primitive process arousing primitive feelings. To bring one's family to life with living, breathing people permits one to stand back and observe the earlier scenes while participating in them at the same time. Through this double vision one may see one's behavior and feelings as a functional part of the total family constellation. Members of the group took the parts of the primary family members of the parents. In doing so they became a part of the emotional interaction of that family often providing valuable insights.

If a parent was having difficulty with a particular child, we asked him to sculpt his family when he himself was the age of that child. This sensitized the parent to the feelings of the child and helped the child to see his parent as a person with his own problems in growing up. Following is an example of an exchange between mother and daughter during a three-generational sculpting in which an emotional bridge was formed between the past and present resulting in a new experience for both.

In Olga Silverstein's group, a fourteen-year-old girl, Giselle, with a severe stutter, sculpted her family, as follows. Father and brother are playing chess at the kitchen table, not talking but just slightly moving the pieces. She and her mother are standing a great distance apart gazing silently at one another. "I can't talk to mother, because I stutter." During the same session, the mother, Eva, sculpted her family of origin, as follows. Her father and brother are sitting silently reading the newspaper. Mother is sitting at the typewriter writing one of her interminable letters to the two sisters who are away from home. She herself is standing next to her mother talking and talking—she says, "Hysterically trying to get some response." Mother never looks up from her typing. As she re-enacted this scene, she said, "It feels so hopeless. I can't reach anybody." The woman playing her mother said, "There is a part of me that is aware of her unhappiness and would like to reach out but I am afraid." When the therapist asked what she would do were she not afraid, she reached over and drew Eva into her arms. This physical contact aroused Eva's longing for a close relationship with her mother and she spoke at length of her loneliness. When she eventually returned to her seat next to her daughter, she looked at her for a long moment and then spontaneously reached over and drew her into her arms. Both cried and sat for the rest of the session close together. An insight had been translated into an action within the session. Since insights are ephemeral and tend to evaporate or remain intellectual, we strove whenever possible to convert them into immediate action. In answer to the question on our periodic questionnaire: "Did you learn anything new about any member of the family from sculpting," Eva responded, "I learned to see my daughter as different and separate from me so I stopped demanding that she talk to me and now we talk quite easily. *I* talk to her." Giselle responded, "I saw that my mother had even more problems in talking to people than I do. I saw how anxious she was and I stopped being so mad at her. I felt good when she hugged me. I didn't think I could like it."

Theme-Centered Discussions

All three therapists work differently using their own individual styles and techniques but with the same concepts and goals in mind. Betty Carter, an experienced group therapist, followed up sculpting with theme-centered discussions. The themes were chosen for the purpose of focusing family members on critical issues of individuation within the context of family relationships. They were used to continue the work opened up by the sculpting without necessarily verbalizing the parallels or having them interpreted.

For example, a woman married to a busy chemist who spent long hours at the laboratory sculpted her original family by putting her father off in a corner with his back to the family. She spoke of his distance, silence, and isolation from her. When asked where she would like to have had him she burst into tears and pulled the person playing her father into the family group saying vehemently, "In the middle here—relating—a big daddy. What I'm always trying to get George (husband) to do in our family." In a discussion centered around "Taking Responsibility for My Life and Letting You Take Responsibility for Yours," she began to examine her angry dependency on her husband and her reluctance to find a life of her own. Referring back to the sculpting, she drew many parallels between her resentment against her father and her husband. She concluded she would stop trying to put George into the center and would, thus, let him be. Subsequently, in a discussion around the theme "Changing Myself," she spoke of the concrete steps she had taken to take charge of her own life. Her husband, feeling relieved of her obsessive demands, became more communicative and began to talk about his own difficulty with closeness, relating this to his own sculpting of his family of origin.

Resistance

These are the encouraging experiences. Not all the families were this responsive to change. Entrenched reactions, as always, were difficult to budge. Sometimes the sculpting was stereotyped and revealed little, or the person was unresponsive to what was revealed. At other times so many issues were opened up with such rapidity we felt as though we had struck oil and were running around with buckets trying to catch it. Some children presented an idealized picture of the family, either out of fear or a desire to protect their parents; it might take several attempts to elicit a meaningful experience. Denial and scapegoating as always were major roadblocks to progress. At times a particular type of interaction was born out of desperation. For example, in Peggy Papp's group a highly intellectualizing doctor sculpted his family of origin denying all connections between the two families, although these were obvious to everyone else in the group. At the same time he was scapegoating his son unmercifully, labeling him a failure, irresponsible, a con man. In his sculpting of his family of origin, he had placed his mother standing very close to him "spoon-feeding him." His father, at a great distance, was charming the world with a smile. "He was an angel on the outside and a devil on the inside. A real con man." He went on to describe the grandfather as a gambler who finally had a run-in with the police, spent some time in jail, had affairs with other women and was seldom home. He denied all feelings regarding this family arrangement.

Several sessions later, however, after a particularly intense blow-up at home between father and son, the father made the following series of remarks to his son during the course of the session: "I do not approve of the way you are conducting your life. . . . As far as I am concerned, you are a complete failure. . . . I am deeply disappointed in you and have been for years. . . . You are irresponsible, a real con man. . . . You have failed to give me the love I expected from you."

When the therapist read over the notes from this meeting (which were taken verbatim), she underlined these remarks and at the next session asked the father to re-create his original sculting repeating all the lines he had said to his son, this time addressing them to the man who was playing his father. She asked the woman who was playing his mother to join him in the chorus, as the mother was obviously collusive in labeling the father and excluding him from the family. At the end of the exercise the father said, "Yes, these are all the things I though about my father but could never say." Following this he was able to discuss some of his real feelings about his father for the first time. The theme of self-disgust which ran through the family and was being passed on to his son, Peter, was now available for examination. Unfortunately, this "insight" had little immediate effect on the father's relationship with his son, as he was unable to integrate it in moments of crisis. However it had an immediate effect on Peter. After raptly observing the above sculpting, Peter exclaimed, "Then all that stuff doesn't belong just to me! Wow, I never knew you felt that way about your father." Peter had been moping about the house all year refusing to work or to go to school. Two weeks later he took his first step to move out of the failure role in the family by making arrangements for a make-up program in school. He graduated from high school at the end of the year.

If a child can be helped to understand the family theme he is acting out, he has the possibility of unhooking himself even though the parent cannot. Having caught just a glimpse of how he was enmeshed in the family net Peter was able to begin a long hard process of extricating himself from it. His efforts were reinforced by the group who saw totally different aspects of him, describing him as "mature, sensitive, bright, and unusually perceptive." They reacted intensely to the father's total renunciation of the boy compelling the father to control some of his irresponsible behavior toward Peter.

Change

The therapeutic emphasis in the groups was heavily and prejudiciously oriented toward changing circular reinforcing behavior. The major question we asked ourselves throughout was "How do insights get translated into action." Insights that did not result in changed behavior or a shift in the family system we considered worthless. Changes in family relationships sometimes came about spontaneously as the result of changed feelings or a new awareness. Sometimes they did not. A common fallacy in every kind of therapy is the assumption that if someone "understands" something he will act on it. All too frequently this has not come to pass. While it is easier to change one's behavior on the basis of insight and a new perspective, it is sometimes necessary simply to change it without waiting for this. Based on Salvadore Minuchin's "First Comes Change, Then Comes Insight," we put into operation what became known as a "de-labeling" program. This was aimed directly at helping family members to "de-label" themselves by changing their predictable behavior within the family. Each family member was taken aside separately by the therapist for brief conferences during which they discussed how they were labeled in the family and how best to go about changing their label. This was based on a diagnostic understanding of the process of labeling within each family that had developed over the months. They were not to let the others know what they intended to do but to observe reactions of the family to the change. The element of surprise was important in assessing the effects on the family and on themselves. One of the most important gains was becoming aware of what they experienced as they tried to change. For example, a husband who had been labeled as the tyrant and critic in the family was asked if he could stop criticizing for one week. "Of course, easy," he stated. The following week the family reported a remarkable change in the home atmosphere. "It was delightful. There was no hostility between us all week!" exclaimed the wife. "It's the first time I've ever seen my father act human," said the son.

The father's endurance lasted three weeks and then he began to waver. The whole family lapsed back into their old ways. "You know this doesn't solve the basic problem in the family anyway," the husband grumbled. When asked what it was, he replied, "It's my wife's sloppy housekeeping, of course." "And how has that been the past few weeks?" asked the therapist. "Well—wonderful. In fact, she's been great. But that's only because I haven't criticized her." Much laughter from the group. Even the father saw the humor in his paradoxical statement. His emotional investment in his label was now open for exploration in terms of action, interaction, and reaction in the total family. His attempted change had made waves in the entire family unit. The wife, relieved at first, found herself getting depressed as her role of being the maligned one was taken away. The son, robbed of the constant bickering, became provocative and picked fights with his father.

It was expected that anxiety would be stirred up as the families were disequilibrated. One seventeen-year-old boy whose mother was the mediator in the family exclaimed, "Don't let my mother stop mediating, or my father and I will kill each other." The mother, however, deciding the role was costing her too much stayed out of the interaction between father and son for a week. She reported, "I was so relieved. When I was in between Bob and his father, they used to argue for several hours at a time. When I wasn't there, they argued for several minutes." Someone in the group suggested, "Maybe you weren't the mediator, maybe you were the trouble-maker." This shifted the family into a new gear of perception.

The de-labeling program had been instituted with some apprehension on the part of the therapist, who feared it might produce some mechanical and short-lived results. It was, therefore, of great interest to learn via the final questionnaire that the group felt this was the single most helpful activity in which they had participated.

Feedback

Questionnaires were used periodically to get feedback and monitor change. We wanted to know from the families themselves what was helpful and what was not. Therapists often theorize about what has produced change without asking those who know the best—the ones who are experiencing it. The questions were directed toward: (a) observing one's behavior in the family and the effect it had on others, (b) understanding the family system and the part each played in it, (c) defining one's own goals, and (d) monitoring one's own change. The families felt the questionnaires had been helpful in forcing them to think about what they were doing and where they were going. They suggested the questionnaires be used at more frequent intervals.

USE OF GROUP

The group was used to create a learning environment in which all the senses were used. Space, movement, and sensory pictures became an integral part of the experience. Body and mind were engaged in reliving past experiences and transforming them into new experiences in the present family scene. The presence of the others bearing witness intensified the experience.

Free interaction among group members was somewhat limited in order to clarify issues in each family. Group process was focused around specific themes and activities. This sometimes required putting aside immediate concerns of families such as the quarrel last night or the battle over the weekend in favor of longer range, overall goals. While taking something away, we felt it added something more important. It reduced the amount of time wasted in superficial discussions and permitted families to participate on a deeper level. Rather than analyzing the process in the group, we analyzed the process within each family.

Despite the fact that our structure cut down on group interaction, the valuable features of a group seemed to have been enhanced rather than lost. "It was so helpful having the others participate in my sculpting. I learned so much about my family that I never knew before." "I gained a great deal from seeing the sculptings of other families and relating their experiences to mine." "It's a comfort to know others have the same problems and to be able to share them."

Socializing was done mainly outside the sessions and we neither encouraged nor discouraged this. The extent of the socializing varied from group to group and was done mainly through and around the children.

SUMMARY AND CONCLUSIONS

This has been a description of an experimental community project aimed at prevention. In searching for an educational, time-limited, self-help method, we experimented with new techniques and approaches. We often felt uncomfortable with the new methods, as they were a departure from our accustomed approach. The primary question we addressed ourselves to was, "How are insights translated into change within the family system?" Much of our thinking changed in the process of asking and seeking the answer to this question. All of our conclusions at this point are tentative and paradoxical: (a) Structuring tends to enhance rather than hamper the spontaneous release of feeling. It provides the possibility for more things happening, not less. (b) Presenting Teaching concepts can lead away from intellectualizing, not toward it. Intellectualizing is usually a defense against anxiety and feeling. The presentation of concepts promotes contemplation, provides perspective, reduces anxiety, and leads towards the release of feelings. (c) Limiting group interaction intensifies rather than diminishes the effect of the group. The focusing of group interaction around specific issues in each family deepens the group experience. (d) Deliberately changing one's behavior such as in the delabeling program need not produce mechanical results, but, on the contrary, can lead to insightful changes.

NONVERBAL TECHNIQUES

The use of nonverbal techniques by a family therapist can be helpful in (a) soliciting additional information from family members, (b) retaining control of the session, (c) showing support, (d) facilitating awareness, (e) inclusion of resistance of withdrawn family members, and (f) continuing the process past a point. Many people may not be aware of the wide variety of creative and effective possibilities available. The articles in this chapter suggest techniques that should accomplish some of the goals listed above. In addition, these tasks are often interesting enough to grasp everyone's attention while reducing anxiety and acting as a stimulant for future verbal exchanges.

Many individuals are seemingly unable to relate only to verbal communications. They find it much easier to respond to "pictures" rather than auditory or kinesthetic messages. "Pictures" are defined as internal mental images as well as external happenings. These techniques allow the therapist to interact with the client's dominant representational system while facilitating the therapeutic process.

Geddes and Medway describe a technique that is useful as a diagnostic, therapeutic, and research tool. The symbolic drawing of the family life space allows the focus to shift away from the scapegoat while helping the therapist to gain additional informational about the family's social networks. The technique also enables the therapist and family members to examine rules, roles, and the structural nature of the family.

Robert Schachter describes kinetic psychotherapy. This technique utilizes a number of social interaction games to illustrate the family's interactional pattern and facilitate communication. In addition, this technique allows family members to become more aware of their previous patterns and suggests possible solutions.

Herta Guttman advises the family therapist to carefully monitor children's nonverbal messages since they are often reluctant to draw attention to themselves during the therapy sessions. She suggests a variety of ways the therapist can understand the child's communication within the context of the family. Examples of methods the child uses to communicate are presented to illustrate behaviors the family therapist should be aware of.

These techniques all appear to be initially nonthreatening and encourage communication by all family members. However, inevitably as families become aware of their patterns, tension will increase and resistance may ensue. These strategies may be used again to help families past these difficult periods while also facilitating change.

Chapter 26

THE SYMBOLIC DRAWING OF THE FAMILY LIFE SPACE

MICHAEL GEDDES AND JOAN MEDWAY

TASK-CENTERED PROCEDURES

Minuchin has developed a number of task-centered situations to facilitate family assessment (11). The familial structure may be explored by asking family members to complete such tasks as replicating a model with a construction block kit or deciding together which family member comes closest to being the most bossy, the biggest crybaby, or the biggest troublemaker. In a similar vein, Watzlawick assesses typical familial interactions by asking the family to plan something they could do together as a unit (21). The simplicity of these tasks is perhaps one of their greatest strengths, as is their ability to highlight the typical patterns of verbal and nonverbal family transactions.

Typical family interaction as well as family fantasy material may be elicited by task assignments employing projective materials. These involve the entire family, producing a group response to a traditionally individual type of test. Loveland et al. employ the Family Rorschach Method in which the family's task includes interpreting the inkblots to each other while attempting to reach some consensus in their responses (10). To compare similarities and differences between the individual's psychological functioning when working independently versus in the family context, Levy and Epstein first administer the Rorschach separately to each family member and then to the family as a unit (8). Though the use of these projective materials is stimulating and relatively standardized, their sophisticated and in-depth nature requires special training, which many family therapists might not have as part and parcel of their therapeutic armamentarium.

From M. Geddes and J. Medway, The Symbolic Drawing of the Family Life Space, *Family Process*, 16:219-28, 1977. Courtesy of *Family Process*.

EXPRESSIVE MODALITIES

Symbolic expressive modalities, blending the cognitive with the experiential, tend to facilitate communication by lowering defenses and allowing an individual to express his concerns in a more or less indirect and nonthreatening manner. Under the guise of "play," an abundance of significant material may be harvested. The most widely used expressive modalities include family sculpture, family art therapy, and family puppet interviews.

Family sculpture, originated by David Kantor and Fred Duhl, is a symbolic nonverbal activity that often serves as a stimulus to verbal interchange (19, 17). The therapist asks each member of the family to spatially arrange the other members in a meaningful configuration. This gestalt is a vivid portrayal of the individual's present family life space. The technique is similar to psychodrama, since it reveals family relationships in terms of space, alliances, attitudes, and underlying feelings. Because of the expressive nature of the technique, many clients may be inhibited, feeling that they must perform as if they were on stage.

Family art therapy, a provocative technique, yet one which may be less inhibiting than family sculpture, has been employed as a natural extension of the analytically oriented individual art therapies (15, 20, 6). Kwiatkowska has the family make a series of sequentially ordered drawings, including a "joint family scribble," in which each member does a quick scribble and then the entire family completes the scribble by making a picture (7). This procedure enables the therapist to perceive the patterning of role allocation within the family and illuminates the family decision-making process. Bing also has family members draw a picture together to graphically represent and come to some consensus on how they see themselves as a family (2). Rubin and Magnussen ask family members to produce a joint mural as well as a two- or three-dimensional family portrait (18). Family art therapy leads to gradual clarification of areas of conflict, but it is much more time-consuming than the use of more primitive graphic symbolism.

Just as family art therapy has been a natural development of anaytically oriented individual art therapy, family puppet interviews are a natural extension of the well-established use of puppets in clinical work with children. Irwin and Malloy offer the family a basket with a large selection of puppets (4). The family is instructed to make up a story using the puppets, while the therapist observes from another room. The therapist returns to the family when the beginning of the story is being planned and has the family act out the story with their puppets. The puppet play is used as a vehicle for associations and as a means of highlighting sources of conflict as well as alliances. Though a wealth of material may be elicited from this expressive technique, it is likely that many individuals will resist the regression.

THE SYMBOLIC DRAWING OF THE FAMILY LIFE SPACE

The Symbolic Drawing of the Family Life Space, primarily a task-centered projective technique, that also possesses many qualities of symbolic expressive modalities, was developed by Dr. Danuta Mostwin[1] as a part of the Short-Term Multidimensional Family Intervention model[2] (12, 13, 1, 16, 5, 14). This technique may be utilized in the first therapeutic encounter with a family or an individual in the following manner.

A large circle is drawn by the therapist on a blackboard or standing easel. The family is told that everything inside this Family Circle represents what they feel is part of their family. Persons and institutions felt not to be part of their family are placed outside the Family Circle in the Environment. The Family Circle and the Environment represent the Family Life Space.[3]

Each member of the family is asked, in turn, to come to the blackboard and place a small circle representing himself within the Family Circle. Therapist judgment and intuition determine the order of choice of family members. Though there are no hard and fast rules, in order to shift the focus from the identified patient to the family unit, it is recommended that the identified patient never be called to the blackboard first.

The authors tend to start with the family member who they sense might be the most cooperative. They continue to make decisions regarding the order of selection guided by process cues from the family. Therefore, the decision regarding the order of selection can never be made before one meets with the family. For example, to a certain extent the first person placing himself on the drawing controls the possibilities for the use of space by the other family members. If mother places herself directly in the center of the family circle and father starts to protest, nonverbally, therapist judgment may deem it wise to call father next to the blackboard. Here, as in all therapeutic encounters, sensitivity and timing are crucial.

---

[1]Dr. Mostwin is on the faculty of the National Catholic School of Social Service of Catholic University.

[2]Short-Term Multidimensional Family Intervention is a time-limited crisis-oriented approach to family treatment. Employed primarily with families having an acting-out adolescent as the identified patient, STMFI is characterized by two main concurrent levels of treatment: individual and family group. An interdisciplinary team first meets with the family group for a forty-five minute session and then breaks into forty-five minute individual sessions—each family member having his own therapist. During the private interviews, the team leader floats from session to session transmitting relevant information to facilitate the therapeutic process. After therapist collaboration, the team and family reconvene for a thirty-minute wrap-up session. Treatment lasts six weeks.

[3]The technique of the Symbolic Drawing inspired by Lewinian Field Theory was also influenced in its development by some of Kwiatkowska's techniques of family art therapy (7).

Each family member proceeds to place himself in the circle, in a position relative to other family members and the Environment. For the sake of clarity, several different colored marking pens or pieces of chalk may be provided, so that each family member can choose a different color. Immediate feedback is given by the therapist to the family member as he places himself, by such remarks as "You feel you're in the center of your family, very far from your parents and brothers."

It is at this point that the authors attempt to gain information about the family member's social network,[4] by asking the following question, "Are there any other people who you feel are important enough to you to be included in this drawing?" The family member then places important others, i.e., *absent* family members and/or friends, deceased or living, somewhere within or outside the family circle, as he perceives them. There is often considerable disagreement among family members about the placement of absent extended family. When this happens, the authors note the perceptual differences diagramatically by asking the dissenting family member to place the person where *he* feels this person should be in the drawing (e.g. see Figure 26-1).

Occasionally, for various reasons, one will find a family that does not include anyone not present in the session. The authors then probe for information regarding at least the paternal and maternal grandparents and siblings. Here one begins to see and learn about multigenerational patterns, family secrets, past traumatic experiences, such as deaths, abortions, etc.

The therapist then asks the client to place significant social institutions (e.g. schools, churches, community agencies, etc.), in the Environment. This differs from any of the aforementioned task-centered or symbolic expressive modalities, since utilization of relevant environmental information is regularly included for a comprehensive diagnosis. Although not stressed enough by most family therapists, consideration of this environmental information is not only consonant with the expertise of the psychosocial therapist but should be also an integral part of his diagnostic process.

After all family members have come to the blackboard to place themselves and significant others, the therapist then instructs the family in the following way: "Now I would like to know how you feel you communicate with the people and institutions on this drawing. By communicate, I mean how you feel you can talk with another person and whether or not that person understands you. In other words, do you get your message across. You have three choices: if you feel that you have 'good' communication with another person, draw a straight line from

---

[4]The reader might be interested in a similar but more standardized mapping technique developed by Dr. Carolyn Attneave, which focuses in a more comprehensive fashion on the social network. See *Family Therapy*, edited by Philip Guerin, New York, Gardner Press, 1976.

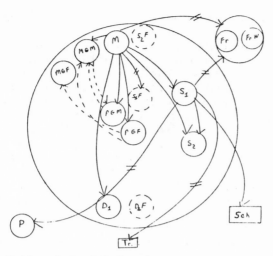

Guide to the Symbolic Drawing

M ......mother
S_1 ......son, age 10, identified patient
D_1 ......daughter, age 7
PGF ....paternal grandfather
MGF ...maternal grandfather as perceived by maternal grandmother
S_2F .....father, as perceived by son
Fr ......friend
Sch .....school
Tr ......training school
F ......father
S_2 ......son, age 8
PGM ...paternal grandmother
MGM ...maternal grandmother
S_1F .....father, as perceived by son
D_1F ....father, as perceived by daughter
FrW ....friend's wife
P ......plaintiff (man who had identified patient arrested)

Fig. 26-1. The Key family – Session 1

you to that person, like this (*Therapist draws an example 0* ⟶ *0*). If you feel that you have 'so-so' communication with another person, sometimes good and sometimes not so good, draw a dotted arrow from you to that person, like this (*therapist draws an example 0* -----→ *0*). Finally, if you feel that you have 'poor' communication or none at all with another person, draw an arrow slashed twice from you to that person, like this (*therapist draws an example 0* —/—/→ *0*). So you have three choices: 'good,' 'so-so,' and 'poor' or no communication at all.''

At this point the therapist recalls each family member, usually in the same order as before, to indicate the quality of his communication with the other members of his family, significant others, and social institutions present in the drawing. Again feedback is provided by the therapist to each member by reflecting the quality of communication he has noted: "You have good communication with your mother" or "So you feel you cannot talk at all to your father" or "You feel you have 'poor' communication with your school."

This constant feedback and clarification of the family members' perceptions, coupled with their own diagrammatic representations of their relationships, actively engages the family in the process of self-observation. For the therapist, the Symbolic Drawing of the Family Life Space serves as:
1. a diagnostic source providing information regarding the structural configuration of a family, i.e., dyadic and triangular alliances, enmeshment, and estrangement;
2. a therapeutic tool gauging the degree of intra-familial congruence, i.e., agreement of perception of spatial position within the family and agreement regarding quality of communication; and
3. a research device providing an effective means for measuring the change of familial structure.

The authors will select examples of symbolic drawings from their work in STMFI to illustrate the functions mentioned above.

STRUCTURAL INFORMATION

The Key family is a white, lower class, urban family of Polish and German descent, referred by the Department of Juvenile Services when the 10-year-old son was placed on probation for destruction of property. At the time of referral, the father, an ex-drug addict, was completing the last two months of a two-year prison sentence for violation of probation. Mrs. Key was, and is, on probation for aiding in narcotics traffic and is on public assistance. Her two younger children, ages 7 and 9, were experiencing difficulties in school. The paternal and maternal grandparents, who lived nearby, seemed to be in the home more than the mother. At this first diagnostic encounter, the following family members were present: mother, her three children, paternal grandparents, and maternal grandparents. Absent, but included in the drawing, were the father and the maternal grandfather.

The structure of the Key family during the first family therapy session shows rather clearly the absence of generational boundaries depicting what is typically termed an "enmeshed family" (see Fig. 26-1). This initial drawing by the Key family accurately represents the lack of intragenerational boundaries within this family, the lack of clear lines of authority resulting from the absence of role differentiation, and the almost entire denial by the family of any impoverishment of communication. By having as its primary goal the reinstatement of the mother and father in their parental positions, the interdisciplinary therapeutic team attempted to discourage and dilute the grandparents' infantilization of their own children, while encouraging them to redefine their roles as supportive elders who occupy positions outside of—but aligned with—the nuclear family. Figure 26-1 indicates the structural relationships in the Key family at the sixth family session and will be discussed later in this article.

The Bings are a white, middle-class, suburban family referred by the school psychologist because of the acting-out behavior of Mrs. Bing's 14-year-old son from a previous marriage. Mr. Bing's drawing of his family in his first individual session portrays the triangulation of the identified patient as well as the tribal-like split in this family, which was formed by the marriage of a divorced father and his two children and a divorced mother and her two children (see Fig. 26-2). Note the coalition of Mr. Bing, his parents, and his two natural children on the right; and the positioning of his wife, her parents, and her natural child on the left. Mr. Bing unconsciously perceived his stepson, the identified patient, as occupying the position through which all the familial tension flows. He has accurately portrayed the identified patient's role as a cohesive force in this family—a force that keeps from awareness the underlying parental conflicts preventing a healthy merger of these two coalitions.

PERCEPTUAL CONGRUENCE

The Symbolic Drawing of the Family Life Space also unearths information regarding the way two people perceive the spatial and communicative aspects of their relationship, i.e., the degree of congruence. The therapist may want to use instances of lack of congruence as springboards for bringing forth hidden feelings, clarifying role conflicts and expectations, and, in so doing, increasing the quality and depth of communication between family members. The following case example shows a lack of spatial congruence within the family.

The Simpsons are a white, lower middle-class, suburban family referred by the school psychologist because of the acting-out behavior of their 14-year-old son. The Simpson family initially presented a schism (9, p. 246) between an extremely passive father and a domineering mother; a dyadic configuration between the mother and the eldest son Bob, age 17, who was increasingly carrying out the father's role; and the acting-out adolescent, who was the identified patient. The interdisciplinary therapeutic team's goals were to realign the parents,

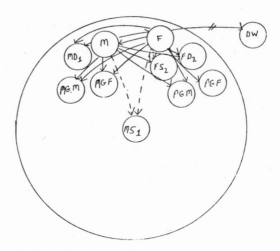

Guide to the Symbolic Drawing
F . . . . . . .father
M . . . . . .mother
MS₁ . . . .mother's son, age 14, identified patient
MD₁ . . . .mother's daughter, age 13
FS₁ . . . . .father's son, age 14
FD₁ . . . .father's daughter, age 13
PGM . . .paternal grandmother
PGF . . . .paternal grandfather
MGM . . .maternal grandmother
MGF . . .maternal grandfather
DW . . . .father's divorced first wife

Fig. 26-2. Father's drawing of the Bing family —
Session 1

support the passive father's role, deparentify the oldest son, Bob[5] (3, p. 151), and create a dyad between the identified patient and the father. In so doing, Bob began to feel obsolete, as his former functions were gradually assumed by a more assertive father. He depicted this in the sixth family session (see Fig. 26-3) by positioning himself outside the nuclear family boundary in the Environment, while saying to his family "You don't need me anymore." His family rushed to clarify the lack of congruence between his perception of his position and theirs, affirming their love for Bob while emphasizing several important functions they

---

[5]Nagy defines parentification as the "subjective distortion of a relationship as if one's partner or even children were his parent." In the Simpson family, Bob became caretaker to his father, rescuing him from bars when he was too drunk to drive hom. He also was the chief source of companionship for his mother, a role his father had abdicated.

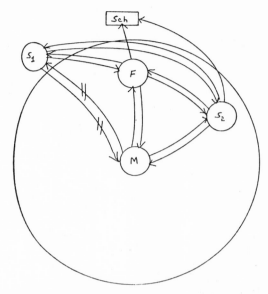

Guide to the Symbolic Drawing

F ...father
M ...mother
S₁ ...son, age 17
S₂ ...son, age 14, identified patient

Fig. 26-3. Oldest son's drawing of the Simpson family
– Session 6

perceived Bob to hold in the family. Mrs. Simpson, in her subsequent individual drawing (the reader is reminded that in the particular model of therapy used with this family, both individual and family group sessions were employed) indicated the incongruence between her perception of Bob's position and his, by placing him well within the nuclear family boundary (see Fig. 26-4).

Visual discrepancies in the depiction of the quality of communication between family members, i.e., communication incongruence, provide family members with new insight regarding their relationships.

The Parker family is a white, lower middle-class suburban family, referred by the school psychologist because of the school phobia of 8-year-old Patty. Mr. Parker, who had two jobs, was physically and mentally removed from the family, while Mrs. Parker centered her entire life around her children.

In this drawing of the Parker family, the communication indicated by the family members is blantantly incongruent with that of the mother

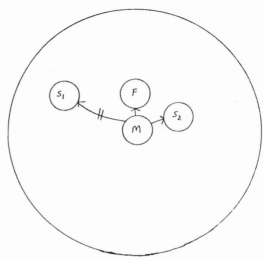

Guide to the Symbolic Drawing

F ...father
M ...mother
S₁ ...son, age 17
S₂ ...son, age 14, identified patient

Fig. 26-4. Mother's drawing of the Simpson family
Session 6

(see Fig. 26-5). All family members indicated good communication with her, while she indicated "so-so" communication with everyone except her youngest son. The mother's unhappiness became increasingly apparent to her husband and four children as they watched her draw symbolic lines of communication that *conflicted* with their own indications of "good" communication.

CHANGE OF FAMILIAL STRUCTURE

The Symbolic Drawing of the Family Life Space, in offering this "bird's-eye view" of familial structure and the degree of spatial and communicative congruence, serves simultaneously as a useful device to measure movement in the family. For example, if one compares the drawing of the first Key family session (see. Fig. 26-1) with the drawing of the sixth and last Key family session (see Fig. 26-6), change in familial structure is apparent. A more clearly differentiated generational boundary has been formed as the paternal grandparents have been cast out into the Environment, no longer occupying the center of a multigenerational

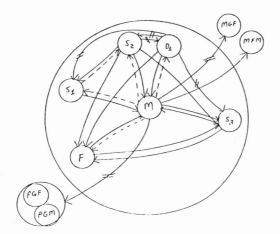

Guide to the Symbolic Drawing

F ......father

S$_1$......son, age 12

S$_3$......son, age 7

MGF ...maternal grandfather as perceived by mother

PGF ...paternal grandfather as perceived by mother

M ......mother

S$_2$......son, age 11

D$_1$ .....daughter, age 8, identified patient

MFM ..maternal foster mother as perceived by mother

PGM ...paternal grandmother as perceived by mother

Fig. 26-5. The Parker Family – Session 1

enmeshed family; the mother has moved closer to the center of her family, symbolically assuming her parental responsibility; and the mother's adulterous relationship with Sam, her boyfriend, which was revealed in the third session, is openly noted.

CONCLUSION

Several innovative task-centered and expressive techniques employed by family therapists have been reviewed. Generally, all of these various techniques are intended to facilitate meaningful communication and interaction among family members while providing a wealth of information for the therapist in a more or less nonthreatening manner.

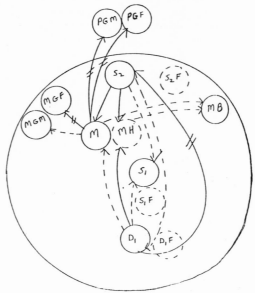

Guide to the Symbolic Drawing

M ......mother
MH ....mother's perception of husband
S_1 ......son, age 10, identified patient
S_2 ......son, age 8
D_1 ......daughter, age 7
PGM ...paternal grandmother as perceived by mother
PGF ....paternal grandfather as perceived by mother
MGM ...maternal grandmother as perceived by mother
MGF ...maternal grandfather as perceived by mother
S_1F ....son's perception of father
S_2F ....son's perception of father
D_1F ....daughter's perception of father
MB ....mother's boyfriend as perceived by mother

Fig. 26-6. The Key family — Session 6

A new technique, developed by Dr. Danuta Mostwin, the Symbolic Drawing of the Family Life Space, has been described and illustrated with case examples.

The authors have observed that this simple technique is an effective device for lowering anxiety and reducing blocks to communication, especially in the complex, initial diagnostic encounter. The task is interesting enough to grasp everyone's attention and reach the subconscious yet does not require family members to perform or expose themselves prematurely. Its simplicity is one of its greatest asssets, as children of five or six years of age have little difficulty in comprehending the directions. By giving the family an achievable and unthreatening task, use of the Symbolic Drawing of the Family Life Space engages the family in therapy before they even realize it.

Use of this technique in a variety of settings is recommended, e.g., inpatient mental health facilities, outpatient mental health clinics, family agencies, and perhaps even the office of the school guidance counselor. The authors have successfully employed this technique with clients diagnosed as having psychotic, neurotic, character, and borderline disorders. However, it has been found that many brain-damaged individuals are unable to engage themselves in this task or at least find it to be very difficult or frustrating. Since use of this technique requires no special training, it is a valuable tool to any mental health practitioner.

REFERENCES

1. Allman, M. and Madigan, M., "The Effectiveness of Short-term Multi-dimensional Family Intervention as a Model of Treatment for Families Presenting an Adolescent as the Identified Patient," Masters Group Research Project, National Catholic School of Social Service, 1974.
2. Bing, E., "The Conjoint Family Drawing," *Family Process*, 9: 173-194, 1970.
3. Boszormenyi-Nagy, I. and Spark, G.M., *Invisible Loyalties* Hagerstown, Md., Harper & Row, 1973.
4. Irwin, E. and Malloy, E., "Family Puppet Interview," *Fam. Proc.* 14: 179-191, 1975.
5. Ives, P., Schwall, R., Henderson, M., "The Effectiveness of Short Term Multidimensional Family Intervention in Working with Families with Adolescent Problems," Masters Group Research Project, National Catholic School of Social Service, 1975.
6. Kramer, E., *Art Therapy in a Children's Community* Springfield, Ill., Charles C Thomas, 1958.
7. Kwiatkowska, H., "Family Art Therapy," *Fam. Proc.* 6: 37-55, 1967.
8. Levy, J. and Epstein, N., "An Application of the Rorschach Test in Family Investigation," *Fam. Proc.* 3:344-376, 1964.
9. Lidz, T., Cornelison, A., Fleck, S., and Terry, D., "Marital Schism and Skew," *Am. J. Psychiat.* 114: 241-248, 1959.
10. Loveland, N., Wynne, L., and Singer, M., "The Family Rorschach: A Method for Studying Family Interaction," *Fam. Proc.* 2: 187-215, 1963.
11. Minuchin, S., Montalvo, B., Guerney, B., Rosman, B., and Schumer, F., *Families of the Slums* New York, Basic Books, 1967.
12. Mostwin, D., "Involving the Family in the Treatment of School Phobia: A Team Approach to Family Casework," Unpublished paper, 1972.

13. Mostwin, D., "Multidimensional Model of Working with the Family," *Soc. Casewk.* 55: 209-215, 1974.
14. Mostwin, D., "Social Work Intervention with Families in Crises of Change," *Soc. Thought* (a publication of the National Conference of Catholic Charities and the National Catholic School of Social Service), 2: 81-99, 1976.
15. Naumburg, M. *Schizophrenic Art: Its Meaning in Psychotherapy* New York, Grune and Stratton, 1953.
16. *Our Family,* National Catholic School of Social Service Seminar on Social Casework in the Field of Family Treatment, The Catholic University of America, 1974.
17. Papp, P., Silverstein, D., and Carter, E., "Family Sculpting in Preventive Work with Well Families," *Fam. Proc.* 12: 197-212, 1973.
18. Rubin, J. and Magnussen, M., "A Family Art Evaluation," *Fam. Proc.* 13: 185-200, 1974.
19. Simon, R., "Sculpting the Family," *Fam. Proc.* 11: 49-57, 1972.
20. Stern, M., "Free Painting as an Auxiliary Technique in Psychoanalysis," in J. Despert and G. Bychowski (Eds.), *Specialized Techniques in Psychotherapy* New York, Basic Books, 1953.
21. Watzlawick, P., "A Structural Family Interview," *Fam. Proc.* 5: 256-271, 1966.

THE CHILD'S PARTICIPATION
IN CONJOINT FAMILY THERAPY

Herta A. Guttmann

Conjoint family therapy developed out of the realization that individual treatment of the preadolescent child can founder when the child is really a presenting symptom, either of a particular parent's malaise or of a family problem. Ultimately, this insight led to focusing on the entire family as a unit, the disturbed child being considered simply as one part of a system in which people reciprocally affect and are affected by one another (Stachowiak, 1968).

Within such a conceptual framework, the child should be considered a significant and integral member of the family, whether or not he is the presenting problem (Augenbraun and Tasem, 1966; Tasem et al., 1965). However, it has been my own and other's experience that family therapists—particularly those who have little or no training in child therapy—do not pay as much attention to the child in actual practice as they do in theory, especially when the child is not the identified patient (Zilbach et al., 1972). His participation is often on a nonverbal level, and he does not usually respond to direct questions which focus on the "family problem." He seems to sit quietly aloof, or alternatively to squirm, wriggle, ask for drinks of water, or ask irrelevant questions. Sometimes such children become wildly uncontrollable, thereby increasing the parents' and the therapist's anxiety and frustration. In such cases, the therapist may muster enough interest to exhort the parents to control the child. As often as not, he concludes that this child's presence is not really serving a useful purpose and asks that he be left at home next time. From then on, the therapist concentrates on the older family members.

The technique of involving the younger child in conjoint family situations is an important but neglected aspect of the teaching of family therapy. It is generally agreed that the ideal way of including him or

From H. Guttmann, The Child's Participation in Conjoint Family Therapy, *Journal of the American Academy of Child Psychiatry, 14:*490-99, 1975. Courtesy of *Journal of American Academy of Child Psychiatry.*

her would involve having play materials at hand, since drawing and other forms of play—as well as movement and vocalization—are his favored mode of communication. However, children's play within the usual office setting is often considered to be disruptive, distracting, and messy. Supervisors of family therapy often communicate to their students that it is best to ignore or eliminate younger children from the therapy situation because it requires inordinate insight, an ultra-large playroom, and lots of equipment to do justice to the child's potential activities. Even those authors who have used art therapy to facilitate and clarify family interaction seem to view this as a group project, rather than as a means of integrating the child's experiences and feelings into the treatment of the family (Kwiatkowska, 1967).

I would like to examine the possibility that a child can help the therapist understand the whole family system as much as, and sometimes more than, other family members. Moreover, the therapist can play an educative role for adult family members by showing them how one may understand and respond to the child's communications as legitimate comments on his satisfactions or dissatisfactions with family functioning. In my opinion, this can be done by any therapist who has a conventional understanding of the possible symbolic significance of children's verbal and nonverbal activity. It does not require a great deal of equipment, and honors in the observance rather than in the breach a commitment to treating the family as a whole.

The following examples illustrate some ways in which the child, in his behavior and play, "acts out" certain family feelings and problems, and some ways in which these communications can be fully integrated into the therapeutic process.

CASE EXAMPLES

Communicating a Family Problem by Changing or Preserving the Seating Arrangement

1. A middle-class family consisting of the parents, the identified patient—a boy of 15—and an 11-year-old daughter, had been in treatment for four months. They had been referred for therapy by the juvenile court because the son had systematically stolen electronic equipment from various houses in his neighborhood over a period of a year. During the first months, the seating arrangement was such that the parents sat on either side of the therapist, with the children between them, the girl nearer the mother and the boy nearer the father. The boy was consistently attacked by the mother, and alternately attacked and protected by his rather pompous father. The parents did not argue directly. The 11-year-old girl was usually silent, but she would become sad and protective toward her mother whenever the latter cried.

As therapy progressed, it became clear that the father would have to confront his wife in order to stop her persistent attacks on the son. This became dramatically obvious on the day that the daughter marched into the office and took her father's chair, thereby forcing him to sit between her brother and mother and really make a choice. The therapist interpreted her behavior accordingly. This enabled the mother to realize that she had an unrealistic fear of losing her husband's affection if he loved his son as well as her. This was probably derived from her early experience with her parents, who doted on her younger brother and excluded her. The father had been afraid of hurting his wife's feelings by coming to the son's rescue. As he better understood the basis of her reaction, he became more courageous about intervening in the mother-son deadlock.

2. In a family consisting of the parents and four children, a dominant theme concerned the mother's closeness to and control over the children, whereas the father was relatively distant and isolated. Usually, the parents sat at either end of a row, with the children between them. It soon became apparent that the state of family affairs could be most accurately gauged by changes in the members' positions. When the father became less isolated in the family, the youngest child, a 4-year old who always sat next to his mother, began sitting next to him.

3. A 14-year-old boy, who had always been the parents' scapegoat, was sitting between them, while his 5-year-old brother played with blocks on the floor. With the therapist's help, the parents began confronting one another about their mutual disappointment. The older boy became restless and anxious, and finally moved to a more peripheral chair, again with the therapist's encouragement. A few minutes later, the younger child left his toys and came to sit in the empty chair, as if he wished to take his brother's vacated position, thereby restoring a safe distance between their warring parents.

Communicating a Family Problem Through Aggressive Play

1. In a family in which a stepfather had recently died, the 10-year-old son was reported to be very aggressive toward other children at school. Mother, son, and 6-year-old daughter came for therapy. During several sessions, the boy repeatedly punched a toy elephant while the therapist and the mother were discussing the family's reaction to their recent bereavement. His behavior became even more aggressive when they discussed the mother's apathy and indifference toward the children since her husband's death. When it was pointed out that the son was punching his elephant as if he was angry with his stepfather for dying, and with his mother for her indifference, his aggressive behavior within and outside therapy sessions decreased markedly.

2. A woman who suffered from a peptic ulcer was referred by a gastroenterologist for a psychiatric opinion on the advisability of performing a gastrectomy. She said that she considered her main

problem to be her 5-year-old son, whom she described as being
"uncontrollable." She had no difficulties with her two older daughters.
It was suggested that she and her husband come with the son for a
conjoint interview.

The boy was mischievous, disobedient, and restless. He so single-
mindedly wished to leave the room that his mother finally had to sit in
front of the office door to prevent him from leaving. Meanwhile, the
father sat rigidly in his chair, physically rejected all the boy's attempts to
play with him, and did nothing to assist the mother in controlling the
child as he became more and more destructive with the office furniture
and furnishings.

The therapist interpreted the child's behavior and the wife's ulcer as
being responses to the father's withdrawal and lack of support,
empathy, or playful involvement with his son or with his wife. At this
interpretation, the wife began to cry and the child quietened. The
husband first denied that his wife was crying at all, then became
increasingly defensive as his behavior was connected with his own
experiences with his distant father. This family subsequently refused
further treatment, and the mother had a gastrectomy.

Clearly, this family's relationships were so maladaptive that it was
difficult to select an intervention which might alter their rigid defenses.
In retrospect, the therapist might have been more effective had she
limited her interpretation to each parent's interaction with the child,
and ignored the parental relationship for the moment. This might have
permitted the mother greater freedom to express her anger and
frustration and to move out of her sacrificial role.

Deflecting Attention Through Provocative Behavior

1. During individual therapy, a young woman constantly complained that her husband would passively withdraw into silence
whenever she became annoyed with him. The therapist asked to see her
together with her husband and 4-year-old daughter. As the therapist
tried to get the parents to discuss their problem, the little girl became
increasingly provocative. She insisted on sitting between her parents, on
her father's chair, and kept pushing her father off his chair so that
interaction between the parents became impossible. The therapist
intervened and pointed out that the child was behaving toward her
father much as her mother did, and that he responded to them both by
withdrawing and thereby increasing their anger and anxiety, rather
than reassuring them by taking a firm stand. When the father became
more forceful and made the child go back to her own chair, she sat
quietly while the parents proceeded to speak to each other.

2. A family with three children was so seated that the 6-year-old
daughter was sitting between her parents. As the mother began to
complain of her husband's dependency, the child repeatedly interposed

herself physically so that the mother's attention was deflected to her and she began scolding her instead of the father. It emerged that this behavior reflected the little girl's fear that she would lose a second father, since her mother and natural father had been divorced a number of years previously.

3. An 8-year-old boy who had made several suicidal gestures by taking aspirin had been treated individually while his parents were concurrently receiving conjoint marital therapy. When the whole family was seen together, the parents began discussing their mutual sadness and disappointment. The identified patient began distracting their and the therapist's attention by grimacing and laughing with his younger sister, much as he had distracted them at home by his suicidal gestures. When this was pointed out, the son was able to tell them how angry and frightened he became when they quarreled, and how he wished to "get away" from having to act as a judge between them.

4. In a family which asked for consultation because of the delinquent behavior of a 15-year-old daughter, her 11-year-old brother kept whispering and diverting his sister's attention by making her laugh. This happened whenever the therapist touched on her wish to be valued by her demanding and perfectionist father, her sadness at being left to fend for herself, and her defense of being "tough." The boy's joking seemed to help his sister sustain this defensiveness, and probably helped him keep his favored position in the family as well.

Communicating Empathy with and Feelings about a Depressed, Preoccupied Parent

1. A family consisting of two parents and three young children had undergone a series of major life crises: the father's father and the mother's two parents had been seriously ill within the last year; the father's brother had died of severe asthma, and the mother's brother had died by apparently accidental drowning; the youngest child, a boy of 8 months, was presently in the hospital with severe asthma. The mother, a constricted, dutiful person, denied that she was still preoccupied with her younger brother's death; yet, as the session progressed and she became more comfortable talking about her feelings, she became obviously depressed and began to weep. At that point, the small 3-year-old boy began to call attention to his shoelaces with a piercing cry ("Mummy, Mummy"), as if to save his mother from her feelings by diverting her attention to himself.

2. An immigrant mother, whose 7-year-old son had a learning problem, blamed herself for not paying sufficient attention to him at the time of immigration when she was very homesick and when there was also a new baby to care for. As she described this, the boy began sucking his thumb while his smaller sister rummaged in the mother's handbag for cookies. Both children seemed to be expressing empathy for the

mother and anxiety about losing her attention (cookies.)

Communicating Feelings of Helplessness and Compensatory Protectiveness

1. A couple, in marital therapy for six months, were both rather immature people, and so egocentrically preoccupied that they had enormous difficulty in developing any mutuality in their relationship, even in helping each other with the practical tasks of everyday life. These problems had become vividly apparent during marital therapy, and the therapist had repeatedly pointed out that they were content with each other only when playing together as children, and never when having to behave as responsible adults.

During the seventh month of therapy, they reported that their 7-year-old daughter had suddenly become afraid to leave the house to go out to play with her friends. A family session was held, during which time the child drew a picture of a royal family. A large princess was sweeping the floor with a broom in the foreground, while her parents, the king and queen, who were much smaller people in the background, were not doing anything. She then added a fourth figure—intermediate size—whom she identified as a prince, the princess's little brother. The little girl agreed with the interpretation that she was afraid to leave the house to play because she felt she had to help her parents, and that she wished for a baby brother who could be her companion. The parents subsequently reported that their daughter had become more outgoing since the interview.

2. A 6-year-old girl repeatedly denied that her mother was sad, although the mother was crying about her frustrations, sadness, and helplessness at having to manage everything alone, without her husband's help. The child finally said, "I don't want Mommy to be sad, and she isn't!"

Communicating Feelings of Guilt

A 7-year-old boy began worrying about the videotape cameras and wondering whether people who knew the family were watching them on TV, when his mother started talking about feeling guilty that she had blamed him for being "bad' rather than sick, before she had realized that he was a hyperactive child and required medication.

Communicating the Identified Patient's Problem of Passive Dependence

1. A 6-year-old girl drew a picture of her 8-year-old brother as a female ballet dancer, dressed in pink, while her parents and the therapist were discussing her brother's babyish behavior and the ways in which the

mother fostered it. Although the mother energetically denied it, the drawing confirmed this more effectively than did anything said by her husband or by the therapist. The son, who had hitherto been plaintive and infantile during the therapy session, became quieter and behaved more appropriately for his age. Although the family refused conjoint therapy, the mother continued in individual treatment, and later reported that this observation had motivated her and her husband to make some changes in their handling of the child.

2. A 6-year-old girl drew a picture in which there was a tiny girl in the distance, whom she identified as her 12-year-old brother, and a larger person in the foreground, whom she identified as herself. This drawing reflected the parent's perception of her being much more independent and mature than her overprotected, whiny, diabetic brother. Later in treatment, this girl drew another picture of her brother as a large boy in the foreground. This reflected a substantial improvement in his independent and autonomous behavior.

Communicating Feelings about Successful Family Therapy

1. The 12-year-old diabetic boy mentioned above drew pictures of various objects in the office, as well as composite portraits of his parents and the therapist during the last family session. The family agreed that the drawing reflected the family's feeling of being in greater harmony, as well as their difficulty in leaving the therapist, whom they wished to incorporate into their family.

2. In the mourning family previously mentioned, both children painted many pictures in black. The boy painted warlike scenes of jet fighters or destroyers, fighting battles and going down in flames. These pictures communicated feelings of sadness mingled with anger at the departed stepfather, who, as it happened, was a black man. As treatment progressed, and the family dealt with their mourning, the paintings gradually became more colorful, and the planes and boats were sent on more peaceful missions.

DISCUSSION

These descriptions demonstrate some of the many ways in which children communicate their own feelings, and participate in defining their family's problems. In many instances, the child tries to preserve family homeostasis by the various behaviors which have been described. It is he who expresses the family's resistance to the therapist's attempts to stimulate confrontation and change. In other instances, the child acts as the primary agent of change within the family because his activity disrupts the family's previous equilibrium. By being constantly aware that the children, as well as adults, preserve or disrupt family homeostasis, the therapist can integrate the child into the treatment situation in a more meaningful way, and can begin exploring the family problem to which the child is drawing attention.

This is a far more empathic and effective method than to direct "Why?" and "How?" questions at a young child (e.g., "Why are you wriggling? How do you feel when mommy and daddy fight?"). Such questions usually increase the child's reluctance to communicate, because he himself often cannot readily use words to describe the "why" and "how" of his perceptions. His behavior, his play, and his art constitute the language through which he must and can be understood, both by the therapist and by the more adult members of the family. Moreover, the therapist can more tactfully convey many potentially painful observations to the parents in his seemingly innocuous and aimless verbal interaction with their children (Whitaker, 1967).

To do this effectively, the therapist must constantly monitor the children's reactions, even while listening to or talking with other family members. He may not immediately draw attention to this information, but he stores it for use at some appropriate moment. Sometimes the therapist's interventions merely integrate the child into the group as a perceptive, contributing family member. Sometimes, he may wish actually to interrupt whatever else is going on, to draw attention to something the child has said or done, and to connect it with the current theme within the interview situation. Often, the child's behavior forms the basis of an interpretation which draws attention to an interpersonal problem within the family.

Although the use of simple toys may facilitate a child's communication, an elaborate playroom setting is certainly not a prerequisite for the emergence of behavioral clues of the kind I have described. Many of the examples which have been cited in this paper were, in fact, observed in a highly unlikely environment: an amphitheater in which family interviews are conducted and videotaped in front of an audience of 80 to 100 people, without any play materials at hand whatever. Nevertheless, it is more desirable and relatively easy to provide paper, crayons, building blocks, and a few simple toys, even in the setting of a private office.

Aside from the more passive therapeutic stance of observing, drawing attention to, or interpreting the young child's behavior, the therapist can play a more active role. He can ask the child to draw a picture of the family, at work or at play. He can have the child take a turn in "sculpting" the family or at participating in a family game (Simon, 1972). Even then, as Ackerman (1970) has cautioned, one does well to keep one's distance at first: the child does not know the therapist and does not immediately accept a strange adult. Moreover, although active and directive methods have their place, the child's spontaneous activity is even more informative, especially at later stages in therapy when the family's relationship with the therapist is well established. It is my experience that children will rapidly become aware that their type of participation is valuable and valued by the therapist, and will quite naturally interject their comments, or will ask for appropriate play materials if they are missing at a particular session because they have learned to define themselves as very important members in the family.

The understanding garnered from the insights of play therapy can thus be profitably combined with family therapy which is more verbally or insight-oriented. Through this technique, the young child becomes an integral part of the situation and makes his own unique, important contribution. The family therapist becomes more meaningfully committed to conjoint family therapy as the treatment of a whole system, and is helpful to all family members in developing ways of understanding and solving their problems.

SUMMARY

Family therapy, to be true to its commitment to systems theory, should be as concerned with the younger child as with all other family members, whether he is the presenting problem or not. As a rule, family therapists do not pay enough attention to the child, because to involve him requires meaningfully integrating his communications into the family system. Since children communicate through play, movement, and seemingly irrelevant remarks, therapists must be taught to understand and use their contributions.

This paper illustrates some ways in which children's communications may be understood within a family context. Such understanding can help educate older family members regarding the children's needs and can be an important tool for meaningful therapeutic intervention in the family system.

REFERENCES

Ackerman, N.W. (1970), Child participation in family therapy. *Fam. Proc.*, 9: 403-410.

Augenbraun, B. & Tasem, M. (1966), Differential techniques in family interviewing with both parents and preschool child. *This Journal*, 5:721-730.

Kwiatkowska, H.Y. (1967), Family art therapy. *Fam. Proc.*, 6:37-55.

Simon, R.M. (1972), Sculpting the family. *Fam. Proc.*, 11:49-57.

Stachowiak, J.G. (1968), Psychological disturbances in children as related to disturbances in family interaction. *J. Marr. Fam.*, 30:123-127.

Tasem, M., Augenbraun, B., & Brown, S.L. (1965), Family group interviewing with the preschool child and both parents. *This Journal*, 4:330-340.

Whitaker, C.A. (1967), The growing edge (interview). In: *Techniques of Family Therapy*, ed. J. Haley & L. Hoffman. New York: Basic Books, pp. 265-360.

Zilbach, J.J., Bergel, E., & Gass, C. (1972), Role of the young child in family therapy. In: *Progress in Group and Family Therapy*, ed. C.J. Sager & H.S. Kaplan. New York: Brunner/Mazel, pp. 385-399.

Chapter 28

KINETIC PSYCHOTHERAPY IN THE TREATMENT OF FAMILIES

Robert S. Schachter

Kinetic Psychotherapy (KPT) was originally developed as a form of group therapy for children and adolescents who have difficulty verbalizing feelings. Recently, this author has been adapting this technique to family therapy. This paper will explore some of the exciting possibilities KPT offers as an approach to working with families, both as treatment and as a consultation tool.

The Field of Family Therapy

Since 1951, family therapy has gradually become a respected force in the field of psychotherapy. It is diverse and still young. The theoretical work and valuable research now being done will doubtless be followed by more detailed analyses of the nature of behavioral development and change in the family. Throughout the literature, several themes emerge regarding the style and focus of this type of therapy. The three most common are: (a) helping the family clarify and learn alternative patterns of communication (Satir, 1965; Jackson, 1967; Bell, 1961; Whitaker, 1967; Zuk, 1966, 1967, 1968); (b) assessing the family's system of functioning and helping to change it (Minuchin & Barcai, 1969; Minuchin, 1974; Tharp, 1963; MacGregor, Ritchie, Serrano, Shuster, McDonald, & Goolishan, 1964); and (c) understanding the individual psychodynamics in the light of the family dynamics (Bowen, 1961, 1965; Ackerman, 1958; Paul, 1965; Paul & Grosser, 1967; Framo, 1970). While these goals differ from each other, they share recognition of the need to assess the family's interaction as a unit rather than focusing merely on individual psychodynamics. Kinetic psychotherapy can serve as a useful determinant of the pattern of interaction in a family, as well as a useful tool for facilitating communication in addition to providing an

From R. Schachter, Kinetic Psychotherapy in the Treatment of Families, *The Family Coordinator*, July 1978, pp. 283-88. Copyrighted 1978 by the National Council on Family Relations. Reprinted by permission.

experiential way to try different patterns of interaction in a nonthreat-ening situation.

KINETIC PSYCHOTHERAPY

As described previously by this author (Schachter, 1974), kinetic psychotherapy utilizes, as its medium, a number of social interactive games. These games are modified to facilitate interaction and mobilize feeling while appearing to be nonthreatening diversions; they are, in reality, situations which stimulate emotional responses analogous to those aroused in threatening real-life situations, such as anger, fear, joy and sadness.

As a person participates in such an exercise, three stages are observed. First, the person begins to experience rising feelings and indicates these through verbal or nonverbal signs. Second, in response to the feeling and the situation, the person engages in his or her characteristic coping behavior such as withdrawal or aggressiveness depending on his usual style. Third, the person associates to other times he has felt a similar way.

Examples of some of the activities in KPT are "Bombardment" and "Freeze-tag". In Bombardment, two teams of two or three persons each stand on opposite sides of a room and throw soft plastic balls at each other. Once each member is hit three times, he is out of the game. Anger is a feeling often apparent in this activity. Joy and sharing are common themes in "freeze tag," a game in which an antagonist attempts to "freeze" the participants by touching them with a soft plastic ball. The "frozen" person can only be freed when another team member tags him. This game places a person in a situation where he or she can ask for and give help. Other games echo feelings of frustration, isolation, fear, anxieties, shared responsibilities, competition and excitement. The games and activities used in KPT are not geared to elicit emotions in the manner of encounter group exercises, but instead serve to catalyze existing feelings at that time which need to be expressed.

Kinetic Psychotherapy and Patterns of Communication

The process of kinetic psychotherapy involves placing participants in a number of the situations described above. As feelings become evident through verbal and nonverbal cues, the therapist *stops the action* and facilitates verbalization. A person is taught the skills to communicate an emotion at the instant it occurs. The individual can also safely experience and practice communication skills.

By this process, family members learn to identify and verbalize feelings together, in a manner conducive to more efficient family interaction. Throughout this situation, the participant is never pres-sured to express emotions and does so at his own pace. A discussion period follows a twenty-minute activity period. In such a session, members can talk about ·feelings in ways probably new to them, allowing patterns of communication previously frozen or immobile to be gradually opened. As participants begin to verbalize emotions, the therapist suggests that they express these directly to the person or persons at whom they most want to direct them. Thus, for example, if a sibling gets angry at another sibling in a "Bombardment" game, he is encouraged to tell the other about it rather than act out his anger. The same procedure is applied to parent-parent or parent-child communication. The participant here has the opportunity to experience an alternative mode of dealing with an affective experience.

Kinetic Psychotherapy and Patterns of Interaction

A second aspect of KPT particularly suited to family therapy is the opportunity to observe, first hand, the characteristic coping patterns of all family members. Patterns of interaction become evident through the game in an undeniable way and, therefore, provide the therapist with an opportunity to stop the game and reflect upon the *observed* behavior. There is no need for interpretation since the experiential awareness gained by the participants as they increasingly gain insight into their behavior, is more powerful, and less defensible than an interpretation. During the activity period, members can also observe behavior of others and provide feedback. As mentioned previously, most behavioral responses in the game are characteristic examples of everyday life. Therefore, the father who avoids positive contact with the identified patient may ignore him in a game until the child provokes an interaction. In the discussion after the activity this pattern can be explored as it exists in real-life situations. Other issues discussed are other interactions observed by participants, their feelings, their responses to these feelings, and their actions. People who take part in these sessions report a high correlation between behavior in the game and behavior at home. This contrasts with behavior in the therapist's office, which is at times disguised and fails to reflect true behavior at home. Furthermore, in a KPT game one can look at one's behavior with less anxiety than in a strictly verbal session. The nonthreatening nature of the activity appears to contribute to both a lower anxiety level and a less defensive posture. Behavior patterns observed in the game, therefore, provide reliable data about the patterns of interaction, alliances and exclusions which exist in a family. In addition, KPT provides an atmosphere promoting open discussion of these currents.

Kinetic Psychotherapy and Experiencing Change

A third aspect of KPT provides a safe arena for experimenting with and experiencing alternative patterns of interaction once awareness of present patterns is gained. The usefulness of structural assessment and realignment has been demonstrated by a number of clinicians and researchers (Minuchin & Barcai, 1969; Minuchin, 1974; Kantor & Lehr, 1975). By helping the family experience alternative coping patterns within the game situation, the therapist can provide a half-way step for family members to experience alternative behavior in nonthreatening situations. Such participation seems to facilitate role changes outside the therapy session.

Additional Advantages of Inclusion of Children

In some settings, the family sessions may take place in a playroom where children can interact with each other and play out unconscious themes and conflicts. In a case described by Ferber and Ranz (1972), the children were invited to bring in toys to use during the session. Zilbach, Bergel and Gass (1972) also see advantages in including children in family sessions.

Since most children have difficulty talking while sitting in chairs, an atmosphere in which they can relate in their own medium appears both merciful and productive. In such a situation the therapist might engage the parents in observing the playing activity, comment on its signifi-cance and then verbally involve the child regarding the playing. While this technique helps bring useful information to the session, it provides little room for direct interaction between parents and children, particu-larly with latency aged children for whom doll play is no longer appropriate. In KPT the child or children and adults directly participate in a game. Thus, the adult is participating in the child's milieu which, in turn, produces a meaningful verbal interchange, with the children fully attentive to the verbal material and participating less defensively in the conversation.

CASE STUDIES

The usefulness of kinetic psychotherapy is implicit in the following three case examples.

Case 1: The "E" Family

Joey, the ten year old identified patient, was referred by a guidance counselor at school because of behavioral difficulties. He would disrupt his class by starting fights with other children and by talking back to teachers. Because of a short attention span and apparent difficulty sitting still Joey had been seen by a prominent neurologist who reported unremarkable neurological findings. After an evaluation consisting of a standard psychiatric history and interview, weekly, family therapy was suggested because of poor communication patterns in the family and the conclusion that Joey's behavior was in response to cues he received at home. The family consists of Mrs. E., a chronically depressed woman who was racked by guilt over an unspoken anger at her failure to rear a youngster who could function adequately in school and in the neighborhood, and Mr. E., an engineer who is also a victim of much unexpressed anger. Locked out by his wife because of her depression, he resents Joey and continually puts the child into a bind by not following through with some punishments and giving the message that his acting out is not bad while reprimanding the boy for his actions. In part, this behavior represents his acting out his angry feelings towards his wife.

The two children in the family are adopted. Joey plays the role of the scapegoat and Mary, who is nine years old, is regarded as the family angel.

The family was seen weekly by the author using a communication-based model of family therapy similar to that described by Satir (1965). After 6 sessions, the family had discussed issues of limit setting and more direct communication. However, this process appeared to be stagnating. The family refused to listen to one another. In one instance, Joey would frequently point out that his sister instigated many situations by teasing him. His parents refused to acknowledge that this was possible and would reprimand Joey for not listening to them.

At this point the therapist felt that he was making little headway in helping the parents to listen to Joey or each other. He suggested a kinetic psychotherapy session to see if this approach would be more helpful. This session was held in a large office 15' x 25' with no furniture in the room. It began with the entire family playing a game euphemistically called "frustration." One participant is in the middle trying to catch the ball. The others stand in a circle and try to keep the ball away from the person in the middle. The one who touches the ball last before it is caught takes the next turn in the middle.

The therapist decided to participate and began in the middle; the game continued until all had had a turn in the center. During the game several behavior patterns became clear to the therapist and the family members. The most apparent was that while Joey was in the center, Mary, who had the ball, began literally to tease him. She approached him with the ball several times and then took it away from him, leaving him angry and frustrated. At this point the therapist stopped the game and asked the family members what they had observed. The father said that Mary was teasing Joey. He admitted his past unawareness of this tendency on her part, her behavior was undeniable and she had to take responsibility for it. Meanwhile, Joey was visibly angry. He was asked if he wanted to express what he felt. (It is extremely important here to point out again that in KPT a person's rights and defenses are respected above all else and he is free to refuse discussion of his feelings.) Joey chose to say he was angry—he verbalized this directly to

Mary. Communication was thereby opened between them. He could express his feeling the moment it occurred and thereby eliminated the need for aggressive behavior to express it. All sat down at this point and began a verbal session around the issues that became evident in the game. Essentially, this was the first time that both parents agreed that Mary could be part of the problem in the home and that Joey could shed his role as scapegoat even if for a brief time. It was also the first time that Joey verbalized his feelings directly to his sister which set a precedent for future verbal transactions between them.

This situation illustrates the process involved in kinetic psycho-therapy:

(a) a behavior pattern can be acknowledged by the participants and
(b) direct communication can be established.

Case 2: The "G" Family

This family consists of the mother, father, 9-year-old sister and 11-year-old brother. The 11-year-old was referred as the identified problem, showing poor attention at school and defiant behavior at home. Additionally, his parents, particularly the father feared that he might be effeminate. On evaluation, the therapist became aware of two issues; (a) there was little communication in the family apart from shouting to which no one listened and (b) the boy and the girl both appeared to bear the brunt of the parents' unhappy living conditions. Since their marriage, 15 years ago, they have lived on the top floor of the maternal grandmother's house. This situation caused much conflict not dealt with by either parents; instead both act out onto the children with unduly harsh criticism of them.

In a game of freeze-tag, the therapist was able to observe a pattern which was verified in later meetings. This game consists of an antagonist, in this case the therapist, who attempts to tag various members with a soft plastic ball. When tagged by the ball, the person must "freeze," until released by someone else on the team (anyone else in the family). The feelings and theme of this game deal with helping—giving help, getting help. As the game began, the father immediately went to save the girl and the boy; he would do this although his wife also was frozen. The boy would go to save his mother. Mother saved no one and the little girl saved both mother and father. As these patterns and alliances were pointed out and discussed, the mother spoke of feeling isolated in the family. At home the father often ignored his wife and stays with the children as they watch television. She resented her husband going off to be with "the kids." When he had free time, he avoided his wife, instead of working out issues about which he was angry. The issue of the difficulties in their relationship was brought to light and discussed during several verbal sessions afterward.

Case 3: The "H" Family

Chris, the 14-year-old identified patient, was referred after seeing two different well-known therapists, who had seen him and his parents separately for several years. Throughout this time his defiant behavior had increased, particularly towards his father. Chris was the second oldest in a family of four children; the others were a boy, age 17, a sister, age 13, and a brother, age 8. He had learned quite early that if he took the role of the "bad child" his parents would be so busy "being concerned" that peace would exist in the family. For this reason family therapy appeared to be an appropriate modality. In a game of "freeze tag," the therapist noticed that several times the boy would save both his mother and father while both of them, particularly the father, would save only the three other siblings. The game was stopped and each was asked how they reacted to the family's behavior. The father had not been aware of this total neglect of Chris and spontaneously began to help him more when the game resumed. The boy complained in the discussion that followed, that he missed having interactions with his father. The following week both father and son reported having gone fishing together, somthing they had not done in years.

DISCUSSION

In the cases mentioned, one can see three possible benefits of KPT. In the last described case, the emerging patterns showed that Chris was neglected by his father. In fact his father's exclusion of him was a primary force in his acting-out behavior. As they both became more aware of this pattern, they moved to change it and investigated its ramifications—why these patterns existed and what could be done to change them. Of course, not all situations are as clear-cut or as easy to improve as this one; however, the general process is illustrated by this example.

In the first case, that of Joey, a pattern denied by the parents, the sister's role in the family problem, was faced and responded to. Joey also had an opportunity to express his feelings directly to his sister, opening communication in the family.

Finally, in the G family, (case 2), the pattern of alliances became clear as well as emerging as a major issue in the family; it brought to focus a disharmonious marital relationship which the mother was willing to speak about openly to the benefit of the therapy and the couple.

Each of the patterns would have taken longer to become visible and possibly to change if the family had not been involved.

SUMMARY

While not a therapeutic panacea, kinetic psychotherapy offers exciting prospects both as a treatment modality and as a tool for consultation, diagnosis, and treatment in family therapy. Originally developed as a form of group therapy for children and adolescents, this process, when applied to work with the family, can help the therapist and family group gain insight into the functional mechanism of the family. By observing the behavior of the members while they participate in a series of games designed to facilitate interaction and mobilize feelings, the therapist can observe these and help the family become aware of their alliances, defense mechanisms, and other patterns of interaction. Another function of KPT is to help the family learn alternative patterns of communication experientially. A third function is to provide a situation in which the family can experiment with different patterns of interaction. Additionally, KPT provides a setting in which children can relate with their parents on their own level.

REFERENCES

Ackerman, N. *The psychodynamics of everyday life.* New York: Basic, 1958.

Bell, J. Family group therapy. U.S. Public Health Service Publication No. 64. Washington, D.C.: U.S. Government Printing Office, 1961.

Bowen, M. Family Psychotherapy. *American Journal of Orthopsychiatry*, 1961, **31**, 40-60.

Bowen, M. Family psychotherapy with schizophrenia in the hospital and private practice. In I. Nagy & J. Framo (Eds.), *Intensive family therapy.* New York: Harper, 1965.

Ferber, A. & Ranz, J. How to succeed in family therapy: Set reachable goals— give workable tasks. In A. Ferber, M. Mendelsohn, & A. Napier (Eds.), *The book of family therapy.* New York: Science House, 1972.

Framo, J. Symptoms from a transactional viewpoint. In N. Ackerman (Ed.), *Family therapy in transition.* Boston: Little, Brown, 1970.

Jackson, D. (Ed.) *Communication, family, and marriage.* Palo Alto, Science and Behavior, 1967.

Kantor, D., & Lehr, W. *Inside the family.* San Francisco: Jossey Bass, 1975.

Macgregor, R., Ritchie, A., Serrano, A., Shuster, F., McDonald, E., & Goolishan, H. *Multiple impact therapy with families.* New York: McGraw Hill, 1964.

Minuchin, S., & Barcai, A. Therapeutically induced family crisis. In C. Sager & H.S. Kaplan (Eds.), *Progress in group and family therapy.* New York: Brunner/Mazel, 1972.

Minuchin, S. *Families and family therapy.* Cambridge: Harvard, 1974.

Paul, N., & Grosser, G. Operational mourning and its role in conjoint family therapy. *Community Mental Health Journal*, 1965, 1, 339-345.

Paul, N. The use of empathy in the resolution of grief. *Perspectives in Biology and Medicine*, 1967, 11, 153-169.

Satir, V. *Conjoint family therapy.* Palo Alto: Science and Behavior, 1965.

Schachter, R.S. Kinetic psychotherapy in the treatment of children. *American Journal of Psychotherapy*, 1974, **28**, 430-437.

Tharp, R. Diversions of marriage roles. *Marriage and Family Living,* 1963, **25,** 389-404.

Whitaker, C. The growing edge. In J. Haley & L. Hoffman (Eds.), *Techniques of family therapy.* New York: Basic, 1967.

Zilbach, J., Bergel, E., & Gass, C. The role of the young child in family therapy. In C. Sager & H.S. Kaplan (Eds.), *Progress in group and family therapy.* New York: Brunner/Mazel, 1972.

Zuk, G. The go-between process. *Family Process,* 1966, **5,** 162-178.

Zuk, G. The victim and his silencers: Some pathogenic strategies against being silenced. In G. Zuk & I. Nagy (Eds.), *Family therapy and disturbed families.* Palo Alto: Science and Behavior, 1967.

Zuk, G. The side-taking function in family therapy. *American Journal of Orthopsychiatry,* 1968, **38,** 553-559.

PARADOXICAL INTERVENTIONS

The use of paradoxical tasks in family therapy has become increasingly popular. These methods cut across theoretical orientations. In fact many therapists have used the concept intuitively in their interactions with clients. However, paradoxical intervention has become prominent as an intentional technique to lead to behavior change.

The technique is called paradoxical because the therapist instructs the family to do the very problem behavior that they want to change. The therapist schedules the occurrence of the symptoms so they are exhibited by the family under systematic and specific conditions. The technique involves the therapist expressing agreement with the family members' inappropriate feelings, attitude, and behavior and then encouraging them to exaggerate it.

People may not recognize their inappropriateness, but when it is mirrored back to them they often respond to it as inappropriate. By agreeing with exaggerating the inappropriateness, the therapist incites the family members to take a stand against the intentionality of the therapist's ideas and thus their own position.

The article by Soper and L'Abate reviews the types of paradoxical interventions that may be used in family therapy. They describe prescribing the symptom and reframing, assigning tasks, using written instructions, giving positive interpretations, using paradoxical intention and hypnosis. Hare-Mustin states that using absurd or confounding tasks breaks up the family's usual pattern of behaving and perceiving each other and permits them to achieve some detachment from the disturbing behavior. Several short cases are used to illustrate paradoxical tasks. The Milan group of Mara Selvini Palazzoli and her colleagues reports on the treatment of small children through therapy with their parents. They believe that a family coming to therapy is in crisis and if told to change they would try to ward off the therapy. The technique involves approving the family's behavior, thus being accepted by the family and gaining influence to change the system.

PARADOXICAL TASKS IN FAMILY THERAPY: WHO CAN RESIST?

RACHEL T. HARE-MUSTIN

A paradox is any seemingly self-contradictory or absurd event which in reality expresses a possible truth. Paradoxical tasks are those which appear absurd because they exhibit an apparently contradictory nature, such as requiring clients to do what in fact they have been doing, rather than requiring that they change, which is what everyone else has been demanding.

The systems approach to family treatment based on cybernetics provides a model for understanding the basic problem of change: The more an individual tries to change the system, the more the individual is activating the processes which maintain the system unchanged (Watzlawick, Weakland, & Fisch, 1974). The family members respond in error-activated ways when an individual exceeds a certain limit. As Haley (1963) has pointed out, each member functions as a governor of the others in maintaining the system. The introduction of the therapist into the system does not alter this mechanism, but mobilizes the family to induct the therapist into their ways of interacting and communicating, thus frequently rendering the therapist ineffective in producing change (Umbarger & Hare, 1973).

Paradoxical tasks encourage the individual to carry out and even exaggerate usual behavior. As a consequence, any resistance to the task through the client's exertion of will against the therapist produces change in the desired direction (Erickson, 1973). Of course, having the usual behavior occur under the therapist's guidance makes it a different behavior, and because of the confusion about how to resist, the usual patterns are altered, new perceptions occur, and change results. As Frankl (1960) has pointed out in paradoxical intention, the purpose of replacing the usual restrictions on undesired behavior with intentional

_____

From R. Hare-Mustin, Paradoxical Tasks in Family Therapy: Who Can Resist? *Psychotherapy: Theory, Research and Practice, 13:*128-30, 1976. Courtesy of *Psychotherapy: Theory, Research and Practice.*

and even exaggerated effort is to enable clients to develop detachment and gain distance by laughing at their own behavior.

Greenberg (1973) utilizes exaggeration in an "anti-expectation" technique with resistant clients which involves the therapist joining or echoing and amplifying the client's negative self-comments. Erickson (1958) also uses the unexpected in initially adapting to the client. The use of negative practice by behavior therapists like Wolpe and Lazarus (1966) in treating undesirable habits, or Stampfl's implosive therapy (Stampfl & Levis, 1967) gives the clients a sense of control over their behavior, but does not depend on exaggeration, humor, and the unexpected to shift perceptions or on the use of the client's resistance to produce change.

Tasks in family therapy are particularly appropriate around the parents' complaints about a child. Focusing on and requiring the disturbing behavior rapidly reduces its occurrence and allows the family to be open to a redefinition of the problem in family terms that respond to treatment. When the first tasks assigned to the family are simple and assured of some success, they provide the basis for the family's acceptance of subsequent task assignments. Often it has been found desirable to specify what every family member is to do, even if some are not directly involved with the task, so no one feels left out or is free to sabotage the task.

A Bad Boy

Billy is an eight-year-old boy who was brought by the parents to treatment because he was so bad his mother could no longer deal with his disobedience. The first two family sessions started with a tearful and distraught mother describing her rage and despair at Billy's not minding, and her fear that in losing her temper, she would injure him physically. After attempting to find out any good things Billy did, without success, the therapist assigned a task for the family for the next week. For a specified day, which Billy and his parents agreed to before leaving the session, Billy was to be bad all day. If he tried to be good in any way, his parents were to remind him to be bad, and his brother and sister were not to interfere. The next week when questioned, the family reported that Billy had not been bad. When the therapist asked why the parents had not cooperated in the task, the mother could only say that she did remind him once not to hold the door for her and help her in with the groceries. When Billy was asked why he had not been bad, he responded, "There was nothing to be bad about." Billy's reply and the parents' realization that they could not make him bad for even an entire day when required to struck them as absurd. Their perspective shifted, they became doubtful about what was happening, and their willingness to work for a hopeful change in the family increased.

Do You Love Me?

Martin is a 10-year-old boy whose mother was very concerned about his sleep disturbances. She was recently separated from her husband and depended a great deal on Martin and his 16-year-old sister. She was very annoyed by Martin's asking her every morning in a repetitive way whether she loved him. The therapist pointed out that this was this family's pledge of allegiance to each other every morning before starting the day. They were to continue it without fail, but they were told it would be all right to do it only five days a week if they wished just as the pledge was done at school. The daughter was told to remain in bed during this morning ritual as was her custom. The family very soon reported that they had trouble remembering to do the ritual, and therapy was able to shift from Martin to the basic problem of the lack of appropriate generational distance between this mother and both her children.

Temper Tantrums

In the Browning family, Carl, aged four, and his seven-year-old sister were both very immature. A brother had died shortly before Carl's birth and the parents were overprotective and given to using a "reasoning" approach. They admitted they felt helpless and frantic over Carl's almost daily temper tantrums. The therapist pointed out that what was disturbing about tantrums was that they were not predictable, that they could occur anywhere. The first task was for Carl to have his tantrums, but only in a chosen tantrum place. The family and Carl together decided what should be the tantrum place at home. They were told that if Carl should start to tantrum at any other place, he was to go to, or be taken to, the tantrum place. If he were away from home, such as at the store, when he started to tantrum, he sould be told he would have to wait until he got home to go to the tantrum place. The next week, the task was for Carl to tantrum, but only at a certain time of day (and of course in the tantrum place.) The therapist suggested the family pick a two-hour period that was the most frequent time of occurrence. By the third week, Carl's tantrums had diminished so markedly that he was required to tantrum during the following week, but, as expected, the family failed in this task. Carl's control of his tantrums under the paradoxical task assignments enabled the parents to recognize that they could be more relaxed about giving their children responsibility for controlling their own behavior.

Cry A Little

A family with six children, a semi-invalid father, and a mother who worked part-time felt very beleagured in a decaying part of the city, so that the therapist and the family had come to characterize their home as Fortress O'Sullivan. During treatment, the parents expressed concern because their 14-year-old daughter, Sheila, cried so much. The therapist reassured the family by pointing out that adolescents cry, and further gave Sheila "permission" by assigning the task for her to "cry a little every day." By the next session Sheila's crying had diminished, and she had been able to talk with her mother about what was troubling her.

Trashing

A family with a 12-year-old schizoid son seemed immobilized by the mother's depression and the father's obsessive-compulsive nature in their desire to clean up their house. They all complained that the house was full of boxes, still lying about unpacked from their last move two years ago. When the father further complained that his wife brought in broken things from other people's trash that was waiting to be collected at the curb, the following task was assigned. The family were told that it was not clear whether they were disorderly or not, so when they got home from the session, they were to bring all the broken chairs in the house, basement, and attic to the dining room, and keep them there and consider them carefully for a full week. At the next session it was learned that the husband had rebelled after five days, and on trash collection day had put out all but one of his wife's nine broken chairs to be taken away. His action not only enhanced his self-respect, but also relieved both him and his wife of their indecision about keeping so much junk.

DISCUSSION

The use of paradoxical tasks is a powerful lever in producing change in the family by using the resistance in the family system. The selection of tasks of an absurd or confounding nature breaks up the family's usual ways of behaving and perceiving each other as it enables them to achieve some detachment from the disturbing behavior. In the case of "the bad boy," the paradox is clearly insolvable. If Billy is good when told to be bad, then he is disobeying and being bad. If he is bad as instructed, then he is being good because he is following instructions. Frequently, relabeling is part of the paradoxical task. In the case of Martin's ritualized, "Do you love me?" a bit of behavior was relabeled as a family pledge of allegiance. By making its form explicit, the therapist shifted the meaning of the interaction and it became unnecessary.

Paradoxical task assignments also serve to give permission for certain behaviors, such as Martin's questioning or Sheila's crying so they are no longer a source of anxiety or anger in the family. Such behaviors cease to be reinforced by special attention directed toward stopping them. Being required by someone else to carry on usual behaviors also shifts the source of control and thus the voluntary-involuntary aspect of the behavior. Not only can temper tantrums be reduced by specifying when and where they shall occur (Hare-Mustin, 1975), but crying and many other disruptive behaviors can be rapidly diminished, which then frees the family to be open to a redefinition of the problem that can lead to changes among all the members of the family system.

REFERENCES

Erickson, M.H. Naturalistic techniques of hypnosis. *American Journal of Clinical Hypnosis,* 1958, **1,** 3-8.

Erickson, R.C. "Free will" and clinical research. *Psychotherapy: Theory, Research and Practice,* 1971, **10,** 10-13.

Frankl, V.E. Paradoxical intention: A logotherapeutic technique. *American Journal of Psychotherapy,* 1960, **14,** 520-535.

Greenberg, R.P. Anti-expectation techniques of psychotherapy: The power of negative thinking. *Psychotherapy: Theory, Research and Practice,* 1971, **10,** 145-148.

Haley, J. *Strategies of psychotherapy.* New York: Grune and Stratton, 1963.

Hare-Mustin, R.T. Treatment of temper tantrums by a paradoxical intervention. *Family Process,* 1975, **14,** 485.

Stampfl, P.G. & Levis, D.J. Essentials of implosion therapy: A learning theory-based psychodynamic behavioral therapy. *Journal of Abnormal Psychology,* 1967, **72,** 496-503.

Umbarger, C. & Hare, R.T. A structural approach to patient and therapist disengagement from a schizophrenic family. *American Journal of Psychotherapy,* 1973, **21,** 274-284.

Watzlawick, P., Weakland, J.H., & Fisch, R. *Change.* New York: Norton, 1974.

Wolpe, J. & Lazarus, A.A. *Behavior therapy techniques.* New York: Pergamon Press, 1966.

Chapter 30

THE TREATMENT OF CHILDREN THROUGH BRIEF THERAPY OF THEIR PARENTS

MARA SELVINI PALAZZOLI, LUIGI BOSCOLO,
GIAN FRANCO CECCHIN, AND GIULIANA PRATA

Granted that there does not exist to date a comprehensive theory of family therapy, it seems nevertheless possible to state a common denominator: the trend away from the disturbed individual seen as an artifically isolated monad toward the study and the treatment of dyads, triads, the entire nuclear family and, finally, of the complx network of relationships in which every family is embedded. However, beyond this one point of agreement, workers in our fields are known to hold radically divergent views about questions of epistemology and practice, as described very comprehensively by Beels and Ferber (1). These views range from models based on group dynamics in the psychoanalytic sense to role theory, learning theory, games theory, systems theory, and cybernetics.

After various trials and errors, our research team at the Center for the Study of the Family in Milan began to adopt in 1971 the theoretical model proposed in the late 50s and early 60s by the so-called Palo Alto Group under Gregory Bateson's theoretical leadership and the extensions of this model developed by Jay Haley in Philadelphia and by the Brief Therapy Center of the Mental Research Institute in Palo Alto (5). In terms of this model, the family is considered an interacting error-controlled system.

Our method of procedure is to have two co-therapists meet with the entire family (i.e. all members of the nuclear family actually living together) from the first session. The remainder of the team observes the sessions from behind a one-way vision screen and after each session meets with the therapists to devise the interventions for the next session. The families are informed of this arrangement.

From M.S. Palazzoli, L. Boscolo, G.F. Cecchin, and G. Prata, The Treatment of Children Through Brief Therapy of Their Parents, *Family Process,* 13:429-42, 1974. Courtesy of *Family Process.*

As a general principle, all sessions are with the entire family, except when in the course of treatment it seems appropriate to deviate from this rule for the purpose of observing one of its sub-systems or of making a specific intervention. In particular, there is one exception to this rule that we consider especially important. It has to do with those parents who seek therapy for behavioral problems in very young children (two to four years) or in older children who have already been traumatized by numerous medical and psychiatric interventions and are therefore already labeled as "sick"—a label we do not wish to attach to them even more firmly. To this one may object that the convocation of the entire family is in and of itself an implicit communication that the problem is one of the family and not just of the identified patient. It is our experience, however, that the parents often inform their child of the forthcoming first visit with the implied message, "We have to go there because of you." It sometimes also happens that families are referred to us on the strength of some misconception about the Center and contact us in the belief that they should "hand over" their youngster for individual treatment.

Since our first contact with the family is usually by telephone, we have set aside special hours for these calls so that we may talk to them at length and thereby avoid many mistakes and misunderstandings that may otherwise occur due to lack of time. The fact that treatment (and often also its outcome) begins with this first telephone contact can hardly be stressed too much. The member of the team who takes the calls tries to obtain as much information as possible and immediately enters it on a fact sheet. He especially attempts to elicit as accurate a definition of the problem as possible, as well as other information about the family's present situation and their real reasons for seeking help.[1]

If the call comes from the parents of a very young child, whose problem, in our view, is almost always the expression of a marital problem of the parents or from the parents of a child who has already been traumatized by unsuccessful treatments, we usually invite only the parents to the first session in order to observe their interaction.[2]

---

[1]This first telephone contact deserves special study. It already enables us to observe, and to note, a number of phenomena: disturbed communication, tone of voice, general attitude, peremptory demands for all kinds of information, immediate attempts at manipulation by requesting a certain date and hour for the interview or by imposing certain conditions, thus attempting a role reversal and making it appear as if it were the therapists who are "looking for" the family. Except for a very few special cases, we have generally found it counterproductive to schedule the family for an emergency session.

[2]An exception are those families whose treatment has been discussed beforehand with a referring colleague who is seeing the child in individual therapy. In these cases the families have already been informed by the referring therapist that he considers it necessary for them to meet together for the purpose of observing them as a family group. This is, for instance, the case with autistic children.

During the first visit the therapists collect the information necessary to decide whether they should continue to work with the parents alone or whether the child should participate. In the following two cases, the team decided to continue the therapy with the parents alone. The reasons will soon become evident.

A CONTRACT FOR A CASE OF STOOL INCONTINENCE[3]

An anxious mother called the Center with regard to problems with her youngest child, Tonino, who was nine years old. Since early childhood Tonino had had a problem with encopresis of moderate degree, which until recently the mother was prepared to tolerate. The reason she now needed help was that in recent months the incontinence had worsened to an intolerable degree (almost daily he "craps in his pants" at school) and the child had developed other "strange" behaviors, in addition, that finally prompted the teacher to call his mother. Tonino not only entertained his school friends by telling them incredible stories in which he always played the role of the hero and which he firmly insisted were true, but he also "lied" in his in-class compositions. For some time these papers had been full of grammatical and spelling mistakes and he had been writing about "things which are neither here nor there."

In the first session the parents brought along two such composiions. In one of them, entitled "An Important Event in My Life," Tonino described with the verve (and the bad grammar) of a sports reporter his overwhelming victory at an imaginary Italian swimming championship for eight-year-old boys, allegedly held in Florence. In the other essay, with the title "How to Help Others," Tonino described at length his ferocious battle with a wolf during a recent Sunday trip into the mountains. He explained how, alerted by the screams of his oldest brother, he rushed into a nearby forest and there, after a wild struggle, managed to strangle this huge wolf that had sunk its teeth into the brother's arm and bitten it off. "That evening," concluded his essay, "I was pleased with my good deed, but somewhat dissatisfied because my brother had lost his arm."

The "mendacious" accounts that had so greatly shocked the elderly teacher thus revealed a Tonino for whom there was no other space or method to assert himself in life. The parents explained that physically Tonino was the least fortunate of their four sons. He was short, puny, cross-eyed, and seemed to have spent a large part of his young life in "repair shops." He underwent an operation for his strabismus at an early age and had since been wearing clumsy prescription glasses

---

[3]These two cases have been published in the journal *Neuropsichiatria Infantile* (46:539-554, 1973) and we wish to thank the Editor for his permission to include them here.

(which he frequently lost and which the mother promptly replaced with a new pair despite the considerable expense involved). Every week he was taken to an orthoptic specialist to exercise his eyes. As he also suffered from a knock-kneed condition, he had been made to wear, since age four, heavy orthopedic shoes that were laced all the way up above his ankles. And now, the mother reported, it also turned out that his permanent teeth were growing irregularly and a radical program was under way to have a dentist pull some and straighten out the others. It goes without saying that with all these treatments and other measures Tonino had been largely deprived of the psychophysical freedom necessary for a child's normal development. His brothers, on the other hand, were all handsome, healthy, and strong boys, especially the oldest (the one who had his arm bitten off).

The observations reported by the parents, the description of their relationships with their respective families of origin, and much of what we could intuit about their relationship with Tonino, all seemed highly significant. Upon Tonino there seemed to converge a series of problems that the parents had been unable to resolve in their own lives. The mother, still young and attractive, came from a family in which religious observance was pushed to almost fanatical extremes. When she fell in love and decided to marry her present husband, she followed his example of refusing certain religious practices, whereupon her mother cursed her, saying the God would punish her: never would living children issue from her womb!

The first three years of her marriage were spent in increasing anxiety over this curse since, indeed, she did not become pregnant. After many unsuccessful attempts to receive specialist help, she eventually turned to Padre Pio, a famous wonder healer, and received from him a great consolation: "Go in peace," he told her, and children would soon come, like flowers in spring. The prediction turned out to be only too true: she had three sons, with only ten months between one birth and the next. After that much grace, the spouses agreed (albeit with a great sense of guilt on the wife's part) to use a birth-control method. But not even that worked: there ensued the totally unwanted conception of Tonino. With great embarrassment, the mother confessed that at first she had even felt the temptation to have an abortion. But eventually she resigned herself to her fate and hoped for the arrival of a baby girl. Who did arrive, however, but that ugly gosling, Tonino, the result of "grave sins" that logically demanded heavy "retributions." The father, himself homely, puny, and cross-eyed, stated that he saw in Tonino all those negative aspects that made his own life miserable. He came from a broken family in which he had never received any affection and thus not only grieved for having passed on to Tonino his own physical defects, but stated he felt a great need to protect and help him and to spare him his own suffering. On account of this he always agreed to whatever steps, regardless of cost, his wife would propose to "repair" Tonino.

At this juncture, then, the latest treatment program, orthodontics, was to be followed by yet another and far more dramatic one: psychiatry. It was for this reason that we decided to spare Tonino an additional humiliation and to treat only the parents. Our expectations were quite optimistic since the marital relationship seemed basically good. The parents appeared to respect each other, to be deeply concerned with Tonino's well-being, and sufficiently motivated to follow any prescriptions given them by the therapists. The opportunity for a decisive intervention came about after the third session. A few days before their next session the mother called in a state of great anxiety, informing us that she had taken Tonino to his orthoptic appointment and waited for him outside. After a while the ophthalmologist came out of the exercise room alone and asked her to follow her into another office. She told the mother that she was very worried about Tonino's mental state and that he probably needed psychiatric help. It turned out that Tonino had willingly sat down in front of the viewer into which she had introduced the slides that the child was supposed to describe. What he did see, however, was something totally different, and he insisted that this was what he really saw. Thus, on viewing the last slide, showing a St. Bernard, Tonino looked up at her and stated delightedly, "I see . . . a large flock of colorful birds."

When the parents came to their fourth session, the mother was asked to call the ophthalmologist to find out whether the orthoptic exercises were still indispensable. The answer was no, since the condition had remained unchanged for quite some time and did not seem to be amenable to further improvement. The therapists then decided to have the parents enter into a contract with Tonino which was to be solemnly signed by all three parties. This contract was a kind of barter. The parents were to take Tonino aside and tell him in all frankness that they were fully aware how thoroughly fed up he was with treatments and specialists. They were also aware of the fact that he was now grown up and about to become a man. For this reason they had decided to cancel the appointment with the orthodontist; after all, it was not important for a male to have teeth as regular and perfect as those of the young ladies in toothpaste commercials. They were also willing to replace the special eye glasses with normal ones and to terminate the sessions with the eye doctor. All this, however, was on condition that Tonino would recognize himself that he was now grown up and that he would once and for all agree not to soil himself anymore. If he accepted these conditions, the contract was to be drawn up by the father and signed by all three of them.

We were told that Tonino did not hesitate for a moment; he immediately accepted the conditions and signed the document with his full signature, i.e., his two Christian names *and* his last name. The contract became valid at once and produced the expected results: the encopresis stopped immediately.

In the following session, and in addition to the terms of the contract, it was agreed that the father would initiate a sports program that was within Tonino's physical capabilities and from which his brothers were to be rigorously excluded. It was also considered necessary for the parents to inform the teacher of these decisions and of their purpose, hoping that Tonino would thus gradually also abandon his exhibitions at school.

Treatment was terminated after the seventh session and it was agreed that the parents would call us in three months. This they did punctually, informing us that everything was going well. Tonino was very proud to have joined a group of hikers who were training for a mountain camp. This telephone conversation served as our follow-up. If the parents had told us that things were not going well, we would then have taken the entire family into treatment, as the absence of progress would have indicated that we were indeed faced with a more complex and rigid problem than we had originally assumed.

A FUNERAL RITE FOR AN ANORECTIC GIRL

A young married couple requested help for their daughter, Marella, who was two years and two months old and had been suffering from anorexia for the last six months. The call to us was made by the mother who sounded anxious but controlled. In this very first contact, she already linked Marella's anorexia with the birth of a baby brother whom Marella had not yet seen. The reason for this was that he had remained in the hospital with septicemia, contracted four days after his birth, which left him severely brain-damaged. Now, seven months later, he was still alive, but there was no hope for his survival. "For Marella he is only a sort of phantom"; this was how the mother literally described the situation. Her request for help was due to a sudden worsening of Marella's eating problem. For the last two weeks, she had been on a veritable hunger strike, accepting only very small quantities of baby food and even those few spoonfuls only from persons other than her parents.

In the first session with the parents, their relationship pattern soon became evident: they maintained a complementary relationship in which the husband, whom we shall call Edoardo, clearly occupied the superior position. He was thirty years old, good-looking, dressed with casual elegance, and came from a wealthy family of local patricians, a large clan comprising four generations, complexly interrelated and headed by a centenarian grandmother. He worked with great indifference in one of the family's several business enterprises, but otherwise devoted every free moment to electronic music, his exclusive passion. He spent entire days in his music room, recording and composing, neglecting all social relations and talking very little. He came on as the "artist," with his head always in the clouds, thus signaling that he was not available for any request, especially not for a practical one.

The wife, whom we shall call Lucia, was extremely graceful and dressed with refined taste. She was emotional and vivacious and tried very cautiously but unsuccessfully to obtain from her husband some appropriate recognition of, and reaction to, her feelings. She came from a middle-class family, and it appeared that Edoardo married her more or less out of gratitude for having cured him of impotence. It was quite evident that Lucia tried very hard to adapt herself to the style of the husband's "great" family and to be accepted by them as a full member in her own right, but it also seemed that these efforts were rather unsuccessful.

Lucia was an only child and her parents' marriage was marred by a long neurological infirmity of her father. From adolescence on, Lucia seemed to have assumed the role of "somebody who thinks of everybody else and asks nothing for herself," who was efficient and always there when needed. She never failed to help her mother who came to depend heavily on her and demanded that she assume certain functions as head of the family. In keeping with this role, Lucia also obtained a diploma as Red Cross nurse.

She had continued to perform this role as a member of the husband's large clan. It was she who came running when a need arose, who patiently listened to and cheered up the old melancholy aunts, who kept reins on the servants staffing the family's large country estate where everybody got together during the summer months. All of this was very convenient for everybody, including the husband, but it did not seem to confer upon Lucia any sign of distinction. From some indications that emerged in the first session, it appeared that the noble family referred to her at best as "our dear Lucia." In this system of rigid complementarity, Lucia's increasingly frantic attempts to gain the desired recognition only served to reinforce in the members of the clan that very attitude of seignorial condescension that she wanted to change.

Her husband's relationship to her was not very different from that of the extended family. He was certainly not rude, quite the opposite—but he treated her with that slightly annoyed and condescending or amused mien that a grandseigneur would put on when disturbed in his elevated thoughts by the petty preoccupations of his butler.

As a result of this interaction, Lucia had turned all her attention to Marella, employing her usual style of omnipresent helper. The father, on the other hand, respected the little girl as being the mother's exclusive territory. It turned out the Marella had developed the habit of calling him in the shrillest of voices even when he was silently sitting next to her—it seemed that difficult to attract his attention.

The birth of the brain-damaged baby had upset this precarious balance. Marella had been separated from her mother for many days, which were spent at her maternal grandmother's, and after the mother returned, Marella saw her disappear every afternoon to spend several hours at the hospital. What was amazing, but at the same time perfectly in keeping with Lucia's role, was that in order to protect Marella she had decided not to tell her about the baby brother's birth, let alone to let her see him. She therefore explained to Marella that she went to the hospital to look after the child of a poor friend. "Since Matteo will not live," she said, "There is no need to complicate Marella's life." As far as the members of the clan were concerned, they had almost ignored Lucia's misfortune and after a few telephone calls had shown no further interest in it. Edoardo was certainly upset but could not, or did not want to, show his feelings to his wife.

The sudden worsening of Marella's anorexia, which had seriously reduced her weight, coincided with the family's return from a vacation with the clan. There was reason to assume that this visit had left Lucia exasperated, but she did not dare to say so. In the next session she expressed only her suffering in connection with her husband, who left every burden and every decision to her. The girl refused all food from the parents. It became necessary to take her for every meal to the "little restaurant," i.e. the apartment of the maternal grandmother who managed to make her swallow a few spoonfuls of mush.

During the three sessions following the initial interview, the therapist showed little interest in the girl's plight and cautiously tried to focus their attention on the marital relationship. The spouses, however, appeared extremely defensive and very adept at changing the subject as soon as sensitive arguments were touched upon. The decisive moment occurred in the fifth session. The spouses reported that Matteo had died a few days ago and had been buried in the family tomb. The mother, therefore, did not go to the hospital anymore, but Marella, whom the mother had again decided to leave in the dark, was eating even less. This time the father also seemed worried. It was obvious to us that the child, with her unusual sensitivity and intelligence, had understood a great deal from the very beginning. Her determination not to eat was now reinforced by this further conspiracy of silence.

We therefore decided to have the parents tell Marella the truth. But mere words would have obviously been insufficient. What was needed was a dramatization, a rite involving all three family members and designed to convey to Marella, who was only at the beginning of the verbal phase of her development, a clear and unequivocal message. Such a rite, it seemed to us, was also indispensable, in view of the father's emotional distance, for the purpose of involving him in a dramatic, emotional experience consistent with that of his wife and daughter. We therefore prescribed that on the following day the official exequies for the deceased child would take place in the garden of their house: Papa had to explain to Marella in simple terms everything that had taken place. He had to explain the reasons for the pitiful lie, tell her that she had indeed had a little brother by the name of Matteo and that he been the very ill baby that mama used to help in the hospital. Now her baby brother was dead; he was no longer there but was buried in the family tomb at the cemetery. But it was important to bury also his clothes, because Matteo was dead and did not need them anymore. The parents agreed to carry out this ritual.[4]

They went into the garden, where Papa dug a fairly deep hole into which, one after the other, Mama slowly laid the baby's clothes. Marella herself took a pair of little shoes and gently placed it on top of them. The parents were quite moved, as if it were a real funeral. Finally Papa took the shovel again, filled the hole, and planted a tree on top of it.

That same afternoon Marella was found playing in her room chewing with great appetite a large piece of bread which she had fetched from the kitchen. Since the phantom was not there anymore, there was no longer any need to compete with it by means of eating "mush." On the following day, Marella not only ate normally but showed further signs of great improvement. She stopped being whiny and clinging to her mother's skirts but for many days kept talking almost obsessively about her little brother, as if to reassure herself that it was finally possible to talk about him and to receive an answer. One day she asked her mother why she had never told her that the baby at the hospital was Matteo. When the mother said, "Because he was never here at home and would never have come," Marella exclaimed, "But he *was* here, in that big tummy of yours," leaving mother speechless.

In spite of the confidence the spouses gained through this rapid success (five sessions), they signaled in various indirect ways that they were not willing, for the time being, to deal with the core problem of their marriage and their relationship with the extended family.

After discussing this in a staff meeting, the team decided to respect their resistance. Our experience has indeed taught us that these joint resistances are insurmountable. Any attempt to meet them head on leads to negative results. One thus has to be modest and content with the successes achieved over the presenting complaint. Moreover, in this particular case, we were convinced that by respecting their reluctance we would strengthen their rapport with the therapists and this, of course, was an indispensable condition for any further course of treatment.

The couple indeed came to see us again six months later. Marella had continued to do very well, and the wall of silence was broken. In this session, it was decided to have the wife meet with one of the co-therapists for some individual sessions to overcome the difficulties of her relationship with her husband's family.

---

[4]Family rituals of this kind are among the most important and effective therapeutic techniques that we devised in the course of our research into rapid and decisive intervention with dysfunctional families. We have presented their rationale in detail in another publication (3).

DISCUSSION

The problem of deciding at what point to suspend or terminate treatment is specifically examined by our team in every single case. We have often wondered if it is indeed right and honest to terminate therapy shortly after the disappearance of the identified patient's symptom. Have we perhaps worsened the situation? Have we perhaps deprived the family group of the indicator of its dysfunction? At this juncture we can only say that therapeutic interventions in family therapy do not merely affect one individual, but the system as a whole: the disappearance of the symptom is always the expression of a certain change in the family's modes of interaction. It is, of course, possible that this change may be insufficient to guarantee further improvement. If so, it is up to the team to take this possibility into account and to make allowance for it. In the above-mentioned case, we decided to respect the couple's resistance and in doing so to convey to the spouses an implicit message intended to strengthen their feelings of trust, freedom, and spontaneity toward us. In other cases, we prefer to have the spouses call us or to come to a session at an appointed date within a few months. By means of this expedient we maintain the family "in therapy" and implicitly assure them of our continued interest and availability.

As far as the technique of our approach is concerned, it should be pointed out that it is not based on the use of interpretations. While our experience may permit us to infer the past causes of a family's present behavior, we do not verbalize this, just as we do not point out to the family members what we see going on in the interviews or what their patterns of interaction are. We keep these observations to ourselves and utilize them in the design of our therapeutic interventions. As should be evident from the above-mentioned examples, our interventions are of an active-prescriptive nature and through them we set out to change the interaction of the family as a whole. Obviously, they vary from one family to the next. But how do we go about changing these patterns?

In the course of our research we have discovered a kind of intervention that offers more than encouraging results, and we have provisionally called this intervention, to be applied very early in the course of treatment, the *positive connotation*.[5] It consists of approving all observed behaviors of the identified patient or the other family members, and especially those behaviors that are traditionally considered pathological. For instance, in the cases described above we

---

[5]We are quite aware that from a systems theoretical point of view this term is incorrect. On the other hand, conditioned as we are by the linear-linguistic model, "positive" helps to make ourselves clear to others, at least until we hit upon a better name. In essence, the positive connotation is nothing but a metacommunication (about the system) that has the property of a *confirmation*.

praised the attitude of the parents as admirable expressions of affection and concern. From sad experience we have learned that any criticism directed at the parents (which, incidentally, is "culturally" expected and secretly feared) can have no other effect than to produce indignant and negative reactions or, worse, depressive maneuvers of the "we-have-completely-failed" type, which then reduce the therapists to impotence.[6]

We do not consider this *positive connotation* a ploy or a trick. Quite the contrary, its application is all the more our method of choice since the acceptance of the systems model has enabled us to go beyond the casual-moralistic bounds of traditional psychiatry. We therefore consider the observable behavior of a family in therapy as self-corrective and thus tending to maintain the equilibrium of the system. A family who comes into therapy is usually a family in crisis, frightened by the possible loss of homeostasis and therefore anxious to maintain it at all cost. If we were to tell them explicitly that they must change, it would make them enter into a virtually monolithic coalition in order to ward us off. To be accepted into the family system, it is necessary for us to approve their behavior, no matter what it is, since it is directed at a more than understandable goal: the cohesion of the family. (Let us mention as an aside that none of our dysfunctional families has ever challenged this point of view).

Through the *positive connotation* we implicitly declare ourselves as allies of the family's striving for homeostasis, and we do this at the moment that the family feels it is most threatened. By thus strengthening the homeostatic tendency, we gain influence over the ability to change that is inherent in every living system.

Homeostatic tendencies and the ability to undergo change are, indeed, essential characteristics of living systems. Neither of these two properties is in and of itself better or worse than the other; rather, the one cannot exist without the other. It is, therefore, not a question of "better or worse," but of "more or less."

Thus, it seems to us that the *positive connotation* is a therapeutic intervention of prime importance to bring about change in a family system. Change does not come about automatically, but rather as a result of a behavior prescription that is accepted and carried out (thereby triggering the desired change) precisely because, paradoxically, the therapists have aligned themselves with the homeostatic tendency. The therapeutic problem presented by each separate case is thus the design of a specific behavior prescription. Invariably, this prescription will be different for every family and will depend on its particular way of conceptualizing its problem.

---

[6] In this connection, we feel that the gist of Braulio Montalvo's and Jay Haley's article, "In Defense of Child Therapy" (2) relates to this fundamental problem, i.e. how to avoid making the parents feel that they are being accused.

REFERENCES

1. Beels, C.C., and Ferber, A., "Family Therapy: A View," *Fam. Proc.*, 8:280-314, 1969.
2. Montalvo, B., and Haley, J., "In Defense of Child Therapy," *Fam. Proc.*, 12:227-44, 1973.
3. Palazzoli, M.S., *Self-Starvation—From the Intrapsychic to the Transpersonal Approach to Anorexia Nervosa*, London, Chaucer Pub. Co., 1974.
4. Palazzoli, M.S., Boscolo, L., Cecchin, G.F., Prata, G., *Paradosse e Contro-Paradosso. Per un Nuovo Modello Concettuale e Metodologico nella Terapia della Famiglia a Transazione Schizofrenica*, Milano, Feltrinelli, 1975.
5. Watzlawick, P., Weakland, J.H., and Fisch, R., *Change*, New York, W.W. Norton & Co., 1974.

PARADOX AS A THERAPEUTIC TECHNIQUE: A REVIEW

PATRICIA H. SOPER AND LUCIANO L'ABATE

Paradox has been a philosophical curiosity since Epimenedes of Megara devised the paradox of the liar and Zeno of Elea produced the paradoxes of infinity (Hughes and Brecht, 1975). Interest in paradox waned until the late nineteenth century revival of logic (Edwards, 1967). Recently, family therapists have developed an interest in pragmatic paradoxes leaving logical and semantic paradoxes to the domain of philosophers and linguists.

A paradox is defined as a "contradiction that follows correct deduction from consistent premises" (Watzlawick, Beavin, & Jackson, 1967). Watzlawick et al. (1967) viewed pragmatic paradoxes as most important in the study of human interaction because these paradoxes arise in ongoing interactions and determine behavior. Haley (1955) pointed out that a paradoxical behavior has two levels of abstraction. One level denies the assertion of the other; the second statement of the paradox is about the first but is at a different level of abstraction. Haley went on to say that this type of paradox is inevitable in the process of communication.

This paper is concerned with the nature of paradox as a therapeutic intervention from an historical and theoretical perspective. Included is a review of types of paradoxical interventions as well as a brief review of related approaches with heavy paradoxical overtones. Major emphasis is on the use of paradox in family therapy through relevant individual approaches such as paradoxical intention and hypnosis.

THE THERAPEUTIC DOUBLE BIND

The Palo Alto group (including both the Bateson project and the Mental Research Institute) is credited with the recognition of pathological

From P. Soper and L. L'Abate, Paradox as a Therapeutic Technique: A Review, *International Journal of Family Counseling*, 5:10-21, 1977. Courtesy of Brunner/Mazel Publishers.

aspects of paradoxical communication in their work on the double bind (Bateson et al., 1956; Bateson et al., 1963; Watzlawick, 1963). The direct outgrowth of their work is the therapeutic double bind which is a mirror image of the pathological bind (Watzlawick, et al., 1967). The therapeutic double bind presupposes an intense relationship between the therapist and client. The therapist enjoins the client to change while remaining unchanged with the implication that the injunction is the agent of change. The client is in the position either of changing and demonstrating control over his pathology or of resisting by behaving nonsymptomatically. Thus, the client is bound to change. The therapeutic setting dissuades the client from leaving the field by withdrawing or commenting on the paradox (Watzlawick et al., 1967; Feldman, 1976).

PRESCRIBING THE SYMPTOM AND REFRAMING

Varieties of therapeutic double binds that are closely associated with the Palo Alto group are: (1) prescribing the symptom and (2) reframing. Prescribing the symptom is quite simply instructing the client to maintain or exaggerate his symptomatic behavior. Watzlawick et al. (1967) view making the client behave as he has been behaving as applying a "be spontaneous" paradox. If the client is asked to display his symptom which is a nondeliberate, spontaneous behavior, then he cannot be spontaneous any more since the demand precludes spontaneity.

A number of practitioners report the use of this paradoxical instruction to bringing about change in clients. Farrelly (1974) frequently encourages his clients to continue with their symptoms to an absurd degree to "prove" the client's irrational contentions about himself. Montalvo and Haley (1973) report that the child therapist may even encourage a symptom as a means of bringing about change. Fischer (1974) and Prosky (1974) make reference to the usefulness of enlisting the family's oppositional feelings against the therapist. Andolfi (1974) reports that Jackson utilized prescribing the symptom with paranoid patients by teaching them to be more suspicious. In families disrupted by divorce, Peck (1974) instructs the partial family to take their incompleteness more seriously which resolves the members' ambivalence.

Feldman (1976) cites the usefulness of the technique of prescribing the symptom in dealing with a depressed client. The therapist may *implicitly* encourage the client to remain depressed by commenting, "It's a wonder you aren't more depressed." The client can respond by remaining depressed, and thus acknowledging control over his symptom, or evidence decreased depression, which also acknowledges control over his symptom. The therapist can follow through by trying to change or to circumscribe the situation further, suggesting, for instance, that the client spread out his depression throughout the week as opposed to being depressed only on the weekends.

Weakland et al. gave an example of a client who was complaining of headaches. She was told to make every effort to have more headaches at specified periods in the coming week. Again, regardless of whether the headaches got worse or disappeared, the client was bound to demonstrate that the apparently unchangeable problem could change. Weakland et al. (1974) reported that the most effective manner to give such paradoxical instructions is to play onedown or to act ignorant or confused in order to have the advice accepted. When the therapist came on strong with the paradoxical instructions, the client tended to ignore the advice.

An additional example of prescribing the symptom is a case involving a middle-aged woman and her schizophrenic son who were in a power struggle over the son's allowance (Fisch et al., 1972). The mother was reluctant to hand over much money due to her son's unstable mental state while the son was never sure he was able to meet expenses. The mother judged the amount of money she gave the son by the amount of psychotic behavior she perceived in him. The therapist instructed the son to use his psychotic behavior deliberately with the mother who was even more fearful of an expensive rehospitalization of the son that she was of his possible squandering of his allowance. The mother came through with a larger amount paid of a regular basis from which the son saved enough money to buy himself a car, thus giving himself greater independence from his mother.

Reframing, also a therapeutic double bind, involves changing the entire meaning of a situation by altering both or either its conceptual and/or emotional context in such a manner that the entire situation is experienced as completely different, i.e., the situation has been placed in a new frame (Watzlawick, Weakland, & Fisch, 1974). The therapist may frame the therapy procedures so he can work effectively, reinterpret messages from family members in a positive light (Jackson & Weakland, 1961), take a psychotic client's metaphors literally and interpreting it as evidence of his sanity (Kantor & Hoffman, 1966), define all events as being for the good of the family (Haley, 1972), and turn a family member into an observer (Minuchin, 1965). Haley (1963) used the term relabeling which essentially is a synonym for reframing. He makes the point that relabeling maladaptive patterns (or reframing) in couples therapy makes continuing those patterns more of an ordeal than changing.

The concept of reframing may be further clarified by the following examples. DeShazer (1975) reports the tactic of having an uninvolved father formally assigned the chore of keeping score in fights between the mother and child. In another case (Andolfi, 1974), a young couple whose relationship was characterized by frequent fighting was told that their fights were demonstrations of their love. They were directed to fight on a regular schedule. The couple was determined to prove the therapist was wrong, ceased fighting, and consequently began to get along better.

Luthman (1974) reports a case involving a family where the father was progressively going blind. She inquired whether he was learning Braille. The father defensively replied he was "as good a man as anyone else." She asked him, "How does it come about that the possible adding of new knowledge and skills to your repertoire would make you feel less in some way?"

The therapist may employ reframing in his own family. Guerin (Guerin & Fogarty, 1972), a Bowen trainee, reversed his usual tactic of interrogating his wife about what was the matter when she was distant. He began commenting to her that it sure is peaceful to live with someone who does not burden me with personal thoughts and feelings. Or he said, "I cannot stand people who are always talking about their troubles." He would immediately leave the room before she could reply. His wife began to broach the issues that were bothering her to her husband.

TASKS

The therapeutic double bind may be in the form of an assignment or task. The therapist utilizes his clients resistance when assigning a task (Jackson & Weakland, 1961; Camp, 1973). Haley (1973) presents a case of Erickson's involving the breaking of an overt-involved mother-son dyad. The son wet his bed almost on a nightly basis. The exasperated mother brought him to Erickson who assigned a task to the two of them. The mother was to get up between 4:00 a.m. and 5:00 a.m. each morning to check her son's bed. If it was wet, he had to get up and practice his handwriting with his mother supervising him. If the bed was dry, his mother still had to get up and check. The boy went along with the task because his mother would like it less than he. The boy ended up with a dry bed, beautiful handwriting, an admiring mother, and even increased involvement with his father who now played ball with him. Hare-Mustin (1975) used a similar strategy with a four-year-old boy who threw spectacular and frequent temper tantrums. She instructed the boy to continue having his tantrums but only in a special tantrum place at home. The child and his family decided on the specific location. In the following session, the child picked a time of day he would tantrum. By the third session the tantrums had decreased to a bare minimum. Hare-Mustin expressed concern over the rapid change and asked the child to choose a day for a tantrum the following week. The child had no further tantrums.

DeShazer (1974) presents an excellent example of a task in his use of the functions of the presenting symptom in the family's interaction. A family brought in their 14-year-old son who had a stealing problem. The therapist instructed the father and son as a team to hide 5 one dollar bills around the house. If the son resisted stealing the money for one week, he was to be allowed to come in for a previously denied private session with the therapist. Otherwise the whole family was to come in. The son did come in alone and received instructions to steal two of the bills but to delay his usual dramatic confession until the next family session. At this time the son went trough a dramatic display of guilt and sinfulness gaining the full attention of his family, but this time the father's open complicity was known to all. The father was able to recognize his part in his son's stealing episodes as were other family members.

The junior author remembers a difficult case with a couple where the husband demanded intercourse two or three times a week from his wife who felt resentful and angry at being used. Intercourse had become an ordeal for both. Other courses of action such as treatment of sexual attitudes and behaviors had failed. The husband was instructed to give up sex completely for the time being. The husband was reluctant, but the wife expressed great enthusiasm at the idea. For this couple the advantages of the husband's curtailment of his sexual behavior began to become apparent: (1) the pressure would be off both parties to perform sexually; (2) the wife could feel loved for herself rather than for her body; (3) the husband would be forced to think about his sexual behavior in relationship to his wife rather than take the usual route of unreflectively following his impulses; (4) by lowering the husband's dominance the couple could establish equilibrium in the relationship; and (5) the wife, who had been protesting that it was not sex *per se* that turned her off, but the manner in which her husband approached her for intercourse, would be on the spot. It would now be up to her to initiate any sexual activity.

WRITTEN INSTRUCTIONS

Both Selvini-Palazzoli et al. (1975) and L'Abate et al. (1976) have experimented with the effectiveness of using paradoxical written messages for presentation to the clients generally at the end of a session. The advantages of such a procedure are: (1) the message can be systematically thought out in advance and would serve as the major, important interpretation of the session; (2) the message would be more difficult to distort or forget by the clients than a verbal interpretation and thus assure repercussions in marital or familial homeostasis; and (3) copies of the messages could serve as progress notes for the therapist as well as a source of research data. For instance, a paradoxical message was presented to a couple whom the junior author and his wife had seen in therapy for approximately one year with minimal results. Previously, the couple had been in therapy numerous times over the years with a variety of therapists in different towns.

Dear B and J:

On the basis of our detailed and prolonged observation of your marriage and after a great deal of thought and deliberation, we have come to the conclusion that you both love each other so deeply and so dearly that any change for the better in the other is interpreted as a sign of rejection and a demonstration of disloyalty. You both are so loyal to each other that neither one can change for fear of disappointing the other one.

We can see and understand then, how it is impossible for each of you to change for the better, since changing for the better would be a sign of disloyalty and rejection. We really wonder whether each of you can change for the better without disappointing the other.

We would like for each of you to read this note each day but not to talk about it too much. We will talk about it next time we meet.

Cordially yours,
Luciano L'Abate and Bess L. L'Abate

POSITIVE INTERPRETATION

With this technique the therapist takes the stance of stressing the positive aspects of behaviors rather than the negative aspects (L'Abate, 1975; Otto, 1963). Stressing the positives is a form of relabeling or reframing.

Selvini-Palazzoli and her co-workers (1974, 1975) make use of positive connotation in their work with families. The therapists declare themselves as allies of the family and approve the behaviors of the family members—particularly those traditionally considered scapegoated by making them the family heroes, i.e., "By drawing attention to himself Giovanni has protected the whole family and especially father and mother, from looking at themselves and how they behave."

Change is produced by the therapist paradoxically aligning themselves with the family's homeostatic tendency (Selvini-Palazzoli, et al., 1974, 1975). They report a case in which the martyr-like mother of a schizophrenic six-year-old boy declares herself as changed in an early session and no longer wanting to suffer. The therapist expressed concern over her premature change and described the importance of her suffering as a commendable virtue without which she would be at a severe loss. The therapist further described the husband and son as protecting the mother from suffering more than she had to, i.e., keeping her at the status quo. In essence, the therapist posed a paradox which was a metacommunication or confirmation of the pathogenic paradox by prescribing the symptom. Since the family always tries to disqualify the therapist, they must now change their game.

L'Abate (1975) writes of the choice available to the therapist in interpreting behaviors to the family and to himself. He may choose a traditional, negative orientation based on the pathology being presented to him and view the behaviors as a deficit or liability. On the other hand, the therapist may also choose to view the behaviors in terms of assets or strengths. The family expresses many strengths if the therapist is open to recognizing them and pointing them out to the family: Asking for help is a strength, expressing hurt through tears is a strength, caring for oneself and one's family is expressed by the family's presence in the therapist's office, and sharing hurt is a sign of caring. Paradoxically, the use of positive labeling can disrupt fixed, negative views the family takes for granted. For example, the parents of a ten-year-old girl complained that she is making new demands on them. Since she was initially shy and undemonstrative, the therapist praised her new demands as an indication of her positive self-assertion and increased self-esteem.

PARADOXICAL INTENTION

Paradoxical intention, a technique devised by Victor Frankl (1965, 1975a, 1976) has been used successfully in the treatment of phobias, obsessive-compulsive disorders, and anxiety states (Gerz, 1962; Solyom et al., 1972; Hand & Lamontagne, 1974). The technique is similar to that of prescribing the symptom. The therapist instructs the client to train himself to experience his symptom to an extreme degree as frequently as possible. The symptom has run its course when the client recognizes its absurdity and gains sufficient self-detachment to laugh at the symptom. Frankl (1975, 1975b) described the viciously circular nature of symptom which brings forth a fear of recurrence or anticipatory anxiety. The anxiety provokes the symptom whose recurrence reinforces the anxiety or fear. The technique of paradoxical intention is aimed at the phobic's flight from his fear and the obsessive's tendency to fight his fears. In short, the client is instructed to give up the mechanisms of resistance he has developed to avoid giving in to his fears and to face his fears head on. Frankl (1975b) reported the case of a woman who had suffered from severe claustrophobia for 15 years. She feared riding in all modes and transportation and entering buildings. She would become anxious and would fear that she would suffocate and die upon entry into a closed, confined space. As part of her desensitization treatment, she was encouraged to let the symptoms become as bad as possible and to seek out the places where her symptom had previously occurred. Within a week, she was able to enter symptom-free innumerable places, first with her husband and then by herself, that she had previousy been under considerable duress to enter.

HYPNOSIS

Hypnosis employs many of the paradoxical procedures mentioned in this article. The hypnotist uses reframing, emphasizing the positive, resistance, and a variety of double binds. A paradoxical injunction is given to the subject by the hypnotist who communicates two levels of messages: (1) Do as I say; (2) Don't do as I say but behave spontaneously. The subject adapts to the conflicting set of directives by undergoing a change and behaving in a way described as trance behavior (Sander, 1974; Andolfi, 1974; Haley, 1973, Haley, 1963). The hypnotist's techniques are very similar to those of the therapist who first directs his client to do things he can voluntarily do and then requests or communicates an expectation of spontaneous change (Haley, 1973).

Erickson and Rossi (1975) have identified a number of double binds used in hypnosis as well as therapy. The first involves offering a free choice among comparable alternatives, one of which must be chosen, (i.e., "Would you like to go into a trance now or later?"). In a second, rather complex double bind, a request ostensibly made at the conscious level effects a change at the unconscious or subconscious level (e.g., "If your unconscious wants you to enter a trance, your right hand will lift. Otherwise your left hand will lift.") A third double bind uses time as a binding agent (e.g., "Do you want to get over that habit this week or next? That may seem too soon. Perhaps you'd like a longer period of time like three or four weeks?"). The fourth double bind—the reverse set double bind—is frequently used by Erickson in enabling patients to reveal material by enjoining them not to. The fifth therapeutic double bind used by Erickson is the *nonsequitur* double bind where he casually inserts a variety of increasingly absurd comments in a binding form. There is a similarity in the content of the alternatives offered by no logical connection (e.g., "Do you wish to take a bath before going to bed, or would you rather put your pajamas on in the bathroom?").

Not every case involves formal hypnosis. Joe, the eight-year-son of a divorcee, had become the neighborhood and family terror (Erickson, 1963). His mother brought him to see Erickson who assured Joe he would change his behavior "all by himself." His mother would be told some simple things she could do so he could change himself, and he was to guess what they were. The next day, Joe arose, demanded breakfast, and when it was not forthcoming, began to tantrum. His mother prepared for the occasion with books and food for herself, sat on Joe explaining she would get up when she thought of a way to change his behavior, but unfortunately as the day progressed, she did not think she would come up with anything so it was all up to him. Joe struggled, pleaded, screamed to no avail for most of the day. He was sent to bed without supper since he had missed lunch and breakfast had to be eaten before lunch. The next day, Joe was fed oatmeal which he hated for breakfast and had the leftover oatmeal for lunch. He accepted it gratefully. That day he spontaneously cleaned his room, canvassed the neighborhood, apologizing to the neighbors for his past behavior and making arrangements for amends. He spent the rest of the day with his schoolbooks and voluntarily went to bed. The mother explained to him she expected him to behave like a normal eight-year-old boy. All went well with the exception of one relapse dealt with by Erickson several months later. Otherwise, Joe behaved like a normal eight-year-old.

RELATED APPROACHES

Other therapists use paradoxical approaches without labeling their techniques as being paradoxical *per se*. Nelson, and her colleagues (1968) used the term "paradigm" to denote the interactions in which the therapist attempts to foster insight in the client by siding with his resistance and avoiding making interpretations. Sapirstein (1955) emphasized the importance of unconscious processes in the maintenance of paradoxical behavior. Farrelly and Brandsma (1974) labeled their brand of therapy as "Provocative Therapy" using symptom prescription and other double binding maneuvers.

Many of Rosen's (1953) techniques of direct therapy with psychotics involved a therapeutic double bind. When Rosen felt sufficient progress had been made, i.e., the client begins to let the therapist into his unconscious, a variety of techniques acknowledging the psychosis were intially employed. When a client began to make unsuccessful efforts at stopping his visions or voices, Rosen used magical gestures to stop the voices (e.g., repetitive strokes in the air, jumping and shouting, or drawings of antiwitchcraft figures posted on the wall). The client was intent on what Rosen was doing and did not hear the voices. After the client achieved some sense of reality, Rosen employed the technique of *reduction ad absurdum* which is an outright attack on the delusional system or suicidal impulses. He would observe loudly and with annoyance in front of the client who still insisted on dressing as Christ, "Isn't this the fourth Jesus Christ who's been here today?" He would portray the suicide attempt to the client who was no longer suicidal as the most absurd action he could have possibly taken. Both Haley (1955) and Andolfi (1974) viewed this technique in terms of a deliberate confusion of the symbol and the object symbolized. Rosen took his client's metaphorical statements seriously and then insisted they do the same. This technique dramatized the differences between metaphorical and literal messages leading to a clarification of the situation for the client who learned to discriminate between the two levels of messages. Haley (1955) emphasized the importance of reframing in this technique. A second technique employed by Rosen was re-enacting an aspect of the psychosis that bears some similarity to prescribing the symptom. Rosen would instruct a client who no longer heard voices but who was still in a rather shaky state to hear the voices again. The client, if all went well, insisted he did not hear anything while Rosen insisted he did. The client's coming back indignantly was a sure sign of a cure.

THE STATUS OF PARADOX—
THEORETICAL AND OTHER CONSIDERATIONS

Paradox as a therapeutic technique appears to have spotty recognition. In several recent reviews of psychotherapy, paradox was not mentioned (Usdin, 1975; Barter & Barter, 1973; Bergin & Barfield, 1971). Even more surprising is the absence of mention of paradox in recent family therapy publications (Bell, 1975; Howells, 1975, Flick & Kessler, 1974; Andrews, 1974; Zuk, 1971). Fox (Weiner, 1976) also did not mention paradox as a therapeutic technique but does mention the pathological double bind as a historical note. Friedman (1974) did, however, mention prescribing the symptom and relabeling in his alphabet of family therapy techniques. Dolliver (1972) also recognized the importance of paradoxical techniques in the conceptualization of opposites in pschotherapy.

THE WHY OF USING PARADOX

Regardless of the recognition or lack of recognition by psychotherapists, important questions surround the usage of paradoxical techniques: How are paradoxes formed; how does one deliver a paradox successfully; and theoretically, why do paradoxes work? Practitioners and theorists offer a variety of answers to the questions posed which will be briefly reviewed in this section.

The basic appeal of paradox is novelty. Straightforward interpretations by the therapist, particularly with families, have little chance of "shaking-up" the family system. Straightforward interpretations are frequently expected, and, therefore, easily ignored. A paradoxical communication, by presenting the familiar in a new unexpected light, has a greater chance of being heard and, by virtue of this novelty, has a greater potential for evoking change.

A second characteristic of a paradoxical communication is the apparent craziness of the suggestion. The communication seemingly goes against common sense and can even be termed nonsense. How can a client or clients be persuaded to follow a nonsensical directive? One obvious predisposing condition is the desperateness of the client(s). Hare-Mustin (1975) reports spending a great deal of time with her inquiry about the details of the presenting symptom. After laying this ground work, she begins prescribing the symptom. Rossi (1973) points out that the therapist sets up binding conditions prior to the paradoxical prescription. For example, the client promises in advance he will follow the therapist's directive without protest. Weakland et al. (1974) comment that a high pressure approach to presenting the paradox does not work, but a confused, ignorant stance on the part of the therapist seems to facilitate client compliance. Selvini-Palazzoli et al. (1975) observe that paradoxical interventions are more effective if spaced out over time.

There are many theoretical explanations as to how paradoxes work. Social psychology contributes some explanations. Attribution theory (Jones, 1971) is concerned with how an individual explains his world. People tend to think in terms of a linear, cause-effect context and employ social consensus as a criterion for validation of explanations. The presentation of a paradox in therapy provides an alternate, circular explanation or attribution of meaning for a given event. This "re-framing" affects the client's subsequent feelings and behavior about that event. The therapist and changed reactions of other family members are the social context for validating the new explanation of the event.

Laing's use of attribution and mystification in pathological situations (1963, 1971) can be translated into therapeutic paradoxes. The therapist attributes an alternate explanation of the behavior sequence at hand and then offers a cryptic prescription which he refuses to elaborate upon. The attribution denies the family's usual negative explanations of the given behavior and the mystification of the prescription keeps the clients in a state of confusion which circumvents their ignoring of what the therapist has said. Whitaker (1975) writes of the potency of the therapist's use of obscurity and absurdity in family therapy.

Transactional Analysis (TA) utilizes a straightforward approach to therapy. Steiner (1974) commented that the use of permission giving by the therapist in TA is criticized on the grounds that the client may react paradoxically and do the opposite of what the therapist indicates he should do. Steiner denies that this will result if the therapist is speaking from his Adult. Berger (1976) contends that in a deliberate paradoxical approach, an effective paradoxical message comes from the therapist's positive Parent and the client's Child does not dare comment that the message does not make sense. Hartman and Narboe (1974) reported on the protective aspects of certain pathological catastrophic injunctions.

The most widely held explanation for why the paradox works is based on the idea that some clients come to the therapist for help but are resistant to any help offered, in addition to provoking the therapist to try and fail (Adolfi, 1974). The use of paradox enables the therapist to implicitly tell the client to change by asking him not to change. This paradoxical communication, as derived from the Russellian paradoxes in classification systems (Reusch & Bateson, 1951; Haley, 1963) is not a contradiction in the sense that two levels of communication are involved. The higher level or metacommunication is an attempt to control the definition of the relationships (Anderson, 1972; Jackson, 1967). Thus, the therapist is perceived by the couple or family (each of whom have been resisting one another's attempts at defining the relationship already) as trying to define the relationship and unit to resist the therapist. To transcend this circular resistance, the therapist must use circular language (Selvini-Palazzoli et al., 1975). He makes his double binding request at the primary conscious level but effect change on the unconscious or metalevel (Erickson & Rossi, 1975).

The criticism can still be leveled that paradox, irregardless of the preceding theoretical explanations, still lies outside of adequate theoretical explanation. Weisskopf-Joelson (1975) points out that aspects of Frankl's technique of paradoxical intention remain outside the existential tenets of Logotherapy.

CONCLUSION

From this review about the use of paradoxical practices in family therapy, it is easy to see that most evidence is still impressionistic, incomplete, and, hence, questionable. One of the greatest needs in the use of paradoxical practices lies in finding more tenable theoretical, clinical, and empirical bases.

REFERENCES

Anderson, E.K. A review of communication theory within the family framework. *Family Therapy*, 1972, 1, 15-34.

Andolfi, M. Paradox in psychotherapy. *American Journal of Psychoanalysis*, 1974, 34, 221-8.

Andrews, E.E. *The emotionally disturbed family and some gratifying alternatives.* New York: Jason Aronson, 1974.

STAGES IN FAMILY THERAPY

Family interaction during therapy is a complex phenomenon with many variables changing simultaneously. Some individuals may feel that events occur in a confused and unpredictable manner, however an experienced therapist can discern order and patterns in the process. There has been considerable attention given to the phases or stages of individual and group therapy. However, the natural stages through which a family therapy system evolves are different from those usually described in other therapies. To cope with this problem, it is helpful to identify specific stages of development of process. Such abstraction is somewhat artificial because it oversimplifies the process and identifies stages that generally do not have sharp transition points from one to another. Even so, many writers believe that an understanding of the life stages can help a therapist place single event in perspective and help him or her to bring order out of the confusion for the family members.

Although several writers present conceptions of the life stages in family therapy, they present some different ideas. Two perspectives of staging in family therapy are presented here. Freeman describes three major phases of family therapy. This conceptualization shows there are significant differences in the processes and stages between individual and family therapy. Solomon proposes staging family therapy to permit the family to deal with their anxiety about therapy, relinquish their labeling of the identified patient and generalize their discomfort, explore how each member participates in the family pathology, plan problem solving, and then move away from the therapist.

413

PHASES OF FAMILY TREATMENT
DAVID S. FREEMAN

This paper discusses the phases or stages of family treatment. There has been a fair amount written on phases of treatment in individual and group work (Northen, 1969, Perlman, 1957, Smalley, 1967). However, this has not been so for work with families. The therapeutic process always has beginning, middle, and ending stages. This is true whether one is working with an individual, a therapeutic group, and/or a family system. In work with families the natural phases through which the system evolves are different from what one would expect in working with individuals. Some of the major differences will be highlighted in the following discussion.

The assumption underlying phases of treatment is that there is an orderly time sequence to work with a system. This time sequence affects how we involve ourselves in relationships, sustain that involvement, and end or terminate relationships. Whenever one moves into a new relationship it is with some degree of anxiety, uncertainty, and ambivalence. After a certain period of time in the relationship these feelings seem to dissipate and a sense of comfort or at least familiarity develops. As this occurs there is more openness about sharing self with another. However, when the relationship appears to be ending the old feelings of ambivalence and uncertainty return. Some of the same dynamics that occurred in the beginning of the relationship appear near the end or the terminating phase of the relationship. The natural phenomena of how people move into and out of relationships is similar to how people move into and out of therapeutic relationships. However, in work with families some additional dynamics seem to appear. Usually families do not seek treatment for their whole system. When a family does appear in treatment it is frequently because of problems within an individual member of the family or particular subsystem of the family, i.e., parent-child problems, spouse problems, sibling difficulties. The individual client who comes into a therapist's office is

_____

From D. Freeman, Phases of Family Treatment, *The Family Coordinator*, 25:265-70, 1976. Courtesy of the National Council on Family Relations.

414

quite clear that his problem rests within himself or if not within himself, in his inability to deal with the environment. Much of his anxiety, ambivalence, and uncertainty about entering therapy is based on his discomfort around being in a dependent relationship.

Families also come in with a defined problem but usually do not see it as a family problem. Thus, the first stage of family therapy consists of redefining the problem. The goal at this stage is to move the family from perceiving the problem as existing within one of its members to recognizing that all members of the family are involved. It's difficult to work with a family system if the family does not recognize that it is operating as a system, e.g., if one part of the system is hurting the whole system is hurting.

BEGINNING PHASE OF FAMILY WORK: REDEFINING THE PROBLEM

The first stage of family work then is to re-orient the family's thinking around what is troubling the family. This is not to say that the family is not coming in with legitimate concerns. Usually the family has evidence, documentation and a long history of experience with the particular problem they present. It is my belief that the family's commitment to their understanding of the problem and their determination to convince the therapist that the way they see the problem is the only way, can be more of a problem than the particular concern they have come in with. The struggle between the family and the therapist to define the problem is the heart of the first stage of family therapy. Carl Whitaker calls this the "struggle for structure."[1] If the family convinces the therapist to see the problem their way then the therapist has little to offer them. Their definition of the problem has already cemented them in a line of attack for dealing with the problem. However, if the therapist can influence the family to redefine what is going on and get a broader sense of the family's experiences there is a chance that new strategies and ideas for dealing with family concerns can be initiated. This first stage sets the foundation for all that is to follow.

A case example illustrating the dynamics of the first stage follows:

The "M" family sought help for Mrs. "M" whom they considered severely disturbed. Mrs. "M", age fifty-three, had been hospitalized off and on in psychiatric hospitals for eight years, with a diagnosis of paranoid schizophrenic. Mr. "M", age fifty-five, had never been in any type of treatment. The only other member of the nuclear family was Peter, age twenty. In the eight years that Mrs. "M" had been hospitalized the nuclear family had never been seen. There had been a number of sessions with Mr. and Mrs. "M", however, those sessions focused on

---

[1] Carl Whitaker discussed this point in a talk he gave at Burnaby Mental Health Centre, Burnaby, British Columbia, in 1972.

discussing Mrs. "M's" problems. The first family session was set up to assess whether this system could be seen as a whole.

When Mr. "M" and Peter were asked what brought them into the family session they referred to Mrs. "M's" craziness, and said they would be willing to do anything they could to help her. Peter was quick to say that he was there because his mother was psychotic and coming in was a way of getting her off his back. He added he had no problems of his own and was not quite sure his being there would help anyway. Mr. "M" reiterated what his son said and pointed out that his hands were full with having a wife he could not depend on. Mrs. "M" was more than willing to take total responsibility for all that was happening to the family and blamed her mental state as being responsible for the family disorder.

During the first session the position I took was to question the family's basic premise that Mrs. "M" was the total problem in the family. I began to ask each member of the family questions about what each wanted out of the family; what each had experienced as individuals within the family; what some of their own major concerns about self were; and whether members of the extended family had problems similar to theirs. As each member of the family began to respond to these questions it became clear that the parents' main concern was not Mrs. "M's" craziness, but rather their twenty year old son's mental state. Apparently, there had been emotional difficulties on both sides of the extended family. Mrs. "M" had an older sister who had been hospitalized in a psychiatric hospital from the age of fifteen until her death at age forty-four. She was also concerned that her son would develop a diabetic problem since her father and oldest sister both had serious diabetic problems. Mr. "M" also spoke of emotional problems in his extended family and was seriously worried about whether it was possible to transmit emotional problems through one's genes. Further discussion revealed that the main reason this couple had only one child was because "we did not want to play Russian roulette. There was mental illness on my wife's side and mental illness on my side, why take any more chances?" As the family began to redefine their concerns, the focus shifted from Mrs. "M" to concerns of other members of the family. As this was happening, Mrs. "M" became stronger, more articulate, and less willing to take all the problems of the family onto her own shoulders. Mr. "M" began to talk more about his son and was quite sure that one of the things he wanted to work on was having a better relationship with him. Mrs. "M" was quite verbal about wanting to have a better relationship with her husband and spoke of her concern about how he showed extreme anxiety and nervousness whenever she demonstrated any doubt or confusion about what she wanted or what her role should be in the family.

One way to assess whether a family has shifted from focusing on one member of the family to seeing concerns in terms of the family unit is to note how they begin each session. When they are still in the beginning stages the session will start with a complaint about a particular member of the family. When family members start the session with concerns about self and/or discussions about what new things they have started to work on, they have shifted from the beginning to the middle stage. I have found in my own clinical work that it takes anywhere from one to four sessions to move on to the middle stage.

MIDDLE PHASE: WORKING THROUGH STAGE

The middle phase of therapy is represented by the family's ability to recognize that as the family works together as a unit it can better meet both individual and group needs. There is less scapegoating, blaming, and reactive behavior. Individual members within the family begin to take more responsibility for their own behavior and the family becomes more of a resource system to itself. The anxiety and ambivalence about being in family therapy is lessened and the therapist is not as likely to be put in the position of mediator, side-taker, and expert.

One characteristic of this period is that the family begins to feel quite good about what is happening and the crises and difficulties that initially brought them to treatment no longer seem to exist. Many families terminate at this point in therapy. I think this is unfortunate because the family has not really learned enough about itself to withstand another crisis when it hits. The task of the therapist during this stage is to help the family further define or in some cases identify for the first time what other issues and concerns they can work on to meet their needs, both individually and collectively.

At this stage the therapist might need to be very active, asking questions which stimulate the family to identify those subsystems within the intra-familial and extra-familial networks that could be worked on. Discussing relationships with extended kin can help identify important areas of work. For example, if things are calm between parents and children in the nuclear family there might be some important work that could be done on the relationships between the adults and other extended family members.

In one family I worked with, the father moved from working successfully on his relationship with his daughter to wanting to become more involved with his oldest brother with whom he had always had a bad relationship. As he made a move towards his older brother, his wife began reevaluating her relationship with her older sister. The parents' work on their extended families was a help to the children in their work on their own sibling relationships. What was particularly interesting in this situation was that besides the poor relationships between parent and child, there was also severe conflict between the siblings. The parents' work on their own sibling relationships indirectly improved the relationships between their own children.

As mentioned previously, it might be crucial during the middle stage for the therapist to introduce new issues to the family. Systems theory teaches that there is a need to have new information entering the system to help the system learn more about itself and its connections with the outside world. The more dysfunctional a family system is the more likely it is to be cut off from the extra-familial relationships.

It is not unusual for a family that is experiencing severe intra-familial conflict to have very few resources available to itself. Most of the effort in these families seems to be around getting family to meet each other's needs. If these members themselves are very needy they tend to resent demands to meet other family members' needs, and serious conflict, dissatisfaction, and anger result. As the family branches out, begins to make contact with other systems and finds viable resources beyond its own intra-familial boundaries, it loosens up the demands for family members themselves to meet all the needs. This extension of boundaries is a major goal during the middle phase of family treatment. Even though the identified problem is no longer a major concern, no one knows for sure what the future holds and unless the family has viable links with extra-familial resources, i.e., extended family kin, peer relationships, etc., it will gradually close itself off again and some of the old problems may be reinstituted.

The middle phase of treatment is the heart of the family therapy process. The new resources that are built into the system, the redefining of what is family, and who is available to the family in times of crises, and the options and choices that the family and individual members within the family have become clear during this stage. If the family is successful in getting to this stage, the last stage, or the terminating stage, will take on a different flavor and display different dynamics than it would at this stage in individual work.

TERMINATING STAGE: THE LETTING GO STAGE

In individual work the terminating stage tends to be a very stressful, anxiety producing one. As mentioned early in the paper, many of the dynamics that were in evidence during the beginning stage appear again in the terminating stage. Their reappearance seems to be related to the issues of dependence, independence, the importance of the therapy structure to the individual and the degree to which the therapist has been responsible for the successes of the client system. In family work these dynamics should not be in evidence, during the ending phase. If, in fact, the therapist was successful in the beginning stage in redefining the problem as a family focused one and was able in the middle phase to help the family recognize that it had resources available outside the family, then the terminating phase will be a natural one. I think that the eventual success of family therapy rests on how naturally the terminating phase is experienced.

I have found that once families begin to expand their boundaries and recognize that there are many resources both within their own boundaries and outside of their boundaries, they no longer see formal family therapy as necessary. This decision is a natural and evolutionary one on their part. The families have moved from a reactive stage to a proactive one. The reactive stage is clearest during the beginning of family work when the family is taking the position that they are not responsible for what is going on and just need help in solving this one particular problem so everything will be O.K. As the process goes on, they move from this point to the proactive point where the family is able to take the position that it has the resources, the skills and the knowledge to get the job done. Their decisions are not reached by feelings of anxiety and panic but rather through thinking and feeling that they are in control of the situation and have the ability to determine what is best for self and the family as a group. When the family reaches this point it becomes quite natural for them to terminate therapy formally. The ambivalence, anxiety, and fear about leaving formal therapy is not in evidence.

A case example of this follows:

The "W" family came in for help because they were experiencing severe difficulties with their oldest son, age eleven. The family consisted of a father, age forty-five, a mother, age forty and two boys, ages eleven and six. This was the "W's" second experience with therapy. The first time the parents had seen a child psychiatrist because of severe behavioral problems in their older son who was then seven. During the initial interview the father was quick to define the problem for the family. He continued to see his older son as the problem, saying he was stubborn and refused to do anything that the family wanted to do. He was also concerned that the boy was not "masculine" enough and felt that most of the activities he was involved in where "feminine."

The mother agreed entirely with the father. They were both convinced that the eleven-year-old boy was the problem and said they had never had any difficulty with their six-year-old child. When family members were asked to talk about their other relationships, it became clear that the father, a senior executive in an aeronautics company, was seldom home. When he did come home, Mrs. "W" told him about all the problems she had with her son and he then proceeded to try to shape his boy up on the basis of what his wife said. There seemed to be very little involvement between husband and wife in their own relationship. Mrs. "W" was very involved with her boys and also had strong ties to her own parents. She divided her time between taking care of her children, meeting her husband's needs when he came home, and taking care of her aging parents. Mr. "W" seemed to have very little time for the family and the little time he did put aside he wanted to be conflict free.

The children, on the other hand, did not really know their father. The eleven-year-old boy complained that he did not know what his father did at work, seldom saw him and felt his father was always angry at him.

This concern was an eye opener to the father who did not realize his son wanted to know him better. Although he was aware that he was spending little time at home, he thought he was available to his whole family when he was there. Mrs. "W" was quick to say that in the past eleven years they had not been out alone and she felt they were growing apart.

By the third session this family had begun to redefine their problems. Rather than talking solely about their concerns over their eleven-year-old boy, they were discussing how they wanted the family to be structured to allow family activities and time for Mr. and Mrs. "W" to spend together without the children. By the fifth session the family was able to see how they had locked themselves into roles with the father being the disciplinarian; the mother, the complainer; the eleven-year-old, the one responsible for all the unhappiness that had accumulated in this family over time; and the six-year-old, the angel. When the family became aware of this pattern, the eleven-year-old said he knew what the problem in the family was. When asked what he meant he explained that whenever he was talking alone with his mother or father and they began to disagree, the other parent would jump in and he was never able to finish what he started with them. He added, "the problem is that we work in triangles." Interestingly, I had never used the term "triangle"[2] with this family but it had become part of their own rethinking process. Although the eleven-year-old was able to point out how each parent got in the middle between him and the other parent, at that point he was not able to recognize that he got in the middle when his mother and father tried to work something out. However, the family had made strides towards taking a more proactive stance to understand what was going on between all members within the family. By the ninth session this family was ready for termination. The father had decided to take his boy to visit his place of work and had dropped his concerns about his boy not being masculine enough. The husband and wife had already made arrangements to go on a short trip without the children.

The six-year-old no longer seemed like an angel. The eleven-year-old's behavior had changed; he was much more involved with the family and less reactive to family planning. At the same time the six-year-old began to act up. The parents were not so quick to see the six-year-old as a behavioral problem but rather interpreted his behavior as evidence of a

---

[2]Although I had never spoken of the triangle concept with this family, I thought in triangles and had, to myself, identified the major triangles in the family. It was interesting how quickly the family picked up and began to use the concept to understand how they operated as a family.

In any triangle, there are two insiders and one outsider. In a state of calm the two insiders are in the favored position. During periods of unrest one or the other of the insiders will make a move to involve the outsider and he is then in the favored position. Triangles are used as a means to stabilize and deal with conflict and unrest within systems. It is the major maneuver used to stabilize emotional systems.

Bowen (1966) provides a detailed explanation of the triangle concept.

shift that was taking place in the family. By giving him more attention and not reacting to his behavior as solely "bad" behavior, they were sure that it would settle down. A follow-up interview four months later demonstrated the wisdom of this thinking. Termination for this family was quite natural. They had assumed responsibility for what was going on in the family and no longer saw family therapy as necessary.

CONCLUSION

In order for the therapist to move through these phases with families there must be the recognition that families have the resources within themselves to resolve many of their own difficulties. When a family is highly anxious, in a stage of crisis and overwhelmed with problems, its tendency is to be reactive and to try to fend off chance. Some of the ways families do this are by scapegoating, by setting up someone outside of the family as the expert to resolve all the family's difficulties, by rallying a number of health services to take over the job of family functioning, and by blaming their misery on others.

Many of these behaviors are in evidence during the beginning phase of therapy. It's crucial for the therapist to recognize this and help the family reduce its anxiety by: broadening the family's understanding of the problem by pointing out who else is involved, bringing to light the resources the family has within itself to deal with its problems, highlighting the family's past successes in dealing with difficulties. Then the family should be able to move on to the next stage where they can begin to demonstrate competence in working on their own difficulties. One of the beautiful things about working with families is that we have built in resources right in front of us. Working with individuals in isolation from significant others makes it more difficult to rally these resources. Hence, a more dependent and intense relationship develops between client and therapist which influences each stage of the treatment process. When the family therapist capitalizes on the resources within the family the emotional intensity is spread throughout the family. The intensity of the therapeutic relationship and dependency on the therapist is not nearly as great. Thus, family systems are able to separate more easily from formal therapy.

REFERENCES

Bowen, M. The use of family theory in practice. *Comprehensive Psychiatry,* 1966, 7, 345-56.

Northen, H. *Social work with groups.* New York: Columbia University Press, 1969.

Perlman, H.H. *Social casework: Problem-solving process.* Chicago: University of Chicago Press, 1957.

Smalley, R. *Theory for social work practice.* New York: Columbia University Press, 1967.

Chapter 33

THE STAGING OF FAMILY TREATMENT: AN APPROACH TO DEVELOPING THE THERAPEUTIC ALLIANCE

MICHAEL A. SOLOMON

The engagement of families in the process of diagnosis and treatment is complex and perplexing. Therapists report an inability to sustain the process long enough for a therapeutic alliance to be formed.

Most theorists on the family have reinforced the need to be concerned about the process by which the therapist engages the family and develops the alliance for treatment. Luthman (1974) describes the need for flexibility and Minuchin (1974) approaches the issue in his discussion of the accommodation.

Family assessment must be staged so as not to prematurely permit the system to expose itself before an alliance which can handle the exposure is developed between the therapist and the family.

Cleghorn and Levin (1973) have alluded to the necessity for staging the treatment with the family. Their work highlights many of the negotiations which must take place between the family and therapist. However, it does not articulate clearly enough the content of the negotiations nor depict the interdependent nature of the stages of treatment.

Over the past five years this author has been engaged in a training effort directed at teaching family diagnosis and treatment to trainees in all of the mental health professions. The following description of the five stages for family treatment has been developed out of this experience.

The five stages must be negotiated in order (i.e., one before two, two before three, etc.). Failure to negotiate a stage in sequence endangers the family's continuance in treatment. Each stage provides a normal termination point for the family if they are unable to negotiate for continuance. Each stage deals specifically with aspects of the formation of the therapeutic alliance and negotiations require an increasing

From M. Solomon, The Staging of Family Treatment: An Approach to Developing the Therapeutic Alliance, *Journal of Marriage and Family Counseling*, 3:59-66, 1977. Courtesy of American Association for Marriage and Family Therapy.

commitment from the family system.

THE STAGES

Stage I—Consensus Among Members of the System to Participate in the Evaluative Procedure: Or, "How Do You Feel About Being Here Together With Me?"

This stage is designed to negotiate around several issues affecting the therapeutic alliance. The first issue is facilitating the family's evaluation of the loss of self esteem which is associated with the development of the problem and the subsequent need to request professional help. Most families have experienced this loss and are quite willing to share their feelings of fear, failure and worthlessness with a sensitive therapist. The empathy and reassurance of the therapist often creates the beginning of an alliance which permits the family to participate in further negotiations with greater ease and less conflict.

Secondly, the therapist must evaluate the basis of the family homeostasis. If the equilibrium of the family rests on the fact that family members remain isolated from one another (maximally distant) in order to avoid the pain and disappointment they associate with closeness, their request for treatment and the ensuing request by the therapist that the family be seen as a unit could create a problem at the outset (Solomon, 1974). The act of convening the family in one room at the same time serves to reduce the possibility that the system has to maintain the degree of isolation that it needed in the past to survive. In families where the homeostasis is characterized by minimal distance between members, the request for family sessions is viewed positively. However, the moment the therapist begins to relate to family members as individuals the tension develops. Often, at the outset of the first session all family members will give lip service to their complicity about attending but further exploration reveals a variety of resistive stances.

The maximally distant family (Solomon, 1974) can often respond to the therapist's inquiry of "How do you feel about being here together?" with fantasies of destruction related to what will happen if people within the family speak their piece. They will agree to participate, asking the therapist to exert control over the destructive possibilities in the interview. By contrast the minimally distant family will respond to this by members expressing the thoughts and feelings of other members, demonstrating that they have rules concerning the degree to which any family member may operate as an individual in the treatment situation.

Fantasies of marital couples usually reflect their wish that the therapist side with each of them against the other. In families with children the parents often view the therapist as an ally against the children and expect that the interview will serve to "shape up" the kids. In families where an identified patient has been selected, other family members are often resistive to identifying themselves as part of the problem. They agree to come if it will be helpful to the patient. The identified patient often receives enough gratification out of his "sick" role to comply with the family and maintain this role at the outset.

The therapist who begins to expose these undercurrents before he plunges into the presenting problem and precipitating factors allows himself to deal with a facet of resistance which is often missed in therapeutic encounters. The therapist at this juncture may spell out his role with the family as he exposes the wish of certain factions within the system to have him as an ally. He can also identify for family members the etiology of their discomfort about family meetings and suggest that a discussion of the problem need not take place until the family decides family sessions are to be the vehicle for such a discussion.

We have come to understand that the dynamics associated with the decision to seek out treatment for the family or one of its members are quite characteristic of the family's natural response to stress of any kind. Exposing the conflicts about coming for treatment lays the groundwork for exploring the non-productive processes utilized by the family.

The Whitlock Family. Mr. and Mrs. W., after 23 years of marriage, began to experience considerable tension with one another and felt the distance between them growing dangerously. In the first interview they were asked, "How do you feel about being here together with me?"

Mr. W., in an animated fashion, answered, "I am so relieved to be here! Ever since my wife had an affair four years ago our relationship has deteriorated." He went on to share intimate details of their sexual and emotional relationship. It appeared as though he could continue non-stop until the end of the hour.

I interrupted to find out how Mrs. W. was feeling about the appointment and their request for treatment as a couple. She spoke slowly and stated, "I am not sure how I feel about this. I am the kind of person who needs to survey a situation before I get involved. I don't know anything about you (speaking to the therapist), what your credentials for this kind of work are, if you are married and have a family. So I am not too sure." One is impressed with the disparity in the "beginnings" of each person. Speculating that, like most patients, each is anxious about the stress of the first meeting, they handle the anxiety in opposite ways. Mr. W. jumps right in overexposing himself without a relationship with the therapist, and Mrs. W. becomes somewhat retentive and withdrawn. The therapist should not ignore this. This disparity is probably present in many of the negotiations which take place within the family. They are demonstrating their characteristic adaptation as they each deal with their anxiety around the treatment question.

I asked Mrs. W. how she felt about the way her husband answered my question. She exploded at him saying, "You had not right to share those kinds of things with him without getting my permission. I'm angry and hurt" (she began to cry). "I feel that you've tricked me."

Mr. W. responded with defensive anger. "I assumed that was why we came here in the first place. If we are not going to talk about our problems, then let's forget the whole damn thing" (he is screaming).

Mrs. W. angrily retorts, "That's just fine with me. This was your idea, not mine." At this point Mr. and Mrs. W. are perched on the edges of their chairs ready for a departure from the office.

Dynamically, what occurred is that both came to the session with considerable anxiety and ambivalence. Their respective responses to these feelings helped them to behave in their characteristic defensive manner. The individual defenses were to the other partner quite threatening and provocative and led them into a collusion of anger which mitigated the part in each of them that had agreed to the appointment and wanted help. What remained was the pre-existing distance between them and their resistance to change, which was reinforced by the argument.

I pointed out that the appointment stimulated considerable feelings which they had neglected to share with one another. They agreed and went on to discuss how anxious they each were, their rationale for not telling the other, and identified that there was a rather significant disagreement between them about how they were going to participate in the treatment. In successive interviews this couple negotiated with one another for a participation plan and developed a consensus which allowed for continuance. Had consensus not developed, termination of the treatment would have been wise.

Stage II—General Discomfort Stage: Or, "How Do You Feel About Being a Member of This Family?"

This stage allows the family to continue to resolve the ambivalence identified in Stage I. The focus, however, is upon the family system and its provision of resources for its members. Whereas in Stage I consensus was developed around the issue that all family members can be present and that it is safe to have family meetings, Stage II is designed to identify that the symptom carriers in the family are expressing a problem that is likely common to all family members. This stage helps the family evaluate the variety of adaptations they use in order to decide if the system is operating effectively and economically for all members. In Stage II the therapist directs the family's attention from the various symptoms apparent in its members to the general conflicts in family members that motivate these symptoms. Often during this stage the symptom bearers relinquish their symptoms, the family becomes disorganized and searches frantically for a new symptom to re-establish the familiar equilibrium. The therapist attempts to direct the family to a new alternative equilibrium. This is accomplished by a series of interventions which identify, a) the common problem for each family member, b) consensus among family members that they agree upon the common problem, and c) that the problem is one which is interfering with the continued growth and development of the family (Solomon, 1973).

It is important to emphasize here that often therapists assume that identification of a common problem indicates consensus and an evaluation of the non-productive nature of the problem. This is not so. The therapist must explore these steps specifically. The following illustrates a family in Stage II of the treatment process.

The Richter Family. The R. family presented with an "allegedly" schizophrenic fourteen year old daughter who had been in psychotherapy with six or seven individual therapists with little or no change. The patient had recently destroyed her room, thrown a television set out of a window, and ripped up all of her clothes. The family consisted of Father, age forty-three; Mother, forty-two; Karen, sixteen; Dora, fourteen (I.P.); Sarah, eleven; and David, nine.

In the first interview the family expressed their willingness to be there and agreed that Dora's problems affected them and that to be seen together seemed reasonable.

In the second interview they began to describe Dora's bizarre behavior (symptoms) as the problem. I stated that when Dora had feelings she handled them by acting them out. I pointed out that the family could always tell what Dora's feelings were by assessing her behavior. I then asked what the rest of them did when they had feelings like Dora's. Mother said, "I would probably leave the house and go to the beauty parlor or take a long drive until the feelings went away." Mr. R. said, "I would probably stay at work for a couple extra hours until I felt better." David said, "I would draw a picture of the person I was angry at, stick it on a tree and throw rocks at it until it was all torn up." Sarah said, "I would probably go to my room, put my head under the pillow and cry until I felt better."

Mother began to see that everyone had ways of dealing with their feelings and that no one depended upon anyone in the family to understand or help them. She began to get anxious and stated, "We haven't heard from Karen. She's the strongest of us and the one whom we all depend upon." Karen's eyes filled with tears and she began to cry. Through her tears she confessed, "I have been thinking about killing myself for the last six weeks." The family was stunned and silent. The therapist pointed out that in many ways each family member could better understand Dora and her inability to talk about how she felt and that she acted it out instead, for each had described how they do very much the same thing. The family went on to discuss their general loneliness. Together they decided the discussion was upsetting and they felt like they wanted to stop coming, but to live this way was intolerable. Consensus about continuing was established.

In this vignette I attempted to divert the family's attention from Dora's symptoms to what motivated them. Next, the family members were asked to evaluate themselves in regard to this issue. The family began to experience the conflict which originally was thought to exist exclusively in Dora. With support from the therapist, the family developed consensus on the definition of the problem and on its significance. Continuation in treatment was negotiated.

Stage III—Specific Discomfort: Or, "How Do You Understand The Hows and Whys of The Roles That You Assume In The Family and How That Fits With the Hows and Whys of The Role Assumption of Other Family Members."

This stage focuses on family members' insight into the etiology of their own behavior, of the behavior of other family members and the complementarity of behavior.

In this stage the therapist directs family members' attention to the transference which characterizes family interaction. The therapist focuses upon positive as well as negative transferences. The goal here is to assist the family in discriminating those specific aspects of their relationship which interfere with the process of continuing growth and development. Much of the work in this stage superficially resembles the work that is done in individual psychotherapy. Certainly as family members review their past life experiences the interactions between family members and therapist are a parallel to the interactions that occur in individual psychotherapy. However, the goal of this introspective exercise is not to share information with the therapist but rather to share information with other family members.

In this sense, a couple who present with the problem of alcoholism of one spouse will be directed away from the symptom to the issue of dependence vs. independence. Both spouses often learn that in their own lives they were never permitted appropriate expression of their needs for dependent relationships. Each sees that they have adapted to this experience in opposite ways. One learns to be inappropriately dependent by drinking and the other adapts by becoming inappropriately independent and caring for the alcoholic.

The identification of the similarity of conflicts and the disparity in adaptation is the essence of this stage. It is out of this discrimination that the capacity develops on the family's part to understand their complementary role relationships. Then the therapist is in a position to guide the family in identifying the general nature and etiology of this complementarity as it appears throughout the process of family interaction.

The Langer Family. Mr. and Mrs. L. and their two children, ages four and eight, came to treatment because of the consistent tension and hostility in the family's daily life. David, aged eight, was a chronic diabetic, prone to frequent difficulties and hospitalizations seemingly related to the family's inability to organize a consistent plan for diet and medication.

In Stage III of the family's treatment, David announced, "I wish I could be hospitalized once a month for the rest of my life!" The family, shocked by this, began to question him. He shared that when he was critically ill his parents seemed to get along fine, each having "jobs" related to caring for him. When he was regulated, they fought a lot or did not speak to one another. I proceeded to help the family explore this with David, who had confessed that he actively sustained himself out of control as a way of establishing some sort of tolerable equilibrium within the family.

The exploration of David's symptom led to the uncovering of the core conflict between Mr. and Mrs. L. Mrs. L. was the product of a family in which dependence was viewed as a "repulsive quality." She and her sister were prematurely encouraged to deny their dependent longings at all cost. Mrs. L. adapted to this by recreating the caretaking situation and always assumed the role of caretaker. She did so with considerable conflict. On the one hand she was gratified by giving to others, on the other, she experienced considerable rage and depletion in the process. Mr. L. was encouraged to avoid independence at all cost. He adapted with a pervasive passivity and participated with considerable conflict. While he appeared quite passive on the surface, his anger and aggressiveness were demonstrated as he acted them out in his passive role. He would often agree to come home at 5:00 p.m. and then forget. He would pursue his own independent interests without having negotiated the time for them with his wife or family. His passive/aggressive behavior often provoked his wife's rage and feelings of depletion.

In Stage III of the L.'s treatment, two levels of complementarity were explored. The first level was related to the complementarity between David's lack of regulation and the balance that it provided for the marital relationship. This uncovered the complementarity in Mr. and Mrs. L.'s adaptation to the conflicts that each had around the area of dependence and independence. Mr. and Mrs. L. had transferred their respective conflicts from their families of origin and had begun to socialize their children to the task of assisting them in sustaining the conflict in an unresolved state.

The family's awareness of this complex system of complementarity was crucial to their making the decision to work together to modify the conflict and develop a consensus among themselves to change the structure of the family.

Stage IV—Change Stage: Or, "Now That You Understand How Uncomfortable You Are and How You Each Participate In Maintaining the Discomfort, What Do You Want To Do About It?"

This stage is designed to help the family in operationalizing the insight developed at Stage III. The therapist must understand that insight does not guarantee change. Many families at the conclusion of Stage III, preparatory to moving into this change stage, experience considerable disorganization and pain. The family often ambivalently defends against change and the concomitant relinquishment of their old homeostasis by regression, the return to old ways of relating or by changing in such a major way that the system becomes overloaded.

Intervention by the therapist can assist family members in processing their change anxiety and proceeding with planned change comensurate with the capacity of the family system.

The Bales Family. The B. family came to treatment around the school problems of their youngest child, Alex, age eleven. The family consisted of Mrs. B., age thirty-nine; Mr. B., forty; Alex, eleven; Sharon, fourteen; and Lisa, sixteen.

During the treatment the family came to understand a great deal about their structure. It became clear that Mr. B., who at age nine had lost his father, had experienced an overbearing relationship with his mother. She was very controlling and needed to know where he was at all times. Mrs. B., on the other hand, had a relationship with her father that was extremely tenuous. He would disappear for months at a time without anyone in the family knowing where he was. Mr. B.'s adaptation to his experience was to be extremely permissive and distant in all relationships in order to avoid the pain he fantasied would be associated with loss. Mrs. B. dealt with the rejection in her relationship with her father by needing to be involved intensely. In the B.'s relationship with one another and with their children, they were always in conflict due to the extreme positions they assumed with regard to autonomy. The family came to understand they all had feelings of wanting to be close to one another and at the same time wanted to be separate. They saw that they had difficulty achieving a satisfactory ground on the matter. Everyone was either isolated from everyone else or too symbiotic and dependent.

This insight was operationalized when Lisa wanted to go on a high school trip with her classmates. Her ambivalence about the trip was demonstrated in two major ways. First, she didn't tell the family until very late. Second, she had difficulty getting herself together to find a job and make money to defray part of the expense of the trip. Mr. B., characteristically was subtly supportive of Lisa and wanted to give her the money to go on the trip. In a sense, he denied the part of Lisa that did not want to go. Mrs. B. was very controlling of Lisa, increased her household responsibilities, making it more difficult for Lisa to get a job. Mrs. B. also verbally kept after Lisa, telling her she did not feel she wanted the trip because she was doing "nothing" to accomplish the financial end of it. Mrs. B. seemed to be denying the part of Lisa that wanted the trip. The other two children split their allegiances. One went to the father's side, one to mother's. Understandably, the family became very disorganized and a crisis developed.

The family was helped to review the insight they had gained in Stage III, to express how frightened they felt that Lisa was "doing her own thing," and how everyone seemed to be handling their fear of the loss of Lisa in old, non-productive ways. The end result was a family plan in which Lisa was to earn less money than previously agreed upon, mother relieved her of the household responsibilities which had to be temporarily assumed by the other two children, and everyone seemed mutually supportive. Lisa was able to take the trip and the family experienced shared satisfaction over their joint accomplishment.

In Stage IV, the family abandoned their insight in favor of a defensive pattern that protected the parents from the pain of earlier rejection and loss, and protected the children from the pain and loss associated with individuation and separation. The therapist assisted the family in dealing with their anxiety about change in order to apply the insight acquired earlier to a present family problem. The operationalization of the insight provided the family with an increased sense of adequacy and system satisfaction.

Stage V—Termination: Or, "We've Got To Stop Meeting Like This!"

Termination of family treatment has similarities to termination of any form of treatment. It is characterized by temporary regressions, denial and sadness. It is crucial in this form of treatment for the therapist to pick up clues to the family's readiness for termination. The family should not be continued to the point that they fantasy that the changes they have made are completely attributed to the presence of the therapist. Since treatment is aimed at a repair of the problem-solving mechanism of the family rather than at the solution of specific problems, the therapist needs to begin to negotiate the termination with the family when it appears that the problem-solving mechanism is productively operational, not when all of the presenting problems have been solved.

It has been my experience that an appropriate termination with a family takes less time than termination with individuals in traditional psychotherapy. This reduction in time is related to the development of relationship resources within the family during the third and fourth stages of treatment. The family, at termination, does not experience the loss of the therapist so significantly because they have connected with one another in a way that mediates the degree to which the loss is experienced.

The Collins Family. Mr. and Mrs. C. had been in family and marital therapy for over a year and a half. One month before termination they experienced a crisis at home having to do with a vacation that Mr. C. had planned with his brother. It encroached on Mrs. C.'s need to have a vacation during which she did not have to concern herself with the needs of others. Mr. C. had planned the vacation with a "bare bones" of negotiation with his wife and she had gone along with this. Before they came in for their marital session they had understood their respective "craziness." They negotiated with one another and planned to spend part of the vacation with Mr. C.'s brother and the rest by themselves. In the session they merely reported the outcome which enabled the therapist to support them in identifying the productiveness of their problem-solving mechanism and to point out to them that the negotiations around the vacation could prove useful on a variety of other issues. The next week they again reported they averted a crisis around budgeting. They observed as they discussed money that the negotiations were similar to what occurred in planning their vacation. In the last half of this session they raised the issue of termination and proceeded to plan to terminate in two weeks.

This example demonstrates a minor regression around the vacation planning and a quick modification of that process. The therapist moved in and supported the modification and suggested a generalization of the family's problem solving method. The family went on to demonstrate without regression their capacity to do this in relation to finances, and termination followed quite logically and quickly.

DISCUSSION

This staging of family treatment is helpful in allowing the therapist to focus his interventions with the family. It permits a gradual development of commitment on the part of the family to understanding the original description of the problem as one involving the entire family network. The gradual development of the understanding does not seem to overload most families.

This conceptualization of the stages of treatment allows for two decidedly different approaches to change in families. If a family is desirous and possesses the capacity, they may progress through all five stages of treatment. The result should be change based upon insight into the etiology of the maladaptive homeostasis which existed prior to the treatment. However, it is important to realize that insight is not the only road to change. Some families do not have the predisposition, the resources or the time for this form of the process. Therefore, it is important for the therapist to be able to offer another route to these families. In this model of the stages of treatment, a family can move from Stage II directly to Stage IV, skipping the insight portion of the treatment. If the family demonstrates that they can make the necessary shift in their structure and sustain these changes, they are demonstrating their lack of need for insight. This should be supported and valued by the therapist.

REFERENCES

Cleghorn, J.M. and Leven, S. Training Family Therapists by Setting Learning Objectives. *American Journal of Orthopsychiatry*, 43(3):440, April, 1973.

Luthman, S.G. and Kirschenbaum, M. *The Dynamic Family*. Palo Alto: Science and Behavior Books, Inc., 1974, 53-65.

Minuchin, S. *Families and Family Therapy*. Cambridge: Harvard University Press, 1974, 124-125.

Solomon, M.A. Typologies of Homeostasis and Their Implications in Diagnosis and Treatment of the Family. *Family Therapy* (The Journal of the Family Therapy Institute of Marin), 1(1):9-18, 1974.

Solomon, M.A. Developmental, Conceptual Premise for Family Therapy. *Family Process*, 12(2):179-188, June, 1973.

LEGAL, VALUES, AND ETHICAL CONSIDERATIONS

It is important for therapists to be aware of their own personal values and to function within the parameters of professional ethics. A therapist's beliefs will certainly influence his or her behavior in family therapy. The goals, activities, and decisions a person makes are reflections of values the person has established. Values are personal criteria that include ideals, goals, norms, and standards of behavior. Values are generally learned from significant others, and when a person encounters new situations conflicts may arise. Therapists must not only be aware of their own values but be sensitive to those of the family and the possibilities for conflict. Ethics are suggested standards of behavior based on a consensus of values. Family therapists have attempted to translate as many values as possible into structural expectations of behavior. These are translations from the professional code of ethics. An understanding of these codes can serve as a guideline for therapists throughout family therapy. The therapist's role presents situations that could result in legal action. The potential for legal action is increasing, and it is important for therapists to be aware of their legal status.

Himes and Hare-Mustin call attention to some of the ethical problems that may arise in family therapy. When the treatment of a family involves several members whose needs conflict, the therapist may face complex ethical issues. Ethical questions arise when reluctant members are required to attend, expression of hostile feelings is encouraged, or the therapist forms an alliance with certain members. They recommend that ethics training include the therapist's own values as well as ethical issues.

Gansheroff, Boszormenyi-Nagy, and Matrullo present guidelines for writing family therapy records that are clinically meaningful but not unnecessarily damaging to a family member or the therapist in case the records are subpoenaed. They suggest that when writing in a record, the therapist remembers that individuals are part of a family. Patient rights to privacy must be safeguarded by omitting potentially damaging or embarrassing material.

Chapter 34

ETHICAL CONCERNS IN FAMILY THERAPY

PAULETTE M. HINES AND RACHEL T. HARE-MUSTIN

Increasing attention is being directed today to the fact that the objectives of change agents may interfere with individual privacy and human rights. The ethical concerns of which psychotherapists must be aware are compounded and made more complex in instances in which they intevene with an entire family in therapy.

This article is an effort to call attention to ethical problems that may arise in the context of family therapy. Family therapy at present is more of an orientation than an agreed upon set of procedures (Montalvo & Haley, 1973); some family therapists conduct interviews with an entire family, others with various subgroups or with subgroups and the entire family concurrent with individual therapy for a given family member. It is important to recognize that the therapeutic relationship with the family implies a contract with and responsibility to each member.

Despite increasing concern about ethical practice and patient rights, a review of the literature yields a surprising dearth of guiding ethical principles that may be used by practicing family therapists. Some principles, such as competence, which is the ethical issue par excellence, apply in all therapies (Hare-Mustin, 1974). Family therapists must first ask themselves what training or supervision they have had in this modality that qualifies them to use it. We have singled out three major areas of ethical concern for consideration: (a) the goal of maximizing the growth of the entire family, (b) the issue of confidentiality, and (c) the myth of valueless thinking.

Maximizing the Growth of the Entire Family

In family therapy, the therapist attempts to maximize the growth of the family as a whole, as well as that of individual family members. Frequently, within the confines of the therapy hour, the therapist may encourage direct expression of negative affect and evoke and escalate

From P. Hines and R. Hare-Mustin, Ethical Concerns in Family Theapy, *Professional Psychology*, 9:165-71, 1978. Copyright 1978 by the American Psychological Association. Reprinted by permission.

family confrontations as well (Minuchin, 1974). Although family members may be fully aware of each other's hostile feelings, they may not be accustomed to direct verbalizations of hatred, especially in the presence of nonfamily members. The therapist who encourages the expression of anger but is not concerned with preventing these behaviors from occurring outside the therapy room (Mace, 1976) runs the risk of promoting family dissolution and early termination of the therapeutic contract. The therapist can guard against family disintegration by inoculation, that is, by altering the family during the initial stage of therapy to the stresses that may be expected in resolving long-term conflicts.

Breaking down a family's mode of interaction, promoting change in one family member, or change in an area of familial functioning may evoke new or increased distress and dysfunction in other family segments. Different family members at various stages may need added support, if not concurrent individual therapy. An alliance with any family member when it is at the expense of other members, regardless of how psychologically healthy they appear to be, must be carefully weighed against overall goals. The therapist may have stated or implied a position of nonalignment when establishing the initial therapeutic contract, which is now being violated.

A frequently voiced question arises from consideration of the family member being seen by the therapist in individual therapy. Whose interest is the therapist ethically bound to serve? Some therapists (Grosser & Paul, 1964) espouse the view that if the progress of the patient seen in individual treatment is of primary concern and is dependent upon family participation, the clinician must try to involve the family in treatment. Family therapists seem not to have given adequate attention to the basic issue of requiring all family members to participate. As Silber (1976) has pointed out, the prevailing "therapeutic ideology" is that we assume all persons can and should benefit from therapy. However, legal questions are being raised as to whether a person has a right *not* to be treated. This could very well apply to reluctant adult and adolescent participants, as well as children brought to family therapy sessions. Recent concern for children's rights is long overdue. Issues of informed consent are especially difficult when children are involved (Smith, 1967). Similar questions arise in cases in which there appear to be irreconcilable differences between family members. The therapist must examine the situation critically, for dissolution of the family unit may prove to be beneficial for some but not for other family members.

Another issue is the possibility that family members may suffer from embarrassment, a high level of anxiety, and a loss of respect in the eyes of other family members as a result of disclosure of failures in family therapy session discussions. Grosser and Paul (1964) considered this to be a quasi-ethical concern. They asserted that parents are often relieved when others in their family realize that they are not omnipotent and faultless. In the case of more controversial subject matter (e.g., sexual difficulties), Minuchin (1974) believed the therapist should protect the spouses' privacy. Therapists differ in the boundaries they wish to place around different subsystems in the family, but they should always be aware of the ethical, as well as the treatment, issues involved in including or excluding various family members.

Confidentiality

Within the family system, different members vary in their capacity to be open and honest. Information may be transmitted to the therapist in family subgroups or individual sessions by persons unwilling to reveal information when the entire family is assembled. Thus, therapists often find themselves in possession of information that could be therapeutically employed for the well-being of the entire family system.

Whether the therapist has avoided or has encouraged a confidential relationship, the issue is, Do family members have the right to question the therapist and receive information about another member? Mariner (1971) advanced the position that prior agreement on the parts of all involved is necessary before communication of information revealed to the therapist is released—and then only to very close family associates. Guidelines for those conducting growth groups suggest that information on such issues as confidentiality should be made available in writing to prospective participants (American Psychological Association, 1973).

There are several modes of action available to therapists who announce their stands on "privileged communications" at the onset of therapy (Committee on the Family, 1970). First, they may state at the beginning of therapy that they will not keep secrets. When family members reveal information that another member or they themselves are in imminent danger, the therapist may need to inform the family in order to elicit their aid. The California Supreme Court recently judged that a therapist must inform an intended victim (Whiteley & Whiteley, 1977), so such disclosure may become a matter of law rather than solely an ethical issue. Whether cases of marital infidelity should be revealed also has ethical as well as treatment implications. Therapists who advocate nonsecrecy may find it hard to maintain such positions when the consequences for all participants are thoroughly examined.

A second option open to the therapist in regard to confidentiality is to accept confidences with the intent of working with a family member's resistance to openly revealing information to the family. The therapist may help such persons to reveal their secrets to the family or may seek the person's permission to use the information in family sessions. The therapist who follows the second line of action, as well as one who encourages or accepts individual confidences and vows to keep secrets isolated from the family, may be confronted with the same dilemma.

Privileged communications cannot help but bias the way the therapist perceives the family, as well as the interventions she or he chooses to make. Thus, it is an open-ended question about how honest the therapist is to promise absolute confidentiality to a family member.

Problems also arise with relatives outside the family therapy group. Mariner (1971) suggested that besides informing the person who phones that his or her information may be used in therapy, the person should be informed that the patient or family must be apprised of the call. Extreme caution in telephone conversations where the caller's identity is not certain is advised.

There appears to be a gap between what therapists perceive their legal position to be and what it actually is in regard to the issue of confidentiality (Marsh & Kinnick, 1970). Privilege refers to immunity from criminal and/or civil action for what one says or refuses to say. It may be absolute or conditional. Recent court decisions (e.g., Ziskin, 1971) leave no room for doubt that the privileges granted to many psychotherapists are at best conditional.

The courts are becoming increasingly involved in conflicts that arise between psychotherapists and their clients. Therapists are being required to support their claims of "accepted and proficient practices" with the establishment of peer review organizations. Although professional groups have developed ethical standards to guide their conduct (see American Psychological Association, 1977), it appears that "unless ethical and professional standards promulgated by professional associations afford adequate safeguards to members of the general public, said standards afford little or no protection to the professional from either criminal prosecution or civil (malpractice) action" (Roston & Sherrer, 1973, p. 271).

The Myth of Valueless Thinking

As London (1977) has pointed out, we can no longer question the powerful influence of the therapist's values but can only decide the manner in which those values are permitted to influence the therapeutic transaction. For a therapist to tell a family what is "good" is different from the therapist's facilitating a family's own ability to clearly assess their options (Engelhart, 1973). "Can the individual family member also be considered a captive of the therapist's notions of how a family should be changed" (Boszormenyi-Nagy & Spark, 1973, p. 363)? The personal and professional values that provide direction for therapists' manipulations (e.g., assertiveness, autonomy, emotional closeness) may conflict not just with one person's value system but with those of the entire family. Therapists are often unaware of the extent to which their own personal and professional values govern therapeutic moves, to the exclusion of recognizing the uniqueness of the family situation and the net effect of disturbing the family system. Behaviors which therapists seek to change may appear pathological when viewed in a traditional context but have adaptive value within the family's own ecological setting.

Dishonesty on the part of therapists may often be fully recognized by clients according to Halleck (1963). Consider, for instance, the suggestion that impulses are easily modified. Adolescents, especially, recognize that success in this world is not dependent upon such restraint and that conformity may or may not lead to resolution of the adolescent's difficulties. Therapists may unwittingly encourage in their clients certain behaviors that would not be in their best interests from a legal point of view. This is especially true when there are marital conflicts or custody issues that might lead to litigation among family members (Hare-Mustin, 1976; Robitscher, 1972).

Therapists need to direct their attention to the impact that stereotypes based on gender, social class, ethnicity, and education may have on their motivation to initiate and continue treatment with a family, on their choice of interventions, and on their interpretation of unsuccessful outcome (Sabshin, Dressenhaus, & Wilkerson, 1970). Patients may be labeled *resistant* and *poor risks for therapy* for numerous reasons. It is ethically incumbent upon therapists to examine how their expectations and biases may ultimately lead to fulfillment of their prophesies. This is not to say that one can ignore empirical evidence and clinical experience which indicate that the personality characteristics of certain clients, especially as they interact in family systems, make them unlikely to benefit from particular methods of psychotherapy. We, however, do feel justified in pointing out the tendency of some therapists to characterize any person or family who does not respond to their method of treatment as psychologically unsophisticated. Therapists must examine the long-term significance of the labels they use and the extent to which these labels follow from an inability to deal with value systems different from their own.

Conclusion

A review of the literature indicated that relatively little attention has been directed to ethical issues in family psychotherapy. This fact is congruent with the lack of systematic ethics training in most graduate programs and the growing involvement of the courts in resolving conflicts between therapists and their clients. Family therapists, in particular, must increase their awareness of the multiple means by which their actions may impinge upon the rights of the persons they seek to serve. As Hobbs (1965) has pointed out, ethics is not just a guide to conduct but "the very essence of the treatment process itself" (p. 1508).

There is not only a need for increased awareness but also for expansion of existing ethical guidelines. Several proposals may be considered toward this end:

1. Ethical training should be an integral part of professional training programs (Shore & Golann, 1969).

2. Workshops, seminars, and in-service training should be employed to facilitate discussion and development of feasible ethical guidelines.

3. Present ethical principles should be spelled out sufficiently to be of value in the day-to-day endeavors of family therapists.

4. Ethical standards are empirically derived and thus become dated; they should be periodically updated (Hobbs, 1965).

5. Therapists must continually scrutinize themselves regarding their honesty, competency, stereotypes, and biases.

6. Family therapists must utilize the knowledge of persons in other disciplines, particularly in regard to the legalities of therapy (Marsh & Kinnick, 1970).

7. The formulation of policies to be presented to legislators should be a major focus of psychotherapy conventions.

In summary, the ethical issues involved when one intervenes in the world of the family are exceedingly complex; they may never be totally agreed upon nor resolved. However, it is ethically incumbent upon family therapists to continually examine the complex ways their interventions can affect the lives of family members.

REFERENCES

American Psychological Association. Guidelines for psychologists conducting growth groups. *American Psychologist*, 1973, *28*, 933.

American Psychological Association. *Ethical standards of psychologists* (Rev. ed.). Washington, D.C.: Author, 1977.

Boszormenyi-Nagy, I., & Spark, G.M. *Invisible loyalties*. New York: Harper & Row, 1973.

Committee on the Family. The field of family therapy. *Group for the Advancement of Psychiatry*, 1970, *78*, 594-603.

Engelhardt, H. Psychotherapy as meta-ethics. *Psychiatry*, 1973, *36*, 440-445.

Grosser, G., & Paul, N. Ethical issues in family group therapy. *American Journal of Orthopsychiatry*, 1964, *34*, 875-884.

Halleck, S. The impact of professional dishonesty on behavior of disturbed adolescents. *Social Work*, 1963, *8*, 48-56.

Hare-Mustin, R.T. Ethical considerations in the use of sexual contact in psychotherapy. *Psychotherapy: Theory, Research and Practice*, 1974, *11*, 308-310.

Hare-Mustin, R.T. The biased professional in divorce litigation. *Psychology of Women Quarterly*, 1976, *1*, 216-222.

Hobbs, N. Ethics in clinical psychology. In B. Wolman (Ed.), *Handbook of clinical psychology*. New York: McGraw-Hill, 1965.

London, P. *Behavior control* (2nd ed.). New York: New American Library, 1977.

Mace, D.R. Marital intimacy and the deadly love-anger cycle. *Journal of Marriage and Family Counseling*, 1976, *2*, 131-137.

Mariner, A. Psychotherapists' communications with patients' relatives and referring professionals. *American Journal of Psychotherapy,* 1971, *25,* 517-529.

Marsh, J., & Kinnick, B. Let's close the confidentiality gap. *Personnel and Guidance Journal,* 1970, *48,* 362-365.

Minuchin, S. *Families and family therapy.* Cambridge, Mass.: Harvard University Press, 1974.

Montalvo, B., & Haley, J. In defense of child therapy. *Family Process,* 1973, *12,* 227-244.

Robitscher, J. The new face of legal psychiatry. *American Journal of Psychiatry,* 1972, 129, 315-321.

Roston, R., & Sherrer, C. Malpractice: What's new? *Professional Psychology,* 1973, *4,* 270-276.

Sabshin, M., Dressenhaus, H., & Wilkerson, R. Dimensions of institutional racism in psychiatry. *American Journal of Psychiatry,* 1970, *127,* 787-793.

Shore, M., & Golann, S. Problems of ethics in community mental health: A survey of community psychologists. *Community Mental Health Journal,* 1969, *5,* 452-460.

Silber, D.E. Ethical relativity and professional psychology. *The Clinical Psychologist,* 1976, *29*(3), 3-5.

Smith, M.B. Conflicting values affecting behavioral research with children. *American Psychologist,* 1967, *22,* 377-382.

Whiteley, J., & Whiteley, R. California court expands privilege debate. *APA Monitor,* February 1977, pp. 5; 6; 18.

Ziskin, J. Psychology and the law. *Professional Psychology.* 1971, *2,* 202-204.

CLINICAL AND LEGAL ISSUES
IN THE FAMILY THERAPY RECORD

NEAL GANSHEROFF, IVAN BOSZORMENYI-NAGY, AND JOHN MATRULLO

I n writing a family therapy record, the therapist must strike a delicate balance between including enough information to make the material clinically meaningful and useful and avoiding, as much as possible, the inclusion of material that may be legally damaging, shameful, or embarrassing to individual members of the family. When he makes an entry, the therapist should remember that the record may not always be left untouched in the file drawer. It may be needed by another therapist for continuity of care or used to satisfy accreditation standards. Or it may be subpoened as evidence in a malpractice or divorce suit or in a child-custody case.

The family psychiatry department of the Eastern Pennsylvania Psychiatric Institute recently revised its format for keeping family charts and established guidelines for writing the charts. Those guidelines emphasize the need for therapists to consider four main, somewhat overlapping, aspects when writing records: hospital accreditation standards, clinical aspects, legal aspects, and respect for patients' privacy.

Therapists working in centers accredited by the Joint Commission on Accreditation of Hospitals must pay special attention to the commission's standards for writing medical records. Every two years the commission inspects those hospitals, including their medical records. If the records are considered completely unacceptable, hospitals can lose, and in fact some have lost, their accreditation. The standards are contained in the *Accreditation Manual for Psychiatric Facilities* and require, among other things, that "The medical record shall contain sufficient information to identify the patient clearly, to justify the

From N. Gansheroff, I. Boszormenyi-Nagy, and J. Matrullo, Clinical and Legal Issues in the Family Therapy Record, *Hospital and Community Psychiatry*, 28:911-13, 1977. Courtesy of the American Psychiatric Association.

diagnosis, to delineate the treatment plan, and to document the results accurately."[1]

CLINICAL ASPECTS

Many therapists who may be quite adept at writing a meaningful, high-quality record for an individual patient have major difficulties organizing and satisfactorily recording the wealth of complex, interrelated data obtained in treating an entire family. It is one thing to write a record on a single patient; it is quite another to write one about two adults, usually parents, and possibly several children that portrays each as an individual and yet conveys their complex nuclear- and extended-family relationships. If the records are to be meaningful, both individual and family data must be recorded.

Two basic questions should be asked to determine if the records will aid in the clinical management of the case and in a possible legal defense: does the chart tell what is happening in the family, and does it justify a particular therapeutic or administrative decision?[2] As an illustration of such a justification, take the case of a therapist who, in the initial sessions, is faced with parents who want to focus only on their symptomatic child. He elects to postpone intensively exploring their marital relationship until later in therapy. He explains in the record that only a minimal marital history was obtained thus far because he felt that therapy might be jeopardized if that area were opened before the resistant parents were ready to discuss it.

Specific guidelines for family charts, as well as formats in which to include clinical material, have been established for the department's recently revised initial family report, progress notes, and closing summary. The formats were designed to be broad enough to be used by most therapists, even those with diverse orientations. Nevertheless, since any formats or guidelines will reflect, to some degree, the viewpoints of those who developed them, there may be some criticisms. The formats and guidelines are not intended to be the final word on family records, but rather elements that can be modified as new ideas are introduced and experience in using them is gained.

Initial family report. This report should contain the name of the family and of the therapist and the dates of the sessions. Under the heading "identifying information," the names and ages of all family members should be given, as well as their occupations, presenting problems, and source of referral. The next section is "history of presenting problem," followed by, unless the material is included

---

[1]Accreditation Council for Psychiatric Facilities, *Accreditation Manual for Psychiatric Facilities,* Joint Commission on Accreditation of Hospitals, Chicago, 1972.

[2]D.H. Mills, "Hidden Legal Dangers of the Hospital Chart," *Hospital Medicine,* Vol. 1, October 1965, pp. 34-35.

elsewhere, one on "marital and family history."

Under the heading "characterization of family members," there should be pertinent information about race, religion, nationality, socioeconomic status, developmental history of each member, the parents' families or origin and current relationships with them, and personality descriptions of each member in therapy. Under the heading "observations of family system" the therapist should record what goes on in the sessions, both verbally and nonverbally, between family members and between the family and the therapist. Main issues and themes should be recorded here, as well as feelings evoked in the therapist.

A section on "dynamics and treatment plan" should include the therapist's understanding of each member, of the family system, and of how the presenting difficulties came about. Psychodynamics, societal, hereditary, and constitutional factors should also be included. The proposed type of treatment—for example, weekly family therapy or chemotherapy—and goals should be stated. Here the therapist may also give a prognosis.

Progress notes. These reports should state what is happening with the family relationships as well as with the individual family members in terms of important events in their lives and their emotional states. It should also include dates of therapy sessions, who attended them, how the members interacted, what was discussed, and the therapeutic approaches used.

Closing summary. This brief summary of the entire case should include an identification of the family members, the presenting problem, the treatment process, the outcome for the family as a whole and for each of the members, the reasons for termination, and the disposition. The data of the initial and final sessions or contact should also be included.

The essence of these formats is that people are individuals in their own right who significantly affect and are affected by their family members. Thus the formats provide for including valuable information about subjective experience and individual psychodynamics as well as description of the family's systemic relationships.

LEGAL ASPECTS

Some therapists think of a clinical record as being used solely for clinical purposes. They should realize, however, that any member of the family may at any time become involved in a legal action. Divorce proceedings, child-custody disputes, and certain other civil as well as criminal cases may arise during or after family therapy. In some instances the records may be subpoenaed.

What protection do therapists and patients have against having the records opened in court? It is the physician's or psychologist's ethical duty to keep confidential the information he has obtained about a patient in his professional capacity. In almost every state, such information is privileged and thus may not be disclosed in a legal proceeding without the patient's consent. A few states have extended the privilege to psychiatric social workers as well as physicians and psychologists.

Regardless of the professional degree of the family therapist or whether he is protected by privileged-communication laws, family therapy and family-based record-keeping raise very special problems and legal issues. Privilege and confidentiality are affected by the type of legal case involved and by the sheer fact that more than one person is involved in the therapy. For example, a husband and wife go to a therapist for marital therapy. One later sues the other for divorce. One raises the issue of mental condition in either the claim or the defense. Most state courts would consider privilege to have been waived. But what if the other party did not want that information to be brought up?

Should one member of the patient-family have the right to waive the privilege to the detriment of other members of the family who may either still be in therapy or simply want their communications with the therapist to remain confidential? That issue has not yet been directly addressed by case law or statute. An argument could be made that the patient is the entire family unit and that each member must waive the privilege before the records can be examined. Although that argument may be used successfully in a divorce case,[3,4] its chances of success in a child-custody case are slim because the court's primary concern is for the best interest of the child. Massachusetts law, in fact, explicitly denies privilege to any therapist in any child-custody case in which either party raises the mental condition of the other party.

In sum, a general principle of law is that the court has a right to every person's evidence. The psychotherapist privilege is a justifiable exception but is strictly construed and is itself exception-laden. Most important, current law as it relates to family therapy, and records in particular, is at best unsettled. According to Slovenko, the test of relevancy—not privilege—governs the right to nondisclosure.[5] Thus a therapist-family communication is best protected from disclosure by showing that the communication would have no relevance to the issues in the case.

Therefore, the therapist should be cautious about what information he includes in the records. For example, the admission by a husband that he is coming to family therapy sessions to make his case stronger in an anticipated child-custody struggle might best be omitted from the

---

[3]*Ellis v. Ellis,* 472 S.W. 2d 741 (Tenn. App. 1971).

[4]*Simrin v. Simrin,* 233 Cal. App. 2d 90, 43 Cal. Rptr. 376.

[5]R. Slovenko, *Psychiatry and Law,* Little, Brown, Boston, 1973, p. 67.

record. If it is mentioned at all, the reference should be a vague one such as "Motivations for therapy were discussed." Certainly incriminating or conclusive statements such as "The wife is an unfit parent" should be avoided. How detailed the records should be will depend upon the setting in which the therapist works, the family problem being treated, and the type of litigation that could arise.

As a final precaution, each adult family member should be asked to sign an agreement that he understands that all of the communications are confidential and that the therapist will not disclose any communication unless all participating members join in the waiver. If each member does sign a release, the therapist must make sure that he did so knowingly and intelligently. But until the legislatures and the courts recognize the need for an absolute privilege for family therapists, this type of written agreement will provide very little protection in the event records are subpoenaed.

The lack of an adequate privilege law for family therapists has led some therapists to question whether they should keep any records at all. To be sure, accurate records are the therapist's best defense agianst a malpractice suit.[6] Perhaps more important, accurate records ensure continuity of care. Nevertheless, many private practitioners keep no charts except the customary record of appointments and billings; others risk perjury by keeping two sets, one to be turned over in case of subpoena and the other for treatment.

PATIENTS' PRIVACY

In the course of an evaluation or therapy, patients may reveal various intimate aspects of their own or their relatives' past or current life. They generally do so with the belief that the information will be used by the therapist to help them and will not be passed on to others except in certain situations related to their treatment. To safeguard the patient's right to privacy, we recommend that certain damaging or embarrassing material not be written in the chart. Such material may include the details of sexual difficulties or an extramarital affair. In deciding how much, if any, of such private material should be included, the therapist should balance the need to have complete, useful records against the patients' right to privacy

The more private the material is, the stronger must be the clinical reason for writing about it. We have found that an adequate description of the therapy process can be given without including details of exceedingly shameful or damaging material. It is more important to be clear about the strategy and management of the therapy than to be detailed about private matters.

---

[6]Mills, *op. cit.*

REFERENCES

Barten, H.H. & Barten, S.S. *Children and their parents in brief therapy. New York: Behavioral Publications, 1973.*

Bateson, G. *The group dynamics of schizophrenia. In L. Appleby, J.M. Scher, and J. Cumming (Eds.), Chronic Schizophrenia.* Glencoe, Ill.: The Free Press, 1960.

Bateson, G., Jackson, D.D., Haley, J., & Weakland, J.H. A note on the double bind—1962. *Family Process,* 1963, 2, 154-61.

Bateson, G., Jackson, D.D., Haley, J., & Weakland, J.H. Toward a theory of schizophrenia. *Behavioral Science,* 1956, 1, 251064.

Bell, J.E. *Family therapy.* New York: Jason Aronson, 1975.

Berger, M. What is done in trust: Conditions underlying the success of paradoxical interventions. Unpublished manuscript, Georgia State University, 1976.

Bergin, H.E., & Garfield, S.L. (Eds.). *Handbook of psychotherapy and behavior change: An empirical analysis.* New York: Wiley, 1971.

Camp, H. Structural family therapy: An outsider's perspective. *Family Process,* 1973, 12, 269-77.

Dolliver, R.H. The place of opposites in psychotherapy. *Journal of Contemporary Psychotherapy,* 1972, 5, 49-54.

Edwards, P. (Ed.) *The encyclopedia of philosophy.* New York: MacMillan Co. and The Free Press, 1967.

Erickson, M.H. The identification of a secure reality. *Family Process,* 1962, 1, 294-303.

Erickson, M.H. The confusion technique in hypnosis. In J. Haley (Ed.), *Advanced techniques of hypnosis and therapy.* New York: Grune & Stratton, 1967.

Erickson, M.H., & Rossi, E.L. Varieties of double bind. *American Journal of Clinical Hypnosis,* 1975, 17, 143-57.

Farrelly, F., & Brandsma, J. *Provocative therapy.* Fort Collins, Co.: Shields Publishing Co., 1974.

Feldman, L.B. Processes of change in family therapy. *Journal of Family Counseling,* 1976, 4, 14-22.

Fisch, R., Watzlawick, P., Weakland, J., & Bodin, A. On unbecoming family therapists. In A. Ferber, M. Mendelsohn and A. Napier (Eds.), *The book of family therapy.* New York: Science House, 1972.

Fischer, J. The Mental Research Institute on family therapy: Review and assessment. *Family Therapy,* 1974, 1, 105-40.

Fox, R.E. Family therapy. In I.B. Weiner (Ed.), *Clinical methods in psychology.* New York: John Wiley & Sons, 1976.

Frankl, V.E. Paradoxical intention and dereflection. *Psychotherapy: Theory, Research and Practice,* 1975, 12, 226-37.

Frankl, V.E. Paradoxical intention and dereflection: Two Logotherapeutic techniques. In S. Arieti and G. Chrzanowski (Eds.), *New dimensions in psychiatry: A world view.* New York: John Wiley & Sons, 1975.

Frankl, V.E. *The doctor and the soul.* New York: Alfred Knopf, 1965.

Friedman, P.H. Outline (alphabet) of 26 techniques of family and marital therapy. *Psychotherapy: Theory, Research and Practice,* 1974, 11, 259-64.

Gerz, H.O. The treatment of the phobic and the obsessive-compulsive patient using paradoxical intention. *Journal of Neuropsychiatry,* 1962, 3, 375-87.

Glick, I.D., & Kessler, D.R. *Marital and family therapy.* New York: Grune & Stratton, 1974.

Guerin, P., & Fogarty, T. Study your own family. In A. Ferber, M. Mendelsohn, and A. Napier (Eds.), *The book of family therapy.* New York, Science House, 1972.

Haley, J. (Ed.). *Changing families.* New York: Grune & Stratton, 1971.

Haley, J. Paradoxes in play, fantasy, and psychotherapy. *Psychiatric Research Reports of the American Psychiatric Association,* 1955, 2, 52-8.

Haley, J. Strategic therapy when a child is presented as the problem. *Journal of the American Academy of Child Psychiatry,* 1973, 12, 641-59.

Haley, J. *Strategies of psychotherapy.* New York: Grune & Stratton, 1963.

Haley, J. *Uncommon therapy.* New York: Ballantine Books, 1973.

Haley, J. Whither family therapy? *Family Process,* 1962, 1, 69-100.

Hand, I., & Lamontagne, Y. L'intention paradoxale et techniques comportementales similaires en psychotherapie a court terme. *Canadian Psychiatric Association Journal,* 1974, 19, 501-7.

Hare-Mustin, R.T. Treatment of temper tantrums by a paradoxical intervention. *Family Process,* 1975, 14, 481-5.

Hartman, C., & Narboe, N. Catastrophic injunctions. *Transactional Analysis Journal,* 1974, 4, 10-12.

Howells, J.G. *Principles of family psychiatry.* New York: Brunner/Mazel, 1975.

Hughes, P., & Bracht, G. *A panoply of paradoxes: Vicious circles and infinity.* New York: Doubleday & Co., 1975.

Jackson, D.D. (Ed.). *Communication, family, and marriage.* Palo Alto: Science & Behavior Books, 1968.

Jackson, D.D. The individual and the larger contexts. *Family process,* 1967, 6, 139-47.

Jackson, D.D., & Weakland, J.H. Conjoint family therapy: Some considerations on theory, technique, and results. *Psychiatry,* 1961, 24, 30-45.

Jones, E.E. (Ed.). *Attribution: Perceiving the causes of behavior.* Morristown, N.J.: General Learning Series, 1971.

Kantor, R.E., and Hoffman, L. Brechtian theater as a model for conjoint family therapy. *Family Process,* 1966, 5, 218-29.

L'Abate, L. A positive approach to marital and familial intervention. In L.R. Wolberg, and M.L. Aronson (Eds.), *Group therapy 1975.* New York: Stratton Intercontinental Medical Book Corp., 1975, 63-75.

L'Abate, L., O'Callaghan, J.B., Biat, T., Dunne, E.E., Margolis, R., Prigge, B., & Lopez, P. Enlarging the scope of intervention with couples and families: Combination of therapy and enrichment. In L.R. Wolberg and M.L.

Aronson (Eds.), *Group therapy 1976: An overview.* New York: Stratton Intercontinental Medical Book Corporation, 1976, 62-73.

Laing, R.D. Mystification, confusion, and conflict. In I. Boszormenyi-Nagy, and J.L. Framo (Eds.), *Intensive family therapy.* Hagerstown, Md.: Harper & Row, 1965.

Laing, R.D. *The politics of the family.* New York: Pantheon Books, 1971.

Luthman, S. Techniques of process therapy. *Family Therapy,* 1974, 1, 141-62.

Minuchin, S. Conflict-resolution family therapy. *Psychiatry,* 1965, 28, 278-86.

Montalvo, B., & Haley, J. In defense of child therapy. *Family Process,* 1973, 12, 227-44.

Nelson, M.C., Nelson, B., Sherman, M.H., & Strean, H.S. *Roles and paradigms in psychotherapy.* New York: Grune & Stratton, 1968.

Otto, H.A. Criteria for assessing family strength. *Family Process,* 1963, 2, 329-38.

Peck, B.B. Psychotherapy with fragmented (father-absent) families. *Family Therapy,* 1974, 1, 27-42.

Prosky, P. Family therapy: An orientation. *Clinical Social Work Journal,* 1974, 2, 45-56.

Rosen, J.N. *Direct analysis.* New York: Grune & Stratton, 1953.

Rossi, E.L. Psychological shocks and creative moments in psychotherapy. *American Journal of Clinical Hypnosis,* 1973, 16, 9-22.

Ruesch, J., & Bateson, G. *Communication: The social matrix of society.* New York: W.W. Norton, 9151.

Sander, F.M. Freid's "A case of successful treatment by hypnotism (1892-1893)": An uncommon therapy? *Family Process,* 1974, 13, 461-68.

Sapirstein, M.R. *Paradoxes of everyday life.* New York: Random House, 1955.

Selvini-Palazzoli, M., Boscolo, L., Cecchin, G.E., & Prata, G. Paradox and counterparadox: A new model for the therapy of the family in schizophrenic transaction. Paper presented at the Fifth International Symposium on Psychotherapy of Schizophrenia. Oslo: August 14-18, 1975.

Selvini-Palazzoli, M. Boscolo, L. Cecchin, G.E., & Prata, G. The treatment of children through brief therapy of their parents. *Family Process,* 1974, 13, 429-42.

Shazer, S. de. Brief therapy: Two's company. *Family Process,* 1975, 14, 79-93.

Shazer, S. de. On getting unstuck: Some change-initiating tactics for getting the family moving. *Family Therapy,* 1974, 1, 19-26

Solyom, L., Garza-Perez, J., Ledwidge, B.L., & Solyom, C. Paradoxical intention in the treatment of obsessive thoughts: A pilot study. *Comprehensive Psychiatry,* 1972, 13, 291-7.

Steiner, C.M. *Scripts people live.* New York: Bantam Books, 1974.

Usdin, G. (Ed.). *Overview of the psychotherapies.* New York: Brunner/Mazel, 1975.

Watzlawick, P. A review of the double bind theory. *Family Process,* 1963, 2, 132-53.

Watzlawick, P., Beavin, J.H., & Jackson, D.D. *Pragmatics of human communication.* New York: W.W. Norton, 1976.

448   *Strategies and Techniques in Family Therapy*

Watzlawick, P., Weakland, J., & Fisch, R. *Change: Principles of problem formation and problem resolution.* New York: W.W. Norton, 1974.

Weakland, J.H., Fisch, R., Watzlawick, P., and Bodin, A.M. Brief therapy: Focused problem resolution. *Family Process,* 1974, 13, 141-68.

Weisskopf-Joelson, E. Logotherapy: Science or faith? *Psychotheapy: Theory, Research and Practice,* 1975, 12, 238-40.

Whitaker, C.A. Psychotherapy of the absurd: With a special emphasis on the psychotherapy of aggression. *Family Process,* 1975, 14, 1-16.

Zuk, G.H. *Family therapy: A triadic based approach.* New York: Behavioral Publications, 1971.